Addison-Wesley's Nursing Examination Review

Special Edition 1981

Addison-Wesley's Nursing Examination Review

Special Edition 1981

Sally L. Lagerquist, editor

Contributing authors

Irene M. Bobak, R.N., M.N., M.S.N.
San Francisco State University, San Francisco

Sandra Forrest Fritz, R.N., M.N.
University of California, Los Angeles

Sally L. Lagerquist, R.N., M.S.
University of California, San Francisco

Mary Jane Sauvé, R.N., M.S.
California State College, Sonoma

Special collaborator in Unit 1, Psychiatric Nursing
Williamina Rose, R.N., M.S.

Addison-Wesley Publishing Company
Medical/Nursing Division
Menlo Park, California • Reading, Massachusetts • London
Amsterdam • Don Mills, Ontario • Sydney

To Lagie

   my collaborator
   my philosopher
   my friend
   my husband

This book is a thank you to you and our children, Elana and Kalen.
Your patience in postponing "fun" and your continual support and
belief in what I was doing was beautiful!
You three are a part of this book.

                                                        Sally

Cover and text photographs by George B. Fry, III.

Special edition 1981

Library of Congress Cataloging in Publication Data
Main entry under title:

Addison-Wesley's nursing examination review.

   Includes bibliographies and index.
   1. Nursing--Outlines, syllabi, etc. 2. Nursing--
Examinations, questions, etc. I. Lagerquist, Sally L.
II. Bobak, Irene M., 1933-   . [DNLM: 1. Nursing--
Examination questions. WY 18 A227]
RT52.A3 1981   610.73'076   81-952
ISBN 0-201-04389-0 (pbk.)   AACR2

       ghij-AL-8987654321

Addison-Wesley Publishing Company
Medical/Nursing Division
2725 Sand Hill Road
Menlo Park, California 94025

Preface

This book has been written to help nurses study for, and score higher on, state board licensure examinations. For those of you who want to fill in memory gaps, concentrate on basic essential information, or review in general, the content presented and the questions and answers in these pages will refresh your understanding of the core content and key principles of nursing.

Presentation

The *Orientation* section of this book discusses the mechanics and format of the RN State Board Test Pool Examination as well as test-taking strategies. This is intended to help alleviate anxiety about taking this examination and to provide you with some suggestions for more effective test-taking techniques.

This book is divided into the five main subject areas that are covered in the RN licensure examination:

Psychiatric Nursing
Medical Nursing
Surgical Nursing
Maternity Nursing
Pediatric Nursing

The content is presented in *outline form*, highlighting principles and guidelines for nursing approaches and key concepts and theories. *Questions* are included following each unit to test your skills in applying concepts and principles to the test-taking situation. For immediate feedback, the answers and rationale for these questions are then provided. Also, the explanation for the correct response is included to point out underlying basic principles and to serve as an aid for applying the same principles to questions that may be phrased dif-

ferently on the examination. To aid you in recording responses to the questions, *pre- and poststudy answer forms* have been provided for the review questions from each unit. These answer forms are located at the rear of the text and have been perforated for easy removal and use.

In addition to the previously described core material in each of these key five study areas, appendix material applicable to each unit of study has been included at the end of the text. These appendices contain specific information that you need to know for state board examinations and are presented in the form of tables and lists to facilitate review, recall, and understanding. Each unit also contains an annotated bibliography to the most readily available basic texts providing resources for further study.

How to Approach This Text

We suggest, first, that you study the entire book. We have found that the five clinical subjects of nursing—psychiatry, medicine, surgery, maternity, and pediatrics—are treated in the licensure exams with considerable overlap. For example, psychiatric-type questions are asked in *all* subjects covered in the exam, and questions on principles of nutrition may be covered in the medical, surgical, maternity, and pediatric nursing tests. Therefore, reviewing only one or two sections of this book may not cover all core content of any particular area. With this in mind, we have integrated the content on nutrition, pharmacology, and basic social and biologic sciences, which is consistent with the treatment of these topics in the state board examinations.

The review questions at the end of each unit are an integral part of the review process. These multiple-choice, situational questions are expressly written to simulate the concepts, theories, and principles likely to be covered in the state board examinations. The questions are directed at your critical problem-solving ability. Following the questions, the answer/rationale section provides an added learning experience by stressing key principles underlying the best answers. This should facilitate your application of similar principles to questions on the state board examination, and your rote memory of answers can be replaced by the understanding of key principles necessary to select the best answer.

Acknowledgments

We are gratified by the manner in which we were able to work together on this challenging venture. Without mutual support, cooperation, and assistance, this book could not have been completed.

We are grateful also to Suzanne Besler, June Keating, and Joan Rowe, who had the formidable task of clearing through our tangle of handwritten pages and of transforming them into a typewritten manuscript, and to Billie Meador and Sandy Winter for their aid in gathering and organizing material.

The task of writing this book has been considerably lightened by the enthusiasm, encouragement, and good counsel of Addison-Wesley's Health Sciences editorial staff.

Sally L. Lagerquist
Irene M. Bobak
Sandra Forrest Fritz
Mary Jane Sauvé

Abbreviated Contents

Complete Contents

Unit 4   Maternity Nursing   203

Addison-Wesley's Nursing Examination Review

Orientation

HOW TO USE THIS REVIEW BOOK AS A STUDY GUIDE

Although nursing students may know that they are academically prepared to take the National State Board Test Pool Examination, many find that reviewing nursing content for the state board examination itself presents special concerns about *what and how to study*.

Some typical concerns about *what to study* are reflected in the following questions:

- Since there are usually only 90 to 125 questions per subject area tested, how does one select what is the most important content for review? How does one narrow the focus of study and pinpoint the relevant from the nonrelevant material?
- What areas should be emphasized?
- How detailed should the review be?
- How does one know what areas to review most?
- Should basic sciences, such as anatomy, physiology, microbiology, and nutrition, be included in the study?

Concerns relating to *how to study* include:

- How does one make the best use of limited review time to go over content that may be in lecture and clinical notes compiled during two to four years of schooling?
- Is it best to review from all the major textbooks used in nursing school?
- Should material be memorized, or should one study from broad principles and concepts?

We have written this nursing review book with the *general* intent of assisting nurses in identifying what it is that they need to study and in using their study time effectively, productively, and efficiently while preparing for the examination.

Each contributing author has selected content and developed a style of presentation that has been tested by thousands of nursing students attending review courses coordinated by the editor in various cities throughout the United States. Addison-Wesley's Nursing Examination Review is the result of this study. This review book can be used in a variety of ways: (1) as a starting point for review of essential content specifically aimed at state board preparation, (2) as an endpoint of studying for the state board examination, (3) as an anxiety reduction tool, and (4) as a general guide and as a refresher for nurses not presently in practice.

As a Starting Point

This text can be used in early review when a longer study period is needed to *fill in gaps* of knowledge. One cannot remember what one does not know or understand. A lengthy review before the exam allows students time to rework and organize notes accumulated from two to four years of basic nursing education. In addition, an early review allows time for *self-evaluation*. We have provided questions and answers to help students identify areas requiring further study and to help them *integrate* unfamiliar material with what they already know.

As an End-point

This text can also be used for a *quick* review to *promote retention* and *recall*. During that time immediately preceding the examination, the main objective might be to *strengthen previous learning* by refreshing the memory. Or a brief overview may serve to *draw together* the isolated points under main concepts and principles in a way that shows their relationships and relative importance.

As an Anxiety Reduction Tool

In some students, anxiety related to taking examinations in general may reach such levels that it causes students to be unproductive in study and to function at a lower level during the actual examination. Sections of this text are directed toward this problem and provide simple, practical approaches to general anxiety reduction. For anxiety specifically related to unknown aspects of the state board examination itself, the section on the structure, format, and mechanics of the board examination might bring relief through its focus on basic examination information.

For anxiety related to lack of confidence or skill in test-taking "know-how," the special section on test-taking techniques may be helpful.

As a General Study Guide and as a Refresher for Nurses not Presently in Practice

Many student nurses will find this review book useful as a general study guide throughout their education. It will help them put information into perspective as they learn it. And nurses who have not been in practice for several years will find it to be a useful reference tool and review device.

Where to Begin

In using this review book to prepare for the licensure examination, the nurse must:

1. Be prepared mentally
   A. Know the purpose of the examination
   B. Know the purpose for reviewing
   C. Anticipate what is to come
   D. Decide on a good study method—set a study goal before beginning a particular subject area (number of pages, for example); plan the length of the review period by the amount of material to be covered, not by the clock
2. Plan the work to be done
   A. Select one subject at a time for review, and establish and follow a sequence for review of each subject
      (1) Using the perforated answer sheets (prestudy) at the back of the book, answer the practice questions following the outline of the selected subject area (set a time limit, as pacing is important)
      (2) Compare your answers with those pro-

vided as a means of evaluating areas of competence
   B. Identify those subjects which will require additional concentrated study in this review book as well as in basic textbooks
   C. Study the review text outlines, noting headings, subheadings, and *italics* and **bold face** type for emphasis on relative importance
   D. Study the content presented in the appendices, which contain much information presented in synthesized format to facilitate memorization and understanding
   E. Repeat the self-evaluation process by taking the test again (poststudy)
   F. Look up the answers for the correct response to the multiple choice questions and read the rationale for *why* it was the correct response (These explanations serve to correct as well as reinforce. Understanding the underlying principles serves also as an aid in applying the same principles to questions that may be phrased differently on the actual examination.)
   G. If necessary, refer to the annotated bibliography for other basic textbooks to relearn aspects of anatomy, physiology, nutrition, or basic nursing procedures that are unclear

While Reviewing

1. Scan the outline for main ideas and topics
   A. Do not try to remember verbatim what is on each page
   B. Paraphrase or explain this material to another person
2. Refer to basic textbooks for details and illustrations as necessary to recall specific information related to basic sciences
3. Integrate reading with experience
   A. Think of examples that illustrate the key concepts and principles
   B. Make meaningful associations
   C. Look for implications for nursing actions as concepts are reviewed
4. Take notes on the review outline—use stars and arrows and underscore and write comments in margins, such as "most important" and "memorize," to reinforce relative importance of points of information

After Reviewing

1. Repeat the self-evaluation process as often as

necessary to gain mastery of content essential for safe nursing practice

2. Continue to refer to major textbooks to fill in gaps where greater detail or in-depth comprehension is required

3. Look for patterns in response selection to the multiple choice practice questions—identify sources of difficulty in choosing the most appropriate answers

KEY POINTS TO RECALL FOR BETTER STUDY

1. *Schedule*—study time should be scheduled so that review is close to the time at which it will be used. Retention is much better following a well-spaced review. It may be helpful to group material into small learning segments. Study goals should be set before beginning each period of study (number of pages, for example).

2. *Overlearn*—many students have better retention of material after they have reorganized and relearned it.

3. *Rephrase and explain*—try to rephrase material just read in your own words or explain it to another person. Reinforce learning through repetition and usage.

4. *Decide on order of importance*—organize study time in terms of importance and familiarity.

5. *Use mechanical memory aids*—mnemonic (memory) devices simplify recall, for example, "On Old Olympus Towering Top a Finn and German Viewed Some Hops." The first letter in each word identifies the first letter of a cranial nerve.

6. *Association*—associate new material with related content from past experience.

7. *Original learning*—if an unfamiliar topic is presented, do more than review. Seek out sources of additional information such as those given in the bibliographies.

8. *Make notes*—look for key words, phrases, and sentences in the outlined review material and mark them for later reference.

9. *Definitions*—look up unfamiliar terms in a dictionary or the glossary of a basic text.

10. *Additional study*—refer to other textbook references for more detailed information.

11. *Distractors*—keep a pad of paper on hand to jot down extraneous thoughts, get them out of the mind and on to the paper.

THE MECHANICS OF THE STATE BOARD LICENSING EXAMINATIONS FOR REGISTERED NURSES

Frequently candidates for the nursing licensing examination have many questions about structure and format of and rules and regulations concerning the examination procedure.

As an aid to reducing apprehension and time spent on speculation, this chapter is intended to provide information that candidates commonly seek. The information in this section was compiled from a survey of responses by each state's board of nursing registration, as well as from literature distributed by the National League for Nursing. If the candidates have other questions, it is suggested that they contact the board of nursing in their state or refer to appropriate *Nursing Outlook* sources for more information.

1. *What is required for admission to the examination center?* In some states a 2 by 2-inch head and shoulders photo of the candidate must be attached to the admission card. The photo must be a recent likeness of the candidate for positive identification. Only those holding these admission cards with photos will be admitted to the examination room.

2. *Can I bring any material into the examination room?* No, do *not* take any study materials, including books or notes, into the building in which the examination is being given.

3. *Can I use my own pen or pencil in blackening the circles?* No, use only the No. 2 pencil provided at the exam; blacken the circle or line area corresponding to the answer you have chosen.

4. *What subjects are usually covered on the first day?* Medical nursing, psychiatric nursing, and obstetrical nursing.

5. *What subjects are usually covered on the second day?* Surgical nursing, nursing of children, and "Test 6."

6. *What is "Test 6"?* Test 6 is an experimental test to establish the validity of questions for licensure examinations.

7. *Will this extra test count toward my total score?* No, the questions on this part of the test will not count toward your total score. These questions are intended to help measure

the validity of the test for licensure purposes, and all states are asked to participate.

8. *Where do the exam questions come from?* The individual state boards send item writers to the National League for Nursing to write questions for the National State Board Test Pool Examination. The National League for Nursing administers the exam under the control of American Nurses' Association Council of State Boards.

9. *Are there any questions with which I may not have had previous experience in my basic nursing program?* Most of the questions are about patients with conditions familiar to you and are representative of common health problems on a national basis. Some questions may relate to nursing problems with which you may not have had prior experience. Their purpose is to test your ability to apply knowledge of specific principles from the physical, biologic, and social sciences to *new* situations.

10. *Will there be questions on nutrition and diet therapy, pharmacology, nursing fundamentals, and communicable diseases?* Yes, in addition to questions related to the five clinical content areas (medical nursing, psychiatric nursing, obstetrical nursing, surgical nursing, and nursing of children) each of these five tests will include questions from such areas as nutrition and diet therapy, pharmacology, fundamentals of nursing, communicable disease nursing, sociologic aspects of nursing, and natural and social sciences.

11. *How many questions does each test contain?* Each test consists of between 60 and 125 questions of the multiple-choice variety.

12. *Are all of the questions multiple choice questions?* Yes, all are multiple choice questions.

13. *How many choices are included?* Four.

14. *Do some questions have more than one answer?* No, only *one* of the four suggested alternatives is the *best* answer. Mark only *one* answer to each question.

15. *What will happen if I mark more than one response to a question?* You will not receive any credit for that question.

16. *Is it advisable to guess when I do not know the answer?* Answer those questions to which you *think* you know the right answer, although you may not be sure. Do not use wild guessing, as this might lower your score.

17. *Will points be deducted for wrong answers?* Yes.

18. *How many points will be deducted for wrong answers?* One-third of a point is subtracted for each incorrect answer.

19. *Will I get partial credit for selecting the next to the best answer?* No.

20. *May I make marks in the test booklet?* No, do *not* make any marks in the test booklet or in the margins of the shaded area of the special answer sheet provided for the examination.

21. *What is the passing score for each test?* The passing or cutoff score changes from time to time and can vary from state to state. At present, it is 350 for each test in most states. The maximum total score ranges from 800 to 999 and varies for each series.

22. *How is the exam scored?* It is scored by machine. Standardization and conversion tables are used to convert raw scores into standard scores.

23. *How much time is usually allowed for each part?* Each test is timed as follows: medical nursing, approximately 2 hours; psychiatric nursing, approximately 1½ hours; obstetrical nursing, approximately 1½ hours; surgical nursing, approximately 2 hours; nursing of children, approximately 2 hours, and Test No. 6, approximately 1 hour. Enough time is allowed for each test for most candidates to attempt most questions.

24. *Is there time for lunch?* Yes, generally one hour.

25. *What if I need to leave my seat during a test?* You must have permission from the examiner or a designee. Without this permission, your papers will not be counted if you leave.

26. *How often is the exam given?* Twice a year.

27. *Do I have to repeat the entire exam if I do not pass only one or two parts?* In most states, only the subjects failed need to be repeated, if done within a stated time period.

28. *Can the exam be retaken before results from the previous exam are known?* No.

29. *How many times can the exam be repeated?* Unlimited within two to three years in 16 states; other states have limits and may require remedial work. Currently, general rules state that an applicant must pass all five sections in not more than three writings within an 18-month period. After that the entire exam must be

retaken as well as evidence given of remedial assistance. However, each state can set its own limits.

30. *Does the exam fee have to be paid each time the test is repeated by an applicant?* It varies from state to state. In some states, if it is within one year from the first sitting, there is no additional fee. After the second try, a new fee is required.

31. *Where can I obtain copies of old exams?* Examinations are not available to anyone but authorized representatives of the board. The board's regulations prohibit unauthorized persons from soliciting, accepting, or compiling information about the specific content of the examination questions either before, after, or during the exam.

32. *Do diploma graduates take the same test as associate or baccalaureate degree graduates?* Yes.

33. *Do the different states have different exams?* A large number of jurisdictions use the examination from the National State Board Test Pool. However, each state decides on the minimum passing score that will best meet the nursing needs of its jurisdiction.

34. *When will the exam results be known?* It varies from three to four weeks to two to four months, with an average time span of six to eight weeks.

35. *Who grants the nursing license?* The state board of nursing in which you wrote the exam.

HOW TO PREPARE FOR AND SCORE HIGHER ON EXAMS

The Psychology of Test Taking

Many nursing students know the nursing material they are being tested on and can demonstrate their nursing skills in practice but do not know how to prepare themselves for, take, and pass the state board licensure examination.

It is not just a matter of taking exams but *knowing how* to take them, making educated guesses, and utilizing the alloted time in the most productive way. You must learn to use strategy and judgment in answering questions when you are not sure of the right answer. This chapter will discuss practical strategies for eliminating wrong answers and for increasing your chances of selecting the better answers.

1. *The first hunch is usually a good one.* Pay attention to your "body vibes," which may signal you as to which answer "feels" best.

2. *If you cannot decide between two choices, make a note of the numbers of the two choices about which you are not sure.* This will narrow down your focus when you come back to this question. Leave the question; do not spend much time on the ones you are in doubt. When you have completed the test, go back and spend more time on those you had trouble with.

3. *Answer the easy ones first.* This is a basic rule for exam-taking. Too often examinees focus on one question for ten minutes, for example, instead of going on to answer 20 additional questions during this time. The main purpose is to answer correctly as many questions as possible.

4. *Be wise about the timing.* Divide your time. For example, if you have 100 questions and 2½ hours for the test, aim for an average of 10 questions to the quarter hour. Keep working! Do not lose time looking back at your answers.

5. *Use care and caution when using electrical answer sheets.* You will receive a sheet separate from the exam booklet containing the test questions; it has about 150 numbered spaces on a side. (An example is given on the following page; we have also provided similar answer sheets for you to record your answers for the questions in this text.) If the question has five possible choices, you need to fill in the space between the numbered spaces as shown. It is essential that you use the special pencil provided by the examiners. This pencil contains lead that the electrical grading impulse will pick up. If you need to erase, erase the shadings completely. A trace of lead in the wrong space might throw out the answer. Be especially cautious in placing your answers by the correct question number. The numbers may go across the page horizontally. If you leave out a question, make sure that you skip that number on the answer sheet. Otherwise, all the other answers may be out of sequence and result in wrong answers by accident. It might be helpful, to say to yourself as you answer each question, "Choice No. 4 to question No. 3," to make sure that the right answer goes with each question.

6. *Stay the entire time allotted.* If you complete the section early, check your answers. On a second look (after you have completed the

NAME__________ LAST __________ FIRST __________ MIDDLE __________ DATE__________

SCHOOL__________ CITY__________

1__________ 2__________

SAMPLE OF PRE- AND POSTSTUDY ANSWER FORM FOR REVIEW QUESTIONS FOLLOWING EACH UNIT.

DIRECTIONS: Read each question and its numbered answers. When you have decided which answer is correct, blacken the corresponding space on this sheet with the special pencil. Make your mark as long as the pair of lines, and move the pencil point up and down firmly to make a heavy black line. If you change your mind, erase your first mark completely. Make no stray marks; they may count against you.

SAMPLE:

1. Chicago is
   1—1 a country
   1—2 a mountain
   1—3 an island
   1—4 a city
   1—5 a state

1 (answer spaces 1 2 3 4 5; space 4 blackened)

1	31	61	91	121
2	32	62	92	122
3	33	63	93	123
4	34	64	94	124
5	35	65	95	125
6	36	66	96	126
7	37	67	97	127
8	38	68	98	128
9	39	69	99	129
10	40	70	100	130
11	41	71	101	131
12	42	72	102	132
13	43	73	103	133
14	44	74	104	134
15	45	75	105	135

BE SURE YOUR MARKS ARE HEAVY AND BLACK.
ERASE COMPLETELY ANY ANSWER YOU WISH TO CHANGE.

16	46	76	106	136
17	47	77	107	137
18	48	78	108	138
19	49	79	109	139
20	50	80	110	140
21	51	81	111	141
22	52	82	112	142
23	53	83	113	143
24	54	84	114	144
25	55	85	115	145
26	56	86	116	146
27	57	87	117	147
28	58	88	118	148
29	59	89	119	149
30	60	90	120	150

Printed by the International Business Machines Corporation, Dayton, N. J., U. S. A.

IBM FORM I.T.S. 1100 B 107

entire section), you may find something that you are now sure you marked in error the first time. Also, look for and erase stray marks. Use leftover time to ponder over the questions in which you were undecided between two possible answers.

7. *It is better not to guess wildly.* Prior to the date of your exam, check with the literature put out by your local nursing state board as to whether or not the practice is still to deduct wrong answers from correct ones. If this is still the current practice, it is safer not to guess, for if the question was left blank, there would be no wrong answer to deduct.

8. *On the morning of the exam, avoid excessive oral intake of products that act as diuretics for you.* If you know that coffee, beer, or cigarettes, for example, increase urgency and frequency, it is best to limit their intake. Undue physiologic discomforts can distract your focus from the exam at hand.

9. *Increase your oral intake of foods high in glucose and protein.* These foods reportedly have been helpful to some examinees for keeping up their blood-sugar level. This may enable greater concentration and problem-solving ability at the times when you most need to function at a high level.

10. *Prior to examination days, avoid eating exotic or highly seasoned foods to which your system may not be accustomed.* Avoid possible gastrointestinal distress when you least need it!

11. *Using hard candy or something similar* during the test may help to relieve the discomfort of a dry mouth related to a state of anxiety.

12. *Wear comfortable clothes that you have worn before.* The day of the exam is not a good time to wear new clothes and footwear that may prove to be constricting, binding, and uncomfortable, especially at the waistline and shoulder seams.

13. Anxiety states can bring about rapid increase and decrease in body temperature. *Wear clothing that can be shed or added on.* For example, you might wear a sweater that can be put on when you feel chilled or removed when your body temperature fluctuates again.

14. *Women need to be prepared for early, irregular, and unanticipated onset of menses on exam day, a time of stress.*

15. Exam jitters can elicit anxietylike reactions, both physiologic and emotional. Since anxiety tends to be contagious, *try to limit your contacts with those who are either also experiencing exam-related anxiety or who elicit those feelings in you.*

16. *The night before the exam is a good time to engage in a pleasurable activity* as a means of anxiety-reduction. The exam involves many hours of endurance for sitting, thinking, and reacting. Give yourself a chance for restful, not energy- or emotion-draining, activities in the days before the exam.

17. *Get an early start* on the day you take the examination to avoid raising your anxiety level before the actual exam starts. Allow yourself time for delays in traffic and in public transportation or for finding a parking place. Even allow for a dead battery, flooded engine, flat tire, or bus breakdown.

18. *Try a relaxation process* (see p. 10) if anxiety reaches an uncomfortable level that cannot be channeled into the service of learning.

19. When you arrive home after the exam, *jot down content areas that were unfamiliar to you.* This may serve as a key focus for review.

20. If your anxiety level is high *after* the exam because you did not answer every question, remember that *you do not need to get all the answers right to pass.* The exam is not designed for obtaining perfect scores. Achieving the highest score on the state boards will not earn you a gold star on your license or a differently designated license.

21. Aim to do as well as you can but avoid the same competitive pressures and strivings to attain an ''A'' grade that you might have previously experienced in working for school or college grades. Good luck!

Strategies in Answering Questions

If you can intelligently eliminate false answers, you can reduce a four-answer question to a two-answer question in which your chances are as good as those in the true-false type of question, in which you have a good chance to guess half of the answers correctly.

We think that the following pointers will assist you to intelligently narrow down your choices.

1. *Always, all, never, none.* Answers that include global words such as these should be viewed

with caution because they imply that there are no exceptions. There are very few instances in which a correct answer is that absolute. Any suggested answer such as

Nurses should exercise caution in interviewing alcoholics because:
(1) Alcoholics *always* exaggerate
(2) Alcoholics are *never* consistent

should be looked at with care because any exception will make that a false response. A more reasonable answer to the preceding might be "Alcoholics may not be reliable historians."

2. *Broad, most comprehensive answers.* Choose the answer that includes all of the others, which is referred to here as the "umbrella effect." For example, in answering the question

A main nursing function in group therapy is to:
(1) Help patients give and receive feedback in the group
(2) Encourage patients to bring up their concerns
(3) Facilitate group interaction among the members
(4) Remind patients to address their comments to the group

Number 3 is the best choice because all other choices go under it.

3. Test how *reasonable* the answer is by posing a specific situation to yourself.

For example, the question might read, "The best approach when interviewing children who have irrational fears is to: (1) help them to analyze why they feel this way." Ask yourself if it is reasonable to use Freudian analysis with 2-year-old children?

4. *Focus on the patient.* Usually the reason for doing something with a patient is not to preserve the good reputation of the doctor, hospital, or nurse, or to enforce rules. Wrong choices would focus on enlisting the patient's cooperation for the purpose of fulfilling orders or because it is the rule. On seeing a patient out of bed against orders, instead of just saying, "It's against doctor's orders for you to get up," you might better respond by focusing on how the patient is reacting to the restriction on his mobility, for example, "I can see that you want to get up and that it is upsetting to you to be in bed now. Let me help you to get back safely to

bed and see what I can do for you."

5. *Eliminate any answer that takes for granted that anyone is unworthy or ignorant.* For example, in the question, "The patient should not be told the full extent of her condition because": a poor response would be, "she would not understand."

6. *Look for the answer that may be different from the others.* For example, if all choices but one are stated in milligrams and that one reads, "1 gm," that choice may be a distractor. In that case, you can narrow your selection to the other choices.

7. Read the question carefully to see if a *negative verb* is used. If the question asks, "Which of the following are *not* applicable," be sure to gear your thinking accordingly.

8. *Do not look for a pattern* in the answers shaded under a given numbered choice. If you have already shaded four successive answers under choice three for each of the four questions, do not be reluctant to shade choice three for the fifth question in a row if you think that it is the correct response.

9. *Look for the choices that you know are either correct or incorrect.* You can save time and narrow your selection by using this strategy.

10. In eliminating potentially wrong answers, remember to look for examples of what has been included in the "nontherapeutic response" list in Unit 1, Psychiatric Nursing.

11. Wrong choices tend to be either *very brief* in response or are *very long* and involved explanatory responses.

12. Better choices to select are those responses that (a) focus on *feelings*, "How did that make you feel?" (b) *reflect* the patient's comments, "You say that made you angry." (c) communicate *acceptance* of the patient by the nurse rather than criticism or a value judgment. (d) *acknowledge* the patient, "I see that you are wincing." and (e) stay in the *here-and-now*, "What will help now?" Examples of better choices can be found in the "therapeutic responses" list in Unit 1, Psychiatric Nursing.

13. Look for the *average, acceptable, safe, common, "garden variety"* responses, not the "exception to the rule," esoteric, and controversial responses.

14. Eliminate the response that may be the best for a *physician* to make. Look for an *RN–role appropriate* response; for example, *psychiatrists analyze* the past, and *nurses* in general focus on *present* feelings and situations.

15. *Look for similarities and groupings* in responses and the one-of-a-kind key idea in multiple-choice responses. For example:

At which activity would it be important to protect the patient who is on phenothiazines from the side effects of this drug?
   (1) Sunday church services
   (2) A twilight concert
   (3) A midday movie in the theater
   (4) A luncheon picnic on the hospital grounds

Choices No. 1, 2, and 3 all involve indoor activities. Choice No. 4 involves outdoor exposure during the height of the sun's rays. Patients need to be protected against photosensitivity and burns when on phenothiazines.

16. Be sure to note if the question asks for what is the *first* or *initial* response to be made or action to be taken by the nurse. The choices listed may all be correct, but in this situation selecting the response with the *highest priority* is important.

17. When you do not know the specific facts called for in the question, use your *skills of reasoning;* for example, when an answer involves amounts or time (mainly numbers) and you do not know the answer and cannot find any basis for reasoning (all else being equal), avoid the extreme responses.

18. *Give special attention to questions in which each word counts.* A purpose of this type of question may not be to test your knowledge alone, but to also see if you can read accurately and look for the main point. In such questions, each answer may be a profusion of words, but there may be one or two words that make the critical difference.

19. All things equal, select the response that you best *understand.* Long-winded statements are likely to be included as distractors and may be a lot of words signifying little or nothing, such as "criteria involved in implementing conceptual referents for standardizing protocol."

20. *Apply skim-reading techniques.* Read the descriptive case quickly. Pick out *key* words (write them down, if that is helpful to you). Translate, into *your own* words, the gist of what is asked in the question. You might close your eyes at this point and see if the answer "pops" into mind. *Then,* skim the choices of answers, looking for that response that corresponds to what first came into your mind. Key ideas or themes to look for in responses have been covered in this section (that is, look for a "feeling response," acceptance, acknowledgment of the patient, and reflection, for example).

HOW TO REDUCE ANXIETY

Most people have untapped inner resources for achieving relaxation and tension release in stressful situations (such as during an examination) when they need to function at their highest potential.

In anxiety-producing settings whenever you feel overwhelmed or blocked, a fantasy experience can be of help in mastering the rising anxiety by promoting a feeling of calm, detached awareness and a sense of deeper personal coping resources. Through the fantasy you can gain access to a zone of tranquility in the center of your being. Guided imagery often carries with it feelings of serenity, warmth, and comfort. The goal of this discussion is to help you experience a self-guided approach to reducing your anxiety level to one that is compatible with learning and high performance.

Fantasy experiences are, of course, highly individual. Techniques that may help one person to experience serenity may frustrate another. Try out the self-guided experiences suggested here, make up your own, and select ones that are best for you. There are endless possibilities for fantasy journeys. The best approach is to work with whatever fantasy occurs to you at the moment. The ideas for a journey presented here are meant to be a springboard for variation of your own.

A fantasy will be more effective if you take a comfortable physical position, with eyes closed and attention focused on the inner experience. Get in touch with physical sensations, your pattern and rate of breathing, your heart beat, and pressure points of your body as it comes in contact with the chair and floor.

When you take a fantasy journey by yourself, it is important for you to read over the instructions several times so that you will be able to recall the over-all structure of the fantasy. *Then,* close your eyes and take your trip without concern for following the instructions in detail.

Instructions

Sit comfortably in a chair. Shut your eyes and chase your thoughts for a minute; go where your thoughts go.

Then, let the words go. Become aware of how you *feel*, here and now, not how you would like to feel.

Shift your awareness to your feet. Do not move them. Become aware of what they are doing.

Spend 20 to 30 seconds focusing progressively on different parts of your body. Relax each part in turn:

Relax each of your toes; the tops of your feet; the arch of each foot; the insteps, balls, and heels; your ankles, calves, knees, thighs, and buttocks. Become aware of how your body is contacting the chair in which you are sitting. Let go of your abdominal and chest muscles; relax your back. Release the tension in your shoulders, arms, elbows, forearms, wrists, hands, and each finger in turn; relax the muscles in your throat, lips, and cheeks. Wrinkle your nose; relax your eyelids and eyebrows (first one and then the other); relax the muscles in your forehead and top and back of your head. Relax your whole body.

Concentrate on your breathing: become aware of how you breathe. Allow yourself to inhale and exhale in your usual way. Become aware of the depth of your breathing. Are you expanding the lungs all the way? Or, are you breathing shallowly? Increase your depth of breathing. Now focus on the rate at which you are breathing. See if you can slow the rate down. When you breathe in, can you feel an inflow of energy that fills your entire body?

Now concentrate on the sounds in the room.
Focus on how you feel right now.
Slowly open your eyes.

Suggestions for Additional Experiential Vignettes

• Imagine yourself leaving the room. In your mind's eye go through the city and over the fields. Come to a meadow covered with fresh, new grass and flowers. Look out on the meadow and focus on what you see, hear, smell, and feel. Walk through the meadow. See the length and greenness of the grass; see the brilliance, and feel the warmth of the sunlight.

• For a more expansive feeling, visualize a mountain in the distance. Fantasize going to the country and slowly ascending a mountain. Walk through a forest. Climb to the top until at last you reach a height where you can see "forever." Experience your awareness.

• Focus on a memory of a beautiful place you have been to and enjoyed and would like to enjoy again. Be there; experience it.

• Imagine that you are floating on your back down a river. It may help to at first breathe deeply and feel yourself sinking. Visualize that you are coming out on a gentle river that is slowly winding its way through a beautiful forest. The sun is out and the rays feel warm on your skin. You pass trees and meadows of beautiful flowers. Smell the grass and flowers. Hear the birds. Look up in the blue sky; see the lazy tufts of clouds floating by. Leave the river and walk across the meadow. Enjoy the grass around your ankles. Come to a large tree. . . .

Fill in the rest of the trip—what do you see now? Where do you want to go from here?

Sally L. Lagerquist

Unit 1 Psychiatric Nursing

Introduction

The chief objective of this chapter is to highlight the most commonly observed disorders in the mental health field. The emphasis is on (1) main characteristics of each, (2) underlying basic concepts and general principles drawn from a psychodynamic and interpersonal theoretical framework, and (3) nursing approaches based on the therapeutic use of self as the cornerstone of a helping process.

I recognize that the categorization of psychiatric-emotional disorders can be complex and controversial. For purposes of clarity and simplicity, an attempt has been made here to capsulize many theoretical principles and component skills of the helping process that these disorders have in *common*.

The underlying organizational framework for this chapter is based on the concept of *anxiety* as a common denominator for the disorders—an umbrella under which most syndromes can be grouped. The disorders are presented in terms of general responses to anxiety: *moving away* (''flight'' response), *moving against* (''fight'' response), and *moving towards*.

In addition, a special section is included on chronic brain disorders; mental health of the aged, the child, and the adolescent; and current developments in treatment modalities, for example, crisis intervention, milieu therapy, behavior modification, activity therapy, group and family therapy, electroconvulsive therapy, and psychopharmacology.

This unit also includes definitions of frequently used and/or misunderstood terms in the mental field, as well as examples of the most common therapeutic and nontherapeutic nurse-patient responses.

Sally L. Lagerquist

Part A Organizational Framework

THE THERAPEUTIC NURSING PROCESS

A *therapeutic nursing process* involves an interaction between the nurse and patient in which the nurse offers a series of planned, goal-directed activities that are useful to a particular patient in relieving discomfort, promoting growth, and satisfying interpersonal relationships.

1. Characteristics of therapeutic nursing
A. Movement from a first contact through a final outcome
   1. Eight general phases occur in a typical unfolding of a natural process of problem solving
   2. The stages are not always in the same sequence
   3. Not all stages are present in a relationship
B. Phases *
   1. *Beginning* the relationship (goal: build trust)
   2. *Formulating* and clarifying a problem and concern (goal: clarify patient's statements)
   3. *Setting a contract* or working agreement (goal: decide on terms of the relationship)
   4. *Building* the relationship (goal: increase depth of relationship and degree of commitment)
   5. *Exploring* goals and solutions, gathering data, expressing feelings [goals: (a) maintain and enhance relationship (trust and safety), (b) explore blocks to goal, (c) expand self-awareness, and (d) learn skills necessary to reach goal]
   6. *Developing action plan* [goals: (a) clarify feelings, (b) settle on alternative choices or plans, and (c) practice new skills]
   7. *Working through* conflicts or disturbing feelings [goals: (a) crystallize earlier discussions into specific course and (b) work through unresolved feelings]
   8. *Ending* the relationship [goals: (a) evaluation of goal attainment and (b) leave taking]

*Lawrence M. Brammer, The HELPING RELATIONSHIP: PROCESS AND SKILLS, © 1973, p. 55. Reprinted by permission of Prentice-Hall, Inc., Englewood Cliffs, N.J.

2. Therapeutic nurse-patient interactions
A. Guidelines
   1. Demonstrate unconditional acceptance, interest, concern, and respect
   2. Make frequent contacts with the patient
   3. Encourage expression of feelings; focus on *feelings*
   4. Use open-ended questions; Ask "how," "what," "where," "who," and "when" questions; avoid "why" questions; avoid questions that can be answered by a yes or no response
   5. Point out reality; help the patient leave "inner world"
   6. Do not change the subject unless the patient is redundant or focusing on physical illness
   7. Develop trust—be consistent and congruent
   8. Focus on nonverbal communication
   9. Focus comments on concerns of patient (patient-centered) not self (social responses)
   10. Avoid verbalizing value judgments, giving personal opinions, or moralizing
   11. Be honest and direct
   12. Remember the psyche has a soma! Do not neglect appropriate physical symptoms
   13. Sometimes talk is not indicated
   14. Avoid false reassurances, clichés, and pat responses
   15. Use feedback or reflective listening
   16. A patient who complains needs attention
   17. Approach, sit, or walk with agitated patients; stay with the patient who is upset
   18. Offer support, security, and empathy, not sympathy
   19. Assist patients in arriving at their own decisions by demonstrating problem-solving or involving them in the process
   20. Set limits on behavior when patient is acting out unacceptable behavior that is self-destructive or harmful to others
   21. Give information at patient's level of understanding
B. Examples of **therapeutic** responses
   1. *Being silent*—Being able to sit in silence with a person can connote acceptance and acknowledgment that the person has the

right to silence (Dangers: the nurse may wrongly give the patient the impression that there is a lack of interest, or the nurse may discourage verbalization if acceptance of this behavior is prolonged.)

2. *Using nonverbal communication*—nodding head, moving closer to the patient, and leaning forward, for example; use as a way to encourage patient to speak

3. Give encouragement to continue with *open-ended leads*—nurse's responses: "Then what?" "Go on," or "For instance,"

4. *Accepting, acknowledging*—nurse's responses: "I hear your anger," or "I see that you are sitting in the corner."

5. *Commenting on nonverbal behavior* of patient—nurse's responses: "I notice that you are swinging your leg," "I see that you are tapping your foot," or "I notice that you are wetting your lips." Patient may respond with, "So what?" If she does, the nurse needs to reply why he commented, for example, "It is distracting," "I am giving the nonverbal behavior meaning," "Swinging your legs makes it difficult for me to concentrate on what you are saying," or "I think when people tap their feet it means they are impatient. Are you impatient?"

6. Encouraging patients to *notice with their senses* what is going on—nurse's response: "What did you see (or hear)?" or "What did you notice?"

7. Encouraging *recall and description* of details of a particular experience—nurse's response: "Give me an example," "Please describe the experience further," "Tell me more," or "What did you say then?"

8. *Giving feedback by reflecting, restating*
   Patient: I cried when he didn't come to see me.
   Nurse: You cried. You were expecting him to come and he didn't?

9. *Picking up on latent content* (what is implied)—Nurse's response: "You were disappointed. I think it may have hurt when he didn't come."

10. *Focusing, pinpointing*, asking "what" questions
    Patient: They didn't come.
    Nurse: Who are 'they'?
    Patient: (Rambling)
    Nurse: Tell it to me in a sentence or two.

What is your main point? What would you say is your main concern?

11. *Clarifying*—nurse's response: "What do you mean by 'they'?" "What caused this?" or "I didn't understand. Please say it again."

12. *Focusing on reality* by expressing doubt on "unreal" perceptions
    Patient: Run! There are giant ants flying around after us.
    Nurse: That is unusual. I don't see giant ants flying.

13. *Focusing on feelings*, encouraging patient to be aware of and describe personal feelings
    Patient: Worms are in my head.
    Nurse: That must be a frightening feeling. What did you feel at that time? Tell me about that feeling.

14. Helping patients to *sort and classify impressions, make speculations*, to *abstract* and to *generalize* by making connections, seeing common elements and similarities, making comparisons, and placing events in logical sequence—nurse's response: "What are the common elements in what you just told me?" "How is this similar to," "What happened just before?" or "What is the connection between this and."

15. *Pointing out discrepancies* between thoughts, feelings, and actions—Nurse's response: "You say you were feeling sad when she yelled at you; yet you laughed. Your feelings and actions do not seem to fit together."

16. *Seeking agreement* on how the issue is seen, *checking out* with the patient to see if the message sent is the same one that was received—nurse's response: "Let me restate what I heard you say," "Are you saying that," "Did I hear you correctly?" "Is this what you mean?" or "It seems that you were saying."

17. *Encouraging patient to consider alternatives*—nurse's response: "What else could you say?" or "Instead of hitting him, what else might you do?"

18. *Planning a course of action*—nurse's response: "Now that we have talked about your on-the-job activities and you have thought of several choices, which are you going to try out?" or "What would you do next time?"

19. *Summing up*—nurse's response: "Today we have talked about your feelings toward

your boss, how you express your anger, and about your fear of being rejected by your family."

20. *Encouraging patient to appraise and evaluate* the experience or outcome—nurse's response: "How did it turn out?" "What was it like?" "What was your part in it?" "What difference did it make?" or "How will this help you later?"

C. Examples of **non-therapeutic** responses
1. *Changing the subject, tangential response,* moves away from problem and/or focuses on incidental, superficial content
Patient: I hate you.
Nurse: Would you like to take your shower now?
Patient: I want to kill myself today.
Nurse: Isn't today the day your mother is supposed to come?
Suggested responses: (a) give open-ended lead (p. 15), (b) give feedback (p. 15), "I hear you saying today that you want to kill yourself," or (c) clarifying, "Tell me more about this feeling of wanting to kill yourself." (p. 15)

2. *Moralizing:* saying with approval or disapproval that the patient's behavior is good or bad, right or wrong; *arguing* with stated belief of patient; directly opposing the patient
Nurse: That's good. It's wrong to shoot yourself.
Patient: I have nothing to live for.
Nurse: You certainly do have a lot!"
Suggested response: similar to those in No. 1

3. *Agreeing with patient's autistic inventions*
Patient: The eggs are flying saucers.
Nurse: Yes, I see. Go on.
Suggested response: use clarifying response first, "I don't understand," and then depending on patient's response, use either *accepting, acknowledging* (p. 15); *focusing on reality* (p. 15), or *focusing on feeling* (p. 15)

4. *Agreeing with patient's negative view of self*
Patient: I have made a mess of my life.
Nurse: Yes, you have.
Suggested response: use clarifying response about "mess of my life"

5. *Complimenting, flattering*
Patient: I have made a mess of my life.

Nurse: How could you? You are such an attractive, intelligent, generous person.
Suggested response: same as that in No. 4

6. *Giving opinions* and *advice* concerning patient's life situation—examples of poor responses include: "In my opinion. . . ." "I think you should. . . ." or "Why not . . .?"

7. *Seeking agreement* from patient with nurse's personal opinion—examples of poor responses include: "I think . . . don't you?" or "Isn't that right?"

8. *Probing* and/or *offering premature solutions and interpretations;* jumping to conclusions
Patient: I can't find a job.
Nurse: You could go to an employment agency.
Patient: I'd rather not talk about it.
Nurse: What are you unconsciously doing when you say that?
What you really mean is.
Patient: I don't want to live alone.
Nurse: Are you afraid of starting to drink again?
Suggested response: use responses that seek clarification and elicit more data

9. *Changing patient's words* without prior validation
Patient: I am *not feeling well* today
Nurse: What makes you so *depressed?*

10. *Following vague content* as if understood or *using vague global* pronouns, adverbs, and adjectives
Patient: *People* are so *unfair.*
Nurse: I know what you mean.
Suggested response: clarify vague referents such as "people" and "unfair"
Patient: I feel sad.
Nurse: *Everyone feels that way* at one time or another.
Suggested response: "What are you sad about?"

11. *Questioning on different topics without waiting for a reply*
Patient: (Remaining silent)
Nurse: What makes you so silent? Are you angry? Would you like to be alone?

12. *Ignoring patient's questions or comments*
Patient: Am I crazy, nurse?
Nurse: (Walking away as if he did not hear her.)

13. *Closing off exploration* with questions that can be answered by yes or no
    Patient: I'll never get better.
    Nurse: Is something making you feel that way?
14. *Using trite clichés* or stereotyped expressions
    Patient: The doctor took away my weekend pass.
    Nurse: The doctor is only doing what's best for you. Doctor knows best. (Comment: also an example of moralizing.)
    Suggested response: Tell me what happened when the doctor took away your weekend pass.
15. *Overloading:* giving too much information at one time
    Nurse: Hello, I'm Ms. Brown. I'm a nurse here. I'll be here today, but I'm off tomorrow. Ms. Anderson will assign you another nurse tomorrow. This unit has five RNs and three LVNs and students from three nursing schools who will all be taking care of you at some time.
16. *Underloading;* not giving enough information so that meaning is not clear; withholding information
    Patient: What are visiting hours like here?
    Nurse: They are flexible and liberal
17. *Saying no without saying no*
    Patient: Can we go for a walk soon?
    Nurse: We'll see.
    Perhaps.
    Maybe.
    Later.
18. *Using double-bind communication;* sending conflicting messages that do not have "mutual fit," are incongruent.
    Nurse (continuing to stay and talk with the patient): It's time for you to rest.
19. *Protecting;* defending someone else while talking with patient; implying patient has no right to personal opinions and feelings
    Patient: This hospital is no good. No one cares here.
    Nurse: This is an excellent hospital. All the staff were chosen for their warmth and concern for patients.
    Suggested response: focus on feeling tone or clarifying information
20. *Asking "why" questions* implies that the person has immediate conscious awareness of the reasons for his feelings and behaviors—examples of this include: "Why don't you," "Why did you do that?" or "Why do you feel this way?"
    Suggested response: ask clarifying questions
21. *Coercion;* using the interaction between people to force someone to do *your* will, with the implication that if you don't "do it for my sake, I won't love you or stay with you."
    Patient: I refuse to talk with him.
    Nurse: *Do it for my sake,* before it's too late.
22. Focusing on *negative* feelings, thoughts, actions
    Patient: I can't sleep; I can't eat; I can't think; I can't do anything.
    Nurse: How long have you not been sleeping, eating, or thinking well?
    Suggested response: What *do* you do?
23. *Rejecting* patient's behavior or ideas
    Patient: Let's talk about incest.
    Nurse: Incest is a bad thing to talk about; I don't want to.
24. *Accusing, belittling*
    Patient: I've had to wait five minutes for you to change my dressing.
    Nurse: Don't be so demanding. Don't you see that I have several patients who need me?
25. *Evading a response* by asking a question in return
    Patient: I want to know your opinion, nurse. Am I crazy?
    Nurse: Do you think you are crazy?
    Suggested response: I don't know. What do you mean by crazy?
26. *Circumstantiality;* communicating in such a way that after many aside comments, details, and additions, the main point is finally made
    Patient: Will you go out on a date with me?
    Nurse: I work every evening. On my day off I go out of town usually. I have a steady boyfriend. Besides that, I am a nurse and you are a patient. Thank you for asking me, but no, I will not date you.
27. *Making assumptions* without checking them out

Patient: (Standing in the kitchen by the sink, peeling onions, with tears in her eyes)

Nurse: What's making you so sad?

Patient: I'm not sad. Peeling onions always make my eyes water.

28. *Giving false reassurance*

Patient: I'm scared.

Nurse: Don't worry; everything will be all right. There's nothing to be afraid of.

ANXIETY

Anxiety is a subjective warning of danger in which the specific nature of the danger is usually not known. It occurs when a person faces a new, unknown, or untried situation. It is a general concept underlying most disease states. In its milder form, anxiety can contribute to learning and is necessary for problem solving. In its severe form, anxiety can impede a patient's treatment and recovery.

It is essential that nurses recognize their own sources of anxiety and behavior in response to anxiety, as well as help patients recognize the manifestations of anxiety in themselves.

1. **Characteristics of anxiety**
A. Physiologic manifestations
    1. Increased heart rate and palpitations
    2. Increased rate and depth of respiration
    3. Increased urinary frequency and diarrhea
    4. Dry mouth
    5. Decreased appetite
    6. Cold sweat and pale appearance
    7. Increased menstrual flow
    8. Increased or decreased body temperature
    9. Increased or decreased blood pressure
    10. Pupils dilated
B. Behavioral manifestations
    1. Mild anxiety
        a. Increased perception (visual and auditory)
        b. Increased awareness of meanings and relationships
        c. Increased alertness (notice more)
        d. Can utilize problem-solving process
    2. Moderate anxiety
        a. Selective inattention (for example, may not hear someone talking)
        b. Decreased perceptual field
        c. Concentrates on relevant data; "tunnel vision"
    3. Severe anxiety
        a. Focus on many fragmented details

b. Not aware of total environment
c. Automatic behavior aimed at getting immediate relief instead of problem solving
d. Poor recall
e. Cannot see connections between details
f. Drastically reduced awareness
    4. Panic state of anxiety
        a. Increased speed of scatter; does not notice what goes on
        b. Increased distortion and exaggeration of details
        c. Feeling of terror
        d. Dissociation occurs (hallucinations, loss of reality, and little memory)
        e. Cannot cope with any problems; no self-control

2. **Concepts and principles of anxiety**
A. Causes of anxiety
    1. Threats to biologic well-being (food, drink, pain, and fever, for example)
    2. Threats to self-esteem
        a. Unmet wishes or expectations
        b. Unmet needs for prestige and status
        c. Inability to cope with environment
        d. Not utilizing own full potential
        e. Alienation
        f. Value conflicts
        g. Anticipated disapproval from a significant other
        h. Guilt
B. Reactions to anxiety
    1. Fight
        a. Aggression
        b. Hostility, derogation, belittling
        c. Anger
    2. Flight
        a. Withdrawal
        b. Depression
    3. Somatization (psychosomatic disorders)
    4. Learning, searching causes for anxiety, and identifying behavior

3. **Nursing approaches to anxiety**
A. Moderate to severe anxiety
    1. Provide motor outlet for tension energy, such as working at a simple, concrete task, walking, or crying
    2. Help patients *recognize* their anxieties by talking about how they are behaving and exploring their underlying feelings
    3. Help the patients *gain insight* into their anxieties by helping them to recognize how their behavior has been an expression of anxiety

and to recognize the threat that lies behind this anxiety

4. Help the patients *cope* with the threat behind their anxieties by reevaluating the threats and learning new ways of dealing with them

B. Panic state
   1. Give simple, clear, concise directions
   2. Avoid decision-making by patient
   3. Stay with the patient; walk
   4. Avoid touching
   5. Do not isolate patient
   6. Do not try to reason with patient as patient is irrational and cannot cooperate
   7. Allow patient to seek motor outlets
   8. Encourage activity that requires no thought

DEFENSE MECHANISMS

Defense mechanisms (ego defense mechanisms or mental mechanisms) consist of all the coping means used by individuals to seek relief from emotional conflict and ward off excessive anxiety.

1. Definitions*

blocking a disturbance in the rate of speech when a person's thoughts and speech are proceeding at an average rate but are very suddenly and completely interrupted, perhaps even in the middle of a sentence. The gap may last several seconds up to a minute. Blocking is often a part of the thought disorder found in schizophrenic reactions.

compensation making up for real or imagined handicap, limitation, or lack of gratification in one area of personality by overemphasis in another area to counter the effects of failure, frustration, and limitation; for example, the blind compensate by increased sensitivity of hearing; the unpopular student becomes an outstanding scholar; and small men compensate for short stature by demanding a great deal of attention and respect.

confabulating filling in gaps of memory by inventing what appear to be suitable memories as replacements. This symptom may occur in variety of organic psychoses but is most often seen in Korsakoff's syndrome (deterioration due to alcohol).

---

*From Kalkman, M.: Psychiatric nursing, ed. 3, New York, 1967, © McGraw-Hill Book Company, pp. 88-93.

conversion psychologic difficulties are translated into physical symptoms without conscious will or knowledge.

denial an intolerable thought, wish, need, or reality factor is disowned automatically.

displacement transferring the emotional component from one idea, object, or situation to another more acceptable one. Displacement occurs because these are painful or dangerous feelings that cannot be expressed toward the original object, for example, kicking the dog after a bad day at school or work.

dissociation splitting off or separation of different elements of the mind from each other. There can be separation of ideas, concepts, emotions, or experiences from the rest of the mind. Dissociated material is deeply repressed and becomes encapsulated and inaccessible to the rest of the mind. This usually occurs as a result of some very painful experience, for example, split of affect from idea in neurotic and schizophrenic.

fixation a state in which personality development is arrested in one or more aspects at a level short of maturity.

identification the wish to be like another person; situation in which qualities of another are unconsciously transferred to oneself; for example, boy identifies with his father and learns to become a man; a woman may fear she will die in childbirth because her mother did.

introjection incorporation into the personality, without assimilation, of emotionally charged impulses or objects: a quality or an attribute of another person is taken into and made part of self; for example, a girl in love introjects the personality of her lover into herself—his ideas become hers, his tastes and wishes are hers; this is also seen in severe depression following death of someone close—patient may assume many of deceased's characteristics.

projection attributes and transfers own feelings, attitudes, impulses, wishes, or thoughts to another person or object in the environment, especially when ideas or impulses are too painful to be acknowledged as belonging to oneself; for example, in hallucinations and delusions by alcoholics; or, "I flunked the course because the teacher doesn't know how to teach," and "I hate him" is reversed into "He hates me."

rationalization justification of behavior by formulating a logical, socially approved reason for past, present, or proposed behavior. Commonly used and may be conscious or unconscious with reason false or real.

reaction formation   going to the opposite extreme from what one wishes to do or is afraid one might do, for example, being overly concerned with cleanliness when one wishes to be messy or being an overly protective mother if fear own hostility to child.

regression   when individuals fail to solve a problem with the usual methods at their command, they may resort to modes of behavior that they have outgrown but that proved themselves successful at an earlier stage of development; retracing developmental steps; going back to earlier interests or modes of gratification.

repression   involuntary exclusion of painful and unacceptable thoughts and impulses from awareness. Forgetting these things solve the situation by not solving it.

sublimation   channeling a destructive or instinctual impulse that cannot be realized into a socially acceptable, practical, and less dangerous outlet, with some relation to the original impulse for emotional satisfaction to be obtained; for example, sublimation of sexual energy in other creative activities (art, music, or literature) or hostility and aggression into sports or business competition.

substitution   occurs when individuals cannot have what they wish and accept something else in its place for symbolic satisfaction, for example, pin-up pictures in absence of sexual object.

suppression   a deliberate process of blocking from the conscious mind thoughts and impulses that are undesirable, for example, "I don't want to talk about it," "Don't mention his name to me," or "I'll think about it some other time."

symbolism   sign language that stands for many related ideas and feelings, conscious and unconscious. Used extensively by children, primitive races, and psychotic patients. There is meaning attached to this sign language that makes it very important to the individual.

2. **Characteristics of defense mechanisms**
A. Defense mechanisms are utilized to some degree by everyone occasionally; they are normal processes by which the ego reestablishes equilibrium unless used to extreme degree, in which case they interfere with maintenance of self-integrity

B. Much overlapping
1. Same behavior can be explained by more than one mechanism
2. May be used in combination—isolation and repression
C. Common defense mechanisms compatible with mental well-being
1. Compensation
2. Compromise
3. Identification
4. Rationalization
5. Sublimation
6. Substitution
D. Typical defense mechanisms in
1. *Paranoid*—projection
2. *Dissociative states*—denial, repression
3. *Obsessive-compulsive*—displacement, reaction-formation, isolation, denial, repression
4. *Phobias*—displacement, rationalization, repression
5. *Conversion reactions*—symbolization, dissociation, repression, isolation, denial
6. *Depression*—displacement
7. *Manic-depressive*—reaction-formation, denial
8. *Schizophrenic*—symbolization, repression, dissociation, denial, fantasy
9. *Organic disorders*—regression
3. **Concepts and principles of defense mechanisms**
A. Unconscious process—they are used as a substitute for more effective problem-solving behavior
B. Main functions—increase *self-esteem*; decrease, inhibit, minimize, alleviate, avoid, or eliminate anxiety; maintain feelings of personal worth and adequacy and soften failures
C. Drawbacks—involve high degree of self-deception and reality distortion; may be maladaptive because they superficially eliminate or disguise conflicts, leaving conflicts unresolved but still influencing behavior
4. **Nursing approaches to defense mechanisms**
A. Accept defense mechanisms as normal
B. Discuss alternative coping mechanisms that may be more compatible with mental health
C. Look beyond the behavior to the need that is expressed by the use of the defense mechanism
D. Assist the patient to translate defensive thinking into nondefensive, direct thinking; a problem-solving approach to conflicts minimizes the need to use defense mechanisms

Part B   Disorders

DEPRESSION

The term depression is used to describe morbid sadness, dejection, or melancholy. Severe depression should be distinguished from grief, which is realistic and proportionate to what has been lost.

1. **Common characteristics of depression**
A. Physical—early morning awakening, insomnia at night, increased need for sleep during the day, constipation, anorexia, loss of sexual interest, psychomotor retardation, physical complaints
B. Psychologic—unable to remember, decreased concentration, slowing or blocking of thought, less interest and involvement with external world, feel worse in the morning or after any sleep, difficulty in enjoying activities, monotone voice, repetitive discussions
C. Emotional—loss of self-esteem, feelings of hopelessness and worthlessness, self-derogation, irritability, despair and futility (leading to suicidal thoughts), alienation, helplessness, powerless, anger may be denied
2. **Differentiation between reactive depression and endogenous depression**
A. Reactive depression
   1. Precipitating event—easy to identify, for example, death of a loved one
   2. Symptom cluster—precipitating event, difficulty getting to sleep at night, feeling worse as day progresses, and weight loss of less than 10 lb.
   3. Response to environment—responds to environmental stimuli.
B. Endogenous depression (internal factors)
   1. Precipitating event—precipitant may not be evident; history shows no clear-cut event
   2. Symptom cluster—retardation of thought and action, substantial weight loss (over 10 lb), feeling of depression came on gradually, feeling worse in morning but better as day progresses, and feelings of worthlessness
   3. Response to environment—does not respond to environmental stimuli
   4. Family history of depression

   5. May be biochemical disturbance
3. **Concepts and principles of depression**
A. Self-limiting—most depressions are self-limiting disturbances, making it important to look for a change in functioning and behavior
B. Theories as to cause of depression
   1. Aggression turned inward
   2. A response to separation or object loss
   3. Genetic and/or neurochemical basis
C. Need to distinguish between normal sadness or grief and depression, anxiety and depression, and schizophrenia and depression
D. Depression is manifested by a disturbance in *affect* (mood), *thought processes* and *content, behavior,* and *self-concept*
E. Normal concern and appropriate cheerfulness will help in reactive depression. This attitude makes the endogenous depressed person more depressed
4. **Nursing approaches to depression**
A. Promote sleep and food intake—take nursing measures to ensure the physical well-being of the patient
B. Encourage outlets for anger that may be underlying the depression; as patients become more verbal with their anger and recognize the origin and results of anger, help them resolve their feelings—allow patients to complain and be demanding in initial phases of depression
C. Encourage patients to assess their goals, unrealistic expectations, and perfectionistic tendencies—patients may need to change their goals or give up some goals that are incompatible with abilities and external situations
D. Provide nonintellectual activities—avoid chess and crossword puzzles, for example, as thinking capacity at this time tends to be circular
E. Discourage redundancy in speech and thought —Redirect focus from a monologue on painful recounts to an appraisal of more neutral or positive attributes and aspects of their situations
F. Postpone decision-making and resumption of duties by patients
   1. Allow more time than usual to complete activity (dressing, eating) or thought process and speech

2. Structure the environment for the patients to help them reestablish a schedule and routine

G. Protect patients from overstimulation and coercion

H. Assist patients to recapture what was lost through substitution of goals, sublimation, or giving up unrealistic goals—Reanchor patients' self-respect to other aspects of their existence; help them free themselves from dependency on one person or single event or idea

I. Focus on *today,* not the past or too far into the future

J. Provide steady company to diminish feelings of loneliness and alienation; build trust in a one-to-one relationship

K. Provide positive reinforcement for patients through exposure to activities in which the patients can experience a sense of success, achievement, and completion to build their self-esteem and self-confidence

L. Interact with the patients on a nonverbal level if that is their immediate mode of communicating; this will promote feelings of being recognized, accepted, and understood

M. Long-term goal: encourage interest in external surroundings, outside of self
1. Encourage purposeful activities
2. Let patients advance to activities at their own pace

N. Reassure patients that their present state is temporary and that they will be protected and helped

O. Indicate to patients that success is possible
1. Explore what steps patients have taken to achieve goals and suggest new or alternate ones
2. Set small, immediate goals
3. Recognize their efforts to mobilize themselves

P. Make the environment unchallenging and nonthreatening
1. Use a kind, firm attitude with warmth
2. See that patients have favorite foods, and respond to their other wishes and likes

MANIC-DEPRESSIVE PSYCHOSIS

Manic-depressive psychosis (also called affective psychosis and cyclothymic reactions) is a major emotional illness characterized by mood swings, alternating from depression to elation, with periods of relative normality between episodes. Some persons experience the manic and depressed phase cyclically; others have recurrent depression or recurrent mania. There is increasing evidence that a biochemical disturbance may exist.

1. **Characteristics of manic-depressive psychosis**
A. Mania and depression are opposite sides of the same coin
1. Both are disturbances of mood and self-esteem
2. Both have underlying aggression and hostility
3. Both are intense
4. Both are self-limited in duration

B. Depression—mild to severe psychomotor *retardation* of movement and speech; preoccupation with *suicide;* feelings of doom and self-degradation; *delusions* of guilt and unworthiness; concern about money and sin, *anorexia* with weight loss, *constipation,* and *insomnia;* may become mute, immobile, and *stuporous*

C. Acute manic reaction—escalating hypomania to irrational state; exhibitionistic and boisterous behavior and dress; rapid speech with rhyming, punning, and *flight of ideas* and *delusions* of grandeur; sarcastic and witty; much physical energy; demanding and attempting to control; does not attend to personal care, food, or sleep; increased sex activity; full of pranks; quarrelsome, haughty, and arrogant

D. Incidence—more prevalent in women 18 to 35 years of age.

E. Prognosis—good, but recurrence is common

2. **Concepts and principles relating to manic-depressive psychosis**
A. The psychodynamics of manic and depressive episodes are related to hostility and guilt

B. The struggle between the unconscious impulses and moral conscience produces feelings of *hostility, guilt,* and *anxiety*

C. To relieve the internal discomfort of these reactions, the person *projects* long-retained hostile feelings onto others or onto objects in the environment during manic phase; during the depressive phase, hostility and guilt are *introjected* toward self

D. Demands, irritability, sarcasm, profanity, destructiveness, and threats are signs of the projection of hostility; guilt is handled through persecutory delusions and accusations

E. Feelings of inferiority and fear of rejection are handled by being gay and amusing

F. Both phases, though appearing distinctly different, have the same objective: to gain attention, approval, and emotional support. These objectives and behaviors are unconsciously determined by the patient; this behavior may be either biochemically determined or may be a mixture of biochemical and unconscious determination

3. **Nursing approaches to manic-depressive psychosis**

A. Manic Phase
   1. Absorb with understanding and without reproach behaviors such as, talkativeness, provocativeness, criticism, sarcasm, dominance, profanity, and dramatic actions
      a. Allow, postpone, or partially fulfill demands and freedom of expression *within limits* of ordinary social rules, comfort, and safety to the patient and others
      b. Do not cut off manic stream of talk as this increases anxiety and the need for release of hostility
   2. Constructively utilize excessive energies with activities that do not call for concentration or follow-through
      a. Outdoor walks, gardening, putting, and ball tossing are therapeutic
      b. Exciting, disturbing, and highly competitive activities should be avoided
      c. Creative occupational therapy activities promote release of hostile impulses, as does creative writing
   3. Attend to patient's personal care
   4. Provide high-calorie beverages, finger foods within sight and reach.
   5. Prevent physical dangers stemming from exhaustion—promote rest, sleep, and intake of nourishment
   6. Reduce outside stimuli

B. Depressive phase
   1. Take routine suicide precautions
   2. Assist in daily decision making until patient regains self-confidence
   3. Prepare warm baths and hot beverages to aid sleep
   4. Give attention to physical needs for food and sleep and to hygiene needs
   5. Select mild exercise and diversionary activities instead of stimulating exercise and competitive games, as they may overtax physical and emotional endurance and lead to feelings of inadequacy and frustration.
   6. Slowly repeat simple, direct information
   7. Do not allow long periods of silence to develop
   8. Initiate frequent contacts; do not allow the patient to remain withdrawn
   9. Use a kind, understanding, but emotionally neutral, approach
   10. Allow dependency in severe depressive phase; since dependency is one of the underlying concerns with depressive patients, if nurses allow dependency to occur as an initial response, they must plan for resolution of the dependency toward them as an example for the patient's other dependent relationships

INVOLUTIONAL DEPRESSION

Involutional depression is a depressive episode that occurs during the menopausal, climacteric or involutional, period of life. (This is also called involutional melancholia or psychosis.)

1. **Characteristics of involutional depression**
A. Involutional depression occurs in women of menopausal age (40 to 55 years) and men (50 to 65 years)
B. *No* prior history of manic-depressive illness
C. Premorbid personality—meticulous, worrisome, rigid, and overconscientious
D. Onset—slow with increase in *hypochondriasis*, leading to *delusions* about body function, *pessimism*, irritability, and nihilistic thoughts
E. Main symptoms—*agitation*, restless activity, fear and apprehension, ideas of reference, *depression*, self-reproach and *guilt* over wrongdoing and sin, delusions of unworthiness
F. High suicide potential

2. **Concepts and principles relating to involutional depression**
A. The depression is a response to a real or fancied loss of loved ones, possessions, health and vigor, or sexual attractiveness
B. The loss results in anger; the anger is turned upon the self
C. It is a reactive psychosis in which the symptoms are exaggerated reactions to a change in life style and body function—physical limitations and social restrictions associated with aging process

3. **Nursing approaches to involutional depression**
A. Prevention of suicide is first priority

B. Respond to patients' need to be understood, helped, and supported when feeling alone and hopeless
C. Encourage interest in simple craft activity
D. Look after physical needs for food, sleep, and protection from self-destruction
E. Guide patient from repetitious complaints and self-accusations by encouraging patient to note normal and cheerful features of surrounding environment; avoid "persuading" patient out of self-accusatory ideas, as this may increase guilt and prolong depression
F. Be prepared to absorb hostile, clinging, demanding behavior

SUICIDE—A "CRY FOR HELP"

1. **Characteristics of suicide***
A. Verbal clues
   1. Direct: "I am going to shoot myself."
   2. Indirect: "It's more than I can bear."
   3. Coded: "This is the last time you'll see me."
B. Behavioral clues
   1. Direct—trial run with pills or razor, for example
   2. Indirect—buying a casket, giving away cherished belongings, and putting affairs in order
C. Situational
   1. Cancer—mutilative
   2. Surgery—fear
   3. Finances—economic pressures
   4. Failing grades—loss of self-esteem
   5. Family problems—alienation
D. Syndromes
   1. Dependent-dissatisfied—emotionally dependent but dislike the dependent state
   2. Depressed—detachment from life; feel life is a burden
   3. Disoriented—delusions or hallucinations, delirium tremens, chronic brain syndromes
   4. Willful-defiant—active need to direct and control environment and life situation, with low frustration tolerance and rigid set
E. Eight out of ten suicide attempts are warnings
F. Suicidal thoughts are self-limited
G. Suicidal tendencies are not inherited

---

*Copyright May 1965, the American Journal of Nursing Company. Reproduced with permission from the American Journal of Nursing Vol. 65, No. 5.

H. Suicide occurs in all races and socioeconomic groups
2. **Concepts and principles relating to suicide**
A. Perceived failure in relationships with others is the most common cause of attempted suicide
   1. The perception may not be accurate, but it is real to the person nevertheless
   2. Significant others need assistance in recognizing difference in perception of alienation between their viewpoint and the patient's
B. Most suicidal behaviors stem from a sense of isolation and from feelings of some intolerable emotion, with suicide as a means to interrupt an intolerable existence
C. One intolerable emotion is that of rejection, which may lead to suicide if not overcome by a feeling of acceptance
D. Suicide may be an act of revenge to elicit guilt and remorse. It may also be self-punishment to handle one's own guilt or to control fate
E. There is an element of extreme hostility in a suicidal act. Suicidal attempts are not only intended to be self-destructive but are also hostile impulses against significant others (the therapist, for example) in the patient's life
F. The key to suicide prevention is awareness of clues to potential suicide and knowledge of how to respond to the "cry for help"
G. Suicide prevention consists essentially of recognizing that the potential victim is balancing between wishes to live and wishes to die, then emphasizing the drive toward life and living
H. There is a strong life-urge in people
I. Often, the nonlethal suicide attempt is meant to communicate deeper suicidal intentions
J. Patients who experience suicidal impulses can gain a certain amount of control over these impulses through the support they gain from meaningful relationships with staff members
K. The period of recovery from depression may be more dangerous than the depression itself; during recovery, patients have more energy to act on their suicidal thoughts and feelings
3. **Nursing approaches to suicide**
A. Long-term goals
   1. Increase the patient's self-reliance
   2. Help the patient achieve more realistic and positive feelings of self-esteem, self-respect, acceptance by others, and sense of belonging
   3. Help the patient experience success, interrupt the failure pattern, and expand views about pleasure

B. Short-term goals
   1. Provide protection from self-destruction until patients are able to assume this responsibility themselves
   2. Allow outward and constructive expression of hostile and aggressive feelings
   3. Provide for physical needs
C. General approaches
   1. Observe patient closely at all times for verbal (direct, indirect, and coded) and behavioral clues (direct, indirect, situational, and syndromes) indicating the suicidal potential
   2. Emphasize protection against self-destruction rather than punishment
   3. Support the part of the patient that wants to live
   4. Reduce environmental hazards
   5. Elicit what is meaningful to the patient at the moment
   6. Avoid imposing your own feelings of reality on the patient
   7. Listen with empathy, but let patient know there are other alternatives to suicide
   8. Structure a plan for coping when next confronted with the need to commit suicide (for example, the patient could call someone, express feeling of anger outwardly, or ask for help)
   9. Demonstrate your concern for the patient as a person
   10. Provide the patient with an opportunity to be useful
   11. Reduce self-centeredness and brooding by planning diversional activities within the patient's capabilities
   12. Make all decisions for patients in severe depression
   13. Progressively, let the patient make simple decisions: what to drink, what to watch on television, etc.
   14. Initiate interactions with the patient, and gradually increase number of interactions with others
   15. Avoid extremes in your own mood when with the patient (especially exaggerated cheerfulness)
   16. Acknowledge suicidal threats with calmness and without reproach—do not ignore or minimize threats
   17. Help the patient to verbalize feelings, especially aggressive and hostile ones
   18. Reduce feelings of alienation by spending time with the patient
   19. Let the patient know that problems are not insoluble and that they can be solved with available help
   20. Do not point out signs of improvement until patient relates this
   21. Help patient to externalize anger in a socially acceptable way, both verbally and through activities

DYING

Too often the process of death has had such frightening aspects that people have suffered alone. Today there has been a vast change in attitudes; death and dying are no longer taboo topics. There is a growing realization that we need to accept death as a natural process. Elisabeth Kübler-Ross has written extensively on the process of dying, describing the stages of *denial, anger, bargaining, depression,* and *acceptance,* with implications for the helping person.

1. **Characteristics of dying**
A. Physical
   1. Observable deterioration of physical and mental capacities—patient is unable to fulfill physiologic needs, such as eating and elimination
   2. Circulatory collapse (blood pressure and pulse)
   3. Renal or hepatic failure
B. Psychosocial
   1. Fear of death is signaled by agitation, restlessness, and sleep disturbances at night
   2. Depression and withdrawal
   3. Introspectiveness and calm acceptance of the inevitable
   4. Anger, agitation, blaming
   5. Morbid self-pity with feelings of defeat and failure
2. **Concepts and principles relating to death and dying**
A. Patients may know or suspect that they are dying and may want to talk about it; often they look for someone to share their fears and the process of dying
B. Fear of death can be reduced by helping patients feel that they are not alone
C. The dying need the opportunity to live their final experiences to the fullest and in their own way

D. People who are dying remain more or less the same as they were during life; their approaches to death are consistent with their approaches to life
E. The need by dying patients to review their lives may be a purposeful attempt to reconcile themselves between what "was" and "what could have been"
F. Four tasks facing a dying person are (1) reviewing life, (2) coping with physical symptoms in the end-stage of life, (3) making a transition from known to unknown state, and (4) reacting to separation from loved ones
G. Three ways of facing death are (1) quiet acceptance with inner strength and peace of mind, (2) restlessness, impatience, anger, and hostility, and (3) depression, withdrawl, and fearfulness
H. Crying and tears are an important aspect of the grief process
I. There are many blocks to providing a helping relationship with the dying and bereaved
   1. Nurses' unwillingness to share the process of dying by minimizing their contacts and blocking out their own feelings
   2. Forgetting that a dying patient may be feeling lonely, abandoned, and afraid of dying
   3. Reacting with irritation and hostility to the patient's frequent calls
   4. Failure by the nurse to seek help and support from team members when feeling afraid, uneasy, and frustrated in caring for a dying patient
   5. Not allowing patient to talk about death and dying
   6. Nurses using technical language or social chit-chat as a defense against their own anxieties

3. Nursing approaches to death and dying
A. Provide care and comfort with relief from pain; do not isolate the patients
B. Allow the patients to express their feelings, fears, and concerns
   1. Avoid pat answers to questions seeking "why"
   2. Pick up on symbolic communication
C. Stay physically close
   1. Use touch
   2. Be available to form a consistent relationship
D. Be alert to cues when patient needs to be alone (disengagement process)
E. Reduce isolation and abandonment by assigning these patients to rooms in which it is less likely to occur and by allowing flexible visiting hours

F. Be aware of reactions and of the normal grief process
   1. Allow patients and their families to do the work of grief and mourning
   2. Allow crying
   3. Permit yourself to cry
G. Leave room for hope
H. Speak in audible tones, not whispers
I. Keep activities in room as near normal as possible
J. Explore your own feelings about death and dying with team members
K. Help patients to die with peace of mind by lending support and providing them an opportunity to express their anger, pain, and fears to someone who will accept them and not censor their verbalizations

GRIEF

Grief is a typical reaction to the loss of a source of psychologic gratification. It is a syndrome with somatic and psychologic symptoms that diminish when grief is resolved. Grief processes have been extensively described by Erich Lindemann and George Engle.*

1. Characteristic stages of grief responses
A. Shock and disbelief
   1. Denial of reality ("No, it can't be.")
   2. Stunned, numb feeling
   3. Feelings of loss, helplessness, impotence
   4. Intellectual acceptance
B. Developing awareness
   1. Anguish about loss
      a. somatic distress
      b. feelings of emptiness
   2. Anger and hostility toward person or circumstances held to be responsible
   3. Guilt feelings—may lead to self-destructive actions
   4. Tears (inwardly, alone, and inability to cry)
C. Restitution
   1. Funeral rituals are an aid to grief resolution by emphasizing the reality of death
   2. Expression and sharing of feelings by gathered family and friends are a source of acknowledgment of grief and support for the bereaved

---

*Engle, G.: Grief and grieving, Am J Nurs **9**(64):93-98, September 1964.

D. Resolving the loss
1. Increase dependency on others as an attempt to deal with painful void
2. More aware of own bodily sensations—may be identical with symptoms of the deceased
3. Complete preoccupation with thoughts and memories of the dead person

E. Idealization
1. All hostile and negative feelings about the dead are repressed
2. Mourner may assume qualities and attributes of the dead
3. Gradual lessening of preoccupation with the dead; reinvesting in others

F. Outcome (takes one year or more)—can remember comfortably and realistically both pleasurable and disappointing aspects of the lost relationship

2. Concepts and principles relating to grief
A. The cause of grief is reaction to loss (real or imaginary, actual or pending)
B. The symptomatology and course is predictable and observable
C. The "healing" process can be interrupted
D. Grief is universal
E. Grief is a self-limiting process
F. Grief responses may vary in degree and kind (for example, absence of grief, delayed grief, and unresolved grief)
G. People go through stages similar to stages of death described by Elisabeth Kübler-Ross
H. Many factors influence "successful" outcome of grieving process
1. The more dependent the person on the lost relationship, the greater the difficulty in resolving the loss
2. A child has less capability to resolve the loss
3. A person with few meaningful relationships has greater difficulty
4. The more losses the person has had in the past, the more affected that person will be, as losses tend to be cumulative
5. The more sudden the loss, the greater the difficulty in resolving the loss
6. The more ambivalence (love-hate feelings, with guilt) there was toward the dead, the more difficult the resolution
7. A loss of a child is harder to resolve than the loss of an older person

3. Nursing approaches to grief
A. Apply crisis theory and interventions (see crises section)

B. Demonstrate respect for cultural, religious, and social mourning customs
C. Utilize knowledge of the stages of grief to anticipate reactions and facilitate the grief process
1. Anticipate and permit expression of different manifestations of shock, disbelief, and denial
   a. News of impending death is best communicated to a family group (rather than an individual) in a private setting
   b. Let mourners see the dead/dying to help them accept reality
2. Accept anger and rage as a common response to coping with guilt and helplessness
   a. Be aware of potential suicide by the bereaved
   b. Permit crying
3. Promote hospital policy that allows gathering of friends and family in a private setting
4. Allow dependency on staff while patient is attempting to resolve the loss
   a. Respond to somatic complaints
   b. Permit reminiscence
5. Begin to encourage new interests and social relations with others by the end of the idealization stage
6. Encourage mourner to relate accounts connected with the lost relationship that reflect positive and negative feelings and remembrances

SCHIZOPHRENIA

Schizophrenia is a group of interrelated symptoms with a number of common features involving disorders of *mood, thought content, feeling, perception,* and *behavior.* The term means "splitting of the mind," alluding to the discrepancy between content of thought processes and the emotional expression; this should *not* be confused with "multiple personality" (dissociative neurotic reaction).

Half of the patients in mental hospitals are diagnosed as schizophrenics; many more live in the community. The onset of symptoms for this disorder generally occurs between 15 to 27 years of age. Causes, psychodynamics, and psychopathology are still a matter of controversy.

1. Ten common subtypes of schizophrenia (without clear-cut differentiation)
simple type insidious disinvolvement with environment; apathetic, indifferent to others.
hebephrenic disordered thinking ("word salad"),

inappropriate affect, regressive behavior, incoherent speech, preoccupied and withdrawn.

catatonic (stupor and excitement phases) disorder of muscle tension, with rigidity, waxy flexibility, posturing, mutism, violent rage outbursts, and frenzied activity.

paranoid disturbed perceptions leading to disturbance in thought content of persecutory, grandiose, or hostile nature; projection is key mechanism, with religion a common preoccupation.

acute undifferentiated a sudden onset, brief confusion, excitement, depression, or fear, with ideas of reference.

latent type clear symptoms of schizophrenia, with no history; also called "borderline."

residual continued difficulty in thinking, mood, perception, and behavior after schizophrenic episode.

schizoaffective manic-depressive elements

childhood symptoms before puberty, characterized by autism, withdrawal, and failure to develop separate ego identity from mother.

chronic undifferentiated unclassifiable schizophreniclike disturbance with mixed symptoms.

2. Characteristics of schizophrenia
A. Eugene Bleuler described four classic and primary symptoms as the "four A's"
   1. Associative looseness—impairment of logical thought progression, resulting in confused, bizarre, and abrupt thinking
      a. neologisms—making up new words or condensing words into one
   2. Affect—exaggerated, apathetic, blunt, flat, inappropriate, inconsistent
   3. Ambivalence—simultaneously conflicting feelings or attitudes toward person or object
      a. Stormy outbursts
      b. Poor, weak interpersonal relations
   4. Autism—withdrawal from external world; preoccupation with fantasies and idiosyncratic thoughts
      a. Delusions—false, fixed belief, not corrected by logic; a defense against intolerable feeling. The two most common delusions are
         (1) Delusions of grandeur—conviction in a belief related to being famous, important, or wealthy
         (2) Delusions of persecution—belief that thoughts, moods, or actions are controlled or influenced by strange

forces or others
      b. Hallucinations—false sensory impressions without observable external stimuli
         (1) Auditory—affecting hearing (hears voices)
         (2) Visual—affecting vision (sees snakes)
         (3) Tactile—affecting touch (feels electric charges in body)
         (4) Olfactory—affecting smell (smells rotting flesh)
         (5) Gustatory—affecting taste (food tastes like poison)
      c. Ideas of reference—patients interpret cues in the environment as having reference to them. Ideas symbolize guilt, insecurity, and alienation; may become delusions, if severe
      d. Depersonalization—feelings of strangeness and unreality about self or environment, or both; difficulty in differentiating boundaries of self from environment
B. Negativism
C. Catatonic stupor—marked decrease in involvement with environment and in spontaneous movements
D. Catatonic excitement—purposeless and stereotyped motor behavior
E. Regression—extreme withdrawal and social isolation

3. Concepts and principles relating to schizophrenia
A. General
   1. Symbolic language used expresses schizophrenic's life, pain, and progress toward health; all symbols used have meaning
   2. Physical care provides media for relationship; nurturance may be initial focus
   3. Consistency, reliability, and empathic understanding build trust
   4. Denial, regression, and projection are key defense mechanisms
   5. Felt anxiety gives rise to distorted thinking
   6. Attempts to engage in verbal communication may result in tension, apprehensiveness, and defensiveness
   7. Patient rejects real world of painful experiences and creates fantasy world through illness
B. Withdrawal
   1. Withdrawal from and resistance to forming

relationships are attempts to reduce anxiety related to:

    a. Loss of ability to experience satisfying human relationships

    b. Fear of rejection

    c. Lack of self-confidence

    d. Protection and restraint against potential destructiveness of hostile impulses (toward self and others)

2. Ambivalence results from need for approaching a relationship and avoidance of it

3. The patient cannot tolerate swift emotional or physical closeness

4. The patient needs more time than usual to establish a relationship; time to test sincerity and interest of nurse

5. Avoidance of patient by others will reinforce withdrawal

C. Hallucinations

1. It is possible to replace hallucinations with satisfying interactions

2. The patient can relearn to focus attention on real things and people

3. Hallucinations originate during extreme emotional stress when the patient is unable to cope

4. Hallucinations are very real to the patient

5. The patient will react as the situation is perceived, regardless of reality or consensus

6. Concrete experiences, not argument or confrontation, will correct sensory distortion

7. Hallucinations are a substitute for human relations

8. Purposes served by or expressed in falsification of reality:

    a. Problem in inner life

    b. Criticism, censure, self-punishment

    c. Promotion of self-esteem

    d. Satisfaction of instinctual strivings

    e. Projection of unacceptable unconscious content in disguised form

9. Perceptions *not* as *totally* disturbed as they seem

10. Patients attempt to restructure reality through hallucinations to protect remaining ego integrity

11. Hallucinations may result from a variety of psychologic and biologic conditions (extreme fatigue, drugs, pyrexia, and organic brain disease, for example)

12. Hallucinating patients need to feel free to describe their perceptions if they are to be understood by the nurse

4. **Nursing approaches to schizophrenia**

A. General

1. Provide distance as patients need to feel safe and to observe nurses for sources of threat or promise of security

2. Anticipate and accept negativism

3. Set climate for free expression of feelings in whatever mode, without fear of retaliation, ridicule, or rejection

4. Set short-range goals, realistic to patients levels of functioning

5. Seek patients out in their own fantasy worlds

6. Help patients to tolerate nurses' presence and to learn to trust the nurses enough to move out of isolation and share painful and often unacceptable (to the patients) feelings and thoughts

7. Try to understand meaning of symbolic language; help patients to communicate less symbolically

8. Use nonverbal level of communication to demonstrate concern, caring, and warmth, as patients often distrust words

9. Avoid joking, abstract terms, and figures of speech when patient's thinking is literal

B. Withdrawn behavior

1. Seek patients out at every chance and establish some bond

    a. Stay with them, in silence

    b. Initiate talk when they are ready

    c. Draw out, but do not demand, response

2. Use simple language, specific words

3. Use an object or activity as media for relationship; initiate activity

4. Focus on everyday experiences

5. Delay decision-making

6. Accept one-sided conversation, with silence from the patients

7. Accept the patients' outward attempts at response and inappropriate social behavior without remarks or disdain; teach the patients social skills

8. Avoid making demands of the patients or exposing the patients to failure

9. Do *not* avoid the patients

10. Protect these patients from aggressive patients and from impulsive attacks on themselves or others

11. Attend to nutrition, elimination, exercise, hygiene, and signs of physical illness

C. Hallucinations
  1. Provide a structured environment with routine activities
  2. Protect the patients against injury to themselves and others resulting from "voices"
  3. Short, frequent contacts initially, increasing social interaction gradually (one person to small groups)
  4. Respond to anything real the patients say, for example, with acknowledgment or reflection
  5. Ask the patients to describe experiences as hallucinations occur
  6. Distract the patients' attention to something real when they hallucinate
  7. Avoid direct confrontation that voices are coming from patients themselves
  8. Clarify who "they" are
     a. Use personal pronouns, avoiding universal and global pronouns
     b. Nurse's own language needs to be clear and unambivalent
  9. Use real objects to keep patients' interest (painting or crafts, for example)
  10. Encourage consensual validation

PARANOID PSYCHOSES

Paranoid psychoses is a disorder with a concrete and pervasive delusional system, usually persecutory. Projection is a chief defense mechanism of this disorder.

1. **Characteristics of paranoid psychoses**
A. Chronically suspicious, distrustful (thinks "People are out to get me.")
B. Distant, but not withdrawn
C. Poor insight; blame others
D. Misinterpret and distort reality
E. Difficulty in admitting own errors and take pride in intelligence and at being correct
F. Maintain false belief despite evidence of proof (may refuse food and medicine and insist they are poisoned)
G. Literal thinking
H. Dominating and provocative
I. Hypercritical and intolerant of others; hostile and quarrelsome
J. Very sensitive in perceiving minor injustices, errors, and contradictions
K. Evasive
2. **Concepts and principles relating to paranoid psychoses**

A. Delusions are attempts to cope with stresses and problems
B. May be a means of allegorical or symbolic communication and a testing of others for their trustworthiness
C. Interactions with others and activities interrupt delusional thinking
D. To establish a rational therapeutic relationship, gross distortions, misorientation, misinterpretation, and misidentification need to be overcome
E. Delusional patients have extreme need to maintain self-esteem
F. False beliefs cannot be changed without first changing experiences
G. A delusion is held because it performs a function
H. When patients who are experiencing delusions become at ease and comfortable with people, delusions will not be needed
I. Delusions are misjudgments of reality based on
  1. Denial followed by
  2. Projection and
  3. Rationalization
J. There is a kernel of truth in delusions
K. Behind the anger and suspicion in a paranoid, there is a lonely, terrified person feeling vulnerable due to feelings of inadequacy
3. **Nursing approaches to paranoid psychoses**
A. Help patients learn to trust *themselves;* help them develop self-confidence and ego assets
B. Help patients *trust others*
  1. Be consistent and honest at all times
  2. Do not whisper or act secretive or laugh with others in these patients' presence when they cannot hear
  3. Do not mix medicines with food
  4. Keep promises
  5. Let patients know ahead of time what they can expect from others
  6. Give reasons and careful, complete, and repetitive explanations
  7. Ask permission to contact others
  8. Consult patients first about all decisions concerning them
C. Help these patients *test reality*
  1. Present and repeat reality of the situation
  2. Do not confirm or approve distortions
  3. Help patients accept responsibility for their own behavior rather than project
  4. Divert patients from delusions to reality-centered focus
  5. Let them know when behavior does not seem appropriate

6. Assume nothing and leave no room for assumptions
7. Structure time and activities to limit delusional thought behavior
8. Set limit for *not* discussing delusional content
9. Look for underlying needs expressed in delusional content
D. Provide outlets for anger and aggressive drives
   1. Listen matter-of-factly to angry outbursts
   2. Accept rebuffs and abusive talk as symptoms
   3. Do not argue, disagree, or debate
   4. Allow expression of negative feelings without fear of punishment
E. Provide *successful group experience*
   1. Avoid competitive sports involving close physical contact
   2. Give recognition to skills and work well done
   3. Utilize managerial talents
   4. Respect the intellect of these patients and engage them in activities with others requiring intellect (chess, puzzles, and scrabble, for example)
F. Limit physical contact

PERSONALITY DISORDERS

A personality disorder, also referred to as *character disorders* or *antisocial, sociopathic,* or *psychopathic personalities,* is a syndrome in which the person's inner difficulties are revealed by a pattern of living that seeks immediate gratification of impulses and instinctual needs without regard for society's laws, mores, and customs and without censorship of personal conscience.

1. **Characteristics of personality disorders**
A. Disorder of *behavior* rather than *feelings*
B. Usually violate laws, mores, and customs
C. Seek immediate gratification of impulses and instinctual needs without regard for society's rules
D. Intolerance of frustration
E. Do not appear to profit from experience; repeat same punishable or antisocial behavior
F. Poor interpersonal relationships, although they are usually very charming, bright, and intelligent
G. Exhibit poor judgment; may have intellectual, but not emotional, insight to guide judgments
H. May have a history of drug abuse and/or habituation
I. Use manipulative behavior patterns in treatment setting
   1. Demanding and controlling

2. Pressuring, coercing
3. Violate rules, routines, procedures
4. Request special privileges
5. Betray confidences and lie
6. Ingratiating
7. Threatening
8. Monopolize conversation

2. **Concepts and principles relating to personality disorders**
A. One defense against severe neuroses or psychoses is "acting up" or dealing with distressful feeling or issues through action
B. Faulty or arrested emotional development in the preoedipal period has interfered with development of adequate social control or superego
C. Since there is a malfunctioning superego, there is little internal demand and therefore no tension between ego and superego to evoke guilt feelings.
D. The defect is not intellectual; patients show a lack of moral responsibilities, an inability to control emotions and impulses and are deficient in normal feeling responses
E. Pleasure principle is dominant
F. The initial stage of treatment is most crucial; the treatment situation is very threatening because it mobilizes their anxiety, and they end treatment abruptly
   1. The key underlying emotion is fear of closeness, with threat of exploitation, control, and abandonment

3. **Nursing approaches to personality disorders**
A. Set fair, firm, consistent limits and follow through on consequences of behavior; let the patients know in explicit terms what they can expect from the staff and what the unit's regulations are, as well as the consequences for violations
B. Avoid the pitfall of staff being played one against the other by a particular patient; the staff should present a unified approach
C. Use group therapy as a means of peer control and multiple feedback about behavior
D. Encourage expression of feelings as an alternative to acting up
E. Change the focus when patients persist in raising inappropriate subjects (e.g., personal life of nurse)
F. Nurses should control their own feelings of anger and defensiveness aroused by any patient's manipulative behavior
G. Aid the patients in realizing and accepting re-

sponsibility for their own actions and social responsibility to others

ADDICTION

Addiction is a state of chronic or recurrent intoxication from the use of a drug and is characterized by *habituation* (need to take the drug), *tolerance* (requires increase in dose to obtain desired effect), and *physical dependency* (withdrawal symptoms occur when abstain).

Only in recent years have alcoholism and drug addiction been viewed as an illness rather than a moral delinquency or criminal behavior. Both are very complex and little understood conditions that have physiologic, psychologic, and social aspects to their causality, dynamics, symptoms, and treatment, where personality disorder has a major part.

Physiologic aspects—current unproven theories include "allergic" reaction to alcohol, disturbance in metabolism, genetic susceptibility to addiction, and hypofunction of adrenal cortex. There are *organic effects* of chronic excessive use.

Psychologic aspects—disrupted parent-child relationship and family dynamics; deleterious effect on ego-function.

Social and cultural aspects—local customs and attitudes vary about what is excessive.

ALCOHOL ADDICTION

Alcohol addiction is a chronic disorder in which the individual is unable, for physical or psychologic reasons, or both, to refrain from frequent consumption of alcohol in quantities that produce intoxication and disrupt health and ability to perform daily functions.

1. **Characteristics of alcohol addiction**
A. Vicious cycle—(1) low tolerance for coping with frustration, tension, guilt, resentment, (2) alcohol for relief, (3) new problems created by drinking, (4) new anxieties, and (5) more drinking
B. Withdrawal symptoms—tremors, diaphoresis, nausea, vomiting, anorexia, restlessness, hallucinations, convulsions, and delirium tremens
C. Complications of Alcoholism
   1. Delirium tremens (DTs)—result of nutritional deficiencies and toxins; requires sedation and constant watchfulness against unintentional suicide and convulsions
      a. Extreme agitation
      b. Fear
      c. Auditory and visual hallucination
      d. Disorientation
      e. Persecutory delusions
      f. Tremor in hands, tongue, and face
      g. Fever and sweats
      h. Leukocytosis
      i. Tachycardia
   2. Korsakoff's syndrome—degenerative neuritis
      a. Impaired thoughts
      b. Confusion
      c. Loss of sense of time and place
      d. Use of confabulation to fill in memory gaps
   3. Wernicke's syndrome
      a. Disturbed vision
      b. Memory loss
      c. Confusion
      d. Mind wandering
      e. Stupor and coma
   4. *Polyneuropathy*—sensory and motor nerve endings are involved, causing pain, itching, and loss of limb control
   5. Others—*gastritis*, esophageal varices, cirrhosis, pancreatitis, diabetes, pneumonia
D. Treatment approaches are multifaceted
   1. Medical
      a. Polyvitamin therapy (especially vitamin B)
      b. Tranquilizers
      c. Diet (high protein, high carbohydrate)
      d. Maintenance of fluid and electrolytes
   2. Alcoholics Anonymous (AA)—a self-help group of addicted drinkers who confront, instruct, and support fellow drinkers in their efforts to stay sober one day at a time through fellowship and acceptance
   3. Alanon—support group for *family* of the alcoholic
   4. Antabuse—drug that produces intense headache, severe flushing, extreme nausea, vomiting, palpitations, hypotension, dyspnea, and blurred vision when alcohol is consumed while patient is taking this drug.
   5. Aversion therapy—patients are subjected to revulsion-producing or pain-inducing stimuli at the same time they take a drink, to establish alcohol-rejection behavior
   6. Group psychotherapy—the goals of group psychotherapy are for the patient to give up alcohol as a tension reliever, identify cause of stress, build different means for coping with stress, and accept drinking as a serious symptom

2. Concepts and principles relating to alcohol addiction

A. Alcohol affects cerebral cortical functions
   1. Memory
   2. Judgment
   3. Reasoning
B. Alcohol is a depressant
   1. Relaxes the individual
   2. Lessens use of repression of unconscious conflict
   3. Releases inhibitions, hostility, and primitive drives
C. Drinking represents a tension-reducing device and a relief from feelings of insecurity
   1. Strength of drinking habit equals degree of anxiety and frustration intolerance
D. Alcoholism is a symptom rather than a disease
E. The spouse of the alcoholic often unconsciously contributes to the drinking behavior because of own emotional needs
F. Underlying fear and anxiety, associated with inner conflict, motivate the alcoholic to drink
G. Alcoholics can never be cured to drink normally; cure is to be a "sober alcoholic," with total abstinence

3. Nursing approaches to alcohol addiction

A. DTs
   1. Gastric lavage to remove alcohol
   2. Bed rest
   3. Sedation and replacement of fluids, carbohydrates, and vitamins C and B complex
   4. Constant supervision and reassurance about fears and hallucinations
   5. Well-lit room to reduce illusions
B. Acute intoxication
   1. IV glucose in saline, with vitamins C and B
   2. Tranquilizers to control motor excitement, nausea, vomiting, and anxiety
   3. Watch for convulsion
C. Recovery-rehabilitation: encourage participation in ward activities; avoid sympathy when patients tend to rationalize their behavior and seek special privileges—use acceptance and a nonjudgmental consistent, firm, but kind, approach; avoid scorn, contempt, moralizing, and advice-giving or punitive and rejecting behaviors, as they may reinforce feelings of worthlessness, self-contempt, hopelessness, and low self-esteem
D. Refer patients from emergency room to community resources for follow-up treatment with social, economic, and psychologic problems to reduce "revolving door" situation in which patients come in, are treated, go out, and come in again the next night

DRUG ADDICTION

Drug addiction is an overpowering desire or need to continue taking a natural or synthetic drug having habit-forming properties, producing tolerance and need to increase dose. Psychologic and sometimes physical dependency results.

1. Characteristics of drug addiction

A. Include both sexes and all levels of education, social, and economic status
B. Effects
   1. Contentment-inducing
   2. Hallucinogenic
   3. Tension-reducing
C. Patients may resort to illegal means to obtain money for ever-increasing drug consumption or to obtain the drug itself
D. Overdose (OD) may result when purity of drug is altered or when after a period of abstinence, individual goes back to former high dose.
E. Commonly abused drugs
   1. Sedatives (barbiturates)—may result in poor concentration, irritability, mood swings, slurred speech, tremor, staggering gait, suicide
   2. Stimulants (amphetamines)—may result in loud, irritable behavior; tremulousness; persecutory delusions
   3. Tranquilizers—prolonged use may lead to dependency; causes same signs as barbiturates
   4. Hallucinogens (LSD, marijuana, STP, peyote)—produce euphoria, relaxation, perceptual impairment, feelings of omnipotence, "bad trip," "flashbacks," suicide
   5. Narcotics (heroin, morphine, demerol)—used by "snorting," skin-popping," and "main-lining"; may lead to abscesses and hepatitis
F. Withdrawal syndrome (narcotics)—begins within 12 hours of last dose, peaks in 24 to 36 hours, subsides in 72 hours, and disappears in 5 to 6 days
   1. Pupils dilate
   2. Muscles twitch and tremor
   3. Goose flesh
   4. Lacrimation
   5. Rhinorrhea
   6. Sneezing

7. Profuse sweating
8. May lead to fever
9. Vomiting
10. Dehydration
11. Abdominal distress
12. Rapid weight loss

G. Differences between alcoholism and drug addiction
   1. Narcotics obtained by illegal means, making it a legal and criminal problem as well as a medical and social problem
   2. Narcotics inhibit aggression, whereas alcohol releases it
   3. As long as they are on large enough doses to avoid withdrawal symptoms, drug addicts are comfortable and function well, whereas chronically intoxicated alcoholics cannot function normally

2. Concepts and principles relating to drug addiction
A. Direct physiologic effects of long-term narcotic addiction are much less than those in chronic alcohol addiction
B. Three interacting key factors give rise to opiate addiction—psychopathology of the individual; frustrating environment; and availability of powerful, addicting, and temporarily satisfying drug
C. According to conditioning principles, drug dependency proceeds in several phases
   1. Use of opiates for relief from daily tensions and discomforts or anticipated withdrawal symptoms
   2. Habit is reinforced with each relief by drug use
   3. Development of dependency—opiate has less and less efficiency in reducing tensions
   4. Dependency is further reinforced as addict fails to maintain adequate drug intake—increase in frequency and duration of periods of tension and discomfort

3. Nursing approaches to drug addiction
A. Generally the same as those used in treating antisocial personality and alcoholism
B. Group therapy is best for peer pressure, support, and identification
C. Treatment
   1. Detoxification (or dechemicalization)
   2. Withdrawal—may be gradual or abrupt ("cold turkey")
   3. Methadone—patient must have been an addict at least two years and have failed at other methods of withdrawal before admission to program of readdiction by methadone
      a. Characteristics
         (1) Synthetic
         (2) Appeases desire for opiates without producing euphoria of narcotics
         (3) Given by mouth
         (4) Distributed under federal control (Narcotic Addict Rehabilitation Act)
         (5) Given with urinary surveillance
      b. Advantages
         (1) Prevents opiate withdrawal reaction
         (2) Tolerance not built up
         (3) Patients remain out of prison
         (4) Lessens felt need for heroin or morphine
   4. Referral to halfway houses and group living (Synanon or Daytop, for example)
   5. Employment as therapy (work training)
D. Expand patient's ranges of interest to relieve characteristic boredom and stimulus hunger
   1. Provide structured environment and planned routine
   2. Provide educational therapy (academic and vocational)
   3. Arrange activities to include current events discussion groups, lectures, drama, music, and art appreciation
E. Achieve role of stabilizer and supportive authoritative figure; this can be achieved through frequent, regular contacts with the same therapist

NEUROTIC DISORDERS

A neurotic or psychoneurotic disorder is a mild to moderately severe functional disorder of personality in which repressed inner conflicts between drives and fears manifest themselves in behavior patterns, including anxiety reaction, phobias, obsessive-compulsive reaction, dissociative hysteria, conversion reactions, hypochondria, and neurasthenia.

1. Characteristics of neurotic disorders
A. Use neurotic behavior to avoid tense situations
B. Have heightened suggestibility, as in conversion reactions
C. Are prone to minor physical complaints, for example, fatigue, headaches, and indigestion, and are reluctant to admit recovery from physical illnesses
D. Have attitude of martyrdom

E. Often feel helpless, insecure, inferior, inadequate.

F. Use repression, displacement, and symbolism as key defense mechanisms

2. Concepts and principles for specific neurotic reaction patterns

A. Anxiety
1. "Free-floating," unknown fears
2. Suffer from guilt feelings, unknown cause
3. Feelings of impending doom
4. Disturbed emotional feeling: worry and apprehension continuously present

B. Phobias
1. Irrational, abnormal fears, for example, acrophobia, hydrophobia, claustrophobia, and agoraphobia
2. Anxiety is displaced from original to symbolic source

C. Obsessive-compulsive
1. Obsessive—persistent, irrational *idea,* for example, death, murder, or suicide
2. Compulsive—bizarre, incomprehensible *actions*
3. Cannot be banished by will
4. Comes into consciousness inappropriately; patients themselves do not understand the irrational idea or action
5. Behavior can be almost disabling
6. Usually a *symbolic,* indirect way of resolving anxiety or repressed desire

D. Dissociative reactions—extreme *repression* of painful reality
1. Amnesia—loss of memory for names, addresses, and past personal experience
2. Fugue—physical flight
3. Multiple personality
   a. Two or more distinct personalities develop that alternate into consciousness
   b. Conflicting motives exist at same time; satisfied only by *repressing* consciousness of one set while gratifying another

E. Hysteria-conversion reaction
1. Emotional distress converted to body disturbance, for example, paralysis or blindness
2. Involves no actual biologic, cellular, or structural changes
3. Symptoms are result of an *unconscious* process
4. *Not* deliberate faking (malingering)
5. Symptoms may or usually disappear under hypnosis

F. Hypochondria
1. Overawareness of body activities and concern with body functions
2. Enjoyment gained from recounting past illnesses and operations in great detail
3. Eager to try quack cure-alls; read all medical literature
4. History of numerous medical visits

G. Neurasthenia
1. Follows depressive state
2. Marked insomnia, weakness, and exhaustion; fear of "going crazy"
3. Symptoms of various organic diseases without existence of organic disease

3. Nursing approaches to neurotic disorders

A. Attitude of acceptance and giving recognition to the person's worth is especially important

B. Patients who are *fearful* and *anxious*
1. Fulfill needs as promptly as possible; listen to and stay with patients
2. Eliminate the need for patients to make decisions or to be in competitive situations
3. Promote rest; decrease environmental stimuli
4. Never force contact with feared object or situation

C. Patients who are *ritualistic*
1. Accept rituals permissively (excessive handwashing, for example)
2. Avoid criticism or "punishment," making demands, or showing impatience with patients
3. Allow extra time for slowness and patient's need for preciseness
4. Protect from rejection by others
5. Protect from self-inflicted harmful acts
6. Engage in nursing therapy after the ritual is over, when patient is most comfortable
7. Redirect patient's actions into substitute outlets

D. Patients who have *dissociative* and *conversion reactions*
1. Remove patients from immediate environment to reduce pressures
2. Divert attention to topics other than physical complaints
3. Avoid pity and oversolicitous approach to patient's "illnesses"
4. Avoid leaving patients isolated; encourage socialization

E. Patients who are *hypochondriacal*
1. Offer empathy without sentimentality

2. Avoid sternness; use good-natured firmness
3. Restore patient's energy
4. Encourage sense of humor and proper evaluation of nonessentials
5. Provide instruction in hobbies, profitable activities, and recreation to occupy interest and decrease time for hypochondriacal thoughts

PSYCHOSOMATIC DISORDERS

Psychosomatic disorders, also called psychophysiologic disorders, are those diseases of various organs and systems in which emotions are expressed by their effect on body organs.

1. Characteristics of psychosomatic disorders
A. Persistent psychosomatic reactions may produce structural organic changes resulting in chronic diseases, which may be *life-threatening* if untreated
B. All body systems are affected
   1. Skin (pruritus and dermatitis for example)
   2. Musculoskeletal (backache, muscle cramps, and rheumatism, for example)
   3. Respiratory (asthma, hiccups, and hay fever, for example)
   4. Gastrointestinal (ulcers, ulcerative colitis, irritable colon, heartburn, constipation, and diarrhea, for example)
   5. Cardiovascular (paroxysmal tachycardia, migraines, palpitations, and hypertension, for example)
   6. Genitourinary (dysuria and dysmenorrhea, for example)
   7. Endocrine (hyperthyroidism, for example)
   8. Nervous system (general fatigue, anorexia, and exhaustion, for example)

2. Concepts and principles relating to psychosomatic disorders
A. Majority of organs involved are usually under control of autonomic nervous system
B. Defense mechanisms
   1. Repression or suppression of unpleasant emotional experiences
   2. Introjection—illness seen as punishment
   3. Projection—Others are blamed for illness
   4. Conversion—Physical symptoms rather than underlying emotional stresses are emphasized.
C. Often exhibit the following underlying needs in excess
   1. Dependency

   2. Attention
   3. Love
   4. Success
   5. Recognition
   6. Security
D. Need to distinguish between
   1. Malingering—deliberate conscious faking of illness to avoid an uncomfortable situation
   2. Psychoneurosis—affecting sensory systems that are usually under voluntary control; generally nonlife-threatening; symptoms are a symbolic solution to anxiety; no demonstrable organic pathology; conversion reaction and hysteria are examples
   3. Psychophysiologic—Under autonomic nervous system control; structural organic changes; may be life-threatening
E. A decrease in emotional security tends to produce an increase in symptoms
F. When treatment is confined to physical symptoms, emotional problems are not usually relieved

3. Nursing approaches to psychosomatic disorders
A. Prompt attention in meeting patients' basic needs, to gratify appropriate need for dependency, attention, and security
B. Do not say, "There is nothing wrong with you," because emotions do in fact cause somatic disabilities
C. Treat organic problems as necessary but without undue emphasis (that is, do not reinforce preoccupation with bodily complaints)
D. Help patients express their feelings, especially anger, hostility, guilt, resentment, and humiliation, which may be related to such issues as sexual difficulties, family problems, religious conflicts, and job difficulties
   1. Help patients recognize that when stress and anxiety are not released through some channel, such as verbal expression, the body will release the tension through "organ language"
   2. Teach patients more effective ways of responding to stressful life situations
E. Maintain an attitude of respect and concern; the patients' pains and worries are very real and upsetting to them; do not belittle the symptoms
F. Provide outlets for release of tensions and diversions from preoccupation with physical complaints
   1. Provide social and recreational activities to decrease time for preoccupation with illness

2. Encourage patients to use physical and intellectual capabilities in constructive ways available to them
G. Help patients feel in control of situations and to be as independent as possible
H. Protect patients from disturbing stimuli; help the healing process in the acute phase of illnesses (myocardial infarct, for example)
I. Be supportive; assist patients in bearing painful feelings through a helping relationship
   1. Teach the family supportive relationships
   2. Encourage expression of conflicts

CHRONIC BRAIN SYNDROME

Chronic brain syndrome is a mental disorder in which organic changes and neuropathology *can* be demonstrated. Organic brain syndromes have been often classified into acute and chronic forms, psychotic and nonpsychotic situations, and by specific syndromes such as Alzheimer's disease, Pick's disease, senile brain disease, cerebral arteriosclerosis, and presenile disease. A number of these syndromes characteristically occur in the elderly.

1. **Characteristics of chronic brain syndrome**
A. Memory impairment, especially names and *recent* events; patients may compensate by confabulating, circumstantiality
B. Mood changes and unstable emotions
   1. Morbid anger outburst (in cerebral arteriosclerosis, for example)
   2. Tearful
C. May have seizures (in Alzheimer's disease and cerebral arteriosclerosis, for example)
D. Confusion, disorientation
E. Intellectual capacities diminished
   1. Difficulty with abstract thought
   2. Compensatory mechanism is to stay with familiar topics; repetition
F. Short concentration periods; motor restlessness
G. Perceptual disturbances
   1. Illusions
   2. Misidentification of other persons and objects; misperception to make unfamiliar more familiar
   3. Visual and tactile hallucinations; auditory hallucinations may be formed images and voices or disorganized light and sound patterns
H. Personality changes

1. Delusions common, often paranoid persecutions
2. Quarrelsome
3. Loss of ego flexibility; adopts more rigid attitudes
4. Withdraws from social contact
5. Becomes ritualistic about daily activities
6. Depression is a frequent reaction to loss of physical and social function
7. Hoarding
8. Somatic preoccupation (hypochondriasis)
9. Judgment impaired, resulting in socially inappropriate behavior (hypersexuality toward inappropriate objects, for example)

2. **Concepts and principles relating to chronic brain syndrome**
A. Course is progressive, with steady deterioration
B. Alternate pathways and compensatory mechanisms may develop to show a clinical picture of remissions and exacerbations

3. **Nursing approaches to chronic brain syndrome**
A. Make brief, frequent contacts, as attention span is short
B. Allow patients time to talk and to complete projects
C. Stimulate associative patterns to improve recall (repeat, summarize, and focus)
D. Allow patients to review their lives
E. Utilize concrete questions in interviewing
F. Reinforce reality-oriented comments
G. Keep environment the same as much as possible (same room and placement of furniture, for example); *routine* is important
H. Recognize the importance of compensatory mechanisms (confabulation, for example) to increase self-esteem
J. Give recognition for each accomplishment

MENTAL HEALTH PROBLEMS OF THE AGED

In general, problems affecting the elderly are *similar* to those affecting persons of any age. This section will highlight the *differences* from the viewpoint of etiology, frequency, and prognosis.

1. **Causative factors of mental disorder in the aged**
A. Nutritional problems and physical ill health related to acute and chronic illness
   1. Cardiovascular diseases (heart failure, stroke, hypertension)
   2. Respiratory infection
   3. Cancer

4. Alcoholism
B. Decreased physical capacity
C. Problems related to loss, grief, and bereavement
D. Retirement
E. Social isolation
F. Financial problems (reduced incomes)
G. Environmental *change* (moving within a community or from home to institution)
H. Attitudes toward condition and circumstances
2. **Principles and concepts relating to mental health problems of the aged**
A. The elderly *do* have a capacity for growth and change
B. Human beings, regardless of their age, need a sense of future and to have hope for things to come
C. An inalienable right of all individuals should be to make or participate in all decisions concerning themselves and their possessions as long as they can
D. Physical disability due to the aging process may enforce dependency, which may be unacceptable to elderly patients and may evoke feelings of anger and ambivalence
E. In an attempt to reduce feelings of loss, elderly patients may cling to concrete things that most represent, in a symbolic sense, all that has been significant to them
F. As memory diminishes, familiar objects in the environment and familiar routines are important in helping to keep the patients oriented and in contact with reality
G. Familiarity of environment brings security; routines bring a sense of security about what is to happen
H. If individuals feel unwanted, they may tell stories about their earlier achievements
I. Many of the traits in the elderly result from the cumulative effect of past experiences of frustrations and the present awareness of limitations rather than from any primary consequences of physiologic deficit
J. Psychologic characteristics of the aged
   1. Increasingly dependent on others, not only for physical needs, but also for emotional security
   2. Concerns focus more and more inward with narrowed outside interests
      a. Decreased emotional energy for concern with social problems unless these issues affect them
      b. Tendency to reminisce

   3. May appear selfish and unsympathetic
   4. Sources of pleasure and gratification are more childlike, food, warmth, and affection, for example
      a. Tangible and frequent evidence of affection is important (letters, cards, and visits, for example)
      b. May hoard articles
   5. Fears of being unloved or forgotten
   6. Attention span and memory are short; may be forgetful and accuse others of stealing
   7. Deprivation of any kind is not tolerated
      a. Easily frustrated
      b. Change is poorly tolerated; need to have favorite chairs and established daily routine, for example
   8. Main fears in the aged include fear of dependency, chronic illness, loneliness, and boredom and fear of being deserted by those close to them
   9. Nocturnal delirium may be due to problems with night vision and their inability to keep their spatial location
K. Psychiatric problems in aging
   1. Loneliness—related to loss of mate, diminishing circle of friends and family through death and geographical separation, decline in physical energy, loss of work (retirement), sharp loss of income, and loss of a life-long life style
   2. Insomnia—pattern of sleep changes in significant ways: disappearance of deep sleep, frequent awakening, daytime sleeping
   3. Hypochondriasis—a shift of anxiety may occur from concern with finances, job, or social prestige to concern about own bodily function
   4. Depression—common problem in the aging, with a high suicide rate; partly because of bodily changes which influence the self-concept, the older persons may direct their hostility toward themselves and therefore may be subject to feelings of depression and loneliness
   5. Senility—four early symptoms
      a. Change in attention span
      b. Memory loss for recent events and names
      c. Altered intellectual capacity
      d. Diminished ability to respond to others
L. Successful aging
   1. Being able to *perceive* signs of aging and

limitations resulting from the aging process
2. *Redefining* life in terms of effects on social and physical aspects of living
3. Seeking *alternatives* for meeting needs and finding sources of pleasure
4. Adopting a *different outlook* about self-worth
5. *Reintegrating* values with goals of life

3. Nursing approaches to mental health problems of the aged

A. Help elderly patients to *preserve* what facet of life they can and/or *regain* that which has already been lost
   1. Help minimize regression as much as possible
   2. Help patients to retain their adult status
   3. Help patients to preserve their self-image as useful individuals
   4. Identify and preserve the patients' abilities to perform, emphasizing what they *can* do
B. Help to reduce hopelessness and helplessness
C. Attempt to prevent loss of dignity and loss of worth—address patients by titles, not "Gramps"
D. Be sensitive to concrete things patients may want to keep
E. Use touch to reduce feelings of alienation and loneliness
F. Provide sensory experiences for those with visual problems
   1. Give patients objects of various textures and consistency to feel
   2. Encourage heightened use of remaining senses to make up for those that are diminished or lost
G. Allow patients to reminisce to reduce depression and feelings of isolation
H. Avoid changes in surroundings and routine
I. Use simple, unhurried conversation
   1. Protect from rush and excitement
   2. Allow patients extra time to organize their thoughts

MENTAL AND EMOTIONAL DISORDERS IN CHILDREN AND ADOLESCENTS

Children have certain developmental tasks to master in the various stages of development (for example, learning to trust, control primary instincts, and resolve basic social roles; see Unit 5, Pediatric Nursing).

1. Characteristics of selected disorders
A. Childhood schizophrenia

1. Disturbance in how perceptual information is processed; normal abilities present
   a. Behave as though they cannot hear, see, etc.
   b. Do not react to external stimulus
   c. Mute or echolalic
2. Lack of self-awareness as a unified whole—may not relate bodily needs or parts as extension of themselves
3. Severe difficulty in communicating with others—may be mute and isolated
4. Bizarre postures and gestures (headbanging, rocking back and forth)
5. Disturbances in learning
6. Etiology is unknown
7. Prognosis depends on severity of symptoms and age of onset

B. Characteristics of brain-injury
   1. Hyperactivity
   2. Explosive outbursts
   3. Distractibility
   4. Impulsiveness
   5. Perceptual difficulties (visual distortions, such as figure-ground distortion and mirror-reading; body-image problems; difficulty in telling left from right)
   6. Receptive or expressive language problems

C. Enuresis—related to feelings of insecurity due to unmet needs of attention and affection; important to preserve their self-esteem

D. School phobias—anxiety about school is accompanied by physical distress. Usually observed with fear of leaving home, rejection by mother, fear of loss of mother, or history of separation from mother in early years

E. Behavior disorders—includes lying, stealing, runaway, truancy, drug addiction, sexual delinquency, vandalism, and fire-setting; chief motivating force is either overt or covert hostility; history of disturbed parent-child relations

2. Concepts and principles relating to mental and emotional disorders in children and adolescents

A. Most emotional disorders of children are related to family dynamics and the place the child occupies in the family group
B. Children must be understood and treated within the context of their *families*
C. Many disorders are related to the phases of development through which the children are passing (Eric Erickson's developmental levels are trust, autonomy, initiative, industry, identity, intimacy, generativity, and integrity)

D. Children are not miniature adults; they have special needs
E. Play and food are important media to make contact with children and help them release emotions in socially acceptable forms, prepare them for traumatic events, and develop skills
F. Children who are physically or emotionally ill regress, giving up previously useful habits
G. Adolescents have special problems relating to need for *control* versus need to *rebel; dependency* versus *independency;* and search for *identity* and *self-realization*
H. They often *act out* their underlying feelings of insecurity, rejection, deprivation, and low self-esteem
I. Strong feelings may be evoked in nurses working with children; these feelings should be expressed, and each nurse should be supported by team members
3. **Nursing approaches to mental and emotional disorders in children and adolescents**
A. Aim: corrective socialization

B. Help children gain self-awareness
C. Provide structured environment to orient children to reality
D. Impose limits on behavior that is destructive toward themselves or others without rejecting the children
   a. *Prevent* destructive behavior
   b. *Stop* destructive behavior
   c. *Redirect* nongrowth behavior into constructive channels
E. Consistency
F. Meet developmental and dependency needs
G. Recognize and encourage each child's strengths, growth behavior, and reverse regression
H. Help these children reach the next step in the social growth and development scale
I. Use play and projective media to aid children in working out feelings and conflicts and in making contact
J. Offer support to parents and strengthen the parent-child relationship

Part C   Treatment Modes

CRISIS INTERVENTION

Crisis intervention is a type of brief psychiatric treatment in which individuals and/or their families are helped in their efforts to forestall the process of mental decompensation in reaction to severe emotional stress by direct and immediate supportive approaches.

1. **Characteristics of crisis intervention**
A. Acute, sudden onset related to a stressful precipitating event of which individual is aware but which immobilizes previous coping abilities
B. Responsive to brief therapy with focus on immediate problem
C. Focus shifted from the psyche in the individual to the individual in the environment; Deemphasis on intrapsychic aspects
D. Crisis period is time-limited (usually up to six weeks)

2. **Concepts and principles relating to crisis intervention**
A. Crises are turning points where changes in behavior patterns and life styles can occur; individuals in crisis are most amenable to altering old and unsuccessful coping mechanisms and are most likely to learn new and more functional behaviors
B. Social milieu and its structure are contributing factors in both the development of psychiatric symptoms and eventual recovery
C. If a crisis is handled effectively, the person's mental stability will be maintained; individual may return to a precrisis state or better
D. If a crisis is not handled effectively, individual may progress to a worse state with exacerbations of earlier conflicts; future crises may not be handled well.
E. There are a number of universal developmental crisis periods in every individual's life

F. Each person tries to maintain equilibrium through use of adaptive behaviors

G. When individuals face a problem they cannot solve, tension, anxiety, narrowed perception, and disorganized functioning occur

H. Immediate relief of symptoms produced by crisis is more urgent than exploring their cause

3. Nursing approaches to crisis intervention

A. Goals
   1. Avoid hospitalization
   2. Return to precrisis level and preserve ability to function
   3. Assist in problem solving, with here-and-now focus

B. Assess the crisis
   1. Identify stressful precipitating events: duration, problems created, and degree of significance
   2. Assess suicidal and homicidal risk
   3. Assess amount of disruption in individual's life and effect on significant others
   4. Assess current coping skills, strengths, and general level of functioning

C. Plan the intervention
   1. Consider past coping mechanisms
   2. Propose alternatives and untried coping methods

D. Intervention approach
   1. Help patient to relate the crisis event to current feelings
   2. Encourage expression of all feelings related to disruption
   3. Explore past coping skills and reinforce adaptive ones
   4. Use all means available in social network to take care of patient's immediate needs (significant others, law enforcement agencies, housing, welfare, employment, medical, and school, for example)
   5. Set limits

MILIEU THERAPY

Milieu therapy consists of treatment by means of controlled modification of the patient's environment to promote positive living experiences.

1. Characteristics of milieu therapy

A. Absence of serious conflict among personnel

B. Opportunity to discuss interpersonal relationships in the unit between patients and between patients and staff (decreased social distance between staff and patients)

C. Friendly, warm, trusting, secure, supportive, comforting atmosphere throughout the unit

D. Maximum of individualization in dealing with the patients, especially regarding treatment and privileges in accordance with the patient's needs

E. Opportunity for the patients to take responsibility for themselves and for the welfare of the unit in gradual steps
   1. Patient government
   2. Patient-planned and patient-directed social activities

F. An optimistic attitude about prognosis of illness

G. Attention to comfort, food, and daily living needs; help with resolving difficulties related to tasks of daily living

H. A program of carefully selected resocialization activities to prevent regression

I. Opportunity to live through and test out situations in a realistic way by providing a setting that is a microcosm of the larger outside world

2. Concepts and principles relating to milieu therapy

A. Everything that happens to patients from the time they are admitted to the hospital or treatment setting has a potential that is either therapeutic or antitherapeutic
   1. Not only the therapists, but all who come in contact with the patients in the treatment setting are important to the patients' recovery
   2. Emphasis is on the social, economic, and cultural dimension, the interpersonal climate, as well as the physical environment

B. Patients have the right, privilege, and responsibility to make decisions about daily living activities in the treatment setting

3. Nursing approaches to milieu therapy

A. New structured relationships—allow patients to develop new abilities and use past skills; support patients through new experiences as needed; help build liaison with others; set limits; help patients modify destructive behavior; encourage group solutions of daily living problems

B. Managerial—inform patients about expectations; preserve orderliness of events

C. Environmental manipulation—regulate the outside environment to alter daily surroundings
   1. Geographically move patients to units more conducive to meeting their needs
   2. Work with families, clergy, employers, etc.
   3. Control visitors

BEHAVIOR MODIFICATION

Behavior modification is a therapeutic approach involving the application of learning principles to change maladaptive behavior

1. Definitions

conditioned avoidance (also, *aversion therapy*) a technique whereby there is a purposeful and systematic production of strongly unpleasant responses in situations to which the patient has been previously attracted but now wishes to avoid.

desensitization frequent exposure in small, but gradually increasing, doses of anxiety-evoking stimuli until undesirable behavior disappears or is lessened (as in phobias)

token economy desired behavior is reinforced by rewards, such as candy, money, and verbal approval.

operant conditioning behavior of a person which operates on the environment to bring about a specific consequence. Operant conditioning is a method designed to reinforce desirable behavior (especially useful in mental retardation).

positive reinforcement giving rewards to elicit or strengthen selected behavior or behaviors.

2. Objectives and process of treatment in behavior modification

A. Emphasis is on changing unacceptable, overt, and observable behavior to that which is acceptable; emphasis is on changed way of *acting* first, not a change in thinking

B. Therapist determines what behavior should be changed and the treatment plan

C. Therapy is based on the knowledge and application of learning principles, that is, stimulus-response, the unlearning or extinction of undesirable behavior, and the reinforcement of desirable behaviors

D. Therapist identifies what events are important in the life history of the patient and arranges situations in which the patient is therapeutically confronted with them

E. Two primary aspects of behavior modification
1. Eliminate unwanted behavior by *punishment* (negative reinforcement) and *ignoring* (withholding positive reinforcement)
2. Create acceptable new responses to an environmental stimulus by positive reinforcement

3. Assumptions of behavioral therapy

A. Behavior is what an organism does

B. Behavior can be observed, described, and recorded

C. It is possible to predict under what conditions the same behavior may recur

D. Undesirable social behavior is not a symptom of mental illness, but is behavior that can be modified

E. Undesirable behaviors are learned disorders that relate to acute anxiety in a given situation

F. Learning process is the same for all; therefore, all conditions (except organic) are accepted for treatment

G. Maladaptive behavior is learned in the same way as adaptive behavior

H. People tend to behave in ways that "pay off"

I. Three ways in which behavior can be reinforced
1. Positive reinforcer (adding something pleasurable)
2. Negative reinforcer (removing something unpleasant)
3. Adverse stimuli (punishment)

J. If an undesired behavior is ignored, it will extinguish

4. Nursing approaches to behavior modification

A. Find out what is a "reward" for the patient

B. Break the goal down into small successive steps

C. Maintain close and continuous observation of the selected behavior or behaviors

D. Be consistent with on-the-spot, immediate intervention and correction of undesirable behavior

E. Record focused observations of behavior frequently

F. Participate in close teamwork with the entire staff

G. Evaluate procedures and results continuously

ACTIVITY THERAPY

Activity therapy consists of a variety of recreational and vocational activities (RT, recreational therapy; OT, occupational therapy; and music, art, and dance therapy) designed to test and examine social skills and serve as adjunctive therapies.

1. Characteristics of activity therapy

A. Usually planned and coordinated by other team members, the recreational therapists or music therapists, for example

B. Goals
1. Encourage socialization in community and social activities
2. Increase self-esteem
3. Teach new skills, help patients find new hobbies
4. Provide pleasurable activities

5. Free and/or strengthen physical and creative abilities
6. Offer graded series of experiences, from passive spectator role and vicarious experiences to more direct and active experiences
7. Help patients release tensions and express feelings

2. Key concepts and principles relating to activity therapy

A. Socialization counters the regressive aspects of illness
B. Activities need to be selected for specific psychosocial reasons to achieve specific effects
C. Nonverbal means of expression as an additional behavioral outlet adds a new dimension to treatment
D. Sublimation of sexual drives are possible through activities

3. Nursing approaches to activity therapy

A. Encourage, support, and cooperate in patient's participation in activities planned by the adjunct therapists
B. Share knowledge of patient's illness, talents, interests, and abilities with others on the team

GROUP THERAPY

Group therapy is a treatment modality in which two or more patients and one or more therapists are interacting in a helping process to bring about relief in emotional difficulties, increase self-esteem and insight, and improve behavior in relations with others.

1. General group aims

A. Provide opportunity for self-expression of ideas and feelings
B. Provide a setting for a variety of relationships
C. Explore current behavioral patterns with others
D. Provide peer and therapist support and source of strength for the individuals to modify present behavior and try out new behaviors
E. Provide on-the-spot multiple feedback (that is, receive reactions of others to behavior), as well as give feedback to others

2. Basic concepts and principles relating to group therapy

A. People's problems usually occur in a social setting, thus they can best be evaluated and corrected in a social setting
B. Not all patients are amenable to group therapies—
   1. Brain damaged

2. Acutely suicidal
3. Acutely psychotic
4. Persons with very passive-dependent behavioral patterns

C. It is best to match group members for *complementarity in behaviors* (verbal with nonverbal, withdrawn with outgoing) but for *similarity in problems* (obesity, predischarge group, cancer patients, prenatal group) to facilitate empathy in the sharing of experiences and to heighten intragroup identification and cohesiveness
D. Feelings of *acceptance*, belonging, respect, and comfort develop in the group and facilitate change and health
E. In a group, members can test reality by giving and receiving *feedback*
F. Patients have a chance to experience in the group that they are not alone (concept of *universality*)
G. Expression and *ventilation* of strong emotional feelings (anger, anxiety, fear, and guilt) in the safe setting of a group is an important aspect of the group process aimed at health and change
H. The group setting and the *interactions* of its members may provide corrective emotional experiences for its members
   1. A key mechanism operating in groups is *transference* (strong emotional attachment of one member to another member, to the therapist, and/or entire group)
I. To the degree that people modify their behavior through corrective experiences and identification with others rather than through personal insight analysis, group therapy may be of special advantage over individual therapy, in that the possible number of interactions is greater in the group and the patterns of behavior are more readily observable
J. There is a higher patient-to-staff ratio, and it is thus less expensive

3. Nursing approaches in the group setting

A. Nurses have different roles and functions in the group, depending on the type of group, its size, its aims, and the stage in the group's life cycle
   1. The multifaceted roles may include
      a. Catalyst
      b. Transference object
      c. Clarifier
      d. Interpreter of "here-and-now"
      e. Role model and resource person
      f. Supporter
B. During the first session, explain the purpose of the group, go over the "contract" (structure,

format, and goals of sessions), and facilitate introductions of group members

C. In subsequent sessions, promote greater group cohesiveness by
1. Focusing on group concerns and group process rather than on intrapsychic dynamics of individuals
2. Demonstrate nonjudgmental acceptance of behaviors within the limits of the group contract
3. Help group members handle their anxiety, especially during the initial phase
4. Encourage silent members to interact at their level of comfort
5. Encourage members to verbally interact without dominating the group discussion
6. Keep the focus of discussion on related themes; set limits and interpret group rules
7. Facilitate sharing and communication between members
8. Provide support to members as they attempt to work through anxiety-provoking ideas and feelings
9. Set the expectation that the members are to take responsibility for carrying the group discussion and exploring issues on their own

D. Termination phase
1. Make early preparation for group termination (ending-point should be announced at the first meeting)
2. Anticipate common reactions by patients to separation anxiety and help each member to work through these reactions
   a. Anger
   b. Acting-out
   c. Regressive behavior
   d. Repression
   e. Feelings of abandonment
   f. Sadness

FAMILY THERAPY

Family therapy is a process, method, and technique of psychotherapy in which the focus is not on an individual but on the total family as an interactional system.

1. **Basic theoretical concepts of family therapy**
A. The ill family member (called the identified patient, or IP), by symptoms, sends a message about the "illness" of the family as a *unit*
B. *Family homeostasis* is the means by which families attempt to maintain the status quo

C. *Scapegoating* is found in disturbed families and is usually focused on one family member at a time, with the intent to keep the family in line
D. Communication and behavior by some family members bring out communication and behavior in other family members
1. Mental illness in the IP is almost always accompanied by emotional illness and disturbance in other family members
2. Changes occurring in one member will produce change in another
E. Human communication is a key to emotional stability and instability—to normal and abnormal health
1. Conjoint family therapy is a communication-centered approach that looks at interactions between family members
F. *Double bind* is a "damned if you do, damned if you don't" situation; it results in helplessness, insecurity, anxiety, fear, frustration, and rage
G. *Symbiotic tie* usually occurs between one parent and a child, where individual ego development is hampered and strong dependence and identification with the parent is fostered (usually the mother)
H. Three basic premises of communication*
1. One cannot *not* communicate
2. Communication is a multilevel phenomenon
3. The message sent is not necessarily the same message that is received

2. **Nursing approaches to family therapy**
A. Establish a family contract (who attends, when, duration of sessions, length of therapy, fee, and other expectations)
B. Encourage family members to identify and clarify own goals
C. Set ground rules
1. Focus is on the family as a whole unit, not on the IP
2. No scapegoating or punishment of members who "reveal all" should be allowed
3. Therapists should not align themselves with issues or individual family members
D. Use self to empathetically respond to family's problems; share own emotions openly and directly; function as a role model of interaction
E. Point out and encourage the family to clarify

---

*From Watzlawick, P.: An anthology of human communication, Palo Alto, California, 1964, Science and Behavior Books, Inc.

unclear, inefficient, and ambiguous family communication patterns
F. Identify family strengths
G. Listen for repetitive interpersonal themes, patterns, and attitudes
H. Attempt to reduce guilt and blame (important to neutralize the scapegoat phenomenon)
I. Present possibility of alternative roles and rules in family interaction styles

ELECTROCONVULSIVE THERAPY (ECT)

Electroconvulsive therapy is a physical treatment that induces grand mal convulsions by application of electric current to the head. It is also called electric shock therapy (EST).

1. Characteristics of electroconvulsive therapy
A. Usually used in treating depression
B. Consists of a series of treatments (6 to 25) over a period of time (three times a week, for example)
C. Patient is asleep through the procedure and for 20 to 30 minutes afterwards
D. Convulsion starts with tonic spasm of entire body, followed by series of clonic, jerking motions, especially in extremities
E. Confusion is present for 30 minutes after treatment
F. Loss of memory occurs for recent events
2. Proposed views concerning success of electroconvulsive therapy
A. Posttreatment sleep as the "curative" factor
B. Shock treatment is seen as punishment, with an accompanying feeling of absolution from guilt
C. Chemical alteration of thought patterns results in memory loss, with decrease in redundancy and awareness of painful memories
3. Nursing approaches to electroconvulsive therapy
A. Always tell the patient of the treatment
B. Inform the patient about temporary memory loss for recent events after the treatment
C. Pretreatment care
  1. Take vital signs
  2. See to patients' toileting
  3. Remove patient's dentures, eyeglasses, or contact lenses
  4. NPO for 8 hours beforehand
  5. Atropine sulfate subcutaneously 30 minutes before treatment to decrease bronchial and tracheal secretions
  6. Anesthetist gives anesthetic and muscle relaxant IV (succinylcholine chloride, or Anec-

tine) and oxygen for two to three minutes and inserts airway
D. During the convulsion the nurse holds the patient firmly to avoid dislocation and fractures
E. Care during recovery stage
  1. Take blood pressure and respirations
  2. Stay with the patient until awake; respond to questions until patient can care for self
  3. Orient patient as to time and place and that the treatment is over
  4. Offer support to help patient feel more secure and relaxed as the confusion and anxiety decrease

PSYCHOPHARMACOLOGY: COMMON PSYCHOTROPIC DRUGS

1. Antipsychotics
A. Phenothiazines (Compazine, Sparine, Thorazine, Mellaril, Stelazine, Trilafon, Vesprin, Prolixin Enanthate)
  1. Use—acute and chronic psychoses; most useful in disorganization of thought or behavior; to decrease panic, fear and hostility, restlessness, aggression, and withdrawal
  2. Side effects
    a. Hypersensitivity effects
      (1) Blood dyscrasia—agranulocytosis, leukopenia, granulocytopenia (watch for signs of sore throat, fever, malaise)
      (2) Skin reactions—photosensitivity, flushing, dermatitis, blue-gray skin
      (3) Obstructive *jaundice*
    b. Extrapyramidal effects—affecting voluntary movement and skeletal muscles
      (1) Parkinson's disease—tremors, rigidity, shuffling gait, pill rolling, masklike facies, salivation, and difficulty in starting muscular movement (dyskinesia)
      (2) Dystonia—limb and neck spasm, extensive rigidity of back muscles, oculogyric crisis, speech and swallowing difficulty, and protrusion of tongue
      (3) Akathisia—motor restlessness, pacing, foottapping, inner tremulousness, and agitation
    c. Potentiates central nervous system depressants

d. Orthostatic hypotension

e. Anticholinergic effects (atropinelike)—dry mouth, stuffy nose, blurred vision, urinary retention, and constipation

f. Ocular changes (lens and corneal opacity)

B. Butyrophenones (Haldol, Innovar, Serenace)—side effects the same as those listed for phenothiazines, but less orthostatic hypotension

C. Thioxanthenes (Taractan, Navane)—chemically related to phenothiazines and have similar therapeutic effects

2. Antidepressants

A. Tricyclic (Tofranil, Elavil, Triavil, Aventyl, Vivactil, Sinequan)—effective in 1 to 3 weeks

1. Side effects

a. Behavioral—psychosis, depression, mania

b. CNS—tremor

c. ANS—dry mouth, aggravation of glaucoma, bowel and bladder control problems, edema, paralysis, ECG changes (arrhythmia severe in overdose)

B. Monoamine-oxidase inhibitors (MAO) (Nardil, Marplan, Parnate, Marsilid, Eutonyl, Niamid)

1. Side effects

a. Behavioral—psychosis, depression, mania, excitement

b. CNS—tremors; *hypertensive crisis* (avoid cheese, coke, caffeine, wine, or other foods high in tyramine or pressor amine, for example, amphetamines, and cold and hay fever medications); *intracerebral hemorrhage*; *hyperpyrexia*

c. ANS—dry mouth, aggravation of glaucoma, bowel and bladder control problems, edema, paralysis. ECG changes (arrhythmia severe in overdose)

d. Allergic hepatocellular jaundice

3. Antianxiety

A. Librium—also used in psychoses and obsession, alcoholism, tension, and irrational fears; has muscle relaxant and anticonvulsant properties

1. Side effects—drowsiness, motor uncoordination, confusion, skin eruptions, edema, menstrual irregularities, constipation, extrapyramidal symptoms, and blurred vision

2. Precautions

a. Habituating (withdrawal convulsions)

b. Potentiates CNS depressants

c. Effect on pregnancy

d. Patients with suicidal tendencies

B. Valium—More of a sedative effect; *not* used in psychotics

1. Side effects—same as those for Librium, plus double or blurred vision, difficult speech, headache, hypotension, incontinence, tremor, and urinary retention

2. Precautions—same as those for Librium

4. Anti-manic

A. Lithium—effect occurs one to three weeks after first dose

1. Use—acute manic attack and to prevent recurrence of cyclic manic-depressive episodes

2. Side effects—tremor, nausea and vomiting, and diarrhea, polyuria, polydipsia, ataxia, motor weakness, headache, edema, and lethargy; signs of severe toxicity: neurological, e.g. twitching, marked drowsiness, slurred speech, athetotic movements, convulsions, coma

3. Precautions—patients on diuretics, patients with disturbed electrolytes (sweating, dehydrated, and postoperative patients), with thyroid problems, those on low-salt diet, patients with congestive heart failure, and impaired renal function.

4. Dosage—therapeutic level 0.8-1.6 mEq/L; dose for maintenance 300-1500 mg/day; toxic level >2.0 mEq/L; blood sample drawn in acute phase 8 to 12 hours after last dose

5. Anti-Parkinson agents

A. Artane

1. Side effects—dry mouth, blurred vision, dizziness, nausea, constipation, drowsiness, urinary hesitancy or retention, pupil dilation, headache, and weakness

2. Precautions—cautious use with cardiac, liver, or kidney disease, glaucoma, or obstructive gastrointestinal-genitourinary disease

B. Cogentin

1. Side effects—same as those for Artane plus

a. Effect on body temperature may result in life-threatening state

b. Gastrointestinal distress (relieved by taking it after or with meals)

c. Inability to concentrate, memory difficulties, and mild confusion (often mistaken for senility)

d. May lead to toxic psychotic reactions

e. Subjective sensations—light or heavy feelings in legs, numbness and tingling of extremities, light headedness or tightness of head, and giddiness

Glossary

affect   feeling or mood.

ambivalence   contradictory (positive and negative) emotions, desires, or attitudes coexisting toward an object or person.

amnesia   loss of memory due to physical or emotional trauma.

anxiety   state of uneasiness or response to a vague, unspecific danger cued by a threat to some value that the individual holds essential to existence (or by a threat of loss of control); the danger may be real or imagined. Physiologic manifestations are increased pulse, respiration, and perspiration, with feeling of "butterflies."

autism   self-preoccupation and absorption in fantasy as found with schizophrenia, with a complete exclusion of reality and loss of interest in and appreciation of others.

catatonia   type of schizophrenia characterized by muscular rigidity, alternating with excitability.

compulsion   an insistent, repetitive, intrusive, and unwanted urge to perform an act that is contrary to ordinary conscious wishes or standards.

cyclothymia   alterations in moods of elation and sadness, with mood swings out of proportion to apparent stimuli.

defense mechanism   device used to ward off anxiety or uncomfortable thoughts and feelings; an activity of the ego that operates out of awareness to hold impulses in check which might cause conflict (repression and regression, for example).

delusion   a false fixed belief, idea, or group of ideas that are contrary to what is thought of as real and cannot be changed by logic; arise out of the individual's needs and are maintained in spite of evidence or facts (grandeur and persecution, for example).

depression   morbid sadness or dejection accompanied by feelings of hopelessness, inadequacy, and unworthiness. Distinguished from grief, which is realistic and in proportion to loss.

disorientation   loss of awareness of the position of self in relation to time, place, or person.

echolalia   automatic repetition of phrases or words heard.

echopraxia   automatic repetition of observed movements.

ego   the "I," "self," and "person" as distinguished from "others"; that part of the personality, according to Freudian theory, that *mediates* between the primitive pleasure-seeking instinctual drives of the id and the self-critical, prohibitive, restraining forces of the super ego; that aspect of the psyche that is *conscious* and most in touch with external reality and is directed by the *reality principle.* The part of the personality that has to make the decision. Most of the ego is conscious and represents the *thinking-feeling* part of a person. The *compromises* worked out on an unconscious level help to resolve intrapsychic conflict by keeping thoughts, interpretations, judgments, and behavior practical and efficient.

electroshock   electroshock treatment (EST) or electroconvulsive treatment (ECT) is the treatment of certain psychiatric disorders (best suited for depression) by therapeutic administration of regulated electrical impulses to the brain to produce convulsions.

empathy   an objective awareness of another's thoughts, feelings, or behavior and their meaning and significance; intellectual identification versus emotional identification (sympathy).

euphoria   exaggerated feeling of physical and emotional well-being not related to external events or stimuli.

fugue   dissociative state involving amnesia and actual physical flight.

hallucination   *false* sensory perception in the absence of an actual external stimulus. May be due to chemicals or inner needs and may occur in any of the five senses.

hypochondriasis   state of morbid preoccupation about one's health (somatic concerns).

id   psychoanalytic term for that division of the psyche that is unconscious, contains instinctual primitive drives that lead to immediate gratification, and is dominated by the *pleasure principle.* The id wants what it wants when it wants it.

ideas of reference   misinterpretation of casual incidents and external events as having a direct reference to oneself.

idealization   overestimation of some admired aspect or attribute of another person.

illusion   misinterpretation of a real, external sensory stimuli. (A person may see a shadow on a floor and think it is a hole, for example.)

insanity   legal term for mental defect or disease that is of sufficient gravity to bring person under special legal restrictions and immunities.

labile   unstable and rapidly shifting emotions.

mental retardation   term for mental deficiency or deficit in normal development in intelligence that makes intellectual abilities lower than normal for chronologic age. May result from a condition present at birth, from injury during or after birth, or from disease after birth.

narcissism   exaggerated self-love.

neologism   newly coined word or condensed combination of several words found in schizophrenia, not readily understood by others.

neurosis   also called psychoneurosis, a term for mild to moderately severe illness in which there is a disorder of feeling or behavior but not gross mental disorganization, delusions, and hallucinations, as in serious psychoses. Typical neurotic reactions include disproportionate anxiety, phobias, and obsessive-compulsive behavior.

obsession   persistent, unwanted, and uncontrollable urge or idea that cannot be banished by logic or will.

organic psychosis   mental disease resulting from defect, damage, infection, tumor, or other physical cause than can be observed in the body tissues.

paranoid   term indicating feelings of suspicion and persecution (one type of schizophrenia).

personality disorder   broad category of illnesses in which inner difficulties are revealed not by specific symptoms, but by antisocial behavior.

phobia   irrational, persistent, abnormal, morbid, and unrealistic dread of external object or situation displaced from unconscious conflict.

premorbid personality   state of an individual's personality before the onset of an illness.

psyche   synonymous with mind or the mental and emotional "self."

psychoanalysis   theory of human development and behavior, a method of research, and a form of treatment described by Freud that attributes abnormal behavior to repressions in the unconscious mind. Treatment involves dream interpretation and free association to bring into awareness the origin and effects of unconscious conflicts to eliminate or diminish them.

psychogenic   symptoms or physical disorders caused by emotional or mental factors, as opposed to organic.

psychopath   older inexact term for one of a variety of personality disorders in which person has poor impulse control, releasing tension through immediate action without a social or moral conscience.

psychosis   severe emotional illness characterized by a disorder of thinking, feeling, and action with the following symptoms: loss of contact, denial of reality, bizarre thinking and behavior, perceptual distortion, delusions, hallucinations, and regression.

schizoid   form of personality disorder characterized by shyness, introspection, introversion, withdrawal, and aloofness.

schizophrenia   severe functional mental illness characterized in general by a disorder in perception, thinking, feeling, behavior, and interpersonal relationships with others.

sociopathic   pertaining to a disorder of behavior in which a person's feelings and behavior are asocial, with impaired judgment and inability to profit from experience; the intellect remains intact. This term is often used interchangeably with "psychopath."

soma   term meaning the body or physical aspects.

superego   in psychoanalysis, that part of the mind that incorporated the parental or societal values, ethics, and standards. It guides, restrains, criticizes, and punishes. It is unconscious and learned and is sometimes equated with the term *conscience.*

Questions   Psychiatric Nursing

Therapeutic Nursing Process

1. One therapeutic psychiatric nursing approach is to be permissive. To convey this attitude, the nurse might
   1. Wait for a patient to initiate contact
   2. Let the patient make decisions
   3. Ignore undesirable behavior
   4. Meet patients at their own levels of functioning
2. When a patient's behavior is considered to be abnormal, the nurse first needs to
   1. Ignore the patient
   2. Serve as a role model
   3. Point out the patient's disturbed behavior
   4. Focus on the feelings communicated by the patient's behavior
3. When a patient is in isolation, it is essential that
   1. Restraints be applied
   2. All the furniture is removed from the isolation room
   3. A staff member have frequent contacts with the patient
   4. The patient be allowed to come out after four hours
4. The major basic function in psychiatric nursing is to
   1. Plan activity programs for patients
   2. Maintain a therapeutic environment
   3. Understand various types of family therapy and psychologic tests and how to interpret them
   4. Advance the science of psychiatry by initiating research and gathering data for current statistics on emotional illness

Therapeutic Responses

5. When interacting with patients who have autistic thinking and speaking patterns, which of the following is likely to pose the *greatest difficulty* for the nurse?
   1. Showing acceptance for their incomprehensible acts and verbalizations
   2. Ignoring their bizarre behavior
   3. Speaking in a way that the patients could understand
   4. Determining what needs of the patients are being met by their autistic expressions
6. The patient was telling the nurse about her parents' impending divorce. She said, "I couldn't believe it, that he was going to leave us for someone else." Which reply by the nurse would be best?
   1. "Was your mother expecting this to happen?"
   2. "Yes, go on."
   3. "Did you cry?"
   4. "I can understand how you must feel."
7. Arnold related angrily to the nurse that his wife says he is selfish. Which would be the most helpful response?
   1. "That's just her opinion."
   2. "I don't think you're that selfish."
   3. "Everybody is a little bit selfish."
   4. "You sound angry—tell me more about what went on."
8. Lynn talks about her daughter who is mentally retarded. "She's really an inspiration to me, do you know what I mean?" What would be the most appropriate initial comment by the nurse?
   1. "What makes her an inspiration?"
   2. "It seems to be important to you to find something positive about her."
   3. "No, explain more about what you mean."
   4. "Tell me more about her."
9. The mother relates to the nurse, "When my baby had asthma five years ago, I thought he was going to die." What could the nurse say that would be the most appropriate?
   1. "What made you think that he was going to die?"
   2. "What did you do?"
   3. "You thought he was dying?"
   4. "How did you feel then?"
10. One effective way to start an interaction with a patient who is silent is to
    1. Tell the patient something about yourself and hope that the patient does the same

2. Remain silent, waiting for the patient to bring up a topic
3. Bring up a controversial topic to elicit the patient's response
4. Introduce a neutral topic, giving the patient a broad opening

11. What might be the most therapeutic response you could make to a student who begins crying on hearing that she failed an exam?
    1. "You'll make it next time."
    2. "Failing an exam is an upsetting thing to happen."
    3. "How close were you to passing?"
    4. "It won't seem so important five years from now."

12. A patient tells you that he has something he wants to say to you but does not want you to tell anyone else. As a nurse, you
    1. Agree not to "tell"
    2. Refuse to agree to this
    3. Say nothing, allowing him to go on
    4. Let him know that you cannot promise this

Anxiety

13. Which nursing intervention is effective when patients are severely anxious?
    1. Encourage group participation
    2. Give detailed instructions ahead of treatment procedure
    3. Impart information succinctly and concretely
    4. Increase opportunities for decision making

14. When a patient tells the nurse that she cannot sleep at night because of fear of dying, what would be the best initial response?
    1. "Don't worry, you won't die. You're just here for some tests."
    2. "Why are you afraid of dying?"
    3. "Try to sleep. You need the rest before tomorrow's test."
    4. "It must be frightening for you to feel that way. Tell me more about it."

15. Which of the following are common physiologic reactions that occur in response to anxiety?
    1. Clammy hands and increased perspiration
    2. Palpitations and pupillary constriction
    3. Diarrhea and vomiting
    4. Pupillary dilation, retention of feces, and urine

16. Which behavior is most characteristic of a panic response?

1. Behavior is goal-directed and aimed at a "flight" response from apparent threat
2. Behavior is automatic, with poor judgment
3. The severity of reaction is not related to the severity of the threat to the self-esteem
4. There is a delayed reaction in perceiving the danger

Defense Mechanisms

17. The most common defense mechanism is
    1. Introjection
    2. Projection
    3. Repression
    4. Rationalization

18. Paranoid patients tend to use projection. What is the main purpose of this action?
    1. To control and manipulate others
    2. To deny reality
    3. To handle feelings and thoughts not acceptable to the ego
    4. To express resentment toward others

19. Reaction formation can be described as
    1. Finding a socially acceptable outlet for impulses from the id
    2. Adopting the feelings and attitudes of a hero
    3. Keeping unacceptable ideas or feelings from awareness
    4. Adopting a feeling or attitude that is the opposite of the original attitude

20. Regression is common in physical and emotional illness. Which of the following best explains this mechanism?
    1. When faced with frustration, conflict, and/or anxiety, people may need to return to a prior level of functioning where they felt secure and comfortable
    2. Immature behavior has secondary benefits
    3. Childlike behavior is a way of getting away with expression of hostility
    4. The individuals enjoy the sympathy and attention they received as children when they were ill

21. Fixation can best be understood as
    1. Reversion to an earlier developmental phase
    2. Behavior persisting into later life that was appropriate at an earlier developmental phase
    3. A disturbance in the rate of speech
    4. The wish to be like another and to assume attributes of the other

22. An angry man channels his hostilities into competitive sports in which there are many opportunities for combat. This can be seen as
    1. Sublimation
    2. Repression
    3. Rationalization
    4. Reaction-formation
23. Repression can be defined as
    1. Selective forgetting and storing unacceptable thoughts, wishes, and impulses in the unconscious mind
    2. Conscious, deliberate forgetting
    3. Transfer to another situation an emotion felt in a previous situation where its expression would not have been acceptable
    4. Unconscious imitation of the manners, behavior, and feelings of another
24. Mary, a patient who attempted suicide recently, remarks to the nurse the next morning, "Let's not think about that now. Maybe I'll feel like thinking about it later." This can be identified as
    1. Blocking
    2. Denial
    3. Suppression
    4. Repression
25. Repetitive handwashing is often seen when a patient is experiencing guilt feelings. This ritualistic behavior can be described as a mechanism whereby the patient attaches significance to the act of washing. This is seen as
    1. Symbolism
    2. Fantasy
    3. Isolation
    4. Conversion
26. The patient shouts at the nurse one morning, "Why do you waste your time on me? I'm not sick; I don't need you. Go talk to Mr. Gomez. He's really sick!" This can be identified as
    1. Reaction formation
    2. Denial
    3. Intellectualization
    4. Rationalization

Manic-Depressive Reaction, Depressive Phase

Mrs. Allen, a 28-year-old woman, is admitted to the psychiatric hospital with symptoms of severe depression. Fourteen months ago, her 9-month-old boy died of crib death. Since then, Mrs. Allen has lost weight, will not eat, spends most of her time immobile, and speaks only in monosyllabic responses. She pays little attention to her appearance.

27. Which one of the following nursing approaches would be best for Mrs. Allen while her symptoms are severe?
    1. Allow her time for quiet thought; remain silent
    2. Ask her to join you and the other patients in the TV lounge
    3. State that you would like to go with her for a short walk around the outside grounds, and assist her with her coat
    4. Give her a choice of recreational activities
28. One afternoon, Mrs. Allen comes to lunch with her hair combed and traces of lipstick. What could a nurse say to reinforce this change in behavior?
    1. "What happened? You combed your hair!"
    2. "This is the first time I've seen you look so good."
    3. "You must be feeling better. You look much better."
    4. "I see that your hair is combed and you have lipstick on."
29. Which of the following are important nursing approaches in depression?
    1. Providing motor outlets for aggressive, hostile feelings
    2. Protecting against harm to others
    3. Reducing interpersonal contacts
    4. Deemphasizing preoccupation with elimination, nourishment, and sleep
30. When Mrs. Allen says to the nurse, "I can't talk; I have nothing to say," and continues being silent, what should the nurse do?
    1. Say, "All right. You don't have to talk. Let's play cards, instead."
    2. Explain that talking is an important sign of getting well and that she is expected to do so
    3. Be silent until Mrs. Allen speaks again
    4. Say, "It may be difficult for you to speak at this time, perhaps you can do so at another time."
31. In working with patients who are depressed, it is essential that the nurse know that depression may stem from
    1. A sense of loss, actual, imaginary, or impending
    2. Revived memories of a painful childhood

3. A confused sexual identity
4. An unresolved oedipal conflict

Manic Depressive Reaction, Manic Phase

Mr. Short, a 35-year-old man, is brought to the psychiatric hospital by his wife. His history included periodic episodes of manic behavior, alternating with depression.

32. Which characteristic is shared by a patient who may be in the depressed phase and one who may be in the manic phase of manic-depressive reaction?
    1. Suicidal tendency
    2. Underlying hostility
    3. Delusions
    4. Flight of ideas
33. A nursing-care plan for a hospitalized hyperactive patient in manic reaction needs to include
    1. Involvement in a group activity and encouragement to talk
    2. Attention to adequate food and fluid intake
    3. Protection against suicide
    4. Permissive acceptance of bizarre behavior
34. One evening the nurse sees Mr. Short in the dayroom without any clothes. He is shouting vulgarities and dancing wildly about the room while other patients are watching TV. The best initial response by the nurse at this time would be:
    1. "Let's sit down with the others and watch TV; I'll put this blanket over you to keep you warm."
    2. "We do not allow this behavior in the hospital. It is embarrassing the other patients."
    3. "Please put your clothes on."
    4. "Come put your clothes on, Mr. Short. I will help you."
35. When talking with a manic patient in the acute phase who has flight of ideas, the nurse primarily needs to
    1. Speak loudly and rapidly to keep the patient's attention, as the patient is easily distracted
    2. Focus on the feelings conveyed rather than the thoughts expressed
    3. Encourage the patient to complete one thought at a time
    4. Allow the patient to talk freely

Involutional Depression (Melancholia)

36. Involutional depression may be differentiated from other depressive states by
    1. The age period in which it is most likely to occur
    2. Its characteristic symptoms of delusions stemming from progressive hypochondria
    3. Premorbid personality profile traits of a compulsive, inhibited, frugal, worrisome person with narrowed interests
    4. All of the above

Suicide

37. The most important considerations in caring for a person who is a suicide risk include the following:
    1. Constant awareness of the patient's whereabouts
    2. As long as the patient is talking about suicide, there will be no attempt
    3. Relax vigilance when the patient seems to be recovering from depression
    4. All of the above
38. John, a new patient admitted *last* night, relates to the nurse in the *morning*, "I was going to kill myself." What is the best initial response by the nurse?
    1. Say nothing. Wait for his next comment.
    2. "What were you going to do this time?"
    3. "Have you felt this way before?"
    4. "You seem upset. I am going to be here with you; perhaps you will want to talk about it."
39. Suicide may occur in
    1. Involutional psychosis
    2. Schizophrenia
    3. Manic-depressive, depressive phase
    4. All of the above
40. A nurse discovers a 19-year-old man crouched in a corner of the psychiatric unit corridor. There is blood on the floor. He is holding on to a gushing wound on his right wrist and looks pale and frightened. A razor is nearby on the floor. What should the nurse do first?
    1. Sit down on the floor next to the patient, and in a quiet reassuring tone, say "You seem frightened. Can I help?"
    2. Ask the aid to watch the patient and run to get the doctor
    3. Apply pressure on the wrist, saying to the patient, "You are hurt. I will help you."

4. Go back down the hall to get the emergency cart

Dying

41. A 10-year-boy, diagnosed with acute leukemia, terminal stage, asks the nurse one morning while she is fixing his bed: "I am going to die, aren't I?" What would be the most appropriate response by the nurse?
    1. "No, you're not. You are getting the latest treatment available and you have a very good doctor. Your white count was better yesterday."
    2. "We are all going to die sometime."
    3. "What did the doctor tell you?"
    4. "I don't know. You have a serious illness. Do you have feelings that you want to talk about now?"
42. Ruth, an acutely ill forty-year-old wife and mother hospitalized for treatment of metastatic lung carcinoma, begs the nurse to ask the doctor to give her a pass to attend her son's high school graduation in a city 100 miles from the hospital. "If only I could be free of pain to just do this one thing, then I'll be ready to die," she says. Which understanding is essential for the nurse to have to consider such a request?
    1. Ruth is being unrealistic and denying the degree of her illness
    2. Ruth is using bargaining as a reaction to death and dying
    3. Ruth is being manipulative to get her way
    4. Ruth doesn't know her diagnosis

Grief

Mrs. Betty Barnes, mother of a 5-year-old girl and an 11-year-old boy and long estranged from her husband, received a letter informing her that her husband had recently died from cancer. Her immediate reaction was stunned silence, followed by expression of anger: "I suppose he didn't have any insurance benefits to leave to the children."

43. Which of the following indicates that the nurse best understands Mrs. Barnes' reaction?
    1. She is experiencing a normal grief reaction
    2. Her reaction can best be understood if more was known about the marital relationship and breakup
    3. The children and the injustice done to them by the father's death are her main concern

4. She is not reacting normally to the news
44. Resolution of grief is most likely to be complicated when
    1. There are ambivalent feelings for the deceased
    2. Death was due to a chronic illness
    3. It is the first loss to be experienced
    4. Little emotional dependency existed on the deceased
45. Mr. Barnes' mother comes to stay with them. Betty notices that her mother-in-law is acting more and more like her deceased son, even complaining of similar physical symptoms that her son had before he died. She is preoccupied solely with thoughts about his positive attributes. Which of the following might be most indicative that she is beginning to work through and resolve her grief?
    1. She encourages Betty to remarry
    2. She is able to talk about both the pleasurable and the painful aspects connected with her son
    3. She tries to make up for his deficiencies, saying, "He would have wanted me to do this for you."
    4. She is finally able to feel anger with her son and agree with Betty that he had failed them all

Schizophrenia

46. The main nursing goal with schizophrenic patients is to
    1. Set limits on their bizarre behavior
    2. Establish a trusting, nonthreatening, reality-based relationship
    3. Quickly establish a warm, close relationship to counteract their aloofness
    4. Protect them from self-destructive impulses
47. Symptoms that are characteristic of schizophrenia include
    1. Symbolization
    2. Impaired reality testing
    3. Depersonalization
    4. All of the above
48. Jean has been having auditory hallucinations. When the nurse approaches her, Jean whispers, "Did you hear that terrible man? He is scarey!" Which would be the best response for the nurse to make initially?
    1. "What is he saying?"
    2. "I didn't hear anything. What scarey things is he saying?"

3. "Who is he? Do you know him?"
4. "I didn't hear a man's voice, but you look scared."

49. In responding to a neologism, it would be best for the nurse to
    1. Divert the patient's attention to an aspect of reality
    2. State that what the patient is saying has not been understood and then divert attention to something that is reality-bound
    3. Acknowledge that the word has some special meaning for the patient
    4. Try to interpret what the patient means

50. Jean looks at a mirror and cries out, "I look like a bird. My face is no longer me." Which would be the best response by the nurse?
    1. "Which bird?"
    2. "That must be a distressing experience; your face doesn't look different to me."
    3. "Maybe it was the light at that particular time. Would you like to use another mirror?"
    4. "What makes you think that your face looks like a bird?"

51. A 23-year-old premedical student, Georgia, is admitted to a psychiatric hospital in a withdrawn catatonic state. She was an honor student and very active in student government and had become progressively withdrawn, silent, and mute. For two days prior to admission, she remained seated in one position without moving or speaking. On the ward, she continues to exhibit waxy flexibility as she sits all day. During the initial phase of hospitalization, what is the nurse's first priority?
    1. Watch for edema and cyanosis of the extremities
    2. Encourage Georgia to discuss her concerns leading to the catatonic state
    3. Provide a warm, nurturing relationship, with therapeutic use of touch
    4. Understand the predisposing factors in her illness

52. Janice seems preoccupied with her own thoughts as she grins, giggles, grimaces, and frowns. Although she is 28 years old, her behavior seems childish and regressed. She is unkempt, voids on the floor, disrobes, and openly masturbates. The initial nursing care for Janice should be directed toward
    1. Improving her social conduct to meet hospital standards

2. Controlling her narcissistic impulses
3. Finding out why she is behaving this way
4. Showing acceptance of her

Paranoid Psychoses

53. Mr. Carlson refuses to eat his meals in the hospital, stating that the food is poisoned. The patient is expressing an example of
    1. Hallucination
    2. Illusion
    3. Delusion
    4. Negativism

54. Mr. Carlson cannot find his slippers. During the community meeting, he accuses patients and staff of stealing them during the night. The most therapeutic approach is to
    1. Listen without reinforcing his belief
    2. Logically point out that he is jumping to conclusions
    3. Inject humor to defuse the intensity
    4. Divert his attention

55. Patients with symptoms such as Mr. Carlson's use projection. This mechanism is chiefly a way to
    1. Provoke anger in others
    2. Control delusional thought
    3. Handle their own unacceptable feeling
    4. Manipulate others

Personality Disorders

Alice, an attractive intelligent 15-year-old girl, has a history of truancy from school, running away from home, and "borrowing" other people's things without their permission. She denies that she steals, rationalizing instead that as long as no one was using the items, she thought it was all right to borrow them. She has been referred by the juvenile court to the local mental health center.

56. Psychodynamically, this behavior may be largely attributed to what developmental defect?
    1. Id
    2. Ego
    3. Super ego
    4. Oedipal

57. In interacting with Alice, what would be the most therapeutic approach, consistent with question No. 56?
    1. Reinforce her self-concept as a young woman
    2. Gratify her inner needs

3. Give her opportunity to test reality
4. Provide external controls

58. A new nursing student reports to the unit. He is assigned to take patients for an outing. Alice approaches him and says, "I like you. I'm glad you'll be the one to take us out. My doctor told me that I can go too." In view of a characteristic behavior of persons with personality disorders, the best initial response by the nurse might be
    1. "Since I am new here and not familiar with unit routine, I will go check with the staff and be back."
    2. "It's a beautiful day, and I'm glad that you have ground privileges now."
    3. "When did the doctor tell you that?"
    4. "You seem pleased."

59. Alice arouses anxiety and frustration in the staff and tends to intimidate by her manipulative patterns. One morning Alice shouts at the nurse, "Since you won't give me a pass, go away, you fat pig or I'll hit you." What is the most effective response by the nurse to a patient who threatens or derogates?
    1. "You are rude and I don't like it. It makes me want to not talk with you."
    2. "That kind of talk will keep you here longer."
    3. "What did I do wrong?"
    4. "I don't like to hear insults and threats. What is the matter?"

Alcohol Addiction

Reva Jones, age 38 years and mother of two children, ages 12 and 14, was brought to the emergency ward at the hospital by her husband, Paul. Her diagnoses was delirium tremens.

60. On admission, the patient is likely to exhibit signs of
    1. Perceptual disorders
    2. Nutritional deficiencies
    3. Insomnia and tremulousness
    4. All of the above

61. To relate therapeutically with Mrs. Jones, it is important that the nurses base their care on the understanding that
    1. Alcoholism is hereditary
    2. Alcoholism is due to lack of will-power and true remorse
    3. Alcoholics always break promises
    4. Alcoholism cannot be cured

62. Physiologic consequences of chronic alcoholism are
    1. Pancreatitis and gastritis
    2. Peripheral neuritis
    3. Brain deterioration
    4. All of the above

Drug Addiction

63. The signs of heroin withdrawal may include
    1. Rhinorrhea, sneezing, and high fever
    2. Pupillary dilation, diaphoresis, and weight loss
    3. Pupillary constriction, vomiting, and pruritus
    4. Choreiform movements and frequent lip wetting

64. Methadone treatment for heroin addiction is likely to
    1. Eliminate craving by blocking the physiologic effects of heroin
    2. Produce nausea, gingivitis, and pruritus
    3. Be addictive in itself
    4. All of the above

65. In establishing a therapeutic nursing approach with a patient who is addicted, the nurse primarily needs to
    1. Promote a permissive, accepting environment
    2. Use a straightforward and confronting approach
    3. Meet the patient's need for a chemical substitute for the drug
    4. Prevent the patient's use of the addictive drug

Neurotic Disorders

Mr. David's behavior has been a source of concern to the staff. He refuses to attend group therapy sessions at 9:00 A.M. because he says he has to wash his hands for at least 45 minutes from 9:00 A.M. until 9:45 A.M. At the team meeting, the staff discuss the problem. They feel it is important for Mr. David to participate in the group therapy sessions to learn more successful methods of interaction with others.

66. Which concepts and principles do the staff need to keep in mind in planning nursing interventions for this patient?
    1. Fears and tensions are often expressed in disguised form through symbolic process
    2. Tension which has accumulated is dis-

charged through ritualistic behavior

3. One reason for ritualistic behavior is that the patient is spared the need to make decisions
4. All of the above

67. To help reduce stress and to aid this patient in using less maladaptive means of handling stress, the nurse could
    1. Provide varied activities on the unit, as change in routine can break a ritualistic pattern
    2. Give him ward assignments that do not require perfection
    3. Tell him of changes in routine at the last minute to avoid build-up of anxiety
    4. Provide an activity in which positive accomplishment can occur and he could gain recognition

68. Which of the following is an example of *limit setting* as an effective nursing intervention in ritualistic behavior patterns?
    1. "I don't want you to wash your hands so often anymore."
    2. "If you continue to wash your hands so frequently, the skin on your hands will break down."
    3. "You may wash your hands before the group therapy meeting if you wish, but not during group therapy."
    4. "The doctor wrote an order that you are to stop washing your hands so often."

69. Mr. David's repetitive handwashing is probably an attempt to
    1. Punish himself for guilt feeling
    2. Control unacceptable impulses or feelings
    3. Do what the voices tell him to do
    4. Seek attention from the staff

In the last five years Alice Adams has gone to a number of different doctors for nonspecific complaints of chest pains without any conclusive findings of an organic disease process. She has collected all the medical literature on the subject of coronary diseases. Most of her time is spent recounting details of her symptoms. Her latest internist has referred her to the local mental health center's day-treatment facility.

70. When meeting Alice for the first time at the day-treatment center, which approach by the nurse would be best initially?
    1. Encourage the patient to describe her physical problems to become familiar with them

2. Comment on a neutral topic instead of the usual conversation opener of "How are you today?"
3. Give the patient a simple but direct explanation of the physiologic basis for her symptoms
4. Let the patient know that you are familiar with her psychogenic problems and guide the discussion to other areas

71. All of the following goals are important for a patient who has the diagnosis of hypochondria. Which would be appropriate for an *initial* nursing goal?
    1. Help the patient learn how to live with her functional organic disturbance without using her symptoms to control others
    2. Assist the patient in developing new and varied interests outside of herself in which she can be successful
    3. Accept the patient as a person who is sick and *needs* help
    4. Help the patient to see how she uses her illness to avoid looking at or dealing with her problems.

72. To formulate an effective care plan for this patient, the nurse *needs* to have an understanding of which of the following psychodynamic principles related to hypochondriac reactions?
    1. The major fundamental mechanism is regression
    2. An extensive, prolonged study of her symptoms will be reassuring to the patient, as she seeks sympathy, attention, and love
    3. The symptoms of hypochondriases are an attempt to adjust to painful life situations or to cope with conflicting sexual, aggressive, or dependent feelings
    4. The patient's symptoms are imaginary and her suffering is faked

73. In what way is malingering different from conversion reaction?
    1. It is a conscious reaction to stress
    2. It provides an escape from a difficult situation
    3. The symptoms occur in organs that usually are under voluntary control
    4. The symptoms may reduce anxiety

74. It would not be helpful for the nurse to use logic and reason to assist the patient with conversion reaction symptoms (such as paralysis of the arm) to give up focus on her physical

state because (choose the best answer)
1. The patient is not in contact with reality and thus is unable to "hear" or understand the nurse
2. The patient may need her symptoms to handle feelings of guilt or aggression
3. The nature of the patient's particular illness makes her suspicious of all medical personnel
4. Paralysis of the arm has become a habitual response to stress

75. The most common defense mechanisms utilized in psychoneurotic reaction are
1. Repression and symbolism
2. Sublimation and regression
3. Substitution and displacement
4. Reaction formation and rationalization

76. Which adaptive behavior by a patient with psychoneurosis might be indicative that the patient is showing the greatest improvement in her condition?
1. She recognizes that her behavior is unreasonable
2. She agrees to go to occupational therapy and recreational therapy every day
3. Her symptoms are replaced by expressions of hostility
4. She is verbalizing how she feels instead of demonstrating it by pathologic body language

Psychosomatic Disorders

77. In caring for a patient with a psychosomatic illness, the nurse needs to know that
1. The symptoms will go away in time
2. The patient has an inadequately formed superego
3. The patient's ability to express emotions appropriately is impaired
4. Attention to the physical illness will alleviate the psychologic difficulties

78. How are psychosomatic disorders different from psychoneurotic ones?
1. They may have long-term reactions
2. They bring about secondary benefits
3. Psychotherapy may be helpful
4. The symptoms may be life-threatening

Mr. Simon, a thirty-five-year-old married clerk, had surgery for ulcerative colitis ten days ago. The physical symptoms have abated, but he continues to angrily complain and be demanding of the nursing staff. He has numerous requests, such as to open or close the windows, to bring him fresh water, and so on.

79. What might Mr. Simon's behavior be saying?
1. "You aren't doing your job."
2. "I am alone and helpless and need to depend on you to take care of me when I need you."
3. "Everyone needs attention."
4. "I'm going to get even with you for thinking I'm a crank by making you work."

80. Mr. Simon's family is ready to make discharge plans jointly with him and the staff. What will have the greatest bearing on his rehabilitation course?
1. The amount of emotional support his family gives him
2. His wife's interest in and ability to take care of his postoperative dietary needs
3. The family's expectations of him to resume his role in the home
4. Mrs. Simon's understanding that the course of his illness may have exacerbations and remissions

81. Mr. Simon's psychophysiologic symptoms will probably show the most improvement when he (select the best response)
1. Accepts the fact that his physical symptoms have an emotional component.
2. Finds more satisfying ways of expressing feelings through verbalization
3. Becomes involved in group activities and focuses less on his symptoms
4. Understands that his current way of reacting to stress is not healthy

82. One day Mr. Simon became angry with a patient who was monopolizing the group therapy meeting. What assessment could be made regarding this noted change in Mr. Simon's behavior that would indicate the nurse's understanding of the dynamics of his psychophysiologic disorder?
1. He is intolerant of others
2. He has strong competitive drives
3. He has his own ideas of how the group members should act
4. He is repressing less of his feelings

83. When Mr. Simon asks his doctor about his prognosis, he becomes alternately depressed and agitated about his impending discharge.

Which nursing approach would be best at this time?

1. "You *are* much better than when you first were hospitalized. You have to decide whether you need to be hospitalized longer or whether you are ready to go home."
2. "You seem to have concerns about going home."
3. "What is it about going home that bothers you?"
4. "You seem sad about going home. Would you like to talk about it?"

84. What would be the most realistic statement about Mr. Simon's prognosis after a course of necessary treatment?
    1. His symptoms will reoccur
    2. His ulcerative lesions will heal, but under stress, the same symptoms may reappear
    3. It is not possible to prognosticate the future course
    4. On-going psychotherapy is going to be essential if he is to be free of symptoms

Chronic Brain Syndrome

85. The main function confabulation serves in patients, especially with chronic brain syndromes, is to
    1. Impress others
    2. Protect their self-esteem
    3. Control others by distance maneuvers
    4. Maintain a sense of humor

86. A key consideration in planning the care of patients with chronic brain syndrome is that
    1. They be protected from suicide attempts
    2. Their capacity for physical activity is diminished
    3. Team effort be aimed at increasing their independence
    4. The staff be sympathetic when patients mention their failing abilities

87. Which of the following most commonly occurs in the clinical picture of chronic brain syndrome?
    1. Memory loss for events in distant past
    2. Quarrelsome behavior directly related to the extent of cerebral arteriosclerosis
    3. Increased resistance to change
    4. Insight into one's situation, its probable causes, and its logical consequences

88. An important part of care for a patient with chronic arteriosclerotic brain syndrome would be

1. Minimizing regression
2. Correcting memory loss
3. Rehabilitating towards independent functioning
4. Preventing further deterioration

89. One morning, Mr. Allen, an 80-year-old patient, said to the nurse, "I'm going to the university today to be their guest lecturer on aerodynamics." Which response by the nurse would be most therapeutic?
    1. "Do you know that you are in the hospital now?"
    2. "Are you saying that you would like to be asked to give a lecture at the university?"
    3. "How about watching a movie on television instead?"
    4. "It's more important that you don't tire yourself out."

Mental Health of the Aged

90. In planning an elderly patient's schedule, it is most important that the daily activities
    1. Are highly structured
    2. Are changed by the nurse each day to meet the patient's needs for variety
    3. Are simplified as much as possible to avoid problems with decision making
    4. Provide many opportunities for making choices to stimulate patient's involvement and interest

91. The mental health of the aged patient is most directly influenced by
    1. The attitude of relatives in providing for the patient's needs
    2. Societal factors such as role change, loss of loved ones, and loss of physical energy
    3. The patient's level of education and economic situation
    4. The attitudes the patient has toward life circumstances

92. Which of the following are common basic needs of the aged?
    1. Sexual outlets and security
    2. Unconditional acceptance by others of their deficits
    3. Preservation of self-esteem
    4. All of the above

93. Erickson's stages of growth and development characterize the task of old age as
    1. Ego integrity versus despair
    2. Autonomy versus shame and doubt
    3. Trust versus mistrust

4. Industry versus inferiority

94. Mrs. Jacobson, a 90-year-old patient who is hard of hearing and in the convalescent home, tells the same story over and over again to all personnel who come to take care of her—about the exciting time when her family came out West in a covered wagon. Which of the following statements would demonstrate understanding of this behavior?
    1. Mrs. Jacobson has better recall for past events than recent
    2. She enjoys reliving pleasurable aspects of her life, since the present and future are bleak
    3. Repeating her stories is one way of interacting, to compensate for a two-way conversation that is difficult for her to sustain
    4. All of the above

95. Mr. Bell has Alzheimer's disease. One night, at 4 A.M., the nurse finds 88-year-old Mr. Bell in the hallway trying to open the door to the fire escape. Which response by the nurse would probably indicate the most accurate assessment of the situation?
    1. "Mr. Bell, you look confused. Would you like to sit down and talk with me?"
    2. "That door leads to the fire escape. Why do you want to go outside now?"
    3. "This is the fire escape door. Are you looking for the bathroom?"
    4. "Something seems to be bothering you. Let's go back to your room and talk about it."

Children and Adolescents

96. According to Erickson's stages of psychosexual development, puberty and adolescence are characterized by what task?
    1. Identity versus role confusion
    2. Initiative versus guilt
    3. Ego integrity versus despair
    4. Intimacy versus isolation

97. Johnny, age 10 years, was admitted to the hospital for a tonsillectomy. In the morning, the nurse notes that the bedding is wet. There are several boys his age in the room. Which initial approach by the nurse would best demonstrate her understanding of the condition and Johnny's stage of growth and development?
    1. While proceeding to change the wet linens,

ask Johnny what sports he likes best, purposefully staying on impersonal topics
    2. Draw the curtains around his bed while changing the linen, saying, "I know that this must be embarrassing to you."
    3. Say nothing while changing the bed; return at another time when the other boys are not in the room and explain to Johnny the medical-emotional reasons for enuresis
    4. Sit down on the bed and convey acceptance of him as a person rather than his symptoms

98. A symptom that characteristically differentiates an autistic child from one with Down's syndrome is
    1. Retardation of activity
    2. Short attention span
    3. Difficulty in responding to a nurturing relationship
    4. Poor academic performance

Crisis

99. The main characteristics of crisis include which of the following
    1. Evidence of a precipitating event
    2. Often seen in stresses of normal stages of growth and development
    3. May need help from a therapist
    4. All of the above

Milieu Therapy

100. A key characteristic feature of milieu therapy is
    1. Inclusion of family therapy in the treatment process
    2. Permissiveness, with lack of rules or structure
    3. Patient-planned, patient-led activities
    4. Staff do not participate in decision making

101. A patient in a therapeutic community setting approached the nurse one weekend evening, complained of being bored, and requested that some activity be provided. Which response by the nurse would be consistent with a milieu therapy approach?
    1. "All right. I'm not busy. How about playing cards with me?"
    2. "I'll go ask the head nurse and see if we can come up with something."
    3. "Why don't you ask Mr. Anderson to play cards with you?"
    4. "Let's get the patients and staff together and discuss this."

Behavior Modification

102. Which of the following are terms commonly associated with behavior therapy?
    1. Conditioned avoidance and positive reinforcement
    2. Token economy and desensitization
    3. Operant conditioning and reciprocal inhibition
    4. All of the above

103. In their role in a behavior therapy program, it is essential that nurses
    1. Ask the patients about the content of their dreams
    2. Only interact with patients who are verbal
    3. Continuously observe the patient behavior and immediately intervene
    4. Obtain a detailed account of each patient's growth and development

104. In setting up a successful behavior modification program it is essential that
    1. There is agreement and support from all personnel involved in daily contact with the patients
    2. That goals be broken down into sequential substeps
    3. The "positive reinforcer" is specifically selected for the individual patient
    4. All of the above

Activity Therapy

105. Which of the following activities would be best for a patient with manic behavior?
    1. Solitary activity, such as reading
    2. Hammering on metal in a jewelry-making class
    3. Playing chess
    4. Competitive games

106. Which of the following activities would be best for a patient who is depressed?
    1. Folding laundry or stapling paper sheets for charts
    2. Playing checkers
    3. Doing a crossword puzzle
    4. Ice skating

Group Therapy

107. The nursing role in group therapy may include being a
    1. Role model and catalyst
    2. Transference object and interpreter
    3. Participant, observer, and facilitator
    4. All of the above

108. Although each of the following have been proposed as advantages of group therapy over individual therapy as a treatment modality, which is the most relevant from a theoretical point of view?
    1. More people can be treated in the same time period
    2. Multiple transference is facilitated in a group setting, and corrective feedback and experiences can be readily provided
    3. Peer group identification occurring in group fosters feelings of relief based on emotional catharsis
    4. Group therapy is less expensive per session to the individual than individual therapy

Family Therapy

109. In family therapy sessions the nurse should
    1. Serve as an arbitrator during disputes
    2. Focus on the person with the presenting problem
    3. Neutralize the scapegoating phenomenon
    4. Use paradoxical communication

110. Family therapy is the choice mode of therapy in the treatment of
    1. Children and adolescents
    2. Alcoholism
    3. Character disorders
    4. Neuroses

Electroconvulsive Therapy

111. Electroconvulsive therapy is ordered as treatment for a patient who is depressed. What is the most important item for the nurse to know to plan immediate posttreatment care?
    1. The patient will not be as depressed as before and therefore will be a high suicide risk
    2. The patient needs to be left alone and needs to sleep
    3. The patient may look bewildered, be confused, and have memory loss
    4. The patient will be hungry after being NPO and will need nourishment on awakening

Psychopharmacologic Therapy

112. The following activities have been planned for Ms. Carson, a patient who is mute and autistic. In which of the following activities will it be important for the nursing staff to take precautionary measures for a common side effect of Thorazine?

1. Shopping in an enclosed mall after lunch
2. Attending the symphony on Wednesday evening
3. A day at the beach, if the weather permits
4. A morning at the art museum

113. Some patients who are on phenothiazines are also given Cogentin. What is the purpose of this practice?
    1. To prevent skin reactions
    2. To increase the effectiveness of the phenothiazines
    3. To decrease motor restlessness
    4. To reduce extrapyramidal side effects

114. Mr. Bill has been on Prolixin, IM, for three years now. He has recently complained of frequent sore throats, and malaise. What potentially serious side effect might these symptoms indicate?

1. Agranulocytosis
2. Akathisia
3. Dystonia
4. Dyskinesia

115. When nialamide (Niamid) or isocarboxazid (Marplan) are administered, what must the nurse know about these drugs?
    1. They lower the threshold for seizures
    2. They potentiate the effects of many other drugs and common foods
    3. They decrease muscular contractions
    4. They commonly cause obstructive jaundice

116. Lithium salts are frequently used to treat mania. What are some frequent side effects?
    1. Slurred speech
    2. Twitching and athetotic movements
    3. Motor weakness
    4. All of the above

Answers / Rationale   Psychiatric Nursing

---

1. (4) If a particular patient is nonverbal, for example, the nurse should not expect that patient to function at a verbal level until ready. In choice No. 1, if the nurse waits for a withdrawn patient, for example, to make contact, it may not be helpful. In No. 2, an ambivalent patient may need assistance in making decisions. In No. 3, the patient's undesirable behavior may be adversely affecting those around.

2. (4) Focusing on feelings is usually the best choice. Ignoring the patient is rarely an acceptable intervention. Pointing out disturbed behavior and role modeling by the nurse are valid, but not as first interventions.

3. (3) Frequent contacts at times of stress are important, especially when a patient is isolated.

4. (2) This is the most neutral answer by process of elimination. The first answer is mainly the function of a recreational-occupational therapist, although nurses participate. The third answer is usually filled by psychologists and social workers, and answer No. 4 is carried out primarily by psychologists or statisticians, although nurses are involved. "Maintenance of a therapeutic environ-

ment" fits more readily into a nursing role than the other professionals because of the number of hours per day a nurse spends with the patients on a unit in comparison with those spent by persons in other disciplines.

5. (4) Decoding symbolic, autistic expressions calls for skill and sensitivity in understanding latent messages. Answer No. 1 is not a good choice since showing "acceptance" is a basic, initial nursing goal that does not require a complexity of skills. No. 2 points out a nontherapeutic nursing action, which is best not to use at all. No. 3 implies that the nurse use short sentences with clear, concise, unambiguous meaning; this can be accomplished with practice. No. 1 and 3 need to be accomplished before No. 4 can occur.

6. (2) Offering a broad opening by giving a general lead is most therapeutic to elicit further description of the patient's reaction and clarify her feelings, which were vaguely stated. No. 1 is a switch of focus from the patient to the mother. No. 3 is nontherapeutic because a question that can be answered by a yes or no often closes off further exploration. No. 4 could be a helpful intervention

but is premature acknowledgment before feelings have been elaborated.

7. (4) It is important to pick up on a feeling tone and encourage exploration of the feelings and the situation.

8. (3) An appropriate direct response to a "you know what I mean" comment is to say you do *not* automatically know what is meant.

9. (4) Attempts to focus on encouraging the patient to describe feelings are important. No. 1 and 2 ask for facts instead of focusing on feelings, and No. 3 is an example of reflecting—a therapeutic response, but in this case it only reflects a *thought*, instead of a feeling.

10. (4) This is the least threatening. The nurse needs to intervene into a pattern of silence. It is not therapeutic for the focus to be on the nurse, and bringing up a controversial topic (such as religion or politics) usually results in an exchange of opinions and arguments.

11. (2) No. 1 and 4 focus on "there-and-then" rather than "here-and-now" feelings and events, and No. 3 is irrelevant because the focus is on a *fact* rather than a feeling.

12. (4) Information that is given to you, the nurse, that may interfere with the patient's recovery needs to be related to other team members.

13. (3) In severe anxiety, the person cannot respond to the social environment; giving detailed information results in overload, as the patient cannot retain and recall data. Only directive information that is brief and specific is effective when the patient cannot focus on what is happening.

14. (4) Acknowledging a feeling tone is the most therapeutic response and provides a broad opening for the patient to elaborate feelings.

15. (1) Common reactions: pupillary dilation, *not* constriction; diarrhea, *not* constipation. Vomiting is not typical of an anxiety response.

16. (2) In panic, a person is highly suggestible and follows "herd instinct" rather than exercising independent judgment and problem solving. The more severe the perceived threat (actual or imaginary), the more intense the reaction to the danger.

17. (4) The first three answers are examples of more pathogenic defenses; that is, they predispose or lead to illness.

18. (3) Projection is a defense mechanism. Most defense mechanisms are aimed at either reducing anxiety to the *self* system or maintaining self-esteem. Although answer No. 2 may be correct at times, it is not so in *all* instances of projection. Denial may operate in *some* cases of projection.

No. 1 and 4 are not good answers because the main focus of defense mechanisms is on *self*, not on others.

19. (4) By definition, No. 1 describes sublimation; No. 2, introjection; and No. 3, repression.

20. (1) It is the most comprehensive, inclusive choice, which may also encompass answers 2 and 4. Since regression is a defense mechanism, we know that the key purpose is to increase self-esteem and/or decrease anxiety; therefore, choice response No. 3 does not fit, as expressing hostility does not necessarily increase esteem and/or decrease anxiety.

21. (2) No. 1 describes regression; No. 3, blocking; and No. 4, identification.

22. (1) By definition, this is the release of energy or impulses into socially-acceptable outlets.

23. (1) By definition, No. 2 is suppression; No. 3, displacement; and No. 4, identification.

24. (3) By definition, this is the conscious deliberate effort to avoid talking or thinking about painful, anxiety-producing experiences.

25. (1) Symbolism is the most clearly descriptive mechanism.

26. (2) Denial is the mind's way of protecting the self-system from a disturbing reality.

27. (3) This will reduce the isolation and withdrawal, while at the same time does not put the burden of decision making on her. She needs a structured routine that is simple. She may not be able to handle close proximity with more than one person at this point, as in No. 2.

28. (4) A simple acknowledgment of what the nurse sees is the best response. Choice No. 3 makes an assumption that she feels better if she looks better. Choices No. 1 and 2 can be taken as a "put-down."

29. (1) It is important to externalize the anger away from self.

30. (4) Meet the patient at her level of functioning, and provide support and encouragement for higher level in the near future.

31. (1) "Loss" is most basic to the development of depression.

32. (2) In the depressed person, anger is turned inward; in the manic, it is noted in sarcasm, demanding behavior, and angry outbursts. No. 3 and 4 occur in the manic phase; No. 1 is a particular problem in depressed phase.

33. (2) The manic patient may be too busy to eat and sleep. Choice No. 1 and 3 are more appropriate for depressed phase; No. 4 is more appropriate for schizophrenia.

34. (4) It is a matter-of-fact statement that is direct, while offering assistance and setting limits on inappropriate behavior.

35. (2) Often the verbalized ideas are jumbled, but the underlying feelings are discernible and need to be acknowledged. Flight of ideas should be curtailed. The patient may not be able to control the internal stimuli to focus on one idea at a time. A louder and more rapid tone by the nurse may only increase the external stimuli for the patient.

36. (4)

37. (1) All suicidal talk and gestures are to be taken seriously. If the patient *talks* about suicide, there *may* be an attempt. Suicide risk is greater when depression is lifting, requiring greater vigilance.

38. (4) The patient may interpret the nurse's silence as discomfort in talking about his suicidal feeling and thoughts. No. 2 focuses on facts too swiftly without providing an opportunity for the patient to express his feelings. Also, No. 2 would be most appropriate in *crisis* intervention when patient was *first* admitted, *not* the next morning. No. 3 moves away from focus on here-and-now to focus on the past.

39. (4) Schizophrenic behavior leading to a suicide act, might be a response to a hallucination or delusion, and No. 1 and 3 are depressive states.

40. (3) In No. 1 and 2 the patient could suffer extensive blood loss if the nurse focuses on feelings at this point or leaves him without first attempting to control the bleeding. In choice No. 4, the patient is left alone, bleeding, frightened, and with a razor still next to him.

41. (4) An honest, direct answer that focuses on feelings is the best approach.

42. (2) Refer to Elisabeth Kubler Ross' emotional stages of death and dying.

43. (1) Shock and anger are commonly the primary initial reactions. Choice No. 2 is irrelevant; and No. 3 is a literal, concrete interpretation of Mrs. Barnes' reaction, not aimed at the possible latent feelings.

44. (1) Reactions to loss tend to be cumulative in effect, in that the more loss experienced in the past, the greater the reaction the next time. Reactivation of feelings connected with previous losses by the current loss accounts for the increased intensity of the reaction. Sudden, unexpected death is harder to resolve, and strong, not little emotional dependency also complicates grief resolution.

45. (2) When the mourner can pass through the idealization stage and be more realistic about the positive and negative aspects of the loss, resolution of grief is beginning.

46. (2) A permissive atmosphere is the key, as well as a *slowly* evolving relationship with room for *distance.* Self-destruction is not a persistent problem requiring major focus for concern.

47. (4)

48. (4) This is a reality-based response, as well as one that acknowledges the patient's nonverbal reaction.

49. (3) Choice No. 1 is not a *direct* response; No. 2 leaves out the importance of the meaning of a neologism to the patient; and No. 4 is less valid and important than *acknowledgment* of the meaning to the patient.

50. (2) This acknowledges the experience and points out reality as the nurse sees it.

51. (1) Circulation may be severely impaired in a patient with waxy flexibility who tends to remain motionless for hours unless moved.

52. (4) The primary initial focus of the nurse-patient relationship is in showing the patient through acceptance that it is *the patient* one is concerned about, *not* the *symptoms.*

53. (3) This is a false belief developed in response to an emotional need.

54. (1) A key consideration in interacting with patients who are suspicious is to avoid the use of logic and argument; humor usually intensifies the anger and suspicions. Changing the topic may serve to reinforce his belief of the guilt of others.

55. (3) Definition of projection as a defense mechanism.

56. (3) This shows a weak sense of moral consciousness.

57. (4)

58. (1) Prevent use of manipulative patterns.

59. (4) Let patient know without anger how you feel, that you are not intimidated, then help her to examine what she is doing and why.

60. (4) Frightening visual hallucinations are especially common, as well as dehydration and vitamin, protein, and caloric deficiencies.

61. (4) Arrest of the disease is possible through abstinent behavior, not a cure through change in psychophysiologic response to alcohol.

62. (4)

63. (2)

64. (4) In addition to those listed here, the most common side effects also include constipation and jaundice.

65. (2) It is important to provide external support in helping to develop the superego and to lessen manipulative behavior.

66. (4) All of these items are important to aid the staff in understanding the underlying psychodynamics of ritualism.

67. (4) The opposite of what is stated in the first three choices is true. The patient seems to do best when (1) routine activities are set up and changes are avoided, which are anxiety-provoking; (2) perfection-type activities bring satisfaction (cleaning and straightening a linen closet, for example); and (3) he knows ahead of time about changes in routine.

68. (3) This is the best example of setting limits on the behavior. Choices No. 1 and 4 may be closely linked to nontherapeutic use of power. Choice No. 2 is more of an example of a punishment approach.

69. (2) A ritual, such as compulsive handwashing, is an attempt to allay anxiety caused by unconscious impulses that are frightening.

70. (1) It shows acceptance by listening to the initial account by the patient about her physical problems. Neither a superficial focus nor a technical explanation of physical problem convey acceptance of the patient as a person; choice No. 4 is too abrupt for an initial response.

71. (3) Showing *acceptance* and gaining trust and confidence are usually the key initial nursing goals.

72. (3) Choice No. 1 is incorrect because conversion, not regression is the major defense mechanism, and No. 2 is incorrect because, if a possible cause is identified and treatment relieves the discomfort, the patient often develops another new symptom. Frequently, patients do not want to be cured of their symptoms because they *need* the symptoms to control the behavior of others or because they do not know how else to get attention. In No. 4, the converse is true.

73. (1) The other choices are all *similarities* between malingering and conversion reaction.

74. (2) This is a better choice than No. 4, which may be true, but is a tangential and irrelevant reason. Choice No. 1 is not correct because the patient *is* aware of reality, but may not understand the *cause* for her conversion reaction. Choice No. 3 is more relevant in a *paranoid* reaction.

75. (1) The original source of conflict, pain, and/or guilt is repressed (pushed out of awareness) only to surface in a symbolic way.

76. (4) This answer also incorporates No. 3. Agreement to attend activities does not indicate the *greatest* improvement. The patient already recognizes that her behavior is irrational but cannot understand the cause nor banish the behavior by will.

77. (3) It is believed at this time that if the patient had another acceptable outlet for emotions (such as verbalizing anger, frustration, and disappointments) the emotions would not directly affect the organs. Choice No. 1 is not correct because some disorders may be life-threatening (ulcers, for example). Choice No. 2 is irrelevant; however, in Freudian terms, the opposite would be more true; No. 4 is incorrect in that it is a well-known situation when one physical illness is "cured," another disorder comes to light.

78. (4) All other responses describe the *similarities* between the two forms of disorders.

79. (2) Characteristic underlying needs in psychophysiologic reactions are dependency, attention, and the need for security through trust.

80. (1) Emotional support is a key need.

81. (2) All the other choices are correct but can be dovetailed into the second choice.

82. (4) One defense mechanism often seen in psychophysiologic reactions is repression. As the patient is better able to handle the anxiety connected with underlying feelings, the need for repression lessens.

83. (2) It reflects the patient's underlying concerns in the most open-ended manner.

84. (3) This answer is the best choice because the other choices seem too certain for a disorder, which although it has a pattern, can be altered if and when the patient adopts different outlets for expressing his emotions.

85. (2) Recognizing that confabulation is a defense mechanism, the best choice is the one that defines one of the main functions of defense mechanisms—to protect self-esteem.

86. (2) An important principle to remember here is that a program of care should not increase physiologic losses by overtaxing the patients' physical capacities. It is important to remember that suicide is the *main* concern of *depression* and not a key concern of chronic brain syndrome.

87. (3) One of the main needs experienced by most elderly patients with chronic brain disorders is the need for most things to be the same. The other choices are wrong for the following reasons: There has been no demonstrable evidence of relationship between any behavior symptom and the extent or severity of pathophysiologic condition; intellectual blunting usually occurs, which interferes with ability to deal with abstract thoughts; and memory loss is for recent events and names.

88. (1) Memory loss is usually permanent; how-

ever, disorientation attributed to loss of memory can be minimized. Patients become usually more dependent in the course of illness and deteriorate progressively. Use of regression as a coping response *can* be minimized.

89. (2) This is the best choice. The other choices are not helpful for the following reasons: Choices No. 3 and 4 switch the focus and ignore the patient's statement; No. 1 is too brusque an attempt to bring patient back to reality.

90. (1) Elderly patients feel more secure when they can count on their environment being the same, predictable, and consistent in detail from day-to-day to compensate for feelings of loss of the familiar in terms of body functions, social environment, and so on.

91. (4) Although all the other choices are valid and important, the fourth answer encompasses them all and is therefore the most comprehensive answer.

92. (4) It is often assumed that sexual activity is no longer a need in the elderly, but research supports the idea that sex *is* a basic need of the aged.

93. (1) Choice No. 2 relates to toddler; No. 3 to infancy; No. 4 to latency period in childhood.

94. (4)

95. (3) Nocturnal urination is a most common need, complicated by disorientation related to the patient's age, his disorder, and an unfamiliar environment by night.

96. (1) Choice No. 2 refers to preschool age, No. 3 is characteristic of "maturity" in later years of life, and No. 4 refers to young adulthood.

97. (4) The goal is to preserve ego strength through acceptance and respect of him as a person. Choice No. 1 focuses on the tangential and irrelevant; choice No. 2 makes the problem more obvious to others in the room and makes an assumption without validation about how Johnny must feel; choice No. 3, it is usually not helpful to give a rational explanation for an emotional difficulty related to enuresis.

98. (3) Most children with Down's are affectionate and enjoy being held and cuddled, whereas the opposite is usually the case with an autistic child.

99. (4) A crisis situation may be a developmental one in which the person's usual means for handling difficulties are not effective at this time, and the situation may call for therapeutic intervention. A stress usually precipitates the crisis.

100. (3) Although families and significant others are brought in when needed, family *therapy* is neither a key feature nor an emphasis in milieu therapy. Structured activities based on members'

needs, rather than permissiveness, is the keynote. Staff participate *with* (not dominate) patients in discussing plans for activities.

101. (4) This calls for joint patient-staff planning and decision making. The other responses are typical of a high degree of direction by the staff, with patients in the passive-dependent role.

102. (4) All are examples of behavior modification and are techniques that emphasize overt behavior, *not* unconscious processes.

103. (3) Focus on dreams is part of Freudian analysis; behavior modification is used in the treatment of mute patients also; and the emphasis of behavioral therapy is in the present and not the past developmental history.

104. (4) A major assumption of behavior therapy is that it *is* possible to predict under what conditions the same behavior may occur if all staff members agree and use the same reinforcer for rewarding each step of approximation toward a specific goal.

105. (2) It will provide energy release without the external stimuli and pressure of competitive games. Reading usually requires sitting, which a manic patient cannot readily do.

106. (1) An undemanding task that the patient could finish would allow a feeling of successful accomplishment. Choices No. 2 and 3 require intellectual activity that is usually slowed down during a depressive phase. Activity No. 4 requires a skill that the patient may not have, and the patient might experience frustration in learning; also, the patient may not have the psychomotor energy for the ice skating.

107. (4)

108. (2) Choices No. 1 and 4 relate to socioeconomic justification for the advantages of group therapy. Choice No. 3 can be incorporated into No. 2 with No. 2 being the more comprehensive and inclusive response. Multiple transference can be therapeutic from the standpoint of eliciting positive as well as negative feelings, not only by seeing similarities between self and others but also by experiencing differences.

109. (3) A contract early in therapy is essential to make expectations clear, which includes no scapegoating or blaming of one family member by another. The opposite of choices No. 2 and 4 are important to practice. It is crucial that nurses not take sides or try to referee a family fight.

110. (1) Alcoholism and character disorders are usually best treated in groups with peers; behavior modification (desensitization) is currently the most

effective mode of treatment in neuroses.

111. (3) The patient will be in a confused state after treatment and will require side rails and the reassuring presence of a nurse.

112. (3) The patient needs to be protected against photosensitivity and dermatitis when exposed to the sun; a sun-screen preparation should be applied to exposed parts of the skin and the patient should wear long sleeves and cover-up clothing.

113. (4) This is the best choice as it encompasses choice No. 3. Choices No. 1 and 2 are definitely wrong.

114. (1) Blood dyscrasias often are overlooked when first symptoms of possible adverse drug effects appear in the form of a minor cold.

115. (2) Hypertensive crisis can be precipitated by combining this drug with common cold medications and foods high in tyramine or pressor amines (yogurt, Chianti wine, cheese, coke, and coffee, for example).

116. (4)

Annotated Bibliography

Burgess, A., and Lazare, A.: Psychiatric nursing in the hospital and the community, Englewood Cliffs, N.J., 1976, Prentice-Hall, Inc.

The most valuable feature of this book is the simple format and writing style. It is not as comprehensive in scope or theory as Kyes and Hofling, or Kalkman and Davis; however, the intent is to devote a major part of the book to the application of basic concepts to nursing management of clinical syndromes. The art work is effective; key points are enumerated in outline form, key phrases are placed in the margins, and end-of-chapter summaries all serve to promote this as a useful book for initial learning and review of major psychiatric conditions.

Hays, J. S., and Larson, K. H.: Interacting with patients, New York, 1963, Macmillan, Inc.

This is a compendium of process recordings with lists and numerous easy-to-understand examples of therapeutic and nontherapeutic responses for beginning students.

Kalkman, M., and Davis, A.: New dimensions in mental health-psychiatric nursing, ed. 4, New York, 1974, McGraw-Hill, Inc.

In addition to chapters on disorders, this text includes chapters concerning group and family therapy, the dying person, and old age. Implications for nursing appear throughout the book.

Kyes, J., and Hofling, C.: Basic psychiatric concepts in nursing, ed. 3, Philadelphia, 1974, J. B. Lippincott Company.

This text is a comprehensive reference covering personality development, neuroses, psychoses, character disorders, psychosomatic disorders, emotional disorders of children and adolescents, and treatment modes. It also includes a glossary and quick reference index. It contains a clear description of theory, is illustrated with case examples, and has suggestions for nursing management.

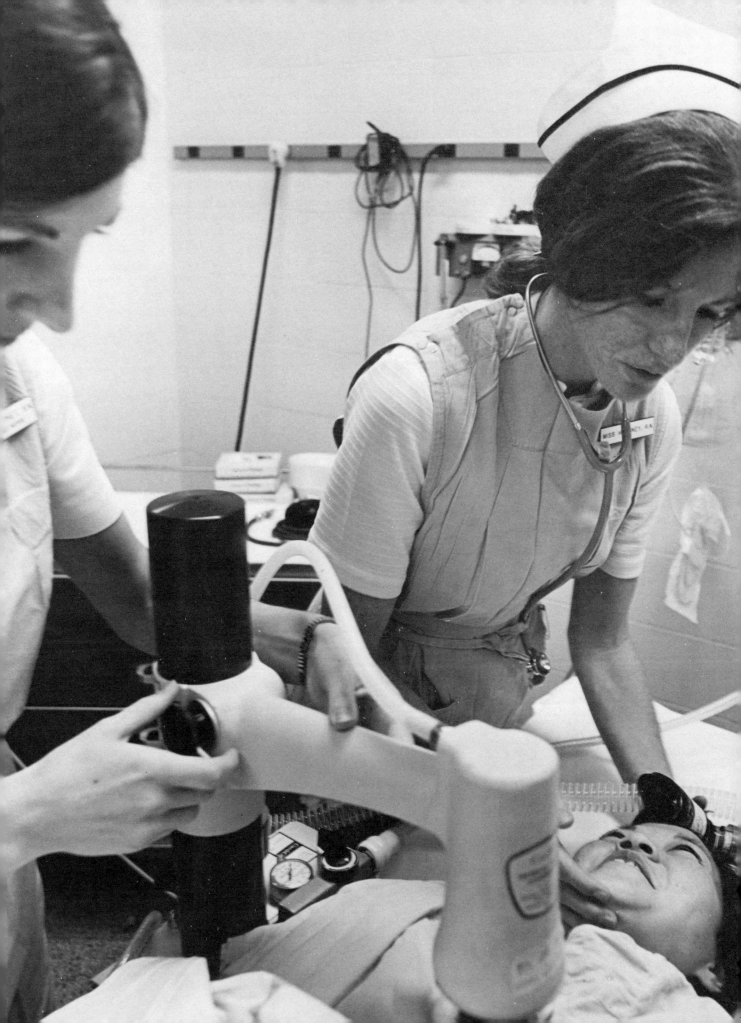

Unit 2　Medical Nursing

Introduction

The primary purpose of this section is to provide a framework that will assist the student in the identification of common medical problems and to provide a rationale for nursing interventions. The content has been organized under five homeostatic processes and cell maturation and reproduction to present the information in terms of commonalities that facilitate understanding rather than the memorization of the signs and symptoms of dysfunctions. Common imbalances are discussed under each of these headings and are related to the physiologic dysfunction. Assessment criteria, objectives of nursing care, and nursing interventions are prioritized to assist the student in systematically analyzing patient data and planning nursing care to promote or maintain wellness.

Mary Jane Sauvé

Part A   Homeostasis

Homeostasis is a term used primarily to describe the coordinated physiologic processes that act to maintain the integrity of the organism and thereby aid in its survival. It may also be applied to the wider range of activities that enable humans to derive satisfaction from their environment and to pursue the process of self-actualization.

A. Survival of cells and maintenance of their function is dependent on the cells' immediate fluid environment
B. The physical and chemical characteristics of the fluid environment, which must be maintained within *narrow limits*, include
   1. Blood pressure
   2. Serum glucose
   3. Fluid and electrolytes
   4. Hydrogen ion concentration
   5. Muscle tone
C. Deviations in the physical or chemical characteristics of the internal environment elicit responses that automatically tend to compensate or counter-balance the deviation
   1. Negative feedback mechanisms act to minimize deviations and to *bring back* the physical and chemical characteristics to a state that is optimum for cellular function
   2. Deviations may be toward excess or deficiency

D. Integration and regulation of homeostatic processes in humans is the function of the autonomic nervous and endocrine systems
   1. The many interconnections of the autonomic nervous system with the central nervous system enable it to detect and evaluate deviations and send impulses to appropriate structures for action
   2. The sympathoadrenal response elicited by these two systems is the body's first-line defense mechanism against changes initiated by internal or external stressors
E. Maintenance of homeostasis is also dependent on the body's ability to regulate the reproduction, maturation, and structure of cells
F. Design of nursing actions
   1. Identify the nature of the stressor—internal and/or external
   2. Identify the system's responses as appropriate, excessive, or deficient
   3. Plan interventions
      a. Reduce stress
      b. Support adaptive behaviors
      c. Strengthen deficient responses
      d. Modify excessive responses
      e. Prevent injury or complications
      f. Promote self-actualizing behaviors
   4. Reappraise stressors and responses and modify interventions as indicated

Part B   Blood Pressure

THE PHYSIOLOGY OF BLOOD PRESSURE

A. The pressure exerted by blood on the walls of the arterial system
B. Acts to maintain adequate transport of nutrients to the tissue and for removal of waste products
C. Arterial pressures are measured indirectly with auscultation of the brachial artery after it has been compressed with the inflatable cuff of a sphygmomanometer
   1. Systolic pressure—first tapping sound
   2. Diastolic sound—first muffled sound
   3. Recorded *systolic/muffling/disappearance of sound*—120/80/76

4. Normal range—100/60 to 140/90
D. The systolic pressure is the maximum pressure of the blood against the artery walls and occurs with left ventricular ejection
   1. Provides information about the force of left ventricular contraction
   2. Is influenced by the total blood volume, blood viscosity, and the distensibility of the major arteries
E. The diastolic pressure represents the lowest force exerted against the artery wall and occurs when the heart is relaxing
   1. Provides information about the condition of peripheral vessels
      a. Narrowed arterioles increase diastolic pressure
      b. Dilated arterioles decrease diastolic pressure
   2. Influenced by kidney function, nervous, and humoral factors
F. The mean arterial pressure is the average pressure circulating the blood volume
   1. Mean pressure is one-third systolic pressure plus two-thirds diastolic pressure
   2. Normal kidney function requires a mean arterial pressure of 70 mm Hg

3. Indicates average stress level to which heart and blood vessels are subjected
G. The pulse pressure is the difference between the systolic and diastolic pressure—averages 40 mm Hg
   1. Diminished with decreased stroke volume or in obstruction of left ventricular output
   2. Increased with increased stroke volume, abnormally rapid runoff of blood and with aortic rigidity
H. Blood pressure therefore is essentially a reflection of the relationship between cardiac output (stroke volume × heart rate) and peripheral resistance, BP = CO × PVR (see also Table 2-1).

IMBALANCES IN BLOOD PRESSURE

1. **Hypotension**—develops as a result of decrease in cardiac output or a decrease in peripheral vascular resistance, or both
A. Decrease in cardiac output—produces signs and symptoms related to homeostatic mechanisms activated to maintain blood pressure
   1. Increased heart rate to maintain stroke volume (tachycardia—rate over 100)

Table 2-1. Factors controlling blood pressure

Components	Influencing factors	Homeostatic regulator
Cardiac output		
Stroke volume	Blood volume	Endocrine system; ADH—aldosterone Kidney
	Venous return	Local blood flow regulators
	Strength of cardiac contraction (inatrophic action)	Sympathetic nervous system
Heart rate	Exercise, anxiety, nervous excitement, eating, metabolic rate, sleep	Autonomic nervous system— sympathetic increases rate and parasympathetic decreases rate
Peripheral vascular resistance		
Elasticity of arterial walls	Age, sclerosis, injury, inflammatory process	
Viscosity of blood	Hematocrit	Hematopoietic system
Caliber of arterioles (vasoconstriction, vasodilation)	Blood volume, cardiac output, arterial oxygen tensions, pH of body fluids, pain, emotional reactions	Autonomic nervous system—Sympathetic nervous system increases vasomotor tone, parasympathetic nervous system decreases vasomotor tone
	Tissue metabolism	Local blood flow regulators

2. Increased peripheral vascular resistance (vasoconstriction) to promote venous return and provide adequate perfusion to heart and brain
   a. Pale, cool, dry, or moist skin
   b. Indigestion, nausea, vomiting
   c. Dyspnea
   d. Decreased urine output
   e. Apprehension, anxiety
B. Etiology of decreased cardiac output
   1. Decreased blood volume
      a. Hemorrhage
      b. Plasma loss—burns, intestinal obstruction
      c. Excessive loss of fluid and electrolytes—vomiting, diarrhea, sweating
      d. Angina pectoris—insufficient coronary blood flow
         (1) Pathophysiology
             (a) Narrowing of coronary arteries due to atherosclerosis, spasm or inflammation
             (b) Decreased coronary blood flow due to hypotension, aortic valve defects, polycythemia
             (c) Increased need for myocardial oxygenation in cardiac hypertrophy, during heavy exertion, or in conditions in which cardiac output is increased, as in anemia and hyperthyroidism
         (2) Assessment findings
             (a) Subjective data
                 i. Pain
                 • *Type—burning, aching, squeezing*
                 • *Location—substernal; may radiate to left shoulder*
                 • *Duration—5 to 20 minutes*
                 • *Precipitated by exertion, emotional stresses, or cold temperatures*
                 • *Relieved by rest or nitroglycerin*
                 ii. Shortness of breath
                 iii. Indigestion
                 iv. Faintness
             (b) Objective data—vital signs
                 i. Blood pressure—normal range
                 ii. Pulse—tachycardia

(3) Nursing care is designed to provide relief during acute attacks, identify precipitating factors, and promote measures that prevent attacks
    (a) Bedrest until pain subsides
    (b) Oxygen as needed
    (c) Nitroglycerin sublingually, as ordered
    (d) Assist in identifying stressful people, activities, and situations
    (e) Involve patient and family in health teaching
        i. Review action, effects, dosage, and administration of medication; carry "fresh" nitroglycerin at all times, as it loses potency after six months
        ii. Encourage weight loss if indicated
        iii. Devise program of regular exercise and rest to promote coronary circulation
        iv. Explain need to avoid physical and emotional stress
        • *Large meals and heavy exercise*
        • *Extremes in temperature*
        • *Stimulants—coffee, smoking*
        • *Sexual relations when fatigued*
2. Inadequate or inefficient myocardial contractility
   a. Myocardial infarction—localized necrosis of myocardium due to sudden cessation of coronary blood flow; a leading cause of death in the United States
      (1) Pathophysiology
          (a) Coronary occlusion due to thrombosis, embolism, or hemorrhage of atheromatous plaque or insufficient blood flow for muscle mass due to cardiac hypertrophy, hemorrhage, shock or severe dehydration
          (b) Asynergic pumping of left ventricle, decreased stroke volume, decreased blood pressure
      (2) Predisposing factors—family history, sex, age, stressful life style, diet, and chronic diseases such as diabetes mellitus and hypertension

(3) Assessment findings
  (a) Subjective data
      i. Pain
         • *Type—severe, crushing, burning*
         • *Location—precordial or substernal often radiating to one or both arms, neck, jaw, or back*
         • *Duration—lasts longer than 30 minutes*
         • *Precipitating factors— unrelated to exercise or respirations and is not relieved by rest or nitroglycerine.*
      ii. Shortness of breath (dyspnea)
      iii. Sweating
      iv. Indigestion, nausea
      v. Severe anxiety—fear of death very strong
  (b) Objective data
      i. Vital signs
         • *Blood pressure—decreased*
         • *Apical pulse—tachycardia (rate over 100); heart sounds diminished*
         • *Peripheral pulse—weak, rapid*
         • *Temperature—elevates within 24 hours (100-103 F)*
         • *Respirations—increased, shallow*
      ii. Skin—pale, cool, diaphoretic
      iii. Emotional status—restless
      iv. Laboratory studies (see Appendix E, Diagnostic tests)
         • *Elevated WBC, sedimentation rate*
         • *Elevated serum enzymes (CPK, SGOT, LDH)*
(4) Nursing care is designed to reduce the cardiac workload, relieve anxiety and pain, prevent complications, and provide support for patient and family
  (a) Bedrest in a semi-Fowler's position, avoiding unnecessary nursing functions
  (b) Humidified oxygen per mask, cannula, or nasal catheter
  (c) Medications, as ordered (see Appendix F, Drugs for action, side effects, observations)
      i. Analagesics—morphine, meperidine (Demerol) HCl
      ii. Sedatives—phenobarbital, diazepam (Valium)
      iii. Antiarrhythmics—lidocaine HCl, quinidine HCl, procaine amide (Pronestyl), Isoproterehol (Isuprel) HCl
      iv. Anticoagulants—heparin sodium, bishydroxycoumarin or dicoumarin
  (d) Institute and maintain parenteral infusions
  (e) Assist with insertion and continuous monitoring of central venous pressure (CVP)
      i. Reflects the pressure exerted by blood returning to the right atrium from the systemic circulation
      ii. Measure central venous pressure (CVP)
         • *Position manometer so that zero is at level of right atrium*
         • *By way of three-way stopcock, allow fluid from infusion bottle to enter the manometer*
         • *CVP is recorded after stopcock has been turned to patient and final height of column in manometer has been reached*
         • *Fluid in manometer should fluctuate with patient's respirations*
         • *Normal CVP is 4 to 10 cm water—increase indicates fluid overload or congestive heart failure; decrease indicates low blood volume and more parenteral infusions are needed*
  (f) Check vital signs and apical pulse every one to two hours and prn
      i. Observe rate, rhythm, and characteristics of pulse
      ii. Observe for pulse deficit—apical pulse greater than radial pulse
  (g) Monitor ECG pattern, observing for ectopic beats and rhythm changes
  (h) Provide emotional support
      i. Stay with anxious patients
      ii. Encourage communication

with families

    iii. Explain procedures and treatments—may be necessary to do frequently with anxious patients

  (i) Maintain tissue nutrition

    i. Parenteral fluids

    ii. Diet—liquid, low-sodium, or low-cholesterol, (see Appendix C, Diets)

  (j) Measure intake and output

    i. Notify physician if urine output falls below 25 ml/hour or specific gravity exceeds 1.020

    ii. Weigh daily, as ordered

    iii. Utilize bedside commode for bowel movements if possible

  (k) Deal with anxiety, loss of body image, sexuality, and fears of dying and death

    i. Allow patient and family to verbalize concerns

    ii. Encourage self-care activities and ambulation, as ordered

    iii. Discuss any activity restrictions with patient and family, clarifying whether they are temporary or long term

    iv. Emphasize importance of maintaining diet restrictions if any, avoidance of caffeine, smoking, large meals

  (l) Discuss medications, purpose, side effects, dosage, scheduling, and precautions

b. Congestive heart failure—clinical syndrome in which heart is unable to maintain normal outflow of blood

c. Myocarditis—inflammation of the cardiac muscle

3. Restriction of heart muscle

a. Acute and chronic pericarditis—inflammation of parietal and/or visceral pericardium

  (1) Pathophysiology

    (a) Compression of heart pumping action by fibrosis of pericardium or accumulation of fluid in pericardium

    (b) Decreased cardiac output results in increased systemic and pulmonic venous pressures

  (2) Etiology

    (a) Bacterial, viral, or fungal infections

    (b) Tuberculosis

    (c) Collagen diseases

    (d) Uremia

    (e) Transmural myocardial infarction

    (f) Trauma

  (3) Assessment findings

    (a) Subjective data

      i. Pain

       • *Type—sharp, moderate to severe*

       • *Location—over wide area of precordium; may radiate down right arm or to jaw and teeth*

       • *Precipitating factors—may be aggravated with movement and with deep inspiration*

      ii. Chills with sweating

      iii. Apprehension, anxiety

      iv. Fatigue

      v. Abdominal pain

      vi. Shortness of breath

    (b) Objective data

      i. Vital signs

       • *Elevated temperature—runs erratic course; may be low grade*

       • *Decreased pulse pressure, tachycardia*

       • *Pericardial friction rub—appears on first day and has wide distribution over precordium*

       • *Pulsus paradoxus—an abnormal drop in systemic blood pressure of more than 8 to 10 mm Hg during inspiration*

      ii. Increased CVP, distended neck veins

      iii. Dependent pitting edema, liver engorgement

      iv. Restlessness

      v. Serum enzymes—SGOT may elevate slightly; elevated WBC (see Appendix E, Diagnostic tests)

      vi. Chest x-ray may indicate cardiac enlargement

(4) Nursing care is designed to reduce discomfort, provide physical and emotional support, and prevent complications
 (a) Bedrest—semi-Fowler's position
 (b) Vital signs every two to four hours and prn
  i. Cooling measures as indicated
  ii. Apical as well as radial pulse—notify physician if heart sounds decrease in amplitude
  iii. Notify physician if pulse pressure narrows
 (c) Parenteral infusions, as ordered
 (d) Strict intake and output records
 (e) Low-sodium diet may be ordered—assist with feedings as needed
 (f) Oxygen, as ordered
 (g) Medications, as ordered
  i. Analgesics—aspirin, morphine sulfate
  ii. Antibiotics
  iii. Digitalis and diuretics if heart failure present
 (h) Assist with aspiration of pericardial sac if needed
 (i) Prepare for pericardectomy (excision of constricting pericardium), as ordered
 (j) Provide continuous emotional support to patient and family
 b. Cardiac tamponade—acute compression of the heart by a rapid accumulation of fluid in the pericardial sac
4. Valvular defects
 a. Mitral stenosis—progressive thickening and calcification of mitral leaflets, which narrows orifice and obstructs blood flow between left atrium and left ventricle
 (1) Pathophysiology
  (a) Blood flow across narrowed orifice; cardiac output is maintained by an elevated atrioventricular pressure gradient
  (b) Elevated left atrial pressure results in elevated pulmonary venous and capillary pressure
  (c) Elevation of pulmonary vascular

resistance may result in eventual right-sided heart failure
 (2) Etiology and incidence
  (a) Most common sequelae of rheumatic heart disease
  (b) Congenital defects
  (c) Patients—75% are women under 45 years of age
 (3) Assessment findings
  (a) Subjective data
   i. Shortness of breath on exertion
   ii. Excessive fatigue
   iii. Cough
   iv. Bloody sputum (hemoptysis)
   v. Sleeps with two or more pillows (orthopnea)
   vi. Breathlessness in sleep (paroxysmal nocturnal dyspnea)
  (b) Objective data
   i. Vital signs
   • *Blood pressure—normal or slightly low*
   • *Pulse—weak, may be irregular*
   • *Respirations—increased, shallow*
   ii. Cardiac palpation, auscultation
   • *Diastolic thrill (palpable murmur) at apex of heart*
   • *Presystolic, low-pitched, rumbling murmur, heard best at apex*
   iii. Severe stenosis with right-side failure
   • *Facial and peripheral cyanosis*
   • *Neck vein distention, liver enlargement, dependent edema*
   iv. Pulmonary function tests (see Appendix E, Diagnostic tests)
   • *Decreased vital capacity*
   • *Decreased total lung capacity*
   v. Left heart catheterization—detects extent of stenosis and chamber pressures
   vi. Ultrasound—detects mobility of mitral valve
 (4) Nursing care is designed to reduce cardiac workload, prevent

complications, and prepare the patient for surgical intervention (commissurotomy or prosthetic valve replacement); see nursing care: (a) congestive heart failure and (b) cardiac surgery

b. Mitral insufficiency or regurgitation—distorted or damaged mitral valve is no longer able to approximate during systole

(1) Pathophysiology

(a) During systole, blood regurgitates from the left ventricle into the left atrium

(b) Compensation consists of rapid left ventricular decompression into the left atrium during early ejection, reducing ventricular size and tension and resulting in more complete emptying of the left ventricle

(c) As the end-diastolic volume (blood in ventricles at end of diastole) increases, left atrial enlargement may occur along with elevation of left atrial pressures and resultant increased pulmonary vascular resistance

(d) As larger quantities of blood are regurgitated into the left atrium, the left ventricle deteriorates, decreasing cardiac output

(2) Etiology and incidence

(a) Chronic rheumatic heart disease—in contrast to stenosis, affects men more frequently than women

(b) Congenital anomaly

(c) Myocardial infarction with ischemia of the papillary muscles

(d) Bacterial endocarditis

(e) Marked ventricular hypertrophy

(3) Assessment findings

(a) Subjective data

i. Fatigue

ii. Shortness of breath on exertion

iii. Sleeping on two or more pillows (orthopnea)

iv. Breathlessness during sleep (paroxysmal nocturnal dyspnea, PND)

v. Weight loss

(b) Objective data

i. Vital signs

• *Blood pressure, temperature, respirations—usually normal*

• *Pulse—regular, characterized by a sharp upstroke*

ii. Precordial inspection, palpation, and auscultation

• *Rocking motion of chest with each cardiac cycle*

• *Systolic thrill palpable at apex*

• *Holosystolic (throughout systole) murmur, which usually radiates to axilla*

iii. Chest x-ray—extreme left atrial enlargement

(4) Nursing care is designed to reduce cardiac workload, prevent complications, and prepare patient for surgical intervention if indicated (prosthetic valve replacement); see nursing care: (a) congestive heart failure and (b) cardiac surgery

c. Aortic stenosis—fibrosis and calcification of aortic valve resulting in narrowing of orifice between left ventricle and the aorta

(1) Pathophysiology

(a) Blood flow is obstructed by narrowing aortic orifice, increasing left ventricular pressures

(b) Increased ventricular pressures result in left ventricular hypertrophy

(c) As ventricular compliance decreases, left atrial contractions become more forceful, raising left ventricular end diastolic volumes to a level necessary to maintain ventricular contraction

(d) Cardiac output and stroke volume maintained at rest but fail to rise during exercise

(e) Ventricular dilatation and failure

(f) Ventricular hypertrophy increases oxygen needs of heart, whereas increasing ventricular pressures compress coronary arteries decreasing cardiac perfusion—ischemic attacks

(2) Etiology and incidence
  (a) Congenital anomaly
  (b) Rheumatic heart disease
  (c) Idiopathic in elderly
  (d) Symptoms usually not manifested until fourth or fifth decade
(3) Assessment findings
  (a) Subjective data
    i. Shortness of breath on exertion
    ii. Chest pain (angina pectoris)
    iii. Fainting
  (b) Objective data
    i. Vital signs
    • *Blood pressure— usually within normal limits*
    • *Pulse—slow rise and delayed peak*
    ii. Precordial examination
    • *Cardiac apex displaced laterally and inferiorly*
    • *Systolic thrill at base of heart and along carotid arteries*
    • *Low-pitched, rasping systolic murmur radiating to carotid arteries*
    iii. Diagnostic tests
    • *Electrocardiogram—nonspecific*
    • *Left heart catheterization*
    • *Angiocardiography*
(4) Nursing care is designed to reduce cardiac stress, promote comfort, and if indicated, prepare patient for surgery (valvular prosthesis or aortic valve homograft); see nursing care for (a) angina pectoris, (b) congestive heart failure, and (c) cardiac surgery

d. Aortic insufficiency or regurgitation—aortic valve leaflets fail to close during ventricular diastole
(1) Pathophysiology
  (a) As aortic pressures increase and ventricular pressures decrease, blood flows backwards into left ventricle
  (b) End-diastolic left ventricular volumes are increased
  (c) Left ventricle dilates and increases its muscle mass to accommodate increased stroke volume and to eject it
  (d) Reflexly peripheral arterioles relax, lowering diastolic pressures
(2) Etiology and incidence
  (a) Rheumatic heart disease
  (b) Bacterial endocarditis
  (c) Congenital anomaly
  (d) Syphilis
  (e) Ankylosing spondylitis
  (f) Patients—75% with pure aortic insufficiency are men
(3) Assessment findings
  (a) Subjective data
    i. Palpitation accompanied by head pounding
    ii. Shortness of breath on exertion
    iii. Chest pains at rest as well as with exertion (angina pectoris)
    iv. Sleeps with two pillows (orthopnea)
    v. Shortness of breath during sleep (PND)
    vi. Excessive sweating
  (b) Objective data
    i. Vital signs
    • *Blood pressure—elevated systolic pressure (up to 300 mm Hg) and widened pulse pressure*
    • *Pulse—rapid rising "water hammer" or "Corrigan's" pulse*
    ii. Abrupt distention and collapse of larger arteries
    iii. Head may bob with each heart beat
    iv. Precordial examination
    • *Forceful apical impulse, which may be displaced laterally and inferiorly*
    • *Diastolic thrill over left sternal border*
    • *High-pitched, blowing, decrescendo diastolic murmur best heard in third intercostal space to left of sternum*
    v. Diagnostic tests (see Appendix E)
    • *ECG—nonspecific*

- *Chest x-ray—varying degrees of left ventricular enlargement*
- *Angiocardiograms*

  (4) Nursing care is designed to support adaptation, reduce cardiac workload, and prepare the patient for surgery if ordered; see nursing care: (a) congestive heart failure, (b) angina pectoris, and (c) cardiac bypass surgery

5. Arrhythmias
   a. Bradyarrhythmias—rates below 60
      (1) Normal in well-trained athletes
      (2) May be secondary to drugs such as digitalis
      (3) Myocardial infarction—vagal response
      (4) Third degree *heart block*
         (a) Pathophysiology
            i. Wave of excitation begun at the SA node is blocked at the AV node and does not pass down to ventricles
            ii. Conductive tissues in ventricles establishes independent rhythm
         (b) Etiology
            i. Atherosclerotic heart disease
            ii. Myocardial infarction
            iii. Congenital heart disease
            iv. Myocarditis
         (c) Assessment findings
            i. Subjective data
            • *Dizziness*
            • *Fainting*
            ii. Objective data
            • *Disorientation—unaware of person, time, place*
            • *Seizures*
            • *Vital signs: (a) increased systolic pressure with widened pulse pressure and (b) pulse—25 to 45 beats/minute, full; rate is regular and increases slightly or not at all with exercise*
         (d) Complications
            i. Heart failure
            ii. Shock
            iii. Stokes-Adams attack—intermittent ventricular standstill or ventricular fibrillation

  (e) Nursing care is designed to promote comfort, prevent complications, and prepare the patient for transvenous (permanent) pacemaker insertion
   i. Limited activity or bedrest to decrease tissue oxygen needs
   ii. Oxygen, as ordered
   iii. Medications, as ordered (see Appendix F, Drugs)
   • *Isoproterenol*
   • *Atropine*
   • *Epinephrine*
   iv. Include patient and family in instructions on transvenous pacemaker insertion—pacing catheter is advanced into right ventricle via jugular or subclavian vein; battery pack is placed subcutaneously beneath clavicle or in axilla
   • *Outline procedure, its duration, equipment utilized, and importance of postinsertion monitoring*
   • *Explain purpose of pacemaker and type: (a) set rate—ventricles stimulated at fixed rate and (b) demand—stimulates ventricles only when patient's heart rate falls below preset time limit*
   • *Practice postinsertion ROM exercises*
   v. Postinsertion care is designed to prevent complications and promote comfort and rehabilitation
   • *Continuous cardiac monitoring*
   • *Report excessive bleeding or signs of infection at insertion site*
   • *Bedrest in position of comfort*
   • *Observe for signs of pacemaker failure: (a) decreased blood pressure, pulse, (b) pallor, cyanosis, fatigue, dyspnea, and (c) ECG, absent or runaway pacemaker blip*
   • *Avoid electrical hazards by grounding all equipment*
   • *Provide opportunities for patient and family to verbalize feelings about living with*

pacemaker
- *Postinsertion teaching should include (a) daily pulse taking, (b) avoidance of stimulants such as tea, coffee, cola, and (c) safety factors—electrical hazards (microwave ovens, radar), extensive dental work, over-the-counter medications*

b. Tachyarrhythmias—rates over 100
  (1) Sinus tachycardia—increased sinus rates due to fever, anxiety, anemia
  (2) Paroxysmal atrial tachycardia—rate 150 to 200 beats/minute
  (3) Atrial fibrillation—rapid atrial contractions (350/minute) with variable AV node block produce ventricular rate of 90 to 110
  (4) Ventricular tachycardia—three or more PVCs in a row
  (5) Ventricular fibrillation—rapid uncoordinated ventricular excitation without effective ventricular pumping action

C. Etiology of decreased peripheral vascular resistance
  1. Inadequate tissue perfusion
    a. Congestive heart failure—combined right- and left-sided heart failure, resulting in decreased tissue perfusion and tissue hypoxia
      (1) Pathophysiology
        (a) Increased cardiac workload or decreased effective myocardial contractility results in inefficient ventricular emptying and decreased cardiac output
        (b) Pulmonic congestion develops due to decreased left ventricular emptying
        (c) Systemic congestion develops due to inability of right atria and ventricle to pump blood into pulmonic circulation
      (2) Etiology of decreased myocardial contractility
        (a) Myocarditis
        (b) Myocardial infarction
        (c) Tachyarrhythmias
        (d) Bacterial endocarditis
        (e) Acute rheumatic fever
      (3) Etiology of increased cardiac workload
        (a) Elevated temperature
        (b) Physical or emotional stress
        (c) Anemia
        (d) Thyrotoxicosis (hyperthyroidism)
        (e) Valvular defects
      (4) Assessment findings
        (a) Subjective data
          i. Shortness of breath
          ii. Sleeps on two or more pillows
          iii. Sudden breathlessness during sleep (PND)
          iv. Swelling of the feet (edema)
          v. Feeling of puffiness (edema)
          vi. Weight gain (edema)
          vii. Fatigue and weakness
        (b) Objective data
          i. Vital signs
          - *Blood pressure—decreasing systolic pressure and narrowing pulse pressure*
          - *Pulse—pulsus alternans (regular rhythm in which there is an alteration between a strong and a weak cardiac contraction) and increased rate*
          - *Respirations and temperature—nonspecific*
          ii. Distention of neck veins
          iii. Lungs—moist inspiratory rales over lung bases
          iv. Heart sound—pulsus alternans
          v. Dependent pitting edema
          vi. Enlarged tender liver
          vii. Chest x-ray
          - *Cardiac enlargement*
          - *Dilatation of pulmonary vessels*
          - *Diffuse interstitial edema in lungs*
      (5) Nursing care is designed to reduce cardiac workload and tissue oxygen needs, increase strength of cardiac contraction, reduce extracellular fluid volumes, and promote physical and mental relaxation
        (a) Bedrest in a semi- or high-Fowler's position
          i. Elastic stockings and leg exercises to prevent

thrombus formation
  ii. Skin care
  iii. Plan periods of rest
(b) Oxygen at low flow rate
  i. Encourage deep breathing
  ii. Auscultate chest for breath sounds
(c) Medications, as ordered (see Appendix F, Drugs)
  i. Digitalis preparations
  ii. Diuretics—thiazides, furosemide, and ethacrynic acid, for example
  iii. Tranquilizers—phenobarbital, diazepam (Valium), and chlordiazepoxide (Librium) HCl
  iv. Stool softeners
(d) Institute and maintain intake and output records
  i. Report output of less than 30 ml/hour
  ii. Estimate insensible water loss in diaphoretic patient
  iii. Weigh daily—same time, clothes, scale
  iv. Utilize microdrip for parenteral infusions to avoid circulatory overloading
(e) Low-sodium diet, as ordered—restriction depends on severity of failure (see Appendix C, Diets)
  i. Offer small frequent feedings—large meals increase anorexia
  ii. Discuss food preferences with patient
(f) Involve patient and family in discharge teaching and planning
  i. Diet restrictions and meal preparation
  ii. Activity restrictions, if any, and planned rest periods
  iii. Medication schedules, purpose, dosage, and side effects
   • *Daily pulse taking*
   • *Daily weights*
   • *Potassium-containing foods*
  (see Appendix C, Diets)
  iv. Refer to community resources as indicated

b. Peripheral circulating failure—circulatory collapse due to a marked fall in cardiac output
c. Hemorrhagic shock—peripheral circulatory collapse due to blood loss
2. Loss of vasomotor tone
  a. Antibody-antigen reaction with histamine release—anaphylactic shock (see Anaphylactic shock in Table 3-1, Postoperative complications)
  b. Toxin release by bacteria (see Septic shock in Table 3-1)
  c. Interruption of sympathetic nervous system outflow
   (1) Deep anesthesia
   (2) Brain trauma
   (3) Spinal cord injuries (see spinal shock, p. 120)

2. Hypertension—a condition that results from abnormal increases in peripheral vascular resistance; systolic and/or diastolic pressures may be elevated
A. Essential hypertension—etiology unknown, affects 90% of hypertensive patients
  1. Etiology and incidence of essential hypertension—present hypotheses include
   a. Hypersensitivity to sympathetic system stimulation
   b. Increased renin-angiotensin release by the kidneys
   c. Failure of kidney to release a vasodepressor substance
   d. Genetic or family predisposition
   e. Higher incidence among Americans and Europeans than among Asians and Africans
   f. Higher incidence among American blacks than among whites
   g. Onset after 30 years of age; more women than men
  2. Phases of essential hypertension
   a. Prehypertensive and/or labile hypertension
    (1) Blood pressure fluctuates
     (a) Elevated during periods of stress
     (b) Near normal or normal at rest
   b. Mild hypertension
    (1) Resting diastolic pressure between 90 mm Hg and 110 mm Hg
    (2) May demonstrate mild changes in the optic fundi and minor cardiac

and renal involvement

   c. Moderate hypertension

     (1) Resting diastolic pressure between 110 mm Hg and 120 mm Hg

     (2) May demonstrate narrowing of retinal arterioles, left ventricular enlargement, and a trace of protein in the urine

   d. Severe hypertension

     (1) Resting diastolic pressures between 120 mm Hg and 140 mm Hg

     (2) May demonstrate advanced retinal changes such as copper and silver wiring and cardiac and renal decompensation (tachycardia, distended neck veins, proteinuria, oliguria)

   e. Malignant hypertension

     (1) Accelerated form of hypertension or one that is unresponsive to therapy

     (2) Diastolic blood pressure above 140 mm Hg

     (3) Encephalopathy (mental confusion, disorientation, seizures), retinal hemorrhages, exudates, and papilledema, congestive heart failure and kidney failure may be present

3. Assessment findings

   a. Subjective data

     (1) Dull, pounding occipital headache on awakening, wears off during day or is relieved by vomiting

     (2) Dizziness

     (3) Weakness

     (4) Palpitations

     (5) Nervousness, mood swings

     (6) Flatulence

     (7) Ringing in the ears

     (8) Nose bleeds (epistaxis)

     (9) Double vision (diplopia)

   b. Objective data

     (1) Vital signs

       (a) Blood pressure—elevated systolic and diastolic

       (b) Pulse, respirations, temperature—noncontributory unless complications present

     (2) Cardiac, cerebral, and renal changes

     (3) Diagnostic tests (see Appendix E)

       (a) Blood tests—complete blood cell count (CBC), hemoglobin, hematocrit, blood urea nitrogen (BUN), serum electrolytes and creatinine, and uric acid; abnormalities may indicate underlying causes or severity of organ involvement

       (b) Urinalysis and urine culture—screen for kidney dysfunction

       (c) 24-hour urine collections—vanillylmandelic acid (VMA) and 17-ketosteroids and 17-hydroxysteroids; screen for pheochromocytoma

       (d) X-ray, intravenous pyelogram (IVP)—detects sclerosis of renal artery

4. Nursing care—designed to encourage patient cooperation with the therapy regimen, to increase understanding of lifestyle modifications, and reduce physical and emotional stress, anxiety, and feelings of insecurity

   a. Individualize nursing approaches

     (1) Provide consistency in nursing procedures

     (2) Reduce situations that increase physical stress and raise blood pressure

     (3) Identify patient misconceptions of hypertension and institute measures to clarify

       (a) Repeat explanations of nature of disease, stressing its chronicity as necessary

       (b) Review purpose, side effects, and administration of drugs; time consistent with patient's daily activities

       (c) Stress importance of reporting even minor symptoms to physician to regulate treatment

       (d) Discuss effects of excess weight on blood pressure and include family in diet instructions

       (e) Discuss value of exercise; encourage walking

   b. Antihypertensive therapy as ordered (see Appendix F, Drugs)

     (1) Antihypertensives—reserpine, methyldopa (Aldomet), guanethidine (Ismelin) SO_4, hydralazine (Apresoline)

     (2) Diuretics—thiazides (Diuril,

Hydrodiuril) chlorthalidone
(Hygroton), furosemide (Lasix),
ethacrynic acid (Edecrin),
spironolactone (Aldactone)
(3) Sedation—phenobarbital, diazepam
(Valium), chlordiazepoxide
(Librium) HCl
c. Diet, as ordered, explaining dietary
restrictions and determining food
preferences
(1) Low calorie—weight reduction
(2) Low fat—indicated with elevated
serum cholesterol or obvious
atherosclerotic disease
(3) Sodium restricted—decreases blood
volumes; occasionally not ordered if
on diuretics
(4) Potassium sources—indicated
particularly with thiazide,
furosemide, or ethacrynic acid
therapy
d. Include patient and family in teaching
and discharge planning
(1) Importance of not smoking
(2) Medication scheduling, side effects
(3) Dietary restrictions
(4) Exercise and rest
(5) Taking own blood pressures if
ordered
(6) Causes and symptoms of
intermittent hypotension
(a) Antihypertensive medications—
caution patient not to rise
quickly from a lying or sitting
position; to sit down if feeling
dizzy; avoid stooping
(b) Alcoholic intake, hot weather
and exercise cause vasodilation
(c) Vomiting and diarrhea deplete
blood volumes
e. Refer to appropriate community
resources for follow-up care
B. Secondary hypertension—affects 10% of hypertensive patients
1. Systolic hypertension
a. Decreased aortic distensibility—aortic
calcification
b. Increased cardiac output—anemia,
thyrotoxicosis, anxiety, fever
(1) Iron deficiency anemia
(hypochromic microcytic
anemia)—inadequate production of

red blood cells due to the lack of
heme (iron)
(a) Pathophysiology
i. Decreased dietary intake,
impaired absorption or
increased utilization of iron
decreases the amount of iron
bound to plasma transferrin
and transported to bone
marrow for hemoglobin
synthesis
ii. Decreased hemoglobin in
erythrocytes decreases
amount of oxygen delivered
to tissues
(b) Etiology and incidence
i. Excessive menstruation
ii. Gastrointestinal (GI)
bleeding—peptic ulcer,
hookworms, tumors
iii. Inadequate diet—anorexia,
diet fads, cultural practices
iv. Deficiencies most common in
infants, pregnant women,
and premenopausal women
(c) Assessment findings
i. Subjective data
• *Increasing fatigue*
• *Headache*
• *Decreased or increased
appetite*
• *Heartburn*
• *Palpitations*
• *Shortness of breath on exertion*
• *Ankle edema*
• *Numb tingling extremities*
• *Flatulence*
• *Menorrhagia*
ii. Objective data
• *Vital signs: (a) blood
pressure—increased systolic,
widened pulse pressure, (b)
pulse—tachycardia, (c)
respirations—tachypnea, and (d)
temperature—normal or
subnormal*
• *Skin and mucous
membranes—pale, dry*
• *Pearly white sclera*
• *Nails—flattened,
longitudinally ridged, brittle*
• *Diagnostic tests:*

Blood—decreased hemoglobin, mean corpuscular volume (MCV), mean corpuscular hemoglobin concentration (MCHC), and mean corpuscular hemoglobin (MCHb) and increased iron-binding capacity

(d) Nursing care is designed to relieve iron deficiency and promote physical and mental equilibrium

   i. Activity to tolerance

   ii. Iron therapy, as ordered

   • *Oral therapy—ferrous sulfate: (a) single dose initially building to three to four tablets daily and (b) give with meals*

   • *Intramuscular therapy—iron dextran: (a) utilize second needle for administration after withdrawal from ampule, (b) use Z-tract method, and (c) inject 0.5 cc of air before removing needle (prevents tissue necrosis)*

   iii. Include patient and family in teaching plan

   • *Diet—food preferences which are high in iron (see Appendix C)*

   • *Iron therapy—purpose, dosage, side effects: (a) black or green stools, (b) constipation, diarrhea, and (c) take with meals to avoid gastric upsets*

   • *Exercise to tolerance with planned rest periods*

(2) Pernicious anemia (hyperchromic macrocytic anemia)

(a) Pathophysiology

   i. Lack of intrinsic factor in gastric mucosa leads to vitamin B_{12} deficiency

   ii. Vitamin B_{12} deficiency alters DNA synthesis needed for cell division

   iii. Delayed cellular division results in an alteration of the nuclear pattern and increases the size of red blood cells (megaloblast)

   iv. Hemoglobin formation proceeds normally in greatly enlarged cell

   v. Ineffective erythropoiesis accounts for increased serum bilirubin and urobilinogen excretion

   vi. The vitamin B_{12} deficiency effects tissues in the mouth, stomach, vagina, and the myelin sheath covering central and peripheral nerve tracts.

(b) Etiology and incidence

   i. Gastric resection

   ii. Atrophy of gastric mucosa

   iii. Gastritis or extensive neoplasia

   iv. Rarely occurs before age 35 years

   v. Affects both sexes equally

   vi. More common in blue-eyed, fair-skinned blonds who gray prematurely

(c) Assessment findings

   i. Subjective data

   • *Tingling and numbing of hands and feet*

   • *Weakness and fatigue*

   • *Sore tongue*

   • *Anorexia*

   • *Diarrhea*

   • *Shortness of breath*

   • *Palpitations*

   • *Difficulties with memory and balance*

   • *Complaints of irritability or mild depression*

   ii. Objective data

   • *Skin—pale, flabby, jaundice*

   • *Sclera—icterus*

   • *Tongue—smooth, glossy, red*

   • *Vital signs: (a) blood pressure—normal or elevated systolic, (b) pulse—tachycardia, and (c) respirations and temperature—nonspecific*

   • *Nervous system—decreased vibratory sense in lower extremities, loss of coordination; Babinski reflex (flaring of toes with stimulation of sole of foot); positive Romberg (lose balance when eyes closed); increased or diminished reflexes*

• *Diagnostic tests (see Appendix E): (a) blood—increased Hb, MCV, MCHC, MCHb; reduced RBCs and platelets; increased bilirubin, (b) gastric analysis—decreased secretions, (c) urine and feces—increased urobilinogen, and (d) Shilling test—decreased*

(d) Nursing measures are designed to promote relief of symptoms and emotional and physical comfort

   i. Bedrest or activities to tolerance—plan care activities with patient and avoid inconsistency

   ii. Vitamin B$_{12}$ therapy, as ordered

   iii. Nutritious diet in six small feedings

   iv. Allow for verbalization of feelings regarding lifelong medical therapy, mood changes, and nervous system changes

   v. Involve family in patient teaching

   • *Importance of diet and rest and exercise to tolerance*

   • *Assure medical therapy will relieve most symptoms*

   • *Teach injection techniques if medication is to be given at home*

(3) Thyrotoxicosis (hyperthyroidism or Graves' disease)—excessive thyroid hormone in the blood

(a) Pathophysiology

   i. Diffuse hyperplasia of thyroid gland results in overproduction of thyroid hormone and increased blood serum levels

   ii. Hormone stimulates mitochondria to increase energy for cellular activities and heat production

   iii. As metabolic rate increases, fat reserves are depleted despite increased appetite and food intake

   iv. Cardiac output is increased to meet increased tissue metabolic needs and peripheral vasodilation occurs in response to increased heat production

   v. Neuromuscular hyperactivity results in accentuation of reflexes, anxiety, and increased alimentary tract mobility

(b) Etiology and incidence

   i. Possible autoimmune response resulting in increase of a gamma globulin called *long-lasting thyroid stimulator* (LATS)

   ii. Occurs generally in third and fourth decade

   iii. Affects women more frequently than men

(c) Assessment findings

   i. Subjective data

   • *Complaints of nervousness, mood swings*

   • *Increased sweating*

   • *Palpitations*

   • *Heat intolerance*

   • *Weight loss despite appetite increase*

   • *Fatigue, muscle weakness, tremors*

   • *Frequent bowel movements*

   ii. Objective data

   • *Vital signs (a) blood pressure—increased systolic pressure and widened pulse pressure, (b) pulse—tachycardia, and (c) temperature, respirations—nonspecific*

   • *Skin—warm, moist, velvety, increased melanin pigmentation*

   • *Eyes—characteristic stare with widened palpebral fissures, lid lag, and failure to wrinkle brow with upward gaze*

   • *Pretibial edema with thickened skin and color changes*

   • *Goiter*

   • *Diagnostic tests (see Appendix E): (a) Blood—increased protein-bound iodine (PBI), T$_4$ and T$_3$ resin uptake and thyroid uptake of radioiodine and (b)*

basal metabolic rate
(BMR)—increased
(d) Nursing actions are designed to
protect patient from stress,
promote physical and emotional
equilibrium, and prevent
complications
   i. Provide quiet environment
that is cool and well
ventilated—reduces
stimulation and lessens
diaphoresis
   ii. Maintain unhurried
appearance and avoid
discrepancies in treatments
and procedures—lessens
patient's nervousness
• *Accept mood swings*
• *Restrict activities and
visitors—prevents undue fatigue*
   iii. Provide eye care as
indicated
• *Sunglasses to protect from
photophobia, wind, dust*
• *Instill protective drops such as
methylcellulose to soothe exposed
cornea*
• *Tape eyelids that do not close
in sleep*
• *Apply cold compresses for
comfort*
   iv. High-caloric, high-protein,
high-vitamin B diet
• *Six full meals per day, as
needed*
• *Weigh daily*
• *Avoid stimulants*
   v. Observe for complications
• *Heart failure*
• *Thyroid storm
(crisis)—hyperthermia, extreme
tachycardia, extreme
restlessness, weakness, and
delirium*
   vi. Medications, as ordered
• *Antithyroid preparations: (a)
propylthiouracil—blocks thyroid
synthesis; usual dosage 100 mg
q8h, initially, patients should be
instructed to report rashes, sore
throat, or fever to physicians
immediately and (b)
methimazole—similar action and*

*side effects; utilized for patients
allergic to propylthiouracil*
• *Iodine preparations—reduce
vascularity of thyroid gland;
used in treatment of thyroid
storm: (a) SSKI—5 gm in H_2O
q 3 to 4 times daily and (b)
Lugol's solution*
   vii. Prepare for thyroidectomy,
as ordered (see Unit 3)
   viii. Prepare for oral radioiodine
therapy (iodine 131), as
ordered
2. Systolic-diastolic hypertension
  a. Kidney disorders—pyelonephritis,
glomerulonephritis, sclerosis of renal
artery
  b. Adrenal gland disorders
    (1) Pheochromocytoma—excess release
of epinephrine and norepinephrine
→ vasoconstriction → increased
peripheral vascular resistance →
increased blood pressure
    (2) Primary hyperaldosteronism—excess
aldosterone secretion → sodium and
water retention → hypercolemia →
increased blood pressure
  c. Central nervous system
dysfunction—increased intracranial
pressure
  d. Decreased elasticity of systemic arterial
walls
    (1) Arteriosclerosis obliterans—a
degenerative and occlusive disorder
of the arterial system in the lower
extremities
    (a) Pathophysiology
      i. Fatty deposits in the intimal
and medial layer of the
arterial walls results in
plaque formation that
narrows arterial lumens and
decreases arterial
distensibility
      ii. Decreased blood flow
through a narrowed and
obstructed artery results in
ischemic changes in the
tissues supplied by that
artery
    (b) Etiology and incidence
      i. Age—more frequent after 50
years of age

ii. Sex—men more commonly affected
iii. Diabetes mellitus
iv. Hyperlipemia—obesity
v. Cigarette smoking
vi. Hypertension
vii. Polycythemia vera

(c) Assessment findings
i. Subjective data
• *Pain: (a) Type—cramplike, (b) location—foot, calf, thigh, and buttocks, (c) duration—variable, may be relieved with rest, and (d) precipitating causes—on exercise (intermittent claudication) and occasionally even at rest*
• *Cold feet and hands*
• *Tingling and numbness in toes and feet*
ii. Objective data
• *Diminished or absent pedal pulses*
• *Lower extremities—shiny, glossy, dry, cold, chalky white skin, decreased or absent hair, ulcers, gangrene*
• *Diagnostic tests: (a) blood—increased serum cholesterol, triglycerides, CBC, platelets and (b) angiography—delineates location and nature of occlusion*

(d) Nursing care is designed to decrease discomfort, promote circulation, and prevent infection
i. Head of bed elevated on blocks, 3 to 6 inches high, gravity aids in perfusion of legs and thighs
ii. Protect extremity from injury with bed cradle, sheepskin, heel pads
iii. Keep extremity warm and avoid chilling; avoid heating pads
iv. Skin care techniques
• *Use mild soap, dry thoroughly*
• *Apply lotions but do not massage as this could release thrombus*
v. Check pedal pulses, skin color, and temperature qid
vi. Medications, as ordered
• *Vasodilators*
• *Anticoagulants—heparin sodium, dicumarol, ASA*
• *Antihyperlipemias—clofibrate, cholestyramine resin, nicotinic acid*
vii. Diet high in vitamins B and C (see Appendix C)
viii. Patient teaching
• *Skin care*
• *Balanced exercise and rest program—exercise increases collateral circulation*
• *Elevate legs when seated*
• *Diet—low fat, high vitamin B and C*
• *Avoid smoking*

e. Increased blood volume—polycythemia vera and volume overload

---

Part C   Serum Glucose Levels

PHYSIOLOGY

A. The physiologic and chemical processes carried out by our body cells require energy; energy for cellular metabolism is supplied by a compound called adenosine triphosphate (ATP)

1. ATP can be utilized to
   a. Synthesize cellular components such as proteins
   b. Facilitate muscle contraction
   c. Transport ions across membranes as in active reabsorption in the kidney tubule

and transmission of nerve impulses
   (1) ATP can also be synthesized from proteins and fats
   (2) The most important source for ATP synthesis is carbohydrates

B. Carbohydrates are absorbed from the gut in the form of the monosaccharides, fructose, glucose, and galactose
  1. These sugars are transported to the liver via portal circulation
  2. Fructose and galactose are converted into glucose in the liver
  3. Glucose is the only sugar of the blood

C. The levels of blood glucose are homeostatically balanced between the energy needs of the body tissues and the sources of glucose in the body—most tissues can shift to fats or proteins for energy, but glucose is the only nutrient that can be utilized for energy by the central nervous system and the red blood cells

MECHANISMS REGULATING BLOOD GLUCOSE CONCENTRATION

1. Glucose-buffer function of the liver
A. Excess glucose is stored in liver as glycogen
B. Deficient serum glucose activates
  1. Glycogenolysis, or breakdown of glycogen in liver, to replenish serum glucose levels
  2. Gluconeogenesis—formation of glucose from amino acids and fats

2. Hormonal regulators
A. Pancreatic hormones
  1. Insulin—produced by the beta cells of the islets of Langerhans
    a. Increases rate of oxidation of glucose in tissues
    b. Increases rate of glycogen formation in the liver
    c. Increases rate of glucose conversion into fat and its storage in adipose tissue
    d. Lowers serum glucose levels
  2. Glucagon—probably produced by the alpha cells in islets of Langerhans
    a. Increases glycogenolysis in liver
    b. Promotes lipolysis in adipose tissue
    c. Increases serum glucose concentration
B. Adrenal hormones
  1. Glucocorticoids
    a. Increase gluconeogenesis
    b. Decrease tissue utilization of glucose
    c. Increase serum glucose levels

  2. Epinephrine
    a. Effects rapid glycogenolysis in liver
    b. Increases utilization of muscle glycogen
    c. May produce transient hyperglycemia
C. Pituitary hormones
  1. Somatotropin (growth hormone)
    a. Increases gluconeogenesis
    b. Antagonizes action of insulin
    c. Stimulates release of glucogen
    d. Increases serum glucose levels
  2. Adrenocorticotropic hormone (ACTH) or corticotropin
    a. Stimulates adrenal cortex to increase secretion of glucocorticoids
    b. Increased serum glucose level
  3. Thyroid hormone
    a. Increases rate of glucose absorption from intestine
    b. Increases tissue utilization of glucose

IMBALANCE IN SERUM GLUCOSE LEVELS

1. Hypoglycemia fasting serum glucose levels below 60 mg/100 ml of blood
A. Functional hypoglycemias—decreased serum glucose without demonstrable disease process
  1. Pathophysiology
    a. Excessive beta cell secretion of insulin
    b. Abnormally high blood insulin level depletes nutrients (glucose, amino acids, fatty acids) in bloodstream by facilitating entry into skeletal muscle, fat, and other tissue cells
    c. Insulin does not facilitate entry of glucose into brain cells, rather their metabolism is dependent on adequate serum glucose levels
    d. Decreasing levels of serum glucose results in depression of cerebral function
    e. Sympathetic nervous system elicits alarm mechanism, which stimulates glycogenolysis in liver to raise serum glucose levels
  2. Etiology and incidence
    a. Reactive functional—excess insulin release in response to normal rises in blood sugar following meals
    b. Reactive secondary to mild diabetes—insulin first delayed then excessive response
    c. Alimentary hypoinsulinism—excessive

insulin release due to rapid emptying of carbohydrates into intestines (dumping syndrome)

d. Alcohol ingestion and poor nutrition—decreased gluconeogenesis and glycogenolysis

3. Assessment findings
   a. Subjective data
      (1) Excessive sweating
      (2) Feelings of apprehension, anxiety, irritability
      (3) Difficulty concentrating
      (4) Weakness, fatigue, fainting
      (5) Excessive hunger
      (6) Nausea, vomiting
      (7) Headache
   b. Objective data
      (1) Vital signs
         (a) Blood pressure—increased
         (b) Pulse—tachycardia, forceful
         (c) Respirations—increased
         (d) Temperature—subnormal
      (2) Pale moist skin
      (3) Hyperreflexia
      (4) Psychotic behavior
      (5) Relief of symptoms with administration of glucose
      (6) Diagnostic tests (see Appendix E)
         (a) Fasting blood sugar—decreased
         (b) Postprandial blood glucose—decreased

4. Nursing care is designed to reduce underlying metabolic disorder and promote adaptive behaviors
   a. Administer and explain rationale for low-carbohydrate, high-protein, and adequate-fat diet divided into six equal feedings
   b. Monitor vital signs and check for neurologic changes—frequent hypoglycemic attacks can result in permanent neurologic changes
      (1) Diplopia
      (2) Babinski reflex
      (3) Hyperreflexia
      (4) Decreased ability to concentrate
   c. Support and promote adaptive behaviors
      (1) Discuss factors predisposing to recurrence of symptoms—large carbohydrate ingestion and stressful situations or people
      (2) Discuss nature of dysfunction and importance of diet therapy
      (3) Provide the patient and family opportunities to verbalize feelings and concerns—behavior changes and mood swings exhibited by patient before therapy may have strained or disrupted communication lines
      (4) Discuss dosage, action, and side effects of medications ordered (see Appendix F)
         (a) Phenobarbital
         (b) Diazepam (Valium)
         (c) Chlordiazepoxide (Librium) HCl
      (5) Refer patient and family to appropriate community resource as indicated

B. Organic hypoglycemias—decreased serum-glucose levels due to disease processes
   1. Decreased glycogen stores
      a. Extensive liver disease, cirrhosis, carcinoma
      b. Hepatic enzyme deficiencies
   2. Hyperinsulinism
      a. Islet cell adenoma
      b. Complication of insulin therapy in diabetes mellitus
   3. Decreased gluconeogenesis
      a. Adrenal cortical hypofunction
         (1) Addison's disease
         (2) Adrenal hemorrhage
         (3) Rapid withdrawal of steroid therapy in septicemia
      b. Hypopituitarism

2. Hyperglycemia—fasting serum glucose levels above 120 mg/100 ml blood

A. Functional hyperglycemia
   1. Excessive intake of carbohydrates at a given meal
   2. Increased glucose formation due to epinephrine
      a. Stress—alarm reaction
      b. Epinephrine administration
   3. Parenteral infusions of glucose

B. Organic hyperglycemia
   1. Endogenous overproduction of glucose
      a. Increased epinephrine release due to hyperactivity of adrenal medulla—pheochromocytoma
      b. Increased release of ACTH from anterior pituitary—Cushing's syndrome
      c. Increased production of growth

hormone—acromegaly
2. Failure of mechanisms for lowering serum glucose
   a. Diabetes mellitus—decreased or absent insulin production resulting in hyperglycemia and in alterations of protein and fat metabolism
      (1) Pathophysiology
         (a) Deficient beta cell activity leads to inadequate blood levels of insulin
         (b) Glucose fails to enter muscle cells, resulting in decreased glucose utilization and hyperglycemia
         (c) Other sources of energy—fats and proteins—are utilized by cells causing excess production of keto acids and metabolic acidosis ($\downarrow HCO_3^-$) → increased ventilation ($\downarrow Pco_2$)
         (d) Increased glomerular filtration of glucose results in osmotic diuresis as transport mechanism for glucose is exceeded → sodium depletion → dehydration → circulatory failure
      (2) Etiology and incidence
         (a) Inherited disorder
         (b) World-wide distribution
      (3) Assessment findings
         (a) Subjective data
            i. Growth onset
            • *Excessive hunger (polyphagia)*
            • *Excessive thirst (polydipsia)*
            • *Excessive urination (polyuria)*
            • *Sudden weight loss*
            • *Loss of strength*
            • *Increased irritability*
            ii. Maturity onset
            • *Weight loss or gain*
            • *Nighttime urination (nocturia)*
            • *Vulvar itching (pruritus)*
            • *Blurring or decreasing vision*
            • *Fatigue*
            • *Tingling or loss of sensation in extremities*
            • *Impotence*
            • *Foot ulcer*
         (b) Objective data
            i. Vital signs
            • *Blood pressure—normal,*
            decreased
            • *Pulse—normal, increased*
            • *Temperature—normal, increased*
            • *Respirations—increased rate and depth; acetone breath, Kussmaul respirations*
            ii. Diagnostic tests (see Appendix E)
            • *Blood: (a) fasting blood sugar—increased, (b) glucose tolerance test—blood glucose elevated after 180 minutes, (c) postprandial blood glucose—elevated blood glucose after 150 minutes, (d) serum ketones—elevated, and (e) CO_2 combining power—decreased*
            • *Urine—positive for sugar and acetone*
      (4) Nursing care is designed to reduce underlying metabolic dysfunction, attain and/or maintain normal weight, and prevent or delay renal, vascular, and neurologic complications
         (a) Institute and explain diet therapy as ordered (check a diabetic exchange list)
            i. Diet based on patient's ideal weight, age, and activity level
            ii. Foods may be interchanged within each list but not switched between lists
            iii. Involve patient and family in planning meals that are varied and contain preference foods
            iv. Discuss coordination of meals with hypoglycemic medication
         (b) Hypoglycemic medications as ordered (see Appendix F)
            i. Oral agents
            • *Sulfonylureas—tolbutamide (Orinase), chlorpropamide (Diabinese), acetohexamide (Dymelor), and tolazamide (Tolinase)*
            • *Biguanides—phenformin (DBI)*
            ii. Insulin preparations

- *Rapid acting—regular or crystalline, zinc suspension (Semilente) insulin*
- *Intermediate acting—isophane insulin (NPH insulin), zinc suspension (Lente) insulin, and globin zinc insulin*
- *Long acting—protamine zinc insulin (PZI) and zinc suspension (Ultralente) insulin*

(c) Assess patient closely to avoid complications
  i. Vital signs frequently
  ii. Intake and output
  - *Administer Parenteral fluids as ordered (see Appendix D) —normal saline, electrolytes, sodium bicarbonate*
  - *Push fluids, as ordered*
  - *Check urine for sugar, acetone, and specific gravity*
  iii. Check for neurologic changes
  - *Blurring of vision, increasing irritability, and confusion indicate ketoacidosis*
  - *Diaphoresis, trembling, headache, and fainting indicate insulin reaction (hypoglycemia)*

(d) Provide comfort measures
  i. Skin care with position changes
  ii. Avoid exposure to cold
  iii. Oral hygiene—keep mouth and lips moist

(e) Support and promote adaptive behaviors
  i. Encourage patient and family to verbalize concerns, fears—deal with feelings of loss of body image, denial, anger
  ii. Discuss nature of diabetes and purpose of treatment with patient and family
  - *Factors that may precipitate recurrence of symptoms—infection, concentrated carbohydrate ingestion, skipped medication*
  - *Signs of hypoglycemia and precipitating causes—missed meals, heavy exercise*
  - *Importance of diet and regular exercise*
  - *Methods of regular urine testing*
  - *Importance of hygiene measures and foot care*
  - *Medications—dosage, purpose, side effects: (a) rotation of injection sites and (b) calculation, scheduling, injection techniques*
  iii. Refer patient and family to appropriate community resource

b. Acute pancreatitis—inflammation of the pancreas resulting in pancreatic congestion, ischemia, and tissue necrosis

Part D   Fluid and Electrolytes

PHYSIOLOGY

1. **Composition of body fluids**
A. Water constitutes 60% to 70% of the total body weight
B. Electrolytes are substances that dissociate and form electrically charged particles, called ions, when dissolved in water

2. **Body fluids are separated by cell membranes into two compartments**
A. Intracellular fluids
  1. Constitutes 55% of total body fluids
  2. Primary electrolytes
     a. Potassium
     b. Phosphate
     c. Magnesium

d. Proteinase
3. Provides medium for chemical reactions within the cell
B. Extracellular fluids
   1. Constitutes 45% of total body fluids
   2. Primary electrolytes
      a. Sodium
      b. Calcium
      c. Chloride
      d. Bicarbonate and plasma proteins
   3. Serves as a transport medium for cellular nutrition and excretion
3. **Body fluids exist in state of dynamic equilibrium**—fluid composition of each compartment remains relatively stable despite a constant interchange of body fluids from one compartment to the other
A. Dynamic equilibrium is dependent on the osmolarity of the fluid compartment and the active transport of ions across the cellular membrane
   1. Osmolarity—the total number of dissolved particles (electrolytes and colloids) per liter of fluid
      a. Effected by electrolyte concentrations, electrolyte shifts, and movement of water from one compartment to the other
         (1) Diffusion—movement of substances from high to low concentrations
         (2) Osmosis—movement of water from high to low concentrations through a semipermeable membrane
   2. Active transport moves substances against concentration, electrical and pressure gradients, that is, from an area of low concentration to one of high concentration
      a. Maintains intracellular potassium concentration and extracellular sodium concentrations
      b. Facilitates active reabsorption of some substances such as sodium in the renal tubules
4. **Concentration gradients**—interchange of body fluid between the intracellular and extracellular compartments is due to concentration gradients
5. **Pressure gradients**—interchange or transport of body fluids between the vascular compartment and the interstitial fluid compartment is due to pressure gradients
A. Capillary hydrostatic pressures
   1. Pressure of blood within capillary
   2. Dependent on blood pressure, blood flow, and venous pressure
   3. Favors outward flow of fluids
B. Interstitial fluid pressures
   1. A negative pressure due to lymphatic drainage of fluid and proteins from interstitial spaces
   2. Favors outward flow of fluid plasma
C. Colloid osmotic pressures
   1. Results from large quantity of plasma proteins in blood
   2. Favors inward flow of fluids
D. Filtration pressures
   1. Difference between capillary hydrostatic pressure and plasma colloidal pressure
   2. Greater at arterial end of capillary—fluid moves outward from capillary to interstitial space
   3. Decreased significantly at venule end—facilitates movement of fluid from interstitial space back into capillary
6. **Fluid transport between the vascular compartment and the interstitial fluid compartment**—designed to keep interstitial fluid pressures negative
A. A change of interstitial fluid pressure from negative to positive results in edema formation
B. Interstitial fluid pressures are kept negative by
   1. The reabsorption of fluid into the circulatory system
   2. Diffusion of excess fluid and protein (net filtration) from interstitial spaces into the lymphatics

HOMEOSTATIC MECHANISMS CONTROLLING FLUID AND ELECTROLYTE BALANCE

1. **The kidney**—a complex organ that has the responsibility of regulating water, sodium, and hydrogen-ion concentrations
A. Actively excretes or reabsorbs Na^+ and H_2O
B. Excretes nitrogenous wastes, drugs, and toxins
C. Excretes excess hydrogen ions to maintain normal pH of body fluids
D. Maintains extracellular fluid osmolarity by
   1. Selective filtration
   2. Active reabsorption of electrolytes
2. **The endocrine system**—secretes hormones that act to conserve various ions and total body water
A. Antidiuretic hormone (ADH)
   1. Synthesized in hypothalamus and secreted by pituitary gland
   2. Acts on distal tubules and collecting ducts of kidney nephron
      a. Promotes water reabsorption

b. Decreases urine output
3. Release stimulated by hyperosmolarity of extracellular fluid

B. Aldosterone
1. Synthesized and secreted by adrenal cortex
2. Increases the rate of sodium reabsorption in all segments of the renal tubule system
   a. Actively conserves sodium—passively conserves water
   b. Regulates blood and extracellular fluid volume
   c. Decreases urine output
3. Stimulated by sodium depletion

3. The cardiovascular system
A. Maintains optimum environment for cells through capillary exchange mechanism
B. Glomerular filtration determined by renal blood flow
   1. Normally increased with increased blood pressure
   2. Decreased blood pressure decreases renal blood flow

4. The gastrointestinal system
A. Primary route of fluid and electrolyte intake
B. Conducts fluid and electrolytes rapidly across intestinal mucosa in both directions

5. The nervous system
A. Manufactures and stores hormones (ADH and ACTH)
B. These hormones decrease urine output and increase extracellular fluid volume

IMBALANCES IN FLUID AND ELECTROLYTES

Imbalances in fluid and electrolytes may be due to changes in the total quantity of either substance (deficit or excess), protein deficiencies and/or extracellular fluid volume shifts

1. Changes in total quantity of fluid and electrolytes
A. Decreased quantities of fluid and electrolytes—may be caused by deficient intake (poor dietary habits, anorexia, and nausea) or excessive output (vomiting, nasogastric suction, and prolonged diarrhea)
   1. Addison's disease—adrenocortical insufficiency
      a. Pathophysiology
         (1) Decreased adrenal cortical secretions of glucocorticoids, mineralocorticoids, and androgenic hormones
            (a) Decreased or absent physiologic

stress response (vascular insufficiency and hypoglycemia)
            (b) Decreased aldosterone secretion (sodium depletion, dehydration)
            (c) Decreased axillary and pubic hair
         (2) Increased ACTH release—excessive skin pigmentation
      b. Etiology and incidence
         (1) Tuberculosis
         (2) Fungal infections
         (3) Autoimmune response
         (4) Iatrogenic (surgical removal)
      c. Assessment findings
         (1) Subjective data
            (a) Muscle weakness
            (b) Fatigue—most evident toward end of day
            (c) Dizziness, fainting
            (d) Weight loss
            (e) Nausea, vomiting, food idiosyncrasies
            (f) Abdominal pain, diarrhea
         (2) Objective data
            (a) Vital signs
               i. Blood pressure—decreased, orthostatic hypotension, narrowed pulse pressure
               ii. Pulse—increased, collapsing, irregularities
               iii. Temperature—subnormal
               iv. Respirations—noncontributory
            (b) Skin—poor turgor, excessive pigmentation
            (c) Diagnostic tests
               i. Blood chemistry
               • *Decreased Na^+, Cl^-, and HCO_3^-*
               • *Increased K^+*
               • *Decreased serum glucose*
               • *Increased hematocrit*
               ii. Urine—decreased or absent 17-ketosteroids and 17-hydroxycorticosteroids
      d. Nursing care is designed to reduce stress and provide physical and emotional comfort
         (1) Provide quiet nondemanding care schedule
         (2) High-sodium, low-potassium diet; frequent carbohydrate nourishment to prevent hypoglycemia
         (3) Force fluids—weighing daily to

assess fluid balance
- (4) Medications, as ordered (see Appendix F)
    - (a) Glucocorticoids (cortisone acetate)
    - (b) Mineralocorticoids (fludrocortisone acetate)
- (5) Involve patient and family in teaching and discharge planning
    - (a) Purpose, dosage, and side effects of medications—how to use emergency kit of injectable steroids, sudden withdrawal of steroid therapy may precipitate adrenal crisis
    - (b) Importance of avoiding stress and need to report to physician conditions that increase stress (flu, dental extractions, fever)

2. Cholelithiasis and cholecystitis—gallstones and inflammation of the gallbladder
    - a. Pathophysiology
        - (1) Liver secretes bile that is supersaturated with cholesterol
        - (2) Cholesterol crystals precipitate in bile, aggregating with other matter to become stones
        - (3) Stones may then occlude duct, which results in distention of gallbladder, with edema, hyperemia, and tissue necrosis
    - b. Etiology and incidence
        - (1) Etiology of gallstones unknown
        - (2) Gallstones most frequent cause of cholecystitis
        - (3) Wide incidence particularly among Caucasians, Chinese, and American Indians
        - (4) Highest incidence between ages 40 and 60 years
        - (5) Affects more women than men
    - c. Assessment findings
        - (1) Subjective data
            - (a) Pain
                - i. Type—moderate to severe
                - ii. Location—upper right quadrant—may radiate to right shoulder
                - iii. Precipitating factors—may be accentuated with deep inspiration
            - (b) Anorexia, nausea, vomiting
        - (2) Objective data
            - (a) Vital signs
                - i. Pulse—increased
                - ii. Temperature—elevated
            - (b) Abdomen—moderate tenderness to rebound
            - (c) Icterus
            - (d) Skin—jaundice
            - (e) Diagnostic studies
                - i. Blood—leukocytosis
                - ii. Urine—urobilin
                - iii. X-ray studies—failure of the gallbladder to visualize after either oral or intravenous administration of radiopaque dye (see Appendix E, Diagnostic tests)
    - d. Nursing care is designed to reduce pain, provide support during diagnostic workup, and prepare patient for surgery (see Unit 3, under Cholecystectomy)

3. Ulcerative colitis—inflammation of mucosa and submucosa of the colon characterized by remissions and exacerbations
    - a. Pathophysiology
        - (1) Specific physiologic response to emotional trauma
        - (2) Edema and hyperemia of colonic mucous membrane → superficial bleeding with peristalsis → shallow ulcerations → abscesses → bowel wall thins and shortens → loses sacculation
        - (3) Increased rate of flow of liquid ileal contents → decrease water absorption → diarrhea
    - b. Etiology and incidence
        - (1) Genetic predisposition
        - (2) Autoimmune response
        - (3) Infections
        - (4) Greatest occurrence in young adults, ages 20 to 40 years
        - (5) More common in urban areas, upper middle incomes, and groups with better educational backgrounds
    - c. Assessment findings
        - (1) Subjective data
            - (a) Frequent diarrhea (10 to 20 times daily)
            - (b) Stools contain mucus, blood, pus
            - (c) Urgency to defecate, particularly when standing
            - (d) Loss of appetite, nausea, vomiting

(e) Colic-like stomach pains

(f) Weight loss

(g) Influenza-like symptoms (malaise, low-grade fever)

(2) Objective data

(a) Temperature—elevated

(b) Stools—small amount of fecal matter mainly blood, pus, mucus

(c) Diagnostic tests

   i. Sigmoidoscopy—extent of rectal involvement

   ii. Barium enema—detects lesions in proximal bowel

   iii. Blood chemistries—increased hematocrit (hemoconcentration—decreased water and excess sodium), decreased potassium

d. Nursing care is designed to reduce psychologic stresses, relieve symptoms, promote physical and psychologic equilibrium, prevent complications, and facilitate remission

(1) Provide quiet supportive environment, encouraging patient to verbalize worries—decreases anxiety

(2) Institute measures designed to control diarrhea, abdominal pain, and tenesmus

(a) Medications (see Appendix F)

   i. Codeine PO_4 (intramuscular) or codeine SO_4 (oral)

   ii. Camphorated tincture of opium (paregoric)

   iii. Tincture of belladonna

   iv. Phenobarbital sodium

   v. Atropine (Lomotil) SO_4

(b) Avoid coarse residue foods, whole milk, cold beverages—stimulate bowel activity

(3) Institute measures designed to improve nutritional and electrolyte balance

(a) Parenteral hyperalimentation (see Appendix D)

(b) High-calorie, high-protein, low-residue diet

(c) Parenteral, intramuscular, or oral vitamin and mineral supplements—potassium, iron, vitamins C and B

(d) Push fluids to 3000 ml/day

(4) Provide comfort measures—skin care, rest periods, diversional activities, sitz baths

(5) Institute and maintain steroid therapy, as ordered—to facilitate remission

(6) Patient and family teaching should include diet, medications, and importance of avoiding stress and maintenance of emotional stability

(7) Refer to appropriate community resource as indicated

(8) If exacerbation continues, assist in preparation for surgery (Ileostomy, see Unit 3)

4. Excessive output also occurs due to

a. Increased insensible water loss—fever, bronchiectasis

b. Lack of ADH production by pituitary—diabetes insipidus

c. Osmotic diuresis—diabetes mellitus

d. Draining fistulas, large wounds, extensive surgery

B. Excessive quantities of fluid and electrolytes—may be due to increased ingestion, tube feedings, intravenous infusions, enemas, or an inability to excrete excesses

1. Acute and chronic renal dysfunctions

a. Acute glomerulonephritis—inflammation of glomeruli characterized by increased permeability and resulting in proteinuria, cylindruria, hematuria, azotemia, hypertension, and anemia (also see Unit 5, Pediatric Nursing)

b. Pyelonephritis—acute or chronic inflammation due to bacterial infection of the parenchyma and the pelvis of the kidney

(1) Pathophysiology

(a) Inflammation of renal medulla or diffuse inflammation of the lining of the renal pelvis

(b) Nephrons are destroyed resulting in hypertrophy of intact nephrons needed to maintain urine output

(c) Dilatation of tubules may result in defects in sodium reabsorption and inability of the

kidney to concentrate urine
(2) Etiology and incidence
   (a) 95% caused by gram-negative enteric bacilli (*Escherichia coli*)
   (b) Occurs more frequently in young women and older men
   (c) Predisposing factors include obstruction, hypertension, hypokalemia, diabetes mellitus, pregnancy, catheterization
(3) Assessment findings
   (a) Subjective data
      i. Flank pain
      ii. Chills and fever
      iii. Loss of appetite
      iv. Night sweats
      v. Pain on urination
   (b) Objective data
      i. Costovertebral angle tenderness
      ii. Diagnostic tests (see Appendix E)
        • *Blood—polymorphonuclear leukocytosis*
        • *Urine—leukocytosis, hematuria, white blood cell casts, proteinuria, (less than 3 gm in 24 hours), positive cultures*
        • *Intravenous pyelogram (IVP)—may manifest structural changes*
(4) Nursing care is designed to alleviate symptoms, identify predisposing factors, and prevent recurrence
   (a) Relieve pain and fever
      i. Administer analgesics—pentazocine lactate (Talwin) and Meperidine (Demerol) HCl
      ii. Administer acetaminophen (Tylenol) to reduce fever
      iii. Institute cooling measures as indicated
   (b) Administer sulfonamides and/or antibiotics to support body defense mechanisms
   (c) Prevent complications
      i. Maintain intake and output—observe urine characteristics
      ii. Monitor vital signs q4h
      iii. Maintain bedrest or activity to tolerance
      iv. Push fluids unless contraindicated—prevents stasis of urine
      v. Avoid tub baths
   (d) Provide emotional support
      i. Include family in care and teaching plans
      ii. Provide diversional activities
      iii. Encourage activities of daily living as tolerated
      iv. Answer patient's questions and discuss concerns
2. Edema and transudation of fluids
  a. Cushing's syndrome—increased cortisol secretion by the adrenal gland
   (1) Pathophysiology
      (a) Excess glucocorticoid production increases gluconeogenesis raising serum glucose levels → glucose in urine and increased fat deposition in face and trunk
      (b) Gluconeogenesis also decreases amino acids, leading to protein deficiencies → muscle wasting → poor antibody response → lack of collagen
   (2) Etiology and incidence
      (a) Adrenal hyperplasia due to dysfunction of hypothalamus or pituitary tumor
      (b) Adrenal adenoma
      (c) Adrenal carcinoma
      (d) Prolonged steroid therapy
   (3) Assessment findings
      (a) Subjective data
        i. Muscle weakness—decreasing work capacity
        ii. Backache
        iii. Weight gain—obesity
        iv. Impotence
        v. Cessation of menstrual flow, clitoral enlargement
        vi. Frequent mood changes—nervousness, depression
      (b) Objective data
        i. Vital signs—elevated blood pressure
        ii. Skin—thin, purple striae over obese areas, red face,

ecchymoses, pitting edema of ankles
iii. Truncal obesity with thin extremities—moon face, buffalo hump
iv. Hirsutism—fine downy hair over face, forehead, upper trunk
v. Diagnostic test
• *Blood—increased 17-hydroxycorticosteriod levels, decreased eosinophils, increased neutrophils, decreased potassium chlorides, metabolic alkalosis*
• *Urine—increased 17-hydroxycorticosteriods, glucosuria*
• *X-rays—osteoporosis particularly of spine and pelvis, adrenal enlargement*
(4) Nursing care is designed to prevent complications, promote patient relaxation, and prepare patient for surgery (see Adrenalectomy in Unit 3)
b. Hepatitis—inflammation of the liver
(1) Pathophysiology
(a) Infection with either hepatitis A (infectious hepatitis) or hepatitis B (serum hepatitis)—produces inflammation, necrosis, and regeneration of liver parenchyma
(b) Hepatocellular injury impairs clearance of urobilinogen → elevated urinary urobilinogen and, as injury increases → conjugated bilirubin does not reach the intestines → decreased urine and fecal urobilinogen → increased serum bilirubin → jaundice
(c) Failure of liver to detoxify products → increased undetoxified products of protein metabolism → gastritis and duodenitis
(2) Etiology, incidence, and epidemiologic comparison between infectious and serum hepatitis
(a) Infectious hepatitis A
i. Incubation—two to six weeks

ii. Transmission—fecal-oral
iii. Sources—crowding, contaminated food, milk or water, asymptomatic carriers
iv. HB antigen—not present
v. Incidence—sporadic epidemics
(b) Serum hepatitis B
i. Incubation—six weeks to six months
ii. Transmission—parenteral
iii. Sources—contaminated needles, syringes, surgical instruments, blood plasma, or transfusions
iv. HB antigen—present
v. Incidence—increased in ages 15 to 29 years, particularly in heroin addiction; occupational hazard for laboratory workers, nurses, physicians
(3) Assessment findings
(a) Subjective data
i. Influenza-like aches (malaise)
ii. Loss of appetite
iii. Nausea, vomiting
iv. Repugnance to food, cigarette smoke, strong odors, alcohol
v. Dull ache in upper right quadrant
vi. Headache, fever
vii. Rash
(b) Objective data
i. Liver—enlarged, tender, smooth
ii. Skin—icterus in sclera of eyes, jaundice
iii. Urine—normal, dark
iv. Stools—normal, clay-colored, loose
v. Diagnostic tests
• *Blood—leukocytosis, increased SGOT, SGPT, and bilirubin levels, alkaline phosphatase*
• *Urine—increased urobilinogen*
(4) Nursing care is designed to reduce discomforts and promote conditions favorable to liver functioning
(a) Bedrest and precaution or

isolation techniques
- (b) Diet as tolerated
  - i. NPO with parenteral infusions
  - ii. High-protein, high-carbohydrate, low-fat diet offered in frequent small meals
  - iii. Push fluids if not contraindicated
- (c) Assess physical and emotional parameters and employ comfort measures
  - i. Intake and output observation for urine and stool changes; weigh daily
  - ii. Observe for increasing jaundice—if pruritus is present, use mild oil-based lotions to reduce itching
  - iii. Provide oral hygiene q1h to q2h and institute ROM exercises
  - iv. Provide opportunities for patient to express concerns and questions
- (d) Discharge planning and teaching
  - i. Instructions on diet and fluid intake to promote liver regeneration
  - ii. Importance of rest and limited activity to reduce metabolic workload of liver
  - iii. Personal hygiene practices to prevent contamination
  - iv. Avoidance of alcohol, blood donations, and individuals with communicable infections
  - v. Refer to appropriate community resource for follow-up care
- c. Cirrhosis—chronic progressive liver disease characterized by degeneration and disorganized regeneration of liver tissue resulting in fibrosis
  - (1) Pathophysiology
    - (a) Decreased cellular function → impaired detoxification → bad breath → abnormal behavior → peripheral vasodilatation → sodium retention → increased

sensitivity to drugs
- (b) Impaired protein synthesis → fall in plasma proteins → decreased oncotic pressures → edema and ascites → decreased clotting factors → increased bleeding tendency
- (c) Decreased glycogenolysis → hypoglycemia
- (d) Decreased bile secretion → malabsorption of fats → deficiencies in fat-soluble vitamins (A, D, and K)
- (e) Impaired bilirubin conjugations → jaundice
- (f) Portal hypertension, causing enlarged spleen → excessive red and white blood cell breakdown → diversion of portal blood → esophageal and rectal varices
- (2) Etiology and incidence
  - (a) Toxins, including alcohol and drugs
  - (b) Hepatitis
  - (c) Obstruction of common bile duct
  - (d) Malnutrition
  - (e) Incidence parallels increased alcohol consumption
  - (f) Ages 45 to 65 years, more men than women, more nonwhites than whites
- (3) Assessment findings
  - (a) Subjective data
    - i. Anorexia, nausea, vomiting, foul breath
    - ii. Weight loss
    - iii. Distended abdomen
    - iv. Low-grade fever
    - v. Flatulence, diarrhea, constipation
    - vi. Impotence, cessation of menstrual flow
  - (b) Objective data
    - i. Enlargement of liver and frequently spleen, ascites
    - ii. Skin—jaundice, spider angiomas, palmar erythema, breast enlargement in males, testicular atrophy and sparse body hair
    - iii. Diagnostic studies (see Appendix E);

Blood—moderate red blood cells, decreased clotting times and serum albumin, increased bromsulphalein (BSP) retention, serum bilirubin, SGOT and SGPT, positive cephalin-cholesterol flocculation test

(4) Nursing care is designed to reduce metabolic activity, provide substitutes for decreased liver function, promote comfort, and prevent or delay liver failure

  (a) Bedrest in position of comfort—turning, coughing, and deep breathing q2h to promote ventilation and prevent venous stasis

  (b) Provide for maintenance of nutrition and fluid and electrolyte balance

    i. NPO—nasogastric suction may be ordered, parenteral infusions with electrolytes and vitamins, as ordered

    ii. No- or low-protein, moderate-carbohydrate and fat diet; liver unable to detoxify proteins

    iii. Low-sodium diet and fluid restrictions if ascites present

    iv. Small frequent meals to avoid anorexia

    v. Diuretics and serum albumin, as ordered—to establish normal fluid volumes

  (c) Observe closely for signs of complications

    i. Monitor intake and output, noting character of urine and stools; report urine output of less than 25-30 ml/hour

    ii. Check vital signs—institute cooling measures if necessary, observe for signs of cardiac decompensation

    iii. Assess neurologic status—awareness of time and place, confusion, decreased response to verbal commands, tremors; report changes to physician

    immediately

    iv. Check gums and injection sites for bleeding

  (d) Assist with paracentesis, as ordered (see Appendix D)

  (e) Promote comfort measures and emotional support—rest, skin care, quiet environment, verbalization of concerns

  (f) Patient teaching includes diet; avoidance of stress, alcohol, and exposure to infections; and referral to appropriate community agencies

  (g) Complications of cirrhosis

    i. Bleeding esophageal varices

    • Sengstaken-Blakemore tube with esophagogastric balloon is utilized to control bleeding

    • Gastric lavage with ice water may also be employed to encourage vasoconstriction

    ii. Hepatic coma—changes in consciousness, flapping tremor, grimacing, and sweet, musty breath odor

2. Protein deficiencies

A. Proteins are basic constituents of living cells and are essential for body growth and maintenance and repair of tissue

  1. Deficiency may result from

    a. Inadequate intake

    b. Severe loss, as in burns or hemorrhage

    c. Increased utilization by the body, as in wound healing or severe injury

    d. Increased catabolism as in hyperthyroidism, fever, infection, and malignancy

B. Blood proteins (albumin, fibrinogen, globulin) are essential for maintenance of oncotic pressures

  1. Deficiencies result from decreased liver function as in cirrhosis or renal dysfunction (glomerulonephritis)

3. Extracellular fluid volume shifts

A. Plasma-to-interstitial fluid shift

  1. Fluid shifts from injured areas to noninjured areas

  2. Fluid shifts from plasma into peritoneum or pleural space

  3. Shift results in

    a. Decreased blood volume

b. Edema of noninjured areas

c. Dehydration of injured areas

B. Interstitial fluid-to-plasma shifts

1. Shift of fluid and electrolytes to vascular compartment, usually after a plasma-to-interstitial fluid shift

2. Burns—wounds caused by exposure to excessive heat, chemicals, fire, steam, radiation, or electricity

   a. Pathophysiology

      (1) Shock due to pain, fright, or terror → fatigue and failure of vasoconstrictor mechanisms → hypotension

      (2) Capillary dilatation and increased permeability → plasma loss creating blisters and edema → hemoconcentration → hypovolemia → hypotension → decreased renal perfusion → renal shutdown

      (3) Interstitial-to-plasma fluid shift → hemodilution → hypervolemia → heart failure → pulmonary edema.

   b. Incidence

      (1) Two million annually in the United States

      (2) Most occur in home owing to carelessness or ignorance

      (3) 8000 deaths annually

      (4) Survival best in ages 15 to 45 years and in burns covering less than 20% of the total body surface

   c. Assessment findings

      (1) Utilize "rule of nine" to ascertain extent of body surface involved—head and both upper extremities, 9% each; front and back of trunk, 18% each; lower extremities, 18% each; and perineum, 1%

         (a) Repeat on second and third days

         (b) Facial, perineal, and hand and feet burns have greater fatality rates

      (2) Estimate depth of burn

         (a) First degree—epidermal tissue only

            i. Usually red

            ii. Not serious unless large areas involved

         (b) Second degree—epidermal and dermal tissue

            i. Blisters formed

            ii. Hospitalization required if over 30% of body (major burn)

         (c) Third degree—destruction of all skin layers and, frequently, fat, muscle, and bone

            i. Requires immediate hospitalization

            ii. 10% of body surface considered major burn

   d. Nursing care of the burned patient is designed to institute measures to save life, reduce discomfort, prevent disability and deformities, and promote rehabilitation and safety measures

      (1) Institute emergency measures

         (a) Apply cold to burn and get patient to hospital

         (b) Cover burn with clean or sterile towel to protect from contamination and reduce pain from contact with air—do not use ointment of any kind

         (c) Irrigate chemical burns with copious amounts of water

         (d) Roll victim whose clothes are on fire on ground and douse with cold water when flames are extinguished

      (2) Alleviate pain, relieve shock, and institute measures to maintain fluid and electrolyte balance

         (a) Administer narcotic while physical examination is being completed; remove burned clothing

         (b) Weigh patient if possible to establish baseline data for fluid therapy

         (c) Institute parenteral therapy (see IV therapy in Appendix D), as ordered, and insert indwelling catheter

            i. Maintain strict intake and output records

            ii. Weigh daily

         (d) Observe physical and emotional parameters and employ measures to prevent complications

            i. Vital signs hourly

            ii. Utilize hematocrit, CVP, and

urinary output to determine cardiovascular status

iii. Administer medications as ordered
- *Tetanus booster*
- *Antibiotics—prevent infections*
- *Sedatives and analgesics*
- *Steroids*
- *Antipyretics—avoid aspirin*

iv. Prevent contractures by utilizing anatomic positioning
- *Stryker frame or circle bed if circumferential trunk burns present*
- *Head and neck burns—no pillows*
- *Hand burns—Use towel rolls or sandbags to align hands*
- *Upper body burns—keep arms at 90° angle from body and slightly above shoulders*
- *Ankles and feet—allow feet to hang at 90° angle from ankles in prone position; utilize footboards to maintain 90° angle in supine position*
- *Utilize traction and splints to maintain positions*
- *Utilize passive and active ROM exercises*

v. Control gastrointestinal disturbances
- *Initial NPO, then juices or carbonated beverages; do not give ice chips or plain water as these may contribute to electrolyte imbalance*
- *As food is tolerated—high-protein high-calorie diet for energy and tissue repair*
- *Observe for Curling's (stress) ulcer—sudden drop in hemoglobin*

vi. Observe for emotional reactions and provide supportive therapy
- *Loss of body image, threat of pain, repeated operations, long convalescence, dependency conflicts*
- *Care by same personnel as much as possible*
- *Involve patient in care plans*
- *Answer questions clearly and accurately*
- *Encourage contact with family and/or significant person*
- *Provide diversional activities and change furnishings or room adornments when possible to prevent perceptual deprivation*
- *Encourage self-care to tolerance*

e. Burn therapies

(1) Open method—exposure of burns to drying effect of air

(a) Advantages
i. Useful in treating burns of neck, face, trunk, and perineum
ii. Eliminates painful dressing changes

(b) Disadvantage—patient must be placed in isolation

(2) Closed method—pressure dressings applied to burned areas, particularly extremities

(a) Silver nitrate method (0.5% solution)
i. Advantages
- *Bacteriostatic*
- *No isolation*
ii. Disadvantages
- *Increased losses of sodium, chloride, potassium, and calcium*
- *Stains skin, linen, furniture*

(b) Bacteriostatic creams
i. Silver sulfadiazine 1%—reduces water evaporation and is relatively nontoxic; may cause rash in healthy tissue
ii. Gentamicin SO_4 0.1%—reduces water evaporation and is useful against wide range of gram-positive and gram-negative bacilli
iii. Mafenide (Sulfamylon) HCl—relatively nontoxic and reduces evaporative water loss; may burn for a few minutes after application

(c) Porcine xenograft (pigskin application)
  i. Advantages—covers wound temporarily preventing plasma and protein loss and reducing risk of infection

  ii. Disadvantages—dries within day or two causing painful pulling sensation; limits ROM, since grafts may loosen with exercise

Part E   Hydrogen Ion Concentration

PHYSIOLOGY

1. **Normal hydrogen ion concentration**—hydrogen ions (H^+) are normally present in body fluids but in far lower concentrations than other ions (0.00004 mEq/liter)
2. **Sources of hydrogen ion in the body**
A. Volatile H^+ of carbonic acid, which is formed during tissue metabolism
   1. Circulates in body fluids as CO_2 and water
   2. Excreted by the lungs
B. Nonvolatile H^+, which is formed from oxidation of sulfur-containing amino acids and phosphoprotein residue or the production of organic acid
   1. Daily dietary intake of balanced diet produces 50 to 100 mEq of nonvolatile H^+
   2. Excreted by the kidneys
3. **pH**—the negative logarithm of the hydrogen ion (H^+) concentration is usually represented by the symbol pH
A. Increases in H^+ concentrations therefore reduce pH—acidemia
B. Decreases in H^+ concentration therefore increase pH—alkalemia
C. pH scale extends from 0 to 14, with 7 being neutral, that is, exact balance between number of hydrogen ions (H^+) and hydroxyl ions (OH^-)
D. pH of body fluids range from 1.0 (gastric juice) to 8.2 (pancreatic juice)
E. pH of blood is 7.4—slightly alkalotic (normal range 7.35 to 7.45)
4. **Biochemical reactions**—the basis for physiologic activity of the cell; dependent on optimum pH (hydrogen ion concentration)
A. Facilitates the function of enzyme systems

B. Essential for the binding of oxygen to hemoglobin

HOMEOSTATIC MECHANISMS THAT REGULATE H^+ CONCENTRATIONS IN THE BODY

1. **Buffers**—solutions of two or more chemical compounds that minimize changes in pH by combining with a strong acid or a strong base to form a weak acid or a weak base
A. Provide the body's first means for regulation of hydrogen ion concentration
B. Buffer systems of the body are composed of a weak acid and the salt of that acid
   1. Bicarbonate buffer system
      a. Consists of carbonic acid (H_2CO_3) and its salt sodium bicarbonate ($NaHCO_3$)
      b. Buffers up to 90% of H^+ in the extracellular fluid
      c. Concentration of these two chemicals is regulated by the lungs and kidney
         (1) CO_2 excreted by respiratory system
         (2) HCO_3 excreted by the kidney
         (3) pH of blood can therefore be shifted up or down by the respiratory and renal systems
         (4) Acid base status ultimately depends on maintenance of a 20:1 ratio of bicarbonate ions to dissolved CO_2
   2. Phosphate buffer system
      a. Composed of sodium diphosphate (NaH_2PO_4) and Disodium phosphate (Na_2HPO_4)
      b. Abundant in cells and kidney tubules
      c. Acts primarily in intracellular fluid
2. **Respiratory regulation of hydrogen ion con-**

centration—the body's second line of defense against alterations in pH
A. Carbon dioxide is constantly being formed by cellular metabolism; it is transported to the lungs in three forms
   1. Dissolved CO_2 in the plasma
   2. As sodium bicarbonate
   3. As carbaminohemoglobin
B. Increases in carbon dioxide concentrations in the body fluids lowers the pH toward the acidic side
   1. The respiratory center in the medulla is stimulated to increase the rate and depth of respirations
   2. Increased rate and depth of respiration increases pulmonary ventilation, thereby decreasing carbon dioxide and returning pH toward optimum
C. Decreases in carbon dioxide concentrations result in decreased pulmonary ventilation
D. Respiratory system is limited in its control of hydrogen ion balance
   1. Can retain or excrete only carbon dioxide
   2. Can compensate only for temporary changes in hydrogen ion concentrations
   3. Can only partially correct deviations in pH

3. Basis of kidney regulation of hydrogen ion concentration
A. Hydrogen ions are secreted by the proximal and distal tubules of the kidney
B. Sodium reabsorption by the kidney tubules
   1. For each sodium ion reabsorbed a hydrogen ion or potassium ion is excreted
   2. An increase in the concentration of hydrogen ion results in more hydrogen ions than potassium ions being exchanged for sodium
C. Bicarbonate ion secretion
   1. An increase in hydrogen ions (acidity) increases bicarbonate reabsorption in the kidney tubule
   2. When relatively more bicarbonate is available than hydrogen ions (alkalinity), $NaHCO_3$ is excreted in the urine
D. Ammonia—synthesized by cells of the proximal and distal renal tubules and collecting ducts
   1. Ammonia (NH_3) diffuses into tubular lumen and combines with excess hydrogen ions to form ammonium (NH_4)
   2. Ammonium (NH_4) combines with chloride (Cl^-) or sulfate ions (SO^-_4) to form a neutral salt
   3. Ammonia mechanism responds quickly to changes in pH and is capable of buffering large amounts of excess acid in a short period of time
   4. Helps prevent tubular pH from falling below 4.5; hydrogen ion secretion ceases below this critical value

IMBALANCES IN HYDROGEN ION CONCENTRATION

1. Metabolic acidosis—result of excess metabolic acid formation or abnormal loss of alkali (sodium bicarbonate) and is partially compensated for by respiratory hyperventilation
A. Loss of pancreatic, biliary, and lower bowel secretions—severe diarrhea, draining fistulas
B. Utilization of stored fats for energy—diabetes mellitus, starvation
C. Increased cellular metabolism—hyperthyroidism, fever, tissue repair
D. Severe tissue hypoxia—congestive heart failure, shock
E. Decreased excretion of metabolic wastes
   1. Acute renal failure—broadly defined as rapid onset of oliguria accompanied by a rising BUN and serum creatinine
      a. Pathophysiology
         (1) Acute renal ischemia → tubular necrosis → decreased urine output
         (2) Renal blood flow remains reduced after an acute attack due to
            (a) Vasoconstriction mediated by juxtaglomerular apparatus, which reduces glomerular filtration
            (b) Interstitial edema in kidney, which reduces filtration rate and collapses tubules by increasing the pressures in the interstitial spaces
         (3) During the oliguric phase, waste products are retained → metabolic acidosis → water and electrolyte imbalances → anemia
         (4) Recovery phase is marked by rapid diuresis → dilute urine → rapid depletion of sodium, chloride, and water → dehydration
      b. Etiology
         (1) Prerenal—occurs due to factors outside of kidney; usually circulatory collapse

(a) Hemorrhage, severe dehydration
(b) Myocardial infarction
(c) Septicemia
(2) Intrinsic renal—parenchymal disease of kidney
  (a) Nephrotoxic agents
    i. Poisons, such as carbon tetrachloride
    ii. Heavy metals—arsenic, mercury
    iii. Antibiotics—kanamycin SO_4, neomycin SO_4
    iv. Incompatible blood transfusion
    v. Alcohol myopathies
  (b) Acute renal disease
    i. Acute glomerulonephritis
    ii. Systemic lupus erythematosus
(3) Postrenal—obstruction in collecting system
  (a) Renal or bladder caliculi
  (b) Tumors of bladder, prostate, or renal pelvis
  (c) Gynecologic or urologic surgery in which ureters are accidentally ligated

c. Assessment findings
(1) Subjective data
  (a) Sudden decrease or cessation of urine output
  (b) Anorexia, nausea, vomiting
  (c) Abdominal bloating, hiccoughs
  (d) Sudden weight gain
(2) Objective data
  (a) Vital signs
    i. Blood pressure—decreased, elevated
    ii. Pulse—tachycardia, irregularities
    iii. Respirations—increased rate and depth, rales, rhonchi
    iv. Temperature—normal, subnormal, elevated
  (b) Central venous pressure—decreased, elevated
  (c) Neurologic—decreasing mentation, unresponsive to verbal or painful stimuli, psychoses, convulsions
  (d) Skin—dry, rashes, purpura
  (e) Diagnostic studies
    i. Blood—increased potassium, BUN, creatinine, decreased pH, bicarbonate, hematocrit, hemoglobin
    ii. Urine—decreased volume and specific gravity, proteins, casts, red and white blood cells

d. Nursing care is designed to continually assess physical parameters and to provide emotional support
(1) Assessment of fluid and electrolyte balance and maintenance of nutrition
  (a) Weigh daily
  (b) Frequent monitoring of vital signs, CVP, and blood chemistries
  (c) Parenteral infusions, as ordered
    i. Blood, plasma, packed cells, electrolyte solutions to replace losses
    ii. Restricted fluids if hypertension is present
  (d) High-calorie low-protein diet if tolerated
    i. Hypertonic glucose solutions if oral feedings are not tolerated—prevent ketosis from fat metabolism
    ii. Intravenous L-amino acids and glucose
  (e) Control of hyperkalemia
    i. Infusions of hypertonic glucose and insulin—forces potassium into cells
    ii. Calcium gluconate (IV)—reduces myocardial irritability
    iii. Sodium bicarbonate (IV)—corrects acidosis
    iv. Polystyrene sodium sulfonate (Kayexalate) or other exchange resins, orally or rectally (enema)—removes excess potassium
    v. Peritoneal or hemodialysis
(2) Utilize assessment and comfort measures to reduce occurrence of complications
  (a) Respiratory system
    i. Monitor rate and depth of respirations, breath sounds,

arterial blood gases
  ii. Encourage turning, coughing, and deep breathing
  iii. Utilize IPPB as indicated
  (b) Provide frequent oral care to prevent stomatitis
  (c) Observe for signs of infection—elevated temperature, localized redness, swelling, heat, or drainage
 (3) Maintain continuous emotional support
  (a) Same care givers, consistency in procedures
  (b) Give opportunities to express concerns, fears
  (c) Allow for family interactions
2. Chronic renal failure—as a result of progressive destruction of kidney tissue, the kidneys are no longer able to maintain their homeostatic functions
 a. Pathophysiology
  (1) Destruction of glomeruli → reduced glomerular filtration rate → retention of metabolic waste products → increased serum urea → osmotic diuresis and release of ammonia in skin and alimentary tract by bacterial interaction with urea → inflammation of mucous membranes
  (2) Retention of phosphate → decreased serum calcium → muscle spasms, tetany and increased parathormone release → demineralization of bone
  (3) Failure of tubular mechanisms to regulate blood bicarbonate → metabolic acidosis → hyperventilation
  (4) Urea osmotic diuresis → flushing effect on tubules → decreased reabsorption of sodium → excess sodium loss → depletion
  (5) Waste-product retention → depressed bone marrow function → decreased circulating RBC's → renal tissue hypoxia → decreased erythropoietin production → further depression of bone marrow → anemia
 b. Etiology
  (1) Polycystic kidney disease
  (2) Chronic glomerulonephritis
  (3) Chronic urinary obstruction, ureteral stricture, calculi, neoplasms
  (4) Chronic pyelonephritis
  (5) Severe hypertension
  (6) Congenital or acquired renal artery stenosis
  (7) Systemic lupus erythematosus
 c. Assessment findings as previously given only gradual in onset and including ammonia breath, bronze-colored skin, and excessive fatigue and weakness
 d. Nursing care in conservative management of chronic renal failure is designed to preserve renal function, reduce fluid and electrolyte imbalances, provide comfort, and postpone or eliminate the need for dialysis
  (1) See preceding guidelines monitoring fluid and electrolyte balance and maintaining nutrition and serum potassium levels—administer diuretics, as ordered—to reduce excess fluid volumes
  (2) Employ comfort measures that reduce distress and support physical function
   (a) Bedrest in position that facilitates ventilation
   (b) Oral hygiene to prevent stomatitis and reduce discomfort from mouth ulcers
   (c) Turn, cough, and deep breath q2h
   (d) Passive and active ROM exercises—promote venous return and prevents thrombi
   (e) Skin care with soothing lotions—reduces pruritus
   (f) Perineal care each shift
   (g) Encourage communication of concerns
3. Dialysis—differential diffusion of solute through a semipermeable membrane that separates two solutions
 a. Indications
  (1) Acute poisonings
  (2) Acute or chronic renal failure
  (3) Hepatic coma
  (4) Metabolic acidosis
  (5) Extensive burns with azotemia
 b. Peritoneal dialysis—involves introduction of a dialysate solution into

the abdomen, where the peritoneum acts as the semipermeable membrane between the solution and blood in abdominal vessels
(1) Advantages
  (a) Fewer problems with fluid and electrolyte imbalance
  (b) Can be instituted quickly and does not require specialized medical and nursing staff
  (c) Does not require heparinization
  (d) Utilized for infants and children and in facilities in which hemodialysis is not available
(2) Disadvantages
  (a) Treatment is slow and not conducive to long-term care
  (b) Increased risk of infection
  (c) Protein loss
  (d) Peritonitis, recent abdominal surgery, or abdominal adhesion prohibit its use
(3) Procedures
  (a) Area around umbilicus is prepped, anesthetized with local anesthetic, and a catheter is inserted into the peritoneal cavity through a trocar; the catheter is then sutured into place to prevent displacement
  (b) Dialysate is then allowed to flow into the peritoneal cavity
    i. Inflow time—5 to 10 minutes
    ii. Two liters of solution are used in each cycle in the adult
    iii. Solutions contain glucose, Na^+, Ca^{++}, Mg^{++}, K^+, Cl^-, and lactate or acetate
  (c) When solution bottle is empty, dwell time or exchange time begins
    i. Dwell time—15 to 45 minutes
    ii. Processes of diffusion, osmosis, and filtration begin to move waste products from blood stream into peritoneal cavity
  (d) Draining of the dialysate begins with the unclamping of the outflow clamp

    i. Drain time—30 minutes
    ii. Collect in large container and measure
    iii. Drainage facilitated by moving the patient from side to side
(4) Complications of peritoneal dialysis
  (a) Peritonitis
  (b) Leaking of fluid into potential spaces in thoracic cavity or scrotum
  (c) Pneumonia, atelectasis
  (d) Hypo- or hypervolemia
  (e) Hyperosmolar coma
  (f) Abdominal adhesions
c. Hemodialysis—circulation of patient's blood through a compartment formed of a semipermeable membrane (cellophane or cuprophane) surrounded by dialysate fluid
(1) Advantages
  (a) Rapid and efficient procedure
  (b) Long-term treatment feasible
(2) Disadvantages
  (a) Fluid and electrolyte derangement
  (b) Requires specialized equipme and staff
  (c) Requires heparinization and maintenance of a shunt
  (d) May necessitate blood transfusions
(3) Types of dialyzers
  (a) Coil-type
  (b) Parallel-plate
  (c) Hollow-fiber
(4) Types of venous access for hemodialysis
  (a) External shunt
    i. Cannula is placed in large vein and a large artery that approximate each other
    ii. Shunt care
    • *Daily cleansing and application of a sterile dressing*
    • *Prevention of physical trauma and avoidance of some activities, such as swimming*
    iii. External shunts, while providing easy and painless access to blood stream, are prone to infection and

clotting and cause erosion of the skin around insertion area

(b) Arteriovenous fistulas

    i. Large artery and vein are sewn together (anastamosed) below the surface of the skin

    ii. Purpose is to create blood vessel that can relieve and receive blood

    iii. Advantage of fistulas include greater activity range and no protective asepsis

    iv. Disadvantage is necessity of two venipunctures with each dialysis

(5) Complications during hemodialysis

(a) Disequilibrium syndrome—rapid removal of urea from blood → reverse osmosis with water moving into brain cells → cerebral edema → may cause headache, nausea, vomiting, confusion, and convulsions

(b) Hypotension—results from excessive ultrafiltration or excessive antihypertensive medications

(c) Hypertension—results from volume overload—water and/or sodium, causing disequilibrium syndrome or anxiety

(d) Transfusion reactions (see Appendix D)

(e) Arrhythmias—occur due to hypotension, fluid overloads, or rapid removal of potassium

(f) Psychologic problems

    i. Patients react to dependency on hemodialysis in varying ways

    ii. The nurse needs to identify patient reactions, defense mechanisms, and employ supportive behaviors

    • *Include patient in care, helping patient and family understand illness and treatment as much as possible; continuous repetition and reinforcement*

    • *Do not interpret patients' behavior for them—for example,*

do not say, "You're being hostile," or "You're acting like a child."

    • *Answer questions honestly regarding the quality and length of life with dialysis and/or transplantation*

    • *Encourage independence as much as possible*

    • *Identify family interactions and encourage family to verbalize concerns, fears, anger*

2. **Respiratory acidosis**—result of alveolar hypoventilation; compensated for by increased hydrogen ion excretion by the kidneys (acidification of urine) and retention of bicarbonate (metabolic alkalosis)

A. Chronic obstructive pulmonary disease

  1. Characteristics

    a. Persistent obstruction of bronchial air flow

    b. Chronic or recurrent productive cough

  2. Bronchitis—inflammatory mononuclear infiltration in bronchial walls, which results in hypertrophy of mucus-producing globlet cells and destruction of cilia (see Unit 3 for signs and symptoms, nursing care)

  3. Asthma—hypersensitive response of trachea and bronchi to various allergens; stimulates contraction of smooth muscle and increases bronchial secretions, which results in narrowed airways filled with tenacious mucus (see Unit 5 for signs, symptoms, and nursing care)

  4. Emphysema—enlargement of air sacs distal to terminal bronchioles with destruction of septum between alveoli

    a. Pathophysiology

    (1) Increased airway resistance during expiration results in air trapping and hyperinflation → increased residual volumes

    (2) Increased dead space → unequal ventilation → perfusion of poorly ventilated alveoli → hypoxia, carbon dioxide retention (hypercapnia)

    (3) Chronic hypercapnia reduces sensitivity of respiratory center → chemoreceptions in aortic arch and carotid sinus become principle regulators of respiratory drive (respond to hypoxia)

(4) Obliteration of capillaries owing to unequal ventilation, hypoxia, and acidosis → increased pulmonary vascular resistance → hypertrophy of the right ventricle → cor pulmonale

b. Etiology and incidence
   (1) Smoking
   (2) Air pollution
   (3) Occupational hazards—fumes, dust
   (4) More common among men than women

c. Assessment findings
   (1) Subjective data
      (a) Shortness of breath on exertion or exposure to cold air
      (b) Wheezing
      (c) Cough, may be productive
      (d) Weakness
      (e) Loss of appetite
      (f) Weight loss
      (g) Feelings of anxiousness
   (2) Objective data
      (a) Vital signs
         i. Blood pressure—normal, elevated
         ii. Pulse—tachycardia
         iii. Respirations—tachypnea
         iv. Temperature—normal, elevated
      (b) Respiratory system
         i. Increases AP diameter of chest
         ii. Diminished chest expansion
         iii. Use of accessory muscles of respirations (pectorals) on inspiration
         iv. Palpation—decreased tactile fremitus
         v. Percussion—hyperresonance
         vi. Auscultation—distant breath sounds, rales, rhonchi, wheeze
      (c) Skin—pale, cyanosis, nail clubbing
      (d) Diagnostic studies
         i. Blood gases—decreased PO_2, increased PCO_2 and bicarbonate levels
         ii. Decreased chlorides

d. Nursing care is designed to promote optimal ventilation, reduce hypercapnia and provide physical and psychologic comfort
   (1) Institute measures designed to decrease airway resistance and enhance gas exchange
      (a) Semi-Fowler's position
      (b) Oxygen with humidification—no more than 2 liters per minute, (see Appendix H, Oxygen therapy)
      (c) Intermittent positive-pressure breathing (IPPB) with nebulization
      (d) Assisted ventilation
      (e) Postural drainage
      (f) Instruction in breathing exercises, such as pursed-lip breathing and diaphragmatic breathing
      (g) Medications, as ordered (see Appendix F, Drugs)
         i. Bronchodilators—aminophylline, isoetharine (Bronkosol), isoproterenal HCl
         ii. Antibiotics—determined by sputum cultures and sensitivity
         iii. Steroids—methylprednisolone sodium succinate (Solu-medrol), dexamethasone (Decadron)
         iv. Expectorants—acetylcysteine (Mucomyst), glyceryl guaiacolate (Robitussin)
   (2) Employ comfort measures and support other body systems
      (a) Oral hygiene prn
      (b) High-protein, high-calorie diet to prevent negative nitrogen balance
         i. Give small frequent meals if patient fatigues easily
         ii. Supplement diet with high-calorie drinks
      (c) Push fluids to 3000 ml per day, unless contraindicated—helps moisten secretions
      (d) Skin care—water bed, air mattress, foam pads to prevent skin breakdown
      (e) Active and passive ROM

exercises to prevent thrombus formation
  i. Antiembolic stockings or Ace bandages may also be applied
  ii. Increase activities to tolerance
  (f) Provide rest and sleep periods—prevents mental disturbances due to sleep deprivation and reduces metabolic rate
  (g) Provide emotional support for patient and family
    i. Identify factors that increase anxiety
    • *Machines that take over bodily functions, fears of mechanical failure*
    • *Loss of body image, fears of dying*
    • *Families who deny illness or react with exceptional concern*
    ii. Do not reinforce denial or encourage over-concern—give accurate, up-to-date information on patient's condition
    iii. Be open to questioning and ascertain answers if possible
    iv. Encourage patient-family communication
    v. Provide appropriate diversional activities
B. Decreased lung expansion—restrictive lung disease
  1. Characteristics
    a. Decreased or asymmetrical lung expansion
    b. Rapid, shallow respirations
  2. Pulmonary consolidation (pneumonias)—inflammation of lung parenchyma—results in air being replaced by exudates in the alveoli (see Unit 3 for pathophysiology, assessment findings, and nursing care)
    a. Etiology
      (1) Gram-positive and gram-negative bacteria
      (2) Viruses
      (3) Fungi
      (4) Protozol agents
      (5) Cancer

3. Pulmonary fibrosis—excessive amount of connective tissue in all or part of the lung due to infections, noxious fumes, or aspirations, which cause inflammation and necrosis of tissue
4. Pulmonary abscess and cavitation—tuberculosis invasion of lung tissue by tubercle bacillus
  a. Pathophysiology
    (1) Inhalation of *Mycobacterium tuberculosis* results in invasion of tissue and localized consolidation
    (2) Infection spreads by way of lymphatics to hilus → antibodies are released → fibrosis → calcification or
    (3) Inflammation → exudate formation → caseous necrosis → liquification of caseous material → cavitation
  b. Etiology and incidence
    (1) *Mycobacterium tuberculosis*
    (2) Greatly declined since beginning of century, although decline less rapid in past ten years
    (3) Occurs more frequently in urban areas
  c. Assessment findings
    (1) Subjective data
      (a) Loss of appetite
      (b) Weight loss
      (c) Weakness, fatigue, loss of energy
      (d) Night sweats
      (e) Fever—low-grade, frequently in late afternoon
      (f) Cough—green or yellow sputum, bloody
      (g) Knifelike chest pain (pleuritic)
    (2) Objective data
      (a) Vital signs
        i. Blood pressure—noncontributory
        ii. Pulse—tachycardia
        iii. Temperature—normal, elevated
        iv. Respiration—normal rate and depth, increased rate
      (b) Respiratory exam
        i. Asymmetrical lung expansion
        ii. Increased tactile fremitus over area of lesion
        iii. Dullness to precussion

iv. Auscultation—rales following short cough
(c) Diagnostic studies
   i. Chest x-ray—infiltration, cavitations
   ii. Blood—decreased RBCs, WBC in normal limits, elevated sedimentation rate
   iii. Sputum—positive acid-fast smear and cultures
   iv. Positive tuberculin test
d. Nursing care is designed to reduce spread of the bacteria and to promote the patient's physical and psychologic equilibrium
  (1) Respiratory precautions—isolation may be ordered
   (a) Avoid direct contact with sputum
   (b) Teach cough and tissue techniques
    i. Cough into tissue
    ii. Place tissues in disposable container
    iii. Have patient wear mask if unable to follow directions
  (2) Administer drug therapy,
   (a) Isonicotinic acid hydrazide (INH) 300 mg—supplemental pyridoxine HCl (Vitamin B_6) should be administered to prevent polyneuritis
   (b) Streptomycin 1 gm, IM—periodically check hearing and balance; toxicity affects vestibular nerve and occasionally causes renal impairment
   (c) Para-aminosalicylic acid (PAS) 16 to 20 gm
    i. Utilized in combination with INH
    ii. Give after meals to prevent GI irritation
  (3) Promote physical equilibrium
   (a) Provide high-protein, high-calorie diet in frequent small feedings
   (b) Force fluids
   (c) Exercise to tolerance—avoid fatigue
  (4) Provide emotional support
   (a) Include patient and family in

teaching plan about disease process, diagnostic and treatment program, and communicability
   (b) Encourage patient and family to verbalize concerns—many people still believe tuberculosis is a deadly disease
   (c) Provide diversional activities and encourage communications with family
  (5) Refer to appropriate community health agency for follow-up
C. Disturbances in pulmonary vascularity
  1. Characteristics
   a. Exertional dyspnea, dyspnea, weakness
   b. Chest pain may or may not be present
  2. Pulmonary emboli and infarction—occlusion of a pulmonary artery or arteriole by a substance, usually a blood clot, resulting in obstruction of blood flow and tissue necrosis (see Unit 3)
  3. Pulmonary edema—sudden transudation of fluid from pulmonary capillaries into alveoli
   a. Pathophysiology
    (1) Increased blood hydrostatic pressures or increased pulmonary capillary permeability → increased filtration of fluids into interstitial space
    (2) As interstitial fluid pressures become positive, fluid begins to move into alveoli
    (3) Fluid accumulation in alveoli increases air-fluid interface → decreases compliance → decreases diffusion of gases → hypoxia and hypercapnia
   b. Etiology and incidence
    (1) Left ventricular heart failure due to hypertension, aortic valve disease, or myocardial infarction
    (2) Overinfusion of blood, dextran, saline
    (3) Renal shutdown
    (4) High altitudes
    (5) Silo-filler's disease (inhalation of corn gas)
    (6) Transfusion reaction
    (7) Drug sensitivities
   c. Assessment findings
    (1) Subjective data

(a) Extreme shortness of breath
(b) Feelings of smothering
(c) Palpitations
(d) Sweating
(2) Objective data
  (a) Vital signs
    i. Blood pressure—elevated, hypotension
    ii. Temperature—normal, subnormal
    iii. Pulse—tachycardia, pounding, thready
    iv. Respiration—tachypnea, moist bubbly, wheezing
  (b) Skin—pale, cool, diaphoretic, cyanotic
  (c) Respiratory auscultation—rales, coarse rhonchi
  (d) Productive cough—frothy pink-tinged sputum
  (e) Distended neck veins and engorged peripheral veins
  (f) Mental status—restless, anxious, confused, stuporous
d. Nursing care is designed to promote physical and psychologic relaxation, relieve hypoxia, retard venous return, and improve cardiac function
(1) Institute measures to relieve anxiety and slow respirations
  (a) Administer morphine sulfate, as ordered—reduces muscular and respiratory activity; provides sedation
  (b) Remain with patient and encourage slow, deep breathing; assist with coughing
(2) Institute measures to relieve hypoxia
  (a) Apply oxygen with mask
  (b) Utilize IPPB with 100% oxygen
    i. Reduces ventilatory rate
    ii. Provides uniform ventilation
    iii. Reduces venous return by replacing negative intrathoracic pressures with positive pressure
  (c) Administer aminophylline, as ordered
    i. Increases cardiac output
    ii. Lowers venous pressures
(3) Institute measures to retard venous return

(a) Rotating tourniquets
(b) High Fowler's position with extremities in dependent positions
(c) Assist with phlebotomy, as ordered
(4) Institute measures to improve cardiac function
  (a) Digitalis, as ordered
  (b) Diuretics, as ordered
    i. Ethacrynic acid (Edecrin)
    ii. Furosemide (Lasix)
(5) Continuously monitor physical and psychologic parameters to assess effectiveness of therapies
  (a) Vital signs
  (b) Auscultate breath sounds
  (c) Weigh daily
  (d) Intake and output
  (e) Mentation—restless, aware of time and place, not responding
(6) Institute measures to support adaptive mechanisms
  (a) Low-sodium diet (see Appendix C, Diets)
  (b) Fluid restriction, as ordered
  (c) Exercise to tolerance
  (d) Breathing exercises, oral hygiene
  (e) Frequent rest periods
  (f) Patient teaching
    i. Involve family or significant other
    ii. Medications—digitalis, diuretics
     • *Pulse taking*
     • *Side effects*
     • *Potassium supplements if indicated*
    iii. Exercise and rest
    iv. Low-sodium diet
    v. Symptoms of edema that should be reported to physician
D. Disturbances of neurologic innervation of respiratory musculature
1. Poliomyelitis—acute viral infection that attacks anterior horn cells in spinal cord and motor cells in brain stem and cortical levels; results in muscular fasciculations, painful tender muscles, and paralysis
2. Myasthenia gravis—impaired transmission of nerve impulses at myoneural junction

results in excessive muscular fatigability (see Part F, Lower motor neuron lesions)

   3. Tetanus (lockjaw)—an infectious disease characterized by extreme stiffness of the body

3. Metabolic alkalosis—result of an abnormal increase in bicarbonate or a decrease in hydrogen-ion concentration; compensated for by hypoventilation and excretion of large amounts of sodium and potassium bicarbonate in the urine (alkaline urine)

A. Loss of hydrogen ion
   1. Vomiting
   2. Gastric suctioning (particularly with plain-water irrigation)

B. Increase in bicarbonate—excessive ingestion of alkaline drugs
   1. Gastric and duodenal ulcers—circumscribed loss of mucosa, submucosa, and muscle layer in areas of the digestive tract exposed to acid-pepsin gastric juice
     a. Pathophysiology
       (1) Imbalance develops between resistance of mucous membrane lining digestive tract and the secretion of acid-pepsin
       (2) Increased vagal stimulation due to emotional factors (anger, resentment) or stimulants, such as alcohol, increase hydrochloric acid secretion and pepsin formation
       (3) Increased sympathetic nervous system responses to emotional factors or stimulants, such as tobacco, decrease blood supply to gastric mucosa and reduce its resistance to effects of acid-pepsin
     b. Etiology and incidence
       (1) Duodenal ulcer
         (a) Stress and responsibility
         (b) Competitive jobs
         (c) Usually between 25 and 50 years of age
         (d) Twice as many men as women
         (e) Usually well-nourished
         (f) Increased acid secretion
         (g) More frequently are in type O blood group
       (2) Gastric ulcer
         (a) Endocrine factors
         (b) Emotional stress
         (c) Usually over 50 years of age

         (d) Four times as many men as women
         (e) Often malnourished
         (f) Normal to decreased acid production
         (g) No differentiation in blood groups
     c. Assessment finding
       (1) Subjective data
         (a) Pain
           i. Type—dull, gnawing
           ii. Location—Midepigastric, back, may be to right or left upper abdominal area
           iii. Duration—intermittent, continuous one to three hours after eating
           iv. Relieved by ingestion of food or alkali
         (b) Heartburn, belching
         (c) Nausea, vomiting
         (d) Tarry stools
       (2) Objective data
         (a) Diagnostic studies
           i. Stools—positive for occult blood
           ii. Upper GI series—outlines ulcerations in stomach or duodenum
           iii. Gastric analysis—hyperchlorhydria or hypochlorhydria
     d. Nursing care is directed toward reducing stress and controlling gastric acidity
       (1) Institute measures to reduce emotional and physical stress
         (a) Bedrest—position of comfort
         (b) Quiet nonstimulating environment
         (c) Plan procedure times with patient
         (d) Allow time for verbalization of concerns and encourage communication with family
         (e) Restrict visitors who upset patient
       (2) Institute measures to control gastric acidity
         (a) Insert nasogastric tube and attach to low intermittent suction—for nausea and vomiting

(b) Medications, as ordered (see
Appendix F)
   i. Sedatives—phenobarbital,
   diazepam (Valium),
   chlordiazepoxide (Librium)
   HCl
   ii. Anticholinergics—atropine
   SO_4, propantheline
   (Pro-Banthine) Br
   iii. Antacids—magnesium and
   aluminum hydroxide mixture
   (Maalox), magnesium
   trisilicate and aluminum
   hydroxide (Gelusil), Mylanta,
   aluminum hydroxide gel
   (Amphojel)
(c) Bland diet (see Appendix C,
Diets)
(d) Milk and cream therapy (Sippy
diet) may still be ordered but is
no longer considered central to
therapy due to increase in serum
lipids
(3) Monitor effectiveness of therapy
and observe for complication of
ulcers (hemorrhage, perforation,
pyloric obstruction)

(a) Vital signs
(b) Stools for blood after each
movement
(c) Hemoglobin levels
(4) Promote emotional support through
patient teaching
(a) Involve family and patient in
diet teaching and meal planning
(b) Stress need to avoid stimulants,
such as tobacco, alcohol, coffee,
tea
(c) Encourage expression of feelings
(d) Planned exercise and rest
periods
(e) Importance of on-going medical
care

4. **Respiratory alkalosis**—occurs with excessive
secretion of carbon dioxide and is compensated
for by respiratory hypoventilation and retention
of hydrogen ions by the kidney
A. Hyperventilation—anxiety, hysteria, high altitudes, fever
B. Aspirin poisoning—salicylates have a direct
stimulating effect on the respiratory system,
which results in hyperventilation and loss of
carbon dioxide

Part F   Muscle Tone

PHYSIOLOGY

A. Muscle tone is a state of continuous mild contractions of muscles—it is dependent on an
intact nervous system and the inherent contractility and elasticity of muscle
B. Muscle tone is clinically manifested by
   1. Muscles that are resilient, not flabby, at rest
   2. Muscle that will offer some resistance when
   passively stretched by a joint movement

FACTORS AFFECTING MAINTENANCE AND CONTROL OF MUSCLE TONE

1. **The idiomuscular system**—the inherent elastic-

ity, contractility, and extensibility of muscles
themselves
2. **The spinal cord**—lowest level of sensory integration is in the grey matter of the spinal cord
A. Simple stretch reflexes, such as the knee-jerk,
are mitigated through spinal cord centers
B. The spinal cord is capable of eliciting almost
all the muscle movements required for posture
and locomotion
C. Coordination of these patterns, however, requires neuronal control by higher centers in the
central nervous system
3. **The reticular formation of the brain stem**—contains both excitatory and inhibitory centers
A. Excitatory centers, when stimulated, increase

muscle tone throughout the body or in localized areas

B. Inhibitory centers, when stimulated, decrease muscle tone

C. The excitatory impulses transmitted in conjunction with impulses from the vestibular nuclei provide the muscle tone needed by limb muscles to support the body against gravity

4. **The basal ganglia**—consists of the striate bodies and the globus pallidus.

A. Have numerous nerve pathways to the cerebral cortex and reticular formation and among themselves

B. Generally have an inhibitory effect on muscle tone through stimulation of specific areas; can elicit muscle contraction and patterns of movement

5. **The cerebellum**—a deeply fissured structure located behind the brain stem

A. It receives sensory fibers from the spinal cord and thalamus and has motor fibers to the basal ganglia, reticular formation, and cerebral cortex

B. The cerebellum is principally responsible for the coordination and timing of movements

6. **The cerebral cortex**—the highest level for control of muscle tone

A. Frontal lobe of cerebral cortex gives rise to two motor tracts

B. The corticospinal or direct motor pathway from the cortex to the spinal cord

   1. Projects fibers down through the internal capsule to the medulla, where the fibers collect in bundles (pyramids)

   2. Prior to entering the cord, 75% to 90% of the fibers cross over and descend the lateral funiculus on the opposite side of the cord—control of limb musculature is largely contralateral

   3. Initiates and controls discrete muscle movements; also facilitates or lowers the thresholds of anterior motor neurons

C. The extrapyramidal tract—a functional rather than an anatomic unit consisting of those motor nuclei and their fibers outside the corticospinal tract

   1. Nerve fibers reach segmental levels in the cord after making a number of neuronal connections in the basal ganglia, subcortical ganglia, and reticular formation

   2. Principally concerned with associated movements, postural adjustments, and autonomic integration

IMBALANCES OF MUSCLE TONE

1. **Hypertonia** (upper motor neuron lesions)—rigid, spastic muscles that offer resistance to passive movement

A. Lesions of the cerebral cortex

   1. Electrical disturbances (dysrhythmias)

     a. Epilepsies—abnormal electrical activity that produces involuntary muscular contractions and disturbances of consciousness

      (1) Pathophysiology

       (a) Increased excitability of a neuron → may activate adjacent neurons → synchronous discharge of impulses → vigorous involuntary sustained muscle spasms (tonic contractions)

       (b) Onset of neuronal fatigue → intermittent muscle spasms (clonic contractions) → cessation of muscle spasms → sleep

      (2) Etiology and incidence

       (a) Idiopathic or functional

       (b) Brain injury

       (c) Infection (meningitis, encephalitis)

       (d) Water and electrolyte disturbances

       (e) Hypoglycemia

       (f) Tumors

       (g) Vascular disorders (hypoxia or hypocapnia)

      (3) Assessment findings

       (a) Grand mal seizures

         i. Aura—flash of light, peculiar smell, sound, feelings of fear, euphoria

         ii. Convulsive stage—tonic and clonic muscle spasms, loss of consciousness, breath holding, frothing at mouth, biting of tongue, urinary or fecal incontinence

         iii. Postconvulsion—headache, malaise, nausea, vomiting, sore muscles, choking on secretions, aspiration

       (b) Petit mal seizures

         i. Momentary loss of consciousness (10 to 90

seconds), fixation of gaze, blank facial expression

ii. Loss of motor tone—flickering of eyelids, jerking of facial muscle or arm

iii. Postconvulsion—patient resumes action previously being performed

(4) Nursing care in seizure conditions is designed to prevent injury, prevent recurrences, and assist patient in understanding condition and treatment

(a) Institute measures during seizure to prevent injury

i. Place soft object, such as padded tongue blade or handkerchief, between teeth—*Do not force* jaws open during convulsion

ii. Do *not* restrict limbs—support head, turn to side if possible

iii. Loosen constrictive clothing

iv. Note time, level of consciousness, and type and duration of muscle spasms

v. Postseizure care
   • *Oropharyngeal suction as necessary*
   • *Orient to time and place*
   • *Oral hygiene if tongue or cheek injury*
   • *Check vital signs, pupils, level of consciousness*

(b) Prevent or reduce recurrences of seizure activity

i. Encourage patient to identify factors that precipitate seizures

ii. Involve family in instructions, stressing moderation in diet and exercise

iii. Medications, actions, side effects (see Appendix F, Drugs)
   • *Phenobarbital*
   • *Diphenylhydantoin (Dilantin) sodium*
   • *Primidone (Mysoline)*
   • *Trimethadione (Tridione)*

iv. Encourage patients to stay on medications and to have follow-up urinalysis and blood studies

(c) Assist patient in understanding condition
   • *Encourage positive attitude toward life and treatment*
   • *Attempt to clarify misconceptions and fears—especially about insanity, bad genes*
   • *Encourage maintenance of activities, interests—avoiding stress*
   • *Encourage use of Medic Alert band or tag*
   • *Refer to appropriate community resource*

2. Traumatic injuries
   a. Types
      (1) Concussion—transient disorder due to injury in which there is a brief loss of consciousness due to paralysis of neuronal function; recovery is usually total
      (2) Contusion—structural alteration of brain tissue characterized by extravasation of blood cells (bruising); injury may occur on side of impact or on opposite side (opposite side when the cranial contents shift forcibly within the skull with impact)
      (3) Laceration—tearing of brain tissue or blood vessels due to a sharp bone fragment or object or a shearing force
   b. Pathophysiology of impaired central nervous system dysfunction
      (1) Depressed neuronal activity in cerebral cortex → impaired mental ability → inability to concentrate → forgetfulness → emotional instability → inability to interpret significance of sensations (agnosia) → loss of learned motor responses (apraxia)
      (2) Depressed neuronal activity in reticular activating system → depressed consciousness (levels of consciousness)
         (a) Alert—aware of time and place

(b) Stage of automatism—aware of time and place but demonstrates abnormality of mood (euphoria to irritability)

(c) Stage of confusion—inability to think and speak in coherent manner; responds to verbal requests but is unaware of time and place

(d) Stage of delirium—characterized by restlessness and violent activity; may not comply with verbal instructions

(e) Stage of stupor—quiet and uncommunicative; may appear conscious—sits or lies with glazed look; unable to respond to verbal instructions; bladder and rectal incontinence may occur during this stage

(f) Stage of semicoma—unresponsive to verbal instructions but responds to vigorous or painful stimuli

(g) Stage of coma—unresponsive to vigorous or painful stimuli

(3) Depressed neuronal function in lower brain stem and spinal cord → depression of reflex activity → decreased eye movements, unequal pupils → gradual dilation → decreased response to light stimuli → widely dilated and fixed pupils

(a) Superficial and deep reflexes decrease → disappear → absent corneal reflex (eye does not close when touched) → decreased vasoconstriction → decreased blood pressure → circulatory collapse

(b) Decreased muscle activity → vasomotor collapse → decreased body temperature → skin pale and cool

(c) Depression of respiratory center → altered respiratory pattern (Cheyne-Stokes) → decreased rate → respiratory arrest

c. Etiology and incidence

(1) Automobile accidents

(2) Industrial and home accidents

(3) Motorcycle accidents

(4) Military accidents

(5) Affects people of all ages

d. Assessment findings

(1) Subjective data

(a) Headache

(b) Dizziness, loss of balance

(c) Double vision

(d) Nausea, vomiting

(2) Objective data

(a) Lacerations or abrasion around face and head

(b) Drainage from ears or nose

(c) Projectile vomiting, hematemesis

(d) Vital Signs

　i. Blood pressure—elevated, decreased

　ii. Temperature—elevated, decreased

　iii. Pulse—bradycardia, tachycardia

　iv. Respiration—tachypnea, bradypnea, Cheyne-Stokes

(e) Neurologic exam

　i. Altered level of consciousness

　ii. Pupils—equal, round, react to light; unequal, dilated, unresponsive to light

　iii. Extremities—paresis or paralysis

　iv. Reflexes—hypo- or hypertonia, Babinski's

(f) Inability to handle respiratory secretions

e. Nursing care is designed to monitor physical and mental status continuously and to employ measures to sustain vital functions and minimize or prevent complications

(1) Respiratory system

(a) Maintain patent airway— endotracheal tube or tracheostomy may be ordered

(b) Oxygen, IPPB, as ordered— hypoxia increases dysfunction and promotes development of cerebral edema

(c) Position patient in semiprone or prone position with head level—improves gaseous exchange and prevents aspiration—*keep off back*

      (d) Turn from side-to-side—
           prevents stasis of secretions
           in lungs

(2) Neurologic system
    (a) Vital signs
    (b) Neurologic check—pupils, level
        of consciousness, muscle
        strength
    (c) Report changes to physicians
    (d) Maintain seizure
        precautions—padded tongue
        blade at bedside, padded side
        rails
    (e) Medications, as ordered
        i. Steroids—to reduce
           inflammation
        ii. Phenobarbital or
           diphenylhydantoin (Dilantin)
           sodium to control seizures
        iii. Analgesic—To reduce
           discomfort; morphine
           contraindicated
    (f) Institute cooling measures or
        hypothermia for elevated
        temperature
    (g) Assist with diagnostic tests
        i. Lumbar puncture
        ii. Electroencephalogram (EEG)

(3) Nutritional balance
    (a) NPO for 24 hours, progressing
        to clear liquids if awake
    (b) Maintain unconscious patients
        with parenteral infusions,
        nasogastric tube feedings
    (c) Strict intake and output
    (d) Monitor blood chemistries—
        disturbances of sodium
        balance not uncommon with
        head injuries

(4) Provide emotional support and
    utilize comfort measures
    (a) Skin care, oral hygiene,
        sheepskins, wrinkle-free linen
    (b) Lubricate eyes if periocular
        edema present q4h
    (c) Institute passive and active
        ROM exercise, physical therapy
        as tolerated
    (d) Support during periods of
        restlessness—avoid restraints
    (e) Encourage verbalization of
        concerns about changes in body
        image, limitations
    (f) Encourage family
        communication

f. Complications of head injuries
(1) Increased intracranial pressures
    (a) Etiology
        i. Cerebral edema
        ii. Abscess or inflammation
        iii. Tumor or other
           space-occupying lesion
        iv. Increased production or
           blockage of cerebrospinal
           fluid
        v. Hemorrhage
    (b) Clinical indications
        i. Altered level of
           consciousness
        ii. Pupillary changes—unequal,
           dilated, and unresponsive to
           light
        iii. Vital signs—changes variable
        • *Blood pressure—gradual or*
        rapid elevation, widened pulse
        pressure
        • *Pulse—bradycardia,*
        tachycardia, significant sign is
        slowing of pulse as blood
        pressure rises
        • *Respirations—pattern*
        changes, deep and sonorous to
        Cheyne-Stokes
        • *Temperature—moderate*
        elevation
        iv. Complaints of headache,
           nausea
    (c) Nursing actions
        i. Report changes to physician
           at once
        ii. Administer medications, as
           ordered
        • *Hyperosmolar diuretics*
        (mannitol and urea)—reduce
        brain swelling
        • *Steroids (anti-inflammatory)*
        • *Antacids (prevent stress ulcer)*
        • *Anticholinergics (prevent stress*
        ulcer)
        iii. Utilize cooling measures to
           reduce temperature
           elevations
        iv. Prepare for surgical
           intervention as indicated

(2) Subdural hematoma—occurs as a result of torn or ruptured veins between the dura and brain
3. Inflammation of brain tissue
   a. Meningitis—acute inflammation of meninges characterized by severe headache, nuchal rigidity, irritability and restlessness (see Unit 5, Pediatric Nursing)
   b. Encephalitis—inflammation of the brain and its coverings
      (1) Pathophysiology
         (a) Brain tissue injury → release of enzymes increases vascular dilatation and capillary permeability → edema formation
         (b) Edema formation in cerebral tissues increases intracranial pressures → depression of central nervous system function
      (2) Etiology
         (a) Syphilis
         (b) Lead or arsenic poison
         (c) Carbon monoxide
         (d) Typhoid fever
         (e) Measles, chicken pox
         (f) Viruses
      (3) Assessment findings
         (a) Subjective data
            i. Severe headache
            ii. Sudden fever
            iii. Nausea, vomiting
            iv. Sensitivity to light (photophobia)
            v. Difficulty concentrating
         (b) Objective data
            i. Altered levels of consciousness
            ii. Nuchal rigidity
            iii. Tremors
            iv. Facial weakness
            v. Nystagmus
            vi. Elevated temperature
            vii. Diagnostic studies
            • *Blood—slight to moderate leukocytosis*
            • *Cerebrospinal fluid—cloudy, increased neutrophils*
      (4) Nursing care is designed to support physical and emotional relaxation
         (a) Vital signs and neurologic checks

         (b) Institute seizure precautions
         (c) Cooling measures as necessary
         (d) Isolation is not necessary
         (e) Administer mannitol or urea, as ordered—to reduce cerebral edema
B. Lesions of the internal capsule, basal ganglia, pons, and medulla
   1. Vascular lesions
      a. Cerebral vascular accident—interference of cerebral blood flow; this ultimately results in ischemia and necrosis of tissue
         (1) Pathophysiology
            (a) Reduced or interrupted blood flow → interruption of nerve impulses down corticospinal tract → decreased or absent voluntary movement on one side of the body → fine movements are more affected than coarse movement
            (b) Initially reflex activity that is normally facilitated by cortical centers is lost → later reflex centers begin to act autonomously → exaggerated tendon reflexes → increased muscle tone due to gamma efferent neuron activity → spasticity and rigidity of muscles
         (2) Etiology and incidence
            (a) Cerebral thrombosis
            (b) Intracerebral hemorrhage
            (c) Cerebral embolism
            (d) Vascular insufficiency
            (e) Highest incidence in elderly
         (3) Assessment findings
            (a) Subjective data
               i. Weakness
               ii. Sudden or gradual loss of movement of extremities on one side
               iii. Difficulty forming words
               iv. Difficulty swallowing (dysphagia)
               v. Nausea, vomiting
            (b) Objective data
               i. Vital signs
               • *Blood pressure—elevated, widened pulse pressure*
               • *Temperature—elevated*

- *Pulse—normal, slow*
- *Respirations—tachypnea, altered pattern, deep, sonorous, Cheyne-Stokes*
  ii. Neurologic
- *Altered level of consciousness*
- *Pupil inequality*
- *Ptosis of eyelid, drooping mouth*
- *Paresis or paralysis*
- *Loss of sensation and reflexes*
- *Incontinence of urine or feces*
- *Aphasia*

(4) Nursing care is directed toward reducing cerebral anoxia, supporting vital functions, and promoting rehabilitation

(a) Institute measures to reduce hypoxia
  i. Maintain patent airway
  ii. Oxygen therapy, IPPB, as ordered
  iii. Bedrest—position to optimize ventilation
  iv. Naso-oral suctioning as needed to remove secretions and prevent aspiration
  v. Turn, cough, and deep breathe q2h

(b) Institute measures that promote cardiovascular function and maintain cerebral perfusion
  i. Vital signs
  ii. Medications, as ordered
  - *Antihypertensives—prevent rupture*
  - *Anticoagulants—prevent thrombus*
  iii. Parenteral infusions to prevent hemoconcentration
  - *Intake and output*
  - *Weigh daily*

(c) Monitor neurologic parameters
  i. Orient to time and place prn
  ii. Identify grief reaction to changes in body image
  iii. Maintain ROM exercises— prevents contractures, muscle atrophy, and phlebitis

(d) Employ comfort measures to provide for physical and emotional relaxation
  i. Skin care, assist with

feedings, support with pillows when on side, utilize hand rolls and arm slings as ordered
  ii. Involve patient and family, in establishing care plan
  - *Exercise routines*
  - *Diet and rest*
  - *Encourage resumption of care activities*
  - *Use of supportive devices*
  iii. Encourage expression of feelings and concerns

b. Transient ischemic attacks—temporary complete or relatively complete cessation of cerebral blood flow to a localized area of brain, producing symptoms ranging from weakness and numbness to monocular blindness; an important precursor to CVA

2. Degenerative diseases
  a. Parkinson's disease
  (1) Pathophysiology
    (a) Degeneration of basal ganglia and/or substantia nigra → decreased dopamine (neurotransmitter) → decreased and slowed voluntary movement → wooden facies → difficulty initiating walking
    (b) Decreased inhibition of alpha-motoneurons → increased muscle tone → rigidity both of flexor and extensor muscles → development of tremor at rest
  (2) Etiology and incidence
    (a) Unknown cause
    (b) Occurs in ages 50 to 65 years
    (c) Affects both sexes and all races
  (3) Assessment findings
    (a) Subjective data
      i. Tremors of hands and feet
      ii. Stiffness in legs and shoulders
      iii. Loss of coordination—such as in writing
      iv. Insomnia
      v. Weight loss
    (b) Objective data
      i. Neurologic
      - *Gait—initiated slowly, then propulsive*
      - *Speech—slowed, slurred*

• *Facies—wide-eyed, decreased expression, eye blinking, excessive salivation, drooling*
• *Limbs—stiff, offer resistance throughout to passive rotation*
• *Tremor—pill-rolling of fingers, head movement to and fro*

(4) Nursing care is designed to be supportive and to promote maintenance of daily activities

(a) Levodopa therapy, as ordered
  i. Given in increasing doses until patient's tolerance is reached
  ii. Not a cure—decreases rigidity and dyskinesia
  iii. Take vitamin B_6 out of diet—it cancels effect of levodopa
  iv. Side effects include nausea, vomiting, postural hypotension, mental confusion, arrhythmias

(b) Provide emotional and physical support
  i. Encourage activity, physical therapy, warm baths, massage to relax muscles— avoid sitting for long periods of time
  ii. Identify reaction to changing body image; allow for verbalization of feelings; encourage social activities
  iii. High-protein, high-calorie, soft diet; assist with cutting of food if necessary; push fluids, small frequent feedings

b. Huntington's chorea—hereditary disease characterized by progressive dementia and bizarre involuntary movements

3. Demyelinating diseases
a. Multiple sclerosis—progressive neurologic disease characterized by demyelination of the brain and spinal cord

(1) Pathophysiology (see CVA for pathologic description of corticospinal tract interference, p. 117)

(2) Etiology and incidence
  (a) Unknown cause

  (b) Affects males and females equally
  (c) Onset between 20 to 40 years of age
  (d) Greater incidence in Northern latitudes

(3) Assessment findings
  (a) Subjective data
    i. Weakness
    ii. Impaired, blurred, or double vision
    iii. Difficulty in coordination
    iv. Numbness in extremities
  (b) Objective data
    i. Motor system—decreased strength in muscles of lower extremeties
    ii. Decreased visual acuity, nystagmus, weakness of eye muscles
    iii. Gait—ataxic-spastic
    iv. Sensory—decreased sensation to pressure and pinprick, impaired vibratory sense
    v. Mental status: emotionally labile, alteration in consciousness
    vi. Marked by exacerbations, remissions over period of years
    vii. Cerebrospinal fluid— protein count normal or slightly elevated, gamma globulin elevated

(4) Nursing care is designed to maintain function as long as possible and to relieve symptoms
  (a) Institute measures designed to maintain mobility
    i. Muscle stretching exercises
    ii. Avoidance of fatigue, stress
    iii. Encourage to sleep prone to minimize flexor spasms of knees and hips
    iv. Encourage walking to tolerance
    v. Diazepam to relax muscles, as ordered
  (b) Institute measures to avoid injury due to loss of sensation
    i. Avoid temperature extremes
    ii. Teach to walk with feet wide

apart to maintain balance
- (c) Institute bladder training to avoid urinary retention and infection—voiding schedule and manual massage if needed over pubic symphysis
- (d) Establish bowel program
    - i. Regular meals and evacuation time
    - ii. Glycerin suppository 30 minutes before scheduled evacuation time
    - iii. Instruct to assume normal position bearing down with abdominal muscles—apply pressure with hand as indicated
- (e) Steroids during exacerbations, as ordered
- (f) Involve patient and family in care plans
- (g) Identify patient's defense mechanisms and assist with dealing with fears
- (h) Refer to appropriate community resource for follow-up care

b. Encephalomyelitis—an acute process, characterized by symptoms related to damage of the white matter of the brain or spinal cord; may occur following such childhood diseases as measles or chicken pox or following vaccination for rabies or smallpox

2. **Hypotonia**—weak, flaccid muscles that offer less than normal resistance to passive movement
A. Lesions and injuries of the spinal cord
1. Spinal shock—temporary flaccid paralysis and areflexia following a severe injury to the spinal cord
   a. Pathophysiology
   - (1) Squeezing or shearing of the cord due to fractures or dislocation of vertebrae → interruption of sensory tracts → loss of conscious sensation
   - (2) Interruption of motor tracts → loss of voluntary movement → loss of facilitation → loss of reflex activity
   - (3) Loss of reflex activity → loss of muscle tone → stretch reflexes → urine and fecal retention
   - (4) If injury above T-1 to L-2 → loss of sympathetic tone →

decreased blood pressure
   b. Etiology and incidence
   - (1) Trauma—automobile or motorcycle accidents, falls
   - (2) Inflammation in the cord (myelitis)
   - (3) Local restricted blood flow; tumor or protrusion of an intervertebral disk
   c. Assessment findings
   - (1) Subjective data
       - (a) Loss of sensation below level of injury
       - (b) Inability to move extremities
       - (c) Pain at level of injury
   - (2) Objective data
       - (a) Neurologic exam
           - i. Absent pinprick, pressure, and vibratory sensations below level of injury
           - ii. Absent reflexes below injury
           - iii. Muscles—flaccid
       - (b) Vital signs
           - i. Blood pressure—decreased (loss of vasomotor tone below injury)
           - ii. Pulse—tachycardia
           - iii. Respiration—increased rate
           - iv. Temperature—elevated
       - (c) Absence of sweating below injury
       - (d) Urinary retention
       - (e) Abdominal (bowel) distention
   d. Nursing care is designed to support body functions until shock is reduced or relieved
   - (1) Maintain patent airway—intubation and mechanical ventilation may be necessary with cervical cord injuries
   - (2) Monitor vital signs—administer blood transfusions and parenteral infusions, as ordered
   - (3) Relieve bladder distention by inserting catheter that is attached to closed drainage
   - (4) Relieve bowel distention with colon lavage or enemas
   - (5) Maintain nutrition as tolerated; NPO with intravenous infusions—high-protein, high-calorie, high-vitamin diet
   - (6) Prevent contractions—maintain proper body alignment

(7) Frequent skin care, turning (Stryker frame)
2. Amyotrophic lateral sclerosis (Lou Gehrig's disease)—motoneuron degenerative disease
B. Lesions in the muscle or disturbances in synaptic transmission
1. Polymyositis
2. Dystrophies (muscular)
3. Myasthenia gravis—disease characterized by weakness and easy fatigability of facial, oculomotor, pharyngeal, and respiratory muscles
   a. Pathophysiology—inadequate acetylcholine or excessive or altered cholinesterase → impaired transmission of motor impulses at myoneural junction
   b. Etiology and incidence
      (1) Possible autoimmune reaction
      (2) Affects women predominantly, 20 to 40 years of age
   c. Assessment findings
      (1) Subjective data
         (a) Drooping of an eyelid
         (b) Double vision (intermittent)
         (c) Difficulty chewing food
         (d) Choking on food
      (2) Objective data
         (a) Expressionless facies
         (b) Easy fatigability of muscles
         (c) Abnormal speech pattern with high-pitched nasal voice
         (d) Respiratory studies
            i. Decreased vital capacity
            ii. Decreased ability to deep breathe and cough
   d. Nursing care is designed to promote muscle function and provide physical and emotional relaxation
      (1) Institute measures to promote motor function
         (a) Anticholinesterase drugs, as ordered—neostigmine (Prostigmin) Br, Edrophonium (Tensilon) Cl
            i. Give with milk or crackers
            ii. Always give at scheduled time—20 to 30 minutes before meals (ac)
            iii. Side effects—nausea, vomiting, excessive salivation, increased muscle weakness
         (b) Passive and active ROM exercises, increasing activity to tolerance

(c) Suction excessive oral secretions and keep tracheostomy set at bedside
      (2) Institute comfort and safety measures
         (a) Medications
            (a) Keep atropine SO_4 at bedside
            (b) Morphine contraindicated
         (b) Diet as tolerated—tube feedings, pureed, soft
         (c) Oral hygiene after meals (pc) and prn
         (d) Vital signs—check respirations q2h
         (e) Keep call bell within reach—utilize paper and pencil for voice difficulties
         (f) Skin care—sheepskins, back rubs
         (g) Eye care—remove crusts, patch for affected eye, eyedrops
         (h) Encourage independence and provide opportunities to express feelings
      (3) Institute preoperative care if thymectomy is ordered
3. **Impairment of the special senses**
A. Eyes
1. Acute and chronic glaucoma—increased intraocular pressure
   a. Pathophysiology
      (1) Impaired passage of aqueous humor into the circular canal of Schlemm due to closure of the angle between the cornea and the iris (acute or closed-angle glaucoma) or local obstruction of aqueous between the anterior chamber and the canal (open-angle or chronic glaucoma)
      (2) Imbalance between rate of secretion of intraocular fluids and rate of absorption of aqueous → increased aqueous humor pressures → decreased peripheral vision → corneal edema → halos and blurring of vision → blindness
   b. Etiology and incidence
      (1) Unknown, but associated with
         (a) Emotional disturbances
         (b) Hereditary factors
         (c) Allergies
         (d) Vasomotor disturbances
      (2) Affects 2% of the population over 40 years of age
   c. Assessment findings

(1) Subjective data
  (a) Acute
    i. Severe pain in or around eyes
    ii. Headache
    iii. Halos of lights
    iv. Blurring of vision
    v. Nausea and vomiting
  (b) Chronic
    i. Eyes tire easily
    ii. Loss of peripheral vision
(2) Objective data
  (a) Corneal edema
  (b) Decreased peripheral vision
  (c) Increased cupping of optic disc
  (d) Tonometry—pressures over 22 mm Hg

d. Nursing care is directed toward implementation of therapies designed to reduce intraocular pressures and toward patient education

(1) Institute measures designed to reduce intraocular pressures
  (a) Bedrest—semi-Fowler's position; physical activity tends to increase pressures
  (b) Medications (see Appendix F, Drugs)
    i. Miotics—pilocarpine HCl, carbachol
    ii. Carbonic anhydrase inhibitors—acetazolamide—(Diamox)
    iii. Anticholinesterase—demecarium Br (Humorsol); facilitates outflow of aqueous humor
    iv. Contraindicated drugs—atropine
  (c) Provide emotional support
    i. Place patient's personal objects within field of vision
    ii. Assist patient with activities
    iii. Allow opportunities for patient and family to verbalize concerns, fears of blindness, loss of independence
  (d) Institute preoperative measures for iridectomy, as ordered
  (e) Involve patient and family in discharge planning and teaching
    i. Avoid activities and stresses that increase intraocular pressures
      • *Anger, excitement, worry*
      • *Constrictive clothing*
      • *Heavy lifting*
      • *Excessive fluid intake*
      • *Atropine or other mydriatics*
    ii. Encourage activities that reduce intraocular pressures
      • *Medications—purpose, dosage, frequency: (a) teach eyedrop installation and (b) caution to have extra bottle in case of loss or breakage*
      • *Moderate use of eyes*
      • *Moderate exercise—walking*
      • *Regular diet and elimination patterns; straining increases pressures*
    iii. Safety measures
      • *Medi-alert wrist band or tag*
      • *On-going out-patient care—refer to community resources as necessary*
      • *Use other eye medications or washes only with consent of physician*

2. The blind patient
  a. Blindness is legally defined as vision less than 20/200 with the use of corrective lenses or a visual field of no greater than 20 degrees
  b. Etiology and incidence
    (1) Glaucoma
    (2) Cataracts
    (3) Diabetic retinopathy
    (4) Atherosclerosis
    (5) Traumas
    (6) Greatest incidence after age 65 years
  c. Rehabilitation
    (1) Institute measures that are designed to promote independence and provide emotional support
      (a) Familiarize patient with surroundings; encourage use of touch
      (b) Establish communication lines
      (c) Deal with feelings of loss and overprotectiveness by family members
      (d) Answer patient and family questions and make suggestions that can prevent accidents in the

home
- (e) Provide appropriate diversional activities
- (f) Encourage self-care activities and allow patients to vent frustrations when unable to complete activities to their satisfaction
- (2) Institute referrals to appropriate community resources
  - (a) Voluntary agencies
    - i. American Foundation for the Blind—provides catalogs of devices for visually handicapped
    - ii. National Society for the Prevention of Blindness—comprehensive educational program and research
    - iii. Recording for the Blind, Inc.—provides recorded educational books free on loan
    - iv. Lion's Club
    - v. Catholic charities
    - vi. Salvation Army
  - (b) Official agencies
    - i. Social and Rehabilitation Service—counseling and placement services
    - ii. Veteran's Administration—screening and pensions
    - iii. State Welfare Department, Division for the Blind—vocational rehabilitation programs

B. Ears
1. The deaf patient
   a. Hard of hearing—slight or moderate hearing loss that is serviceable for activities of daily living
   b. Deafness—hearing that is nonfunctional for activities of daily living
   c. Etiology and incidence
   - (1) Conductive hearing losses
     - (a) Impacted cerumen (wax)
     - (b) Foreign body in external auditory canal
     - (c) Defects (thickening, scarring) of eardrum
     - (d) Otosclerosis of ossicles
   - (2) Sensory hearing losses
     - (a) Arteriosclerosis
     - (b) Infectious diseases—mumps, measles, meningitis
     - (c) Drug toxicities—quinine, streptomycin, neomycin SO_4
     - (d) Tumors
     - (e) Head traumas
     - (f) High-intensity noises
   - (3) Greatest incidence over age 65 years
   d. Indications of hearing loss
   - (1) Inattentive or strained facial expression
   - (2) Excessive loudness or softness of speech
   - (3) Frequent need to clarify content of conversation or inappropriate responses
   - (4) Tilting of the head while listening
   - (5) Lack of response when spoken to
   e. Rehabilitation
   - (1) Institute measures to maximize hearing ability, support adaptive mechanisms, and provide emotional support
     - (a) Evaluative studies—audiogram
     - (b) Establish communication system
       - i. Speech (lip) reading
       - ii. Sign language
       - iii. Hearing aid
       - iv. Paper and pencil
     - (c) Provide a supportive nonstressful environment
     - (d) Refer to appropriate community resource
       - i. National Association of Hearing and Speech Agencies—counseling services
       - ii. National Association for the Deaf—assists with employment, education, and legislation
       - iii. Alexander Graham Bell Association for the Deaf, Inc.—serves as information center for those working with the deaf
       - iv. American Hearing Society—educational information, employment services, and social clubs

Part G Cellular Maturation and Reproduction

PHYSIOLOGY

A. The process of cellular multiplication is called mitosis

B. Begins with duplication of genes and chromosomes

C. Ends with the formation of two new or daughter cells

D. Phases of mitosis
1. Duplication of centrioles—centrioles move apart and form spindles, which penetrate nucleus
2. Prophase—dissolution of nuclear envelope
3. Metaphase—chromosomes pulled to the center of cell
4. Anaphase—chromosomes broken apart
5. Telophase—two sets of chromosomes pulled completely apart and new nuclear membrane develops around each set; cells pinch in two, midway between the two new nuclei

E. Homeostatic mechanisms controlling cell reproduction have not been specifically identified

NORMAL CELL GROWTH AND REPRODUCTION

1. **Causes of cell growth and reproduction**—as a result of either an intrinsic or extrinsic stimuli

A. Hemorrhage stimulates increased erythrocyte production

B. Physical exercise stimulates increased skeletal muscle mass

2. **Needs of the body**—cell growth and reproduction must be sufficient to meet the needs of the body

A. Continuous replacement of worn-out cells

B. Increased erythrocyte production at high altitudes

C. Increased leukocytosis in response to infection and tissue destruction
1. Venereal diseases—diseases that are acquired through sexual contact or congenitally
   a. Syphilis
   (1) Pathophysiology
      (a) Spirochete enters blood through mucous membrane via the lymphatics
      (b) Incubation 10–90 days
      (c) Primary lesion, chancre, occurs at site of entry and heals spontaneously in two to six weeks
      (d) Secondary phase, rash appears about six weeks later and heals in two to six weeks
      (e) Tertiary phase is detectable only with serology testing
   (2) Etiology and incidence
      (a) Peak age group 20 to 24 years
      (b) Incidence higher in men
      (c) Caused by spirochete, *Treponema pallidum*
   (3) Assessment findings
      (a) Subjective data
         i. Chancre on genitals
         ii. Rash
         iii. Fever
         iv. Headache
         v. Weight loss
      (b) Objective data
         i. Primary
         • *Chancre—a painless, indurated ulcer on mouth or genitals*
         • *Lymphadenopathy*
         • *Positive VDRL*
         • *Spirochete visualized on dark-field examination*
         ii. Secondary
         • *Rash*
         • *Hair loss*
         • *Condyloma latum (moist, pink or gray-white lesion, highly infectious)*
         • *Elevated temperature*
         iii. Tertiary
         • *80% asymptomatic*
         • *Ulcers in heart, lungs, bones, liver, and CNS from breakdown of gummas*
   (4) Nursing care is designed to relieve

symptoms, secure treatment for all infected persons, and educate the public

- (a) Case-finding and interviewing infected persons and their contacts
- (b) Nurse must maintain a nonjudgmental attitude to be effective
- (c) Education of the public
  - i. Syphilis is a reportable disease
  - ii. Prevention is the best way of combating the spread
  - iii. It is important to obtain and continue treatment
  - iv. The signs and symptoms of possible infection
- (d) Administer appropriate drug therapy
  - i. Penicillin
  - ii. Tetracycline
  - iii. Erythromycin

b. Gonorrhea
- (1) Pathophysiology
  - (a) Begins with local infection after three days to two weeks incubation period
  - (b) Bacteria can penetrate intact mucous membrane and set up inflammatory response (edema, redness)
  - (c) If untreated, the bacteria spreads throughout the reproductive system, causing strictures and adhesions in the recovery phase (which can lead to sterility)
  - (d) Bacteria is drained off by the lymph system and into the blood stream, causing septicemia and spreading the disease to all areas of the body
- (2) Etiology and incidence
  - (a) Most common venereal disease
  - (b) Over 200,000 cases reported annually
  - (c) Caused by bacteria, *Neisseria gonorrhoeae*
- (3) Assessment findings
  - (a) Subjective data
    - i. Burning and pain on urination
    - ii. Yellowish discharge from urethra
    - iii. Fever, chills, and abdominal pain in women
  - (b) Objective data
    - i. Abscessed Skene's or Bartholin's glands
    - ii. Visualization of bacteria on gram stain or in culture
    - iii. Visualization of bacteria by means of immunofluorescence
    - iv. Elevated temperature, salpingitis
- (4) Nursing care (see Syphilis, nursing care)

2. Infectious diseases—diseases acquired from human, animal, or insect carriers
a. Measles and chickenpox
b. Malaria—chronic protozoan disease transmitted by *Anopheles* mosquito
- (1) Pathophysiology
  - (a) Bite of *Anopheles* mosquito introduces the malarial parasite into bloodstream
  - (b) Parasite invades, alters, and destroys red blood cells
- (2) Etiology and incidence
  - (a) Protozoa of species *Plasmodium* are causative organism
  - (b) Incubation period of ten days to six weeks
  - (c) Endemic in many areas of the world
- (3) Assessment findings
  - (a) Subjective data
    - i. Chills
    - ii. Fever
    - iii. Headache
    - iv. Muscle pains
    - v. Profuse sweating
  - (b) Objective data
    - i. Vital signs
    - • *Blood pressure— noncontributory*
    - • *Pulse—tachycardia*
    - • *Respirations—tachypnea*
    - • *Temperature—elevated*
    - ii. Splenomegaly, hepatomegaly
    - iii. Skin—uticaria; moist
    - iv. Attacks occur in paroxysms
    - • *Cold stage—rigor that lasts 20*

to 60 minutes
- *Hot stage—temperature of 104 to 107 F for three to eight hours*
- *Wet stage—profuse diaphoresis*
  v. Diagnostic tests
- Elevated sedimentation rate
- *Demonstrable Protozoa in peripheral smear*
  vi. Decreased Hb, Hct
(4) Nursing care is designed to eradicate the disease and provide symptomatic relief
  (a) Assist with administration of chemotherapy
    i. Chloroquine PO_4 (quinine)
    ii. Pyrimethamine
    iii. Sulfisoxazole or sulfadiazine
  (b) Provide warmth with blankets and clothing during the cold phase
  (c) Provide linen and clothing change during the wet phase
3. **The nature of cell growth**—cells produced should mature into normal functioning tissue
4. **Decrease in cell production**—cell production should decrease when the demand or need for the cells ceases
A. A decrease in adipose tissue results in a decrease in capillary beds
B. Immobilization results in decreased muscle mass

IMBALANCES IN CELLULAR GROWTH AND REPRODUCTION

1. **Inappropriate cellular production in response to intrinsic or extrinsic stimuli**
A. Intrinsic stimuli
  1. Hormones
    a. Acromegaly—a disease of excessive body growth
      (1) Pathophysiology
        (a) Tumor stimulates increased production of the growth hormone, causing continued growth and expansion of bones and soft tissue
      (2) Etiology and incidence
        (a) Eosinophilic adenomas of the posterior pituitary
        (b) Rare disease

        (c) Usually begins about third or fourth decade of life
      (3) Assessment findings
        (a) Subjective
          i. Excessive growth
        (b) Objective data
          i. Coarse, heavy features
          ii. Enlargement and broadening of hands, feet, and head
          iii. Frontal sinuses become particularly pronounced
          iv. Diagnostic tests
        - *Increased basal metabolic rate*
        - *Impaired glucose tolerance test*
        - *Elevated plasma growth hormone*
        - *Elevated serum inorganic phosphorus and alkaline phosphatase*
      (4) Nursing care is designed to alleviate the discomfort of therapy, prepare the patient for surgery, and provide emotional support
        (a) Radiation therapy (see p. 128)
        (b) Pre- and postoperative nursing care (see Unit 3)
        (c) Physical changes are irreversible even with removal of the tumor, and patients need a great deal of support to accept their altered body images
    b. Dwarfism
  2. Immunologic excesses
    a. Systemic lupus erythematosus
    b. Glomerulonephritis
    c. Hodgkin's disease—believed to be an infectious or neoplastic disease of the lymph system
    d. Rheumatoid arthritis—chronic inflammatory disease
      (1) Pathophysiology
        (a) Synovitis, which causes edema
        (b) Various blood materials proliferate and form a pannus
        (c) Pannus invades joint cartilage, destroys it, and replaces it with fibrous tissue (fibrous ankylosis)
        (d) Calcification of fibrous tissue (osseous ankylosis)
        (e) Follows a course of exacerbations and remissions

(2) Etiology and incidence
   (a) Etiology unknown
   (b) Onset at 20 to 40 years of age
   (c) Seen more in women than men
   (d) 2% to 3% of total population
(3) Assessment findings
   (a) Subjective data
      i. Vague pain or stiffness in joints
      ii. Intermittent joint swelling
      iii. Limited function
      iv. Tires easily
   (b) Objective data
      i. Bilateral symmetrical involvement of joints
      ii. Subcutaneous nodules over bony prominences
      iii. Contractures
      iv. Sjögren's syndrome, dry eyes and mouth and patchy hair loss
(4) Nursing care
   (a) Prevent or correct deformities
      i. Active and passive ROM exercises; exercise even during acute phase
      ii. Low-sodium, high-protein, high-calcium diet
   (b) Prevent complication from drug therapy
      i. Instruct patients to report any tarry stools, since aspirin and steroids are an integral part of therapy
      ii. Suggest antacids or milk as necessary for GI upsets
      iii. Instruct patient to drink at least 1500 ml liquid daily to avoid renal calculi
   (c) Assist the patient in dealing with the psychosocial aspects of chronic illness
      i. Altered self-image may lead to exaggeration or denial of disease
      ii. Altered functioning may lead to change in life style
      iii. Disease may necessitate retirement and cause financial hardships
      iv. Loss of libido and/or satisfactory sexual relations

B. Extrinsic stimuli
   1. Carcinogenic agents, such as nickle, ultraviolet light, viruses, cigarette smoking
   2. Habits and customs
      a. Peptic ulcer disease
      b. Hypertension
      c. Chronic obstructive pulmonary disease (COPD)
      d. Black lung—coal miners
      e. Byssinosis—textile workers
   3. Allergens
      a. Asthma (see Unit 5, Pediatric Nursing)
      b. Migraine headaches
      c. Contact dermatitis—acute skin inflammation caused by contact with external irritating factors
2. **Cellular production that is insufficient or excessive in relation to body's need**
A. Anemia
B. Polycythemia
3. **Nonhomogeneous cellular production that results in abnormal growth of new tissue**
A. Benign tumors
   1. Neoplastic cells that resemble healthy cells
   2. Tumors that are well differentiated
   3. Papilloma, fibroma, adenoma, lipoma, and astrocytoma are examples
B. Malignant tumors
   1. Bear little or no resemblance to tissue from which they arise
   2. Tend to be primitive
   3. Disorganized, poorly differentiated cellular growth
   4. Drain the nutritional resources of the host tissue
   5. Able to metastasize through lymph channels to other sites favorable to multiplication
   6. Adenocarcinoma, malignant melanoma, and fibrosarcoma are examples

NURSING ASSESSMENT IN TUMOR REPRODUCTION

A. General
   1. Pain—usually a late symptom, but depends on organ involved; tumors growing in confined areas such as bone produce a great deal of pain
   2. Skin—changes in nevi, lesions that do not heal, pale, dusky, jaundiced, cool, clammy
   3. Sensorium—drowsy, lethargic, inattentive,

confused, vertigo, syncope, semiconscious, comatose
4. Emotional status—apprehension, restlessness, irritability, agitation, depression, hallucinations, insomnia
B. Neurological system—headaches, dizziness, sensory changes, convulsions, diplopia, blurring of vision, loss of equilibrium, paralysis, personality changes
C. Respiratory system—dyspnea, orthopnea, hoarseness, cough, voice changes, pain, decreased breath sounds
D. Cardiovascular system—bradycardia, tachycardia, palpitations, edema, ascites, neck vein distention, easy fatigability
E. Gastrointestinal system—anorexia, indigestion, nausea, vomiting, change in bowel habits, rectal bleeding, weight loss
F. Musculoskeletal system—muscular weakness, malaise, pain, swelling, stiffness
G. Genitourinary system—change in urinary habits, dysuria, hesitancy, incontinence, hematuria, unusual vaginal discharge, lump, retraction of breast tissue, nipple discharge
H. Laboratory studies
1. Papanicolaou test—utilized to detect early noninvasive cervical cancer
   a. Cells are graded on a five point scale
      (1) Class I—normal
      (2) Class II—probably normal
      (3) Class III—doubtful
      (4) Class IV—probably malignant
      (5) Class V—malignant
2. Biopsy—excision of tissue for microscopic examination
3. X-ray—radiologic studies utilized to detect tumor growth, particularly in the respiratory, gastrointestinal, and renal tracts
4. Alkaline phosphatase—greatly elevated in osteogenic carcinoma
5. Calcium—elevated with multiple myeloma, bone metastases
6. Sodium—decreased with bronchogenic carcinoma
7. Potassium—decreased with extensive liver carcinoma
8. Serum gastrin—test utilized to measure gastric secretion
   a. Decreased in gastric carcinoma
   b. Normal value—40 to 150 pg/ml
9. Complete blood count (CBC)
   a. Anemia

b. Neutrophilic leukocytosis—tumors and carcinomas
c. Eosinophilic leukocytosis—brain tumors, Hodgkin's disease
d. Lymphocytosis—chronic lymphocytic anemia

NURSING CARE—REDUCE SPREAD OF MALIGNANT GROWTH

1. Assisting with radiation therapy
A. Radiation
1. Types—ionizes cell constituents, either directly or indirectly
   a. Alpha particles—stopped by paper
   b. Beta particles—stopped by wood
   c. Gamma rays—stopped by thick concrete
2. Ability to cause injury
   a. Directly proportional to penetrating power
   b. Capable of injuring all living matter
   c. Matter with large numbers of dividing cells are more susceptible
   d. More differentiated cells are less susceptible
3. Effects
   a. Immediate somatic effects
      (1) Nausea
      (2) Vomiting
      (3) Diarrhea
      (4) Depression of bone marrow
      (5) Suppression of immune response
   b. Delayed somatic effects
      (1) Decreased life span
      (2) Induction of malignant neoplasma
   c. Genetic effects
      (1) Genetic mutations
      (2) Sterility
4. Uses in medical therapy
   a. Diagnosis
      (1) X-rays
      (2) Isotopes
         (a) Given intravenously or orally
         (b) Specific isotope used depends on organ or system being studied
   b. Treatment
      (1) Type of radiation used depends on
         (a) Tissue to be treated
         (b) Surrounding tissues
         (c) Available resources
      (2) Local effects of radiation therapy on

skin—reddening, sloughing, pain, edema

(3) Mucous membranes
    (a) Erythema
    (b) Formation of tough gray-white membrane
    (c) Depression or destruction of salivary glands
    (d) Dysphagia

(4) Systemic effects
    (a) Depression of bone marrow
        i. Anemia
        ii. Thrombocytopenia
        iii. Leukopenia
    (b) Gastrointestinal
        i. Nausea
        ii. Vomiting
        iii. Diarrhea

(5) Protective measures for patients and personnel
    (a) Badge sensitive to radioactivity
    (b) Transportation of radioactive materials in lead-shielded containers

(6) Procedure for external radiation therapy
    (a) Usually cobalt or cesium
    (b) Patient placed in room alone
    (c) Patient should lie still during treatment
    (d) Similar to X-ray but equipment is larger
    (e) Marks are made on skin delineating area to be treated

(7) Internal
    (a) Sealed
        i. Usually radium or iridium
        ii. Mouth and cervix common sites
        iii. Exposure only from the source; none from contact with patient's excretions
    (b) Unsealed
        i. Given orally, intravenously or instilled into a cavity as a liquid
        ii. Patient's excretions are a source of exposure
        iii. Usually gold, phosphorus, or iodine

c. Patient support and teaching
  (1) Patients should be instructed not to

wash off marks delineating area to be treated

(2) If patients are well enough, diversional therapy

(3) Instruction concerning the treatment and possible side effects

2. **Administering or assisting with the administration of chemotherapeutic agents** (also see Appendix F, Drugs)
A. Cyclophasphamide (Cytoxan)
B. 5-FU
C. Steroids
D. 6-MP
E. Vincristine

3. **Promoting nutritional, fluid, and electrolyte balance**
A. Administer parenteral fluids, as ordered
B. Provide high-calorie, high-vitamin diet—small attractive feedings
C. Avoid highly seasoned, difficult-to-chew foods
D. Push fluids to 3000 ml per day unless contraindicated

4. **Providing emotional support**
A. Explain pertinent treatments
B. Allow for verbalization of feelings
C. Provide opportunities for socialization, especially for patients isolated for internal radiation therapy
D. Include patient's family or significant others in care plan
E. Support patient seeking spiritual aid
F. Assess level at which patient and family are functioning in relation to stages of grief, loss, or death and devise plans that facilitate their movement through the process
G. Suggest wig or hairpiece for alopecia

5. **Relieving pain and promoting comfort**
A. Administer analgesics and narcotics as ordered
B. Assist with personal hygiene
C. Provide warmth and avoid chilling
D. Promote physical activities within patient's abilities
E. Administer antiemetics as ordered
F. Institute mouth care before and after meals and prn, keeping lips well lubricated
G. Utilize sheepskin and other devices to decrease pressures on dependent areas
H. Use footboard or bed cradle to elevate bed clothing from patient
I. Maintain body alignment
J. Control odors that tend to emanate from radiated tissues

Questions   Medical Nursing

Mr. Marks is a 65-year-old man who complains of weakness and episodes of fainting with minimal exertion. His heart rate is 38/minute, BP 140/70. An electrocardiogram was done, and a diagnosis of complete heart block was made.

1. In complete heart block the
   1. Atria and ventricles beat independently of each other
   2. Pulse pressure is increased
   3. The heart rate may not increase with exercise
   4. All of these are correct
2. What are the drugs of choice in this situation?
   1. Atropine SO_4
   2. Isoproterenol (Isuprel) HCl
   3. Digoxin
   4. 1 and 2 are correct
   5. 2 and 3 are correct
3. Mr. Marks has a permanent-demand pacemaker inserted. The rate is set at 72/minute. Before leaving the hospital, Mr. Marks should be taught how to take his radial pulse. He should be instructed to report which of the following symptoms to his physicians immediately?
   1. A rate of 64/minute
   2. A rate of 84/minute
   3. An irregular pulse
   4. 1 and 3 are correct
   5. 2 and 3 are correct
4. Which of the following hobbies or occupations will Mr. Marks be able to continue?
   1. Ham radio operator
   2. Automobile mechanic
   3. Airplane pilot
   4. Swimming

Mrs. L, a 70-year-old woman, was admitted to the hospital with complaint of dyspnea accompanied by substernal pain after walking short distances. Physical examination revealed a moderately obese older woman with ankle edema and engorged neck veins. Rales were auscultated halfway up the posterior thorax. Vital signs included heart rate-110/minute, BP-110/90, respirations-24, temperature-98 F. Her skin was pale, slightly moist, and cool.

5. The symptoms of congestive heart failure are caused by
   1. Decreased venous return
   2. Accumulation of fluid throughout the body
   3. Inadequate blood flow to the tissues
   4. All of these are correct
   5. 2 and 3 only are correct
6. A decrease in cardiac output activates homeostatic mechanisms in the kidney to
   1. Increase urine output
   2. Retain sodium and water
   3. Decrease urine output
   4. Increase peripheral vascular resistance
   5. All of these except 1 are correct
7. Treatment of congestive heart failure is directed toward
   1. Increasing cardiac output
   2. Reducing tissue demands for oxygen
   3. Elimination of edema
   4. All of these are correct
8. Diuretics given to promote the excretion of sodium and water are best given in
   1. Early morning
   2. Midday
   3. Early evening
   4. Bedtime
9. The most serious side effect of thiazide diuretics is
   1. Dizziness
   2. Nausea
   3. Hypokalemia
   4. Skin rash

Mr. S is a 50-year-old man who owns and operates a small business. He is married and has four children. He is active in community affairs. Ten years ago he developed mild hypertension, which his doctor treated by instructing him to lose weight. Recently, Mr. S's physician placed him on methyldopa (Aldomet).

10. Which of the following is true about hypertension?
    1. Diabetes rarely develops into hypertension

2. It may be symptomless for many years
3. Medications can cure underlying causes
4. Tobacco and stimulants do not affect blood pressure

11. Which of the following symptoms is associated with malignant hypertension?
    1. Papilledema
    2. Fixed pupils
    3. Uremia
    4. Retinal exudates
    5. All except 2 are correct

12. Which of the following types of diets should be ordered for Mr. S?
    1. Low-calorie
    2. Low-salt
    3. Low-cholesterol
    4. Low-protein
    5. All of these except 4 are correct

13. Which of the following health teachings should be emphasized for Mr. S?
    1. Side effects of antihypertensive medications
    2. Weigh daily
    3. Regular care of skin
    4. Limiting physical activity

Last week, while speaking at a city council meeting, Mr. S developed crushing chest pain and was admitted to the local hospital. Admission vitals were BP-190/110, apical pulse-120, respirations-26. Lab studies were CPK-600, SGOT-52, SGPT-100, LDH-280. ECG-sinus tachycardia with occasional PVC. Diagnosis–acute anterior MI.

14. Mr. S's crushing chest pain is due to
    1. Dehydration
    2. Myocardial ischemia
    3. Hypertension
    4. Gastritis

15. Because stress will activate the neural-humoral alarm mechanism, you would expect Mr. S to have all the following symptoms except
    1. Decreased urine output
    2. Increased urine output
    3. Increased heart rate
    4. Cold, clammy, pale skin

16. Three hours after admission to CCU, Mr. S developed ventricular tachycardia. Your first nursing action is
    1. Call the doctor
    2. Administer oxygen
    3. Administer a bolus of lidocaine HCl
    4. Administer atropine

17. After the first few days of hospitalization, Mr. S is likely to experience which fear that he is hesitant to verbalize?
    1. Fear of death
    2. Inability to resume his sex life
    3. Fear of being alone
    4. Fear of going home

18. Which of the following is a complication of myocardial infarction?
    1. Cardiogenic shock
    2. Congestive heart failure
    3. Embolization
    4. All of these

Miss Marble is a 31-year-old woman admitted to the hospital for an arthrotomy. She has had diabetes for two years. On admission her blood-sugar, pH, and electrolytes were normal. Her urine was negative for glucose and acetone. On her first postop day, she began to complain of nausea. Her face was flushed; she appeared listless; respirations were 22 and deep.

19. What is your first nursing action?
    1. Call the attending physician
    2. Check her urine for sugar and acetone
    3. Administer an antiemetic
    4. Change her position in bed

20. Symptoms of diabetes mellitus include
    1. Weight loss
    2. Polydipsia
    3. Irritability
    4. All of these are correct
    5. Only 2 and 3 are correct

21. Which of the following therapies is the foundation of diabetic management?
    1. Exercise
    2. Skin care—expecially the feet
    3. Diet and weight control
    4. Insulin

22. Which of the following is *not* a condition that may precipitate a hypoglycemic reaction to insulin?
    1. Emotional Stress
    2. Excessive exercise
    3. Inadequate food intake
    4. Excessive eating

23. NPH insulin reaches its peak action
    1. Before lunch
    2. Six to twelve hours after injection
    3. Sixteen hours after injection
    4. After supper

24. Nursing interventions in diabetes mellitus are directed toward
    1. Assisting patients in accepting responsibility for following their care plans
    2. Including family members in the diabetic teaching plan
    3. Providing enough time for patients to practice self-care
    4. All of these are correct

25. Which of the following is *not* a symptom of diabetic ketosis?
    1. Cold, clammy, pale skin
    2. Kussmaul respirations
    3. Acetone breath
    4. Highly acidic urine

26. Miss Marble is told she will be discharged on Thursday. She becomes very withdrawn. She spends the entire day in bed, answers only when spoken to and speaks in monosyllables. After lengthy investigation, she tells you Saturday is her birthday. Her family is planning a party with her favorite cake. She says, "And I won't be able to eat any of it." Your reply would be
    1. "That's too bad. You must be very disappointed."
    2. "What is your favorite cake?"
    3. "Do you mean you can't eat cake because you're a diabetic?"
    4. "Happy birthday."

Mr. Noble sustained second-degree burns on his left leg and thigh when his pants caught fire while he was burning leaves. His left ankle was charred and dry. On arrival at the hospital he was in severe pain. BP-96/70, pulse-116, respirations-26. He was restless, diaphoretic, and the unburned areas of skin were cold.

27. Burns are classified according to the depth of tissue destruction. Third-degree burns
    1. Involve the epidermis only
    2. Extend to the dermis and are very painful
    3. Extend to subcutaneous tissues and are painless
    4. Are always extremely painful

28. Equally important in determining severity of burns is the percentage of total body surface involved. Management of fluid and electrolyte balance is critical when burns
    1. Are first degree and cover 18% of body surface
    2. Are second degree and cover 30% of body surface
    3. Are third degree and cover 10% of body surface
    4. 2 and 3 are correct

29. The immediate needs of Mr. N include
    1. Encouragement and explanation of procedures
    2. Removal of burned clothing
    3. Measurement of height and weight
    4. All of the above
    5. All of the above except 3

30. One of the most distressing problems for the patient who is severely burned is
    1. Damage to body image
    2. Dressing changes
    3. Reverse isolation
    4. Limitation of visitors

31. Nursing care in the immediate 24-hours post-burn are directed toward monitoring the adequacy of fluid therapy. Insufficient fluid intake is demonstrated by
    1. Hypotension
    2. Venous distention
    3. Moist rales
    4. Decreased urinary output
    5. 1 and 4 are correct

32. Mr. N's burns are treated by the closed method. His left leg was cleaned and the left ankle debrided. Silver sulfadiazine 1% was applied, and his leg was wrapped in fine mesh gauze. Nursing actions would include
    1. Elevating the left leg
    2. Supporting the left foot with a foot board
    3. Gowning and masking all visitors
    4. 1 and 2 are correct
    5. All of these are correct

Mr. S was admitted to the hospital by his private doctor with complaints of increasing dyspepsia, intermittent bouts of diarrhea, increasing fatigue, and weight loss. Past medical history included pneumonia, viral hepatitis, and low-back syndrome. Examination revealed abdominal distention, enlarged liver and spleen, BP-110/80, pulse-106, respirations-20. Laboratory tests included decreased bromosulphalein (BSP) excretion, increased alkaline phosphatase, SGOT, and SGPT. Serum sodium-135 mEq/liter, serum potassium was normal, and total serum proteins were reduced. Following a liver biopsy, diagnosis was postnecrotic cirrhosis.

33. Plasma proteins are low in hepatic disease because
    1. All plasma proteins except gamma globulin are synthesized by the liver
    2. Jaundice destroys albumin
    3. Leukocytes destroy proteins in liver inflammation
    4. All of these are correct
34. Fluid and electrolyte imbalances develop in cirrhosis due to
    1. Portal hypertension
    2. Hypoproteinemia
    3. Increased levels of circulating aldosterone and ADH
    4. All of these are correct

Mr. S was placed on bedrest and given a high-protein, low-salt diet. Medications included a vitamin supplement and the diuretic spironolactone.

35. One nursing measure that might increase Mr. S's compliance with his diet is
    1. Sit with Mr. S until he has eaten everything
    2. Tell Mr. S that if he doesn't eat he will die
    3. Feed Mr. S yourself
    4. Offer six small feedings instead of three large ones
36. Paracentesis is the mechanical removal of ascites fluid. A serious adverse effect of paracentesis that the nurse should be aware of is
    1. Hypernatremia
    2. Hypertension
    3. Hypotension
    4. Paralytic ileus

Miss Old is a 22-year-old student who was hospitalized with a diagnosis of viral encephalitis. She has a fever of 103 F, a severe headache, and nuchal rigidity. She is restless and irritable, BP–128/80 and pulse–82.

37. The most important sign to watch for with increasing intracranial pressure is
    1. An increase in pulse rate
    2. A decrease in blood pressure
    3. Lethargy
    4. 2 and 3 are correct
    5. All of these are correct
38. The drug of choice in the treatment of cerebral edema with increasing intracranial pressure is
    1. Chlorothiazide (Diuril)

2. Mannitol
3. Cephalothin (Keflin)
4. Caffeine

Mr. Lawson is admitted to the hospital with complaints of fatigue, nausea, and vomiting. A diagnosis of acute renal failure was made.

39. Vomiting results in metabolic alkalosis due to
    1. Excessive Na^+ and K^+ loss
    2. Loss of HCl
    3. Hyperventilation
    4. Increase in H_2CO_3.
40. When the kidney secretes large amounts of potassium into the urine, it tends to conserve which of the following ions?
    1. Hydrogen
    2. Sodium
    3. Glucose
    4. Both 1 and 2 are correct
41. The most common cause of acute renal failure is
    1. Renal calculi
    2. Exposure to nephrotoxic agents
    3. Prolonged renal ischemia
    4. Chronic pyelonephritis
42. The usual symptom of acute renal failure is
    1. Polyuria
    2. Oliguria
    3. Nocturia
    4. All of these
43. Metabolic acidosis is a complication of acute renal failure because the kidney cannot excrete metabolically produced acids. Clinical signs of metabolic acidosis include
    1. Low arterial pH
    2. Hyperventilation
    3. Low-serum bicarbonate levels
    4. All of these
    5. 1 and 2 only are correct
44. The uremic syndrome includes which of the following symptoms?
    1. Nausea and vomiting
    2. Anemia
    3. Muscle twitching
    4. 1 and 3 only are correct
    5. All of these are correct
45. Nursing objectives in the conservative management of acute renal failure include
    1. Monitoring the patient's nutritional state
    2. Monitoring kidney function
    3. Preparing the patient for peritoneal dialysis

4. All of these
5. 1 and 2 only are correct

46. Symptoms of acute glomerulonephritis would *not* include
    1. Diarrhea
    2. Periorbital edema
    3. Albuminuria
    4. Hypertension

47. Patient-teaching objectives would include
    1. Importance of low-protein, low-sodium diet
    2. Need for active exercise (jogging)
    3. Importance of weighing daily at same time of day with same clothing and scales
    4. 1 and 3 only are correct
    5. All of these are correct

J.C. is a 56-year-old man admitted to the hospital with increasing breathlessness for the past five days. He reported that ten days previously he had a runny nose and sneezing with a nonproductive cough. Five days later, the cough became productive of greenish sputum and shortness of breath became more prominent. He has no fever, chills, or chest pain. No orthopnea or paroxysmal nocturnal dyspnea. He was noted to have edema of both ankles. Pulmonary function studies showed a decrease in vital capacity, an increase in residual volume, and an increase in airway resistance. Arterial blood gases were P_{O_2}-58, P_{CO_2}-50, pH-7.34. Normal blood gases are P_{O_2}-80 to 100, P_{CO_2}-40, pH-7.40.

48. A pH of 7.34 and a P_{CO_2} of 50 would indicate JC has
    1. Metabolic acidosis
    2. Metabolic alkalosis
    3. Respiratory acidosis
    4. Respiratory alkalosis

49. As J.C.'s nurse, which of the following would you *not* expect to observe?
    1. Long, slow expirations with pursed lips
    2. Audible expiratory wheezes
    3. Thick yellow-green sputum
    4. Slow, shallow respirations

50. An increased respiratory rate is known as
    1. Hyperventilation
    2. Dyspnea
    3. Tachypnea
    4. Apnea

51. How does the body try to compensate for respiratory acidosis?
    1. Increased respirations
    2. Decreased respiratory effort
    3. Kidneys excrete hydrogen ion and conserve bicarbonate ion
    4. 1 and 3 are correct
    5. 2 and 3 are correct

52. The nurse could increase J.C.'s respiratory efficiency by positioning him
    1. Upright in a position of comfort
    2. Prone
    3. Sitting, up, leaning forward
    4. 1 and 3 are correct

53. J.C.'s teaching objectives would *not* include
    1. Time for verbalization of feelings
    2. Involvement of family in care plan
    3. Instruction in deep-breathing exercises
    4. A discourse on the evils of smoking
    5. Importance of medications, dosage, and possible side effects

Mary Jane is a 29-year-old woman admitted with status epilepticus. She has had epilepsy since age 5 years.

54. Seizures or convulsions result from
    1. Excessive exercise
    2. Excessive, simultaneous, disordered neuronal discharges
    3. Decreased cerebral blood flow
    4. Improper dieting

55. Which of the following characterizes grand mal seizures?
    1. Brief, abrupt loss of consciousness lasting 10 to 20 seconds
    2. Loss of consciousness for several minutes with tonic and clonic convulsions
    3. Tonic contractions of the thumb or hand
    4. Twitching of the facial muscles

56. The drug of choice for long-term control of grand mal seizures is
    1. Phenobarbital
    2. Diazepam (Valium)
    3. Diphenylhydantoin (Denyl, Dilantin) sodium
    4. Trimethadione (Tridione)

57. What are the nursing actions indicated during a seizure episode?
    1. Observe and record the characteristics of the seizure
    2. Take vital signs
    3. Protect patient from injury
    4. Maintain an airway
    5. 1, 3 and 4 are correct

58. Mary Jane tells you she is concerned about her 8-year-old son, who has epilepsy. She is concerned that he may be mentally retarded.

Which of the following statements about epilepsy is *not* true?
1. Epilepsy often follows brain trauma, some infectious diseases, or drug or alcohol intoxication
2. Epilepsy may be inherited in some cases
3. Epileptics are frequently mentally retarded
4. The national epilepsy league has instituted a pharmacy service to provide medication at reduced cost

59. Mrs. L is a 37-year-old housewife with a history of multiple sclerosis. This disease is the result of
1. Excessive dysrhythmic neuronal discharge
2. Degeneration of the basal ganglia
3. Degeneration of the anterior motor neurons
4. Degeneration of the myelin sheaths

Mr. W is a 60-year-old man with complaints of stiffening limbs and tremors of both hands. The nurse notices that the tremor consists of pronating and supinating movements of both hands and forearms, which ceased when Mr. W picked up his pen. Mr. W leans forward when he walks, and his gait is propulsive. Diagnosis: Parkinson's disease.

60. Which of the following is the likely cause of Mr. W's dysfunction?
1. Degeneration of basal ganglia
2. Degeneration of brain white matter
3. Cerebral vascular accident
4. Decreased neurotransmitter at myoneural junction

61. Constipation is a major problem for patients with Parkinson's disease. It is due to
1. Lack of exercise
2. Weakened abdominal muscles used in defecation
3. Inadequate fluid intake
4. All of these are correct

62. Which of the following should be avoided in the nursing care of the patient with Parkinson's disease?
1. Sitting for long periods of time
2. Warm baths and massage
3. Active and passive range of motion exercises
4. Instruction in heel-toe gait

63. Mr. Jones received severe head injuries in an auto accident. A sudden respiratory arrest would indicate pressure or injury to the
1. Thalamus
2. Medulla
3. Hypothalamus
4. Cerebellum

64. Mr. Jones's symptoms include right hemiparesis, aphasia, blood in the cerebrospinal fluid, and disorientation. These symptoms are the result of
1. Injury to the right side of the brain
2. Injury to the left side of the brain
3. Increased intracranial pressure
4. 1 and 3 are correct
5. 2 and 3 are correct

65. Miss Smith is a 56-year-old woman with a five-year history of hypertension. She was admitted to the hospital with complaints of right-sided weakness. Bladder and bowel-control normal. Admission BP-180/110, pulse-76. No loss of speech or comprehension. The most common cause of cerebral vascular accidents is
1. Thrombosis
2. Emboli
3. Intracranial hemorrhage
4. Head trauma

66. Transient ischemic episodes, which may precede CVA, are characterized by
1. Hemiparesis
2. Dizziness
3. Transient aphasia
4. All of these are correct
5. 1 and 2 only are correct

67. Nursing observations in the acute phase of CVA includes
1. Level of consciousness
2. Equality and size of pupils
3. Stiffness or flaccidity of neck
4. Vital signs
5. All of these are correct

68. A nursing action of prime importance to the patient who is unconscious is
1. Assessment of consciousness
2. Establishment of a patent airway
3. Initiation of oxygen with mask
4. Initiation of intravenous therapy

69. The nursing goals for rehabilitation of the stroke patient do not include
1. Prevention of contractures
2. Plans for self-care
3. Use of slings to support weakened arm
4. Regular exercise program

Mrs. Ryan, a 50-year-old librarian, is admitted to the hospital with complaints of postmenopausal bleeding. Following a D & C, a diagnosis of adeno-carcinoma of the uterus was made. Internal radiation therapy was initiated.

70. Mrs. Ryan has cobalt (^{60}Co) seeds implanted. On returning to the unit, she has a vaginal packing and a urinary catheter to dependent drainage. To prevent displacement of the radioactive substance, the patient should be positioned
    1. With the foot of the bed elevated
    2. Flat in bed
    3. With her head elevated 45° (semi-Fowler's)
    4. On her side only

71. Which of the following are precautionary measures to be utilized when caring for a patient being treated with internal radioisotopes?
    1. Maintain distance from patient except when giving necessary care
    2. Limited patient contact
    3. Use of exposure meter to measure emission
    4. 2 and 3 are correct
    5. All of these are correct

72. Which of the following nursing problems would you expect following uterine isotope insertion?
    1. Foul-smelling vaginal discharge
    2. Severe uterine contractions
    3. Bladder atony
    4. 1 and 2 are correct
    5. All of these are correct

73. Mrs. Ryan complains of nausea and a general feeling of weakness. Her stools are loose. You might suspect
    1. Extension of her cancer to the abdominal contents
    2. Radiation syndrome
    3. Electrolyte imbalances
    4. Depression

Jim is a 38-year-old lumberjack who was injured on the job. A tree fell across his lower abdomen and pelvic area. Three days after admission, Jim is excreting less than 100 ml urine per day. Lab data: specific gravity-1.006, creatinine-8.7, BUN-93, K-6.2. A diagnosis of acute renal failure is made.

74. The treatment of choice in this case is
    1. Kayexalate enemas
    2. Peritoneal dialysis
    3. Hemodialysis
    4. Either 2 or 3 is correct

75. The aim of dialysis is to
    1. Remove metabolic waste products from the body
    2. Increase the amount of circulating blood volume
    3. Remove uremia frost from the skin
    4. Improve the patient's mental depression

76. Nursing responsibilities for an arteriovenous cannula include
    1. Observation for signs of inflammation
    2. Careful injection of medications through the cannula
    3. Observation for patency
    4. 1 and 3 only are correct
    5. All of these

Jason is admitted to the hospital for evaluation of thyroid function.

77. The two major manifestations of hypothyroidism are
    1. Cretinism
    2. Myxedema
    3. Exophthalmos
    4. 1 and 2 are correct
    5. 2 and 3 are correct

78. Which of the following is *not* a method of treating hyperthyroidism?
    1. Subtotal thyroidectomy
    2. Therapy with antithyroid preparations
    3. Irradiation
    4. Therapy with thyroid

79. Severe tachycardia, delirium, and extreme irritability in Jason would indicate
    1. Thyrotoxicosis
    2. Thyroid storm
    3. Insulin shock
    4. Adrenal insufficiency

Carol is admitted to the hospital with a diagnosis of Cushing's syndrome.

80. This is a syndrome produced by malfunction of the
    1. Adrenal cortex
    2. Adrenal medulla
    3. Posterior pituitary
    4. Pancreas

81. Carol is depressed and withdrawn one minute and abusive and combative the next. When dealing with this situation the nurse should
    1. Place her in full restraints
    2. Remember this is a normal clinical manifestation of Cushing's syndrome

3. Refer her for psychiatric consultation
4. 2 and 3 only are correct

82. Addison's disease is due to hypofunction of the adrenal glands. Clinical manifestations of this disease are due to
    1. Disturbance of sodium metabolism
    2. Disturbance of potassium metabolism
    3. Deficits of sodium and water
    4. All of these are correct
83. Nursing responsibilities in caring for patients with Addison's disease will *not* include
    1. Observation for signs of addisonian crisis
    2. Maintenance of fluid restrictions
    3. Observation of emotional status
    4. Accurate intake and output
84. Symptoms of iron deficiency anemia would *not* include
    1. Irritability
    2. Fatigue
    3. Flushed complexion
    4. Chest pain
85. The symptoms seen in patients with chronic iron-deficiency anemia will primarily depend on
    1. How chronic the anemia is
    2. The hemoglobin and hematocrit levels
    3. The individual patient's metabolic requirements
    4. Concomitant disease processes
86. Oral iron preparations should be given
    1. With meals
    2. One hour before eating
    3. One hour after eating
    4. Iron preparations should always be given parenterally
87. Mrs. Smith has been taking ferrous sulfate three times a day for three days. She tells you she's very worried because her stools are dark green. Your reply would be
    1. "That's normal."
    2. "Don't worry about it."
    3. "I'll call the doctor immediately."
    4. "Tell your doctor the next time you see her."
88. The essentials of protection in radiation therapy are based on
    1. Shielding
    2. Distance
    3. Time
    4. Time or rays emitted
    5. All of these are correct
89. Which of the following is a benign tumor?
    1. Liposarcoma
    2. Astrocytoma
    3. Glioblastoma
    4. Adenocarcinoma
90. Venereal disease
    1. Is a reportable communicable disease
    2. Can cause widespread and varied systemic damage
    3. Affects only the genitourinary tract
    4. 1 and 2 only are correct
    5. All of these are correct
91. Nursing care of the patient with Hodgkin's disease is designed to
    1. Provide symptomatic relief
    2. Assist in relief of side effects from chemotherapy and radiation therapy
    3. Provide emotional support
    4. All of these are correct

Mrs. X is admitted to the hospital with a diagnosis of acute rheumatoid arthritis. Her medications include aspirin grX qid and prednisone 10 mg qid.

92. A serious side effect of these drugs that the nurse might note is
    1. Black stools
    2. Headaches
    3. numbness in fingers and toes
    4. Diplopia
93. The purpose of the nurse doing passive range of motion to Mrs. X's affected joints is to
    1. Prevent contractures and limited range of motion
    2. Evaluate her limited amount of function
    3. Assess her tolerance for pain
    4. Assess the effectiveness of drug therapy
94. Whole blood expires how soon after donated?
    1. 21 days
    2. 14 days
    3. 2 months
    4. 3 months
95. How rapidly should blood be transfused after it is removed from refrigeration?
    1. Within one hour
    2. Within two hours
    3. Within four hours
    4. Within eight hours
96. People with which of the following conditions are allowed to donate blood?
    1. Syphilis
    2. Female's taking oral contraceptives
    3. Malaria
    4. Persons who have had their ears pierced

nonprofessionally in the preceding six months

97. How long should the nurse observe the patient at the bedside after instituting a transfusion of whole blood?
    1. For the first 15 minutes
    2. For the first 30 minutes
    3. For one hour
    4. Throughout the infusion

98. Signs of a transfusion reaction include
    1. Shortness of breath
    2. Pain in lower back and legs
    3. Polyuria
    4. 1 and 2 only
    5. All of these are correct

Mrs. T is a 44-year-old woman admitted with shortness of breath and tachypnea. BP-110/80, pulse-100, respirations-28. Her PPD is positive.

99. One of the most important measures in eradicating tuberculosis in this country is
    1. Frequent testing with BCG vaccine
    2. Frequent PPD testing
    3. Careful follow-up of all contacts of patients with active disease

4. Chest x-rays every six months

100. The correct interpretation of the available data on Mrs. T is
    1. She has active tuberculosis
    2. She has at some point been infected with tubercle bacilli
    3. She has at some point received a BCG innoculation
    4. No conclusion can be reached
    5. 2 and 3 are correct

101. Important aspects of nursing care for the tuberculosis patient include
    1. Provision for adequate rest and nutrition
    2. Assisting with follow-up of contacts
    3. Prompt administration of chemotherapy
    4. All of these are correct

102. Mrs. T has been treated with rifampin and INH for two weeks. She asks you if she is still contagious. You tell her yes because
    1. There must be three negative cultures before a patient is no longer contagious
    2. She has been inadequately treated with chemotherapy
    3. She will be contagious for at least one year
    4. She has no negative cultures

Answers/Rationale   Medical Nursing

1. (4) Normal stimuli arise in the SA node but are blocked at the AV node. The ventricles adjust by setting up their own rate. The rate is between 20 and 40 beats per minute and does not increase significantly with exercise. Pulse pressures increase due to increased stroke volume, which is caused by increased diastolic filling time.

2. (4) Both atropine and Isoproterenol (Isuprel) HCl are used to increase the ventricular rate in complete heart block. Digoxin is contraindicated because of its effect of slowing the heart rate further.

3. (4) A rate of 64/minute and/or an irregular pulse are both indications of possible pacemaker malfunction that the physician needs to evaluate. A rate of 84/minute does not indicate any malfunction.

4. (4) Patients with permanent pacemakers are

allowed to swim. All sources of high electronic output should be avoided—they may cause pacemaker malfunction. Thus, pacemaker patients are not allowed within 5 feet of radio transmitters; they are not allowed to lean over car engines while the motor is running; and they are cautioned to sit in the back of the plane when flying.

5. (5) Decreased pumping action of the heart decreases tissue perfusion. Also, inability of decompensated heart beat to accept venous return results in venous pooling in the peripheral veins and in the pulmonary veins.

6. (5) The kidney homeostatic mechanisms for maintenance of blood pressure include (1) increased tubular reabsorption of sodium and water, (2) adrenal-cortical secretion of aldosterone, which further increases sodium and water retention, leading to decrease in urine output, and (3) activation

of renin-angiotensin mechanism, which results in peripheral vasoconstriction and, therefore, an increase in peripheral vascular resistance.

7. (4) Bedrest is essential to reduce cardiac workload and tissue metabolism. Bedrest will also facilitate venous return, thus increasing cardiac output and glomerular filtration.

8. (1) Diuretics should be administered early in the morning so that diuresis will not interfere with rest at night.

9. (3) Clinical signs of hypokalemia include weakness and fatigability. Low potassium levels decrease cardiac contractility and may precipitate digitalis toxicity.

10. (2) Over 50% of those people with hypertension are unaware they have it.

11. (4) Malignant hypertension is a severe, rapidly progressive hypertension that results in fibrinoid neurosis of target organs, particularly heart, kidney, brain, and eyes.

12. (5) Diets are suited to individual patient needs. An obese patient with serum cholesterol elevations may have a prescribed diet that is low in calories, cholesterol, and salt.

13. (1) Patient and family need to be aware of symptoms that indicate side effects of antihypertensive drugs. These include lethargy, drowsiness, nausea, vomiting, impotency, and mental depression. These symptoms are often attributed to the patient's general ill health.

14. (2) Pain is perceived only while tissues are dying. Ischemic tissues release toxins such as bradykinin, which stimulates free nerve endings (pain receptors).

15. (2) The neural-humoral alarm mechanism results in widespread vasoconstriction, which results in a cool, clammy, pale skin and a decrease in blood flow to the kidneys. Thus, urine output is decreased due to lowered glomerular filtration. Heart rate is increased due to the chronotropic effect of sympathetic nervous system stimulation.

16. (3) Ventricular tachycardia is a serious arrhythmia. It must be treated at once because it leads to decreased cardiac output and is a precursor of ventricular fibrillation in which there is no cardiac output.

17. (2) Most young and middle-aged men with cardiac disease are afraid they will be sexually inadequate for the rest of their lives. They are hesitant to discuss their sex lives with their physicians.

18. (4) Myocardial infarction results in a decrease in cardiac output because the injured muscle cannot contract synergistically. A drop in cardiac output will result in a drop in blood pressure and may lead to cardiac failure and shock.

19. (2) Check the urine for glucose and acetone before calling the physician. The amount of glucose in the urine will determine the amount of insulin to be administered.

20. (4) Weight loss in diabetes is common because the body will break down fats and proteins to use as an energy source. Polydipsia or excessive thirst is due to the osmotic diuresis accompanying glycosuria. Irritability is a symptom of central nervous system irritation due to increase metabolic end products of protein breakdown.

21. (3) Diet and weight control are the primary therapies for control of diabetes and for preventing many of its complications.

22. (4) Insulin reactions are caused by high blood levels of insulin, which lower blood glucose levels below the needs of body tissues. Emotional stress and heavy exercise increase body glucose needs. Inadequate intake of carbohydrates also results in lowered blood glucose levels.

23. (2) NPH is an intermediate active insulin that reaches its peak action about 6 to 12 hours after injection. Afternoon hypoglycemia may be a problem.

24. (4) The responsibility for treating and controlling diabetes rests with the patient. Therefore, the nurse should facilitate patient learning by beginning a teaching program as soon as the diagnosis is made. This program should involve both the patient and the family and should be tailored to meet each individual's needs.

25. (1) Cold, clammy, pale skin is a symptom of hypoglycemia and is associated with increases in sympathetic nervous system stimulation.

26. (3) Many diabetics get very angry and frustrated trying to manage their diets. Once you have made sure that Miss Marble feels she cannot eat cake because she is a diabetic, you can reassure her that there is nothing she cannot eat in moderation. The "diabetic diet" is the most nutritious and well-balanced diet possible.

27. (3) Third-degree implies destruction of all skin layers and may extend to underlying fat, muscle, and even bone. The skin surface may be either charred and dry or white and moist. Commonly, third-degree burns are painless because nerve endings have been destroyed.

28. (4) Critical burns are classified as second degree over 30% of the body and third degree over 10% of the body. Use "rule of nine" to determine

extent of burn.

29. (4) To reduce the patient's anxiety and stress, the nurse needs to be constantly aware of the patient's real fears and his pain. He needs constant encouragement. The patient's height and weight must be taken on admission, as fluid therapy is based on this baseline information.

30. (1) Persons who are severely burned, especially about the face, suffer a severe blow to body image. The disfigurement and scarring often make them lose all sense of self-respect.

31. (5) Venous distention and moist rales are indicative of fluid overload.

32. (4) One of the advantages of employing the closed method of burn treatment is that isolation is not necessary.

33. (1) The liver synthesizes the plasma proteins albumin, fibrinogen, and alpha and beta globulins. In liver disease, the lymphatics, which synthesize gamma globulins, will try to compensate for decreased plasma proteins by increasing gamma globulin production.

34. (4) In liver disease, connective tissue replaces destroyed liver cells. This tissue clogs the small branches of the portal veins, and a back pressure is created in the vein of the abdomen. Fluid leaks from these veins into the abdominal cavity. In disease, the liver's ability to synthesize plasma proteins is diminished, reducing plasma colloid osmotic pressures and adding to edema formation. Increased circulating levels of ADH and aldosterone accompany liver disease. ADH increases the water load, reduces urinary output, and adds to edema. Aldosterone increases sodium retention and reduces potassium levels.

35. (4) Small, attractively served meals are more likely to be acceptable to the patient with liver disease. Anorexia and nausea due to decreased gastric motility is a frequent problem and large meals may inhibit any appetite he may have.

36. (3) Hypovolemia, hypotension, and shock can occur if fluid from the vascular compartment shifts to the abdomen to replace fluid withdrawn by paracentesis. Pulse and respiratory status should be assessed frequently during the procedure. Observe for color changes and changes in mentation.

37. (3) The patient's level of consciousness is the most important indicator of her condition. Lethargy would indicate increasing intracranial pressure. Changes in vital signs include slowing of pulse to rate of 60 or below; blood pressure increases or widening pulse pressure; respiratory changes may include Cheyne-Stokes or Kussmaul respirations.

38. (2) Mannitol is an osmotic diuretic that is particularly effective in reducing cerebral edema.

39. (2) Large amounts of hydrochloric acid are lost in vomiting stomach contents. This results in metabolic alkalosis first due to excessive loss of hydrogen ions and secondly because the kidney trys to compensate for loss of chloride by conserving bicarbonate ions.

40. (1) Potassium ions and hydrogen ions compete for exchange with sodium ions in the renal tubules. An increase in serum potassium will result in more potassium ions being excreted than hydrogen ions. Hence, hyperkalemia can lead toward hydrogen ion retention or acidosis.

41. (3) Both renal calculi and chronic pyelonephritis lead to chronic rather than acute renal failure. Exposure to nephrotoxic agents, such as mercury and kanamycin SO_4, do cause acute renal failure, but the most common cause seen is renal ischemia.

42. (2) Oliguria or reduced urine output is usually the first sign of acute renal failure when input is normal. It is believed to result from decreased glomerular filtration, even though the glomerulus may not be damaged.

43. (4) Metabolic acidosis decreases body pH and lowers serum bicarbonate levels (H_2CO_3 / $NaHCO_3$ buffer system). Respirations are increased in rate and depth in an effort to reduce hydrogen ion concentration and return normal body pH.

44. (5) The nausea and vomiting result from build-up of waste products in the serum; the anemia results from decreased production of erythropoietin, a bone marrow stimulant and from acidosis, which leads to destruction of red blood cells; the muscle twitching is a result of decreased Ca^{++} levels.

45. (5) Peritoneal dialysis is instituted only if a life-threatening situation develops.

46. (1) Symptoms are due to increased circulating blood volume due to decreased glomerular filtration rate (hypertension) and increased permeability of glomerular capillaries (albumin urea and edema).

47. (4) With evidence of impaired renal function, intake of protein, sodium, and potassium is restricted in an effort to reduce edema and hypertension. Fatigue should be avoided, and nursing care plans should include frequent rest periods.

48. (3) A pH of arterial blood of 7.34 is acidotic. Increased CO_2 would indicate the acidosis was due to the lung's inability to blow off CO_2.

49. (4) Respiratory acidosis increases carbon

dioxide content of blood, which stimulates the medulla to increase the rate and depth of respirations.

50. (3) Tachypnea refers to an increase in rate of respiration. Hyperventilation refers to over-breathing with an increase in rate and depth, which produces hypocapnea.

51. (4) Respiratory centers in the medulla respond to increased CO_2 by increasing rate and depth of respirations. Kidneys will compensate over several hours for carbon dioxide retention by increasing rate of hydrogen ion excretion and reabsorption of bicarbonate ion in tubules.

52. (3) This position allows for complete AP expansion of the lungs and decreases the pressure of abdominal contents on the diaphragm, thereby facilitating diaphragmatic movement.

53. (4) Smoking has been proved to be a toxic agent to lung parenchyma. However, moralizing on the subject of smoking may only increase patient resistance to suggestions to cut down or quit.

54. (2) The basis for seizures appears to be a dysrhythmic electrical discharge of neurons. It may be focal or widely diffused.

55. (2) Grand mal siezures are the most common. Besides loss of consciousness lasting several minutes and tonic and clonic contractions, bowel and bladder incontinence is common.

56. (3) While diphenythydantoin is the drug of choice in grand mal epilepsy, it may be necessary to use other drugs such as barbiturates to control seizures. Side effects include ataxia, drowsiness, and nystagmus.

57. (5) Primary concern of the nurse during a grand mal seizure is to maintain an airway, protect the patient from injury, and observe and record the sequential phenomena of the seizure.

58. (3) There is no relationship between intelligence quotients and epileptic seizures.

59. (4) Multiple sclerosis is a chronic, slowly progressive disease of the CNS, which is characterized by numerous disseminated areas of demyelination of neuronal axons.

60. (1) Besides tremors at rest, limb stiffness, and propulsive gait, Parkinson's disease also affects the facies. The face appears stiff, masklike, and staring; the patient's eyes may be fixed in an upward, downward, or one side position. It is due to degeneration of the basal ganglia and/or substantia nigra motoneurons in the brain.

61. (4) Constipation may be prevented by aiding fluid intake through the use of straws, encouraging daily exercise to strengthen weakened muscles, and establishing regular bowel habits.

62. (1) Decreased activity, particularly sitting, decreases joint movement and increases rigidity.

63. (2) Respiratory centers are located in the medulla. Anoxia to this area may cause sudden cessation of respiration.

64. (5) Control of musculature from brain centers is contralateral; that is, the left hemisphere of the brain controls movements on the right side of the body. Increasing disorientation is a sign of increased intracranial pressures and cerebral anoxia.

65. (1) Thrombosis results from occlusion of a vessel usually from atherosclerosis.

66. (4) Transient ischemic attacks (TIA) are reversible episodes of neurologic dysfunction caused by decreased blood flow to a focal area of the cerebrum or brain stem. The most frequent cause is occlusive vascular disease.

67. (5) Each of these parameters are significant in determining the degree of cerebral damage and indicators of cerebral oxygenation.

68. (2) Establishment and maintenance of a patent airway to ensure maximum respiratory function will help alleviate cerebral hypoxia and hypercapnea, which cause cerebral edema.

69. (3) Patient should be instructed to move the affected arm with the good hand and affect ROM exercises several times daily to prevent contracture development in the paralyzed extremity.

70. (2) To prevent dislodgment of the cobalt, the patient is placed flat in bed and is allowed to turn only from side to side.

71. (5) To reduce exposure to gamma rays, the nurse should not work any closer to the patient than is absolutely necessary. Likewise, the time spent close to the radiating source should be kept to a minimum. One means of protecting yourself from excessive radiation is to wear an exposure meter. The meter will indicate when you have received the maximum dose advocated by the National Committee for Radiation Therapy.

72. (4) Foul-smelling vaginal discharge can be expected due to destruction and sloughing of cells. Good perineal care is essential. Dilatation of the cervix during implantation of the radioactive seeds may cause severe uterine contractions.

73. (2) Common symptoms of radiation syndrome include nausea, vomiting, and diarrhea.

74. (3) Due to his extensive abdominal injuries, peritoneal dialysis is contraindicated. Hemodialysis will decrease the elevated K^+ levels and clear the

body of waste products such as creatinine and BUN.

75. (1) Metabolic waste products are removed by diffusion, osmosis, and filtration across a semipermeable membrane. One aim of dialysis is to reduce circulatory overload, since the patient is unable to excrete excess fluid.

76. (4) Medications should never be given through a cannula since that may result in direct arterial contamination. All blood should be drawn from the shunt to preserve vessels for possible revisions of shunts in the future.

77. (4) Exophthalmos is a manifestation of hyperthyroidism.

78. (4) Therapy with thyroid is a method of treating hypothyroidism.

79. (2) Additional signs of thyroid storm are fever and dehydration. It most commonly occurs when sudden stress is experienced by a person with Graves's disease.

80. (1) Cushing's syndrome is produced by hyperactivity of the adrenal cortex.

81. (4) Mood changes, depression, and psychosis are normal clinical manifestations of Cushing's disease. A psychiatric consultation might help the patient to deal with these changes.

82. (4) Elevated potassium, low blood pressure, weight loss, and decreased sodium are signs of Addison's disease.

83. (2) Because dehydration is a serious problem with these patients, fluids are usually not restricted.

84. (3) Skin color in anemia is usually waxy and pale. There may also be some jaundice.

85. (2) Absolute hemoglobin and hematocrit are directly related to the symptoms exhibited by the patient. However, a patient with a slow loss of red cells is able to utilize compensatory mechanisms to maintain homeostasis, whereas, a patient who sustains a sudden large loss is unable to and, therefore, exhibits more severe symptoms with higher lab values.

86. (1) Oral iron preparations are irritating to gastrointestinal mucosa—should be taken with food.

87. (1) The color of stools varies from dark green to black with patients on iron therapy owing to the effect of iron salts.

88. (5) Minimizing the dangers of radiation exposure depends on the type of radiation being used, the time one is exposed to it, the distance one stands from the source, and the amount of shielding or protection around the source.

89. (2) Astrocytomas are benign tumors of the nervous system, specifically the neuroglia.

90. (4) Venereal disease, if untreated, can cause widespread damage to all areas of the body, especially the cardiovascular and nervous systems. There is a nationwide effort underway to halt the spread of disease, and it is a reportable disease entity.

91. (4) Side effects of chemo-therapy and radiation therapy include nausea, vomiting, skin sensitivities, and hair loss.

92. (1) Black, tarry stools are an indication of gastrointestinal bleeding. This is a side effect of both aspirin and steroid therapy, since both drugs are irritating to the gastrointestinal mucosa.

93. (1) Exercise is done even during the acute phase to prevent further limitation of motion and therefore function. Analgesics are not usually given prior to exercise because of the chance of taxing the joints beyond their capabilities and further injuring them.

94. (1) Whole blood expires 21 days after donated. By this time, hemolysis of the red cells begins, and products are formed that can be harmful if transfused. The platelets deteriorate about 48 hours after blood is donated; therefore, if these are needed fresh whole blood is usually ordered.

95. (3) Blood is an excellent medium for the growth of bacteria. Cold retards this growth, but once blood begins to warm up, the growth can occur. However, it must not be transfused so rapidly that the patient becomes overloaded.

96. (2) Taking oral contraceptives does not preclude donating blood. Due to the possibility of hepatitis, persons who have their ears pierced are not allowed to donate for six months. Due to possible contamination, persons who have had malaria or syphilis are never allowed to donate blood.

97. (1) Most transfusion reactions will begin within the first 15 minutes. The nurse should remain at the bedside during this time to closely observe the patient for signs of a reaction.

98. (4) Oliguria, anuria, or hematuria are the usual urinary signs of transfusion reaction.

99. (3) It has been estimated that each person with active tuberculosis has at least five contacts. Follow up of these contacts and treatment where indicated is of utmost importance in preventing the spread of the disease.

100. (5) The only possible conclusion at this point is that she has been infected at some point with the disease or has been given BCG vaccine.

101. (4) Follow-up of contacts is one of the most

important means of preventing the spread of tuberculosis. Adequate rest, nutrition, and administration of drugs are also very important.

102. (1) There must be at least three negative cultures taken two weeks apart before a patient is considered no longer contagious.

Annotated Bibliography

Beland, I., and Passos, J.: Clinical nursing, ed. 3, New York, 1975, Macmillan Publishing Co.

Text utilizes a conceptual approach. Emphasis is placed on understanding pathophysiologic and psychosocial relationships to assess and intervene in common and complex patient problems. While an excellent reference book for all nurses, the format and index are not conducive for obtaining overviews of specific patient problems.

Brunner, L., and Suddarth, D.: Textbook of medical-surgical nursing, ed. 3, Philadelphia, 1975, J. B. Lippincott Company.

A comprehensive text that focuses on assessment and priority-setting in nursing management of patient problems. Text includes a number of tables that outline procedures, therapies, and complications. Frequent illustrations also aid understanding. Presents a great deal of information in a fairly concise, readable format.

Luckmann, J., and Sorensen, K.: Medical-surgical nursing: a psychophysiologic approach, Philadelphia, 1974, W. B. Saunders Company.

Text offers an in-depth presentation of current medical-surgical nursing practice as well as a discussion of basic concepts such as fluid and electrolyte balance. The mere size and depth of this text may be overwhelming for some students, but it does offer a firm foundation for nursing practice. The authors have included unit objectives and varied learning activities to facilitate mastery of the material and to enhance learning. Referencing is extensive.

Moidel, H., Giblin, E., and Wagner, B.: Nursing care of the patient with medical-surgical disorders, ed. 2, New York, 1976, McGraw-Hill, Inc.

A highly readable text that focuses on the nursing process and provides consistent rationale for nursing interventions. Frequent diagrams, tables, and illustrations facilitate understanding.

Shafer, K., Sawyer, J., McCluskey, A., Beck, E., and Phipps, W.: Medical-surgical nursing, ed. 6, St. Louis, 1975, The C. V. Mosby Co.

A nursing textbook classic. This recently updated edition focuses on assessment and understanding of physiologic disturbances, and approaches nursing interventions in terms of goals and objectives. The format allows for rapid review of common patient problems and nursing interventions.

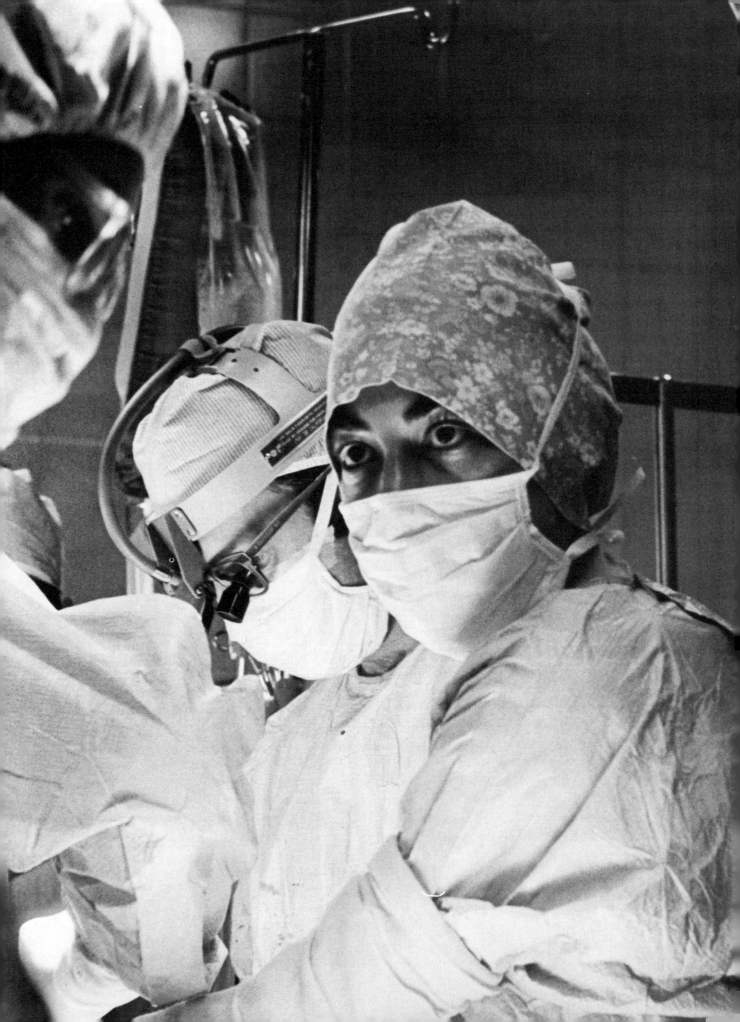

Unit 3 Surgical Nursing

Introduction

This unit, surgical nursing, has been designed, first, to focus on the broad concepts and skills of preoperative and postoperative nursing assessment and care as they apply to all surgical patients and, secondly, to identify and outline assessment criteria and nursing interventions that relate more specifically to individual surgical procedures. While some specific nursing care procedures have been outlined, the overall intent of this unit is to promote understanding of the principles and concepts of care that can be applied to the broad spectrum of patients who may be undergoing the same or similar surgical intervention.

With this in mind, the student will find in the initial pages of this chapter a review of (1) assessment criteria, (2) the implications of specific findings, (3) preoperative breathing and leg exercises, and (4) broad objectives of nursing care that can be individualized to meet specific patient needs. A brief review of the legal implications of the surgical consent follows. The middle portion of this unit contains information relating to specific nursing care functions in the immediate preoperative and postoperative period. A table of surgical complications has been provided which outlines the etiology, pathophysiology, signs and symptoms, and the nursing interventions for complications such as pneumonia, hypovolemic shock, wound dehiscence, and urinary retention.

In the latter portion of this unit the emphasis of the discussion is on nursing interventions in common surgical procedures. The procedures are briefly described and the medical implications for doing the procedures are provided. Nursing care objectives are given for both preoperative and postoperative care, and nursing interventions relating to those objectives are outlined. The student will find several notations to see appendix material, review the table of surgical complications, or to refer to a previous discussion in the unit. This approach has been utilized to minimize duplication of material applicable to a broad spectrum of clinical nursing.

Mary Jane Sauvé

Part A Surgical Therapies

A. Purpose
  1. Curative—procedures in which damaged, diseased, or malformed organs or tissues are repaired or removed (nephrectomy and appendectomy)
  2. Diagnostic—procedures that facilitate making a diagnosis (laparotomy) or which verify suspected diagnosis (biopsy)
  3. Palliative—procedures designed to relieve symptoms but not cure the underlying pathophysiology (sympathectomy)
  4. Reconstructive—procedures that partially or totally restore organ or tissue function or appearance (rhinoplasty)
B. Degree of Risk
  1. High-risk or major surgeries
    a. Involve prolonged anesthesia
    b. Involve handling of vital organs
    c. May incur large losses of blood volume
    d. Have a high probability for the development of postoperative complications
    e. Examples include open-heart surgery, abdominal-perineal resections, and surgeries performed on individuals with other physiologic dysfunctions, such as diabetes mellitus or chronic obstructive pulmonary disease
  2. Low-risk or minor surgeries
    a. Do not involve prolonged anesthesia or may be accomplished with local anesthesia
    b. Postoperative complications are rare for minor surgery
    c. Examples include wart removal, skin biopsies, and closed reduction of fractures
C. Urgency
  1. Emergency procedures—those that must be done to save the patient's life, remove or save a damaged organ or limb, and/or stop excessive bleeding
    a. Performed on short notice
    b. Allow little time for patient preparation
    c. Increase the surgical risk because of the increased physiologic stress and decrease time for physical evaluation
    d. Examples include gun shot wounds, skull fractures, extensive burns
  2. Imperative or required procedures—those that require prompt attention
    a. Should be performed within 24 to 48 hours
    b. Examples include bleeding hemorrhoids, cancer, and kidney or urethral stones
  3. Elective or planned procedures—those that may or may not be necessary but are performed for the patient's well-being
    a. Hospital admission is planned weeks or months in advance
    b. Examples include eye cataracts, tonsillectomies, simple hernia repairs, and cosmetic surgeries

Part B Preoperative Nursing Assessment and Care

PATIENT PROFILE

1. **Age**—children and adults tolerate surgery better than the elderly, who are less able to maintain homeostasis under stress

A. Elderly are more sensitive to drugs such as scopolamine methylbromide and morphine sulfate
B. Elderly are more likely to have one or more chronic diseases

C. Nursing measures are designed to reduce demands on the elderly patient's adaptive capacity
1. Lesser doses of medications
2. Diet high in protein and vitamins
3. Nursing orders designed around habit patterns of patient—sleeping, eating, laxatives, and use of alcohol
2. **Fluid, electrolyte, and nutritional status**—adequate fluid, electrolyte balance, and nutrition is imperative for normal recovery, tissue repair, and avoidance of postoperative complications
A. Deficiencies in fluid, electrolytes, proteins, vitamins, and iron result in poor wound healing and increase the risk of shock and postoperative infection
B. Obesity increases the difficulty of wound approximation and increases the risk of wound dehiscence—fatty tissues are more susceptible to infection and increased demand on heart may lead to cardiac embarrassment
C. Nursing measures are designed to reduce deficiencies and excesses
1. Replace deficits and monitor status
2. A diet high in protein, carbohydrates, and vitamins (B and C)
3. Administer parenteral fluids, as ordered
4. Intake and output records
5. Daily weight
3. **Personal habits**—provide insight and information needed to develop mutually agreeable care plans with the patient
A. Communication—reduction of anxiety and patient cooperation with treatment regimen are dependent on clear communication lines—Does the patient speak English? Is there a speech impediment or disability? Does the patient have a hearing problem?
B. Activities of daily living
1. Identify sleeping, eating, excretory, exercise, and spiritual patterns
2. Identify any abnormalities, such as chronic constipation, diarrhea, incontinence, and decreased mobility
3. Nursing measures are designed to assist patient in the maintenance of the activities of daily living

PHYSICAL AND MENTAL ASSESSMENT

1. **Patient's perception of present illness**
A. Degree of threat patient perceives to physical, psychologic, social, and financial status
B. Patient's perception of the outcome of surgery
C. Patient's behavior in response to the threat of surgery—apprehensive, withdrawn, irritable, agitated, demanding, or happy
D. Nursing measures are designed to alleviate fears and reduce stress
1. Provide information about hospital routines
2. Explain diagnostic procedures
3. Allow patient to ask questions and express concerns
2. **Review of systems**—provides baseline information of preoperative functioning; can be used for comparative purposes during postoperative period; detects presence of disease or other dysfunction
A. Neurological system
1. Note levels of consciousness—alert, attentive, drowsy, stuporous
2. Note cognitive function—aware of time and place, with memory for past events
a. Physiologic causes of decreased cognition—dehydration, electrolyte imbalance, and drugs
b. Nonphysiologic causes of decreased cognition—anxiety, feelings of powerlessness, or a sensory-restricted environment
3. Note responses to stimuli—Are pupils equal and responsive to light and accommodation, Can the patient detect light, touch, temperature, or pain?
4. Note gait, balance, and posture—Is there any tremor, ataxia, spasticity, or rigidity?
5. Neurologic dysfunctions can greatly increase surgical risks—nursing measures are designed to strengthen deficient responses and provide sensory and perceptual stimulation if indicated
a. Frequent visits by family, staff, or friends
b. Clock or calendar can help orient patient to time
c. Move patient to another room or outdoors when possible
B. Cardiovascular system
1. Note blood pressure—low, elevated; if patient is very anxious, repeat blood pressure in 15 to 30 minutes; note difference (blood pressure may be temporarily elevated in persons highly sensitive to sympathetic nervous system stimulation)
2. Note rate, rhythm, and characteristics of apical and radial pulse

a. Increased rate (up to 110) often indicative of response to stress—repeat in 15 to 30 minutes
b. Rate over 110 and below 60 or irregular rhythms may indicate cardiac arrhythmias and should be reported to physician
c. Pulse deficits (apical greater than radial) should also be reported to physician

3. Note signs of edema, pallor, cyanosis (cold or blue extremities), weakness, or fatigue
4. Nursing measures for presurgical patients with cardiovascular disease are designed to strengthen cardiac contractility and prevent circulatory overloading
   a. Diet low in sodium or cholesterol
   b. Cardiac drugs, such as digitalis
   c. Intake and output
   d. Weigh daily
   e. Activity as tolerated to prevent thrombus formation

C. Respiratory system
1. Note presence of any sneezing, coughing, sore throat, or temperature elevation—presence of upper respiratory infection may contraindicate surgery
2. Observe respiratory rate and pattern—thoracic, breathing normal for women; diaphragmatic for men
3. Note any shortness of breath, use of accessory respiratory muscles, coughing with expectoration of copious or purulent mucus, nail clubbing, chest pain, and asymmetrical lung expansion—chronic or severe pulmonary diseases such as emphysema, owing to increased secretions, predispose the patient to respiratory infections
4. Question patient about smoking habits and previous respiratory infections, such as tuberculosis and respiratory allergies
5. Preoperative nursing measures for patients with respiratory dysfunctions are designed to alleviate infection, increase ventilation and gaseous exchange, reduce respiratory secretions, and prevent postoperative complications
   a. Instruct patient in deep breathing and coughing exercises (see p. 150)
   b. Encourage the patient to restrict or avoid smoking
   c. Postural drainage, as ordered
   d. Antibiotics, as ordered
   e. Assist with aerosol treatments
   f. Encourage fluids unless contraindicated
   g. Observe amount, color, and odor of expectorations
   h. Provide frequent mouth care

D. Genitourinary system
1. Note amount, color, clarity, and specific gravity of urine
   a. Kidneys provide for elimination of waste products and are the primary homeostatic control of fluid and electrolyte balance
   b. Urine output should equal fluid intake—report to physician urine outputs below 30 ml per hour in hydrated patients
   c. Specific gravity that remains fixed indicates inability of kidney to concentrate or dilute urine and should be reported to physician
   d. Cloudy urine may indicate infection or a poorly collected sample
   e. Reddish to brown urine may indicate the presence of blood hemoglobin degradation or bilirubin and should be reported to the physician
2. Nursing measures are designed to assess kidney function and maintain urine output
   a. maintain good fluid intake unless contraindicated, as diseased kidneys require more fluid volume to excrete metabolic wastes than do normal kidneys
   b. Maintain strict intake and output records on all patients suspected of renal dysfunction

E. Endocrine system
1. Note history of diabetes mellitus, polyuria, polydipsia, fatigue, tendency to be drowsy after meals, poor wound healing, irritability, nocturia, blurring of vision, or muscle cramps
   a. Diabetes mellitus increases the risk of postoperative infections and predisposes the patient to poor tissue healing
   b. Stress tends to increase hyperglycemia
2. Preoperative nursing measures for the diabetic patient are designed to reduce stress, maintain normal blood sugar levels, and prevent hypoglycemia and fluid and electrolyte imbalances
   a. Provide diabetic diet

b. Observe for signs of hypoglycemia—sweating, trembling, tachycardia, anxiety, weakness, fatigue, and hunger

c. Insulin preparations, as ordered

d. Test urine for sugar and acetone

e. Intake and output

f. Reassure patient that when the diabetic condition is controlled, surgical risk is no greater than that for nondiabetic patient

F. Digestive system

1. Note history of alcoholism, cirrhosis, hepatitis, presence of jaundice, and ascites—nutritional status of patient and ability to control bleeding and repair tissue are largely dependent on the ability of the liver to

   a. Maintain blood glucose levels through glycogenolysis and glyconeogenesis

   b. Synthesize blood proteins, such as albumin and fibrinogen

   c. Form urea from ammonia

   d. Store iron for hemoglobin

   e. Produce prothrombin and other clotting factors

   f. Detoxify drugs

2. Preoperative nursing measures for the patient with hepatic dysfunction are designed to enhance nutritional status of patient and reduce risk of postoperative complications

   a. Diet high in carbohydrates, proteins, and vitamins B and C

   b. Vitamin K to facilitate prothrombin formation

   c. Intake and output records

G. Concurrent or prior drug therapy

1. Ask the patient about drugs presently being taken, including over-the-counter medications, and the frequency of use—serious pathophysiologic dysfunctions, such as circulatory collapse or respiratory depression, can occur when certain drugs interact with anesthetic agents

2. The nursing measure to prevent hazardous drug interaction is to notify the anesthesiologist if the patient is taking any of the following drugs

   a. Antibiotics such as neomycin SO_4, streptomycin SO_4, polymyxin A and B SO_4, colistin SO_4, and kanamycin SO_4—when mixed with curariform muscle relaxant, they interrupt nerve transmission and may cause respiratory paralysis and apnea

   b. Antidepressants—particularly MAO (monoamine oxidase) inhibitors, which increase hypotensive effects of anesthetic agents

   c. Diuretics—particularly thiazide diuretics, which may induce potassium depletion; a potassium deficit may lead to respiratory depression during anesthesia

3. Routine preoperative laboratory studies

   a. Hematology

      (1) Complete blood count—detects presence of anemia, infection, allergy, and leukemia

      (2) Prothrombin time—increase may indicate need for preoperative vitamin K therapy

      (3) Serology (VDRL)—determines presence of syphilitic reagin; a positive reaction may indicate need for antibiotic therapy

   b. Urinalysis

      (1) Specific gravity—measures ability of kidney to concentrate and dilute urine

      (2) Albumin and pus—indicate renal infection

      (3) Sugar and acetone—presence indicative of metabolic disorder (diabetes mellitus)

Part C   Preparing the Patient for Surgery

1. **Legal aspects**—all surgical procedures, however minor, cannot proceed without the voluntary, informed, and written consent of the patient
A. Surgical permits are witnessed by the physician, nurse, or other authorized person
B. Surgical permits protect the patient against unsanctioned surgery and also protect the surgeon and hospital staff against claims of unauthorized operations
C. Informed consent means that the operation has been fully explained to the patient including possible complications and disfigurements, as well as whether any organ or parts of the body are to be removed
D. Adults and emancipated minors may sign their own operative permits if they are mentally competent; permission for surgery of minor children and incompetent or unconscious adults must be obtained from a responsible family member or guardian
E. The signed operative permit is placed in a prominent place on the patient's chart and accompanies the patient to the operating room
2. **Preparatory and preventive teaching**—to reduce operative and postoperative complications, patients need to be taught how to cough, deep breathe, turn, and move their extremities during the postoperative period
A. Diaphragmatic breathing—refers to flattening of diaphragm during inspiration, which results in enlargement of upper abdomen; during expiration the abdominal muscles are contracted, along with the diaphragm
   1. The patient should be in a flat, semi-Fowler's, or side position with knees flexed and hands on the midabdomen
   2. Have the patient take a deep breath through the nose and mouth, letting the abdomen rise
   3. Have the patient exhale through the nose and mouth, squeezing out all the air by contracting the abdominal muscles
   4. Repeat 10 to 15 times with a short rest after each five to prevent hyperventilation
   5. Inform the patient that this exercise will be repeated five to ten times every hour postoperatively
B. Coughing—helps clear chest of secretions and,

although uncomfortable, will not harm incision site
   1. Have the patient lean forward slightly from a sitting position and place the patient's hands over the incisional site; this acts as a splint during coughing
   2. Have the patient inhale and exhale several times
   3. Have the patient inhale deeply and cough sharply three times—the patient's mouth should be slightly open
   4. Tell the patient to inhale again and to cough deeply once or twice
C. Turning and leg exercises—help prevent circulatory stasis, which may lead to thrombus formation and postoperative flatus or "gas pains" as well as respiratory problems
   1. Tell the patient to turn on one side with the upper-most leg flexed; the siderails should be used to facilitate the movement
   2. In a supine position, have the patient bend the upper-most knee and lift the foot; this position should be held for a few seconds, then the leg should be extended and the leg lowered; repeat five times, and turn the patient and do the same with the other leg
   3. Teach the patient to move each foot through full range of motion
3. **Preparing the patient's skin**—the purpose of the bath and skin preparation is to reduce the number of bacteria on the skin to eliminate the transference of these bacteria into the incision
A. The area of the skin prep is always wider and longer than the proposed incision in case a larger incision is necessary
B. The area is gently scrubbed with an antiseptic agent
   1. Soap containing hexachlorophene should be left on the skin for five to ten minutes
   2. When benzalkonium (Zepherin) Cl solution is ordered, do not soap the skin prior to use; soap reduces the effectiveness of zepherin by causing it to precipitate
C. A clean safety razor with a new blade should be used; shave against the grain of the hair shaft
D. Any nicks, cuts, or irritations should be noted;

these are potential infection sites

E. Depilatory creams may also be employed—these are left on the skin for ten minutes then washed off along with the hair; transient rashes are an occasional side effect with their use

4. **Preparing the patient's gastrointestinal tract**—the purpose of this preparation is to reduce the risk of vomiting and aspiration during anesthesia and to prevent contamination of abdominal operative sites by fecal material

A. Food and fluid restriction
   1. Food generally remains in the stomach for six hours after ingestion
   2. Fluids pass far more quickly into the duodenum; but to ensure an empty stomach, fluids are withheld for at least four hours prior to surgery
   3. Nursing measures include
      a. Telling the patient why no food or fluid is allowed
      b. Removing food and water from the bedside
      c. Placing NPO signs on patient's bed or door
      d. Informing the kitchen and the oncoming nursing staff that the patient is NPO in preparation for surgery
   4. Patients who are dehydrated or malnourished may receive IV infusions up to the time of surgery

B. Enemas
   1. An empty bowel is essential to prevent contamination when the proposed surgery involves the intestinal tract and colon; generally two or three enemas are given the evening prior to surgery
   2. Enemas may also be ordered preoperatively if the surgical procedure involves a pelvic organ—an empty bowel enhances the exposure of the operative field and reduces the possibility of injury to the bowel
   3. Surgeries involving the large intestine are usually preceded by three days of bowel cleansing and antibiotic therapy to reduce the colonic flora
   4. Nursing measures are designed to maximize the effectiveness of bowel cleansing and to minimize the physiologic and psychologic discomfort to the patient

C. Gastric or intestinal intubation
   1. Gastric or intestinal tubes may be inserted the evening prior to major abdominal surgery to remove stomach and intestinal contents or to reduce intestinal dilatation
   2. Decompression is accomplished by these tubes when suction is applied
      a. A single-lumen Levin tube is sufficient to remove fluids and gas from the stomach
      b. A long single- or double-lumen tube (Miller-Abbott) is required to remove the contents of the jejunum or ileum
   3. Abdominal suction pressures should not exceed 1.5 pounds of negative pressure—excessive pressures will result in injury to the mucosal lining of the intestine or stomach

5. **Sleep and relaxation**—the evening prior to surgery a barbiturate such as pentobarbital sodium (Nembutal) 0.05 to 0.1 gm or secobarbital (Seconal) sodium 0.1 to 0.2 gm are ordered by the physician to ensure the patient sleeps well and to facilitate reduction of apprehension

Part D The Day of Surgery

1. **The Staff nurse's responsibilities**
A. Be sure that the operative permit has been signed
B. Have the patient shower or bathe or see that it is done
   1. Dress the patient in hospital pajamas
   2. Remove hair pins and cover hair
   3. Remove nail polish—facilitates observation of peripheral perfusion
   4. Remove all jewelry and tape wedding bands securely
   5. Remove pierced earrings and contact lenses
   6. Remove and store dentures and give mouth care
C. Check to see that the patient is wearing the

proper identification

D. Identify relatives or friends who will be awaiting information during the procedure
E. Take the patient's vital signs
F. Have the patient void—prevents distention and possible injury to the bladder
G. Administer the preoperative medication—purpose is to reduce patient anxiety to ensure smooth induction and maintenance of anesthesia
   1. Should be administered 45 to 75 minutes before anesthetic induction
   2. Side rails should be raised, as the patient will begin to feel drowsy and light headed
   3. Tell the patient that it is normal for the mouth to feel dry if atropine SO_4 has been given
   4. Observe for side effects of medication—morphine SO_4 and meperidine (Demerol) HCl may cause nausea and vomiting or drop in blood pressure
   5. Maintain quiet environment until patient is transported to operating room
I. Note the completeness of the chart
   1. Vital signs
   2. Routine laboratory reports
   3. Administration of preoperative medication
   4. Significant patient observations
J. Assist the patient's family in finding the proper waiting room
   1. Inform them that surgeon will contact them after the procedure is over
   2. Explain the length of time the patient is expected to be in the recovery room
   3. Prepare the family for any special equipment or devices that may be needed to care for the patient postoperatively—oxygen, monitoring equipment, or blood transfusions

2. **Anesthesia**—purpose is to block transmission of nerve impulses, suppress reflexes, promote muscular relaxation, and in some instances, achieve unconsciousness
A. Regional anesthesia—purpose is to block pain reception and transmission in a specified area
   1. Agents used in regional anesthesia act by preventing action potentials or impulse formation by inhibiting the movement of sodium into the neuron and preventing potassium from moving out of the neuron
   2. Commonly used drugs are lidocaine HCl, tetracaine HCl, cocaine HCl, and procaine HCl
   3. Regional anesthetics

   a. Topical—applied to mucous membranes or skin; the drug anesthetizes the nerves immediately below the area
   b. Local infiltration—used for minor procedures; the anesthetic drug is injected directly into the area to be incised or manipulated.
   c. Peripheral nerve block—regional anesthesia is achieved by injecting the drug into or around a nerve after it passes from the vertebral column; the procedure is named for the nerve involved such as brachial-plexus block
   d. Field block—a group of nerves are injected as they branch from a major or main nerve trunk
   e. Epidural anesthesia—the anesthetizing drug is injected into the epidural space of the vertebral canal; produces a bandlike anesthesia around body
   f. Spinal anesthesia—the anesthetizing drug is injected into the subarachnoid space and mixes with the spinal fluid; the drug acts on the nerves as they emerge from the spinal cord, thereby inhibiting conduction in the autonomic, sensory, and motor systems; it has a rapid onset and produces excellent muscle relaxation
   g. Intravenous regional anesthesia—utilized on an extremity whose circulation has been interrupted by a tourniquet; the anesthetic is injected into the vein and blockage is presumed to be achieved from the extravascular leakage of anesthetic near a major nerve trunk
B. General anesthesia—a reversible state in which the patient loses consciousness due to the inhibition of neuronal impulses in the brain by a variety of chemical agents
   1. General anesthesia may be administered intravenously, by inhalation, and rectally
   2. Intravenous anesthetics
      a. Thiopental (Pentothal) SO_4—a rapid-acting barbiturate; most frequently used drug for induction of anesthesia
      b. Droperidol (Inapsine) and fentanyl (Innovar and sublimaze)—combine a potent tranquilizer and an analgesic to produce a rapid anesthesia

c. Ketamine HCl—chemically related to the hallucinogens; it produces an anesthesia characterized by a patient who appears awake but who will have no awareness or recollection of the procedure

3. Inhalation anesthesia—produced by inhalation of the vapors of certain gases or volatile liquids
   a. Ether—a volatile, flammable liquid, which while irritating to the mucous membranes, provides excellent muscle relaxation and a wider margin of safety than other anesthetic agents
   b. Nitrous oxide—although irritating to the mucous membranes, it is the most widely used of the gases; it is noninflammable and is frequently combined with oxygen and halothane (side effect—severe liver damage).
   c. Cyclopropane—more potent than nitrous oxide; it is highly flammable but quickly produces unconsciousness and good muscle relaxation
   d. Halothane—a volatile, nonflammable liquid that quickly produces anesthesia and allows for rapid emergence from anesthesia; it has a low incidence of postoperative nausea and vomiting

C. Muscle relaxants—drugs such as curare and succinylcholine (Anectine) Cl are given to supplement general anesthetic agents
   1. Facilitate endotracheal intubation
   2. Provide relaxation of abdominal muscles
   3. Facilitate the administration of lower doses of potent general anesthetic
   4. May cause respiratory depression

D. Hypothermia—a specialized procedure in which the patient's body temperature is lowered to 28 to 30 C (82 to 86 F)
   1. Reduces tissue metabolism and oxygen requirements
   2. Employed in heart surgery, brain surgery, and surgery on major blood vessels
   3. Complications—respiratory depression, cardiac arrest, fat necrosis, edema, and fluid imbalances
   4. Nursing measures are designed to prevent complications
      a. Monitor vital signs
      b. Note levels of consciousness
      c. Record intake and output accurately
      d. Maintain good body alignment

3. **Immediate postanesthesia nursing care**—purpose is to maintain the patient's physiologic and psychologic equilibrium
A. Maintenance of physiologic equilibrium
   1. Position patient on side or on back with head turned to side—prevents obstruction of airway by tongue and allows secretions to drain from mouth
   2. Collect operative data
      a. General condition of patient
      b. Type of operation performed
      c. Pathologic findings
      d. Anesthesia and medications received
      e. Any problems which arose that will affect postoperative course
      f. Amount of intravenous infusion or transfusions received
      g. Any symptoms or complications to be observed
      h. Any symptoms that should be reported immediately
      i. Whether or not patient needs to be attached to a drainage or suction apparatus
   3. Observations
      a. Note patient's level of consciousness
      b. Vital signs
      c. Skin color and dryness
      d. Presence of airway
      e. Status of reflexes
      f. Dressings
      g. Type and rate of intravenous infusion and blood transfusion
      h. Rate, depth, and regularity of respirations
      i. Presence of urinary catheter and, if present, color and amount of urine
   4. Promote a quiet, nonstressful environment—patients need to have siderails up at all times and a nurse in constant attendance
   5. Maintain respiratory function
      a. Leave the oropharyngeal or nasopharyngeal airway in place until patient awakens and begins to eject it—leaving airway in after pharyngeal reflex has returned may initiate gagging and vomiting
      b. After airway is removed, turn patient on side in a lateral position; support upper

arm with a pillow—promotes lung
expansion and reduces risk of aspiration

c. Suction excessive secretions from
mouth and pharynx—prevents
aspiration and obstruction of airway

d. Encourage cough and deep
breathing—increases lung expansion and
promotes gaseous exchange, aids in
upward movement of secretions, and
prevents atelectasis

e. Administer humidified oxygen as
necessary—humidification reduces
respiratory irritation and keeps
bronchotracheal secretions soft and
moist

f. Utilize mechanical ventilation, such as
Bird or Bennet respirator, if needed

6. Maintain cardiovascular function

a. Take vital signs

(1) Compare with preoperative vital
signs

(2) Immediately report a systolic blood
pressure that drops 20 mm Hg or
more, a pressure below 80 mm Hg,
or a pressure that continually drops
5 to 10 mm Hg over several readings

(3) Immediately report pulse rates under
60 or over 110 beats per minute or
that are, or become, irregular

(4) Report respirations over 30 per
minute or those that become
shallow, quiet, slow and in which
the patient uses neck and
diaphragmatic muscles—these are
symptoms of respiratory depression
and artificial respiration is indicated

b. Observe for other alterations in
circulatory function—pallor, thready
pulse, cold moist skin, decreased urine
output, and restlessness

(1) Decreased blood volume →
decreased venous return →
decreased cardiac output →
decreased blood pressure →
increased peripheral vascular
constriction → decreased tissue
perfusion and oxygenation

(2) Immediately report to physician,
initiate oxygen therapy, and place
patient in shock position unless
contraindicated

c. Check time and rate of intravenous
infusions and whether any medications
have been ordered

d. Monitor blood transfusions and observe
for signs of reaction, such as chills,
elevated temperature, urticaria,
laryngeal edema, and wheezing

B. Maintenance of psychologic equilibrium

1. Reassure patient on awakening—orient frequently

2. Explain procedures even though patient does
not appear alert

3. Answer patient questions briefly and accurately

4. Maintain quiet, restful environment

5. Institute comfort measures

a. Maintain good body alignment

b. Support dependent extremities to avoid
pressure areas and possible nerve
damage

c. Check dressings, clothing, and bedding
for constriction

d. Protect arm with intravenous infusion
and check frequently for patency and
signs of infiltration

4. **General postoperative nursing care**—purpose is
to prevent complications and promote recovery
of normal function (see Table 3-1, Postoperative
Complications)

A. Promote lung expansion, gaseous exchange, and
elimination of bronchotracheal secretions

1. Turn, cough, and deep breathe every two
hours

2. Utilize blow bottles, as ordered

3. Administer IPPB, as ordered

4. Encourage hydration—thins mucus secretions

5. Assist in ambulation as soon as allowed

B. Maintain body alignment—promotes functioning of all body organs and enhances drainage
from body cavities

C. Provide relief of pain

1. Assess type, location, intensity, and duration
of pain as well as possible causative factors,
such as poor body alignment or restrictive
bandages

2. Observe and evaluate patient's reaction to
discomfort

3. Utilize comfort measures, such as back rubs
and proper ventilation, staying with patient
and encouraging verbalization

4. Reduce incidence of pain by changing position frequently; supporting dependent extremities with pillows, sandbags, and footboards; and keeping bedding dry and straight

5. Administer analgesics or tranquilizers, as ordered, with verbal assurance that it will help

6. Observe for desired and untoward effects of medication

D. Assist in the promotion of adequate nutrition and fluid and electrolyte balance

1. Administer parenteral fluids, as ordered—monitor blood pressure and intake and output to assess adequate, deficient, or excessive extracellular fluid volume (see Appendix D)

2. Encourage liquid diet when vomiting stops, as ordered

   a. Stimulates gastric juices and promotes gastric motility and peristalsis

   b. Promotes vitamin, mineral, and nitrogen balance

E. Assist patient with elimination

1. Patient should void eight to ten hours after surgery

2. Aid voiding by allowing patient to stand or use commode, if not contraindicated; use other means such as running tap water or soaking feet in warm water to promote micturition

3. Avoid catheterization when possible but utilize if bladder distended and conservative treatments have failed

4. Maintain accurate intake and output records

5. Expect bowel function to return in two to three days

F. Facilitate wound healing and prevent infection

1. Avoid pressure on or around incisional site—enhances venous drainage and prevents edema

2. Elevate injured extremities to reduce swelling and promote venous return

3. Support or splint incision when patient coughs

4. Check dressings every two hours for drainage

5. Change dressings on draining wounds prn and utilize protective ointments to reduce skin irritation

6. If suction is applied to a draining wound, observe carefully for kinking or twisting of the tubes

G. Promote comfort and rest

1. Recognize factors that may cause restlessness—fear, anxiety, pain, oxygen lack, and wet dressings

2. Utilize analgesics or barbiturates or apply oxygen as indicated

3. Change positions, encourage deep breathing, or massage back to reduce restlessness

4. Perform as many care activities at one time as possible, allowing patient to rest in between

5. Administer antiemetic for relief of nausea and vomiting, as ordered

H. Encourage early movement and ambulation—prevents complications of immobilization

1. Assist in turning, coughing, and deep breathing

2. Institute passive and active ROM exercises

3. Encourage leg exercises (see p. 150)

4. Assist with standing or use of commode if allowed

5. Encourage resumption of personal care as soon as possible

6. Assist with ambulation as soon as allowed—note ambulation does not mean getting up and sitting in chair; chair setting should be avoided as it enhances venous pooling and may predispose to thrombophlebitis; patients should ambulate in room and then return to bed

Table 3-1.   Postoperative complications

RESPIRATORY COMPLICATIONS—most common are atelectasis, bronchitis, pneumonias (lobar, bronchial, and hypostatic), and pleurisy; other complications are hemothorax and pneumothorax.

Condition and etiology	Pathophysiology	Signs and symptoms	Nursing interventions
Atelectasis—Undetected preoperative upper respiratory infections, aspiration of vomitus; irritation of the tracheobronchial tree with increased mucus secretions due to intubation and inhalation anesthesia, a history of heavy smoking or chronic obstructive pulmonary disease; severe postoperative pain or high abdominal or thoracic surgery, which inhibits deep breathing; and debilitation or old age, which lowers the patient's resistance.	Clogged bronchi → removal of air from entrapped alveoli by capillaries → collapse of alveoli—may affect all or part of lung	Dyspnea, elevated temperature, absent or diminished breath sounds over affected area, asymmetrical chest expansion, increased respirations and pulse rate, anxiety, and restlessness	1. Position on unaffected side 2. Turn, cough, and deep breathe 3. Postural drainage 4. Nebulization 5. Force fluids if not contraindicated
Bronchitis—see Atelectasis for etiology	Inflammation or infection of mucous membrane lining and/or bronchi → local hyperemia → edema → leukocytic infiltration of submucosa → increased tenacious mucopurulent secretions	Elevated temperature, chills, malaise, nonproductive cough that gradually becomes productive, wheezes, and moist rales	1. Position of comfort—semi-Fowler's 2. Provide humidified air 3. Force fluids to 3000 ml/day 4. Avoid iced drinks 5. Frequent oral hygiene if cough productive 6. Avoid fatigue and chilling 7. Administer bronchodilators, as ordered
Pneumonia—see Atelectasis for etiology	Acute inflammation of alveoli → exudate fill alveoli → consolidation of lung tissue → decreased gaseous exchange	Rapid, shallow, painful respirations; rales; bronchi; diminished or absent breath sounds; asymmetrical lung expansion; chills and fever; productive cough, rust-colored sputum; and circumoral and nailbed cyanosis	1. Position of comfort—semi- to high-Fowler's 2. Force fluids to 3000 ml/day 3. Provide humidification of air and oxygen therapy 4. Oropharyngeal suction prn 5. Assist during coughing 6. Administer antibiotics and analgesics, as ordered 7. Maintain high-calorie diet as tolerated 8. Provide proper disposal of secretions and oral hygiene

Condition/Etiology	Pathophysiology	Signs and symptoms	Nursing interventions
Pleurisy—see Atelectasis for etiology	Inflammation of the pleura	Knifelike chest pain on inspiration; intercostal tenderness; splinting of chest by patient; rapid, shallow respirations; pleural friction rub; elevated temperature; malaise	1. Position patient on affected side to splint the chest 2. Manually splint patient's chest during cough 3. Apply binder or adhesive strapping, as ordered 4. Administer analgesics, as ordered
Hemothorax—chest surgery, gunshot or knife wounds, and multiple fractures of chest wall	Blood from torn vessel fills pleural space inhibiting lobular or total lung expansion → decreased alveolar ventilation → decreased PO_2	Chest pain, increased respiratory rate, dyspnea, decreased or absent breath sounds, decreased blood pressure, trachycardia, and mediastinal shift may occur (heart, trachea, and esophagus great vessels are pushed toward unaffected side)	1. Observe vital signs closely for signs of shock and respiratory distress 2. Assist with thoracentesis (needle aspiration of fluid) 3. Assist with insertion of thoracostomy tube to closed chest drainage (see care of water-seal drainage system)
Pneumothorax, open—see Sucking chest wound (p. 167)			
Pneumothorax, closed or tension—thoracentesis (needle nicks the lung), rupture of aveoli or bronchi due to accidental injury, and chronic obstructive lung disease	Air enters pleural space with each inspiration and is trapped; intrapleural pressures become positive, inhibiting lung expansion and decreasing alveolar ventilation; pressure may collapse lung and cause mediastinal shift, which may result in compression of unaffected lung and great vessels → decreasing venous return and cardiac output	Marked dyspnea, sudden sharp chest pain, subcutaneous emphysema (air in chest wall tissue), cyanosis, tracheal shift to unaffected side, hyperresonance on percussion, decreased or absent breath sounds, increased respiratory rate, tachycardia, asymmetrical chest expansion, feeling of pressure within chest; *mediastinal shift*—severe dyspnea and cyanosis, deviation of larynx and trachea toward unaffected side, deviation either medially or laterally of apex of heart, decreased blood pressure, distended neck veins, and increased pulse and respirations	1. Remain with patient—keep as calm and quiet as possible 2. Place in high-Fowler's (sitting) position 3. Notify physician through another nurse and have thoracentesis equipment brought to bedside 4. Administer oxygen as necessary 5. Take vital signs to evaluate respiratory and cardiac function 6. Assist with thoracentesis 7. Assist with initiation and maintenance of closed-chest drainage

Continued

Table 3-1. Postoperative complications—Continued

CIRCULATORY COMPLICATIONS—Shock, thrombophlebitis, pulmonary embolism, and disseminated intravascular coagulation

Condition and etiology	Pathophysiology	Signs and symptoms	Nursing interventions
Shock, hypovolemic—hemorrhage, sepsis, decreased cardiac contractility (myocardial infarction, cardiac failure, tamponade), drug sensitivities, transfusion reactions, pulmonary embolism, and emotional reaction to pain or deep fear	Decreased venous return due to diminished blood volume (hemorrhage) or plasma loss (intestinal obstruction, burns, or dehydration) → decreased cardiac output → decreased mean systemic pressures → decreased tissue perfusion and oxygenation	Dizziness; fainting; restlessness; anxiety; decreased or falling blood pressure; weak, thready pulse; shallow, rapid respirations; pallor; cool, clammy, pale to cyanotic skin; decreased temperature; thirst; oliguria; and CVP below 5 cm water	1. Position patient with foot of bed raised 20°, keeping knees straight, trunk horizontal, and head slightly elevated; avoid Trendelenburg's position 2. Administer blood transfusions, plasma expanders, and intravenous infusions, as ordered 3. Check vital signs, CVP, and temperature 4. Insert urinary catheter to monitor hourly urine output 5. Administer oxygen, as ordered
Shock, septic—see Hypovolemic shock for etiology	Local or generalized infection → vasodilation, locally then generally → increased cardiac output in response to vasodilation and increased metabolic rate due to fever → red cell agglutination with sludging of blood → decreased venous return → decreased cardiac output → circulatory collapse	As hypovolemic shock, except temperature may be elevated; CVP may elevate over 15 cm water	1. Position as for hypovolemic shock 2. Institute cooling measures if indicated 3. Administer antibiotics, steroids, and intravenous infusions, as ordered 4. Monitor vital signs, CVP, temperature, and urinary output as for hypovolemic shock
Shock, anaphylactic—see Hypovolemic shock for etiology	Antigen-antibody reaction → cellular damage → release of histamine and histaminelike substance → venous dilatation → increased vascular capacity → dilatation of arteriolae → decreased mean systemic blood pressure → decreased venous return → cardiac failure	Flushing; sneezing; itching; urticaria; asthmatic wheezing; decreased or falling blood pressure; edema, particularly laryngeal edema; and weak, thready pulse	1. If patient is receiving a blood transfusion, stop immediately 2. Administer antihistamines and steroids, as ordered 3. Prepare epinephrine in event of respiratory distress 4. Maintain intravenous infusions, as ordered 5. Monitor vital signs, CVP, temperature, and urinary output 6. If transfusion reaction suspected, send blood and urine samples to lab for hemoglobin

Shock, cardiogenic—see Hypovolemic shock for etiology Myocardial infarction → decreased cardiac output → decreased cardiac perfusion → decreased peripheral perfusion → tissue ischemia → release of toxins → increased capillary permeability and vascular dilatation → decreased blood volume and venous pooling → decreased venous return → cardiac depression	As for hypovolemic shock, with orthopnea, irregular or absent peripheral pulses, cardiac arrhythmias, CVP above 15 cm water, heart failure, and pulmonary edema	1. Position for optimal ventilation, semi- or high-Fowler's 2. Avoid routine nursing functions 3. Monitor ECG continuously 4. Administer parenteral infusions, as ordered 5. Administer vasopressors, vasodilators, digitalis preparations, steroids, and narcotics, as ordered 6. Monitor vital signs, CVP, and urine output—axilla for temperature determinations 7. Administer oxygen, as ordered
Thrombophlebitis—injury to vein wall by tight leg straps or leg holders during gynecologic surgery; hemoconcentration due to dehydration or fluid loss; and stasis of blood in extremities due to postoperative circulatory depression Roughened endothelial surface of vessel due to trauma → formation of platelet plug—activation of prothrombin into thrombin, which converts fibrinogen into fibrin threads, which enmesh red blood cells and plasma to form blood clot; slow blood flow → increased concentrations of procoagulants (prothrombin, etc.) in local areas → initiation of clotting mechanism	Calf pain or cramping, redness and swelling (the left leg is affected more frequently than the right), slight fever, chills, Homan's sign, and tenderness over the anteromedian surface of thigh	1. Maintain complete bedrest, avoiding positions that restrict venous return 2. Apply elastic stockings or wrap legs from toes to groin with elastic bandages—prevents swelling and pooling of venous blood 3. Apply warm moist soaks to area, as ordered 4. Administer anticoagulants, as ordered 5. Use bed cradle over affected limb 6. Provide active and passive ROM exercises in unaffected limb
Pulmonary embolism—obstruction of a pulmonary artery by a foreign body in the bloodstream, usually a blood clot that has been dislodged from its original site Embolus, usually from systemic vein, travels to right side of heart → pumped to lungs → total or partial obstruction of pulmonary blood flow → decreased venous return to left side of heart → peripheral circulatory failure may occur; dammed up blood in lungs causes dilatation of right side of heart and engorgement of systemic veins	Sudden, severe stabbing chest pain; severe dyspnea; cyanosis; rapid pulse; anxiety and apprehension; pupillary dilatation; profuse diaphoresis; and loss of consciousness	1. Administer oxygen and inhalants with the patient sitting upright; 2. Maintain bedrest and frequently reassure patient 3. Administer heparin sodium, as ordered 4. Administer analgesics, such as morphine SO_4, to reduce pain and apprehension

Continued

Table 3-1. Postoperative complications—Continued

CIRCULATORY COMPLICATIONS—Shock, thrombophlebitis, pulmonary embolism, and disseminated intravascular coagulation—Continued

Condition and etiology	Pathophysiology	Signs and symptoms	Nursing interventions
Disseminated intravascular coagulation (DIC)—septicemia (gram-negative), severe and prolonged hypotension (shock), toxemia of pregnancy, carcinoma of the prostate, chemotherapy for cancer, acidosis, and liver damage	Tissue injury → activation of coagulation system → thrombin formation reacts with fibrogen to form fibrin → fibrin clots deposited throughout microcirculation in kidneys, brain, and lungs → microinfarcts and tissue necrosis → red blood cells are trapped in fibrin and destroyed → excessive clotting causes consumption of fibrinogen, platelets, and other clotting factors and results in formation of fibrin split products, which inhibit clotting and lead to bleeding	Petechiae and ecchymoses on skin and mucous membranes, cyanosis of fingers, toes, and limbs: wound and venipuncture bleeding; subcutaneous hematomas; severe uncontrollable hemorrhage during surgery and childbirth or from ulcer; oliguria; anuria; convulsions; coma; abnormal coagulation tests (prothrombin time, platelet count, and fibrinogen level)	1. Carry out nursing measures designed to alleviate basic problem (shock, septicemia, and cancer) 2. Administer heparin SO_4, q4–6h, as ordered, to reverse abnormal clotting 3. Monitor and record intake and output, vital signs (oral and axillary temperature), and central venous pressure; report changes to physician 4. Administer blood or plasma, as ordered 5. Avoid administering parenteral medications if possible; this further irritates vein walls and may increase thrombus formation

WOUND COMPLICATIONS—infection, dehiscence, and evisceration

Condition and etiology	Pathophysiology	Signs and symptoms	Nursing interventions
Wound infection—obesity or undernutrition, particularly protein and vitamin deficiencies; decreased antibody production in aged; decreased phagocytosis in newborn; metabolic disorder, such as diabetes mellitus, Cushing's syndrome, malignancies, and shock; breakdown in aseptic technique	Tissue necrosis or decreased local tissue perfusion provide medium for pathogenic growth, eliciting inflammatory response; blood vessels dilate → rapid blood flow → increased filtration pressures → edema; slowing of blood flow → migration of leukocytes to area → phagocytosis	Redness, tenderness, and heat in area of incision; wound drainage; elevated temperature; and increased pulse rate	1. Assist in the cleansing and irrigation of the wound and insertion of a drain 2. Apply hot wet dressings, as ordered 3. Administer antibiotics, as ordered, and observe responses
Wound dehiscence and evisceration—Obesity and undernutrition, particularly protein and vitamin C deficiencies; cancer; liver metabolic disorders; increased intra-abdominal pressures due to	Inadequate tissue nutrition → decreased formation of new or scar tissue → inadequate wound approximation → increased intra-abdominal pressures due to	Slow parting of wound edges with a gush of pinkish serous drainage or rapid parting with coils of intestines escaping onto the abdominal wall; the latter is	1. Maintain bedrest in a low-Fowler's or horizontal position 2. Notify physician immediately 3. Cover exposed coils of

Condition and etiology	Pathophysiology	Signs and symptoms	Nursing interventions
disease; common site is midline abdominal incision, frequently about seven days postoperatively; and precipitating factors include abdominal distention, retching, coughing, hiccups and uncontrolled motor activity	flatus, retching, etc. → splitting of incisional site	accompanied by pain and, often, vomiting	intestines with sterile towels or dressing and keep moist with sterile normal saline 4. Monitor vital signs frequently 5. Remain with the patient, and reassure patient that physician is coming 6. Prepare for physician's arrival by setting up IV equipment, suction equipment, and nasogastric tube and by obtaining sterile gown, mask, gloves, towels, and warmed normal saline 7. Notify surgery that patient will be returning to operating room

URINARY COMPLICATIONS—retention and infections

Condition and etiology	Pathophysiology	Signs and symptoms	Nursing interventions
Urinary retention—obstruction in the bladder or urethra; neurologic disease; mechanical trauma as in childbirth or gynecological surgery; psychologic conditioning that inhibits voiding in bed; and prolonged bedrest	Depression of urinary reflex by general anesthetic and anticholinergic drugs (atropine SO_4) given before surgery → blockage of parasympathetic stimulation → failure of bladder to empty	Inability to void in 10 to 18 hours postsurgery, despite adequate fluid replacement, palpable bladder, frequent voiding of small amounts of urine or dribbling, and suprapubic pain	1. Assist patient to stand or use bedside commode if not contraindicated 2. Provide privacy 3. Reduce tension and provide psychologic support 4. Use warm bedpan 5. Run tap water 6. Place patient's feet in warm water 7. Pour warm water over vulva 8. Catheterize if conservative measures fail
Urinary infections—Urinary retention, bladder distention, repeated or prolonged catheterization.	Slowing of urinary flow and/or presence of foreign body in normally sterile bladder → decreased resistance → increased susceptibility to infection → bladder trigone may show increased vascularity, generalized	Burning and frequency of urination, low-back or flank pain, pyuria, hematuria, elevated temperature, chills, anorexia, and positive urine culture	1. Push fluids to 3000 ml daily unless contraindicated 2. Avoid stimulants such as coffee, tea, and cola beverages 3. Administer antibiotics, sulfonamides, or acidifying agents, as ordered

Continued

Table 3-1.   Postoperative complications—Continued

URINARY COMPLICATIONS—retention and infections—Continued

Condition and etiology	Pathophysiology	Signs and symptoms	Nursing interventions
Urinary infections—Continued	edema, and ulceration; chronic cystitis → bladder may become thick-walled and contracted		4. Maintain meticulous perineal care 5. Administer perianal care after each bowel movement

GASTROINTESTINAL COMPLICATIONS—gastric dilatation, paralytic ileus, and intestinal obstruction

Condition and etiology	Pathophysiology	Signs and symptoms	Nursing interventions
Gastric dilatation—depressed gastric motility due to sympathoadrenal stress response, idiosyncrasy to drugs, emotions, pain, shock, and fluid and electrolyte imbalances	Failure of neuromuscular innervation → decreased motor function (peristalsis) → abdominal distention → thinning of gastric mucosa → decreased blood supply → further decrease in gastric motility	Feeling of fullness, hiccups, overflow vomiting of dark foul-smelling liquid; severe retention leads to decreased blood pressure (due to pressure on vagus nerve) and other symptoms of shock syndrome	1. Report signs to physician immediately 2. Insert or assist in the insertion of a nasogastric tube and attach to intermittent suction 3. Irrigate nasogastric tube with saline (using water will deplete electrolytes and result in metabolic alkalosis) 4. Administer IV infusions with electrolytes, as ordered
Paralytic ileus—see Gastric dilatation	Decreased motor activity (due to toxic or traumatic disturbance of the autonomic nervous system) → decreased peristalsis → increased intestinal retention	Greatly decreased or absent bowel sounds, failure of either gas or feces to be passed by rectum, nausea and vomiting, abdominal tenderness and distention, fever, dehydration	1. Notify physician 2. Insert or assist with insertion of nasogastric tube and attach to intermittent suction 3. Insert rectal tube 4. Administer IV infusion with electrolytes, as ordered 5. Irrigate nasogastric tube with saline 6. Assist with insertion of Miller-Abbott tube if indicated 7. Administer medications to increase peristalsis, as ordered
Intestinal obstruction—poorly functioning anastomosis, hernia, adhesions, and fecal impaction	Moderate obstruction → increased peristalsis above obstruction → stretching of mesentery → severe pain and occasionally reflex vomiting → increased secretion	Severe, colicky abdominal pains, mild to severe abdominal distention, nausea and vomiting, anorexia and malaise, fever, lack of bowel movement, electrolyte	1. Assist with insertion of nasoenteric tube and attach to intermittent suction 2. Maintain IV infusions with electrolytes

Condition and etiology	Pathophysiology	Signs and symptoms	Nursing interventions
	and distention of gut → intestinal paralysis → vascular to intestinal fluid shift due to failure to reabsorb excessive secretions → accumulation of fluids → dehydration → decreased blood volume → increased pulse rate and falling blood pressure	imbalance, and high-pitched tinkling bowel sounds	3. Encourage nasal breathing to avoid air swallowing 4. Check abdomen for distention and bowel sounds every two hours 5. Encourage verbalization 6. Plan rest periods for patient 7. Administer oral hygiene frequently

TRANSFUSION REACTIONS—allergic, febrile, and hemolytic

Condition and etiology	Pathophysiology	Signs and symptoms	Nursing interventions
Allergic and febrile reactions—unidentified antigen or antigens in donor blood or transfusion equipment; previous reaction to transfusions; small thrombi; bacteria; and lysed red cells	Unknown antigen → formation of antibodies → cellular damage → release of histamine and histaminelike substances → vascular dilatation → edema of tissue	Fever to 103 F, may have sudden onset; chills; itching; erythema; urticaria; nausea; vomiting; and dyspnea and wheezing, occasionally	1. Stop transfusion and notify physician 2. Administer antihistamines, as ordered 3. Send STAT urine to lab for analysis 4. Institute cooling measures if indicated 5. Maintain strict input and output records 6. Send remaining blood to lab for analysis and order recipient blood sample for analysis
Hemolytic Reaction—Infusion of incompatible blood	Infusion of incompatible blood → hemolysis (rupture of RBC) of erythrocytes by isoagglutinins in recipient → release of cellular contents microemboli → decreased blood volume → decreased cardiac output → shock	Early chills and fever; feeling of burning in face; hypotension; tachycardia; chest, back, or flank pain; nausea; vomiting; feeling of doom; spontaneous and diffuse bleeding; icterus; oliguria; anuria; and hemoglobinuria	1. Stop infusion immediately, take vital signs, and notify physician 2. Send patient blood sample and unused blood to lab for analysis 3. Send STAT urine to lab 4. Save all urine for observation of discoloration 5. Administer parenteral infusions to combat shock, as ordered 6. Administer medications, as ordered—diuretics, sodium bicarbonate, hydrocortisone, and vasopressors

Continued

Table 3-1. Postoperative complications—Continued

EMOTIONAL COMPLICATIONS

Condition and etiology	Pathophysiology	Signs and symptoms	Nursing interventions
Emotional Disturbances—grief associated with loss of body part or loss of body image; previous emotional problems; decreased sensory and perceptual input; sensory overload; fear and pain; decreased resistance to stress as a result of age, exhaustion, or debilitation	Unknown	Restlessness, insomnia, depression, hallucinations, delusions, agitation, and suicidal thoughts	1. Report symptoms to physician 2. Encourage verbalization of feelings and give realistic assurance 3. Orient to time and place as necessary 4. Provide safety measures, such as siderails 5. Keep room well lighted to reduce incidence of visual hallucinations 6. Administer tranquilizers, as ordered 7. Use restraints as a last resort

Part E   Specific Nursing Observations and Interventions in Common Surgical Procedures

RESPIRATORY SYSTEM

1. **Tonsillectomy and adenoidectomy**—removal of tonsils and adenoids
A. Rationale—chronic tonsillitis and/or adenoiditis, adenoiditis with recurrent episodes of otitis media, severe tonsillar hypertrophy with obstruction of the pharynx
B. Preoperative nursing observations are designed to prevent postoperative complications
   1. Bleeding time
   2. Signs of upper respiratory infection
C. Postoperative nursing measures are designed to reduce incidence of postoperative bleeding, maintain fluid and electrolyte balance, and promote physical and psychologic relaxation
   1. Signs of bleeding—emesis of large amount of bright red or brown liquid, frequent swallowing, increased pulse rate, decreased blood pressure, pallor, and restlessness
   2. Provide ice collar—minimizes bleeding and reduces discomfort
   3. Administer fluids when tolerated, ice chips, water, popsicles, sherbert
   4. Rinse mouth frequently with water to aid in eliminating thick oral mucus
2. **Tracheostomy**—an opening into the trachea, temporary or permanent
A. Rationale—indicated in airway obstruction due to foreign body, edema, tumor, excessive tracheobronchial secretions, respiratory depression, decreased gaseous diffusion at alveolar membrane, or increased dead space as in severe emphysema
B. Preoperative nursing observations and procedures are designed to relieve anxiety and fear
   1. Explain purpose of procedure and equipment
   2. Demonstrate suctioning procedure
   3. Establish a means of postoperative communication—paper and pencil, magic slate, picture cards, and call bell
   4. Remain with patient as much as possible
C. Postoperative nursing measures are designed to maintain a patent airway and alleviate apprehension

   1. Administer mist to tracheostomy—natural humidifying oropharynx pathways have been eliminated
   2. Place patient in a semi-Fowler's position—prevent forward flexion of neck; facilitates respiration, promotes drainage, and minimizes edema
   3. Suction each hour or prn—increased respirations, moist noisy respirations, or nonproductive coughing indicate need for suctioning
      a. Secretions may be slightly blood tinged at first
      b. Strict aseptic technique and sterile suctioning tubes with each aspiration
         (1) Prevent hypoxia by administering 100% oxygen before suctioning unless contraindicated
         (2) Do not suction when inserting suction catheter
         (3) Turn patient's head to right to suction left bronchus; turn patient's head to left to suction right bronchus
         (4) If patient coughs during suctioning, gently remove catheter to permit ejection and suction of mucus
         (5) Apply suction intermittently for no longer than 10 to 15 seconds—prolonged suction decreases arterial oxygen concentrations
         (6) If cuffed tracheostomy cuff is used, deflate for five minutes every hour to prevent damage to trachea
         (7) Clean inner cannula of a silver tube every two to eight hours or as needed, depending on amount and consistency of secretions—do not use hot water as it coagulates the mucus
      c. Remain with patient as much as possible
      d. Encourage patient to communicate feelings, using preestablished communication system
3. **Laryngectomy**—radical neck dissection; consists of removal of entire larynx, lymph nodes,

sternomastoid muscle, and jugular vein on the same side as the lesion
A. Rationale—cancer of the larynx that extends beyond the vocal cords
B. Preoperative nursing care is designed to provide emotional support and optimal physical preparation
   1. Encourage verbalization of fears and answer all questions honestly, particularly about having no voice after surgery
   2. Preoperative care before tracheostomy (see p. 165)
   3. If possible, plan to have a person who has successfully adapted to laryngectomy visit patient
   4. Emphasize the life-saving aspects of the surgery and that it is possible to learn other means to speak again
C. Postoperative nursing measures are designed to maintain a patent airway, maintain fluid and electrolyte balance, prevent aspiration, and promote optimal postoperative physical and psychologic functioning
   1. Place in semi-Fowler's position—preventing forward flexion of neck
   2. Observe for respiratory embarrassment—dyspnea, cyanosis, and changes in vital signs
   3. Institute tracheostomy care
      a. Observe for presence of stridor (coarse high-pitched inspiratory sound)—report to physician immediately
      b. Have stand-by laryngectomy tube available at bedside
   4. If pressure dressings are used, reinforce as ordered
   5. If Hemo-Vac is used, expect 80 to 120 ml of serosanguineous drainage the first postoperative day
      a. Drainage should decrease daily
      b. Observe patency of drainage tubes
   6. Prevent infection by maintaining clean surgical technique
   7. Answer patient call bell immediately, utilizing preestablished means of communication
   8. Reexplain all procedures while giving care
   9. Observe for swallowing difficulties—teach patient to chew food well and to swallow each bite with water to facilitate movement of food to stomach
4. **Thoracic surgeries**—thoracotomy (incision in the chest wall to examine lung tissue and secure biopsy), lobectomy (removal of a lobe of the lung), pneumonectomy (removal of an entire lung)
A. Rationale—bronchogenic and lung carcinomas, lung abscess, tuberculosis, bronchiectasis, emphysematous blebs, and benign tumors
B. Preoperative nursing measures are designed to provide optimal physical and psychologic preparation for the surgical procedure
   1. Minimize pulmonary secretions
      a. Humidify air to moisten secretions
      b. Teach patient to cough against a closed glottis—increases intrapulmonary pressure
      c. Utilize IPPB as ordered to improve ventilation
      d. Administer bronchodilators, expectorants, and antibiotics, as ordered
      e. Utilize postural drainage, cupping, and vibration to mobilize secretions
   2. Instruct in diaphragmatic breathing and coughing (see p. 150)
   3. Instruct and supervise practice of postoperative arm exercises—flexion, abduction, and rotation of shoulder prevents ankylosis and stiffness of the arm on operative side
   4. Explain to the patient that there will be chest tubes, intravenous infusion, and oxygen therapy postoperatively
C. Postoperative nursing measures are designed to maintain a patent airway, promote ventilation and gaseous exchange, maintain fluid and electrolyte balance, prevent complications, and provide physical and mental relaxation
   1. High-Fowler's position
   2. Turn, cough, and deep breathe
      a. Pad area around chest tube when turning on operative side
      b. Do not turn pneumonectomy to unaffected side, as it inhibits lung expansion and interferes with drainage of secretions
      c. Splint chest during coughing
         (1) Support incision—reduces discomfort and incisional stress
         (2) Coughing up sputum is the single most important activity the thoracic patient performs postoperatively
   3. Attach chest tubes to water—seal drainage system
      a. Inserted to drain off excess fluid and air, speed reinflation of lungs, and reestablish normal negative intrapleural pressures
      b. Mark original fluid level on drainage

bottle to facilitate calculation of drainage; mark level, time, and date each time drainage is measured

c. Keep drainage bottles below chest level to prevent backflow of fluid and air into intrapleural space

d. Milk tubing in the direction of drainage bottle each hour to maintain patency and prevent plugging

e. Observe fluctuation of fluid level in the glass tubing—will stop when lung reexpanded or plugged by fibrin or clot

f. Observe and report leaks in the system—constant bubbling in water-seal bottle, leaking trapped air can result in tension pneumothorax

g. Observe and report immediately crepitations, labored or shallow breathing, tachypnea, cyanosis, tracheal deviation, and symptoms of hemorrhage

h. Keep two hemostats at the bedside at all times—if water-seal drainage bottle is broken, immediately clamp chest tube to prevent air from entering chest cavity

4. Auscultate chest for breath sounds—report diminished or absent breath sounds on unaffected side; indicates decreased ventilation and may lead to respiratory embarrassment

5. Administer parenteral infusions slowly—greater threat of pulmonary edema in these patients due to decrease in pulmonary vasculature with removal of lung lobe or whole lung

6. Institute range of motion of operative arm and ambulate as condition permits

5. Chest injuries

A. Flail chest—multiple rib fractures resulting in instability of the chest wall with subsequent paradoxical breathing (portion of lung under injured chest wall moves in on inspiration while remaining lung expands; on expiration it expands while unaffected lung tissue contracts)

1. Signs and symptoms—pain, dyspnea, cyanosis, uneven chest expansion, tachypnea, pneumothorax, hemothorax, and shock

2. Complications of severe chest injuries include hemothorax (blood in pleural cavity) and pneumothorax (air in pleural cavity) (see also p. 157)

3. Nursing measures are designed to stabilize chest wall and promote ventilation

a. Internal stabilization—use of volume-controlled ventilator to control patient's respirations → decreases movement of fractured ribs

b. External stabilization—achieved by skeletal traction applied to broken portion of ribs

c. Assist with chest tube insertion, as ordered

B. Sucking chest wound—penetrating wound of chest wall with hemothorax and pneumothorax, resulting in collapse of lung and mediastinal shift toward the unaffected lung

1. Signs and symptoms—severe dyspnea, weak rapid pulse, clammy cold skin, hypotension, and rush of air through hole in chest with respiration

2. Nursing measures are designed to eliminate positive intrapleural pressures and to restore adequate ventilation

a. Apply pressure bandage over wound as patient exhales forcefully against a closed glottis (Valsalva movement)

(1) Prevents further air from entering pleural cavity

(2) Valsalva movement aids in expanding collapsed lung by creating positive intrapulmonary pressures

b. Assist with insertion of endotracheal tube if needed

c. Assist with thoracentesis and insertion of chest tubes with connection to water-seal drainage as needed

CARDIOVASCULAR SYSTEM

1. **Cardiopulmonary bypass**—blood from cardiac chambers and great vessels is deviated into a pump oxygenator that allows surgical repair of the heart with full visualization and maintains perfusion and metabolic function of the body

A. Rationale—repair of atrial and ventricular septal defects, transposition of great vessels, tetralogy of Fallot, pulmonary and aortic stenosis, coronary artery bypass, and mitral and aortic valve replacement

B. Preoperative nursing care of the cardiac patient is designed to promote optimal physical functioning, reduce anxiety, and enhance coping mechanisms

1. Preoperative teaching

a. Customary procedures as cough, deep breathe, and turn

b. Tour of the intensive care unit

c. Introduction to personnel

  d. Demonstration of postoperative
     equipment that will be utilized
2. Encourage verbalization and questions—
   fear, depression, and overwhelming despair
   are frequent feelings
3. Supportive measures
   a. Provide opportunity for family to visit
      patient on morning of surgery
   b. Provide for religious consultation if
      desired
   c. Explain to the patient that medication
      will be given to reduce pain and that
      patients are awakened frequently
      postoperatively for vital signs, deep
      breathing, coughing, and turning
C. Postoperative nursing measures are designed to
   promote physiologic function of all body systems, maintain fluid and electrolyte balance,
   provide comfort and relief from pain, and prevent postoperative complications
D. Postoperative assessment
   1. Neurologic observations
      a. Levels of consciousness
      b. Pupillary reactions—dilatation of the
         pupils occurs when the blood contains
         excess carbon dioxide
      c. Movement of limbs and
         temperature—failure of patient to
         awaken, hemiplegia, and disorientation
         may be due to cerebral emboli
   2. Respiratory observations
      a. Rate, depth, and symmetry of
         respirations
         (1) Respirations increase in airway
             obstruction, pain
         (2) Respirations decrease in extreme
             carbon dioxide retention
         (3) Respirations are shallow and uneven
             with pain and atelectasis
      b. Skin color
      c. Patency and drainage from chest tubes
      d. Amount and color of sputum
   3. Cardiovascular observations
      a. Blood pressure
         (1) Decrease may indicate low cardiac
             output, tamponade, hemorrhage,
             arrhythmias, and thrombosis
         (2) Increase may indicate anxiety or
             hypervolemia
      b. Radial, apical, and pedal pulses
         (1) Check for rate, rhythm, and quality
         (2) Increased pulse rate (> 100)—

shock, fear, fever, hypoxia,
arrhythmias
         (3) Pulse deficit—atrial fibrillation,
             ectopic beats
         (4) Absent pedal pulse—peripheral
             emboli
      c. Central venous pressure (CVP)
      d. Temperature—normal to two- or
         three-degree elevation during first and
         second postoperative day
   4. Gastrointestinal observations—presence of
      nausea, vomiting, or abdominal distention
      (abdominal distention restricts pulmonary
      expansion and may indicate electrolyte
      imbalances)
   5. Renal system
      a. Observe volume, color, and specific
         gravity of urine
         (1) Report decrease urinary output
             below 25 ml/hour to physician
         (2) Lowered specific gravity—lower
             than 1.010
             (a) Overhydration
             (b) Renal tubular dysfunction
         (3) Elevated specific gravity—greater
             than 1.020
             (a) Dehydration
             (b) Oliguria
             (c) Presence of blood in urine
   6. Employ comfort measures and the judicious
      administration of narcotics to relieve pain
   7. Utilize passive and active range of motion
      exercises to prevent complications—patient
      having coronary artery surgery should be
      positioned in supine position for 48 hours
      to prevent hypotension; after this period, the
      patient may be turned from back to right
      side every two hours
2. Splenectomy—removal of the spleen
A. Rationale—rupture due to trauma, tumor,
   idiopathic thrombocytopenic purpura, and acquired hemolytic anemia
B. Preoperative nursing management
   1. Administer whole blood, as ordered
   2. Insert nasogastric tube to decrease post-
      operative abdominal distention, as ordered
C. Postoperative nursing measures are designed to
   prevent complications
   1. Observe for signs of hemorrhage—increased
      bleeding tendency in patients with thrombo-
      cytopenia purpura due to decreased platelet
      counts

2. Observe for gastrointestinal distention—removal of enlarged spleen may result in distention of stomach and intestines to fill void
3. Recognize that temperature elevation up to 101 F is not unusual for ten or more days after splenectomy
4. Manually splint incision when patient coughs—high incidence of atelectasis and pneumonia due to tendency to decrease diaphragmatic excursion with upper abdominal surgery

3. Vein ligation and stripping
A. Rationale—advancing varicosities, stasis ulcerations, and cosmetic needs of patient
B. Postoperative nursing measures are designed to prevent complications and to promote health habits that help decrease recurrence of varicosities
  1. Assist with early and frequent ambulation—prevents thrombic formation
  2. Check elastic bandages and dressings frequently for signs of bleeding
  3. Review health practices that prevent venous stasis
    a. Weight reduction
    b. Avoid garments that constrict venous flow, such as garters and girdles
    c. Frequent changes of position
      (1) If sitting—walk several minutes each hour to promote circulation
      (2) If standing—sit and elevate legs when they become tired
    d. Utilize support hose or elastic stockings to enhance venous return

GASTROINTESTINAL SYSTEM

1. Gastrostomy—the surgical establishment of a fistulous opening between the stomach and the skin to establish a route for administration of food and fluid to the patient
2. Gastric surgeries to relieve complications of peptic ulcers—hemorrhage, perforation, pyloric stenosis or obstruction and/or failure of medical management to promote healing
A. Vagotomy with gastrojejunostomy or pyloroplasty
  1. Ligation of vagas nerve results in decreased secretions and atonicity of stomach muscle, necessitating an additional drainage procedure
  2. Gastrojejunostomy provides a second outlet

for gastric contents through the anastomosis of jejunum to stomach
  3. Pyloroplasty divides the pylorus on gastric and duodenal sides transversely, thus providing a larger opening from the stomach to the duodenum
B. Vagotomy and antrectomy
  1. Resection of vagus nerve and removal of the antral portion of the stomach
  2. Antral portion of stomach produces gastrin, which stimulates acid secretion
  3. Procedure removes more of stomach and prevents later duodenal ulceration due to antral stasis
C. Partial gastrectomy (Billroth I)
  1. Distal one-third to one-half of stomach is removed, and the duodenum is anastomosed to remaining portion
  2. May be done with or without vagotomy
D. Hemigastrectomy and vagotomy (Billroth II)
  1. First part of duodenum, the pylorus, and up to one-half of the stomach are removed
  2. The duodenal stump is closed, and the jejunum is anastomosed to the remaining stomach
E. Preoperative nursing measures are designed to relieve anxiety and to physically prepare the gastrointestinal system for surgery
  1. Allow for verbalization of feelings and fears—aids in identifying factors that produce stress and predispose to ulcer formation
  2. Insert nasogastric tube on morning of surgery to decompress stomach and intestines
    a. Prevents vomiting and flatulence
    b. Reduces stress on suture line
    c. Prevents secretions from infiltrating site of the anastomosis.
  3. Enemas, as ordered
F. Postoperative nursing measures are designed to promote comfort, wound healing, and nutrition and to prevent complications
  1. Administers analgesics, as ordered—assures deep breathing, coughing, and turning, preventing vascular and pulmonary complications
  2. Initiate nasogastric suction
    a. Check drainage—report excessive bleeding to physician; drainage normally bloody for first 10 to 14 hours postsurgery, then turns dark green
    b. Irrigate nasogastric tube with saline, as ordered

c. Relieve discomfort of nasogastric tube with frequent mouth care, applying water-base lubricant or lotion around nostril and properly taping tube to face

d. Maintain low suction to prevent damage to gastric mucosa or suture line

3. Administer parenteral infusions, as ordered—Patient remains NPO one to three days

4. Check dressings for bleeding

5. Check for bowel sounds beginning second postoperative day

   a. Oral fluids are begun after bowel sounds return and adequate healing of suture line has taken place

   b. Feedings progress from 30 ml water to bland diet divided into six feedings

   c. Observe for nausea, vomiting, and distention

6. Instruct the patients in diet modifications to avoid "dumping syndrome"

   a. Dumping syndrome is a hypoglycemic-type attack that occurs when high osmotic fluids pass quickly into the jejunum producing hypovolemia and initiating the sympathoadrenal response; symptoms include fainting, dizziness, sweating, and increased pulse rate

   b. Treatment of dumping syndrome
      1. Avoid foods high in salt and carbohydrates
      2. Eat frequent small meals
      3. Take fluids between rather than with meals
      4. Eat regularly and slowly
      5. Rest after meals

3. **Gastric resection**—treatment of choice for cancer of the stomach

A. Total gastric resection involves complete removal of the stomach and anastomosis of the esophagus and jejunum

   1. Nursing interventions are as given previously for other gastric surgeries, plus measures designed for chest surgery (see p. 160), since the chest cavity is usually entered

   2. Meals are frequent and small to allow absorption in the intestinal tract

   3. Vitamins, particularly vitamin B$_{12}$ and iron, are administered to prevent pernicious anemia

      a. Removal of stomach halts secretion of

"intrinsic factor" needed for absorption of vitamin B$_{12}$

      b. Decreased levels of hydrochloric acid inhibit iron absorption

   4. Primary goal of supportive care is to assist patient to maintain the activities of daily living as long as possible with comfort

B. Partial or subtotal gastric resection is the same as the gastrectomy for ulcer (Billroth II)

4. **Appendectomy**—removal of the appendix

A. Rationale—acute appendicitis

   1. Signs and symptoms
      a. Generalized abdominal pain that localizes gradually in right lower quadrant of abdomen
      b. Low-grade fever
      c. Rebound tenderness and some rigidity in lower right quadrant
      d. Moderate leukocytosis
      e. Anorexia, nausea, and vomiting

B. Preoperative nursing measures are designed to prevent rupture of the appendix

   1. Laxatives and enemas are contraindicated
   2. Utilize conservative nursing measures to relieve pain until diagnosis is made—lying with right knee flexed occasionally relieves pain

C. Postoperative nursing measures are designed to promote comfort and prevent complications (see postoperative care, p. 154)

5. **Herniorraphy**—surgical repair of hernia (protrusion of abdominal contents through a weakened area of abdominal cavity: inguinal, femoral, umbilical, or ventral)

A. Rationale—prevention of strangulation or incarceration of intestines

B. See preoperative care, pp. 147-152

C. Postoperative nursing care is designed to prevent disruption of the repair

   1. Encourage deep breathing and turning more than coughing
      a. Coughing increases intra-abdominal pressures, placing stress on incision
      b. Assist patient to splint incision when coughing

   2. Administer mild cathartics, as ordered—straining during defecation increases intra-abdominal pressures

   3. Should swelling of scrotum occur, utilize ice bags and elevate scrotum on rolled towel to reduce edema

   4. Postoperative teaching
      a. Encourage patient to stand up straight

as stooping will shorten abdominal muscles, making later posture corrections difficult

    b. Remind patient not to lift anything heavy and that strenuous activity must be avoided for three to six weeks

6. Ileostomy—surgical formation of a fistula or artificial anus between the abdominal wall and ileum

A. Rationale—in ulcerative colitis when the patient's condition does not respond to medical regimen or in which there is profuse bleeding, stricture, or perforation of the bowel or carcinoma is suspected

B. Preoperative nursing measures are designed to relieve anxiety and promote a positive self-image in the patient

    1. Provide accurate, brief, and reassuring explanations of all procedures

        a. Allow time for patient to assimilate information emotionally

        b. Plan to repeat explanations as necessary

    2. Allow for verbalizations of fears, fantasies, and questions

    3. Introduce patient to a member of an "Ostomy Club" if possible—provides model for patient of someone who has successfully mastered or adjusted to ileostomy

    4. Additional physical preparation for surgery includes

        a. Fluid, electrolyte, and blood replacement

        b. Low-residue or clear-liquid diet

        c. Neomycin SO_4 or sulfonamides to reduce intestinal flora

        d. Enemas until clear

        e. Insertion of nasogastric tube

C. Postoperative nursing measures are designed to maintain fluid, electrolyte, and nutritional balance, to promote physical and psychologic comfort, and to assist patient in assuming self-care activities

    1. Administer parenteral fluids with electrolytes and vitamins, as ordered

        a. Large amounts of fluid and electrolytes may be lost through ileostomy

        b. Maintain strict intake and output records, as deficits can develop quickly

    2. Initiate ostomy care

        a. Apply temporary ileostomy appliance

            (1) Ileostomy drainage contains digestive enzymes, which can

excoriate skin

            (2) Appliance must be worn at all times

        b. Change appliance prn

            (1) Observe color, consistency, and amount of drainage

            (2) Avoid damaging skin by gently peeling appliance from outside toward midline

        c. Keep skin around stoma clean and dry, applying soothing ointments as necessary

        d. Control odors

            (1) Frequently empty and rinse bag

            (2) Add deodorizing drops to bag

            (3) Administer bismuth or chlorophyll preparation, as ordered

            (4) Ventilate and deodorize room

        e. Recognize that loss of anatomical integrity initiates grieving process

            (1) Accept feelings of depression, silence, apathy, or disinterest

            (2) Assist family in understanding patient behavior

        f. Assist in learning self-management by explaining procedures and why they are done

            (1) Slowly involve patient in procedures as they are being performed

            (2) Encourage movement toward independence in bowel care

            (3) Provide for practice sessions with nursing supervision

    3. Assist patient to identify fears and concerns in home situation—refer patient to community health nurse for follow-up home care

    4. Inform patient of the importance of diet management

        a. Encourage food high in sodium and potassium—bananas, bouillon, and citrus juices

        b. Avoid gas-producing, highly seasoned foods; also nuts, raisins, and raw fruits

    5. Advise patient of possible complications that require medical intervention

        a. Nausea, vomiting, and diarrhea—may lead to fluid and electrolyte imbalance

        b. Abdominal cramps, vomiting, and watery or no discharge—signs of intestinal obstruction

7. Colostomy—the surgical formation of an artificial anus between the surface of the abdominal wall and the colon

A. Rationale—intestinal obstruction, cancer of the colon or rectum, severe diverticulitis, infection, perforation, or trauma

B. Types of colostomies
1. Single-barrel—only one loop of bowel is opened to abdominal surface
   a. Permanent if bowel distal to it has been resected
   b. Permanent colostomy usually done close to the end of the descending colon
2. Double-barreled—consists of two loops of bowel, a proximal and a distal portion, opened to abdominal wall
   a. May be temporary or permanent
   b. Temporary colostomy usually located at midpoint in descending colon or in the transverse colon

C. Preoperative nursing care is designed to alleviate fears and promote a positive self-image in the patient (see preoperative ileostomy care, p. 171)

D. Postoperative nursing measures are designed to promote physiologic and psychologic equilibrium (see p. 154) and to assist patient in assuming self-care of the colostomy
1. Initiate ostomy care
   a. Apply appliance as soon as possible
   b. Measure stoma each day for current appliance size
   c. Change appliance prn
   d. Keep skin around stoma clean and dry, applying protective creams as indicated
   e. Control odors
2. Institute colostomy irrigations seven to ten days after surgery
   a. Aids in controlling elimination and establishing pattern of evacuation
   b. Prevents intestinal obstruction and reduces excoriation of skin
3. Explain irrigation procedure and equipment in a concise, reassuring manner
   a. Involve patient and family with procedure as soon as they are emotionally able
   b. Encourage return demonstrations
4. Observe the following precautions during colostomy irrigation
   a. Place patient in a sitting position in bed or on commode—facilitates the flow of expelled drainage into receptacle or toilet; also some patients find it helps stimulate straining, as if having anal elimination
   b. Insert lubricated catheter gently 4 to 6 inches (10 to 15 cm) allowing solution to flow into colon slowly—slow-flowing solution relaxes the bowel and facilitates insertion of the tube
   c. Clamp tubing and allow patient to rest if cramping occurs—cramps generally occur due to rapid flow or too much solution
   d. Allow 25 to 45 minutes for return of flow—abdominal massage or position change may assist slow return
5. Allow patient to verbalize feelings and reassure that radical changes in life-style are not necessary
   a. Involve in colostomy club if one is available
   b. Refer to community health nurse for follow-up at home
6. Inform patient of foods that might increase flatulence—corn, beans, cabbage, broccoli, and cauliflower
7. Inform patient of signs indicating obstruction—abdominal cramps, vomiting, and watery or no discharge

8. **Gallbladder surgeries**—removal of stones, bile, or pus in the gallbladder itself (cholecystostomy), in the common duct (choledochostomy), or complete removal of the gallbladder (cholecystectomy)

A. Rationale—acute or chronic cholecystitis, cholelithiasis, or obstruction of the bile duct

B. Preoperative nursing management is designed to prepare the patient physically and psychologically for surgical procedure
1. Explain and assist patient with presurgical diagnostic evaluation
   a. Gallbladder x-rays
   b. Blood, urine, and stool specimens
2. Initiate preoperative instructions (see p. 150)

C. Postoperative nursing care is designed to provide for T-tube or cholecystostomy tube drainage, prevent complications, and promote physiologic and psychologic equilibrium (see p. 154)
1. Connect nasogastric tube to intermittent suction, as ordered
2. Connect T-tube to closed gravity drainage
   a. Maintain semi-Fowler's position if not contraindicated—facilitates gravity drainage
   b. Provide enough tubing to allow turning without tension

c. Record bile output every eight hours and report increases

d. Keep dressings clean and dry—apply protective ointment as necessary to protect skin

e. Clamp T-tube, as ordered
   (1) Observe for abdominal distention, pain, nausea, chills, or fever
   (2) If symptoms appear, unclamp T-tube and report to physician

3. Observe skin, sclera, urine, and bowel movements for indication of jaundice

4. Instruct in importance of maintaining a low-fat diet for at least two to three months
   a. Eat only foods allowed
   b. Add fatty foods as tolerated

9. **Hemorrhoidectomy**—removal of all internal and external hemorrhoids by ligation and excision, clamping and cauterization, or other procedure

A. Rationale—bleeding, prolapsed, strangulated, or thrombosed hemorrhoids

B. Preoperative nursing measures are designed to promote comfort and physical equilibrium
   1. Administer low-residue diet—reduces stool formation
   2. Administer cleansing tap-water enemas, as ordered

C. Postoperative nursing measures are designed to reduce pain, promote gastrointestinal function, and prevent complications
   1. Administer ice packs, warm compresses, sitz baths, analgesic ointments, or narcotics to relieve discomfort and pain, as ordered
   2. Assist patient in assuming a position of comfort
   3. Assist with voiding to reduce bladder distention and urinary retention
      a. Assist men patients in standing
      b. Utilize bedside commode for women
      c. Encourage fluids
      d. Administer bethanechol (Urecholine) Cl, as ordered (see Appendix F, Drugs)
      e. Catheterize if necessary
   4. Assist with the reestablishment of normal bowel patterns
      a. Liquid or low-residue diet until successful defecation
         (1) Prevents bowel movement until some healing has taken place
         (2) Modifies consistency of stool
      b. Mineral oil or psyllium (Metamucil) to facilitate elimination, as ordered

c. Low oil-retention enema, as ordered, usually third postoperative day

d. Reduce discomfort of first defecation by administering analgesic 30 minutes before patient attempts defecation
   (1) Provide privacy but remain with patient and observe for dizziness or fainting
   (2) Utilize moist cotton rather than toilet paper to cleanse area

e. Follow each defecation with a warm sitz bath—promotes healing and reduces discomfort

5. Observe for signs of hemorrhage—may occur immediately or four to ten days after surgery

6. Should hemorrhage occur
   a. Place patient on bedrest
   b. Record vital signs
   c. Note amount and color of drainage
   d. Apply pressure dressing and ice pack
   e. Notify physician

GENITOURINARY SYSTEM

1. **Prostatectomies**

A. Types
   1. Transurethral resection of prostate (TUR)—removal of obstructive prostatic tissue by an electric wire (resectoscope) introduced through the urethra
   2. Suprapubic prostatectomy—low midline incision is made directly over the bladder; bladder is opened and prostatic tissue is removed through incision in urethral mucosa
   3. Retropubic prostatectomy—removal of hypertrophied prostatic tissue through a low abdominal incision; bladder is not opened
   4. Perineal prostatectomy—removal of prostatic tissue is accomplished through an incision made between the scrotum and the rectum; usually results in impotency

B. Rationale—to relieve urinary retention and frequency caused by benign prostatic hypertrophy or cancer of the prostate

C. Preoperative nursing measures are designed to facilitate optimal kidney function
   1. Sterile insertion of indwelling urinary catheter or suprapubic cystostomy—to reestablish urinary drainage
   2. Antibiotics, as ordered—to prevent and control infection

3. Push fluids to ensure adequate hydration—patients often limit their own fluid intake because of urinary frequency
   a. Monitor intake and output
   b. Weigh daily
4. Assist with renal function studies—determine if backflow has damaged kidneys
5. Assist with hematologic studies—to identify any clotting defects, as hemorrhage is a major postoperative complication
6. Provide diet high in protein, vitamins, and iron

D. Postoperative nursing care is designed to promote optimal bladder drainage, prevent complications, promote comfort, and assist in rehabilitation
   1. Utilize sterile closed-gravity system for urinary drainage—maintain external traction, as ordered
   2. In suprapubic prostatectomy, connect suprapubic catheter to closed-gravity drainage system—observe character, amount, and flow of urethral and suprapubic catheters
   3. Check dressings
      a. Keep dry and clean
      b. Reinforce if necessary
      c. Notify physician of excess bleeding
   4. Maintain continuous bladder irrigation, as ordered
      a. Helpful in controlling bleeding and keeping clots from forming
      b. Observe frequently for bladder distention
         (1) Distinct mound over pubis
         (2) Slow drop in collecting bottle
         (3) Irrigate catheter, as ordered
      c. Observe for signs of increased bleeding
         (1) Bright red drainage and clots
         (2) Cool clammy skin, pallor, and increased pulse rate
   5. Explain purpose of catheter to patient
      a. Urge to void due to bladder spasm
      b. Pulling on catheter will increase bleeding and clot formation
   6. Administer anticholinergic medications to reduce bladder spasms (see Appendix F, Drugs)
   7. Diet—clear-liquid to regular diet as tolerated
   8. Force fluids to 3000 ml per day unless contraindicated
   9. After removal of suprapubic catheter, observe for urinary drainage q4h for 24 hours
      a. Administer skin care
      b. Report excessive drainage to physician
   10. Ambulate, as ordered, keeping urinary drainage bag dependent
   11. Deal with fears of incontinence and loss of male identity
   12. After urinary catheter is removed
      a. Note time and amount of each voiding
      b. Begin perineal exercises—buttocks are pressed together and held in that position as long as possible; 10 to 20 times each hour; assist patient in regaining urinary control
      c. Inform patient he can expect "dribbling" following catheter removal
   13. Postoperative instructions include avoiding
      a. Long automobile trips—increases tendency to bleed
      b. Alcoholic beverages—causes burning on urination
      c. Tub baths—increases possibility of infections

2. **Nephrectomy**—removal of a kidney; may be done through a flank, retroperitoneal, abdominal, thoracic, or thoracic-abdominal approach
A. Rationale—malignant tumor or severe trauma resulting in nonfunctioning organ
B. Preoperative nursing care is designed to optimize physical and psychologic function (see pp. 147–151 for general preoperative assessment)
   1. Assist in diagnostic studies designed to evaluate renal function
      a. Serum electrolytes, BUN, creatinine, and phenolsulfonphthalein
      b. Intravenous urography
C. Postoperative nursing measures are designed to promote comfort and prevent complications (see p. 154)
   1. Observe for signs of paralytic ileus—a fairly common complication following renal surgery (p. 162)
   2. Assess fluid and electrolyte balance by weighing patient daily—maintain within 2% of preoperative levels
   3. Observe carefully for signs of hemorrhage (see p. 158)

3. **Ureterolithotomy**—key points similar to nephrectomy

4. **Kidney transplantation**—placement of a donor (sibling, parent, cadaver) kidney into the iliac fossa of a recipient and the anastomosis of its ureter to the bladder of the recipient

A. Rationale—end-stage of renal disease
B. Donor selection
  1. Sibling or parent donor—survival rate of kidney is greater and is preferred procedure for transplantation
  2. Cadaver—greater rate of rejection following transplantation, but the majority of transplants are with cadaver kidneys
C. Preoperative nursing care is designed to promote optimal physical and emotional support for patient and family
  1. Patient teaching should include
    a. Nature of surgery and placement of kidney
    b. Possibility of postoperative dialysis
    c. Purpose and effects of immunosuppressive therapy
    d. Rationale for employing reverse isolation and its techniques
    e. Drainage tubes that will be inserted during surgery
    f. Postoperative turning, coughing, and deep breathing exercises
    g. Assurance that medication will be given for relief of pain
  2. Identify and deal with the fears and anxieties of patient and family
  3. Support patient who needs continued dialysis prior to surgery—optimal preoperative physical condition requires removal of waste products and fluid, important to electrolyte and acid-base balance
  4. Begin administration of immunosuppressive drugs
    a. Azathioprine—an antimetabolite that interferes with cellular division
      (1) Results in dysfunction and death of immunologic and other body cells
      (2) Side effects
        (a) Gastrointestinal bleeding
        (b) Bone marrow depression
        (c) Development of malignant neoplasms
        (d) Infection
        (e) Liver damage
    b. Glucocorticoids—believed to effect lymphocyte production by inhibiting nucleic acid synthesis
      (1) Anti-inflammatory action helps prevent tissue damage if rejection occurs
      (2) Side effects

        (a) Stress ulcer with bleeding
        (b) Decreased glucose tolerance
        (c) Muscle weakness
        (d) Osteoporosis
        (e) Moon face
        (f) Acne and striae
        (g) Depression and hallucinations
D. Postoperative nursing measures are designed to maintain urinary output and fluid and electrolyte balance, observe for signs of rejection, prevent infections, and promote physical and emotional comfort
  1. Institute reverse isolation techniques
  2. Attach indwelling catheter to closed drainage system
    a. Monitor color, characteristics, and amount of urinary output
      (1) Kidney may begin to function immediately, putting out large amount of urine
      (2) If kidney does not function within 24 to 48 hours, hemodialysis is instituted
      (3) Kidney may not function for a week or more
      (4) Gross hematuria or clots in urine should be reported immediately to physician
        (a) Carry out perineal care each shift—prevents bacteria from entering meatus and bladder
  3. Institute and maintain respiratory hygiene procedures
    a. Coughing and deep breathing
    b. Clapping
    c. Blow bottles
    d. IPPB
    e. Mouth care
  4. Observe for fluid and electrolyte disturbances
    a. Hypovolemia
      (1) Decreased blood pressure
      (2) Increased pulse rate
      (3) Increased hematocrit (hemoconcentration)
      (4) Confusion, hallucinations, and delirium
    b. Hypervolemia
      (1) Hypertension
      (2) Peripheral and pulmonary edema
      (3) Puffy face
      (4) Distended neck veins

(5) Tachycardia

(6) Increased CVP

c. Hyperkalemia

   (1) Intestinal colic and diarrhea

   (2) Muscle weakness

   (3) Flaccid paralysis

d. Azotemia and acidosis

   (1) Increased rate and depth of respirations

   (2) Irritability, lethargy

   (3) Decreasing ability to carry on a conversation

5. Observe for early signs and symptoms of rejection

  a. In functioning and nonfunctioning kidneys

   (1) Low-grade fever

   (2) Tenderness and/or pain over graft site

  b. In functioning kidney

   (1) Decreasing urine output

   (2) Decreased creatinine clearance

   (3) Increasing serum potassium and BUN

   (4) Decreasing urinary sodium

   (5) Increased proteinuria

6. Observe for side effects of immunosuppressive therapy

7. Promote psychosocial adjustment

  a. Assure patient that feelings of depression may be drug related

  b. Allow verbalization of fears

  c. Deal with feelings due to transition from chronically ill state to relative state of wellness

   (1) Reassumption of role responsibilities

   (2) Alteration of dependent habits and life-style

   (3) Sexual adjustments

    (a) Problems of contraception

    (b) Normal sexual development and attendant confusion in adolescents

   (4) Bodily changes due to steroid therapy

   (5) Reemployment or new employment

8. Postoperative teachings include

  a. Dietary limitations, as ordered

  b. Timing, dosage, and side effects of medications

  c. Precautions and activity restrictions

  d. How to measure intake and output and keep records of daily weight

  e. How to take and record temperature

  f. Means of collecting 24-hour urine specimens

  g. Importance of follow-up visits

  h. Signs and symptoms of rejection and infection

SURGERIES OF FEMALE REPRODUCTIVE SYSTEM

1. Hysterectomy—removal of the uterus

A. Types

  1. Total hysterectomy—removal of entire uterus, may be done abdominally or vaginally

  2. Panhysterectomy—removal of uterus, tubes, and ovaries

B. Rationale—cancer of the cervix, severe endometritis, cancer of the uterus, uterine prolapse, and fibroid tumors

C. Preoperative nursing measures are designed to reduce anxiety and depression and promote optimal physical and psychologic functions

  1. Allow verbalization of feelings

   a. Many women fear the loss of femininity and changes in secondary sex characteristics

   b. Patient may fear cancer or the discovery of venereal disease

   c. Disappointment may be acute if woman has not had children

  2. Assess relationships with husband, family, and significant others

  3. Administer vaginal douche or enemas, as ordered

D. Postoperative nursing measures are designed to prevent complications and support coping mechanisms (see p. 154)

  1. Catheter care—temporary bladder atony may be present as a result of edema or nerve trauma

  2. Observe for abdominal distention

   a. Utilize rectal tube to decrease flatus

   b. Auscultate abdomen for bowel sounds

   c. Encourage early ambulation

  3. Utilize measures to decrease pelvic congestion and prevent venous stasis

   a. Avoid high-Fowler's position

   b. Apply antiembolic stockings, as ordered

   c. Institute passive leg exercises

  4. Apply abdominal support, as ordered

  5. Allow for verbalization of feelings

6. Discharge teachings include
   a. Avoidance of coitus or vaginal douching until advised by physician
   b. Avoidance of heavy lifting for at least two months
   c. Explain hormonal replacement therapy if applicable
   d. Avoidance of sitting for long periods of time and of wearing constrictive clothing, which tend to increase pelvic congestion
   e. Explain that menstruation will no longer occur
   f. Explain importance of reporting symptoms such as fever, increased or bloody vaginal discharge, and hot flashes to physician
2. **Radical mastectomy**—surgical removal of the entire breast; subclavicular, apical, pectoral, and axillary nodes; and the pectoralis major and minor muscles; there are several modifications to this procedure
A. Rationale—carcinoma of the breast, intraductal papillomas, and Paget's disease
B. Preoperative nursing measures are designed to support the patient and family (see pp. 147–152)
   1. Allow for verbalization of fears and feelings and dispelling misconceptions
   2. Answer all questions clearly and concisely
   3. Institute preoperative instruction
C. Postoperative nursing measures are designed to minimize complications and facilitate physical and psychologic functioning (see postoperative care, p. 154)
   1. Observe pressure dressings, axilla and under shoulder, for bleeding
      a. Report excessive drainage or bloody drainage
      b. Do not remove dressings but reinforce if necessary
   2. Connect drainage tubes to suction machine or portable suction (Hemo-Vac)—drains serum and blood, allowing skin flap to adhere to chest wall
   3. Facilitate venous and lymphatic drainage
      a. Place patient in semi-Fowler's position
      b. Elevate arm above right atrium with pillows
   4. Maintain joint mobility
      a. Flexion and extension of fingers and elbows
      b. Initiate active ROM exercises as soon as

ordered to prevent ankylosis—exercises should not be painful
   c. Encourage self-care activities, as ordered
5. If skin graft has been performed, check donor site every four hours—limit active arm exercises
6. Assist with emotional response to changes in body image
   a. Encourage patient to look at scar
   b. Involve patient in incision care as tolerated
   c. Refer to "Reach for Recovery" program of American Cancer Society
7. Inform patient about occurrences of postoperative edema and importance of avoiding even minor injury to the arm, since removal of lymph nodes decreases the body's ability to combat infection

ENDOCRINE SYSTEM

1. **Thyroidectomy**—partial or total removal of the thyroid gland
A. Rationale—total removal if malignancy is present; partial removal (five-sixths) to correct hyperthyroidism
B. Preoperative nursing care is designed to promote normal thyroid function and reduce side effects of thyrotoxicosis
   1. Provide quiet, nonstimulating, stable environment
      a. Avoid discrepancies in timing and performance of procedures
      b. Restrict visitors if indicated
      c. Assist with activities that are difficult due to tremors—pouring beverages or tying shoes
   2. Provide high-protein, high-carbohydrate, high-vitamin B diet—to rebuild lost tissue and meet increased energy needs
      a. Avoid stimulating beverages such as coffee, tea, and colas
      b. Provide food choices when possible
   3. Administer medications, as ordered
      a. Antithyroid preparations—propylthiouracil and methimazole (Tapazole)
         (1) Slow-acting chemicals that inhibit synthesis of thyroxine
         (2) Important to time and space dosages to maintain therapeutic levels

(3) Side effects
  (a) Sore throat
  (b) Fever
  (c) Rash
  (d) Jaundice
b. Iodine preparations—Lugol's solution
  (1) Iodine preparations reduce thyroid vascularity and help prevent postoperative hemorrhage
  (2) Measure solution accurately
  (3) Add drops to fruit juice or milk to disguise unpleasant taste
C. Postoperative nursing care is designed to promote physical and emotional equilibrium and to prevent complications
  1. Place patient in semi-Fowler's position, immobilizing head with pillows or sandbags
    a. Prevents flexion or hyperextension of neck, thus reducing stress on sutures
    b. Reduces edema and promotes venous return
  2. Support patient's neck by placing a hand on either side during position changes
    a. As soon as patients are able, teach them to support weight of the head by placing their hands at back of the neck while moving in bed
    b. After sutures are removed, institute ROM exercises (flexion, lateral movement, and hyperextension), as ordered—prevents contractures
  3. Prevent or relieve complications
    a. Hemorrhage
      (1) Check vital signs
      (2) Check dressings for drainage
      (3) Reinforce dressing as needed
      (4) Report excess drainage to physician
    b. Respiratory obstruction
      (1) Turn, cough, and deep breathe
      (2) Apply ice packs to incision, as ordered—to promote comfort and reduce edema
    c. Hoarseness and weakness of voice due to laryngeal nerve damage
      (1) Check quality of voice
      (2) Avoid unnecessary talking
      (3) Establish alternate means of communication—pencil and paper
    d. Hypocalcemia and tetany due to accidental removal of parathyroid gland
      (1) Check reflexes q2h and report any muscle twitching immediately

    (a) Chvostek's sign—tapping of the face in front of the ear produces spasm of ipsilateral facial muscles
    (b) Trousseau's sign—compression of upper arm elicits carpal (wrist) spasm
  4. Promote comfort measures
    a. Administer narcotics, as ordered
    b. Offer iced fluids (if preferred and tolerated)—soothes sore throat
  5. Ambulation and diet as tolerated
2. Adrenalectomy—surgical excision of adrenal tumor
A. Rationale—pheochromocytoma, primary aldosteronism, and Cushing's syndrome; bilateral adrenalectomy may be done for cancer of the breast or prostate with metastasis
B. Preoperative nursing measures are designed to reduce risk of postoperative complications
  1. Steroid therapy is discontinued to prevent postoperative infection
  2. Antihypertensive drugs are discontinued as surgery may result in severe hypotension
  3. Administer phenobarbital for sedation, as ordered
  4. Institute general preoperative care
C. Postoperative nursing care is designed to promote hormonal balance and prevent postoperative complications
  1. Administer hydrocortisone parenteral therapy, as ordered—rate dictated by fluid and electrolyte balance, blood sugar, and blood pressure
  2. Monitor vital signs per protocol and prn for 48 hours or until stability is regained
  3. If on vasopressor drugs such as metaraminol (Aramine) bitartrate are used, check vital signs every 15 minutes
    a. Maintain flow rate, as ordered
    b. Notify physician of significant changes
    c. Readings that are normotensive for some may be hypotensive for patient who has been hypertensive
    d. Observe for signs of decreased perfusion—confusion, oliguria, tachycardia, and increased pulse and respiratory rate
  4. NPO—attach nasogastric tube to intermittent suction; abdominal distention is common side effect of this surgery
  5. Promote respiratory hygiene and prevent

complications
   a. Turn, cough, and deep breathe
   b. Splint flank incision with coughing
   c. Administer narcotic 30 minutes before coughing—as flank incision is close to diaphragm, coughing may be extremely painful
   d. Place in flat or semi-Fowler's position
   e. Auscultate breath sounds q2h—decreased or absent breath sounds, sudden chest pain, and dyspnea should be reported immediately, as spontaneous pneumothorax can occur
   f. Administer frequent mouth care
6. Check dressings, reinforcing as needed
7. Ambulate, as ordered
   a. Check blood pressure every 15 minutes when ambulation is first attempted
   b. Apply elastic stockings to lower extremities to enhance stability of vascular system
8. Maintain diet as tolerated after nasogastric tube is removed
9. Postoperative teachings should include
   a. Signs and symptoms of adrenal crisis
      (1) Rapid, weak, or thready pulse
      (2) Elevated temperature
      (3) Restlessness
      (4) Severe weakness and lethargy
      (5) Headache
      (6) Convulsions
   b. Importance of maintaining steroid therapy schedule—to ensure therapeutic serum level
      (1) Weigh daily
      (2) Clinitest daily
      (3) Report undesirable side effects to physician
   c. Importance of avoiding persons with infections—decreased resistance
   d. Importance of adequate rest, moderate exercise, and good nutrition
3. **Hypophysectomy**—complete removal of hypophysis or pituitary gland

NEUROLOGICAL SYSTEM—EYE AND EAR

1. **Cataract removal**—removal of opacified lens; opacity may be due to degeneration with age, toxic, metabolic, or traumatic injuries
A. Rationale—loss of vision
B. Preoperative nursing care is designed to reduce

patient anxiety
1. Preoperative teaching
   a. Instruct patient not to rub, touch, or squeeze eyes shut after surgery
   b. Inform patient that eye patches will be on after surgery
   c. Reassure patient that assistance will be given for needs
2. Administer mydriatic eye drops prior to surgery (see Appendix F, Drugs)
   a. Note dilatation of pupils
   b. Avoid glaring lights
3. Determine degree of sight by testing visual fields and acuity
C. Postoperative nursing measures are designed to reduce stress on the sutures, prevent hemorrhage, and promote psychologic well being
1. Maintain bedrest up to 24 hours in a flat or low-Fowler's position
2. Patient may lie on back and turn to *unoperated* side—turning to operative side increases pressures
3. Avoid activities that may increase intraocular pressures
   a. Antiemetic for nausea, avoid vomiting if possible
   b. Deep breathe but avoid coughing
   c. Brushing teeth, hair, shaving, bending, and stooping are usually forbidden
      (1) Provide mouth wash
      (2) Provide hair care
      (3) Place equipment and personal items within easy reach
      (4) Utilize "step-in" slippers
4. Provide frequent contacts with elderly to prevent development of emotional disturbances associated with sensory deprivation
5. Diet and ambulation, as ordered
6. Assist patient in adjusting to temporary cataract spectacle lenses
   a. Explain about magnification of objects, perceptual distortion, and blind areas in peripheral vision
   b. Guide patients through some activities with glasses on to help them adjust to distortions and spatial relationships
   c. To decrease distortion, instruct patient to look through the central portion of the lens and to turn head to the side when looking to the side
7. Involve patient and family in postoperative teaching

a. Instillation of eye drops
b. Signs and symptoms of infections
   (1) Redness and pain
   (2) Edema and drainage
c. Need to continue wearing eye shield at night to prevent injury
d. Avoidance of heavy lifting
e. Encouraging independence in the performance of self-care activities

2. **Retinal detachment**—separation of retina from choroid as the result of trauma or degeneration; vision becomes blurred, patchy, and may be totally lost
A. Surgical interventions
   1. Electrodiathermy—electrode needle is passed through sclera, draining the subretinal fluid; retina will then adhere to the choroid
   2. Cryosurgery—super-cooled probe is applied to the sclera, causing a scar, which pulls the choroid and retina together
   3. Laser beam—a beam of intense light from a carbon arc is directed through the dilated pupil onto the retina; effect is the same as in electrodiathermy
   4. Sclera buckling—the sclera is resected or shortened to enhance the contact between the choroid and retina
B. Preoperative nursing care is designed to orient the patient to environment and to reduce anxiety
   1. Encourage verbalization of feelings and answer all questions, reinforce physician's explanation of surgical procedures
   2. Prevent further detachment by keeping patient quiet in bed
      a. Eyes are usually covered to reduce stress and provide rest
      b. Position so that retinal hole is in the lowest position
   3. Administer medications, as ordered
      a. Cycloplegic or mydriatics
      b. Keep pupils widely dilated
C. Postoperative nursing care is designed to reduce intraocular stress, prevent hemorrhage, and support the patient's coping mechanisms
   1. Bedrest in flat or low-Fowler's position—sandbags may be used to position head
   2. Movements that increase intraocular pressures are usually restricted (see p. 179)
   3. Administer medications, as ordered (see Appendix F, Drugs)
      a. Mydriatics
      b. Antibiotics—prevent infections

c. Corticosteroids—reduce inflammation
4. Employ ROM exercises and apply elastic stockings to legs to avoid thrombus formation during period of bedrest
5. To allay anxiety, plan all care with the patient
   a. Allow patient to verbalize feelings and fears
   b. Encourage family interaction and diversional activities

3. **Stapedectomy**—removal of the stapes and its replacement with a prosthesis
A. Rationale—deafness due to otosclerosis, which fixes the stapes, preventing it from oscillating and transmitting vibrations to the fluids in the inner ear
B. Preoperative nursing care is designed to provide emotional support and to assist patient in understanding the nature of the procedure
   1. Preoperative teaching includes
      a. Informing patient of the importance of keeping head in position ordered by physician postoperatively
      b. Necessity of avoiding activities such as sneezing, blowing the nose, and vomiting, which increase pressure in eustachian tubes
      c. Breathing exercises
C. Postoperative nursing care is designed to promote physical and psychologic equilibrium
   1. Place patient in position ordered by physician—this varies according to preference
   2. Raise siderails as vertigo is a common experience
   3. Check ear dressings frequently
   4. Administer medications, as ordered
      a. Antiemetic to control vomiting
      b. Analgesics to control pain
      c. Antibiotics to control infection
   5. Provide emotional support to patient and family—reassure patient that reduction in hearing is normal and that hearing may not immediately improve following surgery
   6. Assist with ambulation and avoid rapid turning—reduces vertigo
   7. Postoperative teaching principles
      a. Keep ear covered outdoors
      b. Keep outer ear plug clean, dry, and changed
      c. Avoid washing hair for two weeks
      d. Avoid air travel and swimming for six months
      e. Avoid individuals with upper respiratory

infections
  f. Avoid heavy lifting

SKELETAL SYSTEM

1. **Fractures**—a disruption in the continuity of bone as the result of trauma or various disease processes, such as Cushing's syndrome, which weaken the bone structure
A. Types of fractures
    1. Open or compound—the fractured bone extends through to the skin and mucous membranes; increased potential for infection
    2. Closed or simple fracture—fractured bone does not protrude through the skin
    3. Complete fracture—fracture extends through the entire bone, disrupting the periosteum on both sides of the bone
    4. Incomplete fracture—the fracture extends only part way through the bone; bone continuity is not totally interrupted
    5. Greenstick or willow of hickory stick—fracture of one side of bone, the other side merely bends
    6. Impacted or telescoped—fracture in which bone fragments are forcibly driven into other or adjacent bone structures
    7. Comminuted—fracture having more than one fracture line and with bone fragments broken into several pieces
    8. Depressed—fractures in which bone or bone fragments are driven inward, as in skull or facial fractures
B. Signs and symptoms of bone fracture
    1. Deformity
    2. Pain
    3. Swelling and bruising
    4. Abnormal or impaired mobility
    5. Crepitus—grating sensations heard or felt as bone fragments rub against each other
C. Treatment measures for fractures are designed to restore function to the affected part, prevent complications, and obtain normal (cosmetic) appearance
    1. Reduction or setting of the bone—restores bone alignment as nearly as possible
        a. Closed reduction—manual traction or manipulation
            (1) Usually done under general anesthesia to reduce pain and muscle spasm
            (2) Maintenance of reduction and

immobilization is accomplished by casting
        b. Open reduction—operative procedure utilized to achieve bone alignment; pins, wire, nails, or rods may be used to secure bone fragments in position
        c. Traction reduction—force is applied in two directions to obtain alignment
            (1) Used for fractures of long bones
            (2) May be applied by
                (a) Skin traction—secured by adhesive or moleskin strips
                (b) Skeletal traction—secured by wires, pins, or tongs placed through the bone
    2. Immobilization—maintains reduction and promotes healing of bone fragments
        a. External fixation or immobilization is achieved by application of casts, splints, or continuous traction
        b. Internal fixation is achieved by utilizing nails, rods, and wires in joining bone fragments
    3. Rehabilitation and prevention of complications
        a. Active range of motion of joints above and below cast
        b. Isometric exercises of muscle covered by cast
        c. Active exercises or physical therapy after removal of cast
        d. Ambulation techniques with crutches, cane, or walker
    4. Complications of fractures (see Tables 3-1 and 3-2)
        a. Shock
        b. Fat embolism
        c. Thrombophlebitis
        d. Infection
        e. Peripheral nerve damage
        f. Nonunion and avascular necrosis
D. Nursing care of the patient in a cast
    1. Main purpose of cast is immobilization, but it is also used to support body tissues and to prevent or correct deformities—in fractures, the joint above and the joint below the injury are immobilized
    2. Types of casts
        a. Spica—applied to immobilize hip or shoulder joints
        b. Body cast—applied to trunk
        c. Short leg cast—applied to lower leg,

Table 3-2. Complications of fractures

CARDIOVASCULAR COMPLICATIONS—Shock, thrombophlebitis (see Table 3-1, Postoperative complications), and fat emboli

Condition and etiology	Pathophysiology	Signs and symptoms	Nursing interventions
Fat emboli—multiple injuries, fracture of long bones, severe burns, soft tissue injury, and orthopedic procedures	Fat released from marrow of fractured bones → alteration of fat emulsion due to catecholamines → minute globules of fat carried in blood stream → embolization in vascular system in vital organs	*Respiratory*—dyspnea, cyanosis (in black patients, skin becomes slate gray), tachypnea, and severe chest pain *Cerebral*—pupillary changes, muscle twitching, change from alertness to confusion, agitation, and loss of consciousness *Skin*—petechiae over chest and shoulders, axilla, and soft palate *Extremity*—pale, cold, numb, and cold to touch; nausea; vomiting; faintness; and shock	1. Place in high-Fowler's position to relieve respiratory symptoms 2. Administer oxygen at once—relieves anoxia and reduces surface tension of fat globules 3. Institute respiratory support measures, as ordered—IPPB and respirator 4. Observe closely for heart failure and shock 5. Administer parenteral fluids, as ordered: (a) IV alcohol and (b) blood and fluid replacement 6. Administer medications, as ordered: (a) corticosteroids, (b) digitalis, (c) aminophylline, and (d) heparin sodium

ankle, and foot
  d. Long leg cast—applied to midthigh, leg, and foot
  e. Short arm cast—applied from forearm to palmar crease, may include thumb
  f. Long arm cast—applied from upper level of axillary fold to palmar crease immobilizing elbow at right angle
3. Precasting nursing care is designed to reduce anxiety and promote physical and psychologic comfort
  a. Inform patient that cast will feel hot during application and for several hours afterwards
  b. Allow patient to verbalize fears
  c. Clean skin with antiseptic soap
  d. Administer an analgesic, as ordered
4. Nursing care of the patient in a cast is designed to maintain reduction and prevent complications of pressure and immobility
  a. Observations
    (1) Signs of circulatory impairment—

reduced blood flow and venous return
    (a) Weak or absent pulses
    (b) Color, temperature, or sensation changes
    (c) Swelling and numbness
  (2) Signs of decreased innervation
    (a) Decreased mobility of toes and fingers
    (b) Increasing or constant pain
    (c) Smarting or burning sensation under cast
    (d) Numbness
  (3) Signs of tissue necrosis
    (a) Foul odor from cast
    (b) Drainage through the cast
    (c) Decubitus formation around edges of cast
    (d) Elevated temperature
  (4) For patient in spica cast—observe for duodenal distress
    (a) Anorexia, nausea, and

abdominal pain
    i. Report to physician immediately
    ii. Place patient in prone position to relieve pressure
    iii. Have cast cutters and nasogastric suction available

E. Interventions
1. Expose cast to air until dry—avoid the use of plastic or disposable diapers (Chux) containing plastic, which inhibit drying
2. Casts on extremities should be elevated on pillows, each joint higher than preceding joint, to promote venous return and reduce swelling
3. Patients with spica casts should remain supine until cast is dry
    a. Mattress firm and level; bed boards may be used—reduces muscle spasm
    b. Maintain warmth by covering uncasted areas only
    c. Avoid turning for eight hours
    d. When turning is allowed, utilize enough personnel so that patient is entirely turned at one time
    e. Support chest and cast with pillows
    f. Observe for signs of respiratory distress
4. If blood or drainage appears on cast mark the spot with a circle
    a. Note date and time and continue observations
    b. Report further drainage to physician
5. Promote skin care
    a. Apply lotion or cornstarch—no powders
    b. Tape edges of cast to reduce irritation
    c. Inspect skin under cast frequently for signs of irritation
    d. Caution patient not to stick anything down cast in an effort to scratch—skin abrasion may lead to decubitus ulcer
6. Promote motor function by initiating active range of motion exercises to unaffected extremities
    a. Use footboard to prevent footdrop
    b. Encourage use of trapeze if applicable
    c. Isometric exercises, as ordered
    d. Flex hand or foot of affected extremity—passive and active
7. Ambulate patients in extremity casts
    a. Support arm cast as needed
    b. Allow no weight bearing on leg cast unless ordered

8. Instruct in crutch-walking techniques if applicable
    a. When one leg only can bear weight
      (1) Swing-to gait—crutches forward swing body to crutches
      (2) Swing-through gait—crutches forward swing body through crutches
      (3) Three-point gait—crutches and effected extremity forward; swing forward placing good foot ahead or between crutches
    b. When both legs can move separately and bear some weight
      (1) Four-point gait—right crutch forward, left foot forward; swing weight to right side while bringing left crutch forward then right foot forward; gait simulates normal walking
      (2) Two-point gait—as four-point gait but faster; one crutch and opposite leg moving forward at same time
    c. Utilize tripod gait when the patient is unable to walk—crutches forward at a wide distance, drag legs to point just behind crutches, balance, and repeat
    d. Measure crutches accurately
      (1) Subtract 16 inches from total height
      (2) Complete extension of the elbows should be possible without pressure of axillary bar into the axilla
      (3) Handgrip should be adjusted so that complete wrist extension is possible
    e. Instruct in body alignment
      (1) Head erect
      (2) Back straight
      (3) Chest forward
      (4) Feet 6 to 8 inches apart—wide base for support
    f. Instruct in safety measures
      (1) Weight bearing on hands not axilla
      (2) Position crutches 4 inches to side and 4 inches to front
      (3) Use short strides, looking ahead not at feet
      (4) If patient should begin to fall, crutches should be thrown to the side to prevent falling on them
      (5) If patient should begin to fall, the body should be relaxed, "go limp," to prevent injury

(6) Check floors for potential hazards—water, oil spots, extension cords, and throw rugs

F. Nursing care of the patient in traction
1. Purpose—utilizing a system of ropes, pulleys, and weights, force is applied in two directions to
   a. Obtain and maintain normal alignment
   b. Reduce fractures and decrease muscle spasm
   c. Prevent deformities
2. Types of traction
   a. Continuous—used with fracture or dislocation of bones or joints
   b. Intermittent—employed to reduce flexion contractures or lessen pain and muscle spasm
   c. Skin—traction applied to the skin by using adhesive, plastic, or moleskin strip bound to the extremity by elastic bandage
      (1) Exerts indirect traction on muscles and bone
      (2) Nursing measures include
         (a) Shave extremity and apply tincture of benzoin—improves adherance of strip and reduces skin itching
         (b) Check all bony prominences for evidence of pressure
         (c) Check bandage for slippage, bunching, and replace prn
   d. Skeletal—direct traction applied to bone using pins (Steinmann), wires (Kirschner), or tongs (Crutchfield), which are inserted through the bone in or close to the involved area
      (1) Most effective tractions
      (2) Utilized for fractures of long bones
   e. Cervical traction—direct traction applied to cervical vertebrae using Crutchfield and Vinke tongs that are inserted into the skull
      (1) Traction is increased with weights until vertebrae move into position and alignment is regained
      (2) After reduction is obtained, weights are decreased to the amount needed to maintain reduction
      (3) Nursing measures
         (a) Elevation of head of bed—patient's body serves as a counterweight to traction weight
         (b) Keep tongs free from bed and keep weight hanging freely
   f. Balanced-suspension traction—countertraction produced by a force other than the patient's body weight; the extremity is suspended in a traction apparatus that maintains the line of traction despite changes in the patient's position, for example, Russell's leg traction, the Thomas splint, and Pearson's attachment
      (1) Patient may move as desired, turn slightly (no more than 30° to unaffected side), and may have head of bed elevated
      (2) The heel of the affected leg must remain free of the bed
      (3) Nursing measures are designed to maintain alignment and countertraction
         (a) 20° angle between thigh and bed
         (b) Check for pressure from sling in popliteal area
         (c) Provide foot support to prevent footdrop
         (d) Maintain abduction of extremity
         (e) Check for signs of infection
   g. Running traction—traction that exerts a pull in one plane; countertraction is supplied by the weight of the patient's body or can be increased through the use of weights and pulleys in the opposite direction
      (1) Patient must be kept well centered in the bed
      (2) Head of bed can only be elevated to the point of countertraction
      (3) Patient may not turn from side to side, as this will result in rubbing of the bony fragments
      (4) Check toes or fingers frequently for decreased circulation
      (5) Provide regular back care
   h. General traction care and precautions
      (1) Maintain straight line—ropes taut and riding freely over pulleys
      (2) Never remove or lift weights
      (3) Add trapeze to bed if upper extremities are unaffected
      (4) Initiate active range of motion of unaffected limbs and isometric

exercises in affected limb
  (5) Administer diet high in protein and low in carbohydrates
  (6) Encourage fluids—long immobilization increases occurrence of kidney stones
  (7) Provide activities to reduce perceptual deprivation

2. Total hip replacement—femoral head and acetabulum are replaced by a prosthesis, which is cemented into the bone with a plastic cement

A. Rationale—painful degenerative joint disease, such as rheumatoid arthritis and osteoarthritis; may also be done for complications of femoral neck fractures and congenital hip disease

B. Purpose—to restore or improve mobilization of the hip joint that has limited and painful function due to bony ankylosis

C. Preoperative nursing measures are designed to optimize physical and psychologic functioning (see pp. 147-151) and prevent postoperative complications
  1. Fit patient with antiembolic stockings—thrombophlebitis and pulmonary emboli are frequent complications of this type of surgery
  2. Administer antibiotics, as ordered—commonly given prophylactically
  3. Patient teachings include
    a. Isometric exercises—gluteal, abdominal, and quadricep setting
    b. Dorsiflexion and plantar flexion of the feet
    c. Use of trapeze
    d. Explanation of positioning of the operative leg and hip postoperatively to prevent adduction and flexion
    e. Transfer techniques—bed to chair and chair to crutches
  4. Assist patient with skin scrubs with antibacterial soap

D. Postoperative nursing measures are designed to maintain abduction of the affected joint (prevents dislocation of the prosthesis), promote physical and mental comfort, and prevent complications (see general postoperative care, p. 152, and care of the patient in casts or traction, pp. 182 and 184)
  1. Maintain abduction of affected leg
    a. Buck's extension or Russell's traction may be applied
    b. Plaster booties with an abduction bar may be utilized

    c. Place Charnley wedge pillow between the knees and lower legs
    d. Place two to three pillows or sandbags between patient's legs
  2. Avoid external hip rotation by placing sandbags along upper outer aspects of thigh
  3. Initiate skin care
    a. Alternating pressure mattress
    b. Back care q2h
    c. Sheepskin when supine
  4. Check dressings, drainage tubes (Hemo-Vac), and vital signs
  5. Elevate head of bed and turn per individual physician's orders—if turning is allowed, turn to unaffected side with pillows between legs to maintain abduction
  6. Initiate isometric exercises and dorsiflexion and plantar flexion of foot as soon as allowed
  7. Initiate progressive ambulation, as ordered
  8. Be sure patient lies flat in bed several times each day—prevents hip flexion contractures and strengthens hip muscles
  9. Postoperative and discharge teachings include
    a. Detailed exercise program and list of activity restrictions
    b. Placing pillow between legs when in bed for several weeks—to prevent hip adduction when turning
    c. Avoidance of sitting for more than an hour—patient should stand, stretch, and walk frequently to prevent hip flexion contractures
    d. Informing patient that hip flexion should not exceed 90° or dislocation may occur
      (1) May need assistance putting on shoes and stockings
      (2) Sit in straight-back chairs only
      (3) Use raised toilet seat
      (4) Avoid crossing legs
      (5) Avoid driving car for at least six weeks
    e. Continue to wear support hose for at least six weeks to enhance venous return and avoid thrombus formation

3. Above-the-knee amputation—severence of a portion of the leg through surgery

A. Rationale—peripheral vascular disease, malignant bone tumors, bone infections, complications from diabetes mellitus, traumas, and thermal, chemical, or electrical injuries

B. Preoperative nursing measures are designed to

promote psychologic adjustment to changes in body image and to optimize physical condition of patient (see general preoperative care pp. 147–151)

1. Preoperative teachings include
   a. Reiterating explanations of operative procedures
   b. Explaining phantom-limb sensation
   c. Utilization of prosthesis
   d. Preparation for rehabilitation
      (1) Crutch-walking
      (2) Exercises to increase upper body strength, such as push-ups, using weights while flexing and extending arms, and isometric sitting exercises
      (3) Use of overhead trapeze
2. Allow for verbalization of feelings about changes in body image
   a. Identify behaviors associated with grieving process (denial, aggression, anger, and hostility)
   b. Involve patient and family in preoperative teaching to facilitate understanding
   c. Stress the importance of patients' remaining capabilities
   d. Clarify for the patient and family that, following surgery and rehabilitation, the patient should still be able to carry out the activities of daily living and maintain independence

C. Postoperative nursing measures are designed to prevent complications, provide physical and emotional support, and promote rehabilitation (see p. 152 for immediate and general postoperative care)
   1. Elevate stump on pillow for first 24 to 48 hours to reduce edema and prevent hemorrhage; remove after 24 to 48 hours as prolonged elevation may lead to hip flexion contractures
   2. Observe for signs of hemorrhage frequently
      a. Outline any drainage on dressing, marking date and time
      b. Reinforce dressing prn
      c. Have heavy tourniquet on bed at all times to apply in case of sudden hemorrhage
   3. If open amputation has been done, maintain Buck's traction
      a. Traction prevents skin retraction and flexion contractures
      b. Pulley should be centered to permit turning to abdomen
   4. Avoid external rotation of hip by placing sandbags or trochanter roll along outer side of stump
   5. Initiate cast care (pp. 182–183) if plaster dressing has been applied—report any slippage to physician
   6. Administer pain medications, as ordered
   7. Initiate active range of motion exercises on unaffected limb and provide footboard to prevent foot drop
   8. Reposition patient every two hours while on bedrest, turning to the prone position several hours each day—prevents flexion contractures
   9. Initiate range of motion bed, chair, and stand up exercises as ordered to prevent abduction and flexion contractures
   10. Apply elastic bandage to stump after healed to produce shrinkage and conical shape
   11. Begin stump-strengthening exercises, as ordered
      a. Push stump against pillow
      b. Push stump against harder surface
      c. Massage stump (toward suture line)—decreases tenderness, improves vascularity, and aids in "toughening" stump
   12. Encourage patient and family to verbalize their feelings—recognize that it will take the patient time to adjust to altered body image and modifications in activities
   13. Keep patient as active as possible during postoperative and rehabilitative phases, as activity tends to reduce occurrence of phantom-limb pain

Questions Surgical Nursing

1. The elderly are generally considered high-risk surgical patients because
   1. They are frequently less able to cope with hospital regimens
   2. They are more likely to have one or more chronic diseases
   3. They have a higher probability of developing postoperative complications
   4. 2 and 3 are correct
   5. All of these are correct
2. Mrs. Smith, a 50-year-old married housewife, has been admitted to the hospital for a right breast biopsy and possible radical mastectomy. Your preoperative nursing assessment should include
   1. Ascertaining the degree of threat she perceives to her physical, emotional, and social well being
   2. A detailed explanation of hospital policies
   3. Sending a urine specimen to the lab
   4. Having her sign her operative permit
   5. All of these are correct
3. Mrs. Smith appears very apprehensive. She is talking rapidly and is constantly straightening the bed cloths. Her vital signs are BP-186/110, pulse-90 and strong, and respirations-22. Your first nursing action is
   1. Notify the surgeon immediately
   2. Check her pupils to see if they are equal and responsive to light
   3. Sit down and talk with Mrs. Smith for a few minutes
   4. Check for signs of peripheral edema
4. A half hour later you retake Mrs. Smith's vital signs. They are now BP-138/86, pulse-80, and respirations-16. Mrs. Smith's elevated blood pressure indicates
   1. She may be an individual who is highly sensitive to sympathetic nervous system stimulation
   2. She is emotionally unstable
   3. She is not psychologically prepared for surgery
   4. She is denying the possible loss of her breast

5. While you are taking her nursing history, Mrs. Smith reports she was diagnosed as mildly diabetic six months ago. She states she is controlled by diet and is not taking medication at this time. In checking Mrs. Smith's urine you note sugar 1+ and acetone 0. You recognize
   1. Mrs. Smith's diabetic condition has deteriorated
   2. Stress tends to increase hyperglycemia
   3. Mrs. Smith needs to be retaught how to check her urine
   4. Diet alone cannot control diabetes mellitus
6. Which of the following postoperative complications are more likely to occur as the result of diabetes mellitus?
   1. Poor wound healing
   2. Infection
   3. Shock
   4. 1 and 2 are correct
   5. All of these are correct
7. Preoperative teaching for Mrs. Smith included diaphragmatic breathing and coughing. Which of the following is not part of this instruction?
   1. Informing Mrs. Smith that she will be expected to repeat this exercise five to ten times every hour postoperatively
   2. Having Mrs. Smith practice the exercises
   3. Instructing Mrs. Smith to inhale through both her nose and mouth
   4. Instructing Mrs. Smith to repeat the breathing exercises until she is feeling lightheaded
8. Mrs. Smith's surgeon has ordered a preoperative skin prep with hexachlorophene (pHisoHex). This soap
   1. Should be left on the skin five to ten minutes to reduce skin bacteria
   2. Enhances the bacteriostatic effect of benzalkonium Cl
   3. Should never be applied with friction
   4. Acts as a depilatory
9. On the morning of surgery you are assigned to assist Mrs. Smith in the final preparations before going to the operating room. Before

going in to see Mrs. Smith, your first action is to

1. Prepare her preoperative medication
2. Check to be sure the operative permit has been signed
3. Check to see if the preoperative laboratory reports are on the chart
4. Prepare a bath

10. The preoperative medication ordered for Mrs. Smith by the anesthesiologist is morphine SO_4 gr $\frac{1}{6}$ and atropine SO_4 gr 1/200. This medication should be given
    1. Right before the patient leaves for surgery
    2. At least 45 minutes before anesthetic induction
    3. In a Z-tract
    4. Deep IM

11. Side effects of these preoperative medications include
    1. Nausea and vomiting
    2. Hypotension
    3. Dryness of the mouth
    4. 1 and 3 are correct
    5. All of these are correct

12. Mr. Smith has arrived early to be with his wife before surgery. After his wife leaves for the operating room, you should
    1. Assist him to find the proper waiting room
    2. Inform him that the surgeon will contact him after the procedure is over
    3. Explain that his wife will be in the recovery room for awhile after surgery
    4. All of these are correct

13. On admission to the recovery room, Mrs. Smith is very restless. Her respirations are deep and somewhat irregular; she startles and begins to moan when you touch her. Your nursing action is
    1. Continue to stimulate her by telling her the operation is over
    2. Raise the siderails and remain quietly in attendance
    3. Administer meperidine (Demerol) Hcl 100 mg IM
    4. Check her nail beds for cyanosis

14. Mrs. Smith has an airway in place and is in a supine position. To prevent airway obstruction you should
    1. Leave the airway in and turn her head to the side
    2. Maintain her present position
    3. Remove the airway and turn her head to the side
    4. Remove the airway and maintain a prone position

15. You are monitoring Mrs. Smith's vital signs every 15 minutes. Which of the following changes should be reported immediately to the surgeon?
    1. Dry, cool skin
    2. A systolic blood pressure that drops 20 mm Hg or more
    3. A diastolic pressure below 70
    4. A pulse rate that increases and decreases with respirations

16. Mrs. Smith has a unit of blood infusing in her left arm. Signs of transfusion reactions include
    1. Chills and elevated temperature
    2. Urticaria
    3. Wheezing
    4. 1 and 2 are correct
    5. All of these are correct

17. Mrs. Smith has had a modified radical mastectomy. She has a pressure dressing and two drains attached to a Hemo-Vac pump. Arm positions that facilitate venous return and reduce edema are
    1. Semi-Fowler's position with elevation of the whole arm on pillows so that the hand is slightly higher than the elbow and the elbow is slightly higher than the shoulder
    2. Semi-Fowler's position with the elbow flexed and the arm across the chest
    3. Abduction of the shoulder, flexion of the forearm and elbow with elevation, and the hand placed above the head
    4. 1 and 2 are correct
    5. 1 and 3 are correct

18. Nursing observations and care of the patient with a Hemo-Vac include
    1. Observing the amount and color of drainage
    2. Maintaining suction by emptying and recompressing the apparatus regularly
    3. Maintaining suction by attaching Hemo Vac to wall suction as the drainage increases
    4. 1 and 2 are correct
    5. 1 and 3 are correct

19. The pressure dressing encircles the chest and fits very snugly. You can anticipate difficulty in which of the following postoperative nursing functions?
    1. Maintaining good body alignment
    2. Initiating arm exercises

3. Promoting deep breathing and coughing
4. Taking vital signs
20. On turning Mrs. Smith to her left side, you note a moderately large amount of serosanguineous drainage on the bedsheets. You should
   1. Remove the dressing to ascertain the origin of the bleeding
   2. Milk the Hemo Vac tubing using an upward motion
   3. Note vital signs, reinforce the dressing, and notify the surgeon immediately
   4. Recognize that this is a normal occurrence with this type of surgery
21. Bleeding and hemorrhage are very serious complications of surgery and may lead to shock. Which of the following is not a sign or symptom of shock?
   1. Decreased blood pressure
   2. Polyuria
   3. Weak thready pulse
   4. Pale clammy skin
22. If Mrs. Smith begins to demonstrate some early signs of shock, such as increased pulse, cool clammy skin, and restlessness, you could enhance venous return by
   1. Administering oxygen to reduce restlessness
   2. Raising the foot of the bed 20° keeping her knees straight, trunk horizontal, and head slightly elevated
   3. Placing her in Trendelenburg's position
   4. Wrapping her in blankets
23. Postoperative voiding should occur in eight to ten hours after surgery. The nurse can assist the patient in voiding by
   1. Placing her on the bedpan each time she is coughed and deep breathed
   2. Running tap water while the patient is attempting to void
   3. Assisting her to a bedside commode if not contraindicated
   4. 2 and 3 are correct
   5. All of these are correct
24. Depending on the extent of the surgery and the attending physician's orders, it is possible to initiate arm exercises as early as 24 hours after surgery. Which of the following measures will be most useful in restoring range of motion to Mrs. Smith's right arm and shoulder during the early postoperative period?
   1. Feeding herself and combing her hair

2. Flexion and extension of the elbow every hour
3. Abduction of the arm and external rotation of the shoulder
4. Pendulum arm swings every four hours
25. Shoulder and arm edema is a frequent complication and complaint of postmastectomy patients. In planning for discharge, Mrs. Smith should be informed of actions that might increase lymphedema. Which of the following is most likely to result in edema formation?
   1. Wearing rubber gloves when washing dishes
   2. Having her blood pressure taken in her right arm
   3. Wearing a thimble when sewing
   4. Applying hand cream several times a day

Mr. Hill is a 63-year-old man with bronchogenic carcinoma of the right lower lung. He has a smoking history of two packs per day for 30 years, although he has not smoked for the last six months. He is scheduled for a right lower lobectomy in two days. Preoperative teaching for Mr. Hill includes coughing, deep breathing, and arm and leg exercises.

26. The most important activity that the postoperative thoracic patient performs is
   1. Deep breathing
   2. Coughing up sputum
   3. Arm exercises to prevent stiffening of the shoulder
   4. Leg exercises to prevent thrombophlebitis
27. In preparing Mr. Hill psychologically for his surgery and convalescence you should
   1. Explain to the patient that he will be surrounded by equipment, such as chest drainage tubes, oxygen, and IV infusions, and that these are routine
   2. Tell him he will not have long periods of rest, but will be awakened frequently to turn, cough, and deep breathe
   3. Tell him he will receive medication that will relieve some of his discomfort
   4. 1 and 2 are correct
   5. All of these are correct
28. Preoperative nursing measures designed to prevent postoperative respiratory infections include
   1. Postural drainage
   2. Frequent oral hygiene with antiseptic mouth washes
   3. Utilizing a vaporizer to humidify air and moisten bronchotracheal secretions

4. 1 and 3 are correct
5. All of these are correct

29. On returning from surgery, Mr. Hill has a chest tube connected to a water-seal drainage system. The purpose of this drainage system is
   1. To reestablish normal negative intrapleural pressures
   2. Drain off excess fluid and air in the pleural space
   3. Prevent deflation of the lung
   4. 1 and 2 are correct
   5. 2 and 3 are correct

30. On the second postoperative day, the fluid in the chest tube ceases to fluctuate. This may indicate
   1. The tube is plugged by fibrin or a clot
   2. There is an air leak in the system
   3. Pulmonary edema has developed
   4. All the excess fluid has been successfully drained off

31. Milking the chest tube refers to
   1. The process of stripping the chest tube in a downward motion toward the drainage bottle
   2. The process of stripping the chest tube with an upward motion toward the incision
   3. Keeping the water-seal drainage bottle below chest level
   4. Clamping the chest tube when an air leak occurs

32. Passive arm exercises are instituted on Mr. Hill's right arm four hours after surgery. These exercises are designed to prevent which of the following dysfunctions?
   1. Wrist drop
   2. Ankylosis
   3. Flexion of the elbow
   4. Kyphosis

Miss K is a 41-year-old waitress with severe varicose veins in both legs. She is admitted for vein stripping of her right leg.

33. Indications for vein stripping include
   1. Progressively advancing varicosities
   2. Stasis ulceration
   3. Cosmetic needs
   4. 1 and 2 only are correct
   5. All of these are correct

34. Vein stripping is usually done under what type of anesthesia?
   1. Local
   2. Topical

3. Regional
4. General

35. Which of the following is *not* part of the surgical procedure?
   1. Ligation of saphenous vein at the groin
   2. An incision at the ankle
   3. An incision in the popliteal fossa
   4. Threading a wire from groin to ankle

36. Postoperative measures would not include
   1. Administration of analgesics
   2. Elastic stockings from toe to groin
   3. Sitting in a chair for long periods
   4. Ambulation on the day of surgery

37. Elevation of the foot of the bed postoperatively is utilized to
   1. Decrease pain
   2. Aid venous return
   3. Increase blood supply to feet
   4. Make the patient more comfortable

Mrs. A is a 55-year-old woman with acute respiratory failure. She has been receiving continuous ventilation via a nasotracheal tube. This morning she is going to surgery for a tracheostomy. She is alert and well oriented.

38. A preoperative nursing priority for Mrs. A is
   1. Establishing a means of postoperative communication
   2. Drawing blood for serum electrolytes
   3. Elevating the head of the bed
   4. Removing the nasotracheal tube

39. The purpose of a tracheostomy is to
   1. Remove secretions the patient is unable to handle
   2. Sedate the patient
   3. Facilitate feeding the patient
   4. Facilitate nursing care since trachea tubes are easier to care for than nasotracheal tubes

40. Cuffs on trachea tubes should be deflated at least five minutes every hour. The purpose of this is to
   1. Prevent hemorrhage
   2. Prevent tracheal stenosis
   3. Allow the patient to talk
   4. Allow the patient to eat

41. Oxygen delivered via trachea tubes should be
   1. Intermittent
   2. Continuous
   3. Humidified
   4. 1 and 3 are correct

5. 2 and 3 are correct

42. The inner cannula (if present) should be cleansed with hydrogen peroxide and normal saline
    1. Only as necessary
    2. Every two to four hours
    3. Once a day
    4. Do not remove the inner cannula for any reason

43. The rationale for using humidified oxygen with trachea tubes is
    1. It is a traditional procedure
    2. It is a means of providing fluid intake
    3. It decreases insensible water loss
    4. The natural humidifying pathway is bypassed

44. Turning the patient's head from side to side when suctioning
    1. Provides passive exercise for the sterno-cleidomastoid and trapezius muscles
    2. Prevents nuchal rigidity
    3. Facilitates entry into the main right and left bronchus
    4. Decreases airway resistance, making catheter insertion easier

45. The proper method of suctioning includes
    1. Suctioning only while inserting the catheter
    2. Suctioning only while withdrawing the catheter
    3. Suctioning during both insertion and withdrawal of the catheter
    4. All of these depend on the amount of secretions

46. Observation of Mrs. A when she returns from surgery reveals signs of respiratory embarrassment. These include
    1. Restlessness
    2. Apprehension
    3. An air leak
    4. 1 and 2 are correct
    5. 1 and 3 are correct

47. Crepitus in Mrs. A's neck and upper chest is a sign of
    1. Subcutaneous emphysema from displaced trachea tube
    2. An inadequately inflated cuff
    3. An overinflated cuff
    4. Edema from the trauma of surgery

Mr. L is a 51-year-old man admitted for recurrent hemorrhage from a gastric ulcer. The decision is made to do a gastrectomy.

48. When a partial gastrectomy is performed, the antrum is usually removed because
    1. It secretes HCL
    2. It regulates the production of HCl
    3. It is technically the easiest portion to remove
    4. It is the upper portion of the stomach

49. The mixture of digestive enzymes and food in the stomach is called
    1. Chyme
    2. Pepsin
    3. Trypsin
    4. Chorion

50. Pernicious anemia may be a problem after gastrectomy because
    1. The extrinsic factor is produced in the stomach
    2. The extrinsic factor is absorbed in the stomach
    3. The intrinsic factor is produced in the stomach
    4. There is a high incidence of hemorrhage

51. Drainage of blood from the nasogastric tube after surgery is abnormal if
    1. It occurs after the first 24 hours
    2. It remains bright red
    3. It occurs 6 to 12 hours after surgery
    4. 1 and 2 are correct
    5. 2 and 3 are correct

52. Ambulation of the postgastrectomy patient usually begins
    1. The day after surgery
    2. Two to four days after surgery
    3. After four days bedrest
    4. Immediately upon awakening

53. Dumping syndrome is a significant problem for
    1. 70% to 80% of patients having gastrectomies
    2. 50% of patients having gastrectomies
    3. 25% of patients having gastrectomies
    4. 5% to 10% of patients having gastrectomies

54. Small frequent feedings of which type of diet are recommended?
    1. Low-protein, high-fat, low-carbohydrate diet
    2. High-protein, high-fat, high-carbohydrate diet
    3. High-protein, high-fat, low-carbohydrate diet
    4. Low-protein, low-fat, high-carbohydrate diet

55. Patients suffering from dumping syndrome should be advised to
    1. Drink liquids between meals
    2. Drink liquids only with meals
    3. Drink liquids anytime they want
    4. Avoid all liquids
56. Which of the following is not a symptom of dumping syndrome?
    1. Dizziness
    2. Profuse perspiration
    3. Epigastric fullness
    4. Hunger
57. Patients should be told that the symptoms of dumping syndrome
    1. Are something they must adjust to
    2. Will disappear
    3. Are a symptom of a complication of surgery
    4. Are very unusual and should be reported to the physician

Mr. S, a 38-year-old married public relations officer with cancer of the colon, is admitted for surgery involving a colostomy.

58. Preoperative preparation of Mr. S includes administration of neomycin SO_4 to
    1. Combat infection
    2. Decrease bacterial count of the colon
    3. Reduce the size of the cancer before surgery
    4. Stimulate peristalsis and facilitate action of cleansing enemas
59. A colostomy begins functioning
    1. Immediately
    2. Two to three days postoperative
    3. One week postoperative
    4. Two weeks postoperative
60. Colostomy irrigations should be done
    1. Before breakfast
    2. Before lunch
    3. Before dinner
    4. At the time closest to the patient's normal defecation pattern
61. The purpose of colostomy irrigations is to
    1. Stimulate peristalsis
    2. Relieve constipation
    3. Relieve diarrhea
    4. Remove bacteria
62. Control of colostomy odor can be accomplished with
    1. Dietary control
    2. Charcoal
    3. Bismuth subcarbonate
    4. All of these are correct

63. Diets for patients with colostomies may include
    1. Green salads
    2. Fresh fruits
    3. Prunes
    4. All of these are correct
64. Lack of acceptance of a colostomy is usually related to
    1. Feelings of shame
    2. Nonacceptance by spouse
    3. Threat to body image
    4. All of these are correct
65. Problems that may be very severe for the patient with a colostomy include
    1. Diarrhea
    2. Excoriation of the skin
    3. Electrolyte imbalance
    4. All of these are correct
66. Agencies in the community to which you might refer Mr. S for help include
    1. United Ostomy Association
    2. Aid to the Totally Disabled
    3. Crippled Children's Association
    4. Social Services
67. A frequent major psychological problem for colostomy patients is
    1. Financial
    2. Special diets
    3. Sexual ability
    4. Transportation

Mrs. B is a 44-year-old obese female admitted for upper abdominal pain and inability to tolerate fatty foods. She is scheduled for a cholecystectomy and exploration of the common bile ducts. She has been a heavy smoker for 25 years and experiences some shortness of breath when exercising.

68. The incidence of gallbladder disease is highest in
    1. Obese men over 40
    2. Obese women over 40
    3. Thin men under 40
    4. Thin women under 40
69. The function of the gallbladder is
    1. Production of bile
    2. Storage of bile
    3. Dilution of bile
    4. All of these are correct
70. The common bile duct empties directly into the
    1. Stomach
    2. Liver

3. Duodenum

4. Jejunum

71. Mrs. B's inability to tolerate fatty foods may be due to
    1. Inadequate bile production by the liver
    2. Obstruction of the common bile duct from stones preventing emptying of bile into the duodenum
    3. The fact that fatty foods are difficult to digest
    4. Inadequate bile production by the gallbladder

72. The purpose of inserting a T–tube into the common bile duct after surgery is to
    1. Prevent excoriation of the skin
    2. Collect the bile for testing by the lab
    3. Assure the physician that bile production has stopped
    4. Promote drainage of bile until normal flow is established

73. Yellow skin and sclera in a postoperative cholecystectomy patient would indicate
    1. Viral hepatitis
    2. Infectious hepatitis
    3. Bile flow obstruction
    4. Normal recovery

74. Postoperative patient teaching with Mrs. B would include
    1. Weight loss
    2. Diet
    3. Importance of follow up visits with her physician
    4. All of these are correct

75. When teaching Mrs. B about her diet, you tell her that she
    1. Must never eat fatty foods again
    2. May slowly add fatty foods
    3. May eat only polyunsaturated fats
    4. May have only 20 gm of fat a day

76. Postoperative coughing and deep breathing is especially important in Mrs. B's case because of her
    1. Obesity
    2. Upper abdominal surgery
    3. Decreased respiratory function
    4. Postoperative pain

77. Mrs. B refuses to cough "because it hurts." Your action would *not* be to
    1. Administer analgesics and wait a few minutes
    2. Use a scultetus binder or pillows to splint the incision

3. Help her sit on the side of the bed

4. Let her sleep today; she's tired from surgery

78. Mr. V is a 35-year-old man admitted for right nephrectomy of a hypernephroma. Which of the following is *not* an approach for surgical removal of a kidney?
    1. Lumbar or flank
    2. Peritoneal
    3. Thoracic abdominal
    4. Abdominal

79. The postoperative nephrectomy patient should be very carefully observed for hemorrhage because
    1. The sutures may not be tight enough
    2. There is a very high incidence of postoperative hemorrhage
    3. The renal vessels may be difficult to ligate
    4. All of these are correct

80. The postoperative nephrectomy patient should also be closely observed for
    1. Spontaneous pneumothorax
    2. Copious urine output
    3. Hyperkalemia
    4. Respiratory acidosis

81. Mr. V. is very depressed. In talking to him you discover he is concerned about having only one kidney. You might suggest that
    1. He seek psychiatric counseling
    2. All nephrectomy patients become depressed
    3. He is acting childishly
    4. His remaining kidney is sufficient to perform normal renal function

82. An important part of Mr. V's postoperative care includes
    1. Daily weights
    2. Ambulation
    3. Administration of analgesics
    4. Maintaining intravenous patency

Mr. Robert Mackey, a 19-year-old college sophomore, sustained a transverse fracture of his right tibia and fibula when he tripped playing football. His fractures were reduced in the emergency room and his right leg immobilized in a long leg cast, which extended from his groin to his toes, with the knee slightly flexed.

83. On admission to the orthopedic unit Mr. Mackey's cast is damp and he is complaining that it feels very hot. You should
    1. Explain to Mr. Mackey that the cast will feel hot for several hours as the moisture

evaporates and the cast hardens
2. Recognize that this is a sign of excessive pressure on the soft tissues and notify the physician
3. Tell Mr. Mackey not to worry as this is a common complaint
4. Administer meperidine (Demerol) HCl 50 mg IM to relieve his discomfort

84. After elevating Mr. Mackey's leg, you check his toes for circulation and motor activity. Which of the following is not an indication of circulatory constriction?
1. Swelling and numbness of toes
2. Inability to move toes
3. Blanching or cyanosis of toes
4. Appearance of bloody drainage on cast

85. Several hours after Mr. Mackey is admitted you notice his toes have become edematous. The physician decides to bivalve the cast. This procedure
1. Requires recasting after 24 hours
2. Includes splitting and spreading the cast down the middle to relieve constriction
3. Includes splitting and spreading the cast on each side and cutting the underlying padding
4. Should be followed by placing the patient's leg in a dependent position

86. Appropriate exercises for Mr. Mackey to prevent complications of immobility include
1. Wiggling his toes
2. Quadriceps setting
3. Passive range of motion of hip
4. 1 and 3 are correct
5. All of these are correct

87. A week later, on entering Mr. Mackey's room, you find he is using a long pencil to scratch the skin under his cast. You should
1. Ask the physician for a medication order to relieve itching
2. Explain to the patient that scratching under the cast is prohibited as it may break the skin and cause an infection to develop
3. Assist Mr. Mackey by gently rolling the casted leg in the palmar surfaces of your hand
4. Take the pencil away from Mr. Mackey

88. The doctor has ordered ambulation on crutches with no weight bearing on the affected limb. An appropriate crutch gait for you to teach Mr. Mackey would be
1. Two-point gait
2. Three-point gait
3. Four-point gait
4. Tripod gait

89. Which of the following instructions is *not* appropriate when teaching a patient to use crutches?
1. Utilize axilla to help carry weight
2. Use short strides to maintain maximum mobility
3. Keep feet 6-8 inches apart to provide a wide base for support
4. If he should begin to fall, throw crutches to the side to prevent falling on them

Mrs. Bertha Franz, a 69-year-old retired bookkeeper, has been admitted for a total hip replacement. She has had rheumatoid arthritis for many years. She has limited range of motion in her left hip and states that her hip causes her constant pain.

90. The purpose of total hip replacement is
1. Prophylactic relief of pain
2. To restore or improve mobilization of an ankylotic joint
3. To relieve contractures
4. To prolong the patient's life

91. Preoperative nursing assessment of Mrs. Franz is directed toward ascertaining
1. Her level of independent functioning
2. The range of motion of her other joints
3. The duration of her pain and limited hip function
4. 1 and 2 are correct
5. 2 and 3 are correct

92. Mrs. Franz is afraid she will have to have a urinary catheter inserted after surgery. You should
1. Assure Mrs. Franz if that occurs it is nothing to be ashamed about
2. Encourage Mrs. Franz to tell you why this idea disturbs her
3. Have Mrs. Franz practice using a bedpan in the recumbent position
4. 1 and 2 are correct
5. 2 and 3 are correct

93. Which of the following would *not* be a part of your preoperative teaching plan?
1. Gluteal and abdominal setting
2. Dorsi flexion and plantar flexion of her left foot
3. Internal and external rotation of the left hip
4. Three-point crutch walking

94. On her return from surgery Mrs. Franz's left leg is placed in a balanced suspension traction. To maintain traction you should
    1. Keep a 20° angle between the thigh and the bed
    2. Keep the heel of the affected leg on the bed for countertraction
    3. Never allow the patient to turn from side to side
    4. Keep the patient flat in bed at all times
95. A primary nursing responsibility following total hip replacement is
    1. Maintaining abduction of the affected leg
    2. Maintaining adduction of the affected leg
    3. Encouraging internal and external hip rotation
    4. Instituting early ambulation
96. Which of the following surgical complications is most likely to affect Mrs. Franz?
    1. Pneumonia
    2. Thrombophlebitis
    3. Paralytic ileus
    4. Urinary infection
97. Which of the following activities is most helpful in preventing hip flexion contractures?
    1. Sitting in a reclining chair
    2. Placing a pillow between the knees
    3. Lying flat in bed either supine or prone
    4. Utilizing sandbags along the outer aspects of the thigh

Mr. Edwards, a 70-year-old retired engineer, is admitted to the hospital for removal of a cataract from his left eye.

98. Nursing measures for Mr. Edwards preoperatively include
    1. Keeping him flat in bed
    2. Applying eye patches to both eyes
    3. Orienting him to his environment and nursing personnel
    4. Teaching him eyedrop instillation
99. Postoperatively Mr. Edwards should be positioned
    1. In a semi-Fowler's position
    2. In a prone position only
    3. On his back or on the unoperated side
    4. On his operative side
100. Which of the following activities must Mr. Edwards avoid to prevent complications during the early postoperative period?
    A. Deep breathing exercises
    B. Coughing
    C. Brushing his teeth
    D. Shaving
    E. Blowing his nose

    1. A is correct
    2. B, C, and D are correct
    3. A and B are correct
    4. C, D, and E are correct

Answers/Rationale   Surgical Nursing

1. (4) The elderly are far more likely to have one or more chronic diseases that decrease their physiologic reserves and their ability to cope with stress; they are therefore less able to tolerate physiologic disturbances and become more prone to the development of postoperative complications.

2. (1) Assessment is a process in which data is gathered and evaluated. The patient's perceptions of the surgery, its possible outcomes, and its effect on her life are extremely important factors that directly affect her ability to tolerate surgery and to recover quickly.

3. (3) A primary objective of preoperative nursing care is to reduce stress. Take the time to talk with the patient and encourage her to verbalize her fears. Retake the blood pressure in 30 minutes, and if it is still elevated, notify the surgeon.

4. (1) The physiologic response to stress of any nature—physical, psychologic, or social—is stimulation of the sympathetic nervous system. Signs of sympathetic nervous system stimulation include elevation of blood pressure, pulse, and respiration, as well as increased perspiration and pale cool extremities.

5. (2) During periods of stress the liver acts to break down glycogen stores (glycogenolysis) into glucose. The glucosuria, however mild, should be reported to the physician.

6. (4) Patients with well-controlled maturity-onset diabetes generally undergo surgery with only slightly more risk than nondiabetic patients. Hyperglycemia, however, does increase the risk of infection and poor wound healing.

7. (4) Deep breathing to the point of hyperventilation is contraindicated. The patient should be instructed to rest for a short period after every five deep respirations.

8. (1) The bacteriocidal effect of hexachlorophene is greatly enhanced if it is left on the skin for five to ten minutes. Many surgeons advise their patients to wash with this preparation for several days prior to surgery.

9. (2) No surgical procedures, however minor, can proceed without the voluntary, informed, written consent of the patient.

10. (2) To reduce anxiety and ensure ease of induction, a preoperative medication should be administered 45 to 75 minutes prior to anesthesia. Siderails should be raised after administration of medication, as the patient will begin to feel drowsy and lightheaded.

11. (5) Side effects of morphine include nausea, vomiting, hypotension, and in some patients, depression of respirations and the gag reflex. Atropine is an anticholinergic drug that decreases oral and tracheobronchial secretions, giving the patient the sensation of a very dry, cotton-like mouth.

12. (4) Supporting the patient's family at this time is extremely important. Be sure to clarify for the family that the length of time the patient is in the operating suite is not a criterion for the seriousness of an operation. Delays occur, and the induction and the period of emergence from anesthesia take time.

13. (2) Anesthesia is divided into four stages. Most surgical procedures are carried out in Stage III, during which the patient is unconscious and her reflexes are depressed. As the patient eliminates the anesthetic agent, she goes into Stage II, which is the stage of delirium or excitement. Respirations are exaggerated and irregular, and muscle tone is increased. To prevent injury during this stage, the nursing measures are designed to reduce stimulation by maintaining a quiet, well-regulated environment.

14. (1) The airway should remain in place and the patient's head turned to the side to prevent obstruction of the airway by the tongue and allow secretions to drain from the mouth.

15. (2) A drop in the systolic blood pressure of 20 mm Hg or more below preoperative blood pressure readings is indicative of impending shock. Shock may be due to hemorrhage, vasodilation caused by anesthesia, insufficient fluid replacement, or abnormal clotting.

16. (5) Allergic reactions to transfusions may be due to infusion of incompatible blood (always be sure to match blood and patient identification twice before superimposing an IV) or a reaction to unidentified antigens from the donor. Should symptoms develop, stop transfusion, notify the physician to assess care, and send a STAT urine specimen for analysis.

17. (5) Promotion of venous return is always enhanced when dependent extremities are supported and/or elevated. The specific positioning of the arm after a radical mastectomy may vary according to the extent of the surgery and the physician's preference.

18. (4) The Hemo Vac is a portable suction that provides low negative pressure (30–45 mm Hg) to gently remove excess fluid and debris from the wound. It does not require attachment to any other suction system.

19. (3) Tight pressure dressing, discomfort, and fear of tearing the incision tend to limit chest expansion and the patient's willingness to cough. The nurse can assist the patient in this procedure by helping her to sit upright and by supporting both the anterior and posterior chest wall at the incisional site with her hand. Frequent turning will also facilitate mobilization of secretion and the prevention of atelectasis.

20. (3) Pressure dressings are never removed but, if saturated, should be reinforced with sterile dressings. The possibility of hemorrhage is ever present and signs of increased bleeding should be immediately reported to the surgeon.

21. (2) Polyuria is defined as the passage of excessive amounts of urine. Oliguria and anuria (decreased or absent urine output) are indicative of shock and are due to poor kidney perfusion.

22. (2) The head slightly elevated, the legs elevated in a straight line, and the trunk horizontal improves venous return to the heart and prevents abdominal viscera from impinging on the diaphragm. The Trendelenburg position, after initially increasing blood flow to the brain, initiates a reflex mechanism that causes cerebral vasoconstriction.

Wrapping the patient in blankets will cause dilatation of the peripheral vasculature, which will further decrease venous return.

23. (4) Conservative measures should always be employed before catheterization. Running water, warmed bedpans, placing the feet in warmed water, or assisting the patient to a bedside commode are measures that will provide the support the patient needs to initiate micturation.

24. (1) Activities of daily living are the most useful in restoring range of motion to the affected arm and shoulder after breast surgery.

25. (2) Patients who have had a radical mastectomy need to avoid activities that constrict the tissues of the arm on the affected side. Effort should also be made to avoid cuts, scratches, hangnails, or strong detergent that lead to infection and increase swelling.

26. (2) Coughing up sputum is extremely important in that it reduces bronchotracheal secretions, prevents atelectasis, and promotes adequate ventilation.

27. (5) Preoperative teaching should include a thorough explanation of what the patient can expect in the postoperative period. This process prevents the patient from thinking his condition is poorer than he thought, allays apprehensions, and enables the patient to take an active part in the healing process.

28. (5) Even though Mr. Hill has not smoked for six months, chronic changes such as increased mucus production will have developed over the years. It is extremely important preoperatively to loosen and mobilize these secretions. Frequent oral hygiene with antiseptic mouth washes reduces the number of pathogens in the upper respiratory tract.

29. (4) Chest tubes attached to water-seal drainage drain off excess fluid and air in the pleural space, speed reinflation of the lung, help in reestablishing normal negative intrapleural pressure, and prevent the development of pneumothorax.

30. (1) Fluid in the chest tube will cease to fluctuate when the tubing is plugged or the lung has reexpanded.

31. (1) Chest tubes are milked fairly frequently (every hour) in the early postoperative period. Maintenance of chest tube patency facilitates lung reinflation and reduces the occurrence of complications.

32. (2) Ankylosis or stiffness of the shoulder is the result of immobilization of shoulder joint and disease of injured muscles. Arm and shoulder exer-

cises are designed to maintain normal range of motion, reeducate injured or unused muscle, and to prevent the over-development or strengthening of contralateral muscles (those on the other side), which produces deformity.

33. (5) Vein stripping is done for all of these situations.

34. (4) This is a painful and tiresome procedure, and for patient comfort is done under general anesthesia.

35. (3) Incisions are made only at the groin and ankle.

36. (3) Sitting in a chair is contraindicated due to pressure behind the knees and at the hips, which impedes venous return.

37. (2) Elevation of the foot of the bed aids venous return by the force of gravity.

38. (1) A tracheostomy renders the patient unable to talk and the patient will need a means of communicating her needs to the staff.

39. (1) When patients are unable to handle their secretions some form of intubation is mandatory to prevent aspiration and further complications.

40. (2) Deflation of the cuff removes pressure and allows oxygen and nutrients to be delivered to that area of the trachea.

41. (5) The natural pathway of humidification, the oropharynx, has been bypassed. An artificial means must be used to prevent "drying" of the lung tissue.

42. (2) Especially during the first few days after surgery, it is important the cannula be kept clean, since it is the only means of the patient obtaining oxygen.

43. (4) See rationale for No. 41.

44. (3) Turning the head to the left facilitates entry into the right bronchus and turning to the right facilitates entry into the left.

45. (2) Never suction while inserting the catheter. The only thing this accomplishes is removal of oxygen from the patient's respiratory tract.

46. (4) Restlessness and apprehension are early signs of respiratory distress usually due to hypoxia and/or hypercapnia. An air leak is not a sign of respiratory distress.

47. (1) The trachea tube is no longer in the trachea but is delivering oxygen into the interstitial spaces (under added pressure due to the ventilator).

48. (2) A substance produced in the antrum stimulates the production of HCl.

49. (1) Trypsin and pepsin are digestive enzymes. Chorion is part of a developing embryo.

50. (3) The intrinsic factor necessary for the utili-

zation of vitamin B_{12} is produced in the stomach.

51. (4) It is normal to expect some blood in the nasogastric tube for 12–24 hours after surgery.

52. (1) Ambulation is begun early to prevent complications of bedrest; ambulation can begin as soon as 24 hours.

53. (4) 70–80% of patients suffer from this syndrome, but it is a significant problem for only a small percentage.

53. (3) This type of diet reduces the distress of dumping syndrome. A diet high in carbohydrates is rapidly converted into a concentrated solution that causes first a hyperglycemia and then a hypoglycemia. A diet that is high in protein and fat will compensate for the carbohydrate restriction.

55. (1) Drinking liquids between and not with meals also reduces distress from dumping syndrome by reducing the amount of bulk and allows more food to be taken.

56. (4) Patients with dumping syndrome have a feeling of fullness rather than hunger. These symptoms are believed to result from entrance of food into the jejunum without undergoing the usual changes in the stomach. This stimulates an intrinsic gastrocolic reflex.

57. (2) With time and dietary management, the distress will decrease and usually disappear.

58. (2) Neomycin SO_4 decreases the bacterial count of the colon and reduces the risk of secondary or postoperative infection.

59. (2) The colostomy must be opened wider by removing the clamps or cautery before it can function. This is not done until two to four days postoperative.

60. (4) All colostomy care should be adjusted to meet the needs and convenience of the patient. Irrigations must be adjusted to fit the individual's normal body routine.

61. (1) Distention of the bowel with fluid stimulates normal waves of peristalsis.

62. (4) Charcoal and bismuth subcarbonate may be placed in the colostomy bag. Dietary control consists of discovering which foods produce gas and odor for the individual on a trial-and-error basis.

63. (4) There are no specific foods that must not be used. Generally, anything the patient was unable to tolerate preoperatively, he or she will be unable to tolerate postoperatively. Adjustment of the diet is on an individual, trial-and-error basis.

64. (4) People often connect feces with dirt and are ashamed of this "dirty surgery." As with any surgery, there is a threat to the self-image. Lack of acceptance by the spouse makes the patient's problem of acceptance much greater.

65. (4) All of these problems may become more severe more rapidly in patients with colostomies.

66. (1) United Ostomy Association has local chapters in most communities. These are composed of people who themselves have colostomies. They do counseling and teaching for colostomy patients and their families.

67. (3) Sexual intimacy, even in long-established relationships, is frequently difficult to establish when the bowel is emptying onto the abdomen.

68. (2) Obese women over 40 have the highest rate of gallbladder disease.

69. (2) The gallbladder stores and concentrates but does not produce bile.

70. (3) The common bile duct empties directly into the duodenum, where bile begins the emulsification of fats.

71. (2) Obstruction of the common bile duct would prevent emptying of bile into the duodenum. Since bile is essential for the digestion of fats, the patient would experience discomfort.

72. (4) Normal flow of bile will usually be established within two weeks. Excoriation of the skin is prevented by the dressings and drainage bag, and not the T–tube.

73. (3) Hepatitis might be suspected, but the most common cause of jaundice in gallbladder disease is obstruction to the flow of bile.

74. (4) Weight and dietary management are important both preoperatively and postoperatively. As with any surgical patient, follow-up checks with the physician are very important during the convalescent phase.

75. (2) After an otherwise regular diet has been resumed, these patients may slowly add fatty foods on a trial-and-error basis, depending on individual tolerance.

76. (3) Mrs. B's decreased respiratory function makes her a higher risk for postoperative infection, atelectasis, pneumonia, and respiratory failure because of general anesthesia and the tendency to splint her chest from the pain of upper abdominal surgery.

77. (4) The first three choices are all common methods to facilitate her ability to cough. Coughing and deep breathing are important for anyone who has had general anesthesia and especially so for Mrs. B because of her respiratory function (see rationale for No. 76). You definitely would *not* let her sleep for the day.

78. (2) Surgical approaches for nephrectomies may be lumbar, retroperitoneal, abdominal, thoracic, or thoracic-abdominal.

79. (4) The renal vessels are short and are often involved in the tumor mass, which makes them difficult to ligate in surgery.

80. (1) The pleura may be accidentally perforated during surgery. When thoracic or thoracic-abdominal approaches are used, chest tubes are inserted and connected to water-seal drainage.

81. (4) Only one-third of the kidney mass is needed to perform normal physiologic function. Some consideration might be given to the fact that all major surgery is a threat to body image.

82. (1) Daily weights are an important aspect of postoperative care, since the patient should lose no more than 2% of his preoperative weight.

83. (1) A freshly applied cast generates heat as moisture evaporates and cast hardens. To facilitate drying, keep it exposed to the air. Do not use plastic covers or Chux on pillows used to elevate the limb as these tend to slow drying.

84. (4) Signs of circulatory constriction would include tingling and numbness, swelling toes, blanching or cyanosis, constant pain, loss of mobility, and temperature changes.

85. (3) Bivalving the cast involves full-length splitting of the cast on each side. The underlying padding is also cut as blood soaked padding shrinks and can also cause circulatory constriction. After the cast is cut, it is spread sufficiently to relieve constriction. This procedure does not disturb reduction of the bone.

86. (5) Exercises for the individual in a leg cast include moving both the hip and the toes. Isometric exercises such as quadriceps setting are initiated.

87. (2) It is not safe to insert any foreign object under a cast or to scratch the skin under a cast as the skin may be broken and become infected. Scratching also disturbs the padded surface under the cast, causing it to become wrinkled, which may lead to skin irritation and breakdown.

88. (2) The three-point gait is appropriate when weight bearing is not allowed on the affected limb. The swing-to and swing-through crutch gaits may also be used when only one leg can be utilized for weight bearing.

89. (1) In the use of crutches, all weight bearing should be on the hands. Constant pressure in the axilla from weight bearing can lead to damage of the brachial plexus nerves and produce crutch paralysis.

90. (2) The purpose of total hip replacement is to restore, improve, or maintain mobilization of a hip joint that has limited function due to bony ankylosis.

91. (2) A comprehensive nursing assessment of the patient's motor function is essential in the development of plans for rehabilitation.

92. (5) Negating a patient's fears or concerns is inappropriate. An effort should be made to ascertain the basis of the fears. Teaching the patient to utilize the bedpan preoperatively may reduce the probability of postoperative catheterization.

93. (3) Internal and external rotation of the hip is contraindicated during the postoperative period as these movements may dislocate the prosthesis.

94. (1) To maintain countertraction when a balanced suspension traction is utilized, the angle between the thigh and the bed should be kept at 20°. The heel of the affected limb must also be kept free of the bed. Usually with a balanced suspension traction, the patient may turn slightly and have the head of the bed elevated. Depending on the physician, the head of the bed of a patient with total hip replacement is generally not raised above 45°.

95. (1) Maintaining abduction of the affected leg is of primary importance in total hip replacement. This may be accomplished with traction, plaster booties with an abduction bar, a Charnley wedge pillow or with two or three pillows or sandbags placed between the patient's leg.

96. (2) Thrombophlebitis is a frequent complication following total hip replacement because of postoperative immobility. Precautions include using antiembolitic stockings, administering anticoagulants and aspirin, and initiating isometric exercises to improve muscle tone and activate the venous pump.

97. (3) Lying flat in either a supine or prone position results in extension of the hip and the strengthening of hip muscles.

98. (3) Even though Mr. Edwards will have only one eye patched after surgery, familiarization with the physical arrangement of his room and with nursing personnel will decrease the occurrence of disorientation, which affects many elderly patients.

99. (3) Postoperatively the cataract patient may be placed in a flat or low-Fowler's position on his back or turned to the unoperated side. Turning the patient to the operative side or raising the head of the bed increases the stress on the sutures and may lead to hemorrhage.

100. (2) Coughing, brushing the teeth, and shaving are activities that tend to increase intraocular pressures and are, therefore, restricted during the early postoperative period. Other activities to be avoided include vomiting, bending, and stooping.

Annotated Bibliography

Beland, I., and Passos, J.: Clinical nursing, ed. 3, New York, 1975, Macmillan Publishing Co., Inc.

Provides an excellent chapter on the broad concepts of preoperative and postoperative nursing care. A holistic approach is utilized that promotes understanding of the many factors affecting the patient's response to health and illness and to medical and nursing interventions. However, the book does not present a wide range of surgical nursing situations. Those presented are offered in a case study format that while helpful in understanding the total care, makes gleaning specific information somewhat time consuming

Brunner, L. and Suddarth, D.: Textbook of Medical-surgical nursing, ed. 3, Philadelphia, 1975, J. B. Lippincott Company.

A very comprehensive text presented in an easily read format. Patient assessment, pathophysiology, and rationale of care are consistently presented throughout. Tables and drawings are interspersed throughout the text and are a definite aid to understanding.

Luckmann, J., and Sorensen, K.: Medical-surgical nursing: a psychophysiologic approach, Philadelphia, 1974, W. B. Saunders Company.

The very size and comprehensiveness of this text may inhibit some students. However, the text presents an excellent unit on general surgical nursing principles. Assessment and nursing care are consistently related to underlying psychophysiologic principles. A wide range of specific surgical interventions are discussed in varying depths. Occasionally, nursing interventions are not discussed with the same thoroughness as the surgical procedure. The chapter on the care of the cardiac surgery patient is excellent.

Moidel, H., Giblin, E., and Wagner, B.: Nursing care of the patient with medical-surgical disorders; ed. 2, New York, 1976, McGraw-Hill Book Co.

A well-written, easily read text that presents material clearly and succinctly. Emphasis is on nursing objectives and approaches. The chapter on surgical nursing is very good.

Shafer, K., Sawyer, J., McCluskey, A., Beck, E., and Phipps, W.: Medical-surgical nursing; ed. 6, St. Louis, 1975, The C. V. Mosby Co.

A classic medical-surgical text that has incorporated physiologic rationale for assessment findings and nursing interventions. The format is easily read and emphasis is on nursing care.

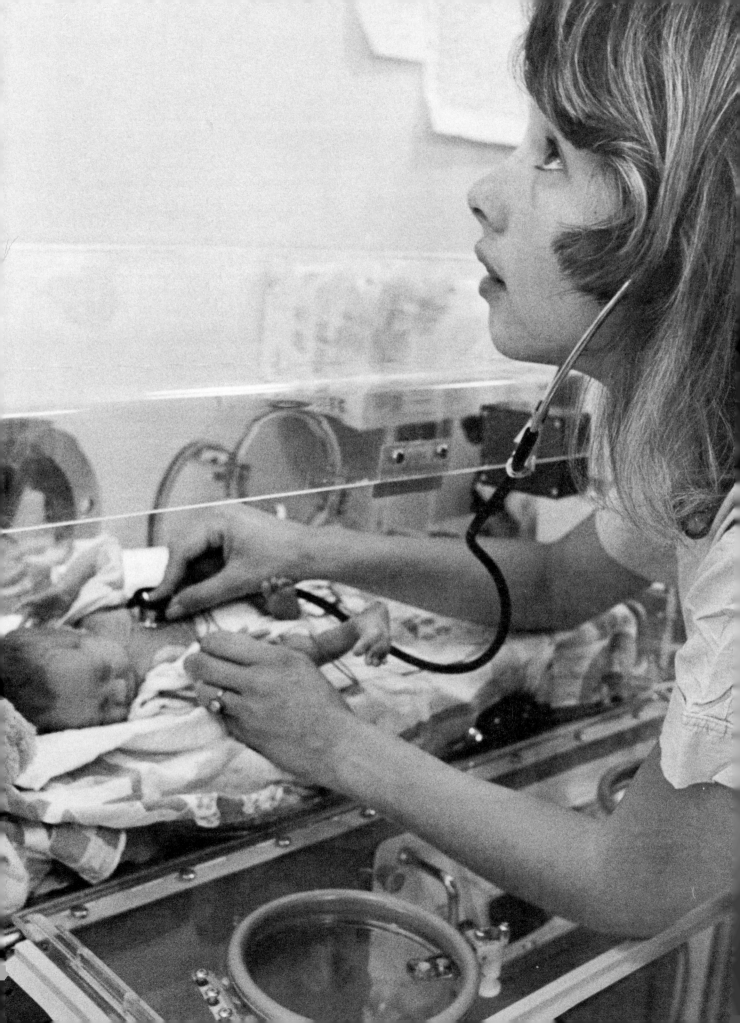

Unit 4 Maternity Nursing

Introduction

The maternity nursing unit reflects the pertinent current theoretical bases (biophysical and psychosocial) and their nursing application. Content is presented in a study outline format with numerous charts and tables, wherein content is synthesized, condensed, and grouped for optimum comparison and contrast to facilitate review, retention, and recall.

Nutrition and pharmacology relevant to maternity are integrated throughout. Key physiologic concepts and measures are included wherever pertinent, but the reader is referred to a basic textbook for review of anatomy.

The maternity nursing unit is divided into three parts:

1. Normal pregnancy—labor, delivery, and postpartum
2. Complications of childbearing and the high-risk neonate
3. The reproductive system in women and men

The review questions contained in this unit are intended for self-evaluation. One hundred and five questions are constructed in a format similar to that of the state board examinations. Fifteen questions require discrimination among several variables and priority-setting.

Special features of this unit include planning for parenthood, when the nurse must deliver the infant, and the pregnant adolescent.

Irene M. Bobak

Part A   Normal Pregnancy

THE MENSTRUAL CYCLE

1. **Central nervous system regulation**—the hypothalamus and anterior pituitary regulate the cyclic activities of the ovary and the endometrium of the uterus
   A. Follicle-stimulating hormone (FSH)—produced during the first half of the cycle, stimulates a graafian follicle in the ovary to begin to ripen an ovum
   B. Luteinizing hormone (LH)—produced during the second half of the cycle
      1. Stimulates release of the mature ovum from the follicle (ovulation)
      2. Maintains corpus luteum (the former graafian follicle) during the last half of the cycle; and, if conception occurs, maintains the corpus luteum during the first two to three months of gestation
2. **Ovarian regulation**—ovarian hormones regulate the hypothalamus and anterior pituitary
   A. Estrogen—produced by the graafian follicle during the first half of the cycle, increases to a peak blood level just before ovulation (day 13 in a 28-day cycle), halting the production of FSH and triggering the release of LH
      1. First half of cycle varies in length
      2. Estrogen begins preparation of endometrium by stimulating the development of the spiral arteries
   B. Progesterone—produced by the corpus luteum, prepares the endometrium to receive a fertilized egg
      1. Develops and stimulates secretion from endometrial glands
      2. Increases basal body temperature
      3. Affects the movement of the fertilized egg through the fallopian tube
      4. Decreases irritability of uterine muscle during pregnancy
      5. In the absence of conception and implantation, progesterone and estrogen levels fall, triggering production of FSH by anterior pituitary; vasoconstriction of spiral arteries in the endometrium results in sloughing of the lining, menstrual flow contains nutrient fluid, cells, and approximately 1 to 2 ounces of blood
      6. The second half of the cycle, from ovulation to the beginning of menstrual flow, is fairly constant at 14 days duration

PLANNING FOR PARENTHOOD

1. **Trends**
   A. Smaller families
   B. Alternative life-style families—single parenthood or commune
   C. Rising divorce rates
   D. Earlier sexual experimentation—availability of assistance to emancipated minors
   E. Legalization of abortion; availability to emancipated minors
2. **General considerations**
   A. Attitude toward use of contraceptives
      1. Religious objections
      2. Social objection—many teens state that "being prepared" negates spontaneity
      3. Magical thinking—"It can't happen to me."
      4. Psychologic need to confirm virility or fertility
   B. Ignorance of methods available
   C. Choice of method (see also Table 4-1)
      1. Safety of method
      2. Degree of effectiveness
      3. Amount of involvement each (man or woman) is willing to have
3. **Interruption of pregnancy**—elective, voluntary, or therapeutic (see also Table 4-2)
   A. Legal aspects
      1. 1973 Supreme Court decision to legalize abortion
      2. Stipulations
         a. First trimester—patient and physician make decision
         b. Second trimester—patient and physician make decision, individual state may stipulate where and how abortion may be performed
         c. Third trimester—increased state regulation, abortion may be prohibited

except when health of mother is jeopardized

3. Menstrual aspiration (extraction) has no legal restriction

B. Postabortion psychologic impact
1. Majority—relieved and happy
2. Small number (5% to 10%)—negative feelings, such as guilt or low self-esteem

C. Nursing care
1. Assist patient in problem solving concerning decision about this pregnancy
2. Explain procedure and encourage ventilation
3. Explain and assist with preoperative preparation
   a. Lab work—blood, urine, and pregnancy test
   b. Laminaria insertion 24 hours prior to procedure
   c. Vital signs and voiding
   d. Medication, if any
4. Provide and explain postoperative care
   a. Monitor bleeding, vital signs, and IVs
   b. Medications—Rho (D antigen) immune globlin (RhoGAM) if indicated; oxytocin, as ordered
5. Predischarge anticipatory guidance
   a. Cramping or bleeding
   b. Signs of infection
   c. Whom to call with questions
   d. Postabortal check-up

PREGNANCY

1. General considerations
A. The life span of the sperm is 48 to 72 hours after ejaculation into the female reproductive tract
B. The life span of the ovum is about 24 to 36 hours after ovulation
C. Conception usually occurs 12 to 24 hours after ovulation, within the distal two thirds of the fallopian tube
D. Implantation occurs within seven days (six to nine days) or about day 20 of a 28-day cycle
2. Pregnancy tests
A. Enough human chorionic gonadotropin (HCG) is produced to give a positive pregnancy test (Gravindex and UCG) within two weeks after implantation or the end of the fifth week (if the cycle were to have been 28 days in length)
B. The Friedman and A-Z (Aschheim-Zondek) tests are no longer done (take longer, cost more, and

require the sacrifice of animals)

3. Estimating gestational age (See also Tables 4-3 and 4-10)
A. Nägele's rule—the estimated date of confinement (EDC) is calculated by noting the first day of the last menstrual cycle (LMP), counting back three months, and adding seven days; length of gestation—280 days, ten lunar months, or nine calendar months plus one week, for example, LMP January 15, EDC October 22
B. Haase's rule—fetal length by lunar months; this is frequently used to determine age of abortus

Month No. $1 \times 1 = 1$ cm (4 weeks)
$2 \times 2 = 4$ cm (8 weeks)
$3 \times 3 = 9$ cm (12 weeks)
$4 \times 4 = 16$ cm (16 weeks)
$5 \times 5 = 25$ cm (20 weeks)
$6 \times 5 = 30$ cm (24 weeks)
$7 \times 5 = 35$ cm (28 weeks)
$8 \times 5 = 40$ cm (32 weeks)
$9 \times 5 = 45$ cm (36 weeks)
$10 \times 5 = 50$ cm (term)

C. Fundal height: cm above the symphysis pubis (SP)
12 weeks—at SP
16 weeks—7.5 cm above SP
20 weeks—13 cm above SP (just below umbilicus)
24 weeks—18 cm above SP
28 weeks—22 cm above SP
32 weeks—25 cm above SP
36 weeks—at ensiform cartilage
38-40 weeks—below ensiform cartilage after lightening
D. Quickening—"feeling life," usually first noted about 18 to 20 weeks gestation
E. Sonography—"A" scan is used to measure the biparietal diameter, starting with week 16
4. Summary of development by week and trimester in calendar months—see Table 4-3
5. Fetal development
A. Environmental influences
1. Teratogens—"monster formers," environmental agents that interfere with normal cell differentiation during the period of organogenesis (the first trimester); proven teratogens are X-ray, rubella (German or three-day measles), and thalidomide
2. Harmful drugs—drugs primarily affect physiologic response when the fetus is exposed during the second and third trimesters

Table 4-1.   Contraceptive methods

Oral medication

Contraceptive Method	Action	Advantages	Disadvantages and Side Effects	Effectiveness
1. (a) Combination of estrogen and progesterone or (b) sequential—estrogen during first half of cycle; progesterone during second half of cycle, for example	1. Suppresses ovulation by suppressing production of FSH and LH; needs to be taken for full month initially before woman is "safe"; a second form of contraceptive should be used during first month of use 2. If dosage is inadequate, ovulation and conception may occur	1. Easy to take for those motivated to remember to take pill as directed 2. Disassociated from sex act 3. Helps regulate cycle for woman who wishes to conceive later 4. Menstrual cycles are predictable 5. No egg matures, so conception is not possible	1. Discomforts simulating those of pregnancy include breast tenderness, water retention, nausea, chloasma—may persist even after discontinuing the pill, and fatigue 2. Hazards include thrombus formation, thrombophlebitis, pulmonary embolus, and hypertension 3. Contraindicated in hypertension, sickle cell disease, heavy smokers, diabetes, and migraine headaches 4. Closure of epiphyses of the long bones	1. Most efficient form of contraception 2. If one pill is missed, it should be taken when woman remembers; next pill should be taken as scheduled 3. If two pills are missed, follow directions above; in addition, a second form of contraceptive should be used for rest of that month 4. If more than two pills are missed, pills should be discontinued for rest of month and another form of contraceptive used; pill-taking schedule should be resumed on fifth day of menstrual cycle
2. Minipill—progesterone (norethindrone 0.35 mg daily)	1. Antifertility effect 2. Makes cervical mucous impervious to sperm or alters endometrium 3. Ovulation does occur	1. Supposedly reduces side effects found with other oral preparations	1. Menstrual irregularity 2. Lumps in breast	1. Undetermined
3. Morning-after pill—estrogen in very high levels (25 mg)	1. Suppresses anterior pituitary or alters endometrium 2. Menstruation within five days	1. Can be taken within 24 hours after coitus; two tablets should be taken each day for five days	1. Nausea and vomiting 2. Dilatation and curettage (D & C) if no menstruation ensues 3. Predisposes fetus to reproductive tract cancer in adulthood	1. 100% effective only when followed by D & C

Intrauterine devices (IUD)

Contraceptive Method	Action	Advantages	Disadvantages and Side Effects	Effectiveness
1. The following are made of soft plastic and/or nickel-chromium alloy, a nonreactive metal: Lippes Loop, Saf-T-Coil, and the Cu-7	1. Interferes with fertilization 2. Alters rate of egg's passage through the fallopian tube 3. Or, discourages implantation by altering endometrium, preventing sperm from entry into fallopian tube	1. No interference with hormonal regulation of the menstrual cycle 2. No need to remember to take a pill each day or engage in other manipulation prior to or between coitus 3. May be removed by physician when pregnancy is desired	1. Hazards—Unnoticed expulsion, must check for presence of IUD after each menses; uterine perforation with intra-abdominal trauma and/or intrauterine or fallopian infection 2. Side effects—heavy flow, spotting between periods, and cramping, especially during early months of use 3. May increase the incidence of tubal pregnancy	1. Not as effective as the pill 2. Failure rate—during first year, about 2% to 3%; later, under 2%

Not recommended

Contraceptive method	Action	Advantages	Disadvantages and Side Effects	Effectiveness
1. Coitus interruptus	1. Avoids ejaculation of sperm into vagina	1. None	1. Requires discipline 2. Psychologically unsound—strains the sexual relationship 3. Preejaculatory drops contain sperm 4. Sperm deposited anywhere near the vagina may lead to conception	1. Low rate of effectiveness
2. Douching	1. Washes out the vagina	1. None	1. Sperm enter cervix as it dips into the ejaculatory pool in the vagina during orgasm 2. Douching may force more sperm into the cervix	1. Ineffective

Continued

Table 4-1.   Contraceptive methods—Continued

Sterilization

Contraceptive Method	Action	Advantages	Disadvantages and Side Effects	Effectiveness
1. Men	1. Vasectomy—vas deferens is ligated and severed, interrupting passage of sperm	1. Relatively simple surgical procedure 2. Does not affect endocrine function, production of testosterone 3. Does not alter volume of ejaculate	1. Some men become impotent due to their psychologic response to the procedure 2. Reversible in 20%–40% of cases	1. 100% effective after the ejaculate is free of sperm that was in the vas deferens (about three months or ten ejaculations)
2. Women	1. Tubal ligation—both fallopian tubes are ligated and severed preventing the passage of eggs	1. Abdominal surgery utilizing 1-inch incisions and laparoscopy	1. Major surgery (if done by laparotomy) with possible complications of anesthesia, infection, hemorrhage, and trauma to other organs 2. Psychologic trauma in some	1. 100% effective if ligatures do not slip
	2. Hysterectomy with salpingo-oophorectomy, no egg is produced	1. No possibility of pregnancy 2. No further menstruation	1. Abrupt loss of ovarian hormones simulating menopause 2. Major surgery complications 3. Psychologic trauma in some—loss of femininity and sexuality	1. 100% effective

Mechanical barriers

Contraceptive Method	Action	Advantages	Disadvantages and Side Effects	Effectiveness
1. Diaphragm—rubber device that fits over cervix	1. Barrier preventing sperm from entering cervix if it is correct size and correctly placed; refitted for size after each baby, and/or every two years	1. Safety—no side effects 2. May be inserted several hours before intercourse and is left in place for six hours afterward	1. Some women find insertion and removal objectionable 2. Requires washing with warm water and soap; careful drying; storage away from heat; and checking for tears	1. Failure rate—10 to 15 pregnancies per 100 users per year 2. Effectiveness is improved somewhat if a spermicidal foam, jelly, or cream is also used

Contraceptive Method	Action	Advantages	Disadvantages and Side Effects	Effectiveness
2. Condom—thin stretchable rubber sheath to cover the penis	1. Barrier preventing sperm from entering the vagina 2. Is applied over the erect penis	1. Safety—no side effects 2. Protective measure against the spread of venereal disease to some extent	1. Some couples object to taking time to apply sheath on erect penis 2. Preejaculatory drops also contain sperm; conception possible even if drops fall around *external* vaginal opening 3. Sheath may tear during intercourse	1. Failure rate—3% if spermicidal foam, jelly, or cream is also used and sheath is held in place as penis is withdrawn to prevent emptying of sperm in or near vagina

Chemical barriers

Contraceptive Method	Action	Advantages	Disadvantages and Side Effects	Effectiveness
1. Spermicide, tartaric acid, and bicarbonate—foam, jelly, cream, or vaginal suppository	1. Kills sperm 2. Decreases sperm motility 3. Sperm cannot pass through chemical barrier	1. Increases effectiveness of mechanical barriers 2. Ease of application 3. Aids lubrication of vagina 4. Does not harm delicate vaginal tissue	1. Described as "messy" by some 2. If it is the only method being used, each intercourse should be preceded by a fresh application 3. Felt to decrease tactile sensation by some users	1. High failure rate, especially when used without diaphragm and condom

Other methods

Contraceptive Method	Action	Advantages	Disadvantages and Side Effects	
1. Rhythm—rectal temperature each morning before *any* physical activity	1. Conception is avoided by sexual abstinence during woman's fertile period; no sperm may be present while egg is present 2. The "fertile" period includes three days before ovulation plus one day after; sperm may live up to three days; the egg from 24 to 36 hours	1. Physically safe to use—no drugs or appliances are used 2. Meets requirements of some religions	1. Effectiveness depends on the following: high level of motivation and diligence, daily temperature-taking and record-keeping for duration of childbearing years, and willingness to abstain 2. Requires fairly predictable menstrual cycle 3. Ovulation usually	1. Very low rate of effectiveness 2. Temperature varies with tension, infection, staying up late the night before, or any prior activity 3. Irregular cycles require long periods of abstinence 4. Effectiveness may be increased by using litmus paper and/or

Continued

Table 4-1. Contraceptive methods—Continued

Other methods

Contraceptive method	Action	Advantages	Disadvantages and Side Effects	Effectiveness
			occurs 14 days *before* the next menstrual flow 4. Ovulation may occur at atypical times	checking changes in cervical mucous 5. Failure rate—14% to 40%
2. Litmus paper—when oral mucous turns paper blue (basic), couple must abstain for five days	1. Identifies fertile period so that the couple knows when to prevent conception or to get pregnant	1. Physically safe 2. Acceptable to certain religions	1. Effectiveness unknown 2. Requires daily check of oral mucous	1. Unknown at present
3. Observe for change in cervical mucous—ovulation method	1. Identifies fertile period	1. Physically safe 2. Acceptable to certain religions	1. Requires the couple to learn cervical mucous changes and engage in the internal vaginal manipulation necessary to assess mucous	1. Unknown at present

a. Anticoagulants—hemorrhage and death of fetus
b. Aspirin (even one dose during week prior to birth)—increased tendency to hemorrhage
c. Sedatives (excessive amounts)—hemorrhage and death
d. Sulfonamides—kernicterus
e. Smoking—small-for-age babies and possible increased tendencies toward respiratory tract illnesses

3. Infections—many infections are hazardous to the fetus during the second and third trimesters
   a. Rubella—causes small-for-gestational-age baby, bleeding tendency, enlarged liver and spleen, hepatitis (often with jaundice), bone lesions, encephalitis, pneumonia, abnormal EKGs, and abnormal fingerprints and palm creases
   b. Herpes simplex II (genital herpes)—may be lethal to fetus, skin eruptions on newborn, and septicemia with respiratory and circulatory failure
   c. Syphilis—snuffles (rhinitis), rhagades (scars around mouth), hydrocephaly, and corneal opacity; later: saddle nose, saber shin, Hutchinson's teeth (notched, tapered canines), and diabetes; no residual fetal-newborn effects if mother is treated adequately before fifth month
   d. Gonorrhea—ophthalmia neonatorum acquired during passage through birth canal and neonatal sepsis with temperature instability, hypotonia, poor feeding, and jaundice; may be cause of premature labor, premature rupture of membranes, maternal fever, and chorioamnionitis
   e. Cytomegalic inclusion disease (virus in parotid glands) and toxoplasmosis (protozoan disease frequently acquired from household cats)—both produce similar symptoms: microcephaly, chorioretinitis, and cerebral calcification with seizures, progressive anemia, and hepatomegaly
   f. Mumps—abortion, premature labor, fetal death, and congenital anomalies

B. Placenta
   1. Development
      a. Primitive placenta—24 hours after

implantation, syncytiotrophoblast begins to invade the endometrium; HCG production begins; and exchange between mother and embryo begins

  b. Decidua—hypertrophied endometrium of pregnancy; sloughed off in lochia following delivery

    (1) Decidua basalis— lies between embryo and decidua

    (2) Decidua capsularis—covers developing embryo

  c. Chorion—outermost fetal membrane continuous with the placenta

  d. Amnion—innermost fetal membrane, contains amniotic fluid and the fetus

  e. Placenta (afterbirth)

    (1) Developed from the decidua basalis and chorion of the embryo

    (2) Formed by the end of the third month of gestation

    (3) Cotyledon—subdivision of placenta on maternal surface

    (4) At term—one-sixth weight of the neonate; rounded, flat, approximately 1 to 1½ lb, 1 inch thick in center, and 7 to 8 inches in diameter

    (5) Fetal surface—glistening grayish (Schultz)

    (6) Maternal surface—beefy red and rough; cotyledons evident (Duncan)

  2. Function

    a. Transfer of gases, nutrients, wastes, antibodies, drugs, and microorganisms between mother and fetus across the placenta is by diffusion and osmosis

    b. Maternal and fetal blood does not mix

    c. Endocrine hormone production

      (1) Human chorionic gonadotropin (HCG)

      (2) Estradiol, estriol—estrogens of pregnancy; estriol is excreted in urine and level is an indicator of fetal condition; in last trimester, 4 mg or less indicative of fetal demise; 4 to 12 mg, fetal distress (24-hour urine specimens)

      (3) Pregnanediol—progesterone

      (4) Human placental lactogen (HPL)—growth hormonelike activity

C. Fetal circulation

  1. Fetal structures—four intrauterine struc-

tures differ from extrauterine structures

  a. Foramen ovale—allows fetal blood to bypass fetal lungs

  b. Ductus arteriosus—allows fetal blood to bypass fetal lungs

  c. Ductus venosus—allows most of the blood to bypass the liver on the way to the ascending vena cava, from the umbilical vein

  d. Umbilical arteries (two)—return deoxygenated blood to the placenta

  2. Umbilical cord—extends from the fetus to the center (usually) of the placenta; it is usually 50 cm (20 inches) long and 1 to 2 cm (½ to 1 inch) in diameter; It contains

  a. Wharton's jelly

  b. One vein—carries oxygen and nutrients from placenta to fetus

  c. Two arteries—carry deoxygenated blood and fetal wastes from fetus to placenta; absence of one artery signals need to examine newborn to rule out intra-abdominal anomalies

6. Maternal changes

A. Physiologic-anatomic adjustments (see also Table 4-3)

  1. Bases of functional alteration

    a. Hormonal—estrogen, progesterone, lactogen, HCG, and relaxin

    b. Mechanical—enlarging uterus causes displacement and pressure; increased weight of uterus and breasts causes changes in posture and pressure

  2. Reproductive organs

    a. Uterus (see Table 4-3)—growth due to hypertrophy and some hyperplasia

      (1) Existing muscle cells and connective tissue increase in size

      (2) New muscle cells and connective tissue

      (3) Increased vascularity

      (4) Three muscle fiber layers

        (a) Outer—hoodlike over fundus

        (b) Middle—figure-of-eight (loops go around fallopian tubes); this layer contains the blood vessels

        (c) Inner—circle the orifices to fallopian tubes and cervix

    b. Cervix

      (1) Increase in vascularity

      (2) Thickening of mucous lining

      (3) Edema, hyperplasia, and increased

Table 4-2. Interruption of pregnancy

First trimester

Methods	Advantages	Disadvantages and Side Effects	Effectiveness
1. Menstrual extraction—forced endometrial extraction	1. Performed stat after missed period	1. Cervical trauma may occur, may lead to incompetence 2. Hemorrhage	1. 100%
2. Prostaglandin—IV or injection into cul-de-sac of Douglas	1. Stimulates contraction of smooth muscle	1. About 24 hours to work 2. May cause vomiting, diarrhea, chills, local tissue reaction (retained placenta necessitates D & C)	1. 100%
3. Vacuum extraction—cannula suction following cervical dilatation under local anesthesia	1. Effective with relatively few complications—minimal bleeding, minimal discomfort 2. 5 to 15-minute duration 3. Done on come-and-go basis	1. Pregnancy ten weeks or less 2. Cervical trauma may occur (decreased if dilatation by laminaria inserted 24 hours prior to procedure)	1. 100%
4. Dilatation and curettage (D & C)—cervix dilated with metal sounds; endometrium is scraped with a spoonlike instrument	1. 15-minute duration 2. Usually complications are few 3. May be done under local anesthesia	1. Pregnancy 12 weeks or less 2. Hazards—uterine perforation, infection (25%), effects of general anesthesia	1. 100%

Second trimester

Methods	Advantages	Disadvantages and Side Effects	Effectiveness
1. Saline abortion—after week 16 (uterus in abdominal cavity and sufficient amniotic fluid present); transabdominal extraction of amniotic fluid and replacement with equal amount of saline (or combination of urea/prostaglandin)	1. Only method available during this period of gestation 2. Does not require laparotomy 3. Patient may ambulate until labor starts (within 24 hours) and during early labor	1. Complications increase proportionately with weeks of gestation 2. Hazards—requires hospitalization; 6% readmitted 3. Reaction to saline—tinnitus, tachycardia, and headache 4. Water intoxication symptoms—edema, oliguria ($\leq$200 ml/8 hours), dyspnea, thirst, and restlessness 5. Hemorrhage; may require postabortal D & C or vacuum extraction as well; fever 6. Experiences labor	1. Fetal death within one hour of injection

Continued

Table 4-2. Interruption of pregnancy—Continued

Second and third trimester

Methods	Advantages	Disadvantages and Side Effects	Effectiveness
1. Hysterotomy—cesarean section	1. Preferred method if woman wishes a tubal ligation or hysterectomy to follow	1. Post-major-surgery complications—hemorrhage and infection 2. Fetus may be born alive, opening ethical, moral, religious, and legal problems 3. Mortality risk—combination hysterotomy-hysterectomy 40% greater than with D & C	1. 100%

mucus gland production, formation of mucus plug by end of month two
   (4) Becomes shorter, thicker, and more elastic
   (5) Chadwick's sign—deepened blue-purple coloration of cervix and vagina
   (6) Goodell's sign—cervical softening
 c. Vagina
   (1) Hypertrophy and thickening of walls
   (2) Relaxation of connective tissue
   (3) Increased vascularity
   (4) Chadwick's sign
   (5) pH—acidic
   (6) Leukorrhea
 d. Perineum
   (1) Increase in size—hypertrophy of muscle cells, edema, and relaxation of elastic tissue
   (2) Deepened color—increased vascularization
   (3) Varices
3. Breasts (see Table 4-3)
4. Metabolism
 a. Weight gain 20 to 30 lb (average gain 24 lb)
 b. Increased water retention
 c. Protein—increased need for fetal and uterine growth and maternal blood (500 gm needed for hemoglobin and plasma protein)
 d. Basal metabolic rate (BMR) increases as pregnancy progresses due to increased oxygen consumption
 e. Carbohydrates

   (1) Need increased amount to spare protein stores and intake
   (2) Pregnancy aggravates existing diabetes mellitus
   (3) Gestational diabetes may occur
   (4) Plasma insulin levels (in normal pregnancy) are higher, coupled with a more rapid destruction of insulin
 f. Fat—levels of plasma lipids rise
 g. Iron—circulating erythrocytes in maternal blood increase by 450 ml, necessitating an added 500 mg; supplementation recommended
5. Cardiovascular system
 a. Heart displaced upward and to the left; systolic murmurs common
 b. Circulation
   (1) Cardiac volume increases by 30% to 50% during the last two trimesters
   (2) Cardiac output
     (a) Increased by 35% during last two trimesters
     (b) Heart rate increases five to ten beats/minute
     (c) Labor—with each contraction, cardiac output increases by 15% to 20% regardless of regional anesthesia
 c. Red blood cell volume and hematocrit and hemoglobin values diminish approximately 10% in the last two trimesters (physiologic anemia)
 d. Vena caval syndrome or supine hypotensive syndrome—bradycardia, reduced cardiac output, and a drop in

systolic blood pressure from uterine compression of inferior vena cava when the mother is supine; additional maternal symptoms include faintness, sweating, and nausea; fetal symptoms include marked bradycardia (deceleration)

6. Urinary tract
   a. Relaxation of smooth muscles (see Musculoskeletal system)—leads to dilatation of ureters (especially on right side) and decreased bladder tone, increasing possibility of urinary stasis and infection; persists between four to six weeks after delivery
   b. Glucosuria evident and normal; later, lactosuria as well (urine glucose level is not a reliable index of diabetic status)
   c. Frequency during early and late pregnancy
   d. Glomerular filtration rate increases by 50% during last two trimesters without a similar rise in renal plasma flow; increases efficiency without raising blood pressure

7. Gastrointestinal tract
   a. Gingivae soften and enlarge and have a greater tendency to bleed due to increased vascularity
   b. Ptyalism—increased salivation
   c. General decrease in smooth muscle tone and motility
      (1) Movement of food slows
      (2) Stomach—emptying time is delayed
      (3) Cardiac sphincter relaxes
      (4) Increasing size of uterus and displacement of intra-abdominal organs results in constipation, heartburn, and flatulence

8. Respiratory tract
   a. Increased ventilation with increased oxygen consumption; increased sensitivity to CO_2 levels; may be short of breath with normal exertion at times
   b. Respiratory rate—relatively unchanged, 16/minute (woman breathes deeper, not faster)
   c. Diaphragm is elevated and anterior-posterior diameter of rib cage is increased
   d. Vital capacity—unchanged

9. Endocrine system
   a. Progressive increase in BMR
   b. Increase in size and activity of some glands—pituitary, thyroid, and adrenals, for example

10. Integument
    a. Increased pigmentation from second trimester of pregnancy—linea nigra, chloasma, and areola
    b. Striae gravidarum (stretch marks)
    c. Increased sebaceous and sweat gland activity

11. Musculoskeletal system
    a. Progesterone- and relaxin-induced relaxation of joints, cartilage, and ligaments
       (1) Feeling of pelvic looseness
       (2) Duck-waddle walk
    b. Posture—increasing weight of uterus tilts the pelvis forward; the woman throws her head and shoulders backward to compensate, exaggerating the lumbar spinal curvature
       (1) Causes—leg and back strain and fatigue
       (2) Treatment
          (a) Good body alignment—tuck pelvis under baby; tighten abdominal muscles
          (b) Squat, bend at the knees not with the back
          (c) Low heeled, sturdy shoes
          (d) Pelvic rock exercise

B. Emotional Changes
   1. Physical bases of changes
      a. Increased metabolic demands may lead to fatigue and anemia
      b. Increased levels of hormones—steroids, estrogen, and progesterone
   2. Types
      a. First trimester—mood swings; emotional lability may be disturbing to self and significant others
      b. Ambivalence toward pregnancy now—usually gives way to acceptance when fetal movements are felt; introversion and passivity usually begin in second trimester
         (1) Old unresolved conflicts emerge—feelings toward mother, sexual intimacy, and masturbation; movement toward resolution is possible now

Table 4-3. Summary of development by week and trimester in calendar months*

Gestational age	Embryo-fetus development	Uterine changes	Possible maternal signs and physiologic changes in pregnancy
Month one			
Menstruation			
Week 1		Weight—57 gm (2 oz); length—6.5 cm (2½ inches); and capacity—30 ml (1 oz)	
Week 2		Phase—estrogenic, preovulatory, or proliferative	
Fertilization-conception			
Week 3		Phase—progestational, secretory, or luteal	Basal body temperature remains elevated, decreased appetite due to decreased gastric motility
Implantation			
Week 4	Digestive system forming, germ layers differentiated, 1 cm long	Mucosa invaded by trophoblasts, endometrium becomes *Decidua*	Nausea, fatigue, and breasts tense and tingling
Month two			
Amenorrhea			
Week 5	Brain, nervous system, and reproductive system forming; heart developing and beginning to beat	Human chorionic gonadotropin (HCG) secreted in quantity by chorionic villi	Basal temperature constant, blood sugar low, and endocrine test (for HCG) positive
Week 6	0.5 cm (3/16 inch) long, facial features forming, and circulation starts	Mild contractions start; cervix and vagina blue—Chadwick's sign; lower uterine segment soft—Hegar's sign	Pressure on bladder and urinary frequency
Week 7	1/2 inch (1¼ cm) long, arm and leg buds appear, and umbilical cord forming	Mucus plug forming in cervical canal	Profuse vaginal secretions, thick and acid; nausea subsiding
Week 8	Hands, feet, fingers, and toes forming (with thalidomide, phocomelia); 4 cm (1½ inches) long; thin skin covers body		Salivation (ptyalism), breasts larger and nodular, and Montgomery's follicles appear
Month three			
Week 9	Eyelids forming, and genital ridge visible but sexless in character as yet	*Placenta* is now secreting progesterone (corpus luteum is decreasing function)	

*Study this chart primarily by *trimester*, not week by week

Continued

Table 4-3.   Summary of development by week and trimester in calendar months—Continued

Gestational age	Embryo-fetus development	Uterine changes	Possible maternal signs and physiologic changes in pregnancy
Week 10	Human appearance, respiratory activity evident, can swallow, and kidneys excrete	Placenta covers one-third of uterine wall	
Week 11	Eyelids fused, sex is *distinguishable*, 20 tooth buds forming, 4¼ to 5 cm (2 inches) long		Colostrum may be expressed from nipples
Week 12	Now a *fetus*, skeleton becoming bone; Length—7½ to 9 cm (3 inches); weight—28 gm (1 oz) and nails forming	Size of orange, fundus at level of symphysis pubis	Nausea and vomiting rare now
Week 13	Muscles contract occasionally, weak	Rising from pelvic cavity	Bladder pressure less and blood sugar up

End of first trimester—period of organogenesis (organ differentiation) and (hyperplasia) ends; fetus is less susceptible to teratogenic effect from now on; and growth continues primarily by hypertrophy (increase in cell size)

Month four

Week 14	Nearly 10 cm (4 inches) long, sex easily distinguishable	Becoming an abdominal organ	Blood volume starts to increase, cardiac output is 24% to 50% greater, and heart size increases
Week 15	*Lanugo* appearing, head hair forming, and human appearance	Enough amniotic fluid (200 ml) to permit aminocentesis	Physiologic anemia; free HCl in gastric declines, making it harder to absorb iron; and blood pressure lower
Week 16	Weight—114 gm (4 oz); length—16 cm (6½ inches); and muscles contract more vigorously	Uterine contractions, but not yet palpable; fundal height—7.5 cm above SP	Increased fibrinogen, plasma volume, and RBC; decreased hemoglobin concentration; and a few mothers may experience quickening
Week 17	Skeleton visible on X-ray, positive sign of pregnancy	Uterine souffle	

Month five

Week 18	*Vernix* caseosa forming on skin and *meconium* collecting	Walls thin	Decisive increase in blood volume (30%) starts; nitrogen storage increasing due to increased metabolic demands for new tissue formation and increased steroids causing retention of Na and water; increase in vascular system
Week 19	Onset of rapid growth; iron starts to be stored; enamel-dentin deposited		Quickening—mother feels fetal movement

Continued

Table 4-3. Summary of development by week and trimester in calendar months—Continued

Gestational age	Embryo-fetus development	Uterine changes	Possible maternal signs and physiologic changes in pregnancy
Week 20	Length—25 cm (10 inches); weight—340 gm (12 oz); fetal heart may be heard with fetoscope		Secondary areola appear and internal ballottement may be felt
Week 21	Eyebrows and eye lashes visible	Fundal height—at the umbilicus, 14 to 15 cm above SP	Umbilicus flush with skin and relaxation of smooth muscle, veins, bladder, etc.
Month six			
Week 22	Body and head more proportionate		External ballottement may be felt
Week 23	25 mg of iron stored		Ureteral dilatation marked and *linea nigra* and *chloasma* (mask of pregnancy) may appear
Week 24	Length—30 cm (12 inches); weight—680 gm (1½ lb); may be viable	Fundal height—18 cm above SP (just above umbilicus)	Period of greatest weight gain starts (4 to 5 lb/month); abdomen slightly distended
Week 25	Skin red and shiny and face wrinkled		*Striae gravidarum* may appear
Week 26	Outline may be felt abdominally, positive sign of pregnancy	Amniotic fluid—1000 to 1500 ml	Period of lowest hemoglobin starts—iron therapy may be started
End second trimester			
Month seven			
Week 27	Much iron stored, storage of subcutaneous fat starts, and testes descend	Wall soft and yielding and start of placental senility	Weight gain continues—4 lb/month
Week 28	Length—35 cm (14 inches); weight—1134 gm (2½ lb); eyelids open; fingerprints set; in female—all eggs are present and have completed first stage of development; viable now	Fundus—22 cm above SP and elastic tissue wall thickening	Period of lowest hemoglobin continues
Month seven			
Weeks 29 to 30	Weak cry, more rapid growth starts, much calcium deposit-storage	Braxton Hicks contractions palpable	Marked protein storage; blood volume highest—30% to 50% over nonpregnant amounts
Month eight			
Week 31	15.5 mg nitrogen is stored, lanugo begins to be shed, and fingernails grow rapidly	Fundus—25 cm above SP, halfway between umbilicus and ensiform cartilage	Large amount of calcium lost to fetus; BMR—+2

Continued

Table 4-3. Summary of development by week and trimester in calendar months—Continued

Gestational age	Embryo-fetus development	Uterine changes	Possible maternal signs and physiologic changes in pregnancy
Week 32	Length—40 cm (16 inches); weight—1800 gm (4 lb); presentation—usually vertex, 3% breech; chance of extrauterine survival greater now		3 to 4 lb gained this month; striae gravidarum more marked; pelvic joints more relaxed—mother may feel her pelvis is loose, duck-waddle walk common
Weeks 33 to 35	227.6 mg iron stored; 31.6 mg nitrogen; and largest deposit of calcium starts	Braxton Hicks contractions stronger	Large amount of iron lost, stomach flaccid and on top of uterus, heartburn
Month nine			
Week 36	Length—45 cm (18 inches); weight—2268 gm (5+ lb); increased amount of subcutaneous fat, storage of minerals and vitamins; and acquisition of immune bodies from mother	Fundus—at ensiform cartilage	Umbilicus protrudes, shortness of breath, Hgb starts to rise, BP rises a bit, BMR—+4
Weeks 37 to 38	58.5 mg nitrogen stored, high Hgb, low O_2 tension (cyanotic), and body well-formed	Engaged (nullipara): fundus—slightly below ensiform cartilage	*lightening* (nullipara), breathing easier, varicosities, ankle edema, and frequency
Weeks 39 to 40	246.2 mg iron stored; lanugo shed; length—50 cm (20 inches); weight—3175 to 3400 gm (7 to 7½ lb)	Weight—1000 gm (2 lb); Capacity—4000 ml; Length—32 cm; Amniotic fluid—500 to 1000 ml	Lightening with start of labor in multigravida
End third trimester	Survival at term—optimal	Placenta—⅙ of fetal weight	BMR +7
Over week 42	Postmature—subcutaneous fat and glycogen reserves decrease; hypoxia with passage of meconium; skin dry and wrinkled; nails long; survival jeopardized	Placenta progressively more senile—efficiency of exchange of nutrients, O_2/CO_2, decreases	Increased fatigue and danger of dystocia

   (2) Reevaluates herself, her life-style, and her marriage
   (3) Daydreams, fantasizes herself as "mother," may acquire pet or babysit, or seek out other pregnant women or new mothers
 c. Third trimester fears
   (1) Loss of body image
   (2) Bodily mutilation—growth and stretching of body tissues, especially birth canal; episiotomy; and cesarean section

   (3) Loss of control of body function—ptyalism, leaking of colostrum, leukorrhea, frequency, and constipation
   (4) For child—deformity or death
   (5) Pain
   (6) Exposing fears and thoughts to others
3. Spouse
 a. Frequently shares her fears and period of introspection, but often each is unaware of this fact

b. Requires same nursing interventions as she does
  (1) Reassurance that these fears and feelings are expected and acceptable
  (2) Assistance in opening or keeping open lines of communication
  (3) Opportunity to ventilate feelings and concerns
  (4) Validation that it is normal for the father to experience some discomforts of pregnancy too

C. Terms
  1. Gravida—a pregnant woman
    a. Primigravida—the woman's first pregnancy
    b. Multigravida—the woman's second and later pregnancies
  2. Para—refers to past pregnancies that had reached viability, whether or not the infant was born alive
    a. Multipara—delivered of two or more pregnancies that had reached viability
    b. Any pregnancy resulting in twins who reach the age of viability, increases her parity by two; therefore, a first pregnancy resulting in viable twins makes her para 2, gravida 1

7. Nursing care and obstetrical support during the antepartal period
A. Nutrition for childbearing
  1. Recommended daily allowance (RDA) for nonpregnant, pregnant, and lactating women of different ages (See Appendix C)
  2. Weight gain—average, 24 lb
    a. If underweight at conception, gravida should gain more than 24 lb
    b. If obese at conception, gravida should *not diet* now; she should gain about 24 lb
    c. Appropriate weight-gain pattern
      (1) First trimester—2 to 4 lb
      (2) Second and third trimesters—0.9 lb per week
    d. Consequent of this weight increase and pattern of weight gain is the lowest incidence of toxemia, small-for-gestational age infants, and perinatal mortality
  3. "Basic four" food groups (see Appendix C)
  4. Fluids—at least four glasses per day (about 1 liter)
  5. Sodium-restriction diets
    a. Degrees of restriction per 24 hours
      (1) Mild—2 to 4 gm (2000 to 4000 mg)
      (2) Moderate—1000 mg (1 gm)
      (3) Strict—500 mg
    b. Care must be taken with these diets since sodium needs normally increase during pregnancy; protein foods of high biologic value contain large amounts of sodium; therefore, two needed nutrients are compromised; these diets in toxemia

Table 4-4. Signs and symptoms of pregnancy

Presumptive (she experiences)	Probable (examiner identifies)	Positive (second trimester)
1. Amenorrhea—more than ten days past missed period	1. Positive pregnancy test	1. Fetal heart tones
2. Breast changes	2. Enlargement of abdomen (after third month)	a. Doptone—12 weeks
3. Nausea and vomiting	3. Reproductive organ changes (after sixth week)	b. Fetoscope—20 weeks
4. Striae gravidarum, linea nigra, chloasma, and quickening (after week 16)	a. Hager's sign—softening of lower uterine segment	2. Examiner feels fetal movements
5. Urinary frequency	b. Goodell's sign—cervix softening	3. X-ray of fetal skeleton (4+ months)
6. Fatigue	c. Chadwick's sign—vagina bluish	4. Sonographic examination (after week 16 when fetal head is sufficiently developed to assure accurate diagnosis)
7. Deeper vulvar color	4. Ballottement (after fourth to fifth month)	
8. Braxton Hicks contractions	5. Outline of fetus palpated through abdominal wall (after fourth to fifth month)	
	6. Braxton Hicks contractions	

are falling out of favor for patients since toxemia may be a disease of malnutrition (diets low in good protein)

   c. Many studies show prevention and cure of toxemia by increasing protein (and, therefore, sodium) in diets

   d. It is wise to limit excess table salt and potato chips, cokes, etc.; caloric value of these is high, the nutritional value low and salt intake excessive

B. Discomforts of pregnancy (see Table 4-5)

C. Danger signs and symptoms during pregnancy
1. Visual disturbances—blurring, double vision, and spots
2. Swelling of face or fingers
3. Severe and continuous headaches
4. Persistent vomiting beyond first trimester or severe vomiting any time
5. Fluid discharge from vagina—bleeding or amniotic fluid (anything other than leukorrhea)
6. Fever or chills
7. Severe pain in the abdomen
8. Absence of fetal movements after quickening

D. Prenatal supervision
1. Initial examination—baseline for health supervision, teaching, emotional support, and/or for referrals (for genetic counseling, voluntary abortion, family planning, and social services)
2. Physical aspects
   a. Weight
   b. Vital signs
   c. Blood work—hematocrit and hemoglobin for anemia; type and Rh; tests for sickle cell trait, syphilis, and rubella antibody titer
   d. Urinalysis—glucose, albumin, signs of infection, and pregnancy test (HCG)
   e. History
     (1) Familial—inheritable diseases and reproductive problems
     (2) Personal, medical, and past obstetrical
     (3) Present pregnancy—LMP and calculation of EDC, symptoms, drugs taken, and exposure to X-ray or infectious diseases
   f. Pelvic examination
     (1) Signs of pregnancy
     (2) Adequacy of pelvis and pelvic structures
     (3) Size and position of uterus
     (4) Papanicolaou's smear (see p. 269)
     (5) Smears for monilial and trichomonal infections (see p. 267)
     (6) Signs of pelvic inflammatory disease (see p. 268)
3. Psychosocial aspects
   a. Note whether pregnancy was planned or not, whether wanted or not; ascertain the plans for this pregnancy (voluntary abortion, desire for pregnancy, and relinquishment for adoption)
   b. Provide anticipatory guidance and support for ambivalent feelings, negative feelings, and mood swings and changes
   c. Support both partners
     (1) Encourage mutuality between them
     (2) Increases the tendency for the mother to turn to the father as the most significant person (as opposed to turning toward the obstetrician)
     (3) Decreases the probability of postpartum psychologic problems
   d. If the couple is unwed, encourage both to participate in the decision regarding this pregnancy

E. Sexuality and sexual expression during pregnancy and postpartum
1. Sexual appetite may increase or decrease during pregnancy; because of the perineal vasocongestion, some women are orgasmic for the first time during pregnancy
2. First trimester
   a. Decline in interest, usually—nausea, fatigue, breast tenderness
   b. If woman is an habitual aborter, it may be wise to avoid intercourse during the times when she would normally be having her menstrual period; however, orgasm has not been proved to cause abortion
3. Midtrimester
   a. A relative increase in orgasmic activity and sexual interest occurs
   b. Women may feel a responsibility to show interest to keep their men at home
   c. Some men are repulsed by the increased vaginal show (leukorrhea)
4. Late pregnancy
   a. In the absence of pathology, bleeding, or ruptured membranes, there is no

Table 4-5.   Discomforts of pregnancy

Discomfort and cause	Prevention	Treatment
Morning sickness—first three months; nausea and vomiting; may occur anytime, day or night; *cause:* hormonal, psychologic, and empty stomach	Do eat—five to six times daily, small amounts; avoid empty stomach, offending odors, and food difficult to digest (food high in fat, for example)	Alternate dry carbohydrate one hour, fluids (hot tea, or mild clear coffee) next hour; take dry carbohydrate before rising, stay in bed 15 more minutes
Fatigue (sleep hunger)—first three months; *cause:* hormones? Often returns late pregnancy when physical load is great	Not preventable—may be modified with rest and diet (prevent anemia)	Iron supplement if anemic—foods high in iron, folic acid, and protein of high biologic value
Fainting (syncope)—early pregnancy, due to slight decrease arterial blood pressure; late pregnancy, due to venous stasis in lower extremities	When standing, do not lock knees; avoid prolonged standing; may come with prolonged fasting	Elevate feet; sit down when necessary
Urinary frequency—enlarging uterus presses on bladder; relieved somewhat as it rises from pelvis; recurs with lightening	Unpreventable—modified by Kegal's exercises	Kegal's exercises; limit fluids just before bedtime to ensure rest
Vaginal discharge—months two to nine; mucusy, acid, and increases in amount	Not preventable; cleanliness important	Treatable only if infection sets in; douche only with prescription
Hot flashes—heat intolerance, increased metabolism, increased sweating	None	No treatment or prevention is necessary—alter clothing, bathing, and environmental temperature as necessary
Headache—cause unknown; blood pressure change? nutritional? tension? (unless associated with toxemia)	Be aware of sources of tension; practice relaxing; eat adequate diet	If pain relief needed, consult physician (avoid aspirin without prescription)
Nasal stuffiness—·due to increased vascularization; allergic rhinitis of pregnancy	Not avoidable if woman has this tendency; will return to normal postpartum	Antihistamines and nasal sprays by prescription only
Heartburn—not related to heart; enlarging uterus and hormones slow digestion; progesterone causes reverse peristaltic waves resulting in reflux of stomach contents into esophagus	Instead of leaning over, bend at the knees, keeping torso straight; sit on firm chairs; limit fatty and fried foods in diet; small frequent meals	Sips of milk may provide temporary relief; physician may prescribe an antacid; "flying exercise"; avoid use of baking soda or seltzers
Flatulence—altered digestion from enlarging uterus and hormones	Not preventable—maintain regular bowel habits, avoid foods that are gas formers	Same as prevention; antiflatulent may be prescribed
Insomnia—fetal movements, fears or concerns, and general body discomfort from heavy uterus	Exercise; side-lying positions of comfort with pillow supports; change position often; backrubs from spouse; time to ventilate feelings	Same as prevention; medication by prescription only

Continued

Table 4-5. Discomforts of pregnancy—Continued

Discomfort and cause	Prevention	Treatment
Shortness of breath—enlarging uterus limits expansion of diaphragm	Not preventable—relieved with delivery	Good posture; cut down on smoking, position—supine and upright
Backache—increased elasticity of connective tissue, increased weight of uterus, and increased lumbar curvature	Avoid fatigue; eat good diet; posture; low-heeled wide-base shoes; pelvic rock; good body mechanics	Correct posture, shoes, and diet; do pelvic rock often, on hands and knees; tuck pelvis under the baby
Pelvic joint pain—hormone relaxin relaxes connective tissue and joints and allows movement within joints	Not preventable—needed to increase the birth passage	Rest; good posture; will go away after delivery, in six to eight weeks
Leg cramps—pressure of enlarging uterus on nerve supplying legs; lack of calcium? Fatigue, chilling, and tension?	Avoid pointing toes, especially when arising; rest legs; keep warm; maintain recommended daily intake of calcium	Stretch affected muscle and hold until it subsides; *do not rub* (may release a blood clot, if present)
Constipation—decreased motility (hormones enlarging uterus) and increased absorption of water; iron therapy (oral)	Diet—prunes, fruits, vegetables, roughage, and fluids; regular habits; exercise; sit on toilet with knees up	Same as for prevention—avoid enemas (damages mucosa, hemorrhoids); never use mineral oil, inhibits vitamin absorption
Hemorrhoids—varicosities around anus; aggravated by pushing with stool and by uterus pressing on blood vessels supplying lower body	Avoid constipation; do not strain at stool, sit on toilet with feet on foot stool	Pure Vaseline or Desitin are mild and sometimes soothing; use any other preparation with prescription only
Ankle edema—normal and nonpitting: gravity	Rest legs often during day with legs and hips raised	Same as prevention
Varicose veins—lower legs, vulva, pelvis: pressure of heavy uterus; relaxation of connective tissue in vein walls; hereditary	Progressively worse with subsequent pregnancies and obesity; elevate legs on pillows above level of heart; support hose may help	Same as prevention; avoid restrictive clothing (knee-high hose); avoid long periods of standing
Cramp in side or groin—round ligament pain; stretching of round ligament with cramping	To get out of bed, turn to side, use arm and upper body and push up to sitting position	Same as for prevention

proven reason why sexual activity cannot continue until labor begins or membranes rupture

b. Positions need to be varied to accommodate enlarging abdomen; may prefer mutual masturbation at this time

c. Men may experience an aversion to viewing a pregnant body or to feeling fetal movement or may express concern regarding fetal welfare and therefore prefer nonintercourse sexual expression

d. Avoid oral-genital manipulation—for example, man blowing into vagina, as

this may cause an air embolus and possible maternal death

5. Postpartum

a. May resume intercourse after lochia stops, about the third week

b. May have some dyspareunia with first intercourse after delivery due to "dry" vaginal mucosa from hormone deprivation between birth of placenta and resumption of menstrual cyclic activity; episiotomy and other trauma to the birth canal should be healed by now

c. To check vaginal readiness, partner

should coat one finger with K-Y jelly
and insert into vagina gently, then two
fingers; if no discomfort, intercourse
should not be painful

d. Use some form of contraception

6. Sexual arousal during breast feeding (see
Infant-Feeding, Breast-feeding, and Lactation)

F. Natural childbirth—education for childbirth

1. Grantly-Dick Read

a. Basic premises—childbirth is a natural
event, tension plus fear equals increased
pain and increased pain perception

b. Tension and fear are often reduced in
prepared couples if the gravida
comprehends contractions and the work
and physiology of labor

c. Breathing techniques help the work of
uterine contractions and relax the
perineum for the birth process

2. Psychoprophylactic childbirth—LaMaze
method

a. Basic premises—a conditioned response
to stimuli occupies nerve pathways thus
dulling pain perception; education for
the birth process replaces
misconceptions and superstitions

b. Conditioned responses
(1) Concentration on a focal point
(2) Breathing techniques to cope with
and to assist contractions, to prevent
bearing down too soon by panting or
use of pant-blow and to bear down
when appropriate; the first and last
breaths should be cleansing breaths

c. The gravida and her coach (husband or
other) are also taught physiology and
anatomy, psychology (of man and
woman), and what to expect in the
hospital setting

d. The gravida requires active coaching to
enable her to use breathing techniques
appropriate for the phase of labor and
to prevent hyperventilation
(1) Stage I—active phase before 10 cm
dilated: pant-breathe to prevent
pushing
(2) Stage II—while head is being born,
to prevent its popping out: panting
(see When the nurse must deliver
the baby)

THE LABOR PROCESS

1. **Terms**
A. Dilatation—process of being opened, as the
cervix enlarging from 0 to 10 cm
B. Effacement—process of thinning out, pulling
up, or shortening of the cervix
C. Lightening—process of "dropping" or sinking
of the fetus into the pelvic inlet with the accompanying descent of the uterus (see Engagement)
1. Effects—pressure on diaphragm alleviated
and breathing is easier; pressure in pelvis
increases with return of urinary frequency
and a worsening of varices (legs, vulva, and
perianal)
D. Engagement—widest diameter of presenting
part has passed through the pelvic inlet, for
example, biparietal diameter of fetal head;
usually occurs two to three weeks before term
in primigravida and during labor in multiparas;
if not, cause should be determined
E. Station—relationship of presenting part to the
level of the ischial spines (IS)
1. Floating—presenting part is still in false
pelvis, above the inlet
2. Dipping—presenting part is entering true
pelvis, but is not yet engaged
3. Station -5 to -1—presenting part above IS
4. Station 0—presenting part at the IS
5. Station $+1$ to $+5$—presenting part has descended to level of ischial tuberosities
F. Fetal head
1. Bones—one occiput, one frontal, two pari-
etals, and two temporals
2. Suture—line of junction or closure between
bones: sagittal (longitudinal), coronal (anterior), and lambdoidal (posterior)
3. Fontanels—membranous space between
cranial bones during fetal life and infancy
a. Anterior "soft spot"—diamond shaped;
2.5 cm × 2.5 cm; forms junction with
coronal and sagittal sutures; ossifies
(closes) in 12 to 18 months
b. Posterior—triangular shaped; 1 cm;
junction of the sagittal and lambdoidal
sutures; ossifies in approximately two
months
6. Maternal pelvis
1. False—lying above the linea terminalis (the
line travels across top of symphysis pubis

around to the sacral promontory); it supports the gravid uterus during gestation
2. True—lies below linea terminalis; divided into
   a. Inlet—"brim," demarcated by linea terminalis; transverse diameter is widest at 13.5 cm; anterior-posterior (or true conjugate from the top of symphysis to sacral promontory) diameter is 11 cm
   b. Pelvic cavity
   c. Outlet—anterior-posterior diameter is widest measurement, thereby facilitating delivery in occiput anterior (OA) position
3. Classifications—structure and configuration of inlet
   a. Gynecoid—true female pelvis; circular
   b. Android—triangular or wedge shaped
   c. Anthropoid—oval
   d. Platypelloid—transverse oval
H. Fetal lie—relationship of fetal axis to maternal axis (spine)
1. Transverse—shoulder presents
2. Longitudinal—vertex or breech presents
I. Presentation—that fetal part which enters the inlet first
1. Cephalic—vertex (most common), face, or brow
2. Breech
   a. Complete—feet and legs are flexed on thighs; buttocks and feet presenting
   b. Frank—legs extended so feet are up by shoulder; buttocks present
   c. Footling—single foot; double or two feet; or both knees
3. Shoulder
J. Attitude—flexion or extension of fetal parts on itself

K. Position—the quadrant of the pelvis in which the presenting occiput, mentum, or sacrum is located; could be located on maternal left, anterior or posterior, or on her right side, anterior or posterior; examples: LOA, most frequent; LMA; LSA; determined by Leopold's maneuvers and rectal or vaginal examination
L. Denominator—occiput, mentum, or sacrum
2. **Initiation of labor**—exact mechanism unknown
A. Overdistention of uterus
B. Altered levels of estrogen and progesterone
C. Progressive degeneration of placenta
D. High levels of prostaglandins
E. Fetal hormone secretion
F. Combination of two or more of these mechanisms
3. **False and True Labor**—see Table 4-6
4. **Stages of labor**—see Table 4-7
A. First—from beginning to complete dilatation and effacement, from 0 to 10 cm
B. Second—from 10 cm through birth of infant
C. Third—from birth of infant through birth of placenta
D. Fourth—from birth of placenta until mother's condition is stabilized (one to four hours)
5. **Mechanisms of labor—vertex presentation**
A. Descent—head engages and proceeds down birth canal
B. Flexion—head flexes on chest, allowing smallest diameter of vertex to present
C. Internal rotation—during second stage of labor, transverse diameter of fetal head enters pelvis; occiput rotates 90° to bring back of neck under symphysis pubis, for example, LOT to LOA to OA for delivery
D. Extension—back of neck pivots under symphysis pubis to allow head to be born by extension
E. Restitution—head turns 45° back to normal

Table 4-6. False and true labor

Characteristic	False	True
Contractions	Braxton Hicks contractions intensify (or seem to) at night	Fairly regular; may be 20 to 30 minutes apart at first, with frequency, duration, and intensity increasing
	Short and irregular	
	Stop with a change in position or activity	Not stopped by moderate analgesia, change of position, or activity
	Abdominal discomfort may be due to GI upset or bladder spasms	Felt in lower back, radiating to abdomen
Dilatation, effacement	None or no progress if some cervical change is present	Progressive

Table 4-7. Maternal behavior during labor

Phases of first stage	*Expected maternal behaviors*

0 to 4 cm—latent phase and early active phase
1. Time—nullipara 8-10 hours, average
 	
2. Contractions—regular, mild 5-10 minutes apart, 20-30 seconds duration
3. Low back pain and abdominal discomfort with contractions
4. Cervix thins; some bloody show
5. Station
   Multipara——2 to +1
   Nullipara—0
	1. Usually comfortable, euphoric, excited, talkative, and energetic or may be fearful and withdrawn
	2. Relieved or apprehensive that labor has begun
	
	3. Alert, usually receptive to teaching and coaching and diversion and anticipatory guidance

4 to 8 cm—midactive phase, phase of most rapid dilatation 1. Average time—nullipara 1-2 hours 2. Contractions—2 to 5 minutes apart, 30-40 seconds duration, intensity increasing 3. Membranes may rupture now 4. Increased bloody show 5. Station——1 to 0	1. Tired, less talkative, and less energetic 2. More serious, malar flush between 5 and 6 cm, tendency to hyperventilate, may need analgesia, needs constant coaching

8 to 10 cm—transition, deceleration period of active phase
1. Average time
   Nullipara—40 minutes to 1 hour
   Multipara—20 minutes
2. Contractions—1½-2 minutes 60-90 seconds, strong intensity
3. Increased vaginal show; rectal pressure with beginning urge to bear down
4. Station—+3 to +4
	1. If not under regional anesthesia, more introverted; may be amnesiac between contractions
	
	2. Feeling she cannot make it; increased irritability, crying, nausea, vomiting, and belching; increased perspiration over upper lip and between breasts; leg tremors; and shaking

position with shoulders; with LOA, after restitution, infant faces mother's right thigh
F. External rotation—shoulders rotate 45° so that upper shoulder delivers under symphysis pubis
G. Expulsion—delivery of neonate is completed
6. Examining the gravida in labor
A. Leopold's maneuvers or abdominal palpation
  1. First—place fingers just above symphysis pubis to feel presenting part (head presents in 90% of cases)
  2. Second—locate fetal back and small parts by running hands up sides of abdomen
  3. Third—bring hands over fundus to feel fetal breech; breech in fundus feels softer, not as round or mobile as the head would be
  4. Fourth—while facing gravida's feet, run hands down sides of abdomen to symphysis to check for cephalic prominence (usually on gravida's left side) and whether head is floating or engaged

B. Vaginal examination
  1. Condition of cervix—soft or rigid
  2. Dilatation and effacement
  3. Station and position of presenting part
  4. Palpable fontanels, and sutures, and caput succedaneum, if vertex
  5. Membranes
    a. Intact
    b. Ruptured—fluid should be opaque (milky) with white flecks and have no offensive odor; test with litmus (Nitrazine) paper: amniotic fluid is alkaline (blue on litmus)
C. Locate and monitor fetal heart rate (FHR)
  1. Location of most audible FHR and fetal position
    a. Breech presentation—usually *above* the umbilicus

b. Vertex presentation—usually *below* the umbilicus

2. Rate—between 120 and 160/minute; bradycardia, ≤ 100/minute

3. Factors affecting audibility
   a. FHR heard best through fetal back or chest; harder if arms and legs intervene
   b. Polyhydramnios
   c. Obesity
   d. Faulty equipment
   e. Noise in room
   f. Maternal position
   g. Maternal gastrointestinal sounds
   h. Loud uterine bruit—maternal origin, blood moving through uterine vessels, synchronous with maternal pulse
   i. Loud funic souffle—fetal origin, hissing of blood through umbilical arteries, synchronous with FHR

D. Contractions—involuntary intermittent contractile activity of the uterine muscle
   1. Purpose
      a. Move presenting part forward
      b. Efface and dilate cervix
   2. Effect of contractions
      a. Raises maternal blood pressure due to increased peripheral arteriole pressure
      b. Decreases blood flow to fetus
   3. Assessing contractions
      a. Place finger tips over fundus, use gentle pressure
      b. Contraction is felt as a tensing or hardening (acrement), reaching a peak intensity (acme), then diminishing slowly (decrement)
      c. Report if contraction begins other than in fundus
   4. Assessing intensity
      a. Weak—fingers easily indent into fundus
      b. Moderate—fingers indent slightly; some tension felt
      c. Strong—fingers cannot indent fundus
   5. Timing contractions
      a. Frequency—time from beginning of one contraction to beginning of the next
      b. Duration—time from the beginning until the end of a contraction

7. First stage of labor

A. Psychosocial care
   1. Respect gravida's desires concerning management of labor—degree of participation by self and significant other (husband or friend)

and breathing and relaxation techniques
   2. Nurse the patient versus the equipment
   3. Women in labor fear and dread being left alone
   4. Keep patient and family informed of progress
   5. Foster rest—keep noise level down and eliminate unnecessary talking

B. Physical care
   1. Careful evaluation of prenatal history—genetic and familial problems; concurrent medical condition; infectious diseases, past and present; blood type, Rh, serology; EDC; past obstetric history
   2. Perform examinations, as described previously
   3. Continue to monitor labor—on-going assessment of
      a. Contractions—check every 30 minutes
      b. Fetal response to labor—check every 15 to 20 minutes for FHR, fetal activity level, and amniotic fluid
      c. Maternal response to labor (see Table 4-7)
      d. Maternal vital signs
         (1) Obtain between contractions
         (2) Response to pain or use of special breathing technique alters the pulse and respiration
         (3) BP if normotensive, take on admission, then every four hours and prn; after regional anesthesia, every 30 minutes
         (4) TPR on admission, then every four hours and prn if within normal range
         (5) Prior to and after analgesia-anesthesia
         (6) After rupture of membranes (see Amniotic fluid embolism)
      e. Observe character and amount of show
   4. Perineal prep—shaving the perineum is still being done in some hospitals for cleanliness
   5. Enema—soapsuds enema should never be given as it is potentially dangerous; if needed, a Fleet's enema or equivalent is physiologically compatible; enema is *never* given if
      a. There is vaginal bleeding
      b. In presence of premature labor
      c. Fetus is in abnormal presentation or position
   6. Encourage emptying of bladder
      a. Obtain admission urine (if membranes are intact) and send for routine

evaluation
  b. Check for glucose and acetone
  c. Palpate abdomen just above symphysis to check for filling
  d. A full bladder may impede progress, or result in trauma to bladder
7. Encourage gravida to lie on side when she must be in bed
  a. Allows gravity to help in anterior rotation of fetal head
  b. Promotes relaxation
  c. Prevents supine hypotension syndrome
8. Coaching
  a. Discourage bearing down until second stage
  b. Assist with breathing technique suitable for patient
9. Observe for signs of second stage
  a. Increased bloody mucus vaginal drainage
  b. The mother saying, "It's coming!"
  c. Bulging perineum
10. Rupture of membranes—note and record-report
  a. Time—danger of infection if ruptured more than 24 hours
  b. FHRs stat and ten minutes later (to check for prolapsed cord)
  c. Amount—*polyhydramnios* (excessive fluid) is associated with anomalous development, high gastrointestinal tract obstruction, for example; *oligoamnios* is associated with anomalous development of urinary tract
  d. Character—thick consistency and/or odor suggests infection
  e. Color
    (1) *Yellow* fluid may represent fetal distress about 36 hours previous, or Rh or ABO incompatibility
    (2) *Green* fluid and fetus in vertex position may indicate recent or current hypoxia
    (3) *Port-wine* colored fluid may indicate abruptio placentae
  f. Check perineum for prolapsed cord and signs of imminent birth (crowning or bulging perineum)
  g. Vaginal exam—effacement, dilatation, and check for cord
11. Food and fluids per hospital and physician preference

  a. Natural childbirth—may have clear fluids throughout
  b. Ice chips or sips of water until delivery
  c. NPO with IV
  d. IV if regional anesthesia is started
C. Normal time limits for phases of first stage
  1. Nullipara
    a. Latent—8½ hours, normal; 20 hours, upper limit
    b. Active—5 hours, normal; 13 hours, upper limit
  2. Multipara
    a. Latent—5 to 6 hours, normal; 12 hours, upper limit
    b. Active—2½ hours, normal; 10 hours, upper limit
  3. Normal—S—curve on Friedman chart
  4. Dystocia—exaggeration or prolongation of normal S—curve
8. **Second stage of labor**—10 cm to complete delivery of neonate
A. Characteristics
  1. Average time—two minutes to one hour
  2. Vaginal discharge increases
  3. If regional anesthesia has not been given, reflex bearing down occurs with grunting sounds; may experience nausea, vomiting, shaking, and amnesia between contractions
  4. Perineum bulges with contractions—fetal head crowns, then head is born by extension
  5. Episiotomy may be performed now (medial or mediolateral) and head may be delivered by low forceps
  6. After restitution and external rotation of head, first shoulders, then rest of baby slips out with a gush of amniotic fluid
  7. Expulsion is accomplished by abdominal muscles (bearing down) and uterine contractions every 1½ to 3 minutes, lasting 60 to 90 seconds
  8. Fetal oropharynx and nasopharynx are aspirated or drained
  9. Infant is usually held on same level as placenta until pulsation stops before cord is clamped and cut—to prevent fetal blood loss or overloading fetal cardiovascular system
  10. Infant's Apgar score is noted and infant is quickly dried and put in warmer
B. Nursing care of mother
  1. Keep mother and her spouse informed; see that father is comfortable; reassure regarding mother's behavior if she is unanesthetized

2. Never leave mother and spouse alone now, whether she is in labor or delivery room
   a. Monitor FHR continuously by electronic monitor or by fetoscope after each contraction
   b. Time contractions and check BP every five minutes if mother has received regional anesthesia to check for slowing of labor and hypotension
   c. Watch perineum for increased vaginal mucus, bulging, or crowning
   d. Coach breathing, bearing down with each contraction; encourage; adjust mirror so she can see bulging or crowning
3. Precautions in putting legs in stirrups
   a. Never put legs in stirrups if there are extensive varicosities
   b. Avoid pressure points to popliteal veins, pad stirrups
   c. Assure proper alignment by adjusting stirrups
   d. Move legs simultaneously when putting them into and taking them out of stirrups to avoid nerve, ligament, and muscle strain
4. Cleanse perineum, thighs, and lower abdomen, using sterile technique

9. **Third stage of labor**—time between the delivery of the neonate and the complete delivery of the placenta
A. Average time—five minutes
B. Signs of placental separation
   1. Increase in bleeding
   2. Cord lengthens
   3. Uterus changes from a discoid to a globular shape

C. Types of delivery
   1. Schultz—"shiny"; shiny fetal surface presents; most common
   2. Duncan—"dirty"; maternal surface presents
D. Check for intactness and the number of vessels in the cord
E. If mother is to bottle feed, the drug to suppress lactation is given as the placenta is delivered; otherwise, birth of placenta triggers the production of lactogenic hormone by the anterior pituitary

10. **Fourth stage of labor**—first hour postpartum (see p. 236)

11. **Newborn care in the delivery room**
A. Note Apgar score at one and at five minutes, record (see Table 4-8)
   1. Score of 7-10—infant in good condition
   2. Score 4-6—infant is in fair condition; clear airway, give O_2 as needed; assess for CNS depression
   3. Score of 0-3—Infant is in poor condition; requires resuscitative measures immediately
B. Maintain body temperature—quickly dry and warm infant
   1. Conserves energy and preserves store of brown fat
   2. Decreases need for oxygen and prevents acidosis
   3. Assists respiratory efforts or resuscitative measures
C. Ensure patent airway
   1. Suction mouth first, then nose; sensitive receptors around entrance to nares, when stimulated, initiate a gasp, therefore mouth should be free of mucus
   2. Suction with bulb syringe
   3. If deeper suctioning is needed, use a DeLee

Table 4-8. Apgar score

Sign	0	1	2
Heart rate	Absent	Below 100	Over 100
Respiratory effort	Absent	Slow and irregular	Good and crying
Muscle tone	Flaccid	Some flexion of extremities	Active motion
Reflex irritability	No response	Weak cry or grimace	Cry
Color	Blue, pale	Body pink, extremities blue	Completely pink

mucus trap; long and vigorous suctioning should be avoided because

    a. Laryngospasm may result

    b. Oxygen and air may be removed

    c. Tissue trauma may result with edema and bleeding

    d. Cardiac arrhythmia may occur

  4. Trendelenburg's and side-lying position—assist gravity drainage of fluids

D. Identify infant by identiband or beads and footprints

E. Prevent eye infection—silver nitrate, 1% (2 drops in each eye) or penicillin ophthalmic ointment to prevent gonorrheal ophthalmia neonatorum

F. Assess neonate's condition—gross, incomplete assessment at this time; record and report findings

  1. Check cord for one vein and two arteries

  2. Note any malformations and birth trauma (dislocated shoulder, lacerations, or scalp edema)

  3. Identify the preterm or postterm neonate

  4. Note meconium staining—umbilical cord, skin, and nails

  5. Note neonate's cry—presence, pitch, and quality

  6. Note respirations and respiratory effort (nasal flaring, retractions, and expiratory grunt)

  7. Neurologic status

G. Record significant data from mother's chart, diabetes, hypertension, course of labor, and fetal distress, for example; record delivery events

12. Analgesia-anesthesia—see Table 4-9

13. When the nurse must deliver the baby

A. Nursing function when *mother* is giving birth

  1. Reassure her

  2. Assist infant with respirations—mucus, warmth, and resuscitative measures

  3. Protect mother from injury, infection, and hemorrhage

B. Follow these steps until physician arrives or you can get the mother and newborn to a medical facility; use aseptic technique if possible or be as clean as is possible; do not touch birth canal without aseptic conditions prevailing

  1. Delivery of the head—with clean or sterile towel, if available

    a. Place gentle pressure on the head as it emerges from the introitus and ask mother to pant-breathe to prevent rapid perineal stretching and perhaps lacerations and to prevent injury to fetal head

    b. As head emerges, feel with finger down nape of neck for cord; slip it over the head if possible, or down over the shoulders; if it is tight and you have sterile ties and scissors, tie the cord in two places, cut between the ties, unwrap cord, and proceed with delivery of shoulders

    c. If membranes are not yet ruptured, as head is emerging, tear the membranes (caul) at the neck quickly so that the infant's first breath is in air; note color and character of fluid

  2. Delivery of shoulders—hold head in both hands; after restitution, apply gentle pressure downward to deliver the anterior shoulder under the symphysis pubis, and then raise head gently to deliver the posterior shoulder

  3. Support infant as rest of body slips out with a gush of amniotic fluid

  4. Hold infant with head down—*do not hold by ankles or feet* as this may cause injury to cerebral capillaries by gravity and to the spine by over extension; do Apgar score

    a. Infant can be cradled in arms while being held head down to allow drainage of fluids to prevent aspiration; hold infant at same level as placenta until cord stops pulsating; cradling also provides warmth

    b. Milking the trachea is ineffectual

    c. Suction mouth and nose with bulb syringe, if available

    d. Cover infant with what is available; lay infant over mother's abdomen on side with head dependent—provides for drainage and warmth as well as stimulating uterus to contract and separate placenta

  5. Delivery of placenta

    a. *Never* tug or pull on cord

    b. Wait for signs of placental separation (see p. 228), then pull gently to deliver

    c. Cord stops pulsating within one to two minutes following birth by the expansion of Wharton's jelly in cord and by the initiation of infant respiration; therefore, it need not be cut or even tied

  6. For added warmth, wrap infant and placenta

Table 4-9. Analgesia-anesthesia during childbirth

Types	Characteristics	Nursing care
Natural childbirth Read LaMaze		Know method so as to be able to assist patient
Analgesic	Relieves pain or its perception	Explain expected action of drug; *safety measures*—side rails and call bell; *record*—amount, route given, time, and patient response; *Monitor labor*—vital signs, contractions, bladder filling, and FHR; augment effect with comfort measures
Barbiturates Secobarbital (Seconal) sodium Pentobarbital sodium (Nembutal) Amobarbital (Amytal)	Sedation; may depress neonate; produces excitement if given alone in presence of pain	Best given in early latent phase of first stage of labor; must *not* be given with existing maternal or renal disorders
Ataractics Promethazine HCl (Phenergan) Propiomazine (Largon) Hydroxyzine pamoate (Vistaril) Promazine HCl (Sparine)	Tranquillity and sedation; potentiate narcotic; antiemetic	Same as for Analgesic
Narcotics Meperidine (Demerol) HCl	Slows labor, or accelerates labor as mother relaxes; may depress neonate; sedation	Given in active phase, first stage, but *not* when delivery is expected in two hours; maternal vital signs and FHR before and every 15 to 30 minutes after administering
Amnesics Scopolamine (belladonna alkaloid)	Dulls memory and parasympathetic nervous system	Not recommended in LaMaze; give with narcotic to decrease possibility of excitation and hallucinations; stay with patient
Trichlorethylene (Trilene)	Given by inhalation, self-administered (usually) from a capsule and mask strapped to wrist; may cause cardiac arrhythmias	Stay with patient; note pulse every 30 minutes and FHR every 15 minutes
Anesthesia	Produces local or general loss of sensibility to touch, pain, or other stimulation	Explain to patient; note history of allergy
General Nitrous oxide (N_2O)—40%	Mother is not awake; *danger*—aspiration and respiratory depression; safer than regional anesthesia for hypovolemic patients; does not depress neonate unless mother is anesthetized deeply	NPO with IVs

Continued

Table 4-9. Analgesia-anesthesia during childbirth—Continued

Types	Characteristics	Nursing care
Halothane (Flouthane)	Relaxes uterus quickly—facilitates intrauterine manipulation: version and extraction	Observe for postpartum hemorrhage (from uterine atony); recovery room care
Thiopental (Pentothal) sodium	Produces rapid induction of anesthesia; depresses neonate	Recovery room care
Regional analgesia-anesthesia		
Common agents in 0.5–1.0% solution Procaine HCl (Novocaine) Lidocaine (Xylocaine) Bupivacaine (Marcaine) HCl Tetracaine (Pontocaine) HCl Mepivacaine HCl (Carbocaine)	Used with epinephrine (or other vasoconstrictor drug) to (a) delay absorption, (b) prolong anesthetic effect, and (c) decrease chance of hypotension	Note any history of allergy; note patient response: (a) allergic reaction, (b) hypotension, and (c) lack of anesthetic effect or wearing off of effect
Peripheral nerve block Pudendal (5–10 ml each side) anesthetizes lower two-thirds of vagina and perineum	Perineal anesthesia of short duration (30 minutes) given for delivery and repair; local anesthesia; may be done by physician; simple and safe; does not depress neonate; may inhibit bearing-down reflex	Explain to patient to get her cooperation during procedure
Paracervical block (5–10 ml given into each side) anesthetizes cervix and upper two-thirds of vagina	May be given between 3 and 8 cm by physician when patient is having at least three contractions in ten minutes; lasts 45–90 minutes, during which time patient may rest; can be repeated in 90 minutes; can be followed by local, epidural, or other; may cause temporary fetal bradycardia, which does not respond to treatment	Explain to patient, especially length and type of needle; take maternal vital signs and FHR; have patient void; help position patient; monitor FHR continuously; monitor contractions; and watch for return of pain
Local infiltration	Useful for perineal repairs	No special nursing care
Nerve root block	(a) Need trained anesthesiologist, (b) with proper administration, relieves pain completely, (c) may prolong labor if given too early, (d) hypotension from vasodilation (below anesthesia level) is likely, (e) fetal bradycardia from maternal hypotension, (f) bearing-down reflex is partially or completely eliminated, necessitating outlet forceps at delivery, (g) postanesthesia headache if medication mixes with cerebrospinal fluid, (h) fosters postpartum uterine and bladder atony, (i) patient is awake, and	Note history of allergy, skin infection over back, previous neural or spinal injury or disease, and attitude toward anesthesia; explain to patient: (a) expected feeling as anesthesia begins, warm toes and as it wears off, tingling, (b) positioning—help position patient, offering reassurance and support; take maternal vital signs and FHR; have patient void; monitor labor; siderails; record; observe for return of pain

Continued

Table 4-9. Analgesia-anesthesia during childbirth—Continued

Types	Characteristics	Nursing care
	(j) can be used for patients with metabolic, lung, and heart diseases	
Caudal	Useful during first and second stages; can be given "one-shot" or continuously; given in peridural space through sacral hiatus	Treatment of hypotension (with resultant fetal bradycardia): (a) turn from supine to lateral, or elevate legs, (b) administer humidified oxygen by mask at 6–8 liters/minute, (c) increase rate of IV fluids
Epidural	Useful during first and second stages; can be given "one-shot" or continuously; given on top of (or over) dura through 3rd, 4th, or 5th lumbar interspace; risk of dura puncture	Same as for Caudal
Saddle (low spinal or subarachnoid)	Usually given "one-shot" when head is on perineum; medication is mixed with cerebrospinal fluid in subarachnoid space; injected through 3rd, 4th or 5th lumbar interspace	Postdelivery: encourage oral fluids; lying flat in bed for 8 to 12 hours; observe for headache and bladder and uterine atony

together and give to mother
7. To prevent maternal hemorrhage
    a. Put infant to breast
    b. Gently massage fundus; express clots gently when uterus is contracted
    c. If mother's bladder is full, have her void
8. Record the events of delivery
9. Stay with mother and child until assistance arrives; give appropriate praise to mother for her efforts, encourage her to talk about the experience with you if she wishes
10. If placenta does not separate *do not pull on cord*
    a. If no sterile supplies are available, *do not cut cord;* take mother to medical facility
    b. Place baby in mother's arms and at breast if cord is long enough—may stimulate placental separation
    c. Place baby on mother's abdomen or between legs if cord is short
    d. Rationale
        (1) Pulling on cord before placenta separates may invert uterus and result in infection and massive hemorrhage
        (2) Abnormal implantation of placenta
            (a) Placenta accreta has partially grown into myometrium;

treatment—hysterectomy
            (b) Placenta increta has completely grown into myometrium (no decidua present); treatment—hysterectomy
11. If neonate does not breathe spontaneously
    a. Maintain body temperature—dry and cover
    b. Clear airway—turn head to side, lower head, and clear mouth with finger
    c. Stimulate gently—rub back and flick soles of feet
    d. Slightly extend neck to "sniffing position," place mouth over neonate's nose and mouth and exhale air in cheeks, saying "ho" (prevents excessive pressure)
    e. If in hospital, use other techniques, p. 261
14. **Operative obstetrics**—surgical procedures during labor or delivery
A. Episiotomy—incision of perineum to facilitate the birth of the infant
    1. Types
        a. Midline—greater chance of extension into anal sphincter than mediolateral
        b. Mediolateral—healing is more painful than midline
    2. Rationale
        a. Substitutes a surgical incision for a

possible laceration

b. Easier to heal than a laceration

c. Protect infant's head from being forced against a resistant perineum (as in premature delivery)

d. Shortens second stage

3. Nursing care

a. Cleanliness

b. Ice bag during first hour postpartum to decrease edema formation and discomfort

c. Analgesics, topical sprays, Tucks, and sitz baths for comfort and to promote healing

d. Observe and assess for hematoma and infection

e. Evaluate pain in area—if excessive and episiotomy is not the source, report immediately; a vulvar, paravaginal, or ischiorectal abscess or hematoma may be the underlying cause of the pain

B. Forceps delivery—delivery of the head with the aid of forceps

1. Types

a. Low—outlet forceps

b. Mid—applied after head is engaged

c. High—applied before engagement has taken place; rarely done; very hazardous

d. Piper—applied on the after-coming head in breech deliveries

2. Conditions for applying forceps

a. Engaged fetal head

b. Ruptured membranes

c. Full dilatation

d. Absence of cephalopelvic disproportion

e. Some anesthesia has been given

f. Empty bladder and rectum

3. Indications for forceps delivery

a. Fetal distress

b. Maternal need

(1) Exhaustion

(2) Concurrent disease condition such as cardiac disorder

(3) Poorly progressing second stage, secondary inertia, for example

(4) Persistent transverse or posterior fetal position

4. Possible complications

a. Maternal—lacerations of birth canal, rectum-bladder injury, or uterine rupture

b. Fetal injury—cephalhematoma, skull fracture, brain damage, intracranial hemorrhage, facial paralysis, cord compression, and direct tissue trauma (abrasions and ecchymoses)

5. Nursing care

a. Listen to FHRs after forceps application—forceps blade may compress cord

b. Observation of mother-newborn for complications or injury

c. Support mother who may feel baby was taken from her rather than giving birth to baby

d. Support for the parents if bruising or complications occur

C. Cesarean section—incision through abdominal wall and uterus to deliver the products of conception

1. Types

a. Low segment—preferred method, transverse incision into lower uterine segment, and skin incision is longitudinal or transverse

(1) Fewer immediate complications—less blood loss, more comfortable convalescence, and less intestinal obstruction

(2) Future complications less—less chance of uterine rupture and less adhesion formation

b. Classical—longitudinal incision through skin and into body of uterus

(1) More bleeding, scar tissue, and adhesion formation

(2) Necessary for anterior placenta previa and transverse lie

c. Extraperitoneal—transverse incision through skin and into lower uterine segment without entering peritoneal cavity; used less now with availability of blood replacement and antibiotic therapy

d. Porro's—hysterotomy followed by hysterectomy—necessary in presence of hemorrhage from atony, placenta previa, abruptio placentae, placenta accreta, ruptured uterus, fibromyomata, or cancer of cervix or ovary

2. Indications

a. Cephalopelvic disproportion (CPD)

b. Previous surgery on uterus

c. Uterine dysfunction
d. Placental condition—placenta previa and abruptio placentae with Couvelaire uterus
e. Maternal disease—diabetes and toxemia
f. Malposition or malpresentation of fetus—some favor a cesarean section for all nulliparae with a breech presentation
g. Fetal distress
h. Postterm pregnancy
i. Neoplasms of the birth canal or uterus
j. Fetal jeopardy—Rh incompatibility and diabetic or toxemic mother
k. Prolapsed cord

3. Nursing care—same as for other patients preoperative and postoperative except for
a. Monitoring FHR prior to surgery
b. Alerting pediatrician for delivery
c. Postpartum check (see p. 236)

D. *Induction of Labor*—initiation or stimulation of labor
1. Indications for induction
a. Maternal
(1) Woman with history of fast or silent labors or who lives far from the hospital
(2) Premature separation of low-lying placenta with uncontrolled bleeding; after artificial rupture of membranes, presenting part moves down and acts as a tamponade during labor
(3) Uncontrolled progressive toxemia or diabetes
(4) Premature rupture of membranes (PROM) that increases the possibility of intrauterine infection and prolapsed cord
b. Fetal
(1) Maternal diabetes
(2) Rh or ABO incompatibility
(3) Macrosomatia (excessive fetal size)
(4) Postmaturity
(5) Congenital anomaly, anencephaly, for example
2. Conditions for successful induction
a. Absence of CPD, malposition, or malpresentation
b. Engaged vertex of single gestation
c. Close to, or at, term
d. Fetal lung maturity—better survival rate

if 32 weeks or more
e. "Ripe" cervix—softening, partially effaced, or ready for effacement or dilatation if it has not begun as yet
3. Amniotomy
a. Definition—artificial rupture of membranes
(1) Induce labor
(2) Increase efficiency of contractions
(3) Shorten labor
b. Nursing care—same as for spontaneous rupture of membranes
(1) Monitor FHR and assess for fetal distress (p. 254)
(2) Observe for prolapsed cord
(3) Observe fluid (see p. 227)
(3) Assess fetal activity
(a) Excessive activity may indicate fetal distress
(b) Absence of activity may indicate fetal demise
4. Intravenous infusion of oxytocin (Pitocin or Syntocinon)
a. With physician on the unit and with a double set-up running (one bottle of fluid with oxytocin and one without, connected to a three-way stopcock at the point where the needle enters the vein
(1) Monitor drop rate continuously
(2) Monitor each contraction—must not be closer together than two minutes, nor last longer than 90 seconds
(3) Monitor maternal vital signs, especially blood pressure
(4) Monitor FHR either continuously electronically or manually after each contraction—listen during contractions if possible
b. Danger to fetus
(1) Decreased oxygen concentration in cord blood with hypoxia
(2) Anoxia with tetanic contractions; death
(3) Arrhythmias
C. Danger to mother
(1) Uterine rupture
(2) Postpartum hemorrhage
(3) Oxytocin toxicity
(4) Water intoxication following infusion over long periods
(5) Allergic reaction

(6) Hypertensive crisis with possible cerebral hemorrhage

5. Buccal oxytocin (Pitocin)
   a. 200 unit tablet placed between gums and cheek
   b. Rate of absorption unpredictable
   c. Monitor FHR, maternal blood pressure, and contractions
   d. To inactivate tablet, ask patient to spit it out or swallow it; rinse mouth
   e. Toxicity—allergy or hypertension

PUERPERIUM

Puerperium is the period of time spanning from the birth of the placenta through six weeks. It is characterized by anabolic activity of lactation and catabolic activity known as involution

1. **Physiology**—return of body tissues, especially reproductive organs to near prepregnant state
A. Uterus
   1. Reduction in size and weight
      a. Autolysis—breakdown of muscle protein, especially connective tissue collagen and elastin to be excreted in the urine
      b. Lochia—sloughing of the decidua and blood
      c. Size—after delivery 1000 gm (2.2 lb); one week 500 gm (1.1 lb); and two weeks 350 gm (11 oz)
   2. Formation of new endometrium
      a. 21 days—newly formed except for placental site
      b. Six weeks—placental site healed without scarring by process of exfoliation
   3. Height of fundus
      a. After delivery—at umbilicus, size of grapefruit and firm
      b. Day one—one finger above umbilicus
      c. Involutes by one finger each day, until day ten
      d. Day ten—behind symphysis
   4. "After pains"—discomfort of uterine contractions
      a. Primipara—uterus remains contracted, often does not feel "after pains"
      b. Multipara—uterus relaxes and contracts, felt as "after pain"
      c. Increased by breast feeding, after delivering a large baby, and in presence

of retained placental fragments

5. Lochia—blood from placental site, decidua, and mucus
   a. Amount lost in six weeks—225 gm
   b. Days one to three—rubra (bright red)
   c. Days three to seven—serosa (pink to brown)
   d. By day ten—alba (creamy white) contains many microorganisms
   e. Investigate
      (1) If bright red after day three—possible retention of placental fragments
      (2) Clots—hemorrhage
      (3) Putrid odor—infection
      (4) Lochia beyond three weeks—subinvolution
B. Cervix
   1. After delivery—bruised, small tears, and admits a hand
   2. 18 hours—becomes shorter, firmer, and regains its shape
   3. One week—admits two fingers
   4. Never fully returns to prepregnant state
      a. Os is wider
      b. Lacerations heal as scars radiating from os
C. Vagina and pelvic floor
   1. Vagina—never fully returns to prepregnant state
      a. After delivery—thin walled from hormone (estrogen) deprivation; few rugae
      b. Week three—rugae reappear
   2. Pelvic floor
      a. After delivery—infiltrated with blood, stretched, and torn
      b. Month six—considerable tone regained
D. Perineum
   1. After delivery—edematous, may have episiotomy (or repaired lacerations) or hemorrhoids
   2. Hematoma—blood in connective tissue beneath skin; mass is painful, tense, and fluctuant
E. Cardiovascular system
   1. After delivery—increased cardiac load as uterine blood flow is redirected to general circulation
   2. First week—blood volume returns to prepregnant state
   3. Blood values

a. High white cell count of labor returns to normal level within the first few days

b. Week one—hemoglobin, RBC, hematocrit, and elevated fibrinogen return to normal

4. Vital signs

   a. Temperature—normal, except if dehydrated or fatigued; puerperal infection, 38 C (100.4 F) on two postpartal days, starting with day two

   b. Pulse—bradycardia (50 to 70) common on days one and two, but may persist seven to ten days; cause unknown

   c. Blood pressure—generally unchanged

F. Urinary tract

  1. 12 hours to five days—diuresis (daily output may reach 3000 ml)

  2. Urine constituents

   a. Sugar—primarily lactose

   b. Acetonuria—following prolonged labor

   c. Proteinuria for first three days

  3. Edema, trauma, and anesthesia may result in retention with overflow

  4. Dilatation of ureters subsides in a few weeks

G. Integument—skin

  1. Striae—persist as silvery lines

  2. Diastasis recti abdominis—some midline separation may persist

  3. Diaphoresis—excessive perspiration for first few days (approximately five)

H. Weight

  1. After delivery

   a. Loss—fetus, placenta, amniotic fluid, tissue fluid

   b. Abdomen protrudes

   c. Mother weighs more than in prepregnant state

  2. Week six—weight reduction is individual

I. Menstruation and ovarian function

  1. Nonnursing—ovulation four to six weeks and menstruation six to eight weeks

  2. Nursing—anovulatory period varies (39 days to six months or more); some for duration of lactation; some for 8 to 14 months; contraceptive value, very unreliable

J. Breasts

  1. Nonlactating—lactosuppressant, testosterone enanthate and estradiol valerate (Deladumone OB) IM given as placenta starts to separate

  2. Lactating (see p. 242)

K. Postpartal checkup—six weeks

1. Weight, vital signs, urine for albumin, and blood count

2. Breast exam—lactating or not

3. Pelvic exam—involution and position of uterus, perineal healing, and tone of pelvic floor

4. Contraception implemented

2. Nursing Management

A. First hour postpartum—fourth stage of labor

  1. Assessment—every fifteen minutes four times (then every 30 minutes two times or until stable)

   a. Height and firmness of fundus

   b. Blood pressure

   c. Pulse

   d. Lochia—amount, color, number of clots, character, and odor

   e. Perineum—healing and drainage

   f. Bladder fullness

   g. Rate of IV if present; note any added medication

   h. Recovery from analgesia-anesthesia

  2. Interventions—every 15 minutes for one hour

   a. Boggy fundus—gentle massage to avoid uterine fatigue; express clots after fundus is firm

   b. Report increase in blood pressure—decrease IV flow rate if oxytocin has been added; hypotension treatment, see p. 232

   c. Rapid pulse—assess blood pressure, pulse, and bleeding; report

   d. Lochia—more than one soaked pad (100 ml) in one hour; and clots, report to and save for physician; order blood; add oxytocin to IV as ordered; or give oxytocin orally

   e. Perineum—apply covered ice pack over episiotomy; assess for hematoma formation and pain: report to physician and/or medicate prn

   f. Bladder—record voiding or catheterization; character of urine, time, and amount

   g. IV—discontinue when finished or add new bottle if bleeding is excessive or if not fully recovered from anesthesia

   h. Caution patient not to get out of bed (after caudal and epidural); keep patient flat after saddle block for number of hours specified by physician

i. Mate and newborn may visit; newborn may nurse
3. Rationale
  a. Most frequent complication—hemorrhage (leading cause of death); causes, see p. 256
  b. Postpartum toxemia is possible for two days
  c. Full bladder raises and displaces uterus, causing uterine relaxation and bleeding
  d. Ice to perineum discourages edema and numbs the area
  e. Mother-child-father bonding is basic purpose of "rooming-in"
    (1) Mother and father should see, touch, hold, and fondle infant immediately following birth if physically possible to begin bonding or attachment
    (2) Early sustained contact with child facilitates the process of grieving for the loss of the fantasy baby and the identification and acceptance of the real baby
    (3) Nursing at the breast stimulates uterine contractions
B. Subsequent postpartum care
  1. Assessment—minimum two times per day
    a. Vital signs
    b. Fundus, lochia, and perineum
    c. Voiding and bowel function
    d. Breasts
    e. Emotional status and response to baby
  2. Interventions-rationale
    a. Follow prescribed treatment for excessive bleeding, fever, retention, and constipation
    b. Medicate as ordered
      (1) Stool softeners
      (2) Analgesics; sedatives for sleep
      (3) Uterine contraction—ergot products (Methergine, Ergotrate, and Ergonovine); give if patient is normotensive, usually 0.2 mg (1/30 gr) q4h × 6 doses
    c. Perineal care—teach regarding
      (1) Shower for cleanliness
      (2) Wash hands, wipe from front to back once per tissue, apply clean pad from front to back, and wash hands
      (3) Comfort—Tucks, anesthetic sprays,

heat lamp, and sitz baths; keep buttocks together and tightened when in process of standing up, sitting down, and getting out of bed
  d. Breasts—lactating mothers (see p. 242)
  e. Anticipatory guidance
    (1) Process of involution (see p. 235)
    (2) Resumption of intercourse (see p. 222)
    (3) Contraception—pills are resumed *after* first menstrual period (if not breast feeding); use of IUDs or diaphragms is generally determined at six-week checkup (if patient is using diaphragm, size and fit must be readjusted after birth of baby)
  f. Assist with psychologic tasks—maternal role taking
    (1) See bonding, in opposite column
    (2) Need to *integrate* labor and delivery experience by talking about it; need to express disappointment, if any; and need for compliments for what she (and spouse) did well
    (3) Early phase (days one to three)—labeled by R. Rubin as "taking-in" is characterized by passivity; dependency; talkativeness; concern for self needs, such as eating, sleeping, and eliminating; and desire to be taken care of
    (4) "Taking-hold" phase (third day to two weeks)—mother is impatient to have control over own body functions, to learn how to care for own baby ("mothering tasks") with assurance that she is doing a good job now; builds foundation for future success in mother-child relationship
    (5) "Letting-go" phase—begins during pregnancy and continues in the puerperium; mother must give up or "let go" of her former role, professional person, single woman, pregnant woman, or mother of one, and assume her new role; may have concerns about ability or willingness to do it
    (6) "Postpartum blues"
      (a) Thought to be the result of a combination of hormonal

Table 4-10. Clinical estimation of gestational age*

Examination First Hours

WEEKS GESTATION (20–48)

Physical findings		Findings by week of gestation
Vernix		Appears (21) · Covers body, thick layer (24–27) · On back, scalp, in creases (38) · Scant, in creases (40) · No vernix (43)
Breast tissue and areola		Areola and nipple barely visible, no palpable breast tissue (23) · Areola raised (34) · 1–2 mm nodule (36) · 3–5 mm (38) · 5–6 mm (39) · 7–10 mm (40) · ?12 mm (44)
Ear	Form	Flat, shapeless (23) · Beginning incurving superior (34) · Incurving upper 2/3 pinnae (36) · Well-defined incurving to lobe (40)
	Cartilage	Pinna soft, stays folded (22) · Cartilage scant, returns slowly from folding (33) · Thin cartilage, springs back from folding (38) · Pinna firm, remains erect from head (40)
Sole creases		Smooth soles without creases (24) · 1–2 anterior creases (33) · 2–3 anterior creases (35) · Creases anterior 2/3 sole (36) · Creases involving heel (39) · Deeper creases over entire sole (42)
Skin	Thickness & appearance	Thin, translucent skin, plethoric, venules over abdomen, edema (25) · Smooth, thicker, no edema (33) · Pink (37) · Some desquamation pale pink (40) · Thick, pale, desquamation over entire body (42)
	Nail plates	Appear (20) · Nails to finger tips (33) · Nails extend well beyond finger tips (43)
Hair		Appears on head (20) · Eye brows and lashes (23) · Fine, woolly, bunches out from head (28) · Silky, single strands, lays flat (37) · ?Receding hairline or loss of baby hair, short, fine underneath (43)
Lanugo		Appears (20) · Covers entire body (22) · Vanishes from face (33) · Present on shoulders (37) · No lanugo (42)
Genitalia	Testes	Testes palpable in inguinal canal (30) · In upper scrotum (37) · In lower scrotum (40)
	Scrotum	Few rugae (28) · Rugae, anterior portion (36) · Rugae cover (39) · Pendulous (42)
	Labia & clitoris	Prominent clitoris, labia majora small, widely separated (31) · Labia majora larger, nearly cover clitoris (36) · Labia minora and clitoris covered (42)
Skull firmness		Bones are soft (23) · Soft to 1" from anterior fontanelle (29) · Spongy at edges of fontanelle, center firm (35) · Bones hard, sutures easily displaced (38) · Bones hard, cannot be displaced (42)
Posture	Resting	Hypotonic, lateral decubitus (24) · Hypotonic (27) · Beginning flexion, thigh (31) · Stronger hip flexion (33) · Frog-like (35) · Flexion, all limbs (36) · Hypertonic (38) · Very hypertonic (42)
	Recoil - leg	No recoil (20) · Partial recoil (33) · Prompt recoil (38)
	Arm	No recoil (20) · Begin flexion, no recoil (34) · Prompt recoil, may be inhibited (38) · Prompt recoil after 30" inhibition (43)

*An approximation based on published data. Adapted from Lubchenco, L.O.: P Clin N Am 17:125, 1970. Reproduced, with permission, from Kempe, C. H., Silver, H. K., and O'Brien, D., editors: Current pediatric diagnosis and treatment, ed. 4, Los Altos, California, 1976, Lange Medical Publications.

Confirmatory Neurologic Examination To Be Done After 24 Hours

Weeks Gestation

Physical Findings		20	21	22	23	24	25	26	27	28	29	30	31	32	33	34	35	36	37	38	39	40	41	42	43	44	45	46	47	48
Tone	Heel to ear												Some resistance				Impossible													
	Scarf sign	No resistance													Some resistance									Elbow does not reach midline						
	Neck flexors (head lag)	Absent										Elbow passes midline					Elbow at midline													
	Neck extensors														Head begins to right itself from flexed position			Good righting cannot hold it		Head in plane of body		Holds head	Keeps head in line with trunk > 40°		Turns head from side to side					
	Body extensors															Straightening of legs			Straightening of trunk			Straightening of head and trunk together								
	Vertical positions															Arms hold baby, legs extended?			Legs flexed, good support with arms											
	Horizontal positions									When held under arms, body slips through hands			Hypotonic, arms and legs straight						Arms and legs flexed			Head and back even, flexed extremities		Head above back						
Flexion angles	Popliteal	No resistance												150°	110°	100°				90°		80°		A pre-term who has reached 40 weeks still has a 40° angle						
	Ankle													45°				20°				0								
	Wrist (square window)											90°		60°				45°		30°		0								
Reflexes	Sucking												Weak, not synchronized with swallowing	Stronger, synchronized				Perfect		Perfect, hand to mouth				Perfect						
	Rooting												Long latency period slow, imperfect	Hand to mouth				Brisk, complete, durable							Complete						
	Grasp												Finger grasp is good, strength is poor			Stronger				Can lift baby off bed, involves arms						Hands open				
	Moro						Barely apparent						Weak, not elicited every time			Stronger		Complete with arm extension, open fingers, cry		Arm adduction added							?Begins to lose Moro			
	Crossed extension												Flexion and extension in a random, purposeless pattern	Extension, no adduction		Still incomplete		Complete with arm extension		Extension, adduction, fanning of toes				Complete						
	Automatic walk												Minimal	Begins tiptoeing, good support on sole		Begins tiptoeing, good support on sole		Fast tiptoeing		Heel-toe progression, whole sole of foot				A pre-term who has reached 40 weeks walks on toes		?Begins to lose automatic walk				
	Pupillary reflex	Absent										Appears		Present																
	Glabellar tap	Absent												Appears		Present														
	Tonic neck reflex	Absent									Appears			Present																
	Neck-righting	Absent														Appears				Present after 37 weeks										

changes, the realization of the
need to change to take on the
new role and let go of the old,
and the extent of maternal
responsibilities
- (b) This can be frightening, if
unprepared; she and spouse
should be assured that crying
helps (if she chooses to cry)
- (c) May appear by fourth or fifth
day as hormone levels drop
- (7) Lag in experiencing "maternal
feelings"—was first described by
Gerald Caplan; each must be
prepared that this experience is
possible, especially for the
primipara; "maternal lag," with
resultant guilt feelings, may
contribute to "blues"; lag is possible
to extend over six months, but
usually is resolved by four to six
weeks; maternal lag may be greatly
diminished or avoided if the mother
is able to see and hold her newborn
immediately after giving birth

THE NEWBORN INFANT

1. Admission to the nursery
A. Delivery nurse reports significant events from mother's history, labor, and delivery and newborn's condition
B. Place newborn in heated environment, take rectal temperature, weigh, and measure—length and head and chest circumferences; check respirations qlh × 5; take apical pulse qlh × 3; and give IM vitamin K (if ordered) into anterior or lateral thigh muscle
C. Assess for gestational age (see Table 4-10)
D. Do physical assessment of term neonates (see Table 4-11)
E. A bath may be done when temperature is stable

2. Routine nursing care
A. Assess neonate's responses and appearance continuously
B. First feeding
1. Selected infants may breast feed stat after birth
2. Nurse does first feeding otherwise—sterile water (preferable to glucose, which irritates respiratory tree if aspirated); observe infant's

suck-swallow reflex, color, respirations, regurgitation, and fatigability
3. Check infants susceptible to hypoglycemia with Dextrostix at 30 minutes and one, two, and four hours of age; feed if hypoglycemic
4. Start feedings at four to eight hours of age to prevent dehydration, prevent hypoglycemia, keep bilirubin levels lower, and stimulate GI tract
5. May regurgitate mucus and amniotic fluid
C. Weigh daily if bottle fed, or before and after breast feeding
1. May lose 5% to 10% of birth weight in first few days
2. Regain birth weight in 7 to 14 days
D. Note and record all voidings
E. Note and record stools
1. Meconium—deep green-black, sticky, odorless, unformed stools; first day, sterile
2. Transition—greenish yellow and loose (days two to five)
3. Bottle fed (after five days)—firmer, passed less frequently, yellow, pH neutral to alkaline, foul odor, can be normal to have occasional liquid stool
4. Breast fed (after five days)—unformed but not watery, one or two each day or one after each feeding, bright golden yellow, occasionally light green, some odor, pH is acidic
5. Diarrhea—yellowish-green; increased amount of mucus; water ring on diaper around stool; forcefully expelled; causes—overfeeding, infection (usually *Escherichia coli*), or wrong formula
6. Constipation—can be a feature of organic disease, such as obstruction, pyloric stenosis (although usually not until after first month), starvation, megacolon, or rectovaginal fistula
F. Cord care
1. Observe for abnormalities—bleeding, redness, drainage, or odor
2. Keep clean and dry; apply alcohol or thimerosal (Merthiolate) to cord
3. Normal—separates and drops off in seven to ten days
G. Observe for jaundice—sclera, mucosa, and skin
H. Circumcision care—check for bleeding, replace petrolatum gauze prn (if ordered), and keep clean and dry
I. Order PKU test for third day
J. Teach parents characteristics and care of newborn

Table 4-11. Physical assessment of the newborn term neonate

Criterion	Average values and normal variations	Deviations from normal
Vital signs		
Heart rate	120–140 minute, irregular, especially when crying, and functional murmur	Faint sound—pneumomediastinum; and heart rate <100 or >180/minute
Respiratory rate	30–40/minute with short periods of apnea, irregular, cry—vigorous and loud	Distress—chin tug, flaring of nares, retractions, tachypnea, grunting, excessive mucus, < 30 or > 60/minute and weak high-pitched cry
Temperature	Stabilizes about eight to ten hours after birth, 36.5-37 C (97.7-98.6 F, axillary)	Unreliable indicator of infection
Measurements		
Weight	3400 gm (7½ lb)	*See* Table 4-13
Length	50 cm (20 inches)	
Chest circumference	2 cm (¾ inch) less than head circumference	If relationship varies, check for reason
Head circumference	34–36 cm (13½–14½ inches)	Check for microcephalus and macrocephalus
Skin color	Mottling, Harlequin's syndrome, acrocyanosis, and physiologic jaundice	Pallor, plethora, cyanosis, and jaundice within 24 hours of birth
Character	Petechiae (over presenting part), ecchymoses (from forceps), milia, mongolian spotting, telangiectases, lanugo, and vernix caseosa	Petechiae or ecchymoses elsewhere; all rashes, except newborn rash; pigmented nevi; hemangioma; and yellow vernix
Head	Molding of fontanels and suture spaces	Cephalhematoma, caput succedaneum, sunken or bulging fontanels, and closed sutures
Neck	Short, freely movable, and sternocliedomastoid muscles are even	Wry neck, webbed neck
Eyes	Edematous eyelids, conjunctival hemorrhage; dark, slate-colored; usually no tears; uncoordinated movements, although may focus for a few seconds; good placement on face; and white discharge from silver nitrate	Epicanthal folds (in non-Orientals); discharges; agenesis
Nose	Appears to have no bridge; should have no discharge; obligate nose breathers	Discharge and choanal atresia
Mouth	Epstein's pearls on gum ridges	Cleft lip or palate; teeth
Ears	Well-formed, firm; notch of ear should be on straight line with outer canthus	Low placement, clefts; and tags
Face	Symmetrical movements and contours	Facial palsy (seventh cranial nerve)
Muscle tone	Good tone, and generalized flexion	Flaccid, and persistent tremors or twitching
Chest	Enlarged breasts, "witch's milk," barrel shaped, and both sides move synchronously	Misshapen, flattened, funnel chested, and asynchronous movement
Abdomen	Dome shaped, abdominal respirations, soft, and may have small umbilical hernia	Scaphoid shaped, omphalocele, diastasis of rectal abdominal muscles, and distention

Continued

Table 4-11. Physical assessment of the newborn term neonate—Continued

Criterion	Average values and normal variations	Deviations from normal
Genitalia		
Girl	Large labia, may have some bloody discharge per vagina, smegma, and tags	Agenesis and imperforate hymen
Boy	Pendulous scrotum covered with rugae and testes usually descended	Phimosis and epispadias or hypospadias
Extremities	Synchronized movements, freely movable through full range of motion, legs appear bowed, and feet appear flat	Fractures (clavicle and femur), brachial nerve palsy, clubbed foot, phocomelia, webbing of digits, and abnormal palmar creases
Back	Spine straight, easily moveable, and flexible; may have small pilonidal dimple at base of spine	Fusion of vertebrae; pilonidal dimple with tuft of hair, spina bifida, and agenesis of part of vertebral bodies
Anus	patent, well placed, and "wink" reflex present	Imperforate, and absence of "wink" (absence of sphincter muscle)
Stools	Meconium within first 24 hours and transitional—days two to five	Light-colored meconium, inspissated (dry, hard), and absence of with distended abdomen (cystic fibrosis or Hirschsprung's disease)
Reflexes (indicators of neurologic development and musculoskeletal intactness)	Well-developed and complete Moro reflex; tonic neck; grasp—palmar and planter; rooting; suck; swallow; gag; cough; sneeze; stepping; pupillary; Babinski's	Incomplete, absent, or asynchronous responses need to be evaluated
Laboratory values		
Hemoglobin (cord)	13.6–19.6 mg/100 ml blood	Evaluate for anemia, and persistent polycythemia
Serum bilirubin	2–6 mg/100 ml blood	Identify and treat hyperbilirubinemia (term >12 mg and preterm >15 mg) to prevent kernicterus
Blood glucose	≥ 30–40 mg/100 ml blood for term and ≥ 20 mg/100 ml blood for preterm	Identify hypoglycemia prior to overt symptoms if possible—do Dextrostix on all suspects (large- or small-for-gestational-age babies, and babies of diabetic mothers)

3. **Nutrient needs**
   A. Calories—42–50 calories/lb/day
   B. Protein: 1.5–2 gm/lb/day or 3.5 gm/kg/day (1 gm protein = 1 ounce milk)
   C. Fluids—2–3 ounces/lb/day
   D. Vitamin D—400 IU daily for bottle-fed babies after week two
4. **Infant feeding**
   A. Suppression of lactation
      1. Antilactogenic drugs
         a. Testosterone enanthate and estradiol valerate injection (Deladumone

OB)—engorgement, rare
         b. Chlorotrianisene (Tace)—less effective, given in several doses
      2. Other methods—ice bags to breasts, tight binder, and avoid emptying breasts; restricting fluids is unwarranted
      3. Engorgement (see following discussion)
      4. Teach regarding bottle feeding—holding and burping
   B. Breast feeding and lactation
      1. Colostrum (yellowish fluid)—continues for the first two to three days; may have some

antibiotic and nutritive value; infant suckles to give mother and self chance to learn, to meet infant's sucking needs, and to stimulate milk production and "let down" reflex

2. Milk (bluish white, thin-looking)—comes on about the third day; "let down" reflex, a function of the posterior pituitary, stimulates the ejection or release of milk from the alveoli into the nipple ducts

3. Procedure
   a. Teach regarding rooting reflex and putting infant on breast, burping, what to do if infant chokes, and removing infant from breast
   b. Infant must grasp nipple and areola over the location of milk sinuses

4. Factors influencing successful breast feeding—emptying both breasts at each feeding, rest, fluids, relaxation (adrenalin suppresses lactation), and additional calories

5. Infant should nurse at both breasts at each feeding—emptying breasts is best stimulus for milk production; it takes three weeks for supply to meet demand

6. Engorgement—stasis of venous and lymphatic circulation immediately preceding lactation
   a. A painful condition, lasts about 24 hours
   b. Relieved by warm packs, analgesics, emptying breasts, and good supporting bra
   c. Should not be accompanied by fever
   d. Collecting ducts around areola may have to be emptied manually before infant can take hold to suck

7. A restful environment free of emotional and physical discomfort is necessary for adequate milk production

8. Diet—additional calories (120 calories needed to produce 100 ml milk; eventually 1000 ml or more produced per day), protein, minerals, vitamins, and fluids (3000 ml/day); may need to divide this large quantity of food into five or six feedings to manage it

9. Rest—sleep and freedom from emotional stress facilitates milk production

10. Drugs—avoid use except under medical supervision, as drugs and their metabolites appear in breast milk and may affect baby; some drugs (oral contraceptives) may also suppress milk production and predispose to thrombus formation

11. Sexual sensation—some women feel sexual pleasure or are sexually aroused by the nursing process; this natural, pleasurable feeling may upset some women and be a cause to terminate breast feeding

12. During orgasm, milk may squirt out of nipples

13. Contraceptive value of nursing is a *myth*

Part B   Complications of Childbearing and the High-risk Neonate

THE PREGNANT ADOLESCENT

1. **High-risk factors**
A. Psychosocial, emotional, nutritional, and physical demands of pregnancy are compounded by those of adolescence
B. Many pregnant adolescents are also unwed
C. Increased incidence of preeclampsia-eclampsia, premature labor and delivery, and dystocia
2. **Nursing management**
A. Avoid blaming, scolding, and moralizing
B. Nutrition counseling—start where woman is; she may equate "milk and square meal" approach as reverting back to childhood; peer pressure in food preferences; stress value of nutrition for character of skin, hair, return to prepregnant figure
C. Provide atmosphere in which woman may ventilate feelings and fears (during entire childbearing cycle)
D. Involve woman in problem-solving and planning for her future

E. Do not downgrade the father of the child, as this puts the woman down as well
F. Observe for complications
G. Ask her if or what she wishes to know about any contraceptives; inform her where she can get information when she wants it

ANTEPARTAL PERIOD

1. **Reproductive hemorrhagic problems**
A. Spontaneous abortion
   1. Etiology—defective germ plasm, insufficient progesterone production, acute infections, abnormalities of reproductive system, and injuries (physical or emotional)
   2. Types and symptomatology
      a. Threatened—mild bleeding, spotting, cramping, and cervix closed; no loss of fetal parts
      b. Inevitable—moderate bleeding, painful cramping, and cervix dilated; membranes ruptured
      c. Imminent—profuse bleeding, severe cramping, and urge to bear down
      d. Recurrent (habitual)—three or more successive pregnancies lost through spontaneous abortion
      e. Incomplete—fetal parts or fetus expelled and placenta and membranes retained
      f. Complete—all productions of conception expelled
      g. Missed—fetal death with no abortion; may exhibit symptoms of anorexia, malaise, and headache; clotting time may be increased due to hypofibrinogenemia; saline injection via amniocentesis is preferred method to stimulate expulsion of products of conception
   3. Treatment—threatened abortion
      a. Notify physician stat; bring all perineal pads
      b. Bed rest and sedation; reduce physical and emotional stress
      c. Endocrine therapy, progesterone, for example
   4. Treatment—inevitable, imminent, or incomplete abortion
      a. Pain medication
      b. IVs; type and crossmatch to replace blood loss
      c. Prevent (sterile technique) or treat infection
      d. Dilatation and curettage or dilatation and evacuation
      e. IV oxytocin or intrauterine saline induction if abortus is 14 weeks gestation or more
      f. Observe for blood loss, shock, and infection
      g. Administer RhoGAM if woman is Rh negative
      h. Supportive counseling to the woman for the loss
   5. Treatment—habitual or recurrent abortion
      a. Treat as for inevitable, imminent, or incomplete abortion
      b. Diagnose etiology—endocrine, genetic, anomaly or disorder of reproductive tract (uterine fibroma or incompetent cervical os, for example) blood incompatibility, or psychologic
   6. Voluntary or "therapeutic" abortion (see p. 212)
B. Incompetent cervix
   1. Defective cervix (internal os) allowing dilatation and effacement in the middle of the second or early third trimester
   2. Etiologies
      a. Unknown
      b. Injury to cervix during previous birth or repeated cervical dilatation as in abortion (spontaneous or therapeutic)
   3. Succeeding pregnancies may be retained following circlage procedures, such as McDonald or Shirodkar, after the first trimester, may be delivered vaginally (after purse-string suture is cut at onset of labor) or by cesarean section
      a. Supportive care prior to and after surgery
      b. Following procedure—observe for signs of labor and bleeding; generally, no complications are expected
C. Hydatidiform mole
   1. Pathology—anomalous development of placenta in which chorionic villi develop into a grape cluster-like mass of vesicles; may be antecedent to choriocarcinoma, a rapid spreading, highly malignant tumor of the trophoblast
   2. Etiology—incidence 1 out of 2000 pregnancies; seen more frequently in women over

45 years of age
3. Symptoms and diagnosis
   a. Rapid enlargement of uterus not congruous with age of gestation
   b. Brownish discharge, beginning about week 12 of gestation; discharge may contain vesicles
   c. Symptoms of toxemia that appear early in pregnancy (before third trimester)
   d. No fetal parts palpable or seen on X-ray, sonography, or amniography
   e. High HCG levels
4. Medical treatment
   a. Empty the uterus—hysterectomy may be necessary
   b. Chemotherapy (methotrexate) and/or radiation, if malignant cells are seen
   c. Follow-up for one year for HCG levels; persistent HCG level is consistent with choriocarcinoma
   d. Strict contraception for a minimum of one year
5. Nursing management
   a. Observe for hemorrhage, passage of retained vesicles, and abdominal pain or infection (perforation of uterine wall highly probable)
   b. Assist patient in selecting contraceptive method best suited to her and mate
   c. Supportive care for woman after evacuation or hysterectomy and during follow-up care
D. Ectopic pregnancy
1. Pathology—implantation outside of uterine cavity
2. Types—tubal (majority of cases), cervical, abdominal, and ovarian
3. Etiologies
   a. Inflammatory disease—pelvic, salpingitis, and endometriosis
   b. Anomalous tubes or uterus, tubal spasm, and tumors in or pressing on the reproductive organs
   c. Adhesions from pelvic inflammatory disease (PID) or past surgeries
4. Symptoms and diagnosis
   a. Dependent on site of implantation
   b. Early signs—abnormal menstrual period, spotting, and some symptoms of pregnancy; possible dull pain on affected side
   c. Following tubal rupture—pain, usually sudden, in lower abdomen; nausea and vomiting; symptoms of shock, referred pain in shoulder or neck from blood in peritoneal cavity; and blood in cul-de-sac of Douglas
   d. Pain when cervix is touched during pelvic examination
5. Treatment—surgery
6. Nursing management
   a. Usual preoperative and postoperative care (see Unit 3)
   b. Supportive care for
     (1) Loss of a pregnancy
     (2) Loss of a part of the reproductive tract
     (3) Threat to self-image as a woman and as a childbearer
E. Placenta previa
1. Pathology—abnormal implantation of placenta near or over the internal os
2. Types
   a. Low-lying or marginal placenta previa
   b. Partial placenta previa
   c. Complete placenta previa—over the internal os of the cervix; may be accompanied by unusual fetal presentations
3. Etiology
   a. Unknown
   b. Occurs more frequently with multiparity and advanced maternal age
   c. Fibroid tumors or old scars (from cesarean section) or endometriosis may be factors
4. Symptoms
   a. Bleeding that usually appears in the eighth month when there is some cervical effacement and dilatation
   b. Bleeding is usually painless (unless accompanied by abruptio placentae as well) and is not accompanied by uterine contractions; bleeding may be intermittent
   c. Possibility of low implantation may be suspected prior to eighth month by palpating a boggy lower uterine segment during vaginal examination
   d. If in labor, contractions are usually normal
5. Treatment—dependent on location of placenta and amount of bleeding
   a. Vaginal delivery is possible with

low-lying placenta and minimal bleeding,
active labor with good progress, and if
presenting part is acting as a tamponade
  b. Vaginal examination under double
     set-up
     (1) Patient is prepared for cesarean
         section (abdominoperineal
         preparation)
     (2) In an operating room set up for
         emergency cesarean section
  6. Nursing management
     a. Do not permit vaginal or rectal exams
     b. Place on bedrest in high-Fowler's
        position if placenta is marginal
     c. Monitor FHRs continuously
     d. Monitor maternal vital signs and
        bleeding
     e. General preoperative and postoperative
        care (see Unit 3)
     f. Postpartum—observe for hemorrhage;
        placental site is located in a less
        contractile part of uterus
F. Abruptio placentae
   1. Pathology—premature separation of the pla-
      centa; placenta is usually normally implanted
      a. Incidence—1/500 pregnancies
      b. Types
         (1) Partial abruptio placentae—small
             portion of placenta separates
         (2) Complete abruptio placentae—total
             placenta separates
         (3) Abruptio placentae with concealed
             bleeding—blood remains within
             uterus
         (4) Abruptio placentae with external
             bleeding—blood escapes into vagina
      c. Complications possible
         (1) Afibrinogenemia and disseminated
             intravascular disease—result of clot
             formation behind placenta
         (2) Couvelaire uterus—bleeding into
             myometrium, necessitating
             hysterectomy
         (3) Amniotic fluid embolus (see p. 254)
         (4) Hypovolemic shock
   2. Etiologies
      a. Toxemia
      b. Preceding the delivery of second twin
      c. Traction on placenta (short cord or
         impatient accoucheur)
      d. Rupture of membranes
      e. Injudicious use of oxytocin in induction

   f. High parity
   g. Chronic vascular renal disease with
      hypertension
3. Symptoms
   a. Bleeding, concealed or external
      (1) Concealed—central separation; prior
          to onset of labor
      (2) External—marginal separation with
          or without central separation,
          allowing passage of blood through
          cervix; usually during labor
      (3) Amniotic fluid may be port-wine
          colored
   b. Shock is usually more profound than
      amount of observed bleeding would
      support
   c. Pain—often sudden and severe (may
      contribute to shock)
   d. Increased uterine muscle tonus—uterus
      may contract unevenly; does not relax
      completely between contractions
   e. Fetal hyperactivity that may indicate
      fetal distress; bradycardia; or loss of
      fetal heart tones with fetal demise
4. Treatment—medical and nursing management
   a. Control hemorrhage
   b. Control neurogenic and hypovolemic
      shock; maintain in side-lying position to
      avoid pressure on vena cava
   c. Determine clotting ability; give
      fibrinogen if necessary; fibrinogen
      injection is avoided if possible since
      there is a high incidence of hepatitis
      with this treatment
   d. Deliver infant
      (1) Cesarean section
      (2) If vaginal delivery is imminent,
          membranes are ruptured to speed up
          delivery
   e. Postpartum
      (1) Be alert for uterine atony,
          hemorrhage, and puerperal infection
      (2) Monitor urinary output (anuria,
          oliguria) or hematuria from renal
          failure
      (3) Observe for pulmonary emboli (see
          p. 254)
      (4) Give heparin if necessary
      (5) Support the parents
2. **Preeclampsia-eclampsia**—toxemias of pregnancy

A. Pathophysiology
 1. Generalized arteriospasm—results in hypertension and decreased perfusion of tissues
 2. Renal lesion—glomerular capillary endotheliosis
B. Incidence
 1. 7% to 10% of all pregnancies
 2. Develops after week 24 of gestation
 3. Fourth leading cause of maternal mortality in the United States today
C. Symptomatology—results from decreased blood flow to the kidney, brain, and uterus
 1. Kidney
  a. Water and sodium retention—edema
  b. Proteinuria
  c. Hypertension (from kidney release of angiotensin)
  d. Oliguria
 2. Brain
  a. Cerebral and visual disturbances—due to arteriospasm and edema
  b. Convulsions and coma—due to increased irritability of central nervous system (CNS)
 3. Uterus
  a. Small-for-gestational-age baby
  b. Abruptio placentae
D. Types
 1. Preeclampsia—mild
  a. Hypertension—systolic increase of 30 mm Hg or more over baseline and diastolic rise of 15 mm Hg or more over baseline
  b. Proteinuria—more than 1 gm/day
  c. Edema—especially digital and periorbital; weight gain over 0.45 kg (1 lb) per week
 2. Preeclampsia—severe
  a. Increased hypertension—systolic pressure at or above 160 mm Hg or 50 mm Hg above baseline and diastolic, 110 mm Hg or more
  b. Proteinuria—5 gm or more in 24 hours
  c. Oliguria—400 ml or less in 24 hours
  d. Cerebral or visual disturbances, such as disorientation and somnolence; severe frontal headache; increased irritability; and blurring, halo vision, dimness, and blind spots
  e. Persistent vomiting
  f. Epigastric pain—edema of liver capsule
  g. Hemoconcentration

 3. Eclampsia—convulsions (clonic and tonic); a more severe form of toxemia; symptomatology same as preeclampsia, but usually accompanied by convulsions
E. Etiologies
 1. Pregnancy—to initiate and continue this condition, a functioning trophoblast must be present
 2. Age—under 17 and over 35 years; multiple gestation, diabetes, or first pregnancy
 3. Diet—one low in protein
 4. Polyhydramnios
 5. Unknown
F. Prognosis
 1. Good—symptoms mild and respond to treatment
 2. Poor—convulsions (number and duration); persistent coma; hyperthermia; tachycardia, 120 or more; and cyanosis
 3. Terminal—pulmonary edema, congestive cardiac failure, acute renal failure, and cerebral hemorrhage
G. Medical-nursing management—moderate to severe condition
 1. Dietary—improve protein intake to replace low serum protein; low serum protein leads to movement of fluid out of vascular and into interstitial fluid compartments
 2. Drugs (see Appendix F)
  a. Diuretics with pulmonary edema and congestive heart failure
  b. Magnesium sulphate (epsom salts, IM or IV)
 3. Reduce CNS irritability
  a. Drugs—sedatives and magnesium sulphate
  b. Reduce stimuli—light and noise
 4. Monitor progress of preeclampsia
  a. Blood pressure
  b. Weight—evaluation of edema
  c. Intake and output—Foley catheter
  d. Reflex responses
  e. Laboratory values—blood (hematocrit, serum protein) and electrolytes
 5. Monitor fetal status (see Fetus in jeopardy)
 6. Monitor for signs and symptoms of labor
 7. Observe for abruptio placentae (a high blood pressure or a rapid drop may initiate abruptio)
 8. Convulsion care
  a. Maintain patent airway; administer O_2 prn
  b. Observe for signs and symptoms of

impending convulsion—sharp cry;
frontal headache; epigastric pain, and
facial twitching

c. Safety—keep padded tongue blade or
plastic airway on hand; pad siderails

d. Observe, report, and record onset and
progression of convulsion and whether
it was followed by bladder and bowel
evacuation and/or coma

e. *Remain alert* for *48 hours postpartum*
for convulsions, even if no convulsions
occurred prior to delivery

3. Cardiac Disorders

A. *Normal* alterations during normal pregnancy
that mimic cardiac disorder

1. Systolic murmurs, palpitations, tachycardia,
and hyperventilation with some dyspnea with
normal moderate exertion

2. Edema of lower extremities

3. Red blood cell sedimentation rate tends to
rise near term

4. Cardiac enlargement

B. Anticipatory guidance and nursing care of the
gravida with cardiac involvement

1. Signs and symptoms of cardiac decompensation and congestive failure—if any of these
appear, the woman should notify physician
(hospitalization is mandatory)

a. Pedal edema
b. Moist cough
c. Dyspnea with minimal physical activity
d. Rapid weak pulse
e. Cyanosis of lips and nail beds

2. Methods of decreasing work of heart

a. Rest—sleep at least ten hours per night
and rest for half an hour after each meal

b. Avoid heavy housework, excessive
weight gain, and emotional stress

c. Prevent and/or treat anemia

d. Avoid infection—avoid crowds, fatigue,
anemia, and cold drafts; eat
well-balanced diet

e. Avoid situations of reduced ambient O_2,
such as high altitudes, flight in
unpressurized plane, smoking, and
prolonged exposure to a smoke-filled or
highly polluted environment

f. Avoid excessive salt intake

3. Management of labor

a. NPO for foods and fluids

b. Frequent vital signs, especially pulse
(over 110), which is the most sensitive

and reliable indicator of impending
congestive heart failure, and respirations
over 24

c. Semirecumbent position, with arms and
legs supported

d. No bearing down efforts; low outlet
forceps and episiotomy are used to
shorten second stage

e. Regional (conduction) anesthesia such
as epidural, caudal, or saddle block
(inhalation anesthesia is contraindicated)
(1) To relieve stress of pain
(2) To eliminate bearing-down reflex

f. Digitalis prn; diuretics with KCl
supplementation, prn; antibiotics, prn

4. Referral to social services if gravida needs
help in home

C. Medical management

1. Determination of cardiac involvement

a. Class I—least affected; no dyspnea with
ordinary activity for example; best
pregnancy risk

b. Class II—activity somewhat limited

c. Class III—activity markedly limited

d. Class IV—most affected; symptoms
apparent at rest; should not get pregnant

2. Drug therapy (see Appendix F)

a. Diuretics with supplementation for lost
electrolytes

b. Digitalis

c. Antibiotics—prophylaxis

d. Oxygen

3. Hospitalize gravida for several days or weeks
prior to EDC and after delivery

4. Special evaluation and supervision stat after
delivery

a. Delivery results in rapid decrease in
intra-abdominal pressure with resultant
vasocongestion and rapid increase in
cardiac output

b. Blood loss—prevent hypovolemic shock

c. Pain relief—prevent neurogenic shock

d. Rapid alterations in water metabolism
that occur after delivery present an
added stress to the new mother with
heart involvement—observe for
tachycardia and/or respiratory distress

5. Operative procedures, therapeutic abortion
and cesarean section, for example, are
avoided if at all possible

4. Diabetes and prediabetes

A. Pathology—inability of the beta cells of the

islands of Langerhans in the pancreas to produce sufficient insulin to metabolize glucose properly

B. White's classification considers age at onset, duration, and vascular or renal changes if any
1. Class A—abnormal glucose tolerance test (GTT), dietary regulation, no insulin needed
2. Class B—onset after 20 years of age, duration less than ten years, no associated vascular involvement
3. Class C—onset between 10 and 19 years of age, duration of 10 to 19 years, no associated vascular involvement
4. Class D—onset under 10 years of age, duration of more than 20 years, early vascular disease (legs, retina)
5. Class E—X-ray verification of pelvic arteriosclerosis
6. Class F—vascular nephropathy
7. Class G—duration over 20 years, vascular disease and nephropathy, history of many obstetric failures

C. Etiology
1. Heredity—recessive trait
2. Obesity—imposes excessive demands on beta cells
3. Stress—added demands on beta cells with infection, pregnancy, and other emotional and physical trauma
4. Age—incidence increases with age

D. Normal metabolic alterations (during normal pregnancy) that aggravate the diabetic condition
1. Decreased glucose tolerance—changes in metabolic rate; increased production of adrenocortical and pituitary hormones; glucosuria is common
2. Diminished glucose utilization (presence of fetal antagonists)
3. Decreased effectiveness of insulin (placental influence)
4. Increased size and number of islands of Langerhans
5. Decreased CO_2—combining power of blood; an increase in BMR increases the tendency to acidosis

E. Effect of diabetes on pregnancy—increased incidence of
1. Toxemias (occurs in one-third to one-half of cases)
2. Polyhydramnios
3. Spontaneous abortion
4. Stillbirths
5. Infertility

6. Congenital anomalies
7. Premature labor and delivery

F. Medical management
1. Hospitalization frequently required for
a. Regulation of insulin; change from tolbutamide* to insulin (regular) during pregnancy
b. Control of infection (to prevent ketoacidosis)
c. Determination of fetal jeopardy—as basis for possible early termination of pregnancy (see p. 254)
2. Weight gain is strictly supervised to prevent water imbalance
3. Mycotic vaginitis is more common and harder to control (see p. 267)
4. Frequent urine tests for sugar and acetone
5. Delivery by induction or cesarean section by week 36 to prevent intrauterine death

G. Effect of pregnancy on diabetes
1. Nausea and vomiting—predisposes to ketosis and acidosis
2. Insulin requirements—relatively stable during the first trimester; increase rapidly during the second and third trimesters
3. Pathophysiologic sequelae of diabetes—nephropathy, retinopathy, and arteriosclerotic changes, for example, may appear now or existing pathology may be aggravated

H. Labor
1. Increased probability of dystocia due to CPD, a consequence of excessive fetal growth (macrosomatia)
2. Intravenous glucose and water with insulin is required to preserve maternal stores of glycogen in liver and skeletal muscles
3. Electronic fetal monitoring and X-ray pelvimetry may be indicated to identify possible fetal jeopardy and CPD

I. Postpartum
1. Wide fluctuations in insulin requirements are to be expected due to
a. Removal of placental antagonists
b. Serum glucose conversion to lactose
c. Withdrawal of fetal insulin

J. Nursing management—mother
1. On-going care—ambulatory

---

*Tolbutamide, a drug that stimulates islet cells of the pancreas to produce insulin, is contraindicated during pregnancy. It does not protect against ketosis, a complication in diabetic gravida that jeopardizes fetal welfare.

a. Assess patient's knowledge concerning management of disease
b. Record pattern of weight gain; blood pressure; and urine test for glucose, acetone, and protein
c. Encourage patient to report problems such as vomiting and infection
d. Check FHR and height of fundus

2. Antepartal hospitalization
   a. Assist with fractional urine, insulin regulation, and diet
   b. Check FHR, height of fundus, and signs of labor
   c. Vital signs, I & O, and daily weight
   d. Assist with tests for fetal status
   e. Encourage bedrest (if prescribed), provide diversions
   f. Provide atmosphere conducive for expression of feelings and concerns; keep her (and family) informed
   g. Prepare for possiblity of cesarean section
   h. In event of fetal demise, provide emotional support

3. Labor and delivery
   a. Fractional urines, q2-3h; regular insulin
   b. IVs (Ringer's); I & O
   c. Monitor FHR continuously
   d. Order blood sugar to be done q1-3h

4. Postpartum
   a. Observe for hypoglycemia or insulin reaction; assist with regulation of insulin
   b. Fractional urines
   c. Observe for and avoid exposure to infection

K. Infant of the diabetic mother (IDM)—observations
   1. Macrosomia—excessive weight for gestational age due to excessive tissue growth, deposit of subcutaneous fat, and retention of interstitial fluids
      a. Caution—excessive size may mask premature status; evaluate each infant for maturity since function is related to gestational age and not fetal size
      b. Possible etiologies of macrosomatia
         (1) Maternal production of large amounts of pituitary growth hormone and adrenocortical hormones
         (2) Fetal production of large amounts of insulin

   (3) Fetal hyperglycemia reflecting maternal hyperglycemia
   2. Cardiac enlargement; hepatomegaly and splenomegaly
   3. Subject to hypocalcemic tetany, acidosis, hypoglycemia, and hyperbilirubinemia
   4. Increased incidence of respiratory distress syndrome (RDS), which, however, may be more closely related to elective premature delivery than to maternal diabetes
   5. Increased incidence of congenital anomalies or defects (five times the average incidence)

L. Nursing management of infant of diabetic mother
   1. Assess for characteristics of IDM (described previously)
   2. Do Dextrostix (or order lab work) at 30 minutes and 1, 2, 4, 6, 9, 12, and 24 hours of age; feed per order, prn
   3. Observe for behavioral indications of hypoglycemia (see p. 261)
   4. Assess for gestational age; institute premature care prn (incubator care)
   5. Observe for jaundice
   6. If baby is large, assess for birth injuries—fractures (clavicle, humerus), brachial palsy, intracranial hemorrhage (symptoms of increased intracranial pressure), and cephalohematoma

5. **Polyhydramnios**—amniotic fluid in excess of 2000 ml (normal—500 to 1200 ml)
A. Incidence—associated with
   1. Maternal diabetes
   2. Multiple pregnancies
   3. Erythroblastosis fetalis
   4. Preeclampsia-eclampsia
   5. Congenital anomalies—anencephaly and upper GI anomalies, such as esophageal atresia
B. Symptoms
   1. Height of fundus higher than appropriate for gestational age
   2. Fetal parts difficult to feel and small in proportion to size of uterus
   3. Increased discomfort due to large, heavy uterus—increased edema in vulva and legs, shortness of breath, and GI discomfort
C. Medical management
   1. Amniocentesis—to diagnose anomalies, erythroblastosis
   2. Sonogram—diagnose multiple pregnancy; gross fetal anomaly

3. Voluntary abortion or hysterotomy
D. Nursing management
  1. Support of mother for diagnostic or therapeutic procedures, loss of pregnancy, or treatment plan if pregnancy is to be continued
  2. Observe for signs of preeclampsia and premature labor
6. Hyperemesis gravidarum
A. Pathology—intractable vomiting during the first 14 to 16 weeks gestation with a peak incidence at 10 weeks; excessive vomiting any time during pregnancy; potential hazards are
  1. Dehydration with fluid and electrolyte imbalance
  2. Starvation, with loss of 5% or more of body weight
B. Incidence—1 out of 300 pregnancies
C. Etiology
  1. Psychologic—thought to be related to rejection of pregnancy and/or sexual relations
  2. Physiologic—secretion of HCG, decrease in free gastric HCl, reduced gastrointestinal motility, and displacement of stomach
    a. Incidence increases in presence of hydatidiform mole
    b. Incidence increases with twin or multiple gestation because the production of HCG is increased
D. Symptoms and diagnosis
  1. Abdominal pain
  2. Hiccups
  3. Weight loss—dehydration, starvation with metabolic acidosis, and increased BUN
E. Treatment and nursing management
  1. Rule out other diseases, infection and tumors, for example
  2. Mild cases—give emotional support, dry crackers on awakening, frequent small feedings every two hours, prochlorperazine dimaleate (Compazine) or other medication
  3. Severe cases—hospitalization
    a. NPO with intravenous fluids containing calories, vitamins, and minerals for 24 hours, careful I & O records
    b. Antiemetics—promazine HCl (Sparine) IV and prochlorperazine dimaleate (Compazine) IM
    c. Bedrest
    d. Restrict visitors, including mate
    e. Observe for acetone breath
    f. Therapeutic abortion is considered if any of the following conditions appear

      (1) Jaundice
      (2) Neurologic disturbances—somnolence
      (3) Pulse 130 or more per minute
      (4) Fever, after woman is adequately hydrated
      (5) Retinal hemorrhage
  4. Discharge home when gravida demonstrates weight gain

INTRAPARTUM PERIOD

1. Mechanical dystocia
A. Definition—prolonged (over 24 hours), difficult labor
B. Uterine dysfunction
  1. Definition—significant prolongation of descent of fetus, effacement, and dilatation
  2. Types
    a. Inertia—deficient forces of expulsion; hypotonic contractions
      (1) Primary—prolongation of latent phase
        (a) Primigravida—over 20 hours
        (b) Multipara—over 14 hrs
      (2) Secondary—prolongation or abnormality of active phase
        (a) Primigravida—less than 1.2 cm/hour
        (b) Multipara—less than 1.5 cm/hour
    b. Excessive contractions—hypertonic
      (1) Precipitate labor-delivery—under three hours; possible trauma to mother and fetus
      (2) Clonic contractions
      (3) Tetanic contractions—last more than 90 seconds; danger of fetal asphyxia or uterine rupture
    c. Failure of uterine contractions—missed abortion or labor
  3. Inertia
    a. Primary inertia—poor uterine muscle tone; contractions are inefficient from the start
      (1) Cause—"unripe" cervix; early or heavy sedation, especially during latent phase; false labor; cause may be unknown
      (2) Diagnosis—vaginal examination, X-ray pelvimetry; Leopold's

maneuvers for fetal position and station

   (3) Nursing care—stimulate labor through walking, monitor oxytocin (Pitocin) induction, give enema, and assist with artificial rupture of membranes

  a. Secondary inertia—previously normal contractions become ineffectual or stop

   (1) Causes—related to maternal exhaustion, injudicious use of analgesia-anesthesia, minor pelvic contractures, CPD, fetal position, overdistended uterus, overdistended bladder, or cervical rigidity

   (2) Nursing care—careful observation to assist physician diagnosis, morphine rest, reassurance, prepare for cesarean section if labor prolonged beyond 24 hours

4. Excessive contractions—hypertonic dysfunction

  a. Symptoms—incomplete relaxation between contractions and frequent prolonged contractions

  b. Hazards

   (1) Decreased oxygen concentration in cord blood

   (2) Rapid molding of fetal skull may result in intracranial hemorrhage

   (3) Possibility of uterine rupture or lacerations of cervix, vagina, or perineum

  c. Treatment and nursing care

   (1) Supportive care to assist mother to cope with fear, pain, and discouragement

   (2) Careful monitoring of maternal and fetal vital signs

   (3) Oxygen by mask, as necessary

   (4) Morphine to promote rest

   (5) Regional anesthesia to slow down contractions

5. Failure of uterine contractions—hypotonic dysfunction

  a. Cause—etiology unclear

  b. Nursing care

   (1) Assist with X-ray pelvimetry

   (2) Supportive care—explain procedures and remain at bedside

   (3) Monitor contractions during oxytocin infusion induction

   (4) Monitor maternal and fetal vital signs

   (5) Prepare for cesarean section

  c. Dangers to mother

   (1) Maternal fatigue, exhaustion, and dehydration evidenced by an increased pulse rate and temperature

   (2) Infection—preventive treatment includes fluids and antibiotics, especially if membranes are ruptured for prolonged period or if mother has a fever

  d. Dangers to fetus—injury and death

6. Some conditions of the uterus make conception, pregnancy, or labor difficult if not impossible

  a. Anomalous uterus or fallopian tube

  b. Myomata of wall of uterine body or cervix

  c. Pathologic or Bandl's contraction ring

C. Fetal abnormalities or conditions—fetopelvic disproportion and cephalopelvic disproportion

1. Excessively large fetus

  a. Macrosomia—large newborn of a diabetic mother

  b. Large newborn—4500 gm (10+ lb)

  c. Enlarged fetal body—erythroblastosis fetalis (edema)

2. Fetal malformations—hydrocephalus (1 out of 2000 pregnancies)

3. Abnormal presentations of fetus

  a. Breech—3% of term deliveries; labor prolonged, soft buttocks do not dilate cervix as efficiently as hard vertex

  b. Occiput posterior (OP)—labor prolonged; may result in deep transverse arrest

  c. Face or brow—presenting diameter may be too large to negotiate through bony pelvis

  d. Transverse lie-shoulder (scapula) presenting—delivery usually by cesarean section, although spontaneous version may occur

  e. Compound presentation—hand alongside head, for example

4. Multiple births—twinning

  a. Comparison—identical and fraternal (see Table 4-12)

  b. Associated problems—increased risk of

   (1) Preeclampsia-eclampsia

   (2) Premature delivery

   (3) Hyperemesis gravidarum

Table 4-12. Comparison of identical and fraternal twins

Identical (monozygotic)	Fraternal (dizygotic)
Union of one egg and one sperm	Union of two eggs and two sperm
One or two placentas (fused, double)	Two placentas (fused, double)
One or two chorions	Two chorions
Always same sex	Same or different sexes
Usually hereditary	Incidence increases with maternal age
Greater chance of twin-to-twin transfusion (one polycythemic and one anemic)	Fare better than single ovum twins

      (4) Dystocia
      (5) Danger of asphyxia of second fetus (placenta may begin separating or cervix may close after birth of first twin)
      (6) Postpartum hemorrhage
    c. Indications of multiple pregnancy
      (1) Height of fundus—too high for dates
      (2) Sonography
      (3) High urine estriol
  5. Nursing Care—depends on type of dystocia
    a. Observe mother for contour of uterus, presentation (vaginal examination or Leopold's maneuvers), contractions, and location of discomfort to help identify possible CPD early
    b. Relieve back pain with sacral pressure, change of position, and pelvic rock if trial labor is indicated
    c. Discuss with gravida her perceptions and knowledge of old wives' tales, "dry births," for example, which may increase her discomfort
    d. Provide anticipatory guidance, for example, newborn's face will be swollen and discolored in face or occiput posterior delivery
D. Birth canal dystocias
  1. Soft tissue obstacles
    a. Full bladder
    b. Full rectum
    c. Myomata of wall of cervix
  2. Pelvis
    a. Congenital deformities
    b. Diseases of pelvic bone—rickets, tuberculosis, or osteomalacia
    c. Abnormalities of spine—lordosis, scoliosis, or kyphosis
  3. Nursing care
    a. Support patient through a trial labor
    b. Keep bladder and rectum empty
    c. Prepare for cesarean section
E. Common problems associated with dystocia
  1. Prolapse of cord
  2. Prolonged labor
  3. Fetal distress
  4. Postpartum—increased incidence of hemorrhage and infection

2. Uterine rupture
A. Pathology and etiology—uterus ruptures when the strain on muscle exceeds its strength; potential stresses include
  1. Excessive distention—large baby or multiple gestation
  2. Old scars—previous cesarean sections
  3. Contractions against fetus who does not progress through birth canal because of malpresentation or CPD, for example
  4. Injudicious obstetrics—malapplication of forceps or application without full dilatation and effacement
B. Symptoms
  1. Complete rupture
    a. Sudden sharp abdominal pain followed by cessation of contractions; abdominal tenderness
    b. Shock, fetal heart tones cease, and vaginal bleeding
    c. Presenting part not palpable during vaginal examination
  2. Incomplete rupture—progresses over several hours
    a. Contractions continue but are accompanied by abdominal pain and failure to dilate
    b. Symptoms of maternal shock—pallor, tachycardia, air hunger, and exhaustion
    c. May have some vaginal bleeding
    d. Cessation of fetal heart tones
C. Treatment—laparotomy, hysterectomy, transfusions, and antibiotics
D. Nursing care
  1. Prevention
    a. Identify predisposing factors early (see previous discussion)
    b. Judicious initiation and monitoring of oxytocin induction

2. Be alert for predisposing conditions and developing signs of uterine rupture—report stat and initiate shock treatment (positioning, O_2, and IVs)

E. Prognosis
1. Fetus—grave
2. Mother—guarded

3. **Amniotic fluid embolus**—amniotic fluid (with any meconium, lanugo, or vernix), enters maternal circulation through open venous sinuses at placental site and travels to pulmonary arterioles

A. Etiology—rare complication, usually following rupture of membranes with some abruptio placentae and difficult labor

B. Prognosis—poor; usually fatal to mother

C. Symptoms
1. Sudden dyspnea and cyanosis
2. Pulmonary shock due to anaphylactic vascular collapse
3. Developing afibrinogenemia

D. Treatment
1. Assist ventilation—position in semi-Fowler's, suction, oxygen, and mechanical ventilatory assistance
2. Give whole blood transfusion and injections of heparin and fibrinogen
3. Deliver stat—preferably with forceps, vaginally
4. Digitalize

4. **Prolapsed umbilical cord**—descent of cord in advance of presenting part

A. Etiologies
1. Spontaneous or artificial rupture of membranes before engagement of presenting part
2. Excessive force of fluid escaping, as with hydramnios
3. Malposition—breech, compound presentation, and transverse lie
4. Premature or small fetus, allowing space for descent of cord

B. Symptoms
1. Visualization of cord outside or inside vagina
2. Fetal distress—variable deceleration and persistent bradycardia

C. Treatment
1. Place mother on absolute bedrest in exaggerated Trendelenburg's position, knee-chest, or Sims's position with pillows to elevate hips
2. Push presenting part off cord with sterile gloved hand in vagina

3. Cover exposed cord with sterile dressing, preferably with warm saline
4. Oxygen by mask (6-8 liters/minute)
5. Deliver stat
   a. Vaginally with forceps
   b. Cesarean section, if vaginal delivery is not imminent
6. Monitor FHR continuously or every two minutes

5. **Inverted uterus**

A. Pathology and etiology—uterus is turned inside out, usually during birth of placenta when
1. Cord is excessively short
2. Cord is pulled before placental separation
3. Fundal pressure is exerted when uterus is relaxed

B. Symptoms—shock, hemorrhage, and severe pain

C. Treatment—replace uterus, hysterectomy, fluid and blood replacement, antibiotic therapy, and treat for shock

6. **Fetus in jeopardy**

A. Pathology—a compromised fetus suffering from hypoxia, anemia, or ketoacidotic environment

B. Etiologies
1. Maternal toxemia, heart disease, or diabetes
2. Insufficient uteroplacental circulation due to
   a. Maternal hypotension or hypertension
   b. Cord compression
   c. Hemorrhage
   d. Malformation of placenta-cord
   e. Postterm gestation (placental senility)
3. Rh or ABO incompatibility
4. Chorioamnionitis
5. Dystocia

C. Symptoms
1. Fetal heart rate (FHR)
   a. Persistent irregularity
   b. Persistent tachycardia of 160 or more/minute
   c. Persistent bradycardia of 100 or less/minute
   d. Early deceleration—head compression
   e. Late deceleration—uteroplacental insufficiency
   f. Variable deceleration—umbilical cord compression
2. Passage of meconium in vertex position; relaxation of anal sphincter, and gasping are consequences of cerebral anoxia
3. Fetal activity
   a. Hyperactivity—symptom of CO_2

retention
b. Cessation—possible fetal demise
D. Fetal heart rate monitors
1. Stethoscope or fetoscope
2. Phonocardiography with microphone amplification
3. Corometric monitor with probe attached directly to fetus through the dilated cervix after membranes are ruptured
4. Doppler probe using ultrasound flow
5. Cardiotocograph—picks up sound through transducers placed on abdomen
E. Evaluative tests
1. Amniocentesis
a. Definition—transabdominal placement of a needle into the amniotic cavity for the purposes of aspirating or injecting fluid
b. Purposes
(1) Assessment of fetal maturity
(2) Diagnosis of fetal jeopardy
(3) Treatment of fetal hemolytic anemia
(4) Assessment of placental function (sufficiency)
(5) Induction of abortion
c. Preparation
(1) Explain to patient
(2) Assist with sonography (to locate placenta)
(3) Ask patient to empty bladder
(4) Do surgical prep of skin
(5) FHR
d. Studies—the aspirant is contrifuged to separate the cellular components from the supernatant fluid for the purpose of
(1) Cytogenetic study—genetic disorders, such as trisomy 21 (Down's syndrome), fetal sex determination (for sex-linked disorders), and fetal ABO incompatibility
(2) Amniotic fluid study
(a) Spectrophotometric analysis for breakdown products of bilirubin (in presence of ABO or Rh incompatibility)
(b) Lecithin/sphingomyelin ratio ("shake test" or "foam test") for fetal lung maturity—lecithin to sphingomyelin ratio of 2 to 1 (after week 35) indicates lung maturity (sufficient surfactant to

initiate and maintain respirations)
(c) Detection of inborn errors of metabolism—enzyme deficiency disease such as Tay-Sachs disease
(d) Creatine level—2 mg/100 ml at week 36
e. Injection procedures
(1) Saline solution to induce abortion (see Table 4-2)
(2) Radiopaque dye for fetus to swallow prior to transfusion of packed red blood cells, type O, Rh negative into the peritoneal cavity of a fetus compromised by maternal isoimmunization, to relieve fetal anemia (see p. 265)
f. Hazards
(1) Stimulation of labor when not desired
(2) Puncture of fetus—monitor FHR
(3) Puncture of placenta or placental vessels
(4) Infection—request patient to notify physician if fever or malaise develop
2. Evaluation of amniotic fluid after rupture of membranes (see p. 227)
3. Estriol assays
a. Definition—index of placental functioning or sufficiency and fetal well-being; estriol is produced by fetal adrenals, processed by placenta, and excreted by maternal kidney; 24-hour levels increase as pregnancy progresses
(1) Serial studies are begun about week 32
(2) Adequate functioning—12 mg or more per 24 hours
b. Specimens
(1) Urine—if maternal renal function is normal
(2) Blood—not dependent on renal function
4. Oxytocin challenge test (OCT)—determination of FHR response to uterine contractions
a. Gravida is hospitalized; the FHR baseline is recorded; oxytocin induction is started; IV drip is regulated until three contractions occur in every ten minutes, then it is discontinued; contractions and FHR are monitored by

cardiotocograph or corometric monitor
  b. If placental function is normal, fetal oxygenation is unimpaired by contractions
  c. If late or variable deceleration patterns are noted, or FHR falls below 100, fetal lung maturity tests are done and the gravida may be prepared for cesarean section, since fetus is most likely unable to withstand the process of labor
  d. This test is most frequently done on the diabetic or prediabetic gravida
  e. Complication—sustained or continuing uterine contractions
5. Fetal blood sampling
  a. Conditions—ruptured membranes, engaged vertex, and some cervical dilatation
  b. Signs of fetal distress
    (1) pH below 7.20 (normal range is 7.3 to 7.4)
    (2) Increased arterial Pco_2
    (3) Decreased arterial Po_2
6. Summary of tests for estimating fetal maturity
  a. Ultrasound—"A" scan may be done weekly for biparietal diameter after week 16
  b. X-ray—distal femoral epiphyses usually formed by week 36
  c. Hormone levels—estriol and human placental lactogen (HPL) rise with normal pregnancy
  d. Analysis of amniotic fluid (discussed previously)
F. Prevention and treatment of fetal jeopardy
  1. Prenatal care to identify and treat concurrent medical conditions
  2. Positioning gravida on her side for labor to prevent hypotensive syndrome
  3. Judicious initiation and monitoring of induction
  4. Intravenous fluids and oxygen prn
  5. Astute frequent monitoring of fetal-maternal vital signs, labor, and response to labor
  6. Prevention of maternal exhaustion, infection, dehydration, and hemorrhage
7. Summary of danger signs during labor
A. Tonic contractions—every two minutes, lasting more than 90 seconds, with poor relaxation in between,
B. Sudden sharp abdominal pain followed by boardlike abdomen and shock—abruptio placentae or ruptured uterus
C. Bleeding from vagina
D. FHR deceleration—late; variable; bradycardia, below 100; and tachycardia, 160 or more
E. Amniotic fluid—excessive or diminished amount; presence of odor; meconium stained, port-wine-colored, or yellow colored; 24 hours or more since rupture of membranes
F. Wide fluctuation in blood pressure—hypotension or hypertension
G. Increased temperature, pulse, and blood pressure
H. Fetal hyperactivity or cessation of activity
I. Prolapsed cord
J. Dyspnea and cyanosis following rupture of membranes

POSTPARTUM PERIOD

1. Hypofibrinogenemia
A. Pathology—decrease of the clotting factor, fibrinogen in the blood; may be accompanied by disseminated intravascular clotting
B. Etiologies
  1. Missed abortion or missed labor following intrauterine fetal death
  2. Clot formation following abruptio placentae
C. Nursing management
  1. Order blood work
  2. Observe patient for bleeding and clot formation
2. Postpartum hemorrhage
A. Definition—loss of 500 ml blood or more during first 24 hours
B. Etiology (in order of frequency)
  1. Uterine atony—uterine relaxation secondary to
    a. Overdistended pregnant uterus—multiple gestation, large baby, or hydramnios, for example
    b. Multiparity
    c. Prolonged labor or precipitous labor
    d. Anesthesia—deep inhalation or regional anesthesia, especially saddle block
    e. Myomata
    f. Oxytocin induction of labor
    g. Postpartum overmassage of uterus
    h. Distended bladder
  2. Lacerations—cervical, vaginal, or perineal
  3. Retained placental fragments

4. Hematoma—deep pelvic, vaginal, or episiotomy site
C. Symptoms of shock—air hunger, restlessness, anxious facial expression, weak rapid pulse, dropping blood pressure, and tachypnea
D. Nursing care
   1. Note
      a. Lab values on prenatal chart—check for clotting time, hematocrit, and hemoglobin
      b. Estimated blood loss during labor-delivery
      c. Estimated blood loss postpartum
   2. Observe for and report
      a. Lacerations—bright red bleeding; bleeding continues when fundus is firm
      b. Atony—constant dark seepage, large clots expressed after firming fundus, and boggy uterus
      c. Hematoma—pain, discoloration, and swelling; can lose 500 ml or more into hematoma
      d. Retained placental tissue—boggy uterus and dark bleeding
E. Treatment
   1. Uterine atony—primarily nursing responsibility (see Postpartum care)
   2. Lacerations—repair and fluid and blood replacement prn
   3. Retained placental fragments—hemorrhage often occurs after woman is discharged; instruct concerning observation for bleeding, fever, and who and when to call; return to hospital for D & C to remove tissue
   4. Hematoma—evacuation and fluid and blood replacement prn
   5. Prevent infection
   6. Remain with patient—check fundus, bleeding, and vital signs every 15 minutes until stable, then every two to four hours for one day
   7. Keep warm
3. **Postpartum infections**
A. "Childbed fever," puerperal fever—a genital tract infection usually localized in the endometrium
   1. Predisposing conditions
      a. Anemia
      b. Premature rupture of membranes (PROM)
      c. Long labor
      d. Intrauterine manipulation—manual

extraction of placenta; version
      e. Retained placental fragments
      f. Postpartum hemorrhage
      g. Numerous vaginal exams during labor
   2. Symptoms:
      a. Fever 38 C (100.4 F) or more, chills, and malaise
      b. Increased pulse rate
      c. Pain—pelvic or abdominal
      d. Vaginal discharge is foul smelling and profuse
      e. Abscess formation elsewhere in body
      f. Thrombophlebitis
      g. Dysuria
   3. Prevention
      a. Prevent anemia
      b. Aseptic technique during labor and delivery
      c. Labor—avoid prolonged labor, treat long labor or PROM with IVs containing calories and electrolytes, antibiotics, or by cesarean section
      d. Avoid lacerations and retained fragments (allow spontaneous separation of placenta if possible) or diagnose early and treat
      e. Perineal cleanliness
B. Urinary tract infection
   1. Predisposing factors
      a. Birth trauma to bladder, urethra, or meatus
      b. Bladder hypotonia with retention (from anesthesia or birth trauma)
      c. Catheterization
   2. Symptoms may not appear for several days—dysuria, frequency, pus, and fever
   3. Nursing care—prevention
      a. Ice pack to perineum during first hour postpartum to discourage edema and facilitate voiding
      b. Encourage fluids
      c. Aseptic catheterization technique and complete emptying of bladder
   4. Nursing care—treatment
      a. Obtain urine for culture and sensitivity
      b. Instruct patient concerning fluids, medications, general hygiene, and diet
C. Mastitis—inflammation of breast tissue
   1. Cause—commonly caused by *Staphylococcus aureus* from infant's nasopharynx and oropharynx
   2. Symptoms
      a. Fever, chills, and increased pulse

b. Affected breast—tense, warm, reddened, and painful
3. Nursing care—prevention
   a. Nurse should be free of infection and use good handwashing technique
   b. Instruct mother about cleanliness—handwashing, washing breasts and nipples with warm water *only* (so as not to dry out tissues and remove protective oils), and clean baby and linens
   c. Assist mother with good breast feeding technique to prevent fissures
      (1) Proper support of infant at breast
      (2) Gradual increase in infant's nursing time as nipples toughen
      (3) Proper removal of nipple from infant's mouth
3. Nursing care—treatment
   a. Medications and ice packs, as ordered
   b. Encourage wearing of bra or good support
   c. Assist mother to stop nursing, if ordered—encourage ventilation of feelings and treat for engorgement (see p. 242)
   d. If mother is to continue nursing, teach her how to "milk" breast to stimulate continued production of milk until nursing from that breast is resumed
D. Thrombophlebitis—inflammation of a vein
   1. Causes
      a. Extension of infection from uterine cavity (placental site) into pelvic and femoral veins
      b. Clot formation in pelvic veins following cesarean section, or in calf of leg, due to poor circulation
   2. Symptoms
      a. Pelvic—abdominal or pelvic discomfort and tenderness
      b. Calf—positive Homan's sign, pain as foot is flexed while knee is extended
      c. Femoral—leg swelling and pain, fever, chills, or "milk leg"
   3. Nursing care
      a. Support bandage or stocking and elevate hip and/or leg
      b. Medications—antibiotics and anticoagulants
      c. Heat therapy, as ordered
      d. Bedrest with bed cradle to support bedding

   e. Caution mother not to massage "cramp" in leg
E. Endometritis—infection of lining of uterus
   1. Mild, local—no symptoms, or slight fever
   2. Severe
      a. Symptoms of infection—fever, chills, malaise, anorexia, headache, and backache
      b. Uterus—large, boggy, and tender; dark brown lochia having a foul odor
      c. If it remains localized, lasts ten days
      d. Treatment
         (1) Isolate
         (2) Discontinue breast feeding—depletes mother's energy
         (3) Medications—antibiotics and ergot products
         (4) Semi-Fowler's to promote lochial drainage
         (5) High-calorie nourishment, fluids up to 4000 ml/day (oral or IV), and I & O
         (6) Emotional support
4. **Postpartum psychiatric problems**—sometimes seen in both the new mother and the new father

NEONATE AT RISK

1. **Classification of infants by weight and gestational age**
A. Terminology
   1. Preterm or premature—37 weeks gestation or under, usually 2500 gm (5½ lb) or less also
   2. Term—38 to 42 weeks gestation
   3. Postterm or postmature—over 42 weeks
   4. Appropriate for gestational age (AGA)—for each week of gestation, there is a normal expected range of weight
      a. Small for gestational age (SGA) or dysmature—weight falls below normal range for age
         (1) Cause—toxemia, malnutrition, smoking, placental insufficiency, rubella, syphilis, twins, or genetic
         (2) A term infant weighing 2500 gm is usually mature in physiologic functioning and frequently may be discharged with the mother
         (3) If respiratory distress occurs, it is usually due to aspiration syndrome
      b. Large for gestational age (LGA)—above expected weight for age

(1) Cause—diabetic or prediabetic mother, maternal weight gain over 35 lb, maternal obesity, or genetic
(2) A preterm infant weighing 7½ lb should be treated as a premature infant; if respiratory distress occurs, it is usually due to respiratory distress syndrome (RDS)
(3) Associated problems—hypoglycemia, hypocalcemia, hyperbilirubinemia, and birth injury

B. Estimation of gestational age—to plan for adequate care, it is essential to differentiate between the premature and the term infant. For guide to clinical assessment see Tables 4-10 and 4-13

2. **Premature infant**—neonate of 37 weeks gestation or less

A. Etiology
   1. Iatrogenic—EDC is miscalculated for repeat cesarean sections
   2. Placental factors—abruptio placentae, placenta previa, and insufficiency
   3. Uterine factors—multiple gestation, incompetent cervix, and uterine anomalies (including fibroids)
   4. Fetal factors—malformations, infections (rubella, toxoplasmosis and cytomegalic inclusion disease), and erythroblastosis
   5. Maternal factors—malnutrition, overwork, severe physical or emotional trauma, toxemia, hypertension, diabetes, heart disease, and infections (syphilis, leukemia, pyelonephritis, pneumonia, and influenza)
   6. Miscellaneous—close frequency of pregnancy, advanced age of parents, heavy smoking, and high altitudes

B. Cause of mortality (in relative order)
   1. Abnormal pulmonary ventilation
   2. Infection—pneumonia, septicemia, diarrhea, and meningitis
   3. Intracranial hemorrhage
   4. Congenital defects

C. Physiologic disadvantages—infant born before term is anatomically and physiologically disadvantaged; environment and care must be planned to meet special needs
   1. Respiratory system—insufficient surfactant and number and maturity of alveoli; immature musculature and rib cage; *problems:* respiratory distress syndrome, atelectasis, apnea, and poor gag and cough reflex

2. Digestive system—poorly developed suck, swallow, and gag reflexes; small stomach capacity; immature enzyme system; *problems:* aspiration, malabsorption, diarrhea, abdominal distention, and fat intolerance; intake of tocopherol (vitamin E) is adequate in the breast milk-fed neonate, but must be supplemented in the formula-fed neonate; edema and anemia are attributed to a deficiency
3. Heat regulation—unstable
   a. Lack of subcutaneous fat
   b. Large body surface area in proportion to body weight
   c. Small muscle mass
   d. Absent sweat or shiver responses
   e. Poor capillary response to change in environmental temperature
4. Resistance to infection is low—lack of immune bodies from mother (these cross placenta from mother late in pregnancy); inability to produce own immune bodies (immature liver); poor WBC response to infection; thin skin
5. Central nervous system immature—weak or absent reflexes and fluctuating primitive control of vital functions
6. Immature liver—susceptible to hyperbilirubinemia and hypoglycemia; immature production of clotting factors and immune globulins; anemia
7. Retrolental fibroplasia—increased susceptibility of immature retina to high levels of arterial oxygen
8. Immature renal function—cannot concentrate urine; precarious fluid and electrolyte balance
9. Capillary fragility—increased susceptibility to hemorrhage in all tissues, including brain

D. Factors influencing survival of premature newborn
   1. Lung maturity
   2. Anomalies
   3. Size
   4. Gestational age

E. Observations
   1. Voiding and stooling
   2. Feeding behaviors—color changes, abdominal distention, fatigue, and respiratory distress
   3. Jaundice—susceptible to kernicterus at lower bilirubin levels
   4. Symptoms of respiratory distress

Table 4-13. Estimation of gestational age—some common clinical parameters

Physical characteristics	Preterm	Term
Head	Oval—narrow biparietal diameter ($\leq$35 cm, $\leq$13 inches); head large in proportion to body size; face looks like an "old man"	Square-shaped; biparietal prominences; head one-fourth body length
Ears	Soft, flat, and shapeless	Pinna firm; erect from head
Hair	Fine, fuzzy, or wooly; clumped; appears at 20 weeks	Silky; single strands apparent
Sole creases	Starting at ball of foot, one-third covered with creases by 36 weeks; two-thirds by 38 weeks	Entire sole heavily creased
Breast nodules	4 cm by 38 weeks; 0 cm at 36 weeks	4–7 cm or more
Genitalia		
Female	Clitoris large and labia gaping	Labia larger and meet in midline
Male	Small scrotum, rugae on inferior surface only, and testes undescended	Scrotum pendulous and covered with rugae; testes usually descended
Musculoskeletal signs		
Muscle tone	Hypotonia	Hypertonia
Posture	Froglike	Attitude of general flexion
Traction response	Head lags and arms have little or no flexion	Head follows trunk and strong arm flexion
Owl sign	Head capable of being rotated past point of shoulder	Head can only be rotated to point of shoulder
Scarf sign	Elbow is capable of being moved beyond midline	Elbow can only be brought to midline, infant resists
Skin	Thin; capillaries are visible	See Term infant, Table 4-11
Length	Under 47 cm (18½ inches), generally	
Weight	Under 2500 gm (5 lb 5 oz), generally	
Neurologic responses		
Moro reflex	Apparent at 28 weeks; good but no adduction	Complete reflex with adduction, disappears four months postterm
Grasp reflex	Fair at 28 weeks; arm is involved at 32 weeks	Grasp response, strong enough to sustain weight for few seconds when infant is pulled up; hands, arm, and shoulders are involved
Cry	24 weeks, weak; 28 weeks, high pitched; 32 weeks, cry is good	Good cry; lusty and can persist for some time
Vernix	Covers body between 31 to 33 weeks	Small amount at term; absent and skin appears dry and wrinkled postterm
Lanugo	Apparent at 20 weeks; between 33 to 36 weeks, covers shoulders	No lanugo, or minimal amount

5. Congenital anomalies
6. Skin—color, petechiae, ecchymoses, turgor, and edema
F. Respiratory distress syndrome (RDS)
1. Pathophysiology—lack of surfactant (lecithin) and immature alveoli predispose to atelectasis; ventilation is compromised; alveolar ducts and terminal bronchioli become lined with a fibrous glossy membrane
   a. Primarily a function of prematurity
   b. Other predisposing factors
      (1) Fetal hypoxia—from maternal

bleeding or hypotension, for
example
(2) Birth asphyxia
(3) Postnatal hypothermia, metabolic
acidosis, or hypotension
c. Factors protecting neonate from RDS
(1) Chronic fetal stress, from maternal
hypertension, toxemia, and heroin
addiction, for example
(2) Premature rupture of membranes
(PROM)
(3) Maternal ingestion of steroids
(4) Low-grade chorioamnionitis
2. Symptoms
a. Usually appear during first or second
day of life
b. Signs of respiratory distress
(1) Retractions
(2) Tachypnea—60/minute or more
(3) Cyanosis
(4) Expiratory grunt
(5) Chin tug
(6) Increase in number and length of
apneic episodes
(7) Flaring of nares
(8) Increasing exhaustion
c. Hypercapnia with increased CO_2 level
(respiratory acidosis)
d. Metabolic acidosis due to increased
lactic acid
3. Nursing Care—supportive
a. Ensure warmth (isolette at 97.6 F)
b. Provide O_2—amount sufficient to
relieve cyanosis
(1) Warmed, humidified, and at lowest
concentration
(2) Via hood, nasal prongs,
endotracheal tube, bag, or mask
c. Monitor continuous positive airway
pressure (CPAP)—oxygen-air mixture is
given under pressure during inhalation
and exhalation; functions to keep alveoli
open on exhalation
d. Position to support respiratory
efforts—side-lying, or supine with arms
at sides, and neck slightly extended in
''sniffing'' attitude
e. Keep airway clear
(1) Postural drainage and percussion, as
ordered
(2) Suction
f. Suctioning the neonate with an
endotracheal tube

(1) Disconnect tubing at the adaptor
(2) Inject up to 0.5 ml sterile normal
saline
(3) Insert sterile suction tube, start
suction, rotate tube between fingers
and withdraw
(4) Suction up to five seconds
(5) Ventilate neonate with bag and mask
during procedure
(6) Reconnect tubing to adaptor
securely
(7) Take apical pulse and listen to chest
for breath sounds
g. Fluids, electrolytes, calories, vitamins,
and minerals; intake and output records
h. Protect against infections
i. Meet neonate's psychologic
needs—touch without pain; hear soft
voices; see faces; and experience
pleasurable motion, such as rocking
j. Parents need support, information on
condition and progress, and early sight
and touch contact to foster bonding
G. Oxygen toxicity
1. Retrolental fibroplasia—primarily a disease
of immaturity and high levels of arterial
oxygen concentration; arterial oxygen concentrations should be kept between 35-60
mm Hg, if possible and should be measured
by blood gas determinations
2. Bronchopulmonary dysplasia—primarily a
disease of immaturity of the pulmonary system and high levels of arterial oxygen concentrations administered under pressure
(CPAP and CEEP)
3. **Hypoglycemia**—low blood glucose level
A. Symptoms
1. Lethargy and hypotonia or jitteriness; convulsions
2. Sweating; unstable temperature
3. Tachypnea or apneic episodes
4. Cyanosis
5. Shrill cry
6. Feeding difficulty
B. Predisposing conditions
1. Birth asphyxia
2. Gestational malnutrition (placental dysfunction; postmaturity)
3. Stress—infection, respiratory distress, abrupt discontinuation of parenteral fluids, and
chilling
4. Erythroblastosis
5. Maternal disease—renal, cardiac, pre-

eclampsia, and diabetes
C. Nursing care
   1. Diagnose by noting preceding symptoms and predisposing conditions
   2. Diagnose by ordering lab work or doing a heel Dextrostix
   3. Normal lab values
      a. Term neonate—30-40 mg/100 ml blood
      b. Preterm neonate—20 mg/100 ml blood
   4. If hypoglycemic
      a. Feed glucose orally or parenterally, as ordered
      b. Record and report to physician
4. **Drug-dependent neonate**—maternal addiction to heroin or morphine
A. 50% to 90% of drug-dependent neonates show withdrawal
B. Symptoms—degree depends on type and duration of addiction and level of drug in maternal blood at delivery
   1. Hyperactivity, hypertonicity; exaggerated reflexes, tremors, twitching, irritability, and difficulty sleeping
   2. Feeding problems—regurgitation, vomiting, poor feeder, diarrhea, and increased mucus production
   3. Hunger—sucks on fists
   4. Nasal stuffiness and sneezing
   5. Respiratory distress, cyanosis and/or apnea, and pallor
   6. Sweating
   7. Convulsions with abnormal eye rolling and chewing motions
C. Acute nursing care
   1. Monitor apical pulse and respirations
   2. Keep airway open—position on side and suction
   3. Collect all urine during first 24 hours for toxicologic studies
   4. Food-fluids—oral or parenteral, I & O, and weigh daily
   5. Decrease stimuli—keep noise down, handle infrequently, and offer pacifier
   6. Keep warm and swaddle for comfort
   7. Skin care—clean; dry; zinc oxide ointment and karaya powder q2-4h to excoriated buttocks, expose excoriated skin to air; and mitts over hands
   8. Medications, as ordered
      a. Paregoric gtt po, to wean neonate from drug
      b. Phenobarbital

      c. Chlorpromazine (Thorazine)
      d. Diazepam (Valium)—do not give it to jaundiced neonate, as it predisposes to hyperbilirubinemia
   9. Emotional support to mother; encourage visits and participation in care; refer to social service or public health nurse prn
5. **Postterm or postmature neonate**—over 42 weeks gestation
A. Labor may be hazardous for mother and fetus
   1. Large size may contribute to dystocia; diagnosis by ultrasound, "A" scan, and/or X-ray
   2. Placental insufficiency may exist, exposing infant to intrauterine hypoxia; diagnosis by oxytocin challenge test (see p. 255)
B. Neonate may exhibit the following characteristics
   1. Wrinkled dry skin—fetus may have needed to metabolize reserves of fat and glycogen to meet energy needs
   2. Long finger and toe nails
   3. No vernix and no lanugo
   4. Wide-eyed, alert expression, probably due to chronic hypoxia (oxygen hunger)
C. Prognosis—higher incidence of infant morbidity and mortality, especially during labor
D. Nursing care
   1. Emotional support of mother during labor—may require cesarean section for CPD or because fetus cannot tolerate stress of labor contractions
   2. Monitor FHR continuously—report late or variable deceleration stat
   3. Diagnose and treat neonatal hypoglycemia
   4. If delivered vaginally, observe neonate for birth injuries
6. **Congenital disorders**
A. Early recognition and treatment of structural or metabolic problems is a priority
   1. Early repair or treatment
   2. Emotional support of parents who must go through a grieving process soon after birth
   3. Genetic counseling or family planning when appropriate
B. Types frequently seen
   1. Gastrointestinal tract
      a. Cleft lip and/or palate
      b. Tracheoesophageal fistula and/or esophageal atresia
      c. Imperforate anus
      d. Intestinal obstruction

e. Omphalocele—protrusion of abdominal contents into base of umbilical cord

2. Orthopedic problems
   a. Clubbed foot (talipes equinovarus)
   b. Congenital hip dysplasia
   c. Phocomelia—absence of all or part of a limb
   d. Supernumerary digits or polydactyly

3. Central nervous system
   a. Anencephalus—absence of the cerebrum, its overlying bones, skin, and hair
   b. Microcephalus or hydrocephalus
   c. Spina bifida
   d. Intracranial bleeding or lesion (signs of increased intracranial pressure: tremors, eye rolling, convulsion, respiratory distress with cyanosis or apnea, poor feeding and/or sucking, bulging fontanel, high pitched cry, and incomplete or absent Moro reflex)
   e. Dysfunction (evident by absent or abnormal reflexes; respiratory distress with cyanosis or apnea; weak and/or high-pitched, whining cry; poor feeding with regurgitation or vomiting; hypotonia or hypertonia; bradycardia; and hypothermia)

4. Urinary system
   a. Hypospadias or epispadias—urinary meatus on the undersurface or the oversurface of the penis
   b. Exstrophy of the bladder—absence of anterior of bladder wall exposing bladder wall; urine seeps onto abdominal skin
   c. Agenesis—absence of development

5. Respiratory system
   a. Diaphragmatic hernia with scaphoid abdomen—hernia of abdominal contents into thoracic cavity
   b. Choanal atresia—partial or complete blockage of posterior nares

6. Chromosomal aberrations
   a. Down's syndrome (mongolism)
   b. Cri du chat syndrome—cry sounds like meowing of a cat
   c. Turner's or Klinefelter's syndromes

7. Cardiovascular system—congenital heart defects
   a. Examples—tetralogy of Fallot, valvular atresias, and transposition of major vessels
   b. Symptoms—cyanosis that may not respond to O_2; X-ray shows an abnormal heart; respiratory distress; lethargy; hypotonia; easy fatigability; weak cry; poor feeding; sweating with exertion, such as crying or feeding; and edema

8. Metabolic—inborn errors of metabolism
   a. Phenylketonuria (PKU)—missing enzyme (phenylalanine hydroxylase), prevents conversion of phenylalanine (essential amino acid present in all animal protein) to tyrosine
      (1) Inherited as a recessive gene
      (2) Incidence—1 in 10,000 live births
      (3) Build up of phenylalanine results in mental retardation
      (4) Treatment to minimize or prevent mental retardation—phenylalanine-poor diet, Lofenalac infant formula, for example
   b. Galactosemia—inborn error of sugar metabolism, leads to mental retardation

C. Nursing care
   1. Preoperative and postoperative care—prevent infections, ensure adequate nutrition, and assist with laboratory work and other diagnostic tests
   2. Parental support—assist parents to express feelings and ask questions; simplify and clarify physician's explanations; prepare them for sight of neonate and equipment needed for the neonate's care; allow for parents to see, hold, and touch neonate and to assist with nursing care as soon as possible; involve parents in decision-making process; make referrals to community resources as necessary
   3. Emotional support of the neonate at risk (see p. 266)

7. **Hemolytic disease of the neonate**
A. Rh incompatibility
   1. The Rh factor is an antigen that appears on the red blood cells of some people; these people are then Rh-positive; the Rh factor is dominant; a person may be (a) homozygous for Rh factor or (b) heterozygous for Rh factor
   2. An Rh-negative person is homozygous for this recessive trait
   3. Isoimmunization is the process by which the

Rh-negative person develops antibodies against the Rh factor
4. Pregnancy and the Rh factor
   a. An Rh-positive mother may carry either an Rh-negative infant or Rh-positive infant with no consequence for the infant
   b. An Rh-negative mother may carry an Rh-negative infant with no consequence to the infant
   c. An Rh-negative mother carrying her first Rh-positive child usually does not develop antibodies to a level harmful to the fetus unless she was previously sensitized by an inadvertent transfusion with Rh-positive blood, fetal cells usually do not enter the maternal blood stream until the time the placenta separates from the uterus, at abortion, abruptio placentae, and at delivery
   d. After the delivery of an Rh-positive child, some of the child's Rh-positive cells enter the maternal blood stream and the mother begins to develop antibodies to them
   e. The anti-Rh-positive antibodies remain in her blood stream with no consequence to her; but at the time of the next pregnancy with an Rh-positive fetus, these antibodies will cross the placenta and enter the fetal blood stream; hemolysis of fetal red blood cells begins; degree of hemolysis is dependent on amount of maternal antibodies
5. Diagnosis of isoimmunization—presence of antibodies against Rh-positive red blood cells; Rh sensitization
   a. Amniocentesis during pregnancy beginning as early as 26 weeks (see p. 255)
   b. Indirect Coombs' test—to determine titer (amount) of antibodies mother has produced
      (1) Specimen—mother's blood
      (2) Test—mix mother's blood with Rh-positive red blood cells
      (3) Positive test result—Rh-positive red blood cells agglutinate (clump)
   c. Direct Coombs' test
      (1) Specimen—neonate's blood (from umbilical cord)
      (2) Test—fetal red blood cells are "washed" and mixed with Coomb's serum
      (3) Positive test result—neonate's Rh-positive red blood cells agglutinate
6. Summary of factors predisposing Rh incompatibility
   a. Rh-negative woman
   b. Pregnancies with Rh-positive fetuses
   c. Accidental transfusion with Rh-positive blood
   d. Small concealed abruptio placentae where pregnancy continues for several days
7. RhoGAM
   a. This drug is given to Rh-negative mothers of Rh-positive infants within 72 hours of delivery; the mothers should have *no* titer
   b. This drug removes fetal Rh-positive red blood cells that have entered the maternal blood stream; therefore, the mother does not develop antibodies
   c. This drug *does not* remove anti-Rh-positive antibodies from the maternal blood stream; that is, it cannot reverse any sensitization that has already occurred
   d. This drug is given after every abortion and after every birth of an Rh-positive baby
   e. If the fetus requires transfusion, Rh-negative blood is used
B. ABO incompatibility—less severe hemolytic disease, usually
   1. The person with Type O blood carries anti-A and anti-B antibodies
   2. The type O mother carrying a fetus who is type AB passes the anti-A and anti-B antibodies across the placenta to the fetus and hemolysis of fetal red blood cells commences
   3. Because these antibodies are already present, even the first pregnancy with a type AB fetus is jeopardized; this incompatibility usually does not result in the severe hemolytic conditions possible with Rh incompatibility
   4. If the fetus needs a transfusion, type O Rh-negative blood is used
C. Symptoms and signs of hemolytic disease
   1. Spectrophotometric analysis of amniotic fluid (between 26 and 31 weeks gestation)

identifies amount of hemolytic activity as seen by the amount of breakdown products of bilirubin present; this analysis is done after the mother has demonstrated a rising titer by indirect Coomb's test for anti-Rh-positive antibodies or has a history of ABO incompatibility

2. Birth of a child with hydrops fetalis—the most severe form of hemolytic erythroblastosis; infant is grossly *edematous* from severe *anemia* and cardiopulmonary failure; infant is usually stillborn
3. Birth of an icteric infant, most common type
4. Development of *jaundice* within 48 hours of birth, mildest type
5. High bilirubin levels lead to the deposit of the yellow pigment in the basal ganglia of the brain, causing kernicterus; kernicterus may result in death or varying degrees of neuromuscular dysfunction
   a. Early signs—poor feeding, depressed reflexes, and increased muscle tone
   b. Treatment—see following discussion of hyperbilirubinemia; if severe, postnatal blood exchange or intrauterine transfusion is performed

D. Hyperbilirubinemia
1. Pathology—bilirubin, a breakdown product of hemolyzed red blood cells, appears at increased levels in the blood, more than 13–15 mg/100 ml blood; *warning:* there is no set serum bilirubin level that is safe; kernicterus is a function of the bilirubin level and the age and condition of the infant; poor fluid and caloric balance subjects the infant (especially the premature) to kernicterus at low serum levels of bilirubin, for example
2. Etiologies
   a. Rh or ABO incompatibility, during first one or two days
   b. During resolution of an enclosed hemorrhage, such as cephalhematoma
   c. Infection-induced
   d. Drug-induced—injection of vitamin K, maternal ingestion of sulfisoxazole (Gantrisin), and "breast-feeding jaundice" (pregnanediol in milk), for example
   e. Immature liver
3. Identification in the neonate
   a. Jaundice noted after blanching skin to suppress hemoglobin color; or noted in sclera or mucosa of dark-skinned neonates
   b. Blood-level determination—hemoglobin or indirect bilirubin
   c. Pallor
   d. Concentrated, dark urine
   e. Kernicterus—clinical manifestations
      (1) Poor feeding and/or sucking and regurgitation and vomiting
      (2) High-pitched cry
      (3) Temperature instability
      (4) Hypertonicity or hypotonicity
      (5) Progressive lethargy; diminished Moro reflex response
      (6) Respiratory distress
      (7) Cerebral palsy, mental retardation, or death
4. Treatment
   a. Prenatal treatment—transabdominal injection of packed Rh-negative, type O, red blood cells into fetal peritoneal cavity to relieve fetal anemia
   b. Phototherapy—fluorescent light breakdown of bilirubin into water soluble products
   c. Nursing care
      (1) Cover closed eyelids while neonate is under light; with light off, remove eye pads for short periods during feeding or cuddling sessions or when parent visits
      (2) Expose as much skin as possible
      (3) Change position q1h
      (4) Note any loose green stools, provide good skin care, and offer fluids between feedings
   d. Exchange transfusion—Rh incompatibility
      (1) Purpose
         (a) Remove anti-Rh-positive antibodies and fetal Rh-positive red blood cells coated with antibodies; remove bilirubin when 20 mg/100 ml blood in term neonates and 16 mg/100 ml blood in preterm neonates
         (b) Correct anemia with red blood cells that will not be destroyed by maternal antibodies, Rh-negative, type O, for example, maximum amount exchanged is 500 ml; duration of

exchange is 45 to 60 minutes

(2) Hazards

  (a) If blood is not at room temperature—cardiac arrest may occur

  (b) If blood is not fresh—there is an increased possibility of hypocalcemia, tetany and convulsions; to counteract this, have on hand calcium gluconate; 1 ml of calcium gluconate is given after every 100 ml of donor blood transfused

(3) Nursing care during transfusion

  (a) Have equipment in readiness—monitors, resuscitation, radiant heater, and light

  (b) Monitor and record vital signs—baseline and continuous every 15 to 30 minutes

  (c) Record time and amount of blood withdrawn, donor blood injected, and medications given

  (d) Observe for dyspnea, listlessness, bleeding from transfusion site, cyanosis, cyanosis and coolness of lower extremities, and cardio-vascular irregularity or arrest

(4) Nursing care posttransfusion

  (a) In addition to preceding symptoms, observe for jaundice; continued observation for cardiac arrest or irregularities, hypoglycemia, and sepsis

  (b) Keep warm

  (c) Take frequent vital signs

  (d) Give oxygen to relieve cyanosis

  (e) Keep cord moist (in case of repeat transfusion)

  (f) Feed per schedule

8. Neonatal sepsis

A. Etiology

  1. Prolonged rupture of membranes
  2. Long, difficult labor
  3. Resuscitation procedures
  4. Maternal infection
  5. Aspiration—amniotic fluid, formula, or mucus
  6. Iatrogenic (nosocomial)—caused by infected personnel or equipment

B. Symptoms—generalized, usually nonspecific

  1. Respirations—irregular, periods of apnea
  2. Irritability or lethargy
  3. Jaundice or pallor
  4. Poor feeding (and/or sucking), vomiting, diarrhea, weight loss, and dehydration
  5. Hypothermia or hyperthermia

C. Diagnosis

  1. Cultures—skin (before bath), throat, blood, urine, spinal fluid, and umbilicus
  2. Stomach contents—examined for polymor-phonuclear cells

D. Nursing care

  1. Isolate
  2. Keep warm
  3. Medications, as ordered
  4. Vital signs
  5. Oxygen to relieve respiratory distress, prn
  6. Food-fluids, as ordered; I & O; weigh daily; and observe for dehydration (soft eyeballs, sunken fontanels, and poor skin turgor on thighs or abdomen)
  7. Emotional support for neonate and parents

9. Emotional support of the high-risk neonate

A. The neonate at risk has the same developmental needs as the healthy neonate—social and tactile stimulation that interest and comfort and removal of discomforts (hunger and soiling) by a consistent mothering person

B. It is more difficult to meet these needs, as the neonate

  1. Listens to the sound of motors, hiss of oxygen, and sounds of human voices distorted by the incubator
  2. Views the outside world distorted through the incubator and oxygen hood
  3. Feels needle sticks and application and removal of monitors

C. *Some* suggestions to modify effects

  1. Assign the same nurses whenever possible
  2. Arrange times to stroke skin, hold hand, hum or sing to neonate in enface position (nurse looking into neonate's eyes), comfort when crying, and hold during feeding if possible
  3. Avoid loud discordant radio music and loud voices
  4. Arrange for parents to do above as often as possible for them to form attachment and to prevent later child abuse (much higher incidence of child abuse against child who had been a high risk neonate)

D. Signs of emotional ill health of neonate

  1. Does not look at person performing care tasks

2. Does not cry or protest
3. Shows poor weight gain and failure to thrive
10. Neonatal infections
A. General infections (see pp. 210 and 266)
B. Oral thrush—mycotic stomatitis
   1. Etiology
      a. Organism—*Candida albicans*, a fungus
      b. Vulnerable newborns—sick, debilitated newborns; those receiving antibiotic therapy; newborns with cleft lip or palate, neoplasms, or hyperparathyroidism
   2. Spread of infections by direct contact
      a. Maternal birth canal, hands, and linens
      b. Contaminated feeding equipment
      c. Contaminated hands
   3. Symptomatology
      a. Appearance of white patches on oral mucosa, gums, and tongue that bleed when touched
      b. Occasionally, some neonates may have difficulty swallowing
   4. Treatment and nursing management
      a. Cleanliness and good hand-washing technique
      b. Chemotherapy
         (1) Aqueous gentian violet 1% to 2% applied with a swab to infected areas
         (2) Nystatin (Mycostatin) instilled into mouth with a medicine dropper or applied with a swab to lesions, after feedings; prior to medicating, feed sterile water to wash out milk

---

Part C: The Reproductive System in Women and Men

THE REPRODUCTIVE SYSTEM IN WOMEN

1. Menstrual conditions
A. Amenorrhea—absence of menstruation
B. Dysmenorrhea—painful menstruation
C. Menorrhagia—excessive menstrual bleeding
D. Metrorrhagia—bleeding between menstrual periods and after menopause
E. Menopause—cessation of ovulation and menstruation, occurring at approximately 40 to 50 years of age
2. Gynecologic procedures
A. Abortion (see Table 4-2)
B. Cold-knife conization of cervix—rotary coring or excision of the endocervix for removal of diseased or abnormal tissue
C. Colporrhapy—anterior (repair of cystocele) and posterior (repair of rectocele)
D. Colposcopy—visualization of the cul-de-sac for evidence of PID, bleeding, ectopic pregnancy, and ovarian cysts
E. Dilatation and curettage (D & C) (see Table 4-2)
F. Hysterectomy—types
   1. Subtotal—fundus excised; cervical stump remains
   2. Total—entire uterus excised; tubes and ovaries remain
   3. Pan—entire uterus, tubes, and ovaries excised
G. Laparoscopy—visualization of intra-abdominal cavity with a scope inserted through small incision in abdomen
3. Infections
A. Vaginal infections—types and care
   1. *Candida albicans* (moniliasis)
      a. Fungus—likes dark wet environment
      b. Symptoms—pruritus, redness, and thick cheesy discharge
      c. Medications—local, 5% gentian violet; insertion propionate compound (Propion gel), ointment or suppository; nystatin (Mycostatin); and antibiotics
      d. Those more prone—diabetics, those taking oral contraceptives, pregnant women, and those on medications (antibiotics and steroids)
      e. Causes *thrush* in newborn
   2. *Trichomonas vaginalis*

a. Protozoa—thrives in alkaline environment
b. Symptoms—increased vaginal discharge, pruritis, burning, and redness
c. Medication—change pH to acid with vinegar douche; oral medication (for both partners), metronidazole (Flagyl)
3. Nursing care
   a. Instruct patient concerning medications and general hygiene
   b. Instruct concerning douching
   c. Instruct about avoiding intercourse until cured
4. Douching—douche only when prescribed during pregnancy; do not douche until after six-week postdelivery checkup
   a. Fill can or bag with prescribed fluid
      (1) Acidic douche—Massengill or white vinegar, 15 ml to 1000 ml water (1 tbsp to 1 qt water)
      (2) 1000 to 2000 ml warmed to 40 to 43 C (105 to 110 F)
   b. Connect via tubing to vaginal *nozzle* (do not use bulb as this may force fluid into uterus and cause embolus)
   c. Hang bag two feet or less above the hips
   d. Sit in clean tub or on toilet
   e. Void prior to procedure
   f. Insert nozzle 1½ to 2 inches downward and backward; rotate to wash all surfaces
   g. If sitting on toilet, hold labia together, fill vagina, release labia; fluid and debris will be washed out
   h. Continue until required solution is used up
B. Endometriosis—abnormal growth of endometrial tissue outside of the uterus
   1. Etiology—unclear
      a. Embryonic tissue remnants
      b. Transport of endometrial tissue to ectopic sites during surgery, with menstrual flow, or via vasculary system
   2. Symptoms
      a. Infertility or sterility
      b. Abnormal uterine bleeding
      c. Pain—backache, rectal, and dyspareunia (painful intercourse), and dysmenorrhea
   3. Diagnosis
      a. Vaginal-rectal pelvic examination—fixed nodes, ovaries, and uterus; pain

b. Barium enema—adhesions and constrictions
4. Nursing management and treatment
   a. Emotional support
   b. Ovulation suppressants to relieve dysmenorrhea
   c. Surgeries—relieve adhesions, resection of tissue, and total hysterectomy
C. Pelvic inflammatory disease (PID)—inflammation of pelvic contents, which may include fallopian tubes (salpingitis), ovaries (oophoritis), pelvic-vascular system, and peritoneum
   1. Etiology
      a. Pathogens are usually introduced through cervical canal and spread by direct extension and by the lymphatic and vascular systems
      b. Pathogens—*Streptococcus; Staphylococcus;* sexually transmitted (venereal) herpes virus II, syphilis, gonorrhea, and *Trichomonas;* and tubercle bacillus (from lungs via blood stream)
   2. Symptoms—fever and malaise
      a. Abdominal and low back pain
      b. Nausea, vomiting, and diarrhea
      c. Leukocytosis
      d. Foul-smelling vaginal discharge with pruritus
      e. Urinary tract infection
   3. Complications
      a. Chronic discomfort and disease
      b. Sterility—from scar tissue in fallopian tubes
      c. Ectopic pregnancy—passage to uterus blocked by scar tissue
      d. Adhesions—pelvic organs
   4. Nursing care and treatment—acute care
      a. Semi-Fowler's to facilitate drainage
      b. Heat—external to abdomen; internal via douching
      c. Shower preferable to tub bathing
   5. Nursing care and treatment (on-going)
      a. Administer medications
      b. Prevent spread
         (1) Good hand washing by patient and personnel
         (2) Isolation technique for care or disposal of equipment, supplies, linen, and perineal pads
         (3) To handle equipment and supplies, wear gloves and use instruments

(forceps)

    (4) Avoid catheterization

  c. Provide emotional support

  d. Nutrition—fluids to 3000 ml/day

4. Neoplasms

A. Tumors of the breast

  1. Types

    a. Fibroadenoma—benign, firm, round, movable, and painless

    b. Cancer, malignant—leading cause of mortality in women; survival rate, approximately 50%

B. Breast

  1. Incidence—increases in women who are childless, have not breast-fed, have a family history of breast cancer, or have a late menopause

  2. Injuries are not a cause

  3. Symptoms—elevation and asymmetry of breast, bleeding from nipple, orange-peel skin, nipple retraction, and painless lump (especially in upper, outer quadrant)

  4. Diagnosis—breast self-examination (95%), physician examination, mammography, thermography, xerography, and biopsy

  5. Stages and treatment

    a. Stage I (localized nodes negative)—mastectomy with or without radiation

    b. Stage II (localized, axillary nodes positive)—mastectomy with or without radiation

    c. Stage III (local extension, area nodes positive)—mastectomy and excision of large axillary nodes; radiation alone if mass is fixed

    d. Stage IV (distant metastasis)—variable surgery, radiation, hormone treatment, and chemotherapy

  6. Treatment and nursing care

    a. Emotional support

    b. Preoperative and postoperative care

    c. For patients receiving localized radioisotope therapy

      (1) Follow directions on precaution sheet accompanying therapy

      (2) Wear film badge when near patient

      (3) Limit time near patient, provide only essential care, for example

      (4) Limit time spent within 1 m (3 feet) of patient

      (5) Encourage patient to remain in own room

      (6) Watch for loosened or lost implants in bedding, clothing, bedpan, dressings, etc.; *do not pick it up*; call the radiology laboratory

      (7) Follow precautions when handling the following

        [a] Iodine—excreted in urine and sweat; present in blood and vomitus

        [b] Colloidal gold—present in wound seepage; excreted in urine

        [c] Phosphorus—excreted in urine and feces; present in vomitus

    d. Predischarge teaching regarding excercises, follow-up care

C. Cervix—Papanicolaou test (cytology test for cancer)

  1. Class I—normal

  2. Class II—atypical cells, nonmalignant; follow-up with repeat pap smears

  3. Class III—suspicious cells; cytology evaluated by biopsy, D & C

  4. Class IV—abnormal cells; suspicious of malignancy; cytology evaluated by biopsy, D & C

  5. Class V—malignant cells present

  6. Herpesvirus, type II—may be a major etiologic factor in cervical dysplasia, cancer (also may cause fetal death)

D. Uterus

  1. Conditions

    a. Benign fibroid tumors (myomata)—20% to 40% women, aged 25 to 40 years, causes menorrhagia, low back pain, urinary and bowel problems, and infertility or sterility

    b. Malignant tumors—women, aged 30 to 50 years; second highest cause of mortality; metrorrhagia; leukorrhea; surgery may be followed by radiation

    c. Endometrial carcinoma—not revealed by pap smear

  2. Treatment—hysterectomy

THE REPRODUCTIVE SYSTEM IN MEN

1. Anatomy and physiology

A. External genitalia

  1. Penis—organ of copulation and urination

    a. Shaft—body of penis

b. Glans—enlarged end of penis containing many sensitive nerve endings and a urethral meatus at the tip (usually) and covered by the prepuce or foreskin in the uncircumcized man

2. Scrotal sac—a double sac containing the testes and serving to maintain optimum temperature for spermatogenesis (for example, in cold weather, scrotum is drawn up closer to body)

3. Escutcheon—pubic hair

B. Internal organs
   1. Testes—two male gonads or testicles; almond-shaped structures normally situated in the scrotum; organ analogous to ovary
      a. Supplied by internal spermatic arteries
      b. Descend into scrotum during the seventh or eighth month of gestation via inguinal canal
      c. Leydig's or interstitial cells are stimulated by the pituitary interstitial stimulating hormone (ICH) to produce the male sex hormone, testosterone
      d. Sertoli's cells line the one to three-feet long seminiferous tubules where spermatids attach and develop into spermatozoa
      e. Epididymis—20 feet of coiled (convoluted) tubules, situated on top of each testis, that serve as storage place for sperm for the three weeks needed for sperm to mature and become capable of motility
   2. Canal system
      a. Seminiferous tubules—one to three feet long
      b. Epididymis—20 feet long
      c. Vas deferens—18 inches long and about the size of a strand of cooked spaghetti
         (1) Storage site for sperm
         (2) Avenue of sperm transport from epididymis to urethra (Note—vas passes from scrotum over pubic bone)
         (3) Vasectomy interrupts sperm transport
      d. Ejaculatory duct—formed where vas deferens and ducts from seminal vesicles join and enter urethra
      e. Urethra—common duct to transport urine or semen
   3. Accessory structures

      a. Seminal vesicles—two glands, situated just above prostate glands, that produce a thick milky nutrient fluid forming the major constituent of the ejaculate
      b. Prostate glands—two glands, *encircling* the urethra just below the bladder, that produce a clear, thin, and slightly alkaline fluid to maintain sperm motility by neutralizing the normal acidity of the urethra
      c. Bulbourethral or Cowper's glands—two pea-sized glands, located on either side of urethra below the prostate glands, that secrete a clear viscid (sticky) fluid into the urethra to facilitate passage of semen during ejaculation

C. Semen—carrier of spermatozoa and secretions from seminal vesicles, prostate, and Cowper's glands
   1. pH 7.35 to 7.50 (slightly alkaline)
   2. Amount per ejaculate—about 1 tsp or 3 to 4 ml
   3. Sperm count—averages 120 million/ml but may vary from 45 to 200 million/ml; infertility is probable with counts at or below 50 million/ml
   4. Sperm deposited close to the cervix may be found within the cervix 90 seconds after ejaculation
   5. Sperm may remain motile within female genital tract for two to three days but may not be capable of fertilization that long

D. Testicular functioning
   1. Puberty—occurs between the ages of 10 and 16; usually on the average of one year later than that in women
   2. Climacteric—cessation of reproductive (testicular) functioning accompanied by endocrine, somatic, and psychic changes; no specific age in men

2. Conditions affecting the reproductive tract in men

A. Venereal disease
   1. Syphilis—chanchre begins as a dull, red, hard, and insensitive papule on or near glans about three to four weeks after infection; treatment by penicillin or tetracycline
   2. Gonorrhea—causes urethritis, purulent discharge about four to ten days after infection; inflammation of meatus with burning on urination developing; treatment by penicillin or tetracycline

B. Prostate

1. Prostatitis—inflammation caused by bacteria, prostatic stones and urethral stenosis, alcohol, and irregular sexual activity
2. Benign hypertrophy—enlargement due to hyperplasia of normal glandular and muscular tissue (interferes with normal urination)
3. Malignant neoplasm—cancer of the prostate (incidence of this rather rare neoplasm may be increased in men whose mothers were treated with DES during that pregnancy

C. Scrotum
   1. Hydrocele—abnormal accumulation of fluid in scrotum following local trauma, infection (epididymitis or orchitis), tumor, or in conjunction with congestive heart failure or hepatic cirrhosis

D. Testes
   1. Tumor—usually malignant
   2. Epididymitis—inflammation due to infection (prostatic, urinary tract, or septicemia)
   3. Orchitis—inflammation of testes most often due to mumps; mumps orchitis may lead to sterility
   4. Cryptorchidism (cryptorchism)—undescended testes; if one or both testes remain in abdominal cavity, testosterone will be produced, but spermatogenesis will not occur; orchiopexy is best performed at 5 to 7 years of age
   5. Vasectomy—ligation-transection of a section of the vas usually done to sterilize the man
      a. Prevents the transport (but not the production) of sperm
      b. No physical effect on production of testosterone or sexual performance (potency, erection, and ejaculation); seminal fluid continues to be produced by the seminal vesicles and prostate glands; psychologic response may alter sexual performance, however
      c. Reversible in 20% to 40% of cases

E. Penis
   1. Glans—ulceration may be caused by cancer; syphilis; herpes virus, type II (genital); psoriasis; and others
   2. Cancer—rare, usually of prepuce or glans
   3. Balanitis—inflammation of glans penis
   4. Phimosis—constricted prepuce that cannot be retracted over glans; treated by circumcision
   5. Circumcision—excision of prepuce or foreskin

6. Paraphimosis—following retraction, prepuce cannot be brought forward over the glans again; this is a surgical emergency (circumcision) to prevent gangrene of glans

Infertility-sterility

Infertility, or the inability to conceive with unprotected intercourse of a year's duration, occurs in about 12% to 15% of couples. The emotional impact of infertility requires judicious and sensitive counseling and physical evaluation. A complete history and physical examination are necessary. Factors in women are responsible in 40% of cases; factors in men, 50%; couple factors, 10%; no medical factors identified, 5% to 10%

A. Factors in men
   1. A low sperm count (50 mil./cc, or less) is a primary factor in 20% of cases and a contributing factor in another 20%
   2. Occasionally, a man develops autoimmunity to his own sperm; the sperm is altered in such a way that fertilization is not possible (this may occur following vasectomy so that even with reanastamosis, the man may remain sterile)

B. Factors in women
   1. Irregular menstrual cycles or anovulatory cycles may be causative factors; usually during a hospitalization of one or two days, several endocrine tests may be done; one is a urine test for FSH, estrogen, and 17-ketosteroids
   2. Hysterosalpingography is done during the woman's follicular phase to evaluate the uterine cavity and tubal patency (often, this test alone clears any minor obstruction and pregnancy may be possible); tubal patency is assessed by transuterine insufflation with carbon dioxide gas (Rubin test)
   3. The Sims/Huhner test for motility of sperm in vaginal/cervical secretions is performed within 24 hours of intercourse; this postcoital test determines the receptivity of the cervical-vaginal mucus to the sperm
   4. Culdoscopy may reveal any structural anomalies present in the intra-abdominal cavity and reproductive organs
   5. Occasionally a female develops antisperm antibodies to her mate's sperm, thus altering their ability to fertilize

C. Couple factors
1. Immune reactions discussed previously
2. Hypothalamic factors of emotional origin
3. Factors implicated—age of man, age of woman, frequency of intercourse, and length of unprotected exposure
D. Counseling and treatments
1. Medical and surgical intervention for the physical problems
2. Timing of abstinence prior to intercourse

calculated to coincide with ovulation may help when the man has a low sperm count
3. Use of the condom and diaphragm until antibody levels drop (if they drop) may help in immune-based problems
4. Oral contraceptives taken over a period of time may help to regulate the woman's cycle so that conception may occur within a few months after the medication is discontinued
5. Each problem is individual

Questions   Maternity Nursing

Normal Pregnancy

1. Janet's last normal menstrual cycle started on April 20. She experienced some brown spotting on May 18. Her due date, or EDC, is
   1. January 27
   2. January 13
   3. February 25
   4. February 11
2. Janet is anxious to hear when a pregnancy test could be done. Counting from the last menstrual cycle, sufficient HCG is present in the urine to give a positive test by the end of the
   1. Fourth week
   2. Fifth week
   3. Sixth week
   4. Seventh week
3. In a 30-day cycle, ovulation probably occurred on which day of the menstrual period?
   1. Fifth or Sixth day
   2. Day 13 or 14
   3. Day 16 or 17
   4. Day 28 or 29
4. Which of the following is not a normal side-effect of oral contraceptives?
   1. Nausea and weight gain
   2. Chloasma
   3. Leg cramps and headaches
   4. Breast tenderness
5. During the first eight weeks of gestation, progesterone and estrogen are produced

principally by the
   1. Trophoblasts
   2. Placenta
   3. Anterior pituitary
   4. Corpus luteum
6. Inadequate nutrition during pregnancy may contribute to fetal-newborn problems such as
   1. Premature delivery and small-for-gestational-age infants
   2. Oversized fat babies with immature functional responses
   3. Hyperbilirubinemia
   4. Acrocyanosis
7. In addition to one liter of water, an adequate daily minimum intake for women who are within normal weight for age and height when they conceive includes the following (or the equivalents):
   A. 1500 ml milk (six cups)
   B. Two servings of meat and one of egg
   C. Vegetables—two green or yellow (one raw)
   D. Fruits—two fruits (one citrus)
   E. Breads—four slices, whole grain with butter and two servings of other (grits, macaroni, etc.)
   1. A, B, C, and E are correct
   2. C, D, and E are correct
   3. B, C, and D are correct
   4. All of these are correct
8. Ms. M tells you she cannot tolerate citrus fruits in any form. Which of the following foods

are rich in vitamin C (ascorbic acid) and can be taken to meet the daily requirement?
1. Broccoli, papaya, and cantaloupe
2. Dried beans (cooked) and peanut butter
3. Yellow cheeses, spinach, and prunes
4. Egg yolk, winter squash, and enriched bread

9. Ms. M should be advised that the following foods are rich in iron
1. Citrus fruits, sweet potatoes, and bananas
2. Dry beans (cooked), chicken, prunes, and broccoli
3. Enriched bread or cereal, cheddar cheese, and egg
4. Peanut butter, carrots, and cornmeal or corn oil

10. To relieve heartburn, a common discomfort during pregnancy, Ms. M may be advised to do all of the following *except*
1. Eat dry bread products before rising in the morning
2. Bend at the knees not at the waist when reaching down
3. Eat several smaller meals per day and avoid fatty or fried foods
4. Take antacid medication

Indicate for questions 11 to 13 those groupings of physical-emotional changes that are most characteristic of a particular trimester of pregnancy.

11. Umbilicus flush with skin; chloasma and secondary areola appear; external ballottement is felt; and iron therapy is started
1. First trimester
2. Second trimester
3. Third trimester

12. Weight gain about 1 lb per week; pelvic joints relax; varicosities increase; and woman is anxious to be done with pregnancy
1. First trimester
2. Second trimester
3. Third trimester

13. Test for HCG positive; lower uterine segment softens; urinary frequency common; and colostrum appears
1. First trimester
2. Second trimester
3. Third trimester

14. Anticipatory guidance during the prenatal period includes instructing the mother to recognize abnormal symptoms that require immediate notification of the physician; these include

1. Ptyalism, enlarged Montgomery follicles, and leukorrhea
2. Fatigue, nausea, and frequency
3. Ankle edema, enlarging varicies, and heartburn
4. Severe pain in abdomen, fluid discharge from vagina, and fingers swelling

15. Placental functions include all of the following, *except*
1. Secrete HCG, lactogen, estrogen, and progesterone
2. Act as the organ of respiration for the fetus
3. Screen out viruses, large bacteria, and toxins
4. Provide for the passage of nutrients to the fetus and for removal of fetal wastes

16. Antibodies produced by the mother are transmitted to the fetus because
1. Fetal and maternal blood mix in the intervillous spaces
2. Osmotic exchange occurs through capillaries between pooled maternal blood and fetal circulation
3. There is active secretion of the antibodies by the placenta
4. Antibodies cannot cross the placental barrier

In questions 17 to 20, indicate in which period you would expect to find the following groupings of characteristics of fetal-neonatal development.

17. Lanugo and vernix caseosa appear, quickening is first noted, FHR is first heard (with a stethoscope), and enamel and dentin are deposited
1. First trimester
2. Second trimester
3. Third trimester
4. In the postterm neonate

18. Fetus assumes a human appearance and is vulnerable to teratogenic effects, period of organogenesis, and placenta begins to secrete progesterone
1. First trimester
2. Second trimester
3. Third trimester
4. In the postterm neonate

19. Fingernails extend well beyond fingertips, skin is wrinkled and dry, eyes are wide open and appear alert, and vernix and lanugo are absent
1. First trimester
2. Second trimester

3. Third trimester
4. In the postterm neonate

20. Length 20 inches (50 cm), eyes are open, cry is good, testes are descended, lanugo is shed, and storage of fat and nutrients
    1. First trimester
    2. Second trimester
    3. Third trimester
    4. In the postterm neonate

21. All of the following may decrease a gravida's anxiety of labor and delivery, *except*
    1. An introduction to some breathing techniques to practice at home
    2. A tour of maternity unit and meeting the personnel
    3. Preparation for parenthood classes
    4. A description in detail of the events of labor and some common complications and how these are managed

22. Which of the following groups of findings are most indicative of a 20-week gestation?
    1. Lightening, FHR audible with Doptone, and height of fundus at one fingerbreadth below umbilicus
    2. Braxton Hicks contractions, ballottement, and height of fundus at umbilicus
    3. Quickening noted, FHR audible by fetoscope, and height of fundus at the umbilicus
    4. None of the above is correct

23. Douching during pregnancy
    1. Is unnecessary
    2. Should never be done, as it may induce abortion
    3. Becomes a necessity because of the copious vaginal secretions
    4. Depends on the woman's routine of personal hygiene

24. Gravidas should know that labor has progressed sufficiently to go to the hospital when
    1. Contractions are three to five minutes apart, lasting 50 seconds, and a malar flush appears
    2. Contractions are three to five minutes apart and low back pain and urinary frequency is experienced with contractions
    3. Contractions are regular, lasting 30 to 45 seconds or more, with some bloody show
    4. Contractions are two-to three minutes apart lasting 60 to 90 seconds

25. Which of the following symptoms should the gravida report to the physician immediately?

1. Edema of lower extremities, vulval varicies, and copious clear vaginal discharge
2. Heartburn, dyspnea, and anorexia
3. Leg cramps, back pain, and increased pigmentation over bridge of nose and cheeks and in vulval area
4. Headache, feeling of fullness in face and hands, and a few spots of brown discharge from vagina

26. The mechanism that initiates labor is unknown. Which one of the following is *not* a factor?
    1. Decrease in progesterone as placenta matures
    2. Maternal pituitary production of oxytocin and fetal hormonal production
    3. Reflex uterine response to overdistention
    4. Increasing fetal activity

27. During her last month of pregnancy, Ms. L tells you she is "sick and tired of this whole thing. I can hardly wait to get this out of me." The nurse's most appropriate response at this time would be
    1. Refer her to the psychiatric social worker since she should be experiencing a positive response to her infant now
    2. Tell her you know exactly how she feels and that you've been through it all yourself
    3. "Well, it sounds like you are ready for labor. Do you have any questions about your coming labor?"
    4. "Your pregnancy is getting a bit wearisome and the time is dragging?"

28. Ms. L tells you that she is planning to breast feed because "you don't have to take contraceptives until you wean the baby." The nurse's response should be
    1. Lactation does suppress ovulation so you are pretty safe
    2. You are safe just as long as you do not menstruate
    3. When a woman is breast feeding, she may not menstruate, although she may ovulate; it is best to use some type of birth control
    4. You will find that you won't be interested in resuming intercourse until you wean the baby

29. During her pregnancy, Mrs. L developed moniliasis. All of the following are true about moniliasis, *except*
    1. Caused by *Candida albicans*, a fungus
    2. Causes ophthalmia neonatorum in the newborn

3. Treated by drugs such as nystatin (Mycostatin) and gentian violet
4. Most prevalent in women who are taking oral contraceptives or who are diabetic

30. When assessing the frequency, duration, and intensity of contractions, the nurse
    1. Spreads the fingers of one hand lightly over the fundus
    2. Moves the fingers of one hand over the uterus, pressing into the muscle
    3. Holds her hand (fingers and palm) over the area just below the umbilicus
    4. Indents the uterus in several places during and between contractions to check for uniform uterine response

31. Vaginal examinations during labor are done to ascertain all of the following, *except*
    1. Station
    2. Dilatation and effacement
    3. Beginning separation of low-lying placenta
    4. Presenting part and fetal position

32. Mr. S is staying with his wife throughout labor. As Mrs. S progresses in labor, she becomes increasingly irritable with her husband, complaining of back pain and fatigue. The nurse appropriately responds by
    1. Having Mrs. S. turn on her side and giving her a back rub
    2. Asking Mrs. S. if she would like the doctor to give her something for the discomfort
    3. Reassuring Mr. S. that irritability is normal now and teaching him to apply pressure to her low back
    4. Encouraging Mrs. S. to try and get some rest and asking Mr. S. if he would like to take a break for some coffee

33. When the physician checks Mrs. S, she reports that the cervix is dilated to 7 cm. To provide pain relief, the physician gives Mrs. S an epidural block. Which nursing action is vitally important during regional anesthesia?
    1. Monitoring blood pressure for possible hypertension
    2. Giving oxytocin to counteract the effect of the epidural (or caudal) in slowing contractions
    3. Having the gravida lie flat in bed to avoid postanesthesia headache
    4. Monitoring blood pressure for possible hypotension

34. Mrs. M is unmedicated. As she approaches the second stage of labor, her expected behavior may include all of the following, *except*
    1. Becoming more talkative and alert
    2. Shaking legs, nausea, and vomiting
    3. Amnesia between contractions
    4. Increase in bloody show and urge to push

35. During the process of labor, the uterine muscle
    1. Undergoes no change in thickness or size
    2. Becomes longer and thinner in both the upper and lower segments
    3. Thins in the lower uterine segment but remains the same in the upper
    4. Thins in the lower uterine segment and becomes shorter and thicker in the upper

36. On vaginal examination, the fetus is found to be LOA. This means that
    A. A bony prominence can be felt in the left front abdomen just above the symphysis
    B. After the birth of the head, the infant will restitute and face the mother's right thigh
    C. The fetus is breech
    D. A hard, round, movable prominence is felt in the fundal area
    E. The infant may have to be turned with forceps, since it is posterior
    F. The posterior fontanel can be palpated vaginally
    G. Labor will probably be prolonged
    1. A, C, F, and G are correct
    2. B and E are correct
    3. C, D, and G are correct
    4. A, B, and F are correct

The first stage of labor is divided into three phases. Identify the phase described in questions 37, 38, and 39.

37. In this phase, the mother becomes more introspective and irritable; she feels she cannot make it; and increased perspiration is noted on her upper lip and between her breasts
    1. Latent phase
    2. Active phase
    3. Phase of transition
    4. Pushing phase

38. In this phase, the mother is apt to be excited, euphoric, and eager to learn; she likes to walk around
    1. Latent phase
    2. Active phase
    3. Phase of transition
    4. Pushing phase

39. In this phase, the mother becomes increasingly more serious; a malar flush is noted; and she has a tendency to hyperventilate
    1. Latent phase
    2. Active phase
    3. Phase of transition
    4. Pushing phase

40. When the midwife finally says that she can push, Mrs. T feels tremendous relief. Her husband assists her in delivery by supporting her shoulders while she pushes the baby out. When the baby is delivered, the midwife announces that the baby is a boy. Mrs. T asks if he is OK and does he have all his fingers and toes? The nurse would reply most appropriately
    1. "Yes, he looks just fine. I can see that from here."
    2. "Yes, he looks fine. As soon as the cord is cut, you can see for yourself."
    3. "Yes, he looks fine. You can rest assured that the pediatrician will check him over thoroughly."
    4. "Yes, he is fine. There is nothing for you to worry about."

41. During oxytocin induction, discontinue the infusion containing the drug if you observe
    1. Increased amount of bloody show from the vagina
    2. Increased pain over sacral area
    3. Increased fetal heart rate above 145 between contractions
    4. Decrease in fetal heart rate below 100 with contractions

42. All of the following are thought to assist in initiating respirations in the neonate at the moment of birth, *except*
    1. An increase in oxygen and a decrease in carbon dioxide
    2. A drop in oxygen and an increase in carbon dioxide
    3. The change in skin temperature and tactile stimulation to the body
    4. Change from weightlessness to gravity environment

43. After the physician cuts the cord and before the infant is given to the mother to hold, the nurse does all of the following. Rank the actions in order of priority.
    A. Confirm identification of infant and apply bracelets to mother and infant
    B. Examine the infant for any observable abnormalities
    C. Dry the infant in prewarmed blankets and place in warm environment
    D. Instill silver nitrate drops in each eye
    1. A, B, D, then D
    2. D, B, A, then C
    3. C, B, D, then A
    4. B, D, C, then A

44. All of the following factors contribute to rapid heat loss in the normal newborn immediately after birth, *except*
    1. Large body surface compared to body weight
    2. Room temperature of 72° F
    3. Neonate's inability to shiver
    4. Wrapping and placing neonate on mother's abdomen

45. All of the following are normal characteristics of the newborn, *except*
    1. The circumference of the newborn's chest is normally equal to or slightly less than that of the head
    2. Abdomen is dome shaped
    3. The newborn's hemoglobin and hematocrit are equal to or less than that of an adult
    4. Irregular patterns of respiratory activity including occasional short periods of apnea

46. Following a precipitous delivery, the neonate appeared in good condition. The physician's orders: "Observe for subdural hematoma." You would be on the alert for all of the following, *except*
    1. Telangiectases and subconjuctival hemorrhage
    2. Separation of cranial sutures
    3. Repeated vomiting
    4. Bulging fontanel

47. Ms. K is concerned that her 2-day-old infant was losing too much weight. She tells you her baby weighed 7 lb at birth and now weighs only 6 lb 8 oz. What is the maximum number of ounces you could expect this baby to lose and still be within normal limits?
    1. 6 oz
    2. 8 oz
    3. 11 oz
    4. 16 oz

48. The first feeding for a formula-fed baby usually is sterile water rather than glucose water or formula. This is done because
    1. If aspiration occurs, it causes less harm
    2. It is less irritating to the gastric mucosa

3. It is assimilated more easily

4. It stimulates gastric secretions and initiates peristalsis

49. The Moro reflex is a reflex response to all of the following, *except*
    1. Sudden or loud noises
    2. The sensation of falling
    3. A jolt to the crib
    4. Hypoglycemia and hypocalcemia

50. Physiologic jaundice in the newborn is consequent to
    1. Liver immaturity and fetal polycythemia
    2. Oliguria and kidney immaturity
    3. Infection
    4. Dehydration

51. Observations during the "fourth" stage of labor (first hour postpartum) include all of the following, *except*
    1. Checking every 30 minutes
    2. Assessing the condition and height of fundus
    3. Assessing for bladder distention
    4. Observation of the episiotomy, the perineal pad, and the linens under the buttocks

52. During the first postpartum day or two, the new mother may be expected to display which of the following behaviors
    1. Talkativeness, dependency, and passivity
    2. Autonomy and independency; interest in learning to bathe the baby
    3. Interest in her own body functions
    4. 1 and 3 are correct

53. Mrs. P. has been looking at her 2-day-old infant; she has a frown on her face. She turns to you and asks if her baby's looks and actions are normal. You know that the following are normal variations of the newborn
    A. Enlarged breasts
    B. A spot of pink drainage from her baby's vagina
    C. The dark line between the baby's umbilicus and symphysis
    D. The little white dots covering the nose
    E. The dark spotting over her lower back and sacrum
    1. All of these are correct
    2. All but B are correct
    3. A, C, and D are correct
    4. C, D, and E are correct

54. Phyllis calls you over to ask you about the "lump" on the side of her baby's head. You note that the tense lump does not cross suture lines. You know that this is caused by
    1. Bleeding between the periosteum and the parietal bone from pressure against the bony pelvis during delivery
    2. Edema of the scalp from pressure of the vertex against the cervix during dilatation
    3. Intracranial hemorrhage from either the pressure against the bony pelvis or the obstetric forceps
    4. A hemangioma

55. "Afterpains" can be very disturbing, especially in the multipara who is also breast-feeding. Which of the following would you do *first*?
    1. Give her a pain medication as per order
    2. Have her lie on her abdomen with a rolled towel at the level of the fundus
    3. Ask her to walk around for a while
    4. Ask her to empty her bladder

56. For the mother who is breastfeeding, good nipple care includes
    1. Washing nipples and breasts every day with soap and water
    2. Keeping nipples clean with warm water and dry
    3. Applying a diluted alcohol solution on them after each feeding to toughen the nipples
    4. Covering the nipples with a plastic-lined shield to protect clothing

57. During her hospital stay, Mrs. C asks you what she should expect as far as physiologic changes now. She wonders if she is all right. Normal changes that occur during the first three to four postpartum days include all of the following, *except*
    1. Headaches and muscular pains in legs, until hormone and metabolic reversals are accomplished
    2. Diaphoresis and diuresis
    3. Strong uterine contractions
    4. Pulse between 50 and 70/minute

58. Jane wishes to breast feed. On the third day there is no indication that her milk is coming in. The physician's orders are
    1. Testosterone enanthate and estradiol valerate injection (Deladumone OB)
    2. Methylergonovine (Methergine) tartrate or ergonovine (Ergotrate) maleate
    3. Stilbestrol
    4. Oxytocin (Syntocinon, Pitocin)

59. Mrs. Q delivered in the car on the way to the hospital. In the emergency room, the physician examined the mother while the nurse

1. Gently tugged on the cord and massaged the uterus to see if the placenta could be delivered now
2. Clamped and cut the cord with sterile scissors
3. Noted and recorded the Apgar score
4. Cleared the mucus from the neonate's mouth and nose

60. Jennie tells you that she is breast-feeding her son because she can't stand the thought of her newborn having to get vaccinations. You respond
    1. "That's great. Vaccinations are not necessary when you're breast-feeding."
    2. "Oh, you still need to have him vaccinated against DPT, measles, and polio before he is 6 months old."
    3. "You can only protect him against those diseases that you have had yourself."
    4. "The most protection comes from the colostrum right after birth, and you didn't start feeding him until the second day."

61. The infant mortality rate is
    1. The number of deaths during the first four weeks per 1000 live births
    2. The number of deaths before 1 year of age per 1000 live births
    3. Lowest in the United States and Canada
    4. Both 1 and 3 are correct

62. Perinatal mortality is
    1. The number of maternal and fetal-newborn deaths within four weeks after term.
    2. Deaths between 28 weeks gestation (1000 gm or more) and four weeks of age
    3. The number of stillborns between 28 weeks gestation (1000 gm or more) and 40 weeks
    4. The number of deaths occurring in the first four weeks of life per 1000 live births

63. Birthrate refers to the number of births per
    1. 1000 population
    2. 1000 women aged 14 to 44
    3. 100,000 population
    4. 1000 women and men aged 14 to 44

Complications of Childbearing and the High-Risk Neonate

64. Ms. J is an unwed pregnant 14-year-old who is giving her baby up for adoption. Nurses and social workers can help her best if they
    1. Provide a safe environment to facilitate ventilation of her feelings but do not give answers or direction so that she makes her own decisions
    2. Help her understand the existing situation, place it in perspective in terms of her life goals, and begin to plan for the future
    3. Assure her that her decision to place the baby up for adoption is the best suited for her needs
    4. Help her see ways of not making the same mistake again so that she can grow in self-esteem and self-respect

65. Adoption agencies such as the Children's Home Society and Family Service Association carefully screen prospective adoptive parents by evaluating
    1. Ages of spouses, and duration of marriage, and financial stability
    2. Physical and mental health of spouses and motivation underlying desire to adopt
    3. Other children, if any, in the home
    4. All of these are correct

66. Medical and nursing management of moderate to severe hyperemesis gravidarum consists of all of the following, *except*
    1. NPO for 24 hours and parenteral therapy with B complex and C vitamins added
    2. Restriction of visitors, including family
    3. Immediate therapeutic abortion
    4. Observation for jaundice, delirium, and tachycardia

67. Hydatidiform mole may be diagnosed by all of the following clinical features, except
    1. Preeclampsia
    2. Continuous or intermittent brownish discharge, starting about the end of the first trimester
    3. Uterus excessively large for gestational age and high serum levels of HCG
    4. Tenderness and rigidity of abdomen and uterus

68. Mrs. T missed two menstrual periods. One day she experienced a sharp, stabbing pain in her lower abdomen. Entering the emergency room, she began spotting and became dizzy and pale. These clinical manifestations are most probably indicative of
    1. Incompetent cervix
    2. Placenta previa
    3. Abruptio placentae
    4. Ectopic pregnancy

69. The gravida carrying twins must be carefully observed for which of the following frequently associated conditions?

1. Hyperemesis gravidarum
2. Premature labor and/or preeclampsia
3. Dystocia and/or postpartum hemorrhage
4. All of these are correct

70. Identical twins differ from fraternal twins in that
    A. Advanced maternal age is an accepted predisposing factor
    B. They result from the union of one egg and one sperm
    C. They frequently are of the same sex
    D. Each can readily accept tissue transplants one from the other
    E. Each shares the same chromosomes with the other
    1. All of these are correct
    2. All but A are correct
    3. A and D are correct
    4. B, D, and E are correct

71. Abnormal symptoms that require immediate notification of the physician include
    1. Ptyalism, enlarged Montgomery follicles, and leukorrhea
    2. Fatigue, nausea, and frequency
    3. Ankle edema, enlarging varicies, and heartburn
    4. Severe pain in abdomen, fluid discharge from vagina, and fingers swelling

72. A gravida is admitted to the maternity unit directly from the clinic with a blood pressure of 146/98. Without waiting for a physician's order, the nurse would do all of the following, except
    1. Evaluate amount and distribution of edema, if present
    2. Place her on bed rest in a room with three new postpartum patients so that they could call the nurse for her if needed
    3. Take her weight on admission and daily thereafter
    4. Test her urine for protein; start an I & O sheet

73. The hospitalized gravida being treated for severe toxemia is closely observed for which of the following?
    A. Urinary output, reflex response, and respiratory rate
    B. Severe frontal headache and/or epigastric pain
    C. Tone of uterus and sensitivity of abdomen and uterus to touch
    D. Fetal heart tones

    E. Signs and symptoms of labor
    1. All of these are correct
    2. All but C are correct
    3. A, B, and C are correct
    4. B, D, and E are correct

74. The nurse should be alert to possible sequelae of abruptio placentae, which include all of the following, *except*
    1. Fetal hyperactivity or fetal demise
    2. Hypertension
    3. Oliguria and afibrinogenemia
    4. Amniotic fluid embolism

75. Postpartum nursing care of a woman who had preeclampsia is influenced by the following knowledge
    1. This mother may convulse any time during the first 48 hours after delivery, even if she did not convulse before
    2. Once the baby is delivered, the nurse can be assured of an immediate cure of the preeclampsia
    3. The woman should be advised that she will undoubtedly be left with chronic renal damage
    4. The woman should be advised regarding contraceptives since a subsequent pregnancy is hazardous

76. Gravida-nurse-physician relationship is especially important when the gravida is diabetic because her motivation and cooperation in the following is essential
    A. Early identification and treatment of infection
    B. Conversion to use of regular insulin
    C. Coomb's tests every month in the laboratory
    D. Frequent urine tests daily in the home
    E. Restriction of daily activity or exercise
    1. A, B, and D are correct
    2. B, C, and E are correct
    3. All of these are correct
    4. *Only* B and D are correct

77. Obstetrical complications encountered more frequently among diabetic gravida include all of the following, *except*
    1. Spontaneous abortion
    2. Preeclampsia
    3. Dystocia
    4. Erythroblastosis fetalis

78. The diabetic gravida may be hospitalized during pregnancy for all of the following, *except*
    1. Regulation of insulin dosage

2. Determination of placental functioning
3. Control of morning sickness
4. Amniocentesis to determine if fetus carries gene for diabetes

79. Congestive heart failure in the gravida with rheumatic valvular damage may be precipitated by all of the following, *except*
   1. Insufficient physical exercise
   2. Loss of a loved one
   3. Urinary tract infection
   4. Eating peanut butter, canned meats and vegetables, and cheeses

80. A gravida with cardiac failure is admitted to your unit with symptoms of dyspnea following ordinary physical activity, moist cough, and a rapid pulse. "Complete bed rest" for her, consists of all of the following, *except*
   1. Assisting her with grooming and changing
   2. Preparing her food on her tray and feeding her
   3. Bathroom privileges
   4. Assisting her with position changes in bed

81. Nursing care of a gravida with class I cardiac involvement during labor and delivery would include
   A. Helping her maintain a sitting position
   B. Monitoring her pulse more frequently than other vital signs
   C. Providing good oral hygiene since she is NPO
   D. Preparing her for regional anesthesia (epidural or caudal)
   E. After complete dilatation, coaching her to bear down only once per contraction
   1. A and E are correct
   2. B, C, and D are correct
   3. All but E are correct
   4. All of these are correct

82. The early postpartum period for the new mother with cardiac involvement is a critical one. All of the following are essential components of her care, *except*
   1. Administer fluids (oral or parenteral) slowly for first day or two
   2. Force fluids so her water metabolism returns to normal more quickly
   3. Minimize blood loss
   4. Stay with her and monitor vital signs and condition continuously through the first hour postpartum

83. The nurse scans the prenatal record to identify factors that may adversely affect the newborn's immediate adaptation to extrauterine life. Some of these are *factors affecting the vascular supply to the placenta.* Examples include
   1. Syphilis
   2. Hypertension
   3. Anemia
   4. 2 and 3 are correct

84. Which of the following events would alert the nurse to the possibility of postpartum hemmorrhage?
   1. Labor of nine hours, baby weighing 6 lb 10 oz, no anesthesia, and primipara
   2. Second baby, weighing 7 lb 2 oz, and paracervical block with local anesthesia for episiotomy repair
   3. Labor prolonged in latent phase and nitrous oxide for delivery of an 8-lb girl, first baby
   4. Labor of two hours, fourth pregnancy, twins weighing 4 lb 8 oz and 5 lb, and spinal anesthesia

85. If there is a possibility that Mrs. T has retained some placental fragments, which of the following drugs *would not* be given?
   1. Testosterone enanthate and estradiol valerate injection (Deladumone OB)
   2. Methylergonovine (Methergine) or tartrate ergonovine (Ergotrate) maleate
   3. Stilbestrol
   4. Oxytocin (Syntocinon, Pitocin)

86. If the expectant mother's membranes rupture more than 24 hours prior to delivery, the neonate's immediate adaptation may be adversely influenced by the possibility of
   1. Amnionitis
   2. A "dry" birth
   3. Hypofibrinogenemia
   4. Couvelaire uterus

87. In addition to FHR, the nurse is constantly alert to two other signs of fetal distress
   1. Crowning and increased fetal activity
   2. Crowning and secondary uterine inertia
   3. Increased fetal activity and meconium-stained amniotic fluid
   4. Secondary uterine inertia and meconium-stained amniotic fluid

88. Which of the following factors contribute to fetal anoxia?
   1. Contractions of the uterine muscle
   2. Maternal supine position
   3. High or low blood pressure of the mother
   4. All of these contribute

89. In the presence of fetal hypoxia, the amniotic fluid appears
    - A. Opaque with white flecks, if hypoxia is recent
    - B. Opaque with white flecks and some streaks of pink, if hypoxia is more than 36 hours past
    - C. Greenish-black if hypoxia is recent
    - D. Yellowish if hypoxia is more than 36 hours past
    1. A and B are correct
    2. C and D are correct
    3. Only C is correct
    4. None of these are correct

90. Should fetal distress be noted, often the nurse can relieve the distress by taking appropriate actions. These actions include all of the following, *except*
    1. Turn gravida from back to side-lying position
    2. Turn gravida from side to back-lying position
    3. Administer oxygen
    4. Stop oxytocin induction, if in progress, and increase rate of intravenous fluid (without oxytocin) if running (or start an IV)

91. Yellowish vernix on a newborn may indicate
    1. Rh or ABO incompatibility or maternal ingestion of sulfisoxazole (Gantrisin)
    2. A gonorrheal infection
    3. Passage of meconium in utero
    4. 1 and 3 are correct

92. What is the Apgar score of an infant who at one minute after birth has the following characteristics?
    Heart rate over 100
    Respiratory effort—slow and irregular
    Muscle tone—flaccid
    Response to slap on soles of feet—weak cry
    Color—body, pink and extremities, blue
    1. 5
    2. 6
    3. 7
    4. 8

93. Asphyxia neonatorum is a condition that exists when the infant, following birth, gives no indication of breathing within
    1. 30 to 60 seconds
    2. 60 to 90 seconds
    3. Two minutes
    4. Five minutes

94. Hyaline membrane disease or respiratory distress syndrome is most likely to occur in the
    1. Infant 38 weeks gestation and over and who weighs under 2500 gm (5 lb 8 oz)
    2. Infant 38 weeks gestation and over and who weighs over 2500 gm
    3. Infant 37 weeks gestation and under and who weighs under 1500 gm (3 lb 5 oz)
    4. Infant 44 weeks of gestation or more and who weighs 2500 gm

95. The nurse knows the infant has respiratory distress when the infant exhibits all of the following, *except*
    1. Respiratory rate over 60 per minute
    2. Much activity of the intercostal muscles
    3. Expiratory grunting
    4. Absence of flaring of nasal alae

96. An infant begins to show signs of respiratory distress. The nursing actions listed below are all appropriate responses in this situation. Which answer best ranks the nursing actions in priority of care?
    - A. Notify the physician
    - B. Give oxygen if cyanosis occurs
    - C. Record—time, symptoms, degree of symptoms, and whether oxygen relieved symptoms
    - D. Apply electrodes from apnea monitor
    - E. Maintain an open airway
    1. B, A, E, C, and then D
    2. A, E, B, C, and then D
    3. D, B, E, A, and then C
    4. E, B, A, D, and then C

97. Signs and symptoms of RDS include all of the following, *except*
    1. Abdominal or see-saw respirations
    2. Acrocyanosis in room air
    3. Flaring of the nares
    4. Expiratory grunt

98. Prolonged and deep suctioning of the throat with a catheter
    1. Is necessary when the infant has aspirated meconium and amniotic fluid
    2. Can cause pulse irregularities and laryngospasm
    3. Minimizes the development of the respiratory distress syndrome
    4. Is done prior to each feeding of an infant with severe respiratory distress

99. Accurate monitoring of the neonate's temperature in an incubator involves all of the following, *except*

1. Checking and recording the temperature of the infant and incubator frequently
2. Placing incubator away from air-conditioning vents
3. Touching the infant's body and extremities to check for coolness
4. Positioning a gooseneck lamp directly over incubator for better visualization of distress indicative of hypothermia or hyperthermia

100. All of the following may be early signs of kernicterus, *except*
    1. A depressed or absent Moro reflex
    2. Passage of yellowish brown stool
    3. Weak or whiny, high-pitched cry
    4. Refusal or regurgitation of feedings

101. The purposes of an exchange transfusion for Rh incompatibility include
    A. Combat anemia
    B. Remove and dilute maternal antibodies
    C. Increase infant's supply of iron for producing more red blood cells
    D. Decrease serum bilirubin levels
    E. Inactivate the maternal antibodies
    1. All of these are correct
    2. All but B are correct
    3. A, C, and E are correct
    4. A, B, and D are correct

102. RhoGAM is given to mothers who
    A. Are Rh-negative
    B. Are Rh-positive
    C. Have just given birth to an Rh-negative baby
    D. Have just given birth to an Rh-positive baby
    E. Have no titer
    F. Have some titer
    1. A, C, and F are correct
    2. A, D, and E are correct
    3. B, D, and E are correct
    4. B, C, and F are correct

103. Phenylketonuria
    A. Is inherited as a recessive trait
    B. Is a congenital defect
    C. Is due to a viral disease of the mother during the first trimester
    D. Necessitates the infant drink Lofenalac
    E. Necessitates infant feedings with breast milk
    F. Necessitates infant feedings with non-allergenic formulas
    1. A and D are correct
    2. B and E are correct

3. C and F are correct
4. B, C, and F are correct

104. When caring for a premature infant, which of the following precautions should be taken to guard against retrolental fibroplasia?
    A. Maintain the oxygen content in the incubator at less than 40%
    B. When the infant is under the fluorescent light, the eyes should be kept well covered
    C. Maintain at least 50% humidity in the incubator, especially when the infant is receiving oxygen
    D. Regulate the amount of ambient oxygen on the basis of arterial blood levels of oxygen
    E. Order daily serum bilirubin levels; levels above 10 mg/100 ml blood predispose to this disorder
    1. All of these are correct
    2. Only D is correct
    3. B, D, and E are correct
    4. A, C, and E are correct

105. Katey gave birth to a little girl with a cleft lip and palate last night. This morning she tells you that she doesn't want to see her physician. She just knows that the antihistamine she took for her allergy three months ago was wrong. The most appropriate response by the nurse would be
    1. "This kind of problem is very easily repaired. Just wait until you see her after surgery!"
    2. "The antihistamines you took had nothing to do with this. Drugs during the last trimester don't affect babies like this."
    3. "The baby is really quite cute otherwise, and it would be wise to get used to feeding the baby now, while you are still in the hospital with someone to help you."
    4. "It must be very difficult for you to have a baby like this."

106. Baby Kelly is with his mother who is a diabetic. He appeared pink, alert, and his temperature was stable when he left the nursery 15 minutes before. His mother calls you over and brings your attention to his legs. You observe spontaneous jerky movements. Your *first* response is to
    1. Tell his mother this is a normal variation of the newborn
    2. Tell her to feed him his glucose water now

3. Take him back to the nursery to do a Dextrostix
4. Take him back to the nursery and observe him for other behaviors and neurologic symptoms

107. The absence of one umbilical artery is of concern because it is frequently associated with
1. Respiratory distress syndrome
2. Renal agenesis
3. Patent ductus arteriosus
4. Premature ossification of cranial bones

108. Syphilis in the newborn is recognized by all of the following characteristics, *except*
1. Conjunctival hemorrhages and/or telangiectases over the bridge of the nose and at the nape of the neck
2. Superficial ulcerations or cracks surrounding the anus and/or mouth
3. Snuffles
4. A skin rash of rose spots and plantar and palmar lesions or blebs

The Reproductive System in Women and Men

109. Maternal vaginal infection that may cause thrush in the newborn is
1. Leukorrhea
2. Gonorrhea
3. Moniliasis
4. *Trichomonas vaginalis*

110. Cytology report on a Papanicolaou smear reveals cell dysplasia, class III. Your anticipatory guidance includes
1. Preparation of patient for biopsy and D & C
2. Preparation of patient for cold knife conization of cervix
3. Scheduling patient for a repeat pap smear
4. No further diagnostic tests or treatment are needed since the cells are normal

111. In performing nursing care for a patient with a cobalt implant in the cervical canal, the nurse does all of the following, *except*
1. Wears an X-ray film badge
2. Maximizes the time spent with the patient, since she is in isolation and suffers from lack of social stimulation
3. Limits the time spent within 1 m (3 feet) of patient
4. Checks linen, clothes, and bathroom floor for any pencil-shaped object

112. Functions of the seminal vesicles include all of the following, *except*
1. Produce prostaglandin
2. Store sperm until mature and capable of motility
3. Add fluid to semen
4. Add nutrients and favorable pH to semen

113. All of the following statements about vasectomy are true, *except*
1. A small segment of each vas deferens is ligated and excised
2. Testosterone production ceases
3. Sexual potency is maintained
4. Ejaculation and volume of seminal fluid production are unaffected

114. The male climacteric occurs
1. At no specified age
2. Between the ages of 10 and 16
3. Between 55 and 65 years of age
4. In conjunction with benign hypertrophy of the prostate

115. Which reproductive structure in man is analogous to the fallopian tube
1. Vas deferens
2. Epididymis
3. Seminal vesicle
4. Seminiferous tubules

116. Conditions that may lead to infertility or sterility include all of the following, *except*
1. Endometriosis
2. Pelvic inflammatory disease
3. Phimosis
4. Mumps orchitis

117. Diagnostic tests for infertility-sterility include all of the following, *except*
1. Immune reactions
2. Sims/Huhner
3. Rubin test
4. Bioassay for HCG

118. A complete history is taken to identify possible factors implicated in infertility. These factors include all of the following, *except*
1. A menstrual cycle varying from 26 to 28 days
2. Ages of each of the couple
3. Length of unprotected exposure to conception
4. Frequency and pattern of intercourse during the month

119. A complete assessment for suspected sterility includes all of the following, *except*
1. Testicular biopsy
2. Cervical smear for cytology

3. Genetic evaluation
4. Cervical smear for antisperm antibodies
120. All of the following are useful in treating infertility, *except*
    1. Record of basal body temperature (BBT) over a period of several months

2. Use of condom and diaphragm until cervical mucosal antibody titer drops
3. Use of an oral contraceptive over a period of time
4. Engaging in intercourse every day and twice per day at the time of ovulation

Answers / Rationale Maternity Nursing

1. (1) Nägele's rule—count back three months and add seven days. Spotting during the time of the first missed period is not uncommon.
2. (2) HCG can be detected 20 days after fertilization (fifth week of cycle). Test results are more accurate after the sixth week, however.
3. (3) Ovulation occurs most regularly 14 days *prior* to the first day of the next menstrual flow.
4. (3) Headache and leg cramps are possible serious complications that need medical attention.
5. (4) Some spontaneous abortions occur at this time (8 to 12 weeks), when hormonal production by corpus luteum decreases, and this function should be taken up by the developing placenta.
6. (1) Inadequate nutrition depletes maternal stores and subjects her to toxemia and infection and is responsible for a higher incidence of congenital disorders or anomalies.
7. (3) 500 to 1000 ml of milk is adequate. More may interfere with absorption of iron and may cause leg cramps from calcium-phosphorus imbalance. Four to five servings from bread group are adequate.
8. (1) Vitamin C is found in many foods. When working with people of different cultures, evaluate the nutrient content, storage, and preparation of the preferred foods.
9. (2) Many obstetricians think it is best to build up a woman's iron stores prior to and right after pregnancy. There is concern for possible fetotoxicity of any drug ingested by the pregnant woman.
10. (1) Treatment for "morning sickness."
11. (2) The maternal-fetal-placental unit is placing a heavy demand on iron reserves. The National Research Council recommends supplementation.
12. (3) Fetus is gaining weight rapidly while the maternal system is preparing for physical and emo-

tional separation from the fetus.
13. (1) Presumptive and probable signs and symptoms of pregnancy.
14. (4) Anticipatory guidance may relieve anxiety that normal changes may cause.
15. (3) Inhibits passage of large molecules only; viruses and many toxins cross the placenta.
16. (2) The other three statements are false.
17. (2) Data are helpful in anticipatory guidance regarding nutrition and estimating the age of an abortus.
18. (1) It is significant to know that during the period of organogenesis (cell differentiation) fetal malformations may be caused by teratogens (drugs, diseases, and X-ray).
19. (4) Mortality rate is four times that of term infants. Wide-eyed appearance is a consequence of long-term hypoxia.
20. (3) Data are helpful in assessing the gestational age of the neonate. The term infant is generally the least likely to be at risk.
21. (4) Overloading—may seed fears parent(s) may not have thought of before.
22. (3) The three signs and symptoms are used to check the anticipated EDC (and the approximate gestational age of the fetus).
23. (1) Injudicious douching may alter the normal vaginal environment. It does nothing to prevent the copious secretions.
24. (3) These instructions vary with the gravida— distance from the hospital, mode of transportation, previous labor history, and others may modify the individual's directions.
25. (4) No. 1 through 3 are discomforts of pregnancy.
26. (4) It is interesting to note that there is a high

level of prostaglandin in the laboring gravida's circulation. Prostaglandin increases uterine irritability and contractibility.

27. (4) The gravida needs support for feelings and needs to know that this reaction is natural and understandable.

28. (3) The bottle-feeding mother's ovulation and menstrual cycle has been noted to occur as early as 36 days; for the breast-feeding mother, 39 days. In both cases, ovulation usually does not occur until later, however.

29. (2) The disease and the drugs used in treating it are not harmful to the developing fetus. The fetus may pick up the organism during the birth process, however (thrush).

30. (1) Excessive manipulation of the uterus can cause uterine dysfunction.

31. (3) Vaginal (or rectal) examinations should never be done if there is even the slightest indication of a possible placenta previa, since the exam may result in massive hemorrhage.

32. (3) This usually helps to assuage the mate's feelings of guilt, impotence, and helplessness and fosters couple mutuality.

33. (4) Hypotension is a frequent side effect. Maternal hypotension causes fetal bradycardia and hypoxia.

34. (1) More indicative of early first stage.

35. (4) This process is necessary to expel the fetus from the uterus and to propel it through the birth canal.

36. (4) D is suggestive of a breech presentation. The fetus is in the most common position for delivery with the vertex presenting, the head well flexed, and the fetal nape pivoting under the symphysis.

37. (3) Gravida needs constant supportive care as she approaches 10 cm, or complete dilatation.

38. (1) Nursing care at this time may include anticipatory guidance, teaching and having her (them) practice breathing techniques, and providing diversionary activities.

39. (2) Gravida is about 5 cm. These behaviors are not noted in those gravida who have received regional anesthesia.

40. (2) The mother must see her infant herself for reassurance and for beginning the process of bonding or attachment.

41. (4) No. 2 is most probably due to persistent posterior position; No. 3, FHR acceleration is not clinically significant (in current level of knowledge). Also, stop oxytocin drip if contractions last two minutes or longer, or if physician leaves the unit.

42. (1) Anoxia seems to be the most powerful stimulant to initiate respiration if not too prolonged.

43. (3) Heat loss must be minimized. Any anomalies should be identified for early treatment.

44. (4) It has been found that the temperature of the wrapped (normal, full-term) infant in his mother's arms does not differ significantly from the infant in a warmed incubator.

45. (3) These values are very high at birth. The excess red blood cells (needed for the relative hypoxic intrauterine environment) are hemolyzed soon after birth, resulting in "physiologic" jaundice by about the third day.

46. (1) Normal variations of the neonate.

47. (3) Term infants may loose 5% to 10% of body weight. Arithemetic: 7×16 oz $= 112$ oz and 10% of 112 oz $= 11.2$ oz.

48. (1) If aspirated, sterile plain water is less irritating to the respiratory tract.

49. (4) The "startle" reflex is one criterion to assess intactness of the neuromuscular system, below the level of the brain stem.

50. (1) The other choices may cause jaundice, but these are not *physiologic*. If serum bilirubin level is greater than 12 mg% , kernicterus may result even if the process was initially physiologic.

51. (1) She should be checked every 15 minutes since the tendency to hemorrhage is greatest during the first hour following delivery.

52. (4) This mother is in the "taking-in" phase. She is interested in being cared for; needs food, fluids, rest, and praise for a job well done; and needs someone with whom to discuss her delivery experience.

53. (1) The mother needs reassurance regarding normal characteristics. At the same time, she is identifying the "real" baby and separating self and real baby from the intrauterine baby of fantasy.

54. (1) No treatment of condition is necessary as it resolves spontaneously in a few weeks; be alert for increased jaundice as the clot resolves, however.

55. (4) A full bladder may be the direct cause of discomfort.

56. (2) Also have mother nurse with infant in "football hold" position—changes the pressure points from the infant's gums.

57. (1) Leg pain may be indicative of thrombus formation. Headaches may indicate impending postpartum preeclampsia or eclampsia.

58. (4) Stimulates the "let down" reflex but is not always successful, however.

59. (4) A clear airway is the first priority. Never tug on the cord until after the placenta has separated.

60. (3) No. 2 is not correct, since the measles vaccination is ineffectual if given before the first birthday.

61. (2) "Infant" refers to the first year of life.

62. (2) Perinatal refers to the four weeks before and the four weeks after birth.

63. (2) Only women of childbearing age are considered in the birthrate.

64. (2) The adolescent's needs include (a) respect and concern for her welfare and involvement in her care and feelings about her future, including her sexual behavior, and (b) assistance with problem-solving techniques and alternatives for action.

65. (4) "Hard-to-place" infants are usually adopted out to older couples; younger couples get the infants. Adoptions from agencies or in private contracts are not finalized for six months.

66. (3) Considered only if gravida develops jaundice and fever while adequately hydrated, tachycardia of greater than or equal to 130, retinal hemorrhage, and delirium.

67. (4) Symptom of abruptio placentae.

68. (4) This gravida's symptoms appear too early for No. 1, 2, and 3.

69. (4) No. 1 also occurs more frequently in presence of hydatidiform mole.

70. (4) A—a factor in fraternal twinning and C—these infants are always of the same sex.

71. (4) The other symptoms are indicative of possible (a) abruption placentae, (b) rupture of membranes, and (c) preeclampsia.

72. (2) Gravida should be housed in a quiet room near the nurse's station for close, frequent observations.

73. (1) A—to monitor drug therapy and disease status; B—signs heralding imminent convulsions; C and D—abruptio placentae is a common occurence; and E—gravida may be unaware of labor if heavily sedated.

74. (2) Hypertension is a cause of abruptio placentae, not a sequela.

75. (1) The possibility of postpartum eclampsia is often overlooked.

76. (1) C—specific for determining level of anti-Rh antibodies. E—normal moderate activity is needed for circulatory sufficiency.

77. (4) Usually results from Rh incompatibility.

78. (4) Exposure to stress of procedure is unwarranted. Intrauterine diagnosis of fetal diabetes is not possible.

79. (1) Need for rest is paramount. No. 4 lists high-salt foods.

80. (3) Patient should be assisted on and off bedpan or bedside commode.

81. (2) A—semirecumbent position is needed instead. E—urge to bear down is strong and difficult to control and requires considerable exertion; she requires regional anesthesia to eliminate this reflex.

82. (2) Sudden release of intra-abdominal pressure following emptying of uterus may cause collapse in immediate postpartal period.

83. (4) Hypotension also decreases uterine perfusion

84. (4) Precipitate labor, multiparity, overdistention of uterus, and relaxation of uterus by spinal anesthesia predispose this woman to postpartum hemorrhage.

85. (2) Methergine or Ergotrate contract the cervix as well and this would interfere with the expulsion of the fragments.

86. (1) No. 1—protective barrier against ascending infection is lost. Neonate may develop pneumonia. However, if fetus is preterm, the production of surfactant (lecithin) is stimulated and the likelihood of RDS is decreased.

87. (3) Crowning indicates that birth is imminent. Inertia by itself does not result in fetal distress.

88. (4) All of these conditions decrease the supply of blood to the fetus.

89. (2) A and B—normal characteristics of amniotic fluid.

90. (2) Side-lying position improves perfusion of uterus by preventing hypotension from the pressure on the ascending vena cava.

91. (4) Yellow color results from breakdown of hemoglobin and/or bile pigments in meconium.

92. (1) Heart rate, 2; respiratory effort, 1; muscle tone, 0; reflex response, 1; and color, 1. Total Apgar is 5.

93. (1) Definitions of asphyxia vary from 30 to 60 seconds, depending on the author.

94. (3) These infants have a greater tendency to be deficient in surfactant (lecithin) necessary to maintain alveolar stability on exhalation.

95. (4) Flaring is another symptom of respiratory distress.

96. (4) Adequate ventilation is the top priority.

97. (2) A frequent normal finding, but neonate may be chilly.

98. (2) Injudicious suctioning may also decrease the amount of oxygen available to the neonate and cause tissue trauma resulting in bleeding

and/or edema.

99. (4) This may increase the neonate's temperature. Hyperthermia may result in episodes of apnea.

100. (2) This describes a normal transitional stool.

101. (4) C—fetus receives ready-to-use packed red blood cells. E—no such remedy is available.

102. (2) RhoGAM cannot deactivate antibodies already formed. It destroys fetal Rh-positive red blood cells before the mother can produce antibodies against them. Fetal red blood cells enter the mother's blood stream at the time of separation of the placenta or after expelling an abortus.

103. (1) Lofenalac does not contain the amino acid, phenylalanine.

104. (2) Retrolental fibroplasia is a disease of immaturity and high arterial oxygen levels. Visual problems may range from mild to complete blindness with retinal detachment.

105. (4) The mother needs assistance to express her feelings now. Other responses either ignore her feelings or are defensive.

106. (3) Test infant for hypoglycemia, feed him glucose water if this term infant's blood sugar is under 35 mg/100 ml, and call the physician.

107. (2) The infant with one umbilical artery requires a comprehensive physical examination. The prenatal history must be reviewed. The presence of oligoamnios as well is suspicious of renal anomalies.

108. (1) Wear gloves when handling this infant! Snuffles refers to the irritating nasal drainage that often covers the upper lip.

109. (3) *Candida albicans* is the causative agent of thrush and moniliasis.

110. (1) Class III results refer to the presence of suspicious cells. Cytology results are confirmed by biopsy and D & C.

111. (2) The time spent near the patient must be minimized.

112. (2) Sperm are stored in the epididymis until they are mature and capable of motility.

113. (2) Testosterone production continues in the Leydig cells.

114. (1) There is no "usual" age for the appearance of the male climacteric.

115. (1) The vas deferens is the transport canal for spermatozoa.

116. (3) Phimosis, stricture of the prepuce, is not related to infertility.

117. (4) A test for pregnancy.

118. (1) A normal menstrual cycle is usually not implicated in infertility.

119. (2) The cervical smear for cytology (pap smear) is a screening test for cervical cellular dysplasia.

120. (4) A period of abstinence prior to the expected day of ovulation is recommended for men who have a low sperm count.

Annotated Bibliography

Clark, A. L., and Affonso, D.: Childbearing: a nursing perspective, Philadelphia, 1976, F. A. Davis Company.

A comprehensive obstetric nursing textbook. Several notable physicians and nurses contributed to the content of this book, adding considerable depth and breadth to the physical and behavioral bases of nursing care on most topics pertinent to the subject.

Clausen, J. P., Flook, M., and Ford, B.: Maternity nursing today, ed. 2, New York, 1977, McGraw-Hill, Inc.

The psychosocial components of nursing care are stressed in this text. Physical science components of care, although well done in parts, are not consistent throughout the book.

Iorio, J.: Childbirth: family-centered nursing, ed. 3, St. Louis, 1975, The C. V. Mosby Co.

This text provides the necessary basic concepts for the nursing care of the childbearing family.

Reeder, S. R., Mastroianni, L., Martin, L., and Fitzpatrick, E.: Maternity nursing, ed. 13, Philadelphia, 1976, J. B. Lippincott Company.

This edition has been updated to include recent advances in fetology and neonatology, alternative lifestyle family living, family planning, and abortion. It retains features such as posttests and numerous illustrations.

Jensen, M., Benson, R., and Bobak, I.: Maternity care: the nurse and the family, St. Louis, 1977, The C. V. Mosby Co.

A comprehensive nursing text. Psychosocial and biophysical content is presented in depth providing the basis for nursing management. Nursing care plans are organized for ease of application. Content is easily retrieved and well indexed. Unique features—chapters on nutrition, genetics and genetics counseling, fathers, grief and grieving incorporated throughout, identification and management of the high-risk neonate, problem-oriented recording, legal aspects, and human sexuality and sexual expression.

Brunner, L., and Suddarth, D.: Lippincott manual of nursing practice: Philadelphia, 1974, J. B. Lippincott Company.

Well-organized, clearly presented, comprehensive text. Information easily retrievable for quick reference or study. Covers all facets of nursing. Provides theory base, medical management, and nursing application.

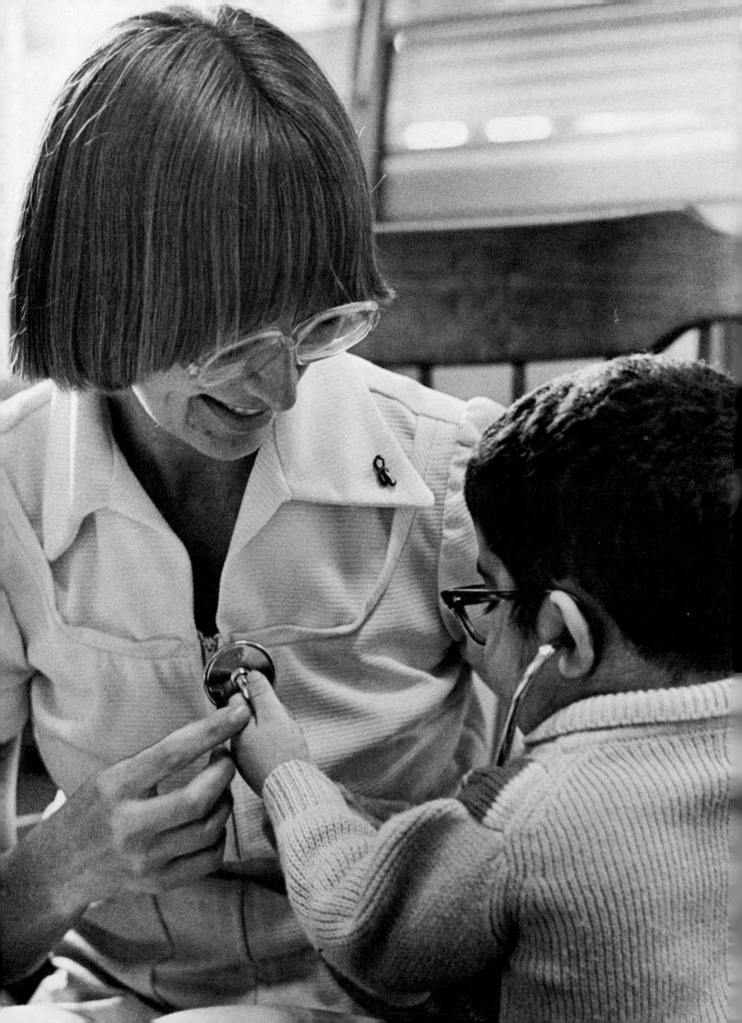

Unit 5 Pediatric Nursing

Introduction

This unit presents a review of basic pediatric principles and concepts, special concerns, and disease entities specific to each of four major age groups.

1. Infancy and toddlers—birth to 2 years
2. Preschoolers—age 3 to 5 years
3. School-age children—age 6 to 12 years
4. Preadolescents and adolescents

It is not meant to be a minipediatric course. For this reason, brief concepts of pathophysiology are included and the nurse is referred to the annotated bibliography at the end of the unit for references to more detailed, in-depth information. This section is to be used as a basis for review of knowledge concerning pediatrics that nursing students have acquired in their education. Questions to test retention of knowledge and ability to reason are found at the end of the unit, with answer/rationale for each question. At times, the nurse is referred to other sections of this text for information that is common to more than one discipline.

Sandra Forrest Fritz

Part A   Infancy and Toddlers—Birth to 2 Years

NORMAL GROWTH AND DEVELOPMENT

1. **Birth to 6 months**
A. Physical development (birth to 6 months)
   1. Height—gains approximately 2.5 cm (1 inch) per month
   2. Weight—gains 150 to 210 gm (5 to 7 oz) per week
   3. Posterior fontanel closes at 2 months
   4. Begins to drool saliva at 4 months
B. Behavior patterns (birth to 6 months)
   1. Motor development (see Table 5-1)
      a. Age 2 months—follows objects horizontally and vertically
      b. Age 3 months—discovers hands and reaches for objects
      c. Age 4 months—recognizes familiar objects and increases body movements at their sight
      d. Age 5 to 6 months—turns over completely and bangs with object held in hand
   2. Socialization and vocalization
      a. Newborn—cries when hungry or uncomfortable
      b. Age 2 months—crying becomes differentiated; smiles in response to another's smile
      c. Age 3 months—babbles and coos
      d. Age 4 months—laughs aloud; recognizes maternal figure and shows interest in other members of family
      e. Age 5 to 6 months—vocalizes displeasure when objects are taken away; vocalizes syllables
C. Nursing implications (birth to 6 months)
   1. Appropriate play activities based on developmental level—child develops cephalocaudally (from head progressing downward and from trunk outward to extremities); each sensory mode must be stimulated to develop perception of that sense organ; deprivation of any sensory mode causes incomplete or lack of development of that modality
      a. Age 1 to 3 months
         (1) Smile, talk, and sing to infant for visual and hearing senses
         (2) Tactile stimulation—hold, pat, caress, cuddle, and touch infant
         (3) Crinkle different kinds of paper, tissue, newsprint, and cellophane, near infant's ear for differentiation of hearing sense
         (4) Use mobiles, wind chimes, and bright dangling objects for visual, hearing, and attention modalities
         (5) Utilize cradle gym and infant seat for posture changes
      b. Age 4 to 6 months
         (1) Use mirror play for increased visual awareness
         (2) Soft squeeze toys in vivid colors and with varying textures for visual and tactile stimulation
         (3) Collect a box of textures—sandpaper, velvet, fur, silk, wood, screening, corrugated cardboard, cotton, and items with smooth, highly polished surfaces; to increase tactile awareness
         (4) Give the infant a very small soft balloon with a jingle bell in it to stimulate tactile and auditory curiosity
   2. Guidance areas
      a. Hold infant during feeding
      b. Support head and back when lifting infant
      c. Allow infant to sleep to get the rest necessary for development
      d. Hold toys in front of infant to encourage reaching
      e. Safety concerns
         (1) Place infant seat where it will not tip over
         (2) Strap infant into high chair or infant seat
         (3) Use toys without buttons, wires, or removable parts
         (4) Bath—avoid scalding infant by checking water with elbow; keep one hand on baby under 4 months;

Table 5-1.   Reflexes of the newborn

Reflex	Description	Presents and/or Disappears
Babinski	Extension of great toe on stroking sole of foot	Disappears at 12 to 18 months
Blinking	Aroused by bright light; protective reflex	Birth
Coughing and sneezing	Clear respiratory tract, rid respiratory system of amniotic fluid, and protect newborn from inhaling foreign substances	Birth
Cry	Protective or defensive; to indicate a need	Birth
Dancing	When held in upright position with feet touching a solid surface, infant responds with prancing movements	Birth, but disappears very soon
Gagging and vomiting	Provide for rejection of irritating or toxic substances from GI tract; gag reflex activated when infant has more in mouth than can successfully be swallowed	
Morro or "startle"	Response to sudden loud noise or jarring causing body to stiffen, legs will draw up with soles of feet turned toward each other, and arms will go up and out, then forward in embracing position; movements are symmetrical	May be *absent first 24 hours* after birth, appear second day, be *strongest* during first *8 weeks* of life, and disappear about *5 months* of age
Neck righting	When head is turned to one side, the shoulder and trunk will turn to that side, followed by the pelvis	Disappears at 9 to 12 months
Palmar grasp	Pressure on palm of hand will elicit grasp	Reflex at birth and later develops into purposeful grasping; reflex disappears at 6 to 7 months
Plantar grasp	Pressure on sole of foot behind toes will cause flexion of toes	Disappears at 9 to 12 months
Pupillary	Ipsilateral constriction to light	Present at birth
Rooting	When corner of mouth is touched and object is moved toward cheek, infant will turn head toward object and open mouth; way of reaching for food	Disappears at 4 months
Shiver	Protective reflex when cold	Present at birth
Sucking	Sucking movements when anything touches lips; necessary for feeding	Present *before* birth
Swallowing	Follows sucking; necessary for ingestion of food substances	Before birth
Tonic neck reflex—"fencing position"	*Postural* reflex of infant lying on back; turns head to one side and extends arm and leg on the side to which infant is facing; arm and leg on opposite side are flexed	Present until 18 to 20 weeks of age; disappears at 5 to 6 months
Yawn	Draws in added supply of oxygen when rate of respiratory exchange is insufficient to meet needs; protective reflex	Present at birth

do not leave 6-month-old infant alone in bath because of danger of drowning

(5) *Do not* leave the infant alone where it is possible for infant to wriggle and roll off

(6) Filmy plastics, harnesses, zippered bags, and pillows can smother or strangle

(7) Use of a good carbed that can be strapped or securely fastened onto the carseat is essential for safety

(8) Keep pins and other sharp objects out of reach

2. Age 6 to 12 months
A. Physical development (6 to 12 months)
  1. Height—66 to 74 cm (26 to 29 inches)
  2. Weight—6 months: twice the birth weight; 12 months: three times the birth weight
  3. Age 12 months—has six teeth (see Table 5-2)
B. Behavior patterns (6 to 12 months)
  1. Motor development
    a. Age 7 to 9 months—plays with feet
    b. Age 6 to 8 months—begins to show good coordination and sits alone
    c. Age 6 to 9 months—transfers toys from one hand to the other
    d. Age 7 to 9 months—begins to crawl and creep
    e. Age 10 to 12 months—pulls self to feet, walks with help and cruises
  2. Socialization and vocalization
    a. Age 6 to 8 months—shows fear of strangers; recognition of individuals other than self and family members
    b. Age 7 to 9 months—cries when scolded
    c. Age 10 to 12 months
      (1) Claps hands on request
      (2) Responds to own name
      (3) Imitative behavior
      (4) Smiles at image in mirror
      (5) Recognizes meaning of no
      (6) Says three words other than Ma-Ma and Da-Da
C. Nursing implications (6 to 12 months)
  1. Appropriate play activities based on developmental level—the child is now acquiring the capacity to differentiate self from environment; there is active exploratory behavior plus a beginning perception of space and depth
    a. Large round nesting toys encourage space and size differentiation
    b. Squeeze toys in bath stimulate curiosity in changes of objects
    c. Peek-a-boo, bye-bye, and pat-a-cake
    d. Toys to stimulate curiosity (milk carton, fabric book, and containers to fill and spill)
    e. Blow bubbles for infant and encourage infant to catch them
    f. Play whistles and horns of different sounds
    g. Table slapping game—encourage imitation
    h. Place several cereal bowls on the table with a different consistency in each one, such as sand, flour, cornflakes, water, cotton balls, sugar, wet coffee grounds, marbles, and beans; help the infant dig into each bowl with both hands so the differences of each material can be felt and learned
  2. Guidance areas
    a. Allow the infant to play with an extra spoon during feeding to prepare for self-feeding
    b. Begin to set limits on areas infant can play in and expected behavior, for example, "no-no" for forbidden behavior
    c. Teething—often causes irritability

Table 5-2. Dentition

	Primary teeth—20 in number			
	Eruption		Shedding	
	Lower	Upper	Lower	Upper
	(age in months)		(age in years)	
Central incisor	6	7½	6	7½
Lateral incisor	7	9	7	8
Cuspid	16	18	9½	11½
First molar	12	14	10	10½
Second molar	20	24	11	10½

| | Permanent teeth eruption—32 in number | |
| | Lower | Upper |
	(age in years)	(age in years)
Central incisors	6–7	7–8
Lateral incisors	7–8	8–9
Cuspids	9–10	11–12
First bicuspids	10–12	10–11
Second bicuspids	11–12	10–12
First molars	6–7	6–7
Second molars	11–13	12–13
Third molars	17–21	17–21

(1) Aids for teething pain—topical ointments, although they may be short acting and cause sensitivity reactions

(2) Teething rings

(3) Aspirin

d. Safety concerns

(1) Fence stairways

(2) Pick up loose objects from floor

(3) Keep hot liquids, hot foods, and electric cords on small appliances out of reach

(4) Tablecloth should not hang within reach of infant

(5) Keep medicines and poisons in a locked cabinet

(6) Place guards in front of open heaters and around registers and floor furnaces

(7) Safety plugs for wall sockets

(8) Keep scissors, knives, and breakable objects out of reach of infant

(9) Easily overturned floor lamps and sharp-edged furniture are dangerous

3. Age 12 to 18 months

A. Physical development (12 to 18 months)

1. Height—76 to 81 cm (30 to 32 inches)

2. Weight—9.5 to 11 kg (21 to 24 lb)

3. Anterior fontanel closed

4. Abdomen protrudes

B. Behavior patterns (12 to 18 months)

1. Motor development

a. Age 12 to 14 months—mimics household chores

b. Age 16 to 18 months—walks and runs with a stiff gait and wide stance

c. Age 14 to 18 months—throws a ball

d. Age 15 to 18 months

(1) Pulls a toy while walking

(2) Climbs stairs and on furniture

(3) Builds a tower up to three blocks

e. Age 16 to 18 months—stoops to pick up toys

f. Age 18 months

(1) Seats self in child's chair by backing into it

(2) Holds cup with two hands

(3) Scribbles; differentiates between circular and straight lines

2. Socialization and vocalization

a. Age 12 to 14 months

(1) Develops new awareness of strangers

(2) Wants to explore everything in reach

(3) Imitates simple things

(4) Hugs a favorite doll or stuffed toy

b. Age 16 to 18 months

(1) Finds security in some object

(2) Knows ten words

c. Age 18 months

(1) Uses phrases

(2) May begin to have temper tantrums

(3) Enjoys solitary play or watching others

(4) May control bowel movements

C. Nursing implications (12 to 18 months)

1. Appropriate play activities based on developmental level—this is a period of increased locomotion as well as one of improving eye-hand coordination; small muscle coordination is steadily becoming differentiated; and verbal communication with the child encourages language development and a meaningful vocabulary

a. Likes pull toys and push toys

b. Likes teddy bears, dolls, pots and pans, telephone, and fabric picture books

c. Collect bells of different tones and have child shake them

d. Give child a pan of warm soapy water in which to splash hands and feet

e. When you pick up the child, say "up" and when you put the child down, say "down"

f. Hold the child around the trunk in front of a mirror and tilt forward, backward, and sideways, telling child the direction of each tilt

g. Put the child in a box and tilt it gently in all directions

h. Age 18 months—collect empty spice bottles to introduce smells to the child by putting various odors on a cotton ball and putting one in each jar

2. Guidance areas

a. Begin teaching infant to brush teeth

b. Read nursery rhymes

c. Readiness factors in toilet training (18 months)

(1) Nervous system growth makes standing possible and child demonstrates need to defecate

(2) Child makes grunting sounds or strains

(3) Tugs at diaper

(4) Tells parents of bowel movement or

brings diaper to them
(5) Bowel movements come at regular times
(6) Child knows what toilet seat or potty chair is for
(7) Child is willing to sit on seat and defecate
  d. Toilet training guidelines
(1) Do not force child to sit on toilet
(2) Small seat or potty chair should be acquired and child allowed to explore it
(3) Supports or height should be adjusted so child's knees are even or above level of anus to allow easy passage of feces and avoid straining and impediment of circulation to lower extremities
(4) Do not shame child for accidents; praise child for success (this is Erickson's stage of autonomy versus shame and doubt)
  e. Safety concerns
(1) Doors that lead to stairways, driveways, and storage areas should be safely fastened
(2) Screens on windows should be locked or nailed
(3) Play yard should be fenced
(4) Pot handles on the stove should be turned to the wall
(5) Matches, furniture polish, and cleaning agents, especially lye and detergents, should be locked up
(6) Toys should have no removable parts and should be unbreakable
(7) Child should never be left alone in the tub or wading pool or around open and frozen bodies of water
(8) Medicines and home products should be stored in child-safe containers
(9) Seat restraints should be used in autos

4. Age 2 years
A. Physical development (2 years)
  1. Height—gains 7.5 to 10.5 cm (3 to 4 inches)
  2. Weight—12 to 13 kg (26 to 28 lb)
  3. Approximately 16 temporary teeth
B. Behavior patterns (2 years)
  1. Motor development
    a. Walks up and down stairs

b. Jumps crudely
c. Opens doors and turns knobs
d. Drinks well with one hand
e. Assists with dressing
f. Imitates vertical stroke when scribbling
g. Uses spoon without spilling
h. Builds a tower of five or more blocks
i. Kicks a ball with one foot without falling
  2. Socialization and vocalization
    a. Uses word "mine" constantly
    b. Has vocabulary of 300 words and makes short sentences or phrases
    c. Fear of separation from parents; has no concept of time, length of separation, or of object permanence when out of sight
    d. Treats other children as objects
    e. Toilet trained in daytime
    f. Helps to undress self; can put on some clothing
    g. Obeys simple commands
    h. Does not know right from wrong
C. Nursing implications (2 years)
  1. Appropriate play activities based on developmental level—the curiousness and the newness of situations are sources of never-ending excitement to this child; the 2-year-old child is aware of self as distinct from other beings and is now striving to gain a sense of autonomy without loss of control; as the child becomes less "babyish" and more demanding of self-rights, behavior problems may arise and maternal figures may become upset about losing a baby and be alarmed by the child's signs of autonomy; manual dexterity is quite refined; and the concept of object permanence is acquired during this year
    a. Likes to investigate small toys
    b. Likes large toys such as wagon or buggy
    c. Manipulation of mud and sand (pounding and patting)
    d. Enjoys hearing stories and being read to
    e. Has short attention span
  2. Guidance areas
    a. Has need for peer companionship, although will not share
    b. Have child eat meals with family
    c. Begin to read to child
    d. Child says "no" even if it is not meant
    e. Be consistent in discipline—parental agreement and consistency concerning when and how to discipline

(1) Excessively strict measures will deflate child's self-image and child may become antagonistic and rebellious or passive with little self-assertion or initiative
(2) Parental example and praise in lieu of excessive discipline
(3) With children under 2 years of age chief use of discipline is to enforce rules for safety, such as removing child from situation
f. Takes doll or toy to bed
g. Delays sleeping by calling for drink of water or asking to go to the bathroom
h. Child is impatient with restraints; provide diversion to achieve cooperation
i. Safety concerns
  (1) Keep child away from the street and driveway with fence and firm discipline
  (2) Supervise play when playmates are present, as they may injure one another with rough play
  (3) Large sturdy toys without sharp edges or small removable parts are safest
  (4) Keep matches and cigarette lighters from child
  (5) Store dangerous tools and garden equipment in safe place
  (6) Child is impatient with restraint, so diversion to achieve cooperation is needed
j. Temper tantrums
  (1) Normal at 3 to 6 years (most frequent during third year)
  (2) Provoked by sudden feeling of frustration
  (3) Recommendations
    (a) Avoid precipitating factor
      i. Avoid abrupt withdrawal from play activities
      ii. Avoid excessive demands on child, especially if child is hungry, tired, or ill
    (b) During tantrum—ignore behavior but stay close so child will not feel abandoned, use distraction
    (c) Parents should be consistent in reactions to temper tantrums and not allow temper tantrums to

modify their behavior or expectation of child

SPECIAL CONCERNS FROM BIRTH TO 2 YEARS

1. **Response to illness and hospitalization**—birth to 2 years
A. Indications of discomfort or pain (birth to 2 years) (see also Table 5-3)
  1. Crying frequently
  2. Excessive irritability
  3. Elevated temperature
  4. Lethargy
  5. Prostration
  6. Decreased appetite
B. Reaction to stage of illness (birth to 2 years)
  1. Initial illness or hospitalization
    a. Expected coping behaviors
      (1) Rejects everyone except mother figure
      (2) Cries loudly—phase one of separation anxiety
    b. Negative behaviors
      (1) Monotonous crying and sad moans—phase two of separation anxiety
      (2) Thumb-sucking, nose-picking, and body-rocking
  2. Prolonged hospitalization and convalescence
    a. Expected coping behaviors
      (1) Demands attention
      (2) May be difficult to handle
      (3) Some regression (toilet-trained toddler begins to wet pants)
    b. Negative behavior
      (1) Indifferent to mother or maternal figure—phase three of separation anxiety
      (2) Preoccupation with material things
      (3) Behaviors do not return to normal
      (4) No protest when mother leaves
      (5) Clings to nurse instead of mother figure
  3. Phases of separation anxiety in toddler*
    a. Phase one—protest
      (1) Lasts a few hours to several days, expressed by violent crying and intense aggression; child may feel

*Based on studies and findings of Bowlby, J.: *Maternal care and mental health*, Geneva, World Health Organization, 1952.

Table 5-3. Vital signs (1 month to 18 years)

Age	Heart rate	Average heart rate	Respirations/minute	Blood pressure
1 month to 1 year	80–180	120–130	26–34	80/60/0
2 years	80–140	110	20–30	
4 years	80–120	100	20–30	85/60
6 years	70–115	100	20–30	90/60
10 years	70–110	90	18–26	100/65
12 to 14 years	60–110	85–90	15–24	110/67
14 to 18 years	50–95	70–75	15–24	118/75

Temperature

Oral—36.4 to 37.2 C (97.6 to 99 F)
Rectal—37 to 37.8 C (98.6 to 100 F)
Axillary—35.9 to 36.7 C (96.6 to 97.8 F)

punished; newly gained sense of control and autonomy is threatened
   (2) Nursing action—important for nurse to be close even though behavior is difficult to tolerate; nurse only needs to remain in visual field, not necessarily attempting to touch or hold child.
  b. Phase two—despair
   (1) Increased hopelessness characterized by sad moans; a perpetually sad countenance; declining activity; thumb-sucking, nose-picking, and body-rocking are seen; few or no demands; and accepts care passively
   (2) Nursing action—encourage social interaction with other children, self, and staff
  C. Phase three—denial
   (1) Often erroneously interpreted as recovery, cheerful, actively interested in ward, indifferent to mother or maternal figure, and preoccupation with material things
   (2) Nursing action—continuity of care is extremely important; help mother to understand situation and encourage her to visit; try to prevent this stage, as it is difficult to cure and may cause long-lasting problems with the child's life
2. **Nutrition and feeding**—birth to 2 years
A. Caloric requirements (birth to 2 years)
  1. Birth to two months—115–120 cal/kg/24 hours

  2. Age 2 to 6 months—110 cal/kg/24 hours
  3. Age 6 to 12 months—100 cal/kg/24 hours
  4. Age 1 to 2 years—1000/24 hours
  5. Age 2 to 3 years—1250/24 hours
B. Normal diets (birth to 2 years)
  1. Infant
   a. Fluid requirement—70 to 130 ml/kg (2 to 3 oz fluid per pound) of body weight per 24 hours
   b. Solid food and supplementary additions—add one new food at a time to observe toleration and sensitivity, rash or diarrhea, for example
   c. Age 1 month—vitamin supplements of A, D, and C once daily
   d. Age 2 to 3 months—cereal and strained cooked fruit twice daily
   e. Age 3 to 4 months—strained cooked vegetables and meat once daily
   f. Age 5 to 7 months—zwieback or hard toast and egg yolk with any feeding
   g. Age 7 to 9 months—meat (broiled or baked and finely chopped) and potato (mashed) twice daily
   h. Since stomach emptying varies, a rigid feeding schedule is not advisable
   i. If infant cries often, reasons other than hunger should be investigated
    (1) Wet diapers
    (2) Fever
    (3) Pain
    (4) Boredom
    (5) Immobilization
   j. Do not force child to eat
   k. Breast-feeding
    (1) Usually mother's preference

(2) Advantages
    (a) Readily available and at proper temperature
    (b) Feeding difficulties are less common
    (c) Antibodies from mother (polio and mumps, for example) transferred to infant, thus providing temporary immunity
    (d) Less expensive
    (e) Promotes good maternal-infant relationship
(3) Disadvantages
    (a) Often inconvenient for parents, lactation diet is necessary for mother, and causes greater fatigue
    (b) May produce jaundice in neonates
(4) Contraindications
    (a) Active tuberculosis in mother
    (b) Severe chronic disease in mother or infant
    (c) Severe maternal malnutrition

2. Toddler
  a. Daily requirements include foods from basic four groups
  b. Spacing of meals coincides with three meals plus snack (crackers, cheese, and pieces of fruit)
  c. Give small portions
  d. Allow child to eat with rest of family
  e. Usual to have decreased appetite due to decreased rate of growth

C. Problems of infant feeding
1. Burping
  a. Infant may swallow air during feeding
  b. Infant should be burped or bubbled at least once during feeding and at end of feeding
  c. Support infant with head elevated (over shoulder) and gently pat or stroke back until infant burps
2. Colic
  a. Recurrent sharp abdominal pain occurring in infants under 3 months of age
  b. Characterized by
    (1) Crying suddenly and loudly
    (2) Face flushes
    (3) Abdominal distention and tenseness
    (4) Legs drawn up to abdomen

  c. Etiology
    (1) Undetermined, with some infants more susceptible than others
    (2) Usually associated with hunger, air-swallowing, overfeeding, and maternal insecurity
    (3) Certain foods may be responsible, but change in diet usually has no effect
  d. Recommendations
    (1) Reassure parents that attacks usually do not occur after 3 months of age
    (2) Hold infant upright over shoulder
    (3) Feed 1 to 2 oz of warm water or weak tea
    (4) Learn feeding and burping techniques
    (5) Establish stable emotional environment
    (6) Sedation *may* be recommended by physician for severe, prolonged attacks
3. Spitting up
  a. Because of immature swallowing mechanism, regurgitation (spitting up) is common for infants for first 6 months
  b. Differentiate from vomiting (emptying of stomach contents)
  c. Unless other symptoms are present and if baby is gaining weight, spitting up should be ignored
4. Vomiting
  a. Most common cause is overfeeding
  b. If accompanied by other symptoms such as fever, decreased urine output, blood in stool, or severe abdominal pain, seek medical attention
5. Diarrhea
  a. Overfeeding of formula may be cause—decrease feeding, give clear fluids (water or apple juice), and offer no solids at next meal or feeding
  b. Frequent watery stools should be referred to physician for possible infectious etiology
  c. Diarrhea that is not stopped within 24 hours should be investigated and treated by physician
6. Constipation
  a. *Hard* stools that are difficult to pass
  b. Increase intake of fluids, such as water or juice

c. If diet is adequate and problem persists, pathology must be ruled out

7. Weaning
   a. About 6 months, offer sips of milk from a cup before and after regular feedings; weaning needs to be gradual process
   b. Most infants are weaned to a cup at about 12 to 14 months of age
   c. Discourage bottle in bed because of the likelihood of causing dental caries; also, older infant does not need the extra calories obtained from the bottle
   d. Since sucking needs differ, infants are not weaned by same age

8. Nutritional anemia (iron deficiency)
   a. Often seen in infants 6 months to 2 years of age
      (1) Infants have iron store from mother to age 6 months
      (2) Most of food intake comes from milk, which is a poor source of iron
      (3) Symptoms—chubby, pale, and irritable
      (4) Sources include iron supplement (may turn stools black) cereal, meat (frankfurters and hamburger are easy for toddlers to eat), egg yolks, peanut butter, and green vegetables

3. Thumb-sucking
A. If prior to mealtime, hunger
B. Between meals—needs more sucking
   1. Breast-fed infants—more time at breast
   2. Bottle-fed infant—fewer and smaller holes in nipple
   3. Nipple comforter or pacifier may be used between meals to satisfy sucking instincts
C. Do not bind arms to side to prevent thumb-sucking
D. Usually disappears by age 2 years
4. Immunizations—see Appendix G

CONDITIONS AND DISEASE ENTITIES FROM BIRTH TO 2 YEARS

1. Congenital diseases
A. Ophthalmia neonatorum (gonorrheal conjunctivitis)
   1. Cause-pathophysiology
      a. Gram negative organism, *Neisseria gonorrhoeae*
      b. Acquired by infant during birth process by direct contact with infected vagina
   2. Signs-symptoms
      a. Redness and swelling of eyelids
      b. Profuse purulent discharge
   3. Nursing approaches
      a. Be absolutely certain to instill eyedrops that are required by law in newborn
      b. Note any of the signs and report them so a smear or culture can be taken
      c. Isolate infected infant
      d. Utilize sterile technique when irrigating infected eye or eyes and move from inner to outer canthus to prevent self-infection
B. Congenital syphilis (Lues)
   1. Cause-pathophysiology
      a. Spirochete, *Treponema pallidum*
      b. Transmitted to fetus by direct innoculation into blood stream through placenta during latter half of pregnancy
   2. Signs-symptoms
      a. Prior to age 6 weeks
         (1) Persistent rhinitis "snuffles"
         (2) Generalized rash, including soles and palms
         (3) Signs of anemia (confirmed by lab)—low hemoglobin count and prolonged bleeding time (see Table 5-4)
         (4) Bleeding ulcerations of mucous membranes
         (5) Pseudoparalysis or pathologic fractures
      b. Later signs and symptoms
         (1) Saddle nose—destruction of nose bones

Table 5-4. Laboratory values in pediatrics

Urine
pH 5-7
Specific gravity
Infant 1.002-1.006
Child 1.005-1.018

Blood	Age	Hemoglobin (Hbg) (gm/100 ml)	Hematocrit (% volume of cells)
	Birth	16-22	53-73
	3 months	11-12	36-38
	6 months	11-12	35-40
	12 months	11-12	35-40
	2 to 8 years	11.5-14	36-43
	8 to 12 years	12-14	37-46

(2) Saber shins—sharp forward curve of tibia

(3) Hutchinson's teeth—permanent central incisors are peg shaped with a notch

(4) Neurosyphilis—characterized by hemiplegia, spastic paralysis, and mental retardation

3. Nursing approaches

a. Prevention of transmission of disease to other infants and staff

b. Strict isolation of infant and use of gown and glove technique

c. Clean infant's nose before feeding because of rhinitis so infant can breathe while eating

d. Handle infant carefully—pain on movement caused by bone lesions

2. Congenital anomalies

A. Congenital heart disease (CHD)—each type will be discussed separately, but generally the signs and symptoms can be explained by understanding the effects of increased pulmonary artery pressure; this results in right to left shunting in the lungs, causing a decrease in the oxygen-carbon dioxide exchange; the infant's rate of respiration increases, which leads to easy fatigability with resultant feeding and weight-gain problems

1. Types

a. Patent ductus arteriosus (PDA)—a vascular connection that directs blood from the pulmonary artery to the aorta during fetal life, normally closes soon after birth; if this connection remains open after birth, the direction of the blood flow in the ductus is reversed by the higher pressure in the aorta; commonly seen in premature infants

(1) Signs and symptoms

(a) Slow weight gain

(b) Murmur heard over pulmonary artery

(c) Feeding difficulties

(d) Pale, scrawny appearance

(e) Usually acyanotic because of mingling of blood between pulmonary and systemic circulations

(f) Low diastolic blood pressure

(2) Treatment

(a) Surgical ligation and division of the patent ductus arteriosus

(b) Usually elective at 2 to 3 years of age, as patency involves risk of bacterial endocarditis

(c) After treatment, the diastolic blood pressure rises but stabilizes four to five days postoperatively

b. Atrial septal defect (ASD)—an abnormal opening between right and left atria, causing left to right shunting of blood; this means that oxygenated blood that flows from the left to the right atrium is recirculated through the lungs, causing an increased total blood flow through the lungs with resultant enlargement of the right heart and distention of the pulmonary vessels

(1) Signs and symptoms

(a) Systolic murmur over pulmonary artery

(b) Enlargement of the heart

(c) Slow weight gain

(d) Usually acyanotic due to mingling of pulmonary and systemic circulations, but may become cyanotic if flow reverses through shunt or defect

(e) Dyspnea with exertion

(f) Tires easily

(g) Frequent respiratory infections

(2) Treatment

(a) Surgical closure by suture or patch

(b) May utilize open-heart or closed technique

c. Ventricular septal defect (VSD)—this is an abnormal opening between right and left ventricles; during systole, there is shunting of blood from left to right, causing an increase in pulmonary arterial pressures

(1) Signs and symptoms

(a) Usually acyanotic, but pulmonary hypertension may occur, causing right to left shunting in lungs and cyanosis

(b) Small defects may be asymptomatic, but large defects develop symptoms at 1 to 2 months

(c) Loud systolic murmur heard

over left lower sternum
  (d) Left ventricular hypertrophy
      evidenced on ECG
      (electro-cardiogram); may have
      right ventricular hypertrophy
  (e) Dyspnea, tires easily
  (f) Repeated respiratory infections
  (g) Feeding difficulties with slow
      weight gain
  (h) Congestive heart failure may
      develop with cardiac
      enlargement and pulmonary
      engorgement
(2) Treatment
  (a) In low septal defects with
      murmur as only symptom, no
      treatment is indicated;
      risk—bacterial endocarditis
  (b) Larger defects require
      open-heart surgery by direct
      closure or by suturing a patch
      into the opening
  (c) Success of treatment depends on
      the amount of resistance that has
      developed in the pulmonary
      vascular bed; if resistance is
      high, child will not do well with
      or without surgery
d. Coarctation of aorta—a narrowed aortic
   lumen producing obstruction to flow of
   blood through aorta, causing increased
   left ventricular pressure and work load;
   the severity of symptoms depends on
   the degree of constriction
   (1) Signs and symptoms
     (a) Elevation of blood pressure in
         arms and low pressure in legs,
         with leg pains; systolic and
         diastolic hypertension
     (b) During later childhood, may
         have slow growth and complain
         of fatigue and weakness in legs
     (c) Headache and nose bleeds due
         to increased upper-body blood
         pressure
     (d) In severe coarctation, the infant
         develops congestive heart failure
         (see p. 304)
   (2) Treatment
     (a) In infancy—treat congestive
         heart failure; surgery only as
         emergency procedure

  (b) Surgery in middle childhood
      consists of excision of
      constricted area and anastomosis
      of excised ends
e. Complete transposition of great
   vessels—the aorta originates from the
   right ventricle and the pulmonary artery
   originates from the left ventricle, thus
   there are two separate circulations; an
   abnormal opening between the two
   circulations must be present to sustain
   life;
   (1) Signs and symptoms
     (a) Severe cyanosis
     (b) Shallow, rapid respirations
     (c) Clubbing of fingers and toes
     (d) Development of congestive heart
         failure (see p. 304)
     (e) Thrombosis
     (f) Severe hypoxia
     (g) Polycythemia and increased
         hemoglobin and hematocrit
         verified by lab tests
   (2) Treatment
     (a) Create opening so two
         circulatory systems can mingle;
         life-saving
         (1) Rashkind—use of balloon
             catheter to create atrial
             septal defect via cardiac
             catheterization
         (2) Blalock-Hanlen—create
             atrial septal defect via
             surgery
     (b) Permanent correction with
         Mustard's procedure—use of
         cardiopulmonary bypass, atrial
         septum is removed and a graft is
         sutured into the atrium to direct
         pulmonary venous blood to right
         ventricle and systemic venous
         blood to left ventricle; usually
         done during preschool years
f. Tetralogy of Fallot—this is
   characterized by pulmonary stenosis,
   ventricular septal defect, overriding
   aorta, and hypertrophy of the right
   ventricle; there is an obstruction of the
   blood from the right ventricle into the
   pulmonary artery; the ventricular septal
   defect allows unoxygenated blood into
   the aorta; high right ventricular pressure

causes right ventricular hypertrophy
(1) Signs and symptoms
    (a) Variable—dependent on the obstruction
    (b) Cyanosis—usually becomes more severe as child gets older and stenosis becomes more severe
    (c) Paroxysmal dyspnea—occurs during first 2 years of life, air hunger, hypoxia, deep cyanosis, and loss of consciousness, with or without convulsions
    (d) Squatting when child reaches walking stage and self-limiting of activities due to fatigue and dyspnea
    (e) Clubbing of fingers and toes
    (f) Slow weight gain
    (g) Dyspnea on exertion
    (h) Usually systolic murmur heard on left sternal border
    (i) Tachycardia
(2) Treatment
    (a) Relieve paroxysmal dyspnea by placing child in knee-chest position to increase cardiac efficiency and administering oxygen to increase oxygen saturation of blood
    (b) Surgery usually between 3 and 14 years, delaying as long as possible to ensure successful outcome
    (c) The following procedures increase pulmonary blood flow by creating a patent ductus arteriosus
        i. Waterston's shunt—anastomosis of ascending aorta and right pulmonary artery
        ii. Blalock-Taussig shunt—anastomosis of branch of aorta (in infants) or sub-clavian artery (in older child) to the right pulmonary artery
        iii. Potts-Smith-Gibson—anastomosis of aorta and left pulmonary artery
    (d) Total correction is achieved by removal of the shunt (one of the preceding procedures), and

repair of ventricular septal defect, and relief of right ventricular obstruction
g. Truncus arteriosus—the aorta and pulmonary artery are fused into a single tube that receives blood from right and left ventricles simultaneously; a VSD is always present
(1) Signs and symptoms
    (a) Degrees of cyanosis, dyspnea, and retarded growth
    (b) Dependent on regulation of blood flow through lungs—the more plentiful the flow, the more mild the symptoms
    (c) Loud murmur heard over truncus point of origin
(2) Treatment
    (a) Symptomatic
    (b) Surgical correction
h. Tricuspid atresia—there is no opening between right atrium and right ventricle; it is characterized by a small right ventricle and a large left ventricle and diminished pulmonary circulation; unless a ventricular septal defect or patent ductus arteriosus is present, there is no way for the blood to circulate through the lungs
(1) Signs and symptoms
    (a) Severely cyanotic infant who does not improve with oxygen
    (b) Dyspnea, lack of energy
    (c) Polycythemia
    (d) Prone to infections
    (e) Failure to thrive
(2) Treatment
    (a) Create a ventricular septal defect or patent ductus arteriosus surgically or via shunt (see Tetralogy of Fallot, see p. 302)
    (b) Most infants do not do well, and many die within first year of life without surgical intervention
2. Nursing approaches
a. Know signs and symptoms of heart defects
(1) Cyanotic type—there is a communication between pulmonary and systemic circulations where the blood is continually flowing from venous to arterial side; the blood

going to the periphery of body is never fully saturated, so tissues have blue tint
- (a) Tetralogy of Fallot
- (b) Tricuspid atresia
- (c) Transposition of great vessels
- (d) Truncus arteriosus

(2) Acyanotic type—there is no abnormal communication between pulmonary and systemic circulations
- (a) Coarctation of the aorta
- (b) Aortic stenosis

(3) Potentially cyanotic—an abnormal communication exists between the pulmonary and systemic circulations, but the pressure is such that blood flows through the shunt from arterial to venous side so that no cyanosis is present; however, it is possible that the flow could reverse direction (unusual stress or myocardial failure) and produce cyanosis by mixing venous blood with arterial blood
- (a) Patent ductus arteriosus
- (b) Atrial septal defects
- (c) Ventricular septal defects

b. Assess child's behavior and physical appearance with accurate recording as a basis for observing and reporting changes
(1) Motor coordination
(2) Muscle development
(3) Skin and mucous membrane coloring—cyanotic or pink
(4) Clubbing of phalanges
(5) Chest—appearance of one-sided prominence
(6) Palpate and record femoral (inguinal area) and brachial pulse
(7) Listen and record type and location of murmur heard or absence of murmur

c. Relieve respiratory distress associated with increased pulmonary blood flow or decreased oxygen available to child
(1) Position child at 45° angle to relieve pressure of organs on the diaphragm and allow expansion of lung volume
(2) Pin diapers loosely to decrease likelihood of pressure on infant
(3) Feed slowly to decrease chance of aspiration due to rapid respirations
(4) Suction mouth and nose if child cannot cough up secretions

d. Provide environment conducive to rest so that less oxygen will be required, thus reducing workload of heart
(1) Organize nursing care to provide periods of undisturbed rest
(2) Avoid excessive crying and expenditure of energy by feeding baby when hungry, use of pacifier, and holding child
(3) Provide diversional activities to avoid fatigue
- (a) Sing to infant
- (b) Read to young child
- (c) Offer books, crayons, or quiet activity appropriate to developmental level

e. Protect child from exposure to infections

f. Explain condition to child and family
(1) Explain condition to child as soon as old enough to understand so child will be more likely to follow restrictions and understand symptoms
(2) Encourage parents to be truthful with child
(3) Help parents understand true limits of child's activities, if any, so they can avoid overprotection and indulgence, as this is common among parents of children with congenital heart disease

g. Observe for signs and symptoms of congestive heart failure (CHF)
(1) Murmurs
(2) Retractions
(3) Tachypnea
(4) Decreased urine output
(5) Tachycardia
(6) Cyanosis or pale color
(7) Weak cry
(8) Poor feeding
(9) Nasal flaring
(10) Periorbital edema in infants; swelling of hands and feet in older children
(11) Irritability
(12) Perspiration, especially with activity, feeding, for example

h. Observe for sign and symptoms of infectious endocarditis
   (1) Spiking fever
   (2) Petechiae
   (3) Anorexia
   (4) Fatigue
   (5) Pallor
 i. Prepare family and child for diagnostic procedures
   (1) Chest X-ray
   (2) Electrocardiography
   (3) Laboratory tests
   (4) Cardiac catheterization
   (5) Angiocardiography
 j. Prepare family and child for planned surgical repair
   (1) Determine from physician what type of repair is planned
   (2) Draw picture for family and child
   (3) Tour ICU or CCU facilities
   (4) Explain preoperative procedures
   (5) Prepare for pain and how child will look and feel on recovering from anesthesia
   (6) Explain that regressive behaviors are normal postoperatively, soiling pants, return to bottle, for example

B. Congenital dislocation of hip
 1. Cause-pathophysiology
   a. Unknown etiology
   b. Malposition or lack of head of femur in acetabulum
 2. Signs-symptoms
   a. Asymmetry of major gluteal folds
   b. Limited ability to abduct leg on affected side to no more than 45° while on back with knees and hips flexed; audible click may be heard, Ortolani's click
   c. Trendelenburg sign—pelvis drops on normal side if child stands on affected leg
   (d) Affected leg shorter
   (e) Delayed walking
   (f) Child limps and abdomen protrudes
 3. Nursing approaches
   a. Report if any of the preceding signs are noted
   b. Special measures while in hip spica cast
   (1) Circulation checks for cyanosis of toes
   (2) Prevention of cast soiling from urine and feces through use of plastic and

by elevation of upper trunk so excrement will not flow into cast
   (3) Petal cast edges and cover with adhesive tape to protect skin
   (4) Maintain in position with upper body elevated
   (5) Space between cast and abdomen should not be constrictive
 c. Provide diversified environment through use of visual and auditory stimulation; no wet toys or toys small enough to fall into cast
 d. Teach parents care of cast and offer suggestions for activities, such as use of wagon to move child

C. Cleft lip
 1. Cause-pathophysiology
   a. Hereditary factor involved
   b. Failure of the embryonic development when fusion of the first brachial arch does not occur
 2. Signs and symptoms
   a. Obvious appearance of incompletely formed lip
   b. May be bilateral or unilateral, involve only lip, or extend to nostril(s) or upper gum
   c. Treatment involves lip surgery, either immediately or within two to three months, or when child weighs 10 lb
 3. Nursing approaches
   a. Preoperatively
   (1) Show acceptance of infant by maintaining composure and not showing shock or disgust when handling
   (2) Anticipate parental grief for perfect infant they did not have
   (3) Feeding
      (a) May feed well with a regular nipple with enlarged holes
      (b) Bubble frequently as infant swallows much air
      (c) Feed in upright position to decrease possibility of aspiration
   (4) Prepare parents for surgery, which may occur several hours after birth rather than later
   b. Postoperatively
   (1) Prevent injury to suture line of lip
      (a) Use elbow restraints
      (b) Logan bow—wire placed cheek to cheek across top of suture

line to prevent lateral tension
   (c) Place infant on side or back, *never* on stomach
   (2) Prevent child from crying, this increases tension
   (3) Maintain nutritional needs with rubber tip dropper or syringe for about three weeks
   (4) Cleanse suture line frequently with wet cotton tip applicator; prevent crusting
   (5) Gently dry mouth by patting
   (6) Observe for respiratory distress—edema of tongue, nostrils, and mouth
   (7) Give water after feeding to rid mouth of milk—decreases bacteria growth and infection
   (8) Teach parents proper care and feeding

D. Cleft palate
   1. Cause-pathophysiology
      a. Hereditary factor involved
      b. Failure of embryonic development when fusion of the first brachial arch does not occur
   2. Signs-symptoms
      a. Opening in roof of mouth
      b. Usually associated with cleft lip
      c. May involve soft palate or soft and hard palate
      d. Sucking difficulties
   3. Nursing approaches
      a. Preoperatively
         (1) Support parents when they see child for the first time; show acceptance of child
         (2) Treatment is done in stages, repair may be begun between 18 and 36 months
         (3) Feeding techniques and equipment
            (a) Hold infant in upright position to decrease chance of aspiration
            (b) Do not allow infant to suck, as this will not be allowed postoperatively
            (c) Equipment—Lamb's nipple, Brecht feeder, and Duckey nipple prior to repair in infant; toddler should drink from cup
         (4) Prevent infection by keeping child away from others with any

infections and by keeping cleft clean
         (5) Teach parents what to expect postoperatively
      b. Postoperatively
         (1) Observe for airway obstruction, shock, and hemorrhage
         (2) Prevent injury to suture line by use of elbow restraints
         (3) Irrigate child's mouth with ear syringe frequently and following meals; child should be sitting and leaning forward
         (4) Do not allow child to suck—feed with rubber tip syringe postoperatively and progress to cup
         (5) Administer antibiotics, as prescribed
         (6) Provide diversion and play activities to maintain normal growth and development
         (7) Be sure parents are aware that follow-up care and repair will be on a *long-term basis*, usually involving plastic surgeon, orthodontist, speech therapist, and possibly others
         (8) Child should be placed on side and back until sutures are removed
         (9) Otitis media is a common complication—any signs of an earache, such as crying and pulling on ear, should be reported immediately

E. Gastrointestinal disorders
   1. Tracheo-esophageal atresia—an abnormal connection between esophagus and trachea; the cause for the failure of this embryonic closure is unknown
      a. Treatment
         (1) Primary repair—surgical esophageal anastomosis and fistula division
         (2) Palliative surgery—gastrostomy and cervical esophagostomy until infant gains weight; usually choice for premature infants
      b. Signs-symptoms
         (1) Excessive amount of secretions exhibited by continual drooling from mouth and nose
         (2) Intermittent cyanosis relieved by suctioning
         (3) Abdominal distention
         (4) Coughing, choking, cyanosis, and return of liquid through nose when

feeding attempted
C. Nursing approaches
  (1) Preoperatively
    (a) Maintain body position in semi-to high-Fowler's to prevent aspiration of gastric juices
    (b) Suction secretions frequently to prevent accumulation in blind pouch
    (c) Administer parenteral feedings to maintain hydration and electrolyte balance
  (2) Postoperatively
    (a) Maintain patent airway to prevent oxygen starvation, apnea, and aspiration of secretions
    (b) Mark suction catheter so it can be inserted to desired depth for suctioning
    (c) Assist in progression of feedings
      i. Parenteral feedings first week
      ii. Oral feeding 7 to 14 days postoperatively; feed slowly, watch for vomiting and difficulty in swallowing, which may indicate stricture of anastomosis site
    (d) Give emotional and physical support to infant and family
      i. Hold infant upright to feed
      ii. Assist mother in feeding her infant
2. Imperforate anus—failure of embryonic development resulting in an intact anal membrane or internal blind pouch of lower bowel
  a. Treatment choices
    (1) Anoplasty
    (2) Abdomino perineal pull-through
    (3) Colostomy with abdominoperineal pull-through when child is older
  b. Signs-symptoms
    (1) No anal opening and inability to insert thermometer or small probe
    (2) Absence of meconium stool
    (3) Gradual increase of abdominal distention
  c. Nursing approaches
    (1) Report any of the preceding signs immediately
    (2) Observe infant for stool-tinged urine

or feces coming from a fistula
    (3) Pass nasogastric tube to prevent abdominal distention
    (4) Explain defect and planned surgical technique to parents
    (5) Postoperatively
      (a) Position child so perineum is exposed for cleaning with minimal irritation, on abdomen or on back with legs suspended at 90° angle to trunk, for example
      (b) Observe for abdominal distention, bleeding from perineum, and respiratory difficulties
      (c) Oral feedings should begin when peristalsis returns
      (d) Perform anal dilatation to prevent stricture at site of anastomosis
3. Pyloric stenosis—congenital hypertrophy of the muscle of the pylorus; the constriction of the lumen of the pyloric canal causes the stomach to become dilated resulting in delayed gastric emptying, which causes vomiting after feeding
  a. Treatment
    (1) Medical treatment—refeeding, use of thickened formula, gastric lavage, and medication to relax pyloric muscle spasm
    (2) Surgical—Fredet-Ramstedt; longitudinal incision in pyloric muscle permitting it to gape
  b. Signs and symptoms
    (1) Nonprojectile progressing to projectile vomiting
    (2) Non-bile-stained vomitus—narrowing located above common bile duct
    (3) Constipation
    (4) Visible left to right peristaltic waves during or after eating
    (5) Excessive hunger
    (6) Dehydration leading to alkalosis
    (7) Weight loss
    (8) Decreased uninary output and number of stools
    (9) Palpable olive-shaped mass in upper right quadrant
C. Nursing approaches
  (1) Preoperatively

(a) Administer IV fluids to restore hydration and electrolyte balance

(b) Record output accurately, including specific gravity of urine

(c) Preventative measures to decrease vomiting, that is, NPO or use of thickened formula

(d) Prepare parents for surgery by explaining procedure and use of gastric tube

(2) Postoperatively

(a) Assist in resuming oral feedings—two to eight hours postoperatively, begin with glucose water and progress from half-strength to regular formula

(b) Elevate head and shoulders after feeding and position on right side to aid in gastric emptying

(c) Encourage parents to care for and feed infant

4. Chalasia—abnormal continual relaxation of lower end of esophagus, cardiac sphincter, causing vomiting; self-limiting; treatment consists of measures to decrease vomiting

a. Signs-symptoms

(1) Regurgitation immediately after feeding

(2) Weight loss

(3) Dehydration

b. Nursing approaches

(1) Administer IV fluids to restore hydration and electrolyte balance

(2) Measures to decrease vomiting

(a) Thickening formula

(b) Place infant upright after feeding

(c) Minimal handling during feeding

(3) Teach parents to play with infant *before* feeding

(4) Explain that problem is self-limiting—usually disappears by 3 months

5. Hirshsprung's disease—the congenital absence or decreased number of ganglion cells in muscle wall of intestinal tract, usually at distal end; no peristalsis in this area; a familial pattern is demonstrated

a. Signs-symptoms

(1) Early infancy

(a) No meconium

(b) Vomiting

(c) Constipation with overflow diarrhea

(d) Anorexia

(2) Later childhood

(a) Progressive distention of abdomen

(b) Peristalsis observable

(c) Constipation with malodorous ribbonlike stool

(d) Failure to grow

b. Treatment

(1) Relieve fecal impaction with enema and digital removal

(2) Medical management—stool softeners and low-residue diet

(3) Surgical intervention by removal of aganglionic area and anastomosis of two ends of colon; sometimes a temporary colostomy is performed with anastomosis performed later

C. Nursing approaches

(1) Preoperatively

(a) Utilize proper measures to empty bowel—enema, digital removal, and liquid diet

(b) Take axillary temperature

(c) Note any abdominal distention

(2) Postoperatively

(a) Observe for any complications—respiratory difficulties, abdominal distention, and hemorrhage

(b) Prevent infections of operative site by careful cleansing

(c) If colostomy is present, keep clean to prevent skin breakdown

(d) Have nasogastric tube available to prevent abdominal distention

(e) Continue axillary temperatures to avoid injury

(f) Observe stools for return to normal pattern

(g) Provide emotional support to child and parents by encouraging them to talk about fears and anxieties and answering their questions

6. Intussusception—the telescoping of a portion of intestine into adjacent distal section; possibly due to increased mobility of intestine and rapid peristalsis; it can lead to gangrene of the bowel

a. Signs-symptoms

(1) Sudden onset in latter half of first year of life
(2) Severe abdominal pain and distention
(3) Currant-jelly-like stools
(4) Vomiting
(5) Absence of stools
(6) Dehydration and fever
b. Treatment
   (1) May reduce spontaneously or be reduced by exerting slight retrograde pressure to barium instilled to confirm diagnosis
   (2) May require emergency surgical intervention to reduce or, if gangrene has set in, to resect portion of colon
c. Nursing approaches
   (1) Maintain IV to restore hydration and electrolyte balance
   (2) Insert nasogastric tube to prevent abdominal distention and vomiting
   (3) Take axillary temperatures to avoid injury and stimulation
   (4) Offer support to family and child to allay fears and anxieties
   (5) Postoperatively—observe for signs of shock and hemorrhage
7. Diarrhea—as a disease entity, diarrhea is an excessive loss of water and electrolytes through repeated passing of unformed stools; it is indicative of some type of condition or disease; it may indicate an infectious process (bacterial or viral infection), non-infectious process (allergic response or metabolic disorder), or a mechanical or congenital disorder (intussusception or Hirschsprung's disease).
a. Signs-symptoms
   (1) Diarrhea of gradual or sudden onset
   (2) Anorexia
   (3) Low-grade fever (below 105 F)
   (4) Rapid respirations
   (5) Dehydration
   (6) Irritability, restlessness, stupor, and/or convulsions
   (7) Signs of metabolic acidosis
b. Treatment goals (see Table 5-5)
   (1) Restore electrolyte balance and hydration
   (2) Laboratory studies to diagnose cause

(a) Serum studies
(b) Urinalysis
(c) Stool cultures
(3) Isolation of infant to protect infant and others from possible pathogens
c. Nursing approaches
   (1) Monitor IV amount and rate to avoid circulatory overload and to restore electrolyte balance and hydration
   (2) Weigh infant daily to determine fluid needs
   (3) Keep child NPO; offer pacifier for sucking needs and observe for abdominal distention (bubbling infant or passage of nasogastric tube may be necessary)
   (4) Talk to and hold child during diagnostic procedures to reassure child
   (5) Explain procedures and treatment to parents
   (6) Skin care to lessen excoriation caused by alkaline stool
F. Neurologic disorders
1. Meningomyelocele—a congenital condition in which both spinal cord and cord membranes protrude through defect in spinal canal; it occurs during the fourth to sixth week of embryonic development, but exact cause is unknown
a. Signs-symptoms
   (1) Round bulging sac on infant's back
   (2) No response to sensation below level of sac
   (3) Constant dripping of urine
   (4) Incontinence or retention of stool
   (5) Spontaneous movements below defect are absent or minimal
   (6) May develop hydrocephalus
b. Treatment
   (1) Surgical correction
      (a) Closure of sac to prevent infection and rupture
      (b) Laminectomy to prevent deterioration of neural functioning
   (2) Orthopedic measures to prevent deformities and ulcerations of lower extremities
      (a) Support ankles with foam or roll to keep toes off bed when infant

Table 5-5. Metabolic and respiratory acidosis-alkalosis

	Metabolic	*Respiratory*
Alkalosis		
Definition	Deficit of acid (H$^+$, hydrogen ions) and excess of base (HCO$_3$, bicarbonate)	Deficit of acid (H$_2$CO$_3$, carbonic acid)
Causes	Vomiting, lavage, and diuretics	Hyperventilation
Signs and symptoms	Nausea, vomiting, diarrhea, tremors, convulsion, and altered degree of alertness	Tachypnea, numbness, tingling of hands and face, and altered degree of alertness
Treatment	Replace fluid loss, especially potassium and chloride	Sedation and have patient hold breath
Nursing approaches	Record intake and output, take seizure precautions, and administer prescribed medications	Give prescribed medications, have child breathe into paper bag, and stay with child to make child feel secure
Acidosis		
Definition	Excess of acid (H$^+$, hydrogen ions) and deficit of base (HCO$_3$, bicarbonate)	Excess of acid (H$_2$CO$_3$, carbonic acid) and elevated P$_{CO_2}$
Causes	Diabetes, renal failure, and diarrhea	Hypoventilation and muscular weakness
Signs and symptoms	Headache, nausea, vomiting, diarrhea, tremors, convulsions, and altered degree of alertness	Decreased respirations, drowsiness, semicomatose, tachycardia, arrhythmia, and altered degree of alertness
Treatment	Treat underlying cause (give glucose, insulin to diabetic); rid body of protein and excess H$^+$ by resins or dialysis; administer oxygen (encourages carbohydrate metabolism); and give bicarbonate IV	Treat cause and take measures to improve ventilation—Intermittent positive pressure breathing (IPPB), antibiotics, postural drainage, suction, endotracheal tube, tracheostomy, and ventilator
Nursing approaches	Administer bicarbonate, take seizure precautions (padded siderails, tongue blade at bedside, and remove toys that could cause injury) and record intake and output; fluid therapy may be forced or restricted	Improve ventilation—semi-Fowler's position, low-flow oxygen, chest physiotherapy (postural drainage), change postions frequently, and encourage coughing

is placed on abdomen; place foam between knees when infant is placed on side
- (b) Casting of clubbed feet—so child can learn to walk with braces when older
- c. Nursing approaches
  - (1) Preoperatively
    - (a) Prevent leakage or rupture of sac by positioning infant on side or abdomen
    - (b) Prevent infection of sac by avoiding contamination
    - (c) Prevent urinary infection by using
      - i. Credé's method to expel urine (apply gentle rolling pressures with hand,

beginning at umbilicus and continue downward under symphysis pubis)
- ii. High vitamin C diet
- iii. Force fluids
- (d) Provide normal handling and sensory stimulation—hold while feeding, hang a mobile over crib, or place a music box near crib, for example
- (e) May use a Bradford frame to ensure good body positions, facilitate gravity flow of urine and feces without contamination, and avoid injury to sac (bedpan is placed in center opening of frame and child can be positioned so sac is in opening

of frame, thus alleviating any pressure)

  (2) Postoperatively

    (a) Prevent postoperative complications

      i. Infection—keep surgical site clean

      ii. Pneumonia—keep airway clear, suction infant, and change position often

    (a) Observe for signs-symptoms of increased intracranial pressure

    (b) Contribute to interdisciplinary approach for planning of infant's future, which will include physical therapy, neurology, orthopedics, and urology

    (c) Provide support for family by referrals to other disciplines and assistance in accepting long-term care of child

2. Hydrocephalus—the inability to absorb cerebrospinal fluid, causing an increase of fluid under pressure, or an obstruction between source of cerebrospinal fluid and area of reabsorption; it may be a sequela to developmental defects, inflammatory reactions (such as meningitis), neoplasm, and hemorrhage (following trauma)

  a. Signs-symptoms

    (1) Rate of increase of more than 1 inch/month in head size

    (2) Tense, bulging, widened fontanel

    (3) Signs-symptoms of increased intracranial pressure (ICP)

    (4) Eventual development of "sunset" eyes and shiny scalp, with noticeable scalp veins

    (5) Developmental lag and failure to thrive

    (6) High-pitched cry in infants

    (7) Hyperactive reflexes

  b. Treatment—involves surgical procedure to insert a tube (shunt) that carries fluid from brain to the bloodstream or some body cavity such as inferior vena cava, peritoneal cavity, or ureter

  c. Nursing approaches

    (1) Preoperatively

      (a) Measure head circumference each day and record

      (b) Provide adequate nutrition by planning of meal times and rest periods as child is anorexic and lethargic, feed after treatment and bath, for example

      (c) Perform range of motion (ROM) exercises to prevent development of contractures

      (d) Prevent skin breakdown of head by frequent turning of infant, as infant may be unable to turn self

    (2) Postoperatively

      (a) Observe infant for respiratory difficulties, increased ICP, sodium imbalance, abdominal distention, and dehydration

      (b) Observe shunt site for obstruction and early signs of infection

        i. Redness

        ii. Swelling

        iii. Tender to touch

        iv. Elevated temperature

        v. Exudate at suture site

3. Cerebral palsy—a nonprogressive disorder of the motor centers and pathways of the brain, causing difficulty in control of voluntary muscles; it is caused by prenatal, natal, and postnatal factors such as maternal anoxia and infections, anoxia or cerebral trauma at birth, and infections or trauma after birth

  a. Signs-symptoms

    (1) Spastic type—fixed postures due to loss of smooth movement of voluntary muscles; scissoring (legs crossed and toes pointed) due to increased deep tendon reflexes; attempts to move a joint causes muscles to contract

    (2) Athetosis—involuntary, uncoordinated, uncontrollable movements of muscle groups due to lesions of basal ganglia

    (3) Dystonia—rigid attitudes; posturing; slow moving; muscles remain semi-contracted and resist movement

    (4) Ataxia—Loss of balance due to cerebellar involvement; visual disturbance

    (5) Early signs

      (a) Asymmetry in motion

      (b) Twitching

(c) Stiffness
(d) Difficulty with sucking and swallowing
(e) Deviation from normal growth and development—no weight gain and persistence or lack of normal reflexes
(f) Delayed or defective speech (often diagnosed as mentally retarded)
(g) Convulsions
(h) Hyperactive gag reflex

b. Nursing approaches
(1) Anticipate possible respiratory problems by having suction machine available
(2) Diet
(a) High-calorie diet as child is likely to eat less than usual for age because of difficulty eating and for increased energy requirements due to motion
(b) Foods that can be easily chewed and swallowed
(c) Relaxed mealtime with little emphasis placed on cleanliness and perfect manners
(3) Provide measures to ensure periods of relaxation, such as quiet activities (reading or listening to music) and organize nursing care to minimize interruptions
(4) Prevent contractures through use of physical therapy, splints, braces, and active motions when playing
(5) Assist child to develop maximum potential by being alert to visual disturbances and hearing and speech problems; often child is of normal intelligence
(6) Help child to play—use puppets, tell stories, or any activities to develop eye-hand coordination
(7) Explain the necessity of long-term care planning with the parents—involves physical therapy, occupational therapy, physicians, speech therapy, and other professionals as needed

G. Mental retardation—term applied to persons with *impaired intelligence* and inadequate development in childhood that affects the ability of the child to adapt to environment (see Appendix B for levels of retardation as developed by the American Association on Mental Deficiency)

1. Causes and frequency (1% of general population)
   a. Before birth (50% to 60% of the 1% total)
      (1) Genetic (Down's syndrome)
      (2) Toxic conditions (Rh or ABO incompatibility)
      (3) Endocrine imbalance (PKU; galactosemia, hypothyroidism, cretinism—early treatment needed to prevent retardation)
      (4) Trauma
      (5) Nutritional
      (6) Anoxemia
      (7) Infections (German measles in first trimester of pregnancy or syphilis)
   b. At birth (8% of 1% total)
      (1) Hemorrhage
      (2) Prolonged and difficult birth
      (3) Forceps delivery (trauma)
      (4) Anoxemia
   c. Following birth (32% to 42% of 1% total)
      (1) Encephalitis or meningitis
      (2) Toxemia
      (3) Malnutrition
      (4) Vitamin deficiency
      (5) Lead poisoning
2. Signs-symptoms
   a. Neuromuscular development does not progress consistently
      (1) Infant does not suck; toddler does not learn to feed self
      (2) Slow to sit, stand, and walk
   b. Unable to learn or profit from experience
   c. May have other sensory defects
      (1) Language disorders
      (2) Speech and language disorders
      (3) Visual and/or hearing defects
   d. Unable to respond in accepted manner in social situations (culturally determined)
   e. Labile emotional reactions—often placid
3. Nursing approaches
   a. If child is hospitalized, obtain a nursing history of child's routine at home so a care plan can be developed to help child feel secure and to minimize regression

(1) Feeding habits—how, when, and what to feed infant
(2) Sleeping—times and any "security" toy
(3) Toilet habits—words used
(4) Play—what activities are usual
b. Plan nursing interventions on child's *developmental level*, not chronologic age
c. Use of three Rs in helping child learn new activities
  (1) Relaxation—provide calm, nonthreatening environment for activity to be learned
  (2) Repetition—the retarded child learns by demonstration and repeated attempts at an activity or behavior
  (3) Reinforcement—positive reinforcement is needed as a reward for behaviors or tasks accomplished or desired
d. Explain to parents necessity of teaching child acceptable standards of behavior
  (1) Establish daily routine so child will know what is expected
  (2) In discipline, use language child can understand to explain misdeed
  (3) If punishment is necessary, it should *immediately* follow the misdeed as child cannot recall past misdeed
  (4) Give child responsibilities that can be mastered (dependent on level of retardation)
e. General goals in management—stimulation needs, motor control, sensory training, sociability, safety, self-care, and independence to maximum developmental not chronologic ability
f. See Behavior modification in Unit 1
H. Down's syndrome—an abnormality resulting from an extra chromosome causing mental retardation; the extra chromosome may be evident as three number 21 chromosomes (trisomy 21) for a total of 47 chromosomes, or the parent may have an abnormal attachment of chromosome 21 to number 15, thus transmitting an extra chromosome 21 plus a normal chromosome 21 (resulting in 46 chromosomes); the latter is therefore inherited but the former is not; chromosomal analysis shows which type of chromosome 21 attachment is present
1. Signs-symptoms

a. Normal fetal growth is affected causing complications
  (1) Congenital heart defects (atrial septal defect is most common)
  (2) Intestinal obstruction
b. Physical findings
  (1) Hypotonia
  (2) Hyperextension of extremity joints
  (3) Inner epicanthic folds of eyes (oriental appearance)
  (4) Flat nasal bridge
  (5) Excess skin on back of neck
  (6) Small low-set ears
  (7) Simian crease—line on hand that goes across palm horizontally
  (8) Shortened fourth finger and flat square hands
  (9) Plantar furrow—line runs vertically down sole of foot
  (10) Brachycephaly with flat occiput
  (11) Mouth open, with thick protruding tongue
2. Nursing approaches
a. Provide nipple that allows minimal sucking effort because of protruding tongue and difficulty swallowing
b. Be aware of abdominal distention as sign of intestinal obstruction
c. Note apical pulse, cyanosis, and respiratory distress as signs of cardiac defects
d. Assist parents to express fears, concerns, disappointments concerning their child by listening and answering questions
e. Utilize previous discussion of mental retardation for further nursing approaches
I. Metabolic disturbances
1. Hypothyroidism (cretinism)—a congenital or acquired endocrine disease; deficient production of thyroid hormone; it is noted at 2 to 3 months of age
a. Signs-symptoms
  (1) Jaundice
  (2) Nasal stuffiness and obstructions
  (3) Episodes of apnea
  (4) Hoarse cry
  (5) Constipation
  (6) Subnormal temperature
  (7) Poor muscle tone and short, stubby extremities

(8) Thick, coarse, dry hair
(9) Thick protruding tongue causing Feeding difficulties, that is, difficulty swallowing and infant takes a long time to eat
(10) Slow motor and mental development and disinterest in · environment
(11) Umbilical hernia

b. Treatment
(1) Oral administration of desiccated thyroid as replacement for deficient thyroid hormone
(2) Untreated child becomes a mentally deficient dwarf; treatment results in normal growth and development if treatment is instituted early, although child may still be slightly retarded

c. Nursing approaches
(1) Administer thyroid as ordered and observe for toxic effects
(a) Tachycardia
(b) Cramps
(c) Diarrhea and vomiting
(d) Elevated temperature
(e) Excitability, hyperactivity
(2) Provide well-balanced diet with special attention to intake of iron, vitamin D, and roughage (see Appendix C)

2. Cystic fibrosis—believed to be hereditary as recessive trait, more often occurring in white males; the secretions of exocrine glands are viscous and tenacious, affecting mainly pulmonary, gastrointestinal, and sweat gland functioning; thick mucus plugs the bronchi and bronchioles cause overinflation of lungs and atelectasis, leading to infections and fibrotic changes in the lungs; thick mucus also plugs the pancreatic ducts, preventing pancreatic enzymes from entering the small intestines and causing impairment of digestion, of fats, in particular

a. Diagnostic test
(1) Sweat test
(2) Stool test for trypsin

b. Signs-symptoms
(1) Infant's skin tastes salty when kissed because secretions contain excessive amount of salt
(2) Coughing and wheezing

(3) Failure to gain weight despite voracious appetite caused by impaired digestion
(4) Stools bulky and foul smelling due to lack of digestive enzymes in small intestine
(5) Protruding abdomen and thin extremities
(6) Recurrent pulmonary infection

c. Treatment
(1) Administration of pancreatic enzymes with meals, pancreatin (Viokase) or pancrelipase capsules (Cotazym), for example
(2) Broad spectrum antibiotics for prophylaxis
(3) Expectorants to thin bronchial mucus secretions
(4) Bronchodilators to increase width of bronchial tubes to allow greater passage of air into lungs

d. Nursing approaches
(1) Administer pancreatic enzymes immediately prior to or with feedings to replace absent pancreatic enzymes—amount of enzyme given is determined by amount of fat in diet
(2) Diet
(a) High-calorie, high-protein, and low-fat diet as absorption of food is incomplete
(b) Water-soluble vitamins (fat absorption is deficit)
(c) Increased salt intake during hot weather to prevent salt depletion because of sweat gland problems
(3) Assist in IPPB therapy and postural drainage to aid in clearing secretions from respiratory tract
(4) Teach breathing exercises to assist in prevention of lung disease and to increase capacity
(5) Assist in parental teaching
(a) Genetic counseling (1 out of 4 children have chance of inheriting disease)
(b) Care and use of IPPB equipment
(c) Coping with insecure, frightened child

3. Celiac disease—an inborn error of metabolism of wheat and rye products, characterized

by chronic intestinal malabsorption causing malnutrition; commonly diagnosed at 6 months of age

a. Signs-symptoms

   (1) Progressive malnutrition symptoms; similar to cystic fibrosis

   (2) Foul, bulky, greasy stools because of malabsorption of food

   (3) Anorexia

   (4) Chronic diarrhea

   (5) Celiac crises, which is an emergency life-threatening complication

     (a) Causes—upper respiratory infection, vomiting, and large watery stools

     (b) Signs-symptoms—drowsy, restless, increased sweating, and extremely cold

b. Treatment is by dietary means

   (1) No wheat and rye products or foodstuffs

   (2) Add foods slowly and one at a time to observe effect

   (3) High-protein, low-fat, and starch-free foods

c. Nursing approaches

   (1) Follow prescribed diet calculations, as suggested in treatment section, precisely and record accurately any reaction to diet

   (2) Use preventive measure to avoid infections

     (a) Avoid exposure

     (b) Keep child warm and dry

   (3) Note any changes in behavior and intervene appropriately

     (a) Whining or crying

     (b) Irritability or restlessness

   (4) Involve parents in care and teach diet and signs-symptoms of celiac crises

4. PKU (phenylketonuria)—a recessively transmitted inborn error of metabolism of phenylalanine caused by lack of an enzyme (phenylalanine hydroxylase); phenylalanine is one of the amino acids in protein; the substance collects in the blood of affected infants after one or two days of milk feedings

a. Signs-symptoms

   (1) High level of blood phenylalanine levels (is correlated later with level of mental retardation)

   (2) Urine contains products of unmetabolized phenylalanine substance verified by a Phenistex test (impregnated paper)

   (3) Signs of mental retardation by age 2 years

   (4) Child is usually blond and blue-eyed because of interference with normal development of pigment

   (5) Eczema

   (6) Convulsions

b. Treatment

   (1) Diet—free of lactose (low-protein and no milk), not very palatable and quite expensive

   (2) Irreparable damage occurs if child is not treated by *6 months* of age; diet therapy useless after *2 years* of age

c. Nursing approaches

   (1) Explain genetic inheritance to parents (1 out of 4) (see Cystic fibrosis)

   (2) Be certain blood and urine test are done on infants

   (3) Refer to dietitian and assist in selection of diet

3. Respiratory conditions

A. Croup

1. Cause-pathophysiology

  a. Epiglottiditis—inflammatory disease of the epiglottis; life-threatening

  b. Laryngotracheitis—inflammatory disease of vocal cords and trachea

2. Signs-symptoms

  a. Epiglottiditis

   (1) Mucous membranes of glottis and epiglottis appear red and swollen

   (2) Airway partially or totally obstructed by inflammation and edema

   (3) Severe inspiratory stridor

   (4) Hoarseness

   (5) Elevated temperature (104 F)

   (6) Cyanosis

  b. Laryngotracheitis

   (1) Early characteristic symptom—inspiratory stridor

   (2) Slightly elevated temperature (below 102 F)

   (3) Cyanosis

   (4) Child restless and frightened

B. Bronchiolitis—an infection of bronchioles and

involves a generalized inflammation of respiratory mucosa, with tenacious exudate in bronchiol lumens

1. Cause-pathophysiology
   a. Infection or virus
   b. Occurs under age 1 year with peak age of 6 months, and mostly in winter and early spring
   c. Air enters alveoli during inspiration; orifice closes, trapping air during expiration, causing atelectasis and expiratory wheezing
2. Signs-symptoms
   a. Expiratory wheezing and sternal retractions
   b. Nonproductive cough
   c. Dyspnea
   d. Cyanosis
   e. Lethargy with fever and restlessness due to oxygen hunger

C. Bronchopneumonia
1. Cause-pathophysiology
   a. Caused by bacteria or virus
   b. Inflammation of the bronchi with exudate formation
2. Signs-symptoms
   a. Anorexia
   b. Vomiting and diarrhea
   c. Cyanosis
   d. Increased pulse and respirations with retractions
   e. Progressive respiratory distress (dyspnea)
   f. Sudden high fever and productive cough
3. Nursing approaches for respiratory conditions
   a. Note respiratory rate and pattern
   b. Note and record presence of cyanosis
   c. Place child in croupette—to provide cool humidified environment with oxygen to alleviate anoxia and liquify secretions
   d. Maintain adequate hydration via IV if in respiratory distress or small sips of *clear liquid* if in no acute distress (use cup or straw)
   e. Record amount and specific gravity of urine to determine hydration
   f. Keep emergency equipment available for intubation and tracheostomy
   g. Reposition frequently and provide postural drainage as necessary—head down, on side

h. Allow child to conserve energy with rest and by adjusting environment
i. Keep constant vigilance on child and promote feelings of security—talk to child and give child comforting toy as appropriate
j. If croup (laryngotracheitis) occurs at home, instruct parent to take child in bathroom, turn on hot-water faucets, and close door to provide wet steamy environment to relieve edema
k. Play in croupette—avoid fatigue, no sharp toys

4. Skin conditions
A. Infantile eczema
1. Cause-pathophysiology
   a. Usually a common early sign of allergy (onset—2 to 6 months of age)
   b. Inflammatory dermatosis
2. Signs-symptoms
   a. Erythematous, papular, weeping lesions involving epidermis
   b. Oozing and crusting of lesions
   c. Pruritus
3. Nursing approaches
   a. Utilize measures to keep child from scratching lesions—prevent irritation and further infection
      (1) Protective devices—elbow or jacket restraints and cotton mitts
      (2) Trimmed nails
      (3) Soft toys
      (4) Medication, as prescribed
      (5) Avoid woolen clothing or blankets
   b. Bathe using prescribed method—*do not use soap* because of allergic response.
   c. Use soaks, paste, and coal tar, as prescribed
   d. Help child adhere to dietary regimen, which is usually an elimination diet (all foods stopped, one new food every two or three days; observe for reaction—hives, further eczema, or itching, for example)
   e. Protect child from sources of infection; place child in protective isolation
   f. Play activities—reading stories or using puppets
   g. Avoid immunizations of live vaccines to child or siblings because of likelihood of overwhelming reaction

B. Oral thrush

1. Cause-pathophysiology
   a. Caused by *Candida Albicans*
   b. Fungus infection of mouth or throat
   c. Often contracted during birth via infected vagina
2. Signs-symptoms
   a. Small white patches on tongue, gums, or oral mucous membranes
   b. Dry mouth
   c. Fever may be present
   d. No pain noted
   e. Most important differentiation—patches rinse away if they are milk particles but will bleed when scraped if fungus
3. Nursing approaches
   a. Look for signs-symptoms in high-risk patients
      (1) Infants who are ill
      (2) Infants receiving antibiotics
      (3) Infants with cleft lip and palate
   b. Prevent spread of disease
      (1) Careful handwashing
      (2) Proper cleansing of nipples
      (3) Apply medication, as ordered
      (4) Prevent infant from putting fingers or toys in mouth

5. Battered child syndrome—the nonaccidental abuse of child, usually by person caring for child

A. Causes
   1. May be result of disciplinary action
   2. Child may not fulfill need of caretaker
   3. Abuser may be under much stress and use child to vent feeling of frustration
   4. Abusive parents—any socioeconomic group; they have often been abused themselves as children; loners, no affiliations with groups; immature emotional responses
B. Signs-symptoms
   1. Incidence
      a. History is incompatible with extent of injury
      b. Victim—child is most likely under 3 years of age, possibly under 6 months
   2. How diagnosed
      a. General characteristics of physical neglect
      b. History of previous emergency-room visits, usually at more than one hospital
      c. Type of lesions
         (1) Welts
         (2) Bruises (coat-hanger marks)
         (3) Wringer fractures caused by twisting or "wringing" extremity
         (4) Burns, especially with characteristic quality, such as those caused by cigarettes
      d. Fractures in different stages of healing (X-ray examination)
      e. Child appears withdrawn; monotonous crying; no or little emotional response
      f. Personality of child becomes happier and no new lesions are present upon hospitalization
C. Nursing approaches
   1. Report any suspicion of abuse to physician
   2. Take a thorough history from person bringing child to hospital
   3. Avoid direct confrontation or accusation of caretaker
   4. Inspect child carefully upon admission and note any lesions (as listed previously, usually bruises) and state of healing
   5. Observe and record caretaker-child relationship—eye contact, comforting measures, manner of talking (gentle or gruff), and body contact, for example
   6. Assign one nurse per shift to care for child in hospital to establish relationship of trust
   7. Foster relationship with caretaker so guidance and help may be provided
   8. Teach caretaker principles of normal growth and development; many caretakers attribute attitudes, thoughts, and behaviors to child of which the child is incapable of developmentally
   9. Refer caretakers for help as appropriate—Parents Anonymous or public health nurse

6. Sudden infant death syndrome (SIDS)

A. Cause-pathophysiology
   1. Exact cause unknown—most common cause of death in first year of life (excluding first week); 1 out of 300
   2. Various theories include suffocation caused by large thymus, cardiac arrhythmia resulting from inappropriate diving reflex (apneic spells), or abnormal respiratory center, which does not respond appropriately
B. Signs-symptoms
   1. An apparently normal infant is found dead in crib
   2. Usually between 2 and 3 months of age, but within first year: rare before 3 weeks or after 8 months

3. Often have history of low-birth weight and often from lower socioeconomic group
4. Most often occurs in late fall or winter

C. Nursing approaches
1. Be aware of nature of SIDS
2. Anticipate parental feelings of guilt and provide factual information to parents
3. SIDS is not thought to be genetically determined, so family counseling may be done with this information
4. Consider referral to community nurse or parent's group

7. Hernia

A. Inguinal
1. Protrusion of abdominal structures into inguinal or scrotal area
2. More common in boys; noticeable 3 to 4 months of age when increased activity causes protrusion on crying or straining
3. Danger—strangulation when protrusion does not retract into abdominal cavity
4. Treatment
   a. Direct pressure and ice pack
   b. Surgical intervention
5. Explain procedure to parents and teach them how to keep dressing clean until wound heals

B. Umbilical or navel
1. Imperfect closure or weakness of umbilical ring
2. Appears at 6 months of age and disappears spontaneously by 5 years of age
3. If large hernia or strangulation occurs, surgical intervention may be indicated
4. Parents should be instructed that taping and use of binder or coin is not necessary and may cause infection or irritation of skin

Part B Preschooler— Age 3 to 5 Years

NORMAL GROWTH AND DEVELOPMENT OF THE PRESCHOOLER

1. The 3 year old

A. Physical development (3 years)
1. Height—grows 5 to 7 cm (2 to 2½ inches) per year; 91 cm (36 inches)
2. Weight—gains less than 2 kg (5 lb); 15 kg (32 lb)
3. Vision—gross testing is 20/30

B. Behavior patterns (3 years)
1. Motor development
   a. Dresses self with supervision
   b. Climbs and jumps well
   c. Can button
   d. Imitates a three-block bridge
   e. Pours fluid from a pitcher
   f. Tries to draw a picture
   g. Can hit large pegs in a pegboard with a hammer
   h. Copies a circle or cross
   i. Can go to toilet
   j. Helps dry dishes and dusts
2. Socialization and vocalization
   a. Can tolerate short separation without undue anxiety
   b. Exaggerates, boasts, and tattles on others
   c. Talks with imaginary companion
   d. Uses language fluently and confidently
   e. Knows first and last name
   f. Can identify longer of two lines
   g. Refers to self as I
   h. Can name figures in a picture
   i. Understands simple explanations of cause and effect
   j. Cautious about common dangers

C. Nursing implications (3 years)
1. Appropriate play activities
   a. Peer-group play
   b. Toys and games—record player, nursery rhymes, housekeeping toys, tricycles, cars, wagons, blocks, blackboard and chalk, easel and brushes, clay, fingerpaints, outside toys (sandbox or swing), books, and drum
2. Guidance areas
   a. Give child small errands to do around

house, such as dusting or drying silverware
  b. Expand world with trips to zoo or market or take child out to lunch
  c. Toileting aids—dress child in simple clothing so child can go to the toilet with little trouble; rarely has accident if reminded to go occasionally
  d. May delay bedtime by ritualistic behaviors—set realistic limits and use night light and/or security toy or doll

2. The 4 year old
A. Physical development (4 years)
  1. Weight—16 to 18 kg (34 to 40 lb), average
  2. Height—approximately 102 cm (42 inches)
  3. Vision—gross testing is 20/20
B. Behavior patterns (4 years)
  1. Motor development
     a. Hops two or more times
     b. Walks upstairs without grasping handrail
     c. Walks backwards
     d. Uses scissors to cut out picture
     e. Throws a ball overhand
     f. Copies a square and a triangle
     g. Can brush teeth
     h. Can lace shoes
     i. Dresses and undresses with little assistance
  2. Socialization, vocalization, and mental development
     a. May have imaginary companion
     b. Can go on errands outside of home
     c. Is obedient and reliable
     d. Has a sense of order
     e. Is developing conscience, which influences behavior
     f. Has increased self-confidence
     g. Is cooperative in playing games
     h. Can name three objects in succession
     i. Knows primary colors
     j. May run away from home
     k. Asks many questions
     l. Has vocabulary—1500 words
     m. Knows own age
     n. Has poor space perception
C. Nursing implications (4 years)
  1. Appropriate play activities
     a. Make use of costumes
     b. Jump rope and skip
     c. Group play and cooperative projects
     d. Simple puzzles
  2. Guidance areas

  a. Quiet time after lunch in lieu of afternoon nap
  b. Prepare for kindergarten by exposing child to other children and allowing child to go on errands outside of home
  c. Loves to hear stories made up by parents
  d. Provide opportunities for group play—invite friends over or send child to preschool for half day several days a week
  e. Allow child to select own food at table and serve self; food jags are common but will soon pass if attention is not drawn to the fact, causes no harm

3. The 5 year old
A. Physical development (5 years)
  1. Height—gains more in inches than pounds so appears taller and slimmer, 104 to 114 cm (43 to 45 inches)
  2. Weight—approximately 19 to 21 kg (42 to 44 lb)
  3. Posture—lordosis has disappeared
B. Behavior patterns (5 years)
  1. Motor development
     a. Begins to attempt riding two-wheel bike
     b. Runs and plays games at same time
     c. Can use hammer to hit nail on head
     d. Can wash self without wetting clothes
     e. Can rollerskate
     f. Puts toys away neatly in box
     g. Can fold paper diagonally
     h. Can form some letters correctly
     i. Prints first name and possibly some other words
     j. Draws recognizable man or woman
  2. Socialization, vocalization, and mental development
     a. Likely to do what is expected
     b. Takes some responsibility for actions
     c. Interested in meaning of relatives (uncle and cousin, for example)
     d. Vocabulary of 2100 words
     e. Talks constantly
     f. Repeats syllables of 10 or more in sentence
     g. Can name at least four colors
     h. Can identify penny, nickel, and dime
     i. Knows names of days of week and week as unit of time
     j. Views death as reversible process
C. Nursing implications (5 years)

1. Appropriate play activities
   a. Plays with other children fairly well
   b. Plays house and begins to imitate firefighters and teachers
   c. Bicycle riding
   d. Games involving large muscles
   e. Have child tell you stories
2. Guidance areas
   a. Starts kindergarten
   b. Allow opportunity for self-expression through talking or play activities
   c. Accepts adult supervision and is interested in conforming to rules and regulations
   d. While children of this age are protective of younger children, they are *not* capable of caring for them and should not be given that responsibility

SPECIAL CONCERNS OF THE PRESCHOOLER

1. **Response to illness and hospitalization—3 to 5 years**
A. Indication of discomfort or pain (3 to 5 years)
   1. Crying
   2. Irritable
   3. Elevated temperature
   4. Decreased appetite
   5. Lethargy
   6. Prostration
   7. Holding affected area
   8. Verbalizations, such as "my tummy hurts"
B. Reaction to stage of illness (3 to 5 years)
   1. Initial illness or hospitalization
      a. Expected coping behaviors—rejects everyone except maternal figure, cries loudly, physical aggression, occasionally withdrawn (not wanting to play), and has fantasies about illness and procedures
      b. Negative behaviors stemming from feeling of abandonment—withdrawal from everyone, monotonous moaning, completely passive or excessively aggressive, and regressive
   2. Prolonged hospitalization and convalescence
      a. Expected coping behaviors—some regression to earlier behaviors, that is, bed-wetting and baby talk; demands attention; wants needs met immediately; and may be difficult to handle
      b. Negative behaviors arising from lack of

trust of anyone meaningful to child—complete rejection of parents, behaviors do not return to normal, and superficial relations with everyone
      c. Nursing implications
         (1) child views illness as punishment for some wrong, real or imagined, so nurse must explain illness or hospitalization to child, emphasizing that child is *not* bad
         (2) Involve child in peer-group activity
         (3) Child is insecure in new or different surroundings—meet needs or demands as soon as possible but help child set limits on behavior, for example, "You can go to the playroom after I put on your new dressing."
         (4) Establish rapport and trust by providing continuity of caretakers; if this is done on admission, most positive behaviors will be maximized and negative behaviors avoided
2. **Nutrition and feeding—3 to 5 years**
A. Calorie requirements (3 to 5 years)
   1. Age 3 to 4 years—1400 cal/24 hours
   2. Age 4 to 6 years—1600 cal/24 hours
B. Normal diet (3 to 5 years)
   1. Transition from baby food to regular diet
      a. Keep variety of nutritious finger foods on hand for snacks, such as cheese, fruit, raw vegetables, crackers, pieces of frankfurter (include raw vegetables and fruits to aid muscle development via chewing)
      b. Allow child to be messy as normal part of learning to eat by self
      c. Since calorie intake needs are lower and growth is slowing child will eat less
      d. Food jags are normal
      e. Call child to meal at least 15 minutes before meal is served to allow time for toilet, handwashing, and settling down from active play
      f. Keep mealtimes pleasant and free from discipline and arguments
      g. Avoid using desserts as rewards
   2. Serve small portions to entice the child to eat more; large portions may appear overwhelming
   3. Accept the fact that child has preferences and offer acceptable substitutes

4. Do not force a child to eat, as it usually results in rebellious behavior

3. Immunizations—3 to 5 years (see Appendix G)

A. Age 4 to 6 years—DPT and TOPV

B. Tuberculin test every one to two years

4. Safety measures—3 to 5 years

A. Keep medicines, gasoline, kerosene, paint products, and *matches* locked up

B. Store tools and equipment in a safe place

C. Check play area for attractive hazards, such as old refrigerators, deep holes, construction, trash heaps, and rickety buildings

D. Check on child's activities frequently

E. Teach child safe ways to handle tools and kitchen equipment

F. Teach child danger of water and start swimming instructions

G. Have child learn rules and dangers of traffic

H. Teach child danger of open flames

5. Fears—3 to 5 years

A. Most often between 2 and 6 years of age

B. Child's fear is real to the child—avoid laughing, strict punishment, or leaving child alone to "get over it"

C. Remain with child until acute fright has subsided, then divert child's attention with toy or talking of something pleasant

D. Common fears
   1. Animals
      a. In time, child will see that the animal is harmless
      b. Hold the animal and allow child to touch, but *not* during child's acute fright
   2. Dark
      a. Part of normal separation anxiety— offer favorite toy or blanket as comfort during bedtime
      b. Use night light or leave door open and talk loudly in another room to assure child of another's presence in the house

CONDITIONS AND DISEASE ENTITIES OF THE PRESCHOOLER

1. Sickle cell disease—severe chronic hemolytic anemia

A. Cause-pathophysiology
   1. Genetically determined, inherited as recessive disorder, and more prevalent in Black and Mediterranean races
   2. Red blood cells sickle (shape of crescent) under low oxygen concentration

B. Signs-symptoms
   1. Sporadic and variable severity of symptoms depending on severity of disease
   2. Anorexia
   3. Paleness
   4. Weakness
   5. Pain in abdomen, legs, and arms due to occlusion of small vessels by sickled red cells
   6. Swelling of joints
   7. Jaundice caused by increased red blood cell destruction
   8. Thrombocytic crisis
      a. Distal ischemia resulting from occluded small vessels
      b. Splenomegaly and abdominal pain
      c. Cerebral occlusion, causing blindness, strokes, and hemiplegia
   9. Sequestration crisis
      a. Blood pools in liver and spleen
      b. Circulatory collapse and death

C. Nursing approaches
   1. Alleviate pain during crisis by producing increased fluid intake to dilute blood
   2. Provide emotional support to child and parents and provide factual information based on child's level of development and parent's knowledge concerning physiology and prognosis (no known cure)
   3. Encourage quiet activities such as reading, puzzles, and table games
   4. Be aware of precipitating factors—dehydration, infection, trauma, extreme fatigue, and overexertion

2. Hemophilia—a congenital blood dyscrasia characterized by absence or malfunction of blood clotting factor

A. Cause-pathophysiology
   1. Hereditary, sex-linked, recessive disease that appears in men but is transmitted by women
   2. Types and clotting factor
      a. Type A (classic)—VIII (antihemophilic factor)
      b. Type B (Christmas disease)—IX
      c. Type C—XI

B. Signs-symptoms
   1. Child is easily bruised
   2. Prolonged bleeding from lacerations or mucous membranes
   3. Intramuscular hematomas from minor trauma
   4. Hemarthrosis causing pain, swelling, and limited movement of affected joint

5. Repeated hemorrhages produce degenerative changes—osteoporosis and muscle atrophy

C. Treatment
1. Immediate or prophylactic (presurgical procedures)—whole blood or plasma (freshly drawn or frozen), contains clotting factor, especially Type VIII, which is not stable for long at regular room or refrigerated temperatures
2. Splinting—decrease excessive motion and further acute bleeding; long-term use causes ankylosis and atrophy

D. Nursing approaches
1. Provide emergency treatement for bleeding wound—cleansing, applying pressure and ice, and immobilization
2. Alleviate pain
   a. Administer prescribed medication, avoid aspirin
   b. Avoid manipulation
   c. Use of bed cradle
3. Prevent further bleeding—oral medications and no sharp toys
4. Prevent permanent deformities and crippling—passive exercise and gentle massage
5. Main danger—avoid overprotection of child
6. Be aware of slow development due to curtailed activities
7. Play—avoid sharp toys or rough play

3. Skin conditions—burns (refer also to Unit 2, Medical Nursing)

A. Cause-pathophysiology
1. Causes vary and include the following
   a. Hot water
   b. Open flames
   c. Electrical burns
   d. Caustic acid or alkali as in household cleaners
   e. Chemicals
   f. Child abuse
   g. Smoke inhalation
2. Types
   a. First degree—superficial epidermis (slight edema, red, and painful)
   b. Second degree—epidermis intradermal (very edematous, red, blistered, moist, painful, and regenerates without grafting)
   c. Third degree—dermis, subdermal, fat, muscle, and bone (marked edema; white, dry, or charred; may or not be painful; and will not regenerate without graft)
3. Physiologic effects
   a. Dilatation of capillaries, increased permeability
   b. Plasma to interstitial fluid shift, resulting in edema around burn area
   c. *Fluid and electrolyte* imbalance—decreased potassium and increased water loss due to damage of evaporative water barrier
   d. Decreased efficiency of temperature control due to water loss
   e. Skin is first line of defense against infections; burn is a medium for bacterial, fungal, and viral invasions
   f. *Circulatory changes*—RBC hemolysis, decreased cardiac output, and decreased blood volume
   g. *Renal changes*—hypotension leads to renal perfusion and renal shutdown → decreased urinary output → increased urinary tract infections
   h. Increase cell volume—increased hematocrit
   i. Gastrointestinal changes—congested capillaries, acute gastric dilatation, paralytic ileus, and hemorrhagic gastritis ("coffee grounds" aspirant)

B. Signs-symptoms
1. Immediate due to fluid shift
   a. Appearance of burned area
   b. Increased pulse rate
   c. Decreased or subnormal temperature
   d. Pallor
   e. Low blood pressure
2. Toxemia development after one to two days due to reduction in blood volume and blocked capillaries
   a. Fever
   b. Rapid pulse
   c. Cyanosis
   d. Vomiting
   e. Edema
3. Respiratory tract signs-symptoms—due to fluid shifts, when neck and face are burned
   a. Dyspnea
   b. Stridor
   c. Rapid respirations
4. Smoke inhalation after 6 to 48 hours
   a. Pulmonary edema
   b. Signs-symptoms of airway obstruction

c. Bronchiolitis
C. Treatment
1. First aid—*do not use ointments or salve*
   a. Apply cold to burn
   b. Cover burn with sterile dressing, clean cloth—prevents contamination and decreases pain by blocking air flow
   c. Irrigate chemical burns
   d. Cover child to prevent body heat loss
   e. Transport to treatment facility for all burns except minor, first-degree
2. Open method—burn area exposed to maintain dry surface, formation of eschar, and less infection
3. Closed method—burn area covered with dressings; dressings can be soaked in solution or applied dry after topical medication is applied to skin
4. Topical agents
   a. Silver nitrate—0.5% solution as a continuous wet soak in combination with large, bulky dressings
   b. Mafenide (Sulfamylon)—"burn butter," applied in even coating to partial and full-thickness burns following initial débridement
   c. Gentamicin cream—specific effect against *Pseudomonas*, applied in even coating
   d. 1% silver sulfadiazine—used in open, semiopen, and closed method; soothing; softens eschar making débridement less painful
D. Nursing approaches
1. Recognize signs-symptoms of shock and hypovolemia—thirst, vomiting, increased pulse, decreased blood pressure, and decreased urine output
2. Urine output is most important sign of fluid balance
3. Accurate intake and output record—circulatory overload is common complication three to five days after burn
4. Administer oxygen via mask, tent, or catheter to combat anoxia
5. Provide source of heat to maintain body temperature
6. Prevent respiratory distress—suction secretions, humidified oxygen, cough, deep breathe, and position and turn child frequently
7. Observe vital signs for increased pulse and temperature
8. Maintain sterility or "super clean" environment to reduce or prevent infection
9. Provide adequate nutrition via high-protein (usually three to four times normal), high-calorie diet (usually two times normal), as metabolic demands are greatly increased
10. Use ingenuity to provide diversion and play for child—use of puppets or act out stories
11. Prevent contractures—keep in body alignment, active-passive ROM, use of whirlpool, and splint extremities in position of function during sleep

4. **Meningitis**—an inflammation of the meninges caused by a bacterial or viral organism
A. Bacterial
1. Preceded by febrile upper respiratory infection
2. Causative agents—*Hemophilus influenzae*, meningococcus, pneumococcus, *Streptococcus*, *Staphylococcus*, or *Escherichia coli*
3. Signs-symptoms—chills, fever, vomiting, headache, stupor, convulsions, and opisthotonos (head and feet touch bed with body arched, caused by tetanic spasm)
B. Viral
1. Causative agents include coxsackievirus B, echovirus, rubella, mumps, or herpesvirus
2. Signs-symptoms—fever, headache, vomiting, lethargy, stupor, and stiff neck
3. Herpesvirus type—rapid onset, severe rapid deterioration, brain damage, and death usually results
C. Diagnosis—symptoms, culture of spinal fluid and nasopharyngeal material, lumbar puncture (increased CSF pressure and cloudy in bacterial)
D. Sequelae—subdural effusion, hydrocephalus, seizure disorders, impaired intelligence, and visual and hearing defects
E. Treatment—IV medications
F. Nursing approaches
1. Observe for convulsions and monitor vital signs for signs and symptoms of increased intracranial pressure
2. Position—flat in bed most comfortable, on side if opisthotonos is present
3. Isolation is not necessary, but excretory precautions should be taken in viral type
4. Adequate hydration—offer fluids in ways not requiring sitting (straw, gelatin dessert, and popsicle)
5. Medications are toxic and irritating to vein—

observe site for inflammation and infiltration
5. **Tuberculosis**—in children, tuberculosis is considered a single disease entity with initial infection of tubercle bacillus, *Mycobacterium tuberculosis*, in the lungs and complications seen in all part of body
A. Pathophysiology
1. Bacillus inhaled through droplets, ingested, and enter through abrasion or mucous membranes
2. Inflammatory area created by bacilli, primary focus
3. Bacilli migrate through lymphatics
4. Incubation two to ten weeks
B. Signs-symptoms—diagnostic procedures
1. Positive skin test
a. Mantoux test—0.1 ml; old tuberculin (OT) or purified protein derivative (PPD) or tuberculin intradermally, results in 48 to 72 hours, 10 mm induration indicates positive reaction
b. Heaf test—PPD injected with gun (six punctures), three to seven days for results, appearance of four or more papules indicates positive reaction
c. Tine test—predipped OT pressed into skin, four tines, 48 to 72 hours, one to two papules 2 mm or larger indicates positive reaction
2. Gastric lavage done after positive skin test—produces bacillus
C. Treatment—arrest condition and prevent complications
1. Isoniazid (INH)—penetrates cell membrane, moves freely into CSF, oral (usual) or intramuscular; neurotoxic
2. Para-aminosalicylic acid (PAS)—bacteriostatic, oral, and causes gastrointestinal disturbances
3. Streptomycin SO_4—inhibits growth of tubercle bacillus, intramuscular, toxicity involves eighth cranial nerve
4. INH and PAS frequently used in combination; streptomycin is used in severe forms, for example, miliary tuberculosis and tubercular meningitis
5. Bacille Calmette-Guérin (BCG) vaccine—lasts ten years, given to child who lives with persons with tuberculosis, given only to child with negative skin test and negative chest X-ray within previous two weeks
D. Nursing approaches

1. Bedrest may be necessary for short period—play activities such as puppets, puzzles, and stories
2. Child on medication and afebrile is not contagious—isolation not necessary
3. Anorexia present—choose favorite, high-nutrition foods (high-calorie, protein, calcium, and phosphorus)
4. *Important on discharge*—stress chemotherapy maintenance
5. Routine skin testing of all children every year if negative
E. Serious types
1. Acute miliary tuberculosis—multiple tubercles develop due to bacilli lodging in capillaries; seen within two weeks on X-ray; 100% mortality if untreated, lower with triple therapy
2. Tubercular meningitis—bacilli in subarachnoid space; convulsion is first sign; 100% mortality unless treated with triple therapy; may still have residual neurologic damage (see Meningitis, p. 323)
6. **Legg-Calvé-Perthes disease**—an aseptic necrosis of capital femoral epiphysis
A. Cause-pathophysiology
1. Unknown etiology, mostly boys 4 to 10 years old
2. Stages—each lasts 9 to 12 months
a. Stage I, aseptic necrosis—femoral head necrotic, swelling of soft tissues, and widening of joint space
b. Stage II, revascularization—epiphysis fragmented and femoral head density increases
c. Stage III, reossification—femoral head reforms, new bone develops, and dead bone is removed and replaced with new bone
d. Stage IV, post recovery period—with treatment, complete recovery; without treatment, femoral head flattens; incongruity between femoral head and acetabulum remains; and degenerative changes occur later in life
B. Signs-symptoms
1. Limping with pain in hip caused by synovitis
2. Referred pain to knee, front of thigh, and groin
3. Limited abduction and rotation of hip
4. Mild to moderate muscle spasm
D. Treatment—avoid weight-bearing on affected

extremity
E. Nursing approaches
1. Due to long-term convalescence (two to five years) and restriction of movement by surgery, cast, or braces, provide carts, wagons, and stretchers for mobility
2. Suggest activity as appropriate to maintain continued development of child while immobilized
3. Teach techniques of skin care and provide opportunity for use and exercise of unaffected limb and upper extremities
4. Provide adequate nutrition, such as high-residue diet, since activity level decreased
5. Teach exercises for lungs—use of blow bottles or blowing up balloons

7. Oncology
A. Wilms' tumor (nephroblastoma)
1. Cause-pathophysiology
   a. Unknown etiology; classified as embryoma
   b. Malignant renal tumor
2. Signs-symptoms
   a. Firm abdominal mass
   b. Abdominal pain occurs as tumor grows and causes pressure, which in turn causes constipation, vomiting, weight loss, hematuria, and interference with kidney function (pressure causes dislocation of pelvis of kidney)
   c. Fever
   d. Hypertension due to kidney ischemia
   e. IVP demonstrates how mass distorts, rather than displaces, collecting system
3. Treatment—usually consists of nephrectomy, radiation therapy, and chemotherapy (see Appendix F)
4. Nursing approaches
   a. Most important nursing measure—avoid manipulation of the abdomen to prevent metastasis
   b. Emotional support of the parents on diagnosis
   c. Be aware that tumor is often encapsulated so prognosis is good
   d. Metastasis is a complication through venous extension or lymphatic channels to any organ
   e. Prepare parents and child for diagnostic tests and surgical procedure (blood drawing, and IVP)
   f. Prepare parents and family for side

effects of radiation—nausea, vomiting, diarrhea, skin irritation, lethargy, and anorexia
   g. Support child and family if tumor metastasizes and child is dying—stay with child, cope with fear of being alone, maintain comfort measures (skin and mouth), and do not leave parents alone at time of death
B. Acute lymphocytic *leukemia*—most common type of leukemia in children
1. Cause-pathophysiology
   a. Exact etiology unknown
   b. Rapid and abnormal proliferation of leukocytes in blood-forming organs and presence of immature leukocytes in peripheral circulation
   c. Peak incidence at 3 to 4 years of age
   d. Types—acute and chronic lymphatic and chronic myelocytic
2. Signs-symptoms
   a. Early—onset usually rapid, two to three months
      (1) Abdominal and bone pain
      (2) Persistent fever
      (3) Enlarged lymph nodes
      (4) Petechiae
      (5) Easily tired and general malaise
      (6) Anemia and pallor
   b. Later
      (1) Oral and rectal ulcers
      (2) Hemorrhage
      (3) Infection
3. Treatment
   a. Treatment is designed to quickly eliminate manifestations of the disease (see Appendix F)
   b. Transfusion of platelets when count is low to avoid hemorrhage
4. Nursing approaches
   a. Be supportive of parents and child on learning diagnosis; do not discuss time limits or offer false hope that child will be okay
   b. Maintain adequate nutrition by making meal a pleasant time—offer food preferences, soft foods because of gum bleeding, and high-protein and high-calorie diet
   c. Record intake and output
   d. Utilize measures to prevent infections
   e. Be alert to signs of hemorrhage

f. Plan nursing care to give child periods of rest

g. Prepare child and parents for return visits to hospital; activity as tolerated during remission

h. Prepare child for tests, transfusions, and IV

i. If death is imminent, be supportive of child and family

8. **Ingestion of poisons and drugs**

A. Cause-pathophysiology
   1. Caused by immaturity of child, availability of substance, or accidental rendering by another person
   2. Ingestion of some substance that harms tissues and disturbs body functioning; two most frequent are aspirin and bleach

B. Signs-symptoms
   1. Gastrointestinal
      a. Abdominal pain and/or distention
      b. Nausea
      c. Vomiting
      d. Diarrhea
      e. Difficulty swallowing
      f. Anorexia; odor of breath
   2. Central nervous system
      a. Convulsions
      b. Coma
      c. Dilated pupils or pinpoint pupils
      d. Restlessness
      e. Delirium
      f. Lethargy
   3. Respiratory
      a. Obstruction
      b. Respiratory depression
      c. Difficulty breathing
   4. Cardiovascular
      a. Increased or decreased rate
      b. Irregular heart rate
      c. Cardiac failure
   5. Skin symptoms
      a. Burns around mouth
      b. Cyanosis

C. Nursing approaches
   1. Determine, if possible, what was ingested and how much
   2. Contact poison control center as necessary to determine treatment; administer antidote as described on product; universal antidote—2 parts burned toast (powdered charcoal), 1 part milk of magnesia, and 1 part strong tea (tannic acid)

3. Remove poison from body
   a. Induce vomiting by sticking finger down throat unless child is convulsing, comatose, or has ingested acid, alkali, kerosene, or gasoline
   b. Gastric lavage—use tap water and follow with cathartic to hasten removal of material from gastrointestinal tract

4. Be aware of signs and symptoms of systems involvement

5. Remain calm and encourage parents to do so also, even though they may feel guilty

6. Measures to decrease occurrence of poisoning
   a. Keep medicines and poisons out of reach
   b. Lock up highly toxic substances such as Drāno
   c. *Do not* store foods, drugs, and poisons in same area
   d. Leave medicines, drugs, and chemicals in original container
   e. *Do not* store dish detergent and cleaning agents under sink
   f. Dispose of poisonous substances where child cannot get to them
   g. Use medicine only for person intended; discard unused portions (for example, flush down toilet)
   h. Do not hide medicine in food for child or tell child that medication is candy
   i. Teach child not to taste or eat unfamiliar foods or substances

9. **Lead poisoning**

A. Occurs most often at 1 to 5 years of age

B. Ingestion of lead-base paint in repainted furniture such as cribs, banisters, and windowsills; certain lead toys, plaster, putty, and face powder; water from lead pipes, fruit covered with insecticides; lead-glazed earthenware pottery; and industrial crayons and oil paints

C. Lead accumulates in body—signs and symptoms
   1. Early—anorexia, crying without reason, listlessness, constipation, vomiting, weight loss, anemia, headache, and insomnia
   2. Later—difficulty in coordination, ataxia, loss of recently acquired developmental skills, (walking and buttoning clothes, for example) joint pains, bradycardia, and encephalopathy

D. Anemia develops due to interference by lead

with metabolism of iron and synthesis of hemoglobin

E. X-rays show lead lines and increased density at end of long bones and along margins of flat bones, indication of temporary cessation of growth

F. Treatment
   1. Excrete lead via kidneys by medication that assists urinary excretions
   2. Remove source of lead ingestion

10. **Otitis media**—Common infection of middle ear, usually a complication of upper respiratory infection in infants and young children because eustachian tube is short and crooked; horizontal position of tube hinders drainage due to usual prone or supine position of infant

A. Signs-symptoms
   1. Fever—may be 104 F
   2. Pain indicated by pulling at ear and crying
   3. Irritability
   4. Rhinorrhea, vomiting, and diarrhea may be present

B. Treatment
   1. Antibiotic, usually ampicillin or penicillin, even after symptoms disappear
   2. Aspirin or acetaminophen may be given to reduce fever
   3. Occasionally, decongestants are also ordered

C. Encourage mother to seek medical care if the preceding symptoms are present

D. If untreated—ruptured tympanic membrane, exudate oozing from ear, scarring, and hearing loss

11. **Tonsillitis (pharyngitis)**
A. Inflammation of structures in pharynx
B. Viral
   1. Gradual onset of fever, malaise, anorexia
   2. White exudate on tonsils
   3. Treatment is symptomatic—aspirin to control fever and soothing throat lozenges or gargling with warm salt water

C. Bacterial (group A, β-hemolytic streptococci)
   1. Abrupt onset of high fever; sore throat; headache; localized, tender, firm cervical nodes; and petechiae on soft palate
   2. Treatment—penicillin (or other antibiotic in case of allergy) for ten days

D. May prefer cool liquids

E. Treatment of bacterial tonsillitis essential to prevent serious complications such as rheumatic fever, scarlet fever, and acute glomerulonephritis

F. Tonsillectomy—surgical removal performed if child has repeated infections; tonsils hypertrophy, causing obstruction (difficulty breathing and swallowing and blockage of eustachian tubes)
   1. Bleeding is most common serious complication—lab tests for clotting time, prothrombin time, and platelets
   2. Preoperatively
      a. Tell child what a hospital is for and why it is necessary to be there
      b. Tell child what will be felt after surgery—sore throat
      c. Take vital signs, check signs of infection (increased temperature), and check for loose teeth to avoid aspiration
   3. Postoperative
      a. Place child in semiprone or prone position to allow patent airway, draining of secretions, and prevent aspiration
      b. When child is alert, offer cool liquids—soothes sore throat and prevents dehydration
      c. Ice collar—to reduce swelling and promote comfort
      d. Signs-symptoms of hemorrhage—frequent swallowing, vomiting bright red blood, rapid pulse, restlessness, and pallor

Part C   School-Age Children— Age 6 to 12 Years

NORMAL GROWTH AND DEVELOPMENT OF SCHOOL-AGE CHILDREN

1. Age 6 to 8 years
A. Physical development
  1. Growth spurt begins
  2. Gains 2 to 4 kg (4 to 7 lb) per year
  3. Begins to lose baby teeth; has 10 to 11 permanent teeth by 8 years of age
  4. Eyes fully developed
  5. At age 8 years, the arms grow longer in proportion to body; some girls may begin to develop secondary sex characteristics
B. Behavior patterns
  1. Motor development
    a. The 6-year-old child is very impulsive and active
    b. Balance and rhythm good
    c. Can throw and catch a ball
    d. Prefers to bathe self
    e. Nervous habits are common
    f. Capable of fine hand movements
    g. Descriptive gestures accompany speech
  2. Social, vocal, and mental development
    a. Plays well alone
    b. Enjoys group play with small groups
    c. Uses telephone
    d. Knows comparative value of coins
    e. Knows right and left
    f. Learns to read
    g. The 7-year-old child counts by 1, 2, 5, and 10s
    h. Aware of differences between own home and that of friends
    i. Begins to tell time; oriented to time and space (day of week and month)
    j. Prefers to play with same sex
    k. Enjoys holiday celebrations; counts days until anticipated event takes place
    l. Has sense of humor
    m. Recognizes property rights
C. Nursing implications
  1. Appropriate play activities
    a. Painting, coloring, pasting, and drawing
    b. Imaginary dramatic play with ''real'' costumes

    c. Table games—tiddlywinks, marbles, and dominoes
    d. Handicrafts
    e. Collections
    f. Radio, TV, records
    g. Magic tricks
    h. Papier-mâché
    i. Cooking sets, erector sets, and tinker toys
    j. Books the child can read
  2. Guidance areas
    a. Give some responsibility for household duties
    b. Teach safety in crossing streets
    c. Aggressiveness is normal
    d. Has quiet days and periods of shyness that should be tolerated as part of growing up
    e. May be subject to nightmares and various fears
    f. Need to be considered important by adults; given small responsibilities
    g. Sex-conscious—requires simple honest answers to questions
    h. Common problems—teasing, quarreling, nail-biting, enuresis, whining, poor manners, and swearing; causes for these behaviors should be investigated and dealt with constructively (for example, trying to find why, substituting other activities, and removing cause), not handled negatively (that is, not using harsh punishment or belittling)

2. Age 9 to 11 years
A. Physical development
  1. Height increases at 9 years
  2. Weight gain may intensify at 10 years
  3. Eye-hand coordination is well developed
  4. Dentition
    a. Shed cuspids and first and second molars
    b. Have approximately 26 permanent teeth by 12 years
  5. Sexual maturation
    a. Girls—breast enlargement, appearance of pubic and axillary hair, and menarche

may begin in girls by age 11 years
   b. Boys—growth spurt, growth of external genitalia, appearance of pubic and axillary hair, change of voice, and transient enlargement of nipples may begin to appear in boys by age 11 years
B. Behavior patterns
   1. Motor development
      a. Constant activity
      b. Plays and works hard
      c. Cares for own physical needs completely
      d. Uses tools fairly well
      e. Uses both hands independently
      f. A marked difference in motor skills according to sex at 10 years
      g. Very active—finger-drumming and foot-tapping, for example
   2. Social and mental development
      a. Play is varied and companionship becomes more important than play
      b. Likes to have secrets
      c. Can do multiplication and division
      d. Sex defferences in play; antagonism between the sexes
      e. Interested in family life
      f. Interested in how things are made
      g. Growing capacity for thought and conceptual organization
      h. Courteous and well-mannered behavior with adults
      i. Seeks others' ideas and opinions
      j. Thinks about social problems and prejudices
      k. Occasional privacy is important
      l. Sees physical qualities as constant despite changes in size, shape, weight, and volume
      m. Has ability to plan ahead
      n. Can be quite critical of own work
      o. An 11-year-old child has hero worship; characters in book become real for child
      p. Operating in Erickson's *sense of industry or accomplishment* versus *feelings of inferiority* stage
C. Nursing implications
   1. Appropriate play activities based on developmental level
      a. Books
      b. Musical instruments
      c. Clubs and organizations
      d. Experiments
      e. Jewelry
      f. Ceramics
      g. Handicrafts—sewing; copper, leather, and metal work, knitting; and crocheting
   2. Guidance areas
      a. Lying and stealing may become a problem; need to investigate cause (gain recognition or remedy inadequacies)
      b. Accept child as is—active or quiet
      c. Encourage participation in organized clubs and youth groups
      d. Give information concerning sex changes
      e. Use "power of suggestion" rather than dictums
      f. Avoid harsh and severe punishment
      g. Support and give democratic guidance as child works through dependence and independence; set realistic limits
      h. Need help channeling energy into purposeful endeavors
      i. Recognize that 11-year-old child may withdraw rather than verbalize
      j. Recognize need to rebel and depreciate others
      k. May feel "picked on" when not in control of situation

SPECIAL CONCERNS OF SCHOOL-AGE CHILDREN

1. **Response to illness and hospitalization**—age 6 to 12 years
A. Indications of discomfort or pain (6 to 12 years)
   1. Expresses that something is wrong, such as, "I feel sick."
   2. Crying
   3. Tells adult of illness so adult can do something about it
B. Reaction to stage of illness (6 to 12 years)
   1. Initial illness or hospitalization
      a. Expected coping behaviors
         (1) Anger
         (2) Guilt
         (3) Fantasies and fears
         (4) Increased activity as response to anxiety
         (5) Reaction to immobility (depression, anger, and crying)
         (6) Increased imagination about surgery or treatments
         (7) Cry or aggressively resist treatment
         (8) Need parents and authority
      b. Negative behaviors—stemming from

loss of control, insecurity, and feelings of inferiority
  (1) Excessive guilt and anger and inability to express it
  (2) Night terrors
  (3) Excessive hyperactivity
  (4) Not talking about experience
  (5) Regression and complete withdrawal
  (6) Excessive dependency
  (7) Insomnia
2. Prolonged hospitalization and convalescence
  a. Expected coping behaviors
    (1) Shows desire to get well
    (2) Wants to do things for self
    (3) Talks about going home
    (4) Shows interest in play, peers, and school
  b. Negative behaviors
    (1) Gives up hope
    (2) Shows no inclination to get well
    (3) Disinterested in happenings outside hospital
C. Nursing approaches (6 to 12 years)
  1. Explain procedures, treatments, and condition to child to allay fears and misconceptions
  2. Encourage child to verbalize feelings so you can discover conceptions, fears, and expectations
  3. If negative behaviors appear, help child explain fears; give punching bag or clay to allow outlet for aggressive feelings
  4. Have same group of nurses care for child to provide security and predictability
  5. Set limits—child expects to be disciplined for misbehavior (taking away a privilege, TV, for example)
2. Nutrition—age 6 to 12 years
A. Age 6 to 8 years—2000-2100 cal/24 hours
B. Age 8 to 10 years—2100-2200 cal/24 hours
C. Age 10 to 12 years—boy, 2500 cal/24 hours; girl, 2250 cal/24 hours
D. Tend to choose own foods; need nutritional education
E. Display good table manners and enjoy having guests eat with them
F. Nutritional snack foods should be kept on hand for extra food during growth spurts
3. Safety concerns—age 6 to 12 years
A. Be role model as safe driver
B. Use safety belts while riding in auto
C. Teach rules of pedestrians
D. Do not allow play in streets or alleys
E. Teach bicycle "rules of the road"
F. Firearms
  1. Store safely
  2. Handle carefully
  3. Teach proper use
G. Provide supervision during sports activities
H. Provide adult supervision and teaching for swimming and boating
I. Teach respect for fire and its dangers
J. Recognize that as part of group, child may try anything once; set good examples for child to follow

CONDITIONS AND DISEASE ENTITIES OF SCHOOL-AGE CHILDREN

1. Acute rheumatic fever
A. Cause-pathophysiology
  1. Most cases preceded by Group A β-hemolytic streptococcal infection
  2. Systemic disease with changes caused by inflammatory lesions of connective tissue and endothelial tissue, specifically of the heart, joints, blood vessels, and subcutaneous tissues
  3. Presence of Aschoff's bodies—cellular response of inflammation to the perivascular connective tissue; nodules; and myocardial lesion
B. Signs-symptoms—modified Jones criteria for diagnosis: two major criteria or one major and two minor criteria present in child
  1. Major criteria
    a. Carditis
    b. Polyarthritis
    c. Chorea
    d. Pink rash (erythema marginatum)
    e. Subcutaneous nodules
  2. Minor criteria
    a. Pain in one or more joints, with no inflammation, tenderness, or limited motion
    b. Fever
    c. Abdominal pain
    d. Rapid pulse during sleep
    e. Anemia
    f. Epistaxis
    g. Malaise
    h. Previous streptococcal infection
    i. Leukocytosis
    j. Elevated erythrocyte sedimentation rate
    k. Prolonged P-R interval on ECG
    l. Positive reactive protein

C. Treatment
1. Major aim—prevent permanent *heart damage*; bedrest during febrile stage
2. Eradication of streptococcal *infection*—penicillin or, if allergic, erythromycin; long-term, *chemoprophylaxis*
3. *Corticosteroids*—used only when congestive heart failure is present
4. *Aspirin*—helps comfort of child when febrile and when joint pain is present

D. Nursing approaches
1. Listen to heart to identify changes in murmur or onset of murmur
2. Provide quiet diversional activity (stories, handicrafts, or TV) while on *bedrest* during febrile stage to prevent cardiac damage
3. When joints are painful, move child carefully, supporting joints; in acute phase—aim is to prevent deformity
4. If febrile, take frequent temperatures; *avoid excessive fluids*, which augment congestive heart failure
5. Low-sodium diet—to prevent fluid retention, should be as palatable as possible so child will eat; offer several small portions rather than three large meals
6. Be aware that two to six months following infection, girls may develop *chorea* (St. Vitus' dance)—muscular twitching, purposeless movements, facial grimacing, and weakness; subsides after period of time; pad bedrails to prevent injury; rectal temperature, as child may bite thermometer if taken orally
7. Recurrence depends on further streptococcal infections; no treatment in acute phase, causing extensive cardiac damage
8. Explain that prognosis depends on amount of cardiac damage
9. Prevent recurrence—long-term antibiotic therapy, avoid exposure to infections, and seek treatment in acute stage

2. Acute glomerulonephritis

A. Cause-pathophysiology
1. Antigen-antibody reaction secondary to initial infection, usually group A β-hemolytic streptococcal infection
2. Causative organism contains antigens similar to basement membrane of renal glomeruli, so antibodies attack organism *and* the glomerular tissue, causing an inflammatory reaction in kidney-glomerulus and resulting in destruction of basement membrane with loss of blood protein due to general vascular disturbances (loss of capillary integrity and spasm of arterioles)

B. Signs-symptoms
1. Hematuria—first sign, oliguria and proteinemia (characteristic symptoms)
2. Headache
3. Malaise
4. Fever—initially over 104 F; stays at approximately 100 F for duration of illness
5. Edema—extremities and cerebrum, presents in most patients (characteristic symptom)
6. Hypertension—present in 50% of patients after four or five days
7. Anorexia and vomiting (characteristic symptom)
8. Bradycardia
9. Congestive heart failure (CHF)

C. Nursing approaches
1. Maintain bedrest to prevent complications—hypertensive encephalopathy and cardiac involvement
2. Protect child from infection—avoid exposure to contagious diseases and upper respiratory infection
3. Hygiene measures
4. Follow dietary regimen and explain modifications to child (low-salt or salt-free diet because of renal failure or decreased potassium or protein, for example)
5. Record exact intake and output to identify fluid retention and prevent fluid overload
6. Weigh child daily—check for fluid retention
7. Limit fluid intake to reduce hypertension
8. Toys—avoid games and articles that require fine eye work
9. Observe for signs of complication indicating decreased kidney function and increase of metabolic end products in blood
   a. Restlessness
   b. Stupor
   c. Convulsions
   d. Severe headache
   e. Visual disturbances
   f. Vomiting
   g. Tachycardia
   h. Dyspnea
   i. Muscular twitching

3. Asthma

A. Cause-pathophysiology
1. Varied etiology
   a. Antigen-antibody response
   b. Infection

c. Irritants
d. Exercise
e. Emotional factors
2. Spasm of bronchial muscle, causing reversible obstruction of air passage by accumulation of thick mucus
3. Status asthmaticus—severe attack not alleviated by treatment

B. Signs-symptoms
1. Gradual increase of nasal congestion and sneezing
2. Wheezing on expiration, nasal flaring, and rales
3. Diaphoresis
4. Coughing and expectoration of viscous mucus secretions
5. Anxiety
6. Paroxysmal dyspnea
7. Cyanosis
8. Increased pulse and respiration
9. Distended neck veins

C. Nursing approaches
1. Observe breathing pattern—shallow rapid respiration, chest retractions, and wheezing
2. Vital signs—observe for nasal flaring; use stethoscope to hear if all areas of chest are aerated
3. Place in high-Fowler's position to allow maximum lung expansion
4. Administer oxygen cautiously, low PO_2 may be necessary for spontaneous breathing
5. Remain with child during acute attack
6. Provide calm, quiet environment
7. Provide adequate hydration to liquify bronchial secretions and maintain electrolyte balance
8. Know effects and side effects of drugs (bronchodilators) administered
9. Teach child and family breathing exercises to increase total lung capacity
10. Teach environmental control of home and child's bedroom (dusting, vacuuming, and cleaning drapes and carpets)
11. Postural drainage
12. Toys—avoid furry materials that could be irritants

4. Skin conditions
A. Tinea capitis (ringworm)
1. Cause-pathophysiology
a. Fungal infection of scalp and hair follicles
b. Fungal infection produces an inflammation of the scalp, which causes alopecia and may produce edema and pustules
2. Signs-symptoms
a. Pruritus
b. Rounded or oval patches covered by scales and broken hairs, disconcerting to child
3. Nursing approaches
a. Recognize lesion and prevent spread of infection through use of sterilized cotton cap
b. Administer prescribed medication (griseofulvin, administered orally) and be aware of side effects—headache, nausea, epigastric pain, diarrhea, and itching
c. Examine child's family to ascertain if others are infected
d. Provide emotional support and stress good hygiene habits—regular shampooing and avoid use of common comb and brush

B. Impetigo
1. Cause-pathophysiology
a. Usually caused by staphylococci or streptococci coupled with poor hygiene
b. Infectious disease of superficial layers of skin
2. Signs-symptoms
a. Reddish-pink macules, progressing to vesicles
b. Progression to pustules, which develop crusts and reddened areas on skin
3. Nursing approaches
a. Be aware of signs and symptoms
b. Prevent secondary infection by use of good hygiene and avoidance of scratching
c. Maintain adequate nutrition
d. Utilize diversionary therapy
e. Teach good hygiene habits to child and family

C. Pediculosis (lice infestation)
1. Cause-pathophysiology
a. Infestation by lice
b. Eggs or nits attach to hair and clothing
2. Signs-symptoms
a. Severe itching of infected area
b. Minute red lesions
c. Observation of nits in hair
3. Nursing approaches

a. Prevent spread of infection—isolate child in hospital
b. Wear gloves and gown when combing or washing child's hair
c. Inspect skin for infection caused by scratching
d. Carry out prescribed treatment
e. Provide for screening of family
f. Teach good hygiene habits

D. Scabies
1. Cause-pathophysiology
a. Caused by parasite—mite
b. Burrowing parasite causes irritation and formation of vesicles
2. Signs-symptoms
a. Itching, primarily at night
b. Burrow lines caused by female mite burrowing into superficial skin to deposit her eggs, most commonly seen between fingers but may occur in any natural folds of body or where elastic on clothing is against skin
3. Nursing approaches
a. Prevent spread of infection by medical asepsis
b. Inspect skin for infection caused by scratching
c. Carry out prescribed treatment, usually gamma benzene hexachloride (Kwell) baths
d. Provide for screening of family
e. Teach good hygiene habits—regular bathing and clean clothes

5. **Intestinal parasites (worms)**
A. Infestation—fecal contamination of food, soil, water, and hands
B. Types
1. Roundworms
a. Eggs hatch in duodenum, larvae pass through intestinal wall to blood stream, liver, lungs, and epiglottis (swallowed).
b. Develop in small intestine—colicky pain, passed in stool as worm
c. Treatment—piperazine citrate, two treatments, two days apart
2. Pinworm
a. Worm attaches to mucosa of cecum and appendix
b. Females deposit eggs on perianal and perineum at night—causes anal itching→child scratches→fingers in mouth→reinfection

C. Measures to prevent reinfection
1. Wash hands after toileting
2. Treat entire family, wash all bedding, and bedclothes
3. Disposing of fecal material in safe hygienic manner (soiled diapers rinsed and disposable diapers in closed container)
4. Avoid putting fingers in mouth

6. **Juvenile diabetes mellitus**—a disorder of abnormal metabolism of fat, protein, and, especially, carbohydrates due to inability to produce insulin
A. Cause-pathophysiology
1. Hereditary—recessive disease
2. Pancreas produces little or no insulin, so body is unable to oxidize glucose properly
3. Glycosuria—serum level of glucose exceeds renal threshold
4. Ketones—in blood because of abnormal fat metabolism, excreted in urine
B. Early signs-symptoms due to osmotic diuresis
1. Three Ps—polydipsia, polyuria, and polyphagia
2. Dry skin
3. Weight loss with nausea and vomiting
4. Glucose and ketones in urine on testing
C. Treatment
1. Diet based on American Diabetes Association exchange method
2. Subcutaneous administration of insulin
D. Complications—arteriosclerosis with hypertension, retinal changes, cataracts, and nephropathy
E. Nursing approaches
1. Recognize signs of diabetic acidosis, refer to Table 5-5 and Appendix F
2. Differentiate between preceding signs and those of insulin reaction, refer to Appendix F
3. Be familiar with child's prescribed diet and assist in teaching child and family
4. Assist child and/or family in administering insulin subcutaneously—practice on sponge and progress in steps; be sure to rotate sites
5. Provide good skin and foot care to prevent infection
6. Teach testing of urine—discard first void in AM; test second, more accurate than residual urine
7. Promote normal growth and development of child—can participate in activities without feeling different; avoid overprotection
8. Have child carry lump of sugar to use in case of insulin reaction

9. Teach relationship between extra activity and stress and food-insulin need

7. **Osteomyelitis**
A. Cause-pathophysiology
   1. 90% are associated with *Staphylococcus aureus* infection
   2. Inflammatory process of long bones
B. Signs-symptoms
   1. Fever and malaise
   2. Pain in bone at the metaphysis, later associated with redness and swelling
   3. Irritability
   4. Weakness
   5. Abrupt onset, usually in boys 5 to 14 years old
C. Nursing approaches
   1. Be aware of signs and symptoms and precipitating primary lesions obtained by history; ask if child had boil or infection recently
   2. Systemic infection—careful handling of discharge material
   3. Monitor vital signs for changes indicating infection—increased pulse, elevated temperature, and increased respiration; and check circulation of affected part or parts
   4. Prepare child and parents for long hospital treatment of IV antibiotics and need for bedrest; provide activities during immobilization
   5. Pain—immobilize limb and give analgesics

8. **Oncology**
A. Brain tumors
   1. Cause-pathophysiology
      a. Etiology unknown
      b. Age 5 to 7 years
      c. Expanding tumor or lesion, most often in the posterior fossa
      d. Most frequent types
         (1) Astrocytoma
         (2) Medulloblastoma
         (3) Ependymoma
   2. Signs-symptoms
      a. Headache
      b. Vomiting without nausea
      c. Delayed response to commands
      d. Blurred or double vision
      e. Change in personality or behavior—lethargy, irritability, hyperactivity, drowsiness, stupor, inattentive, or belligerent
   3. Nursing approaches
      a. Observe for changes in vital signs

b. Convulsive precautions
c. Accurately record and report any headaches
d. Provide emotional support of child and family
e. If surgery is indicated, do preoperative and postoperative preparation, teaching, and care
f. Play activities—avoid bending of head

B. Sarcomas—osteosarcoma and Ewing's sarcoma
   1. Cause-pathophysiology
      a. Cause unknown, but heredity may play a part
      b. Malignant bone tumor
   2. Signs-symptoms
      a. Pain
      b. Weight loss
      c. Palpable mass over site
      d. Swelling of affected part
   3. Nursing approaches
      a. Observe for lung involvement, pain in chest, coughing, and spitting blood, for example
      b. If limb involved is amputated, prepare child and family preoperatively and give appropriate postoperative care
      c. Provide emotional support to child and family

9. **Epilepsy**
A. Cause-pathophysiology
   1. Idiopathic
   2. Organic—trauma, anoxia, infection, degenerative diseases, congenital (PKU and hypoglycemia), and toxic reactions
   3. Recurrent convulsive disorder marked by sudden and periodic lapses of consciousness; disturbances in electrical discharges in the brain
B. Signs-symptoms
   1. Aura type
      a. Small localized seizures; may precede grand mal seizures
      b. Irritability, headache, and nausea
      c. May experience sensation of unusual sounds, colors, and sights
   2. Grand mal
      a. Abrupt onset
      b. Tonic phase (20 to 40 seconds)
         (1) Entire body becomes stiff
         (2) Loses consciousness; may be cyanotic
         (3) Back arched and head usually to one

side
    (4) Incontinence
    (5) Pulse weak and irregular
    (6) Eyes fixed, pupils dilated
    (7) May bite tongue
  c. Clonic phase (variable duration)
    (1) Follows tonic stage and becomes generalized
    (2) Twitching movements of face and extremities
  d. Sleep follows; feels exhausted or has headache on waking
  e. Abnormal EEG
3. Petit mal (30 seconds)
  a. Signs—eyes roll, head lowered, and mild twitching
  b. Will discontinue activity for short period of time and then resume where left off
4. Jacksonian (focal motor)—seen in infants and progresses to grand mal as child gets older; sudden jerking movements of face, arms, and tongue; may remain conscious; sensory or motor voluntary muscles affected, usually clonic
5. Psychomotor
  a. Brief (one minute).
  b. Purposeful, repetitive movements (chewing or picking at clothes), pale, not tonic or clonic
C. Nursing approaches
1. Medications
  a. Side effects
    (1) Phenobarbital—excitement, rash, drowsiness, and vertigo
    (2) Diphenylhydantoin (Dilantin) sodium—hypertrophy of gums (suggest daily gum massage)
2. Observe child for recurrent seizures
3. Protect head from injury with pillow during a convulsive episode; place tongue blade or wad of material (towel) between teeth; move furniture or toys out of way; and loosen clothing around neck
4. To lessen likelihood of seizure—decrease stressful situations, decrease noise level if loud, and avoid blinking light
5. Prepare child for diagnostic tests (EEG and blood studies)
6. Assist parents in raising child as normally as possible; child should attend regular school
7. Educate child and parents about epilepsy—child is not insane or retarded; epilepsy can

be controlled with medication
8. Toys—avoid sharp toys to prevent injury during convulsive episodes

10. **Hyperactivity**
A. Cause-pathophysiology
1. Often used interchangeably with minimal brain damage and hyperkinetic syndrome
2. May be due to brain damage or cerebral dysfunction
3. May be due to other factors
  a. Visual problems
  b. Hearing problems
  c. Emotional problems
  d. Limited intellectual capacity
B. Signs-symptoms
1. Short attention span
2. Inability to sit still for long periods of time
3. Inability to solve problems according to ability of others of same age
C. Nursing approaches
1. Take a good complete history of the child; determine when hyperactivity started
2. Test vision
3. Test hearing
4. Assist in decreasing environmental expectations at home, in school, and in hospital
5. Refer to counselor if parents or teachers are unable to cope with child; to assist them in developing workable plan *for child*

11. **Blindness**
A. Cause-pathophysiology
1. Genetic factors
2. Rubella in pregnant mother (first trimester)
3. Infections (syphilis)
4. Injury or trauma (retrolental fibroplasia)
5. Inflammatory disease
B. Signs-symptoms
1. No eye-to-eye contact
2. Abnormal eye movements
3. Child does not follow objects
4. Child bumps into objects
C. Nursing approaches
1. Be alert to child's responses to light and objects
2. Record child's behavior (eye rubbing and body rocking)
3. When admitting blind child to hospital, familiarize child with surroundings; learn child's usual routine and self-help capabilities
4. Utilize other senses when interacting with child—touch, smell, hearing, and taste
5. Speak to child before touching; let child know

you are in the room; say who you are

12. Impaired eyesight—strabismus—loss of control of eye-movement muscles (intraocular); one or both eyes may deviate rather then function as a unit; untreated condition results in amblyopia, poor vision in affected eye

A. Detection—must be detected by 6 to 8 years of age or visual loss is irreversible (acute visual development occurs at 1 to 6 years of age)

B. Cause
   1. Refractive errors
   2. Corneal scarring
   3. Cataracts
   4. Congenital deformities of orbit of eye or extraocular muscles

C. Treatment
   1. Glasses to correct refractive error and control excess accommodation
   2. Occlusion of straight eye with elastic tape to force other eye into activity
   3. Orthoptic training—exercises for eyes
   4. Surgery
      a. Resection—intraocular muscles shortened
      b. Recession—lengthening intraocular muscles

D. Nursing approaches
   1. Encourage early testing of vision—clinics, day-care centers, and nursery schools
   2. Explain that patch over "good" eye must be worn *constantly*
   3. Surgery
      a. Prepare for eye patches after surgery
      b. *Child should lie flat 24-48 hours after surgery*—restraints may be needed; supply diversion for child, such as familiar tactile and auditory objects in room
      c. Room quiet and dimly lit—for decreased stimulation and greater comfort (decreased light usually more comfortable)
      d. Advance diet slowly—decrease chance of vomiting, causing increased pressure and movement
      e. Use same techniques as for blind child while eyes are patched—speak before touching, explain sounds, and read stories

13. Impaired hearing
A. Cause-pathophysiology
   1. Prenatal factors—rubella and eclampsia
   2. Prematurity
   3. Acute infections of middle ear (otitis media), causing perforation of eardrum
   4. Injury

B. Signs-symptoms
   1. Infant has little or no interest in environment; begins to coo but then vocalizations cease; no response to noise or voices
   2. Toddler uses gestures to indicate needs
   3. School-age child may exhibit intense constant activity, temper tantrums, inattentiveness, and slow learning

C. Nursing approaches
   1. Know how long child has had hearing difficulty, how child has adjusted, and how child communicates
   2. Record observations of behavior during hospitalization
   3. Interview parents at time of admission to learn child's usual routine and method of communicating
   4. Refer for testing any child that is suspected of having a hearing difficulty
   5. Plan activities that will enhance the child's growth and development

14. Appendicitis—acute condition of inflammation of appendix

A. Incidence—more frequent in spring and in boys (school-age and adolescent age groups)

B. Signs-symptoms
   1. Epigastric pain
   2. Anorexia with one or two vomiting episodes
   3. Pain—may become localized after 2 to 12 hours; located in right lower quadrant but remains diffuse in many children; pain increases with ambulation
   4. Constipation
   5. Mild leukocytosis
   6. Fever—99 F to 102 F, usual range

C. Ice bag over painful area may be comforting—*do not use heat or cathartics*, may cause rupture of appendix and peritonitis

D. Treatment—surgical removal

E. Prepare child and parent for surgery and explain postoperative course, such as pain, early ambulation, location of scar, and progression from liquids to solid food

15. Emergency treatment of accidents in children

A. Sprain—apply cold and immobilize and elevate affected part

B. Fractured clavicle—apply sling to immobilize and take child to physician

C. Fractured limb—immobilize with splint (towel, newspaper, or broom handle), apply cold, and take child to physician

D. Abrasions—apply cold and wash with soap and water

E. Dog bite—wash with soap and water, confine dog, and call health authorities

F. Bee sting—remove stinger by scraping, not pulling out, and apply ice

G. Spider bite—apply ice and take child to emergency room if possibility of black widow or brown recluse

H. Minor burn—cold water or ice application, dry dressing

I. Small laceration—clean, apply pressure to stop bleeding, and apply ice

J. Head injury with resultant disorientation and vomiting—do not give liquid or food, keep child quiet and level (flat), and take child to physician

K. Snake bite—rinse; position child so affected part is lower than heart, and take child to emergency room

---

Part D   Preadolescents and Adolescents

NORMAL GROWTH AND DEVELOPMENT OF PREADOLESCENTS AND ADOLESCENTS

1. **Age 12 years or early adolescence**
A. Physical development (early adolescence)
   1. Eruption of bicuspids and second molars
   2. Further development of sex characteristics
B. Behavior patterns (early adolescence)
   1. Motor development
      a. Often awkward, uncoordinated
      b. Displays poor posture
      c. Tires easily
   2. Social and mental development
      a. Increased interest in opposite sex
      b. Peer group extremely important
      c. Becomes hostile toward parents
      d. Forms strong bonds of friendship with one or two peers
      e. Concerned with morality, ethics, religion, and social customs
      f. Great variation in academic interest and ability; girls have increased interest in self, cosmetics, etc.; boys have less interest in hygiene and are more interested in sports or team loyalty
C. Nursing implications (early adolescence)
   1. Appropriate play activities (usual pattern, but any activity may be of interest to boy or girl)
      a. Girls—social functions, romantic TV shows and movies, makeup, cooking, sewing, art, and poetry
      b. Boys—sports, mechanical and electrical devices, and part-time employment
   2. Guidance areas
      a. Require reassurance and help in accepting changing body image
      b. Understanding of conflicts as child attempts to deal with social, moral, and intellectual issues
      c. Set realistic but firm limits on expected behavior
      d. Encourage independence, but allow child to utilize parent when there is a need
      e. Provide opportunity to earn own money—paper route, mow lawns, and begin baby sitting

2. **Late adolescence**
A. Physical development (late adolescence)
   1. Completion of sexual development
   2. Appearance of adult
   3. Has 32 permanent teeth
B. Behavior patterns (late adolescence)
   1. Motor development
      a. More energy as growth spurt tapers
      b. Muscular ability and coordination increase
   2. Social and mental development based on Erikson's stages of adolescence (see Appendix A)—early stage, identity versus self-diffusion; later, intimacy versus isolation

a. More mature, interdependent relationship with parents
b. Romantic love affairs develop as basis for mature relationships
c. Ability to balance responsibility and pleasure
d. Loosened grasp of peer group; an identity concern about self now and self as an adult

C. Nursing implications (late adolescence)
  1. Appropriate play activities
    a. Working for altruistic causes
    b. Sports
    c. Reading
    d. Television
    e. Radio, music, and records
    f. Challenging mental games (chess)
  2. Guidance areas
    a. Provide assistance in selection and preparation for vocation
    b. Provide driver education
    c. Assistance in developing healthy attitude—smoking, drinking, drugs, and nutrition
    d. Parents may need help in adjusting to loss of their dependent child
    e. Assistance in problem solving

SPECIAL CONCERNS OF PREADOLESCENTS AND ADOLESCENTS

1. **Response to illness and hospitalization**—age 12 years to late adolescence
A. Indications of discomfort or pain (preadolescence to adolescence)
  1. Realizes something is wrong and seeks help
  2. Anxiety is present related to body image and dependency
B. Reaction to stage of illness (preadolescence to adolescence)
  1. Initial illness or hospitalization
    a. Expected coping behaviors
      (1) Resistance to accept illness
      (2) Rebellious against authority
      (3) Demands control and independence
      (4) Fearful
      (5) Temporary withdrawal from social scene
      (6) Verbalizes how illness has affected life
    b. Negative behaviors based on loss of self-identity and independence with no hope of redeeming them
      (1) Tries to manipulate staff
      (2) Complete dependence and denial
      (3) Denies fear or concern
      (4) Continued withdrawal
      (5) No verbalization of feelings
  2. Prolonged hospitalization and convalescence
    a. Expected coping behaviors
      (1) Wants to get well
      (2) Seeks out peers
      (3) Impatient to recover
      (4) Gives up dependency
      (5) Concerned about bodily functions and body image
    b. Negative behaviors due to isolation and loss of identity
      (1) Wants to stay in hospital
      (2) Childlike and dependent on parents
    c. Nursing approaches (preadolescence to adolescence)
      (1) Allow adolescent as much control as possible—selection of bath time and selection of menu, for example
      (2) Give independence—let patient chart vital signs and take own medication if possible
      (3) Offer opportunity for peer contact—room where adolescent can meet others (Peds Pad); have ambulatory patient meet in immobilized patient's room
      (4) Assist in maintaining identity—dress in own clothes, provide hair-grooming materials, and encourage makeup if worn
      (5) Listen and validate what you hear from adolescent; encourage patient to discuss feelings
      (6) Explain hospital rules on admission to ensure cooperation and decrease threat of loss of identity and feelings of isolation

2. **Nutrition**—age 12 years to late adolescence
A. Calories
  1. Age 12 to 14 years—boy, 2700/24 hours: girl, 2300/24 hours
  2. Age 15 to 16 years—boy, 3000/24 hours; girl, 2300/24 hours
B. Will select own food and portions; discuss fad diets and eating nonnutritious food
C. Obesity
  1. Most common cause is overeating, usually

accompanied by reduced activity

2. Obese infants tend to become obese older children, who become obese adolescents and adults
3. Recommendations
   a. Diet, exercise, and psychologic factors (stress may be a factor, loneliness, "clean plate" award, and food used as a reward for good behavior)
   b. Involve child in selecting weight-reduction method
   c. Adequate nutrition needs should be calculated as well as decreased calorie intake
   d. Exercise more important than diet in child—walking, active play, bicycling, and swimming
   e. Everyone in family should eat regular meals—*not* in front of television or while engaged in some other activity
   f. Drugs should be used only as a last resort
D. Anemia can be a problem in fad diets; offer acceptable food items high in iron—hamburger, hot dogs, chili with beans, and fortified cereals

CONDITIONS AND DISEASE ENTITIES OF PREADOLESCENTS AND ADOLESCENTS

1. **Juvenile rheumatoid arthritis (Still's Disease)**—chronic systemic disease of unknown etiology; there is a wide range of joint involvement; prognosis is good if only one or two joints are involved
A. Cause-pathophysiology
   1. Inflammation of joint may be due to virus or postsystemic infection
   2. Growth centers next to inflamed joints may produce premature epiphyseal closure or accelerated epiphyseal growth
   3. Synovial tissues, tendon, and tendon sheaths develop inflammatory changes
B. Signs-symptoms
   1. Stiffness and impaired motion of joints (knees, feet, ankles, wrists, and fingers)
   2. Swelling of joints
   3. Spiking fever, malaise, and irritability
   4. Anemia with associated symptoms
   5. Anorexia
   6. Macular rash on trunk and extremities
   7. Hepatosplenomegaly
   8. Lymphadenopathy

9. Eye inflammation with photophobia, nonreactive pupil, and decreased visual acuity
10. Joints—deformed, dislocated, and fused
11. Weak and atrophied muscles near affected joints
C. Treatment
   1. Goal—to preserve good joint function
   2. Drugs to suppress inflammation of joints
      a. Salicylates—antipyretic, anti-inflammatory, and analgesic; given orally or intravenously; side effects are abdominal pain, ringing in ears, hyperventilation in young children, and headaches
      b. Gold salts—exact action unknown; given intramuscularly; side effects are skin rash, nephritis with hematuria or albuminuria, neurotoxicity, and thrombocytopenia
      c. Steroids—anti-inflammatory given orally, intravenously, intramuscularly, and intra-articularly (in the joint); side effects are mask infection, peptic ulcer, vascular disorders, hypertension, blurring or dimming of vision, osteoporosis, euphoria, glycosuria, weight gain secondary to water retention, appetite stimulation, round facial contour, and facial hair
D. Nursing approaches
   1. Encourage exercise and physical therapy to prevent deformities; night splints for wrists and knees
   2. Administer medications (gold salts, salicylates, and steroids)—explain side effects and reversibility when drug discontinued
   3. Hot tub bath prior to exercises promotes relaxation and decreases pain
   4. Encourage normal activity as tolerated
2. **Hyperthyroidism**—endocrine disease manifested by excessive secretion of thyroid hormone
A. Cause-pathophysiology
   1. Exact cause unknown
   2. Long-acting thyroid stimulator (LATS) found in serum—causes iodine accumulation and thyroid hyperplasia independent of pituitary
B. Signs-symptoms
   1. Goiter
   2. Protruding eyeballs
   3. Hyperactivity
   4. Increased appetite with no weight gain
   5. Increased urination

6. Behavior changes
C. Nursing approaches
   1. Provide calm environment to prevent undue excitement
   2. Encourage high-calorie, high-protein diet because of increased need due to increased activity
   3. Know side effects of medication and record any that are noted (propylthiouracil or methimazole); toxic effects include fever, rash, headache, nausea, and pain in joints
   4. Provide emotional support of child and family

3. **Systemic lupus erythematosus**—disease of connective tissue that may affect or involve any organ
A. Cause-pathophysiology
   1. Cause unknown
   2. Connective tissue develops fibrinoid change in collagen and cellular infiltration
   3. Alteration of collagen and thickening of small blood vessel lining obstructs flow of blood
B. Signs-symptoms
   1. Joints may be painful and swollen
   2. Anorexia and loss of weight
   3. Fever
   4. Butterfly rash across nose and cheeks
   5. Hematuria and proteinuria
   6. Weakness
B. Nursing approaches
   1. Know side effects of steroid therapy and explain to child and family the expected changes in appearance
   2. Observe for complications, especially renal involvement (hematuria)
   3. Offer emotional support to child and family
   4. Use measure to prevent infection
   5. Avoid exposure to sun
   6. Maintain adequate nutrition, offer small portions as child is anorexic

4. **Hodgkin's disease**—malignancy of lymphoid system characterized by solid tumors in the lymph nodes
A. Cause-pathophysiology
   1. Etiology unknown
   2. Malignant cell (Reed-Sternberg cell)—large atypical tumor cell invading spleen, bone marrow, and alimentary tract
   3. Peak incidence—age 15 to 29 years
   4. Stages
      a. Stage I—involvement of single lymph node group, excluding mediastinum and abdomen

      b. Stage II—involvement of one or more lymph node systems, limited by diaphragm to either upper or lower half of body
      c. Stage III—involvement above and below diaphragm limited to lymph nodes, spleen, or Waldeyer's throat ring
      d. Stage IV—systemic involvement of organs other than those listed previously (bone marrow, lungs, kidneys, liver gastrointestinal tract, and central nervous system)
B. Signs-symptoms
   1. Enlargement of painless, firm, movable lymph nodes
   2. Fever
   3. Generalized pruritus
   4. Night sweats
   5. Anorexia
   6. General malaise
   7. Rash
C. Nursing approaches
   1. Symptomatic relief of side effects of chemotherapy (see Appendix F)
   2. Maintain adequate nutrition—serve food that child prefers in pleasant surroundings
   3. Have change of clothing available to child for night sweats
   4. Utilize necessary measures, including diversion, to control itching and provide comfort to child
   5. Provide emotional support to child and family
   6. Observe for respiratory problems due to airway compression by enlarged lymph glands or organs

5. **Drug abuse**—the addiction to narcotics, experimentation with many drugs, and self-medication
A. Cause-pathophysiology
   1. Taken to promote physical and psychic changes
   2. Physical dependence
   3. Psychic dependence
   4. Self-medication
B. Signs-symptoms
   1. Hallucinogens
      a. Nausea
      b. Visual imagery
      c. Altered and increased sensory awareness
      d. Anxiety
      e. Uncoordination, impaired judgment
   2. Narcotics

a. CNS depressant

b. Euphoria

c. Long-term use—loss of weight, constipation, anorexia, and addiction

3. Sedatives

a. Sleep-inducing, drowsiness

b. Long-term effects—addiction, irritability, and impaired judgment

4. Stimulants

a. Anorexia

b. Insomnia

c. Decreased fatigue

d. Long-term use—may be habit forming

5. Tranquilizers

a. Decreased anxiety and tension

b. Long-term use—may cause blood dyscrasia, blurred vision, dry mouth, skin rash, and tremors

6. Miscellaneous—glue or catnip

a. Euphoria

b. Impaired judgment and coordination

c. Long-term use—may cause hallucinations or liver or kidney damage

C. Nursing approaches

1. Teach dangers of drugs

2. Try to discover why the adolescent is using drugs and refer to counseling resource if appropriate

3. If overdose, observe for seizures

4. Stay with child who is experiencing withdrawal symptoms—talk to restore reality and reassurrance of care will decrease sense of isolation

5. Ascertain what was ingested if possible—ask patient or friend; check pockets for container, arms for needle marks, and nose for signs of inhalation (sores or foreign substances)

6. Offer support to parents who are experiencing guilt feelings

6. Venereal disease

A. Gonorrhea—inflammation of mucous membrane of genitourinary tract caused by gonococcus, *Neisseria gonorrhoeae*; infection spread by sexual intercourse

1. Called—GC, clap, gleet, strain, and morning dose

2. Incubation—two to eight days

3. Signs-symptoms

a. Women—may not have any

(1) Light, purulent, yellow vaginal discharge

(2) Discomfort, ache in abdomen

(3) Bartholin's glands swollen and painful

(4) May spread to urethra and bladder with burning, urgency, and urinary frequency

(5) Anal area itching, slight discharge

(6) Later stage—pelvic inflammatory disease (PID) may be first noticeable symptom (severe pain, high fever, vomiting, and dysparunia)

b. Men

(1) Thick purulent discharge from penis

(2) Burning on urination

(3) Bladder and prostate involvement (penis red, swollen, and sore)

(4) Inflamed scrotum—hard, swollen, and painful

4. Can cause sterility in both sexes

5. One-half of reported cases are under age 25 years

6. Treatment—aqueous procaine penicillin G, 2.4 million units in one or two doses, IM

B. Syphilis (syph or lues)—caused by spirochete, *Treponema pallidum*, which enters the body during coitus or through cuts and breaks in skin or mucous membranes

1. First sign—chancre at site of infection

2. Incubation period—10 to 60 days, 21 on average

3. Stages

a. Primary—chancre and enlargement of lymph nodes; most infectious stage

b. Secondary—six weeks to six months after primary; skin lesions (macular, papular, follicular, and pustular), arthritic and bone pain, acute iritis, and hoarseness

c. Latent—4 to 20 years after primary if developed at all, most serious; destruction of bone tissue, degenerative skin lesions, blindness, heart disease, and severe crippling or paralysis

4. Diagnosis—serologic, VDRL

5. Treatment—penicillin in first two stages, recovery unpredictable in latent

C. Incidence—increasing due to mobility of population, sexual freedom, promiscuity, and better birth control measures

7. Acne vulgaris—chronic disorder of sebaceous glands

A. Cause-pathophysiology

1. Genetic predisposition
2. Hormonal changes—production of testosterone or progesterone influences size and activity of sebaceous glands
3. Predisposing factors—anxiety, stress, and tension

B. Signs-symptoms
1. Blackheads, whiteheads, pustules, nodules, and cysts
2. Lesions block sebaceous glands, causing pustules and scarring

C. Treatment
1. Prevent follicular obstruction
2. Reduce inflammation
3. Prevent secondary infection
4. Eliminate predisposing factors

D. Nursing approaches in treatment
1. Have patient wash three times a day with mildly abrasive cleaners, shampoo two times a week, and use a brush or rough cloth in bathing
2. Avoid "picking" lesions

3. Expose areas to sunlight
4. Avoid excessive consumption of carbohydrates and fats

8. **Mononucleosis (mono)**—an acute infectious disease thought to be viral

A. Cause-pathophysiology
1. Often seen at 15 to 25 years of age
2. Painful enlargement of cervical lymph nodes
3. Spread through oropharyngeal route

B. Signs-symptoms
1. Fatigue
2. Sore throat
3. Fever and chills
4. Headache
5. Lymphadenopathy
6. Enlarged spleen

C. Nursing approaches
1. Treatment is symptomatic—rest; nutritious, well-balanced diet; and aspirin for fever, chills, and pain
2. Avoid exertion as this may cause rupture of spleen

Questions   Pediatric Nursing

1. The nurse in the newborn receiving nursery suspects that an infant has tracheoesophageal fistula based on the following signs
   1. Drooling, cyanosis, and immediate regurgitation of feedings
   2. Excessive crying, vomiting, and diarrhea
   3. Vomiting, cyanosis, and visible peristaltic waves
   4. Distention, projectile vomiting, and weak cry

2. Based on Mrs. Ks history of Paul, age 3 months, the nurse suspects pyloric stenosis. Paul most likely exhibited the following symptoms
   1. Projectile vomiting beginning abruptly, normal stools, and malnutrition
   2. Rumination of feedings, normal stools, sausagelike abdominal mass
   3. Constant abdominal pain with crying, frequent liquid stools, and firm abdomen

   4. Gradual onset of projectile vomiting, constipation, and weight loss

3. The following statements apply to a patient with Hirschsprung's disease, *except*
   1. Absence of or reduced number of ganglion cells in the intestinal tract muscle wall
   2. No peristalsis occurs in the affected portion of intestine
   3. Abdominal distention and constipation
   4. Colostomy and currant-jelly-like stools

Mr. L is concerned about Eric, his infant son, who "doesn't look right." The doctor suspects Eric has cerebral palsy.

4. A leading diagnostic sign of cerebral palsy is
   1. Drooling
   2. Motor function disorder
   3. Microcephaly
   4. Scissored lower extremities

5. When Mr. L asks what caused the cerebral

palsy, the nurse could explain that a possible cause might be

1. Anoxia at birth
2. Intrauterine infection
3. Prematurity
4. All of these are correct

6. Mr. L could also be told that the following is true of cerebral palsy
   1. It involves a progressive brain lesion
   2. Motor function is not impaired
   3. It involves movement and posture due to a defect or lesion of the brain
   4. Always results in mental retardation

7. Freddy, 4 months old, suffers from chalasia. To minimize vomiting after feeding, the nurse should
   1. Place Freddy on his right side, head elevated
   2. Place Freddy on his left side, head elevated
   3. Place Freddy on his right side, lying flat
   4. Place Freddy on his abdomen, head to one side

8. A newborn baby girl is admitted to the nursery with a sac in her lumbar area. Diagnosis of meningomyelocele is made. The baby exhibits the following clinical signs
   1. Flaccid paralysis of arms and legs and lack of bowel function
   2. Flaccid paralysis of arms, clubbed feet, and lack of bladder function
   3. Flaccid paralysis of legs, clubbed feet, and lack of bowel and bladder function
   4. Flaccid paralysis of arms and legs, hydrocephalus

9. Infants with meningomyelocele often also have hydrocephalus. If hydrocephalus were present, the nurse might observe the following symptoms
   1. Increase in head size, vomiting, irritability, and dilated scalp veins
   2. Decrease in head size, vomiting, and constricted scalp veins
   3. Increase in head size, irritability, constricted scalp veins, and vomiting
   4. Decrease in head size, bulging fontanels, and vomiting

10. As a nurse in the emergency room who is likely to see cases of child abuse, the nurse should be aware that most children who are battered
    1. Are over 6 months of age
    2. Are preschoolers who misbehave
    3. Are under the age of 3 years
    4. Live in underprivileged areas

11. In general, battering parents exhibit all *but* one of the following characteristics
    1. Sensitive about ability and general effectiveness as parents
    2. Like to be alone
    3. Have unrealistic expectations of child behavior
    4. Have no outlet for expression of tension and fear

Tanya T was born with a cleft lip and palate. The lip was repaired soon after birth, but the palate will be repaired in stages.

12. Following repair of the cleft lip, the nurse should do the following
    1. Use a hard nipple for feeding to exercise muscles used for sucking
    2. Not allow the mother to care for the child because of the fragile suture line
    3. Remove the restraints and exercise the child's arms periodically
    4. Change child's position, rotating from side, to abdomen, to back

13. In explaining the cleft palate deformity to Mrs. T, the nurse should explain that one of the following is not affected by cleft palate deformities
    1. Breathing
    2. Swallowing
    3. Neck mobility
    4. Speech

14. When Tanya is readmitted at age 15 months, she would probably enjoy the following activity
    1. Playing with her favorite toy
    2. Constructing a tower of 20 blocks
    3. Listening to popular tunes on the radio
    4. Stringing small beads

15. Mrs. K, a new mother, has several questions about her baby. She has purchased bibs to keep her baby's clothes dry when the baby begins to drool and teethe. The nurse could explain that drooling begins at approximately
    1. Age 1 to 2 months
    2. Age 3 to 4 months
    3. Age 1 to 3 weeks
    4. Age 5 to 6 months

16. Mrs. K questions how she should dress her baby. In counseling Mrs. K on dressing her infant, the nurse should know that normal

infants begin to sweat
1. Right after birth
2. About 1 month of age
3. About 3 months of age
4. About 6 months of age
17. Mrs. K is also concerned about feeding her baby. When the baby is ready to begin solid foods, the nurse explains that foods generally follow a certain progression when introducing them to an infant. The sequence is
1. Fruit, vegetables, and cereal
2. Fruit, meat, and cereal
3. Cereal, fruit, and meat
4. Cereal, meat, and vegetables

Mary, a 5-month-old infant, is admitted to your unit with diffuse areas of reddened papular lesions on her skin. Her mother states that Mary has never been ill before. Mary is fed pureed foods in addition to breast milk and daily vitamin drops. She is presently irritable and attempts to scratch or rub her lesions. She is admitted with a diagnosis of infantile eczema.

18. In response to Mary's mother's questions regarding eczema, you answer that most infants who develop eczema
1. Have it all their lives
2. Outgrow it by the time they reach 4 years of age
3. Outgrow it, but may show allergic reactions or manifestations later in life
4. Will never have another episode of eczema
19. Mary will most likely be placed on
1. A soft diet
2. A high-protein diet
3. A regular diet
4. An elimination diet
20. To prevent Mary from scratching herself and causing irritation and infection, the nurse could
1. Restrain Mary's limbs using clove-hitch restraints, being certain to change her position frequently
2. Allow her free motion after trimming her fingernails and toenails
3. Hold Mary while playing with her, using elbow restraints or mitts as necessary
4. Ask the doctor to prescribe medication for Mary to stop the itching
21. The following toys would be best for Mary
1. Soft washable toys
2. Stuffed toys
3. Puzzles and games

4. Toy cars
22. In bathing Mary, the nurse would most likely use the following regimen
1. Give her a bubble bath
2. Use mineral oil
3. Use only Ivory or castile soap
4. Use baby lotion

As a nurse working in the cardiology unit of a children's hospital, you should be aware of the following facts.

23. Which of the following is not true regarding congenital heart disease?
1. Most infants with congenital heart disease are asymptomatic unless they are blue or in cardiac failure
2. A child with congenital heart disease will set own pace
3. Cardiac failure is a common occurrence over 6 months of age
4. Bacterial endocarditis remains a potential risk
24. You would expect the following to be true of a child with patent ductus arteriosus
1. Becomes cyanotic on exertion
2. Becomes cyanotic when lying flat
3. Is not cyanotic
4. Has difficulty breathing
25. You would expect the following to be true of a child with tetralogy of Fallot
1. Squats a lot, not cyanotic
2. Squats a lot, slightly cyanotic
3. Cyanotic only on exertion, normal activity
4. Not cyanotic, clubbed phalanges
26. Fatigue, cyanosis, clubbed phalanges, and shortness of breath on exertion are clinical manifestations of
1. Patent ductus arteriosus
2. Tetralogy of Fallot
3. Aortic stenosis
4. Congestive heart failure
27. In caring for a child with acute laryngotracheobronchitis, the nurse would observe the following clinical signs
1. Retractions and inspiratory stridor
2. Flaring of nostrils and expiratory wheezing
3. Gradual onset and elevated temperature
4. Rapid onset and inspiratory stridor
28. As a nurse in the pediatric unit, the nurse should be aware that the following causes the highest incidence of morbidity and mortality in infancy

1. Rheumatic fever
2. Infections
3. Congenital heart defects
4. Accidents

29. The nurse should also know that the primary cause of death in children is associated with
    1. Leukemia
    2. Suicides
    3. Accidents
    4. Congenital heart defects

30. Mrs. R is interested in toilet training her 1-year-old daughter. When discussing toilet training, the nurse should keep in mind that this is an automatic function that is placed under voluntary control by
    1. Conditioning and reinforcement
    2. Conditioning and maturation
    3. Trial and error
    4. Imitation and learning

31. Mr. B noticed a mass in his 2-year-old daughter's abdomen while changing her diapers. The doctor has tentatively diagnosed her condition as Wilm's tumor. The nurse must be aware that the most important aspect of caring for this child preoperatively is
    1. Avoid palpating the abdomen
    2. Encouraging the child to eat adequately
    3. Emotional support of the parents
    4. Keeping the child on strict bedrest

32. While caring for Pete, a 5-year-old burn patient, the nurse could best prevent contractures by
    1. Maintaining body alignment
    2. Routine exercises of extremities
    3. Splinting joints
    4. Allowing free motion

33. When caring for Joe, who has just had a tonsillectomy, the following signs should be of concern to the nurse
    1. Frequent swallowing and vomiting dark red blood
    2. Respiratory rate of 20, frequent swallowing, and dry mouth
    3. Frequent swallowing, noisy respirations, and increased pulse
    4. Refusing liquids and complaining of sore throat

34. Certain conditions predispose a child to further problems. Which one of the following is most likely to result in otitis media?
    1. Upper respiratory infection
    2. Bronchiolitis

3. Lobar pneumonia
4. None of these

35. Screening for the sickle cell trait or disease in the United States should be done routinely for the following group of persons
    1. Asians
    2. Negroes
    3. American Indians
    4. Mexican-Americans

36. Lucas O, a two-year-old boy, is admitted in a sickle cell crisis. In addition to loss of appetite, the nurse would expect to see the following signs exhibited by Lucas
    1. Fatigue, infection, and paleness
    2. Alert, jaundice, and pain in abdomen
    3. Mental confusion, weak, and flushed
    4. Weakness, jaundice, and pain in abdomen, legs, or arms

37. Lucas has had many tests and painful procedures. Following these, the nurse could best help Lucas by
    1. Putting him to bed for a nap
    2. Initiate play with use of a puppet
    3. Rock him
    4. Doing funny tricks for him

38. Mrs. O states that Lucas has always been a "good" baby but lately has become very headstrong. The nurse should explain that the most likely reason for negative behavior in a 2-year-old child is
    1. Obstinacy
    2. Spoiled
    3. Seeking independence
    4. Learning right from wrong

Teddy, a 4-year-old boy, has been admitted to the pediatric unit with a diagnosis of acute glomerulonephritis.

39. Teddy and his siblings have recently been ill with scarlet fever. The most likely causative organism is
    1. *Staphylococcus*
    2. Group A β-hemolytic streptococci
    3. Gram negative organism
    4. Tuberculosis organism

40. When Teddy was admitted, the nursing coordinator did *not* place his bed near
    1. Terry, who has leukemia
    2. Tommy, who is mentally retarded
    3. Billy, who has streptococcal tonsillitis
    4. Sean, who has rheumatic fever

41. The most important aspect of Teddy's treat-

ment for glomerulonephritis is
1. Low-protein diet
2. Bedrest
3. Diuretics
4. Increased fluid intake

42. One behavior that would *not* be positive in Teddy while he is hospitalized with his acute condition is
1. Crying loudly when parent leaves
2. Fantasizing about illness
3. Covering head; withdrawal
4. Throwing toys

43. An appropriate play activity for the nurse to suggest for Teddy would be
1. Simple puzzles
2. Water play
3. Watching cartoons on TV
4. Learning to macrame

44. The nurse caring for 5-year-old Bobby, a hemophiliac, following a bleeding episode should
1. Promote quiet and rest for Bobby
2. Exercise his extremities
3. Wrap his joints in cotton batting
4. Administer sedatives to Bobby

45. The nurse should be aware that children with hemophilia often experience the following complication following a bleeding episode
1. Hemarthrosis
2. Bruising scars
3. Hemangioma
4. Anemia

Benjy K, a 5-year-old boy, is admitted with a tentative diagnosis of acute leukemia. He had a cold which seemed to persist. He is pale, apathetic, and losing weight. He also has petechiae on his skin, ulceration of his gums, and large cervical and inguinal lymph nodes. A bone marrow examination to confirm the diagnosis is planned.

46. The sites commonly used for bone marrow punctures are
1. Humerus, sternum, and femur
2. Iliac crest and sternum
3. Sternum and femur
4. Femur and skull

47. The diagnosis is confirmed. The changes producing the symptoms of acute leukemia are
1. Excessive destruction of red blood cells by the liver
2. Abnormal production of white blood cells by the spleen

3. Proliferation of abnormal white blood cells
4. Decreased production of white blood cells

48. Benjy's apathy and pallor are an indication of
1. Anemia
2. Poor nutrition
3. Renal disease
4. Infection

49. The nurse understands that Benjy is especially susceptible to infection because
1. Enlarged lymph nodes are not functional
2. Immature leukocytes are not capable of normal phagocytosis
3. Severe anemia conditions exist
4. Liver cannot detoxify toxins

50. In response to Mrs. K's questions regarding what she could have done to prevent this disease, the nurse should reassure her and explain that the actual etiology of leukemia is
1. Viral
2. Genetic
3. Radiation
4. Unknown

51. Mrs. K is concerned that she did not take Benjy to the doctor when his cold first appeared. The nurse might reply that
1. "It is too late to look back."
2. "Perhaps you should discuss this with your doctor."
3. "The delay did not have any effect on the course of the disease."
4. "We'll never know what could have happened if Benjy was treated sooner."

52. Cortisone acetate is one of the drugs that Benjy is receiving. The nurse should be alert to possible side effects resulting from cortisone administration. These include
1. Increased appetite, edema, and fever
2. Tinnitus and nausea
3. Anorexia and weight gain
4. Hypertension, vomiting, and chills

53. Benjy is readmitted to the hospital after a six-month remission from his disease. He is now in the terminal stage and seems to feel hopeless and afraid. The nurse could best help Benjy by
1. Allowing him to make the decisions for his care
2. Make all his decisions for him
3. Discuss with him the usual fears of dying children

4. Discuss with him the reasons for his fears

54. Benjy has become unconscious and death appears imminent. The nurse should plan to
    1. Avoid Benjy and his parents as much as possible
    2. Spend the usual amount of time with Benjy in his room
    3. Remain with Benjy and his parents as much as possible
    4. Allow Benjy and his parents to have as much time as possible to be alone

55. To cope effectively with Benjy's death, the nurse must first have
    1. Acquired a firm religious belief
    2. Reached the conclusion that death is for the best
    3. Realize that peace comes with death
    4. Coped with personal feelings about death

56. While teaching 9-year-old Karen about diabetes, the nurse should instruct her to carry the following with her at all times
    1. A lump of sugar
    2. A bag of salted nuts
    3. Insulin and syringe
    4. A dime to phone parents in case she feels ill

57. In differentiating between diabetic coma and insulin shock, the nurse needs to know that one of the following is *not* a symptom of insulin shock
    1. Weakness
    2. Pallor
    3. Face flushed
    4. Tremor

Carla, a 10-year-old girl, has been admitted to the pediatric unit where you work with a diagnosis of rheumatic fever. On admission, Carla has an elevated temperature and complains of joint pains. Carla had been ill only a brief time prior to her admission to the hospital.

58. She is fortunate that her illness was diagnosed and treated early because
    1. Manifestations of chorea can be prevented
    2. Spread of infection to other members of her family is minimized
    3. Cardiac damage can be minimized or prevented
    4. She will not have to take large amounts of medicine

59. The most important aspect to which the nurse should adhere in caring for Carla during the acute phase of her illness is
    1. Maintaining contact with Carla's family and friends
    2. Physical and psychologic rest
    3. Continuation of her school work
    4. A nutritious diet

60. Carla has developed carditis, which may cause transient heart murmurs that go away after recovery. The heart valve most often affected in rheumatic fever is
    1. Aortic
    2. Mitral
    3. Tricuspid
    4. Pulmonic

61. The prognosis for Carla depends primarily on the extent of
    1. Chorea
    2. Cardiac damage
    3. Arthritis
    4. Activity

62. Treatment for Carla's rheumatic fever included sodium salicylate. The nurse should be aware of some toxic symptoms, such as
    1. Tinnitus and nausea
    2. Dermatitis and blurred vision
    3. Unconsciousness and acetone odor of breath
    4. Chills and elevation of temperature

63. Sometimes children with rheumatic fever develop chorea during the convalescent stage. The nurse should be aware that signs of chorea include
    1. Random movements and inappropriate facial expressions
    2. Tachycardia and sudden jerky movements
    3. Pain and fever
    4. Mental confusion, retardation, and pain

64. Chorea is usually accompanied by
    1. Carditis
    2. Fever
    3. No other sign of inflammation
    4. Tachycardia

65. According to Erikson's theory of personality development, Carla would have the following core problem
    1. Industry vs inferiority
    2. Autonomy vs shame
    3. Initiative vs guilt
    4. Trust vs mistrust

66. An appropriate activity for Carla while on bedrest would be which of the following
    1. Stringing beads

2. Pillow fight
3. Knitting or crocheting
4. Listening to the radio

Johnny, an 11-year-old boy, is admitted to the pediatric unit in traction with a fractured femur sustained in a motorcycle accident. Johnny's Uncle Joe, who was driving the cycle when the accident occurred, received only minor injuries.

67. When questioning Johnny about the accident, he tells you that his Uncle Joe is not to blame, that he is "the best motorcycle rider in the world." As a nurse, you recognize this as an expression of
    1. Defense mechanisms
    2. Repression
    3. Hero worship
    4. Fantasy
68. The following activity would be *most* suitable for Johnny while he is immobilized by traction in the hospital
    1. Dramatizing with puppets
    2. Building with Popsicle sticks
    3. Watching television
    4. Coloring with crayons or colored pencils
69. If you have a choice in placing Johnny in a room *best* suited for him, you would place him in a room
    1. With a 3-year-old child because Johnny has a 3-year-old sister
    2. With two 11-year-old boys who are ambulatory
    3. With a mentally retarded 14-year-old boy
    4. With another 11-year-old boy who is also confined to bed
70. You notice that Johnny has been squirting other patients and the staff with a syringe filled with water. Recognizing that Johnny has some aggressive feelings, you know that the following activity would probably be *least* helpful to Johnny to release these feelings
    1. Punching bag
    2. Throwing bean bag
    3. Winding music box
    4. Pounding clay
71. According to Erickson, Johnny must develop a sense of industry or he will very likely develop a sense of
    1. Guilt
    2. Inferiority
    3. Shame
    4. Mistrust

72. In caring for 12-year-old Tom, an epileptic, the nurse should know that the type of epileptic seizure seen mainly in children is
    1. Grand mal
    2. Petit mal
    3. Jacksonian-march
    4. Myoclonic
73. Tom's doctor subscribes to dietary control of epilepsy. The type of diet most likely prescribed for Tom would be
    1. Low-salt diet
    2. Soft diet
    3. Ketogenic diet
    4. Low-residue diet
74. Tom has a convulsive seizure while he is in the playroom. The nurse should
    1. Have everyone else leave the room
    2. Ease Tom to the floor and loosen the clothes around his neck
    3. Hold Tom down to keep him from thrashing about
    4. Put something between his teeth

There is some general knowledge the nurse should have when caring for school-age children. The following six questions apply to this.

75. An appropriate activity for a hospitalized 6-year-old child on bedrest might include
    1. Watching a mobile
    2. Reading to self
    3. Handicrafts
    4. Playing musical instrument
76. A 7-year-old child could be expected to
    1. Dress self, know left and right, and cross street by self
    2. Know left and right and build a tower of three blocks
    3. Enjoy parallel play and share toys
    4. Select future vocation
77. The upper central incisors are usually shed at about
    1. Age 6 years
    2. Age 8½ years
    3. Age 7½ years
    4. Age 10 years
78. *All but one* of the following behaviors would be classified as negative during the initial hospitalization of an 8-year-old child
    1. Night terrors
    2. Not talking about experience
    3. Crying outbursts as reaction to immobility
    4. Excessive hyperactivity

79. A common behavioral problem of a 9-year-old child might be
    1. Enuresis
    2. Temper tantrums
    3. Stealing
    4. Vandalism
80. In working with blind children, the nurse should
    1. Speak more frequently
    2. Repeat conversation
    3. Give child extra attention
    4. Speak before touching child
81. Mrs. D is concerned that her son's headaches are caused by a brain tumor rather than eye strain as suggested by the school nurse. As a nurse you should know that signs of possible brain tumor in children include
    1. Headache, lethargy, and vomiting
    2. Increased pulse and head-banging behavior
    3. Convulsions and myopia
    4. Vomiting and fever
82. As a nurse assigned to the adolescent unit, you should know that a "normal" or positive reaction of an adolescent to hospitalization is one that
    1. Holds in feeling about illness
    2. Manipulates staff
    3. Demands control and independence
    4. Shows dependence on parents
83. Mrs. C, who is concerned about her adolescent daughter's daydreaming, should be counseled by a nurse who is aware that
    1. Her daughter is trying to evade responsibilities
    2. Her daughter is most probably schizophrenic
    3. This is typical adolescent behavior
    4. Adolescents tire easily and prefer to sit
84. Sixteen-year-old Burt is quite conscious of his acne. He asks the nurse what causes acne. Her answer is that acne vulgaris is caused primarily by
    1. Erratic diet of the adolescent
    2. Changes in the skin during adolescence
    3. Irritation of the skin due to habit of picking face
    4. Allergy to foods containing chocolate
85. Some adolescents develop scoliosis. The type of scoliosis is called
    1. Idiopathic
    2. Psychologic
    3. Postural
    4. Physiologic
86. You are working in a drug abuse clinic that sees mostly adolescents. In reviewing the history of drugs, you discover that a well-known and long-used mind-altering drug is
    1. Heroin
    2. Marihuana
    3. Mescaline
    4. Nicotine
87. An adolescent who is admitted with an overdose of "speed" has most likely been using
    1. Barbiturates
    2. Marihuana
    3. Amphetamines
    4. Narcotics
88. The major sign of barbiturate overdose is
    1. Clammy skin
    2. Pinpoint pupils
    3. Tachycardia
    4. Dilated pupils
89. A preadolescent boy admitted in a state of mental confusion, ataxic, and with red swollen nasal mucous membranes most probably has been using
    1. Marihuana
    2. Glue
    3. LSD
    4. Aspirin
90. A high school group has asked the nurse to lead a discussion on venereal disease. She could point out that a fairly common complication of gonorrhea in women is
    1. Endometriosis
    2. Infertility
    3. Pelvic inflammatory disease (PID)
    4. Ovarian cysts
91. The incubation period of syphilis is
    1. Approximately one week
    2. About three weeks
    3. About three months
    4. Three to six months
92. Syphilis is most highly contagious during the
    1. Incubation period
    2. Secondary stage
    3. Tertiary stage
    4. Onset of primary stage

As team leader of the pediatric unit, the nurse must be knowledgeable about administration of drugs. The following questions relate to this.

93. The most important responsibility of the nurse when caring for an infant receiving intravenous

therapy is to

1. Remove the needle as soon as the fluid that has been ordered has run into the vein
2. Change the bed linen promptly if it becomes moistened from the intravenous solution
3. Check frequently the number of drops of solution running into the vein and regulate the flow of solution as ordered
4. Add a new bottle of solution when the present one is empty, with or without a physician's order

94. Two preferred sites for parenteral administration of intramuscular medication in infants are
    1. Deltoid and laterofemoral
    2. Laterofemoral and anteriofemoral
    3. Dorsogluteal and deltoid
    4. Dorsogluteal and ventrogluteal

95. Eyedrops are instilled by tilting the head so that the drops flow from
    1. Outer to inner canthus
    2. Inner to outer canthus
    3. Upper to lower lid
    4. Lower to upper lid

96. The nurse should instill eyedrops into the
    1. Center of the eye
    2. Conjunctival sac
    3. Outer corner of the eye
    4. Lower eyelid

97. Ophthalmic ointments are applied to
    1. The cornea
    2. The conjunctival sac
    3. The lower eyelid
    4. The upper eyelid

98. When instilling eardrops in children under three years of age, the nurse should hold the earlobe
    1. Up and back
    2. Down and back
    3. Against the head
    4. Straight out

99. When instilling eardrops in older children, the nurse should hold the earlobe
    1. Up and back
    2. Down and back
    3. Against the head
    4. Straight out

In the following three questions, you will need to ascertain if the dosages given are too much, too little, or correct.

100. For a 12-kg boy, ampicillin, 250 mg po q6h is ordered. The *Physician's Desk Reference* (PDR) says maximum dosage is 50 mg/ kg/day, in 6- to 8-hour intervals
     1. Too much
     2. Too little
     3. Correct

101. For a 32-lb girl, Keflin, 250 mg IV q6h is ordered. The PDR says dosage range is 50 to 80 mg/kg/day, in divided doses
     1. Too much
     2. Too little
     3. Correct

102. For a 17-lb girl, Kanamycin SO_4, 80 mg IM q12h is ordered. The drug insert says maximum dosage is 15 mg/kg divided into two doses daily
     1. Too little
     2. Too much
     3. Correct

103. After 4-year-old Pam had received an IM injection, she said to the nurse, "I hate you. Go away." The nurse should answer
     1. "What a naughty girl you are."
     2. "You seem angry with me."
     3. "I bet your mother would be sad to hear you talk like that."
     4. "I'm sorry you hate me. I like you."

The nurse who is working in an outpatient clinic should be knowledgeable about immunizations and communicable diseases. The following questions concern this information.

104. Immunizations should be started when a child is
     1. Age 6 months
     2. Age 2 months
     3. Age 12 months
     4. Age 2 weeks

105. Infants do not receive passive immunization against the following
     1. Tetanus
     2. Diphtheria
     3. Pertussis
     4. Tetanus and diphtheria

106. There is no active immunization for which one of the following
     1. Measles
     2. Smallpox
     3. Chicken pox
     4. Mumps

107. DPT is used to immunize children against
     1. Diphtheria, polio, and tetanus
     2. Diphtheria, polio, and typhoid
     3. Diphtheria, pertussis, and tetanus
     4. Diptheria, pertussis, and typhoid

108. After administering DPT the nurse should
    1. Massage the site and apply a bandage
    2. Avoid massage and apply a bandage
    3. Avoid massage and press sponge on skin over needle
    4. Apply gauze over area and give aspirin for pain
109. Booster doses of DPT should be given at
    1. Age 4 months and 12 months
    2. Age 6 months and 18 months
    3. Age 18 months and 4 to 6 years
    4. Age 4 to 6 years and 10 years
110. The name of the sensitivity test for diphtheria is
    1. Dick
    2. Schick
    3. Babinsky
    4. Towle
111. Regular tuberculin testing should be done annually
    1. During the first 10 years of life
    2. In the first 5 years of life
    3. Until the test shows positive results
    4. Until a child graduates from high school
112. The results of a tuberculin test should be read
    1. Within 24 hours
    2. Within 48 hours
    3. Within 72 hours
    4. Within 96 hours
113. Mumps vaccine is recommended for the following group
    1. All children 1 to 12 years of age
    2. Pubescent men
    3. Adult men who have not had mumps
    4. All of these are correct
114. Children with scarlet fever display
    1. White spots on skin
    2. White, strawberry tongue
    3. Koplik's spots
    4. Alopecia

An important aspect of staying well and of encouraging healing is good nutrition. Some diets are prescribed for specific diseases. The following questions relate to nutrition.

115. For children through adolescence, the most essential element of the diet is
    1. Fats
    2. Water
    3. Carbohydrates
    4. Protein
116. The following foods are highest in calcium
    1. Liver, raisins, and prunes
    2. Milk, leafy vegetables, fish, and cheese
    3. Milk, spaghetti, and prunes
    4. Leafy vegetables, bread, and cereal
117. In suggesting foods high in protein, the nurse would recommend
    1. Spinach, eggs, dried fruit, and apples
    2. Fish, beef, peanut butter, and chicken
    3. Beef, chicken, eggs, and dried fruit
    4. Milk, bread, fish, and carrots
118. Foods richest in iodine would be
    1. Fruits
    2. Seafoods
    3. Vegetables
    4. Cereals
119. Cereal, bread, and macaroni are rich sources of
    1. Minerals
    2. Calcium
    3. Carbohydrates
    4. Fats
120. The nurse could suggest liver, raisin, and prunes as a rich source of
    1. Vitamin C
    2. Protein
    3. Iron
    4. Vitamin A
121. Obesity is a major problem in the United States. Causes of obesity in children might include
    1. Giving food as reward for behavior
    2. "Clean plate" award at mealtime
    3. Need for attention
    4. All of these are correct
122. Jeff, a 12-year-old boy, has a caloric intake of 3200 per day. To lose 1 lb per week, he will need to decrease his daily intake to
    1. 3100
    2. 3000
    3. 2700
    4. 2200
123. Phenylketonuria (PKU) is an inborn error of metabolism that is managed by a special diet. Diagnosis of PKU is made by
    1. Urine culture
    2. Blood test
    3. Sweat analysis
    4. Genetic history
124. Congenital cretinism is a condition in infants that can be treated by
    1. Addition of salt in the diet
    2. Increased iron intake
    3. Ingestion of desiccated thyroid
    4. High-protein diet

Answers / Rationale   Pediatric Nursing

1. (1) Tracheoesophageal fistula is a connection between the esophagus and the trachea that produces these symptoms, particularly when feeding is attempted.

2. (4) The infant may be a chronic "spitter" after feedings, which develops into projectile vomiting, and infant may become severely malnourished.

3. (4) Colostomy is temporary and constipation is seen. Currant-jelly-like stools are seen in intussusception.

4. (2) This is due to a static brain lesion.

5. (4) Prenatal, perinatal, and postnatal factors can contribute to cerebral palsy.

6. (3) The other statements are untrue; lesion is not progressive, motor function is impaired, and many children have normal intellect.

7. (1) The greater curvature of the stomach is towards the left side, so this position affords less pressure.

8. (3) The area below the meningomyelocele is affected.

9. (1) As the head continues to enlarge, the infant becomes more helpless and unable to raise the head.

10. (3) Studies show that 80% of these children are under the age of 3 years; and one-half of those are under 6 months of age.

11. (2) Although they tend to be loners, they do not like to be alone.

12. (3) This will improve the circulation. The other three answers are contraindicated.

13. (3) Neck mobility is not affected by this condition.

14. (1) Something familiar at this age helps the child adjust to the hospital environment.

15. (2) Infants drool for several months before they learn to swallow their saliva.

16. (2) Body temperature is still very labile.

17. (3) General progression is cereal, fruits, vegetables, meat, and egg yolk, taking care to introduce only one food at a time.

18. (3) Eczema is a frequent indication of allergy in infants.

19. (4) Because of the likelihood of allergies.

20. (3) Gives the infant security of being held, yet allows some freedom while utilizing diversion with play, which also promotes the infant's normal growth and development.

21. (1) Toys should be smooth and of nonallergenic nature.

22. (2) Less irritating and promotes softening of crusts on lesions.

23. (3) Cardiac failure rarely occurs after age 6 months.

24. (3) Is not cyanotic, but may become short of breath on exertion.

25. (2) Lack of oxygen in the arterial blood causes bluish tint, and child feels better in a squatting position because of the strain when standing.

26. (2) These signs are seen in older child rather than infant.

27. (2) Also accompanied with dyspnea; onset is sudden.

28. (3) 5 out of 1000 infants are born with congenital heart defect.

29. (3) Accidents outnumber all other causes of death in children.

30. (2) The infant can first be conditioned to perform elimination on the toilet but must mature before placing this under voluntary control and assume responsibility for this.

31. (1) Palpating the abdomen can cause metastasis.

32. (1) Prevention of contractures during the healing stage is essential.

33. (3) These signs are indicative of hemorrhage.

34. (1) The eustachian tubes may become plugged; infection may occur because of the close proximity.

35. (2) It is more prevalent in the black race; 10% possibly have the trait and 1 out of 400 black Americans have sickle cell anemia.

36. (4) Precipitating factors include extreme fatigue. Pain is due to occlusion of small blood vessels by sickled red cells.

37. (2) The child will need to express his feelings and puppets would be an appropriate way to promote this in a 2-year-old child.

38. (3) He is beginning to distinguish his own action from that of others.

39. (2) This is the causative organism of scarlet fever, and the glomerulonephritis is a complication

of the prior infection.

40. (1) Since the primary infection was probably *Streptococcus*, it is extremely important to isolate Terry from this child because he is highly susceptible to infections.

41. (2) Bedrest is indicated during the acute phase. Treatment is symptomatic; no specific measures.

42. (3) This would be a negative behavior that should be investigated.

43. (1) This is appropriate for a 4-year-old child to promote his developing sense of initiative while in the hospital.

44. (1) Anxiety may predispose the child to further bleeding.

45. (1) Bleeding into the joints is a common complication.

46. (2) The iliac crest and sternum are the sites used in children.

47. (3) These abnormal cells displace or replace normal bone marrow elements.

48. (1) Decrease in the red blood cells carrying hemoglobin causes anemia and the resultant symptoms.

49. (2) Infection most frequently occurs in the lungs, gastrointestinal tract, or skin.

50. (4) Certain factors are felt to be related in some patients, but the exact etiology remains unknown.

51. (3) There is no way to predict that this child would develop leukemia based on his early symptoms; treatment of a cold will not prevent leukemia or alter the course of the disease.

52. (1) Increased appetite may be welcome effect; however, discontinuation of steroids results in rapid decrease in appetite.

53. (4) The other answers are not indicated for this child; he needs to have his fears discussed to make it easier to accept them and not feel abnormal.

54. (3) They need support at this time, not abandonment.

55. (4) By understanding and acknowledging her own feelings, the nurse is then in a position to help others.

56. (1) School-age children are active and may need the extra glucose.

57. (3) This is a symptom of acidosis or diabetic coma.

58. (3) This is the only correct answer. Early detection and bedrest can minimize the effects upon the heart.

59. (2) These are the main factors in preventing complications and extensive damage during the acute phase.

60. (2) Carditis leads to aortic insufficiency and mitral stenosis resulting in fibrosis of the mitral valve.

61. (2) The younger the child, the poorer the prognosis in those children who develop carditis.

62. (1) Notify the physician if these symptoms develop.

63. (1) Most common in girls of school age.

64. (3) Occurs after the attack of rheumatic fever symptoms subside.

65. (1) Successful accomplishment of tasks is necessary for this age group.

66. (3) This is appropriate for bedrest for a school-age girl; promotes her sense of industry.

67. (3) Hero worship is very common in this age group.

68. (2) This fosters his sense of industry and can be done while in bed.

69. (4) Sense of competition is strong in this age group, and another child who is confined to bed would be more easily acceptable.

70. (3) This would not be active enough to promote release of aggressive feelings.

71. (2) It is necessary for the school-age child to be successful in his tasks. Unrealistic expectations can lead to feelings of inferiority.

72. (2) After the age of 3 years these occur more often in girls than boys; duration is approximately 30 seconds.

73. (3) A diet high in fats and reduction of fluid intake tend to prevent seizures.

74. (2) The nurse should also prevent the child from hurting himself but should not restrain his movements.

75. (3) This would be appropriate for this age child.

76. (1) Tower of three blocks or parallel play is seen in toddlers, selection of future vocation is part of adolescence, and sharing toys is preschool.

77. (3) They can be shed at 7 to 8 years of age.

78. (3) This would be an anticipated behavior because of the restriction of activity.

79. (3) Stems from a need to gain recognition.

80. (4) This allows the child to know someone is present and avoids startling the child.

81. (1) Signs that indicate increased intracranial pressure.

82. (3) The other behaviors would be negative behaviors that should be investigated or explored.

83. (3) Adolescents need time to formulate their philosophies of life, to learn to know themselves, and to plan for their future.

84. (2) Increased secretion of hormones increase

oil-gland activity.

85. (1) It is most frequent during rapid periods of growth, usually between 12 and 16 years of age.

86. (3) Comes from the peyote cactus and is said to have been used by some Indian tribes during ceremonies.

87. (3) Sometimes called uppers, they elevate the mood for depressed people.

88. (2) In association with drug abuse, this is a classic sign.

89. (2) Other effects include hallucinations and intense exhilaration.

90. (3) Often the symptoms are absent until there is an inflammatory process of great magnitude.

91. (2) The limits are 10 to 60 days.

92. (2) The secondary stage is manifested by a generalized eruption that lasts two to six weeks.

93. (3) Flow should be carefully regulated to avoid circulatory overload.

94. (2) Gluteal muscles should not be used until the child has been walking to develop these muscles; deltoid is used in older children.

95. (2) To derive the greatest benefit and avoid infecting the tear ducts.

96. (2) Correct place for proper utilization.

97. (3) Easy to administer and necessary to ensure correct usage.

98. (2) Because of the immature physiology of the ear.

99. (1) Facilitates passage of fluid onto the drum.

100. (1) 1000 mg/day is ordered; maximum for this boy is 600 mg/day.

101. (3) This is within the maximum allowable amount (note: to compute this, the pounds must be converted to kg).

102. (2) 160 mg/day is ordered; maximum dosage for a child of this weight is 125 mg/day.

103. (4) It is normal to get this response from a preschooler; the other responses from the nurse for this age group are inappropriate.

104. (2) Recommended by the American Academy of Pediatrics; based on acquired protection in utero.

105. (3) They do receive passive immunization for the other two for up to six months, if the mother is immune.

106. (3) As yet, there is no immunization for chicken pox.

107. (3) Diphtheria and tetanus toxoids with pertussis vaccine.

108. (3) Important to avoid massage for best reaction and prevent backflow from needle.

109. (3) Initial doses are given at 2, 4, and 6 months; pertussis is not necessary for children over age 6 years.

110. (2) This is a toxoid sensitivity test.

111. (2) TB is still an important disease in the United States.

112. (3) A true reading is not possible until the third day.

113. (4) These are all high-risk groups; men who get mumps run risk of orchiepididymitis, leading to sterility.

114. (2) Classic sign that occurs on second to third day.

115. (2) Necessary for variety of cellular functions, metabolic transport, and regulation of body temperature.

116. (2) Calcium needs increase during periods of rapid growth.

117. (2) These foods contain high-protein content, which is particularly important to the older child.

118. (2) Iodine is essential for thyroxin production.

119. (3) Starchy foods tend to contain higher amounts of carbohydrates.

120. (3) Iron is necessary to prevent or combat anemia.

121. (4) There is usually more than one cause for obesity.

122. (3) To lose 1 lb per week, intake must be reduced by 500 calories daily.

123. (2) When the plasma phenylalanine level rises, phenylketone bodies appear in the urine.

124. (3) Cretinism is an endocrine disease resulting from deficient production of thyroid hormone.

Annotated Bibliography

Brunner, L., and Suddarth, D.: The Lippincott manual of nursing practice, Philadelphia, 1974, J. B. Lippincott Company.

A quick reference guide for medical-surgical nursing, maternity nursing, and pediatric nursing. Outline form allows easy access to information needed by the practicing nurse.

Marlow, D. R.: Textbook of pediatric nursing, Philadelphia, 1973, W. B. Saunders Company.

A basic textbook for pediatric nursing students. It includes growth and development of children from infancy through adolescence and includes diseases specific to each age group.

Petrillo, M., and Sanger, S.: Emotional care of hospitalized children: an environmental approach, Philadelphia, 1972, J. B. Lippincott Company.

A paperback book that discusses behaviors of children who are hospitalized for conditions or procedures. Case studies included effectively illustrate certain behaviors. Specific guidelines for preparation of children for procedures are given.

Scipien, G., and Bernard, M., Chard, M., Howe, J., and Phillips, P.: Comprehensive pediatric nursing, New York, 1975, McGraw-Hill Book Co.

An extensive textbook that includes the nursing process, growth and development, effects of illness on children of each age group, discussion of body systems, and current trends in pediatric nursing practice.

Williams, S. R.: Mowry's basic nutrition and diet therapy, ed. 5, St. Louis, 1975, The C. V. Mosby Co.

A paperback book that is divided into three sections: basic principles of nutrition, variables influencing nutrition of specific populations, and diet therapy. Specific examples of various types of diets are given for both normal and special diet needs.

Nursing Trends

Introduction

The primary purpose of this section is to include practice questions that are modeled after the individual test items generally included at the end of the five subject areas in the National State Board Test Pool Examinations.

The content covered in these items focuses on epidemiology of health and illness (incidence, distribution, prevalence, and control of disorders), historical developments and trends, professional responsibilities, and ethical and legal issues with implications for nursing.

Questions   Nursing Trends

1. The main purpose for revising the laws concerning involuntary hospitalization of patients in mental hospitals is to
   1. Give the patients time to adjust to the community when discharged
   2. Ensure that the patients complete their therapy
   3. Extend the civil rights of the mental patients
   4. Provide for the safety of the public
2. If a nurse is convicted of illegally using narcotics, who revokes that nurse's license to practice nursing?
   1. Hospital or agency that employs that nurse
   2. Department of Health, Education, and Welfare
   3. American Nurses' Association
   4. State Board of Registered Nursing
3. Federal funds for promoting teaching and research in psychiatric nursing are administered by
   1. National Institute for Mental Health
   2. National Mental Health Association
   3. Western Interstate Commission for Higher Education in Nursing
   4. American Nurses' Association
4. Which organization has the major responsibility for granting accreditation to schools of nursing in the United States?
   1. National League for Nursing
   2. American Nurses' Association
   3. Council for Higher Education in Nursing
   4. State board of nursing in each state
5. The increasing use of day and night treatment centers as a community mental health service is a recent trend. The main purpose of these centers is to
   1. Offer crisis intervention around the clock
   2. Provide vocational rehabilitation near the patient's home
   3. Assess and diagnose patients in their own communities
   4. Offer out-patient treatment for a designated period of time
6. Which of the following is *not* a reportable communicable disease?
   1. Syphilis
   2. Tuberculosis
   3. Pneumonia
   4. Smallpox
7. Good samaritan laws permit RNs to
   1. Perform surgery without fear of being sued
   2. Prescribe drugs outside the hospital setting
   3. Receive two Sundays off per month to attend church
   4. Give emergency care without fear of being sued
8. Which of the following persons was not a pioneer in nursing?
   1. Florence Nightingale
   2. Sue Barton
   3. Clara Barton
   4. Dorothea Dix
9. According to the ANA position statement of 1965, what type of preparation should be required for the professional nurse?
   1. Diploma
   2. Associate
   3. Baccalaureate
   4. Master
10. What determines legality of nursing interventions?
    1. The AMA and ANA Joint Statement
    2. Each state's Nurse Practice Act
    3. State boards of registration and licensure
    4. The written hospital policy manuals
11. The American College of Nurse Midwifery was founded in
    1. 1932
    2. 1955
    3. 1972
    4. None of these are correct; the Maternity Center of New York is the official organization of nurse midwives in the United States
12. The most significant consequence of the development of alternative life-styles in the United States is evidenced in
    1. The increase in numbers of babies of all races who are placed for adoption
    2. The growing numbers of couples who live together until pregnancy is confirmed and then marry
    3. The trend for unmarried women (or men) to raise the child (or children) in a single parent family

4. The sharp decline in unwed pregnancies, especially in the "under 17" age group

13. In 1973, the U.S. Supreme Court legalized abortion during the first trimester, ruling all of the following, *except*
    1. The man has a part in the decision-making process
    2. The woman has the sole voice in the decision to abort or not
    3. The conceptus, whether a zygote or embryo, is not legally a "person"
    4. The fetus is not legally a "person"

14. In 1916, the first birth-control clinic in the United States was opened in a slum of Brooklyn, New York, by
    1. Mary Breckinredge
    2. Marjorie Karmel
    3. Grantly Dick-Read
    4. Margaret Sanger

15. Each of the states in the United States has laws requiring that the following tests or procedures be performed on mothers-to-be or neonates, *except*
    1. Test for *Treponema pallidum*
    2. Prophylaxis against ophthalmia neonatorum
    3. Test for phenylketonuria
    4. Rubella antibody titer

16. One of the turning points in recognizing the importance of improved care for children in the United States was the establishment of
    1. White House Conference on Children
    2. World Health Organization (WHO)
    3. Children's Bureau
    4. United Nations International Children's Emergency Fund (UNICEF)

17. The agency that administers Project Headstart is
    1. Children's Bureau
    2. Local public welfare office
    3. Office of Economic Opportunity
    4. Family Service Association

18. The state government uses funds from the Rehabilitation Services Administration to administer
    1. Hot-lunch program in schools
    2. Crippled Children's Program
    3. Project Headstart
    4. Day care centers

19. Which of the following programs provides full or part-time experience and training for children 16 to 21 years of age?
    1. Job Corps
    2. Vista Volunteers
    3. Project Headstart
    4. Neighborhood Youth Corps

20. The nurse is protected from *legal action* when she
    1. Administers first aid to an auto accident victim
    2. Uses heroic life-saving measures on a drownded child who later dies
    3. Reports suspected child abuse to authorities
    4. Dispenses birth control devices to a minor youth

Answers / Rationale

Nursing Trends

1. (3) Promotion of civil rights is an important national concern: patients in mental hospitals were previously denied such rights as voting.

2. (4) The agency that grants the nursing license also has the responsibility to revoke, suspend, and deny license to a practicing nurse.

3. (1) NIMH is the official national agency that administers such funds. No. 2 is a *voluntary* agency and is involved in public education. No. 3 is *regional*, not federal, group. And, No. 4 is a *professional* organization that represents and acts as a voice for nurses.

4. (1)

5. (4) No. 1 and No. 2 are types of community mental health services in themselves. No. 3 is the main function of an *intake* service within the community mental health structure.

6. (3) Syphilis, tuberculosis, and smallpox are reportable communicable diseases.

7. (4) The good Samaritan laws permit RNs (and other medical and paramedical personnel) to give emergency care at the scene of an accident without

fear of civil or criminal charges providing they perform only those procedures for which they have been trained.

8. (2) Sue Barton is a fictional character. She is a stereotype that the profession is currently trying to eradicate.

9. (3) According to the ANA's position paper, baccalaureate preparation should be the minimum requirement for the professional nurse.

10. (2) Each state's Nurse Practice Act is the only legal determinant of nursing interventions. The AMA, ANA, and state boards of registration and licensure can make recommendations only. Written policy manuals must follow the legal guidelines set out by the Nurse Practice Acts.

11. (2) The American College of Nurse Midwifery was founded in 1955 and was admitted to the International Confederation of Midwives in 1957. There are about 12 nurse midwifery programs in the United States today; some confer a certificate, whereas others prepare the nurse midwife at the master's level. Each state legislates the standards, duties, and responsibilities of nurse midwifery practice.

12. (3) Although there is still some stigma attached, severe societal rejection is lessening, and the numbers of unwed women (and men) having and keeping their babies to raise is increasing.

13. (1) The man has no claim to the conceptus and therefore is not entitled to codecide its fate; the decision to abort rests entirely between the woman and her physician.

14. (4) Margaret Sanger was responsible for the birth control center. The Research Bureau, founded in 1923, focused on infertility, contraception, and marriage counseling. Ms. Sanger was responsible for the Planned Parenthood Federation of America, Inc., established in 1942, as well.

15. (4) In many states, there is now legislation requiring the woman to be tested for rubella antibody titer when the couple applies for a marriage license. PKU became mandatory in 1965. Carolyn Van Blarcom was the nurse partly responsible for the law requiring eye prophylaxes.

16. (1) The White House Conferences on Children began in 1909 and provides for continuing "well-being of children." The Children's Bureau was established in 1912 and focuses on investigating and reporting all matters pertaining to children of all socioeconomic strata. UNICEF aids children all over the world. And, WHO was established by UN as a special agency headquartered in Geneva.

17. (3) Office of Economic Opportunity. The program was begun to enable culturally deprived children to prepare for entry to kindergarten or first grade.

18. (2) Crippled Children's Program provides diagnostic services, medical care, hospitalization, and follow-up care to handicapped children.

19. (1) Job Corps. Youth of both sexes are provided training in jobs, such as auto mechanics, home repair, graphic arts, and child care.

20. (3) Reports suspected child abuse to authorities. A nurse, physician, or neighbor are all protected by law from legal action by the parents-care-takers suspected of child abuse. A nurse is not protected from a suit filed by persons in No. 1 or 2. In answer No. 4, the nurse does not have a license to prescribe, only to follow a medical prescription.

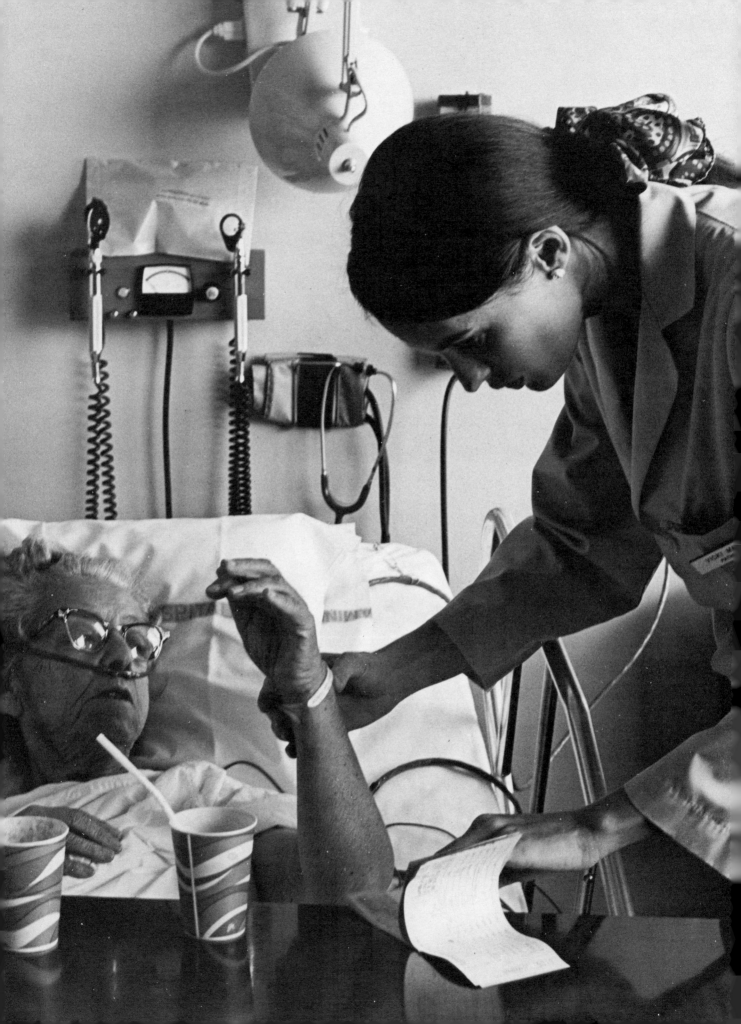

Appendices

Appendix A   Erikson's Stages of Personality Development*

Stage	Approximate age (years)	Central problem	Influencing persons
Infancy	0–1	Trust versus mistrust†	Maternal figure
Toddler	2–3	Autonomy versus shame, doubt	Parental figures
Preschool	4–5	Initiative versus guilt	Basic family unit
School	6–12	Industry versus inferiority	School and neighborhood figures
Puberty and early adolescence	12–18	Identity versus role-diffusion	Peers and leadership models
Late adolescence Young adult	18–25	Intimacy, solidarity versus isolation	Chosen partners of same and opposite sex
Middle-age adult		Generativity versus self-absorption, stagnation	Shared household
Elderly adult		Ego integrity versus despair	''Mankind''

*Reprinted from Childhood and Society, 2nd Edition, by Erik H. Erikson. By permission of W. W. Norton & Company, Inc. Copyright 1950, © 1963 by W. W. Norton & Company, Inc.

†The central problem of each stage must be successfully solved to provide a basis for the solution of the next problem. It should be noted that each problem is not completely solved for each stage but that habits of both continuums remain with most people throughout life.

Appendix B   Mental Deficiency*

Level (IQ)	Preschool (0–5 years)—maturation and development	School age (6–21 years)—training and education	Adult (21 years and over)—social and vocational adequacy
Profound: 0–19	Gross retardation; minimal capacity for functioning in sensorimotor areas; need nursing care	Obvious delays in all areas of development; show basic emotional responses; may respond to skillful training in use of legs, hands, and jaws; need close supervision	May walk, need nursing care, have primitive speech; usually benefit from regular physical activity; incapable of self-maintenance
Severe: 20–35	Marked delay in motor development; little or no communication skills; may respond to training in elementary self-help, for example, self-feeding	Usually walk, barring specific disability; have some understanding of speech and some response; can profit from systematic habit training	Can conform to daily routines and repetitive activities; need continuing direction and supervision in protective environment

*Classification developed by the American Association of Mental Deficiency.

Continued

APPENDIX B-MENTAL DEFICIENCY—continued

Level (IQ)	Preschool (0-5 years)—maturation and development	School age (6-21 years)—training and education	Adult (21 years and over)—social and vocational adequacy
Moderate: 36–51	Noticeable delays in motor development, especially in speech; responds to training in various self-help activities	Can learn simple communication, elementary health and safety habits, and simple manual skills; does not progress in functional reading or arithmetic	Can perform simple tasks under sheltered conditions; participate in simple recreation; travel alone in familiar places; usually incapable of self-maintenance
Mild: 52–67	Often not noticed as retarded by casual observer but are slower to walk, feed self, and talk than most children	Can acquire practical skills and useful reading and arithmetic to a third to sixth grade level with special education; can be guided toward social conformity	Can usually achieve social and vocational skills adequate to self-maintenance; may need occasional guidance and support when under unusual social or economic stress

Appendix C   Diets

NUTRITION DURING PREGNANCY AND LACTATION

1. **Milk group**—important for calcium, protein of high biologic value, and other vitamins and minerals
   Pregnancy—three to four servings
   Lactation—four servings
   Count as one serving—1 cup milk; ½ cup undiluted evaporated milk; ¼ cup dry milk; 1¼ cup cottage cheese; 1½ cup cheddar or Swiss cheese; or 1½ cup ice cream

2. **Meat group**—important for protein, iron, and many B vitamins
   Pregnancy—three to four servings
   Lactation—three servings
   Count as one serving (12-14 gm protein)—2 oz lean meat, fish, or poultry; 2 eggs; 2 frankfurters; 4 tbsp peanut butter; or 1 cup cooked dry beans, dry peas, or lentils

3. **Vegetable and fruit group**—vitamins and minerals (especially A and C) and roughage
   Pregnancy—four to five servings
   Lactation—five servings
   Count as one serving—½ medium grapefruit; 1 medium apple, banana, or orange; ¾ cup fruit juice
   Good sources (vitamin C)—citruses, cantaloupe, mango, papaya, strawberries, broccoli, and green and red chili peppers
   Fair sources (vitamin C)—tomatoes, honeydew melon, asparagus tips, raw cabbage, collards, kale, mustard greens, potatoes (white and sweet), spinach, and turnip greens
   Good sources (vitamin A)—dark green or deep yellow vegetables and a few fruits (apricots, broccoli, pumpkin, sweet potato, spinach, cantaloupe, carrots, and winter squash)
   Good sources of folic acid—dark green foliage-type vegetables

4. **Bread and cereal group**—good for thiamine, iron, niacin, and other vitamins and minerals
   Pregnancy—four to five servings
   Lactation—four to five servings
   Count as one serving—1 slice bread, 1 oz ready-to-eat cereal, ½ to ¾ cup cooked cereal, cornmeal, grits, macaroni, noodles, rice, or spaghetti

SPECIAL PEDIATRIC DIETS

1. **Low-carbohydrate diet**—avoid cream sauces and soups
   A. For obesity; reducing
   B. For diabetics—controlled amounts of carbohydrates, fats, and proteins
   C. For epilepsy—Ketogenic: low-carbohydrate, high-fat

2. **Gluten-free diet**—elimination of all foods made from wheat and rye, used for celiac disease

3. **High-protein diet**—lean meat, cheese, and green vegetables
   A. Infectious hepatitis
   B. Malabsorption (for example, ulcerative colitis)
   C. Malnutrition
   D. Patients with extensive burns
   E. Nephrotic syndrome (may also be on low-sodium diet)
   F. Acute leukemia (combined with high-calorie and soft-food diets)
   G. Neoplastic disease

4. **Low-protein diet**—eggs, fruit (apples, applesauce), and vegetables (carrots, potatoes)
   A. Usually accompanied by high-carbohydrate diet and normal fats and calories
   B. Acute nephritis
   C. Uremia
   D. Anuria
   E. Renal failure

5. **Low-sodium diet**—avoid canned vegetables and fruits
   A. Acute nephritis
   B. Nephrotic syndrome
   C. Congestive heart failure

6. **High-roughage, residue diet**—raw vegetables and fruit
   A. Constipation
   B. Long-term immobilization

7. **Inborn errors of metabolism diets**—based on specific disease or condition, as ordered

COMMON THERAPEUTIC DIETS*

Clear-liquid diet
Purpose: Relieve thirst and help maintain fluid balance.
Use: Postsurgically and following acute vomiting or diarrhea.
Food allowed: Carbonated beverages, coffee (caffeinated and decaffeinated), tea, fruit-flavored drinks, fruit juices, clear flavored gelatins, broth, consommé, sugar, and hard candy.
Foods avoided: Milk and milk products, fruit juices with pulp, and fruit.

---

*Clear-liquid, full-liquid, soft, sodium-restricted, renal, high-protein high-carbohydrate, purine-restricted, bland, and low-fat cholesterol-restricted diets were reprinted by permission from *Recent Advances in Therapeutic Diets*, Second Edition, by Staff of the Department of Nutrition, The University of Iowa © 1973 by the Iowa State University Press, Ames, Iowa.

Sample menu

Breakfast	*Lunch*	*Dinner*
$^3/_4$ c cranberry juice	1 c apple juice	1 c orange drink
$^1/_2$ c broth	$^3/_4$ c bouillon	$^3/_4$ c consommé
$^1/_2$ c lime jello	$^1/_2$ c cherry jello	$^1/_2$ c lemon jello
2 tsp sugar	1 tsp sugar	2 sticks hard candy
Coffee or tea	Coffee or tea	Coffee or tea

Between-meal nourishment: $^3/_4$ c gingerale or Seven-Up

Full-liquid diet

Purpose: Provide an adequately nutritious diet for patients who cannot chew or are too ill to do so.

Use: Acute infection with fever, gastrointestinal upsets, after surgery as a progression from *clear liquids*.

Foods allowed: Clear liquid, milk drinks, cooked cereals, custards, ice cream, sherbets, eggnog, all fruit juices, vegetable juices, creamed vegetable soups, mashed potatoes, mild cheese sauce or pureed meat, and seasonings.

Foods avoided: Nuts, seeds, coconut, fruit, jam, and marmalade.

Sample Menu: Diet offered in six feedings or more.

Breakfast	*Lunch*	*Dinner*
$^1/_2$ c strained orange juice	$^3/_4$ c cream of tomato soup	$^3/_4$ c broth
$^1/_2$ c strained oatmeal with butter, hot milk, sugar	$^1/_2$ c apricot nectar	$^3/_4$ c eggnog
1 c milk	1 scoop vanilla ice cream	$^1/_2$ c strawberry jello with whipped cream
Coffee or tea with cream and sugar	1 c milk	1 c milk
	Coffee or tea with cream and sugar	Coffee or tea with sugar
Midmorning snack	*Midafternoon snack*	*Evening snack*
$^1/_2$ c egg custard	Vanilla milkshake	1 c hot chocolate

Soft diet

Purpose: Provide adequate nutrition for those who have trouble chewing.

Use: Patients with no teeth or ill-fitting dentures; transition from full-liquid to general diet; and for those who cannot tolerate highly seasoned, fried, or raw foods following acute infections or gastrointestinal disturbances, such as gastric ulcer or cholelithiasis.

Foods allowed: Very tender minced, ground, baked, broiled, roasted, stewed, or creamed beef, lamb, veal, liver, poultry, or fish; crisp bacon or sweetbreads; cooked vegetables; pasta; all fruit juices; soft raw fruits; soft breads and cereals; all desserts that are soft; and cheeses.

Foods avoided: Coarse whole-grain cereals and breads; nuts; raisins; coconut; fruits with small seeds; fried foods; high-fat gravies or sauces; spicy salad dressings; pickled meat, fish, or poultry; strong cheeses; brown or wild rice; raw vegetables as well as lima beans and corn; spices such as horseradish, mustard, and catsup; and popcorn.

Sample menu

Breakfast	*Lunch*	*Dinner*
Orange sections	1 c tomato bouillon	Grapefruit sections
1 egg, soft-boiled	1 biscuit	3 oz beef patty
$^1/_2$ c oatmeal	3 oz roast chicken	$^1/_4$ c beef broth gravy
1 slice toast	$^1/_2$ c green beans	$^1/_4$ c cooked carrots
1 tsp butter	$^1/_2$ c buttered rice	Baked potato, without skin, buttered
1 c milk	1 slice angel-food cake	1 dinner roll
2 tsp sugar	1 c milk	1 tsp butter
Coffee or tea	Coffee or tea with sugar	1 slice custard pie
		Coffee or tea

Sodium-restricted diet

Purpose: Reduce sodium content in the tissues and promote excretion of water.

Use: Congestive heart failure, hypertension, renal disease, cirrhosis, toxemia of pregnancy, and in cortisone therapy.

Modifications: Mildly restrictive 2-gm sodium diet to extremely restricted 200-mg sodium diet.

Foods Avoided: Table salt; all commercial soups including bouillon, gravy, catsup, mustard, meat sauces, soy sauce, buttermilk, ice cream, sherbet, sodas, beet greens, carrots, celery, chard, sauerkraut, spinach, all canned vegetables, frozen peas, all baked products containing salt, baking powder, or baking soda, potato chips, popcorn, fresh or canned shell fish, all cheeses, smoked or commercially prepared meats, salted butter or margarine, bacon, olives, and commercially prepared salad dressings.

Sample menu: 500 mg strict salt-restricted diet—
milk or milk drinks limited to two cups per day

Breakfast	*Lunch*	*Dinner*
1/2 c frozen orange juice	Saladbowl: lettuce, endive, raw cauliflower, green pepper, tomato wedges, sliced chicken strips	Roast beef, 4 oz
1/2 c farina		1 baked potato
1 egg, soft-boiled		2 tsp chive butter
1 slice toast, enriched unsalted bread		1/2 c fresh peas and mushrooms
1 tsp unsalted butter	1 tbsp 1000 Island dressing, unsalted	1 roll and butter, unsalted
1 tbsp peach jelly	1 roll, unsalted	1/2 banana, sliced
1 c milk	1 tsp butter, unsalted	1 c milk
Coffee or tea with sugar	1 peach, fresh and sliced	Coffee or tea with sugar

Renal diet

Purpose: Control protein, potassium, sodium, and fluid levels in body.

Use: Acute and chronic renal failure, hemodialysis.

Food allowed: High-biologic proteins such as meat, fowl, fish, cheese, and dairy products—range between 20 and 60 mg per day. Potassium is usually limited to 40 mEq per day. Vegetables such as cabbage, cucumber, and peas are lowest in potassium. Sodium is restricted to 500 mg per day. See sodium-restricted diet. Fluid intake is restricted to the daily urine volume plus 500 ml, which represents insensible water loss. Fluid intake measures water in fruit, vegetables, milk, and meat.

Food avoided: Cereals, bread, macaroni, noodles, spaghetti, avocados, kidney beans, potato chips, raw fries, yams, soybeans, nuts, gingerbread, apricots, bananas, figs, grapefruit, oranges, percolated coffee, Coca-Cola, Orange Crush, Gatorade, and breakfast drinks such as Tang or Awake.

Sample menu: Contains 60 gm protein, 60 mEq potassium, 35 mEq sodium, and 1000 ml fluid

Breakfast	*Lunch*	*Dinner*
1/2 c peach nectar	1 oz chicken unsalted	2 oz roast beef, sirloin
1 egg, soft-cooked	1/2 c green beans, unsalted, drained	1/2 c cubed white potato, drained, unsalted
1 slice toast, white, enriched, unsalted	1 slice bread, unsalted, white, enriched	2 halves canned pears, drained
2 tsp butter, unsalted	3 tsp butter, unsalted	3/4 c tossed lettuce salad
1 tbsp grape jelly	1 tbsp grape jelly	2 tbsp oil & vinegar dressing
2 tsp sugar	1/2 small banana	2 tsp butter, unsalted
1 c Sanka	3/4 c Kool-Aid	1 tsp sugar
		1 c tea
Midmorning snack	*Midafternoon snack*	*Evening snack*
1 c puffed wheat	1/2 c unsalted gelatin	1 slice bread, enriched, unsalted, white
1/2 c milk	10 vanilla wafers	1 oz turkey, unsalted
1 tsp sugar		2 tsp butter, unsalted
1 small apple		1/2 c gingerale
		2 tsp sugar

High-protein, high-carbohydrate diet

Purpose: Corrects large protein losses and raises the level of blood albumin. May be modified to include low-fat, low-sodium, and low-cholesterol diets.

Use: Burns, hepatitis, cirrhosis, pregnancy, hyperthyroidism, mononucleosis, protein deficiency due to poor eating habits, geriatric patients with poor food intake, nephritis, nephrosis, and liver and gallbladder disorders.

Foods allowed: General diet with added protein. In adults, high-protein diets usually contain 135 to 150 gm protein.

Foods avoided: Restrictions are dependent on added modifications to the diet. These modifications are determined by the patient's condition.

Sample menu

Breakfast	*Lunch*	*Dinner*
½ c apple juice	3 oz grilled hamburger on bun	6 oz club steak
¾ c Cream of Wheat	½ sliced tomato on lettuce	½ c mashed potatoes
2 eggs, scrambled	¼ c cottage cheese	½ c buttered carrots
1 slice, whole-wheat toast	2 tsp butter	½ c coleslaw
2 tsp butter	1 slice angel-food cake	1 dinner roll
1 tbsp grape jelly	1 scoop strawberry ice cream	2 tsp butter
1 c milk	Coffee, tea, or milk	½ c sherbet
2 tsp sugar		4 vanilla wafers
Coffee or tea		1 c milk
		Coffee or tea

Midmorning snack	*Midafternoon snack*	*Evening snack*
1 c milk	½ c egg custard	Vanilla milkshake

Purine-restricted diet

Purpose: Designed to reduce the amount of consumed uric acid-producing foods.

Use: High–uric acid retention, uric acid renal stones, and gout.

Foods allowed: General diet plus two to three quarts of liquid daily.

Foods avoided: Cheese containing spices or nuts, fried eggs, meat, liver, seafood, lentils, dried peas and beans, broth, bouillon, gravies, oatmeal and whole wheats, pasta, noodles, and alcoholic beverages. Limited quantities meat, fish, and seafood.

Sample menu

Breakfast	*Lunch*	*Dinner*
½ c orange juice	1 c tomato soup	3 oz Swiss steak
½ c corn flakes	Sandwich:	1 baked potato
2 eggs, soft-boiled	2 oz chicken	½ c string beans
2 slices toast, white	2 slices white bread	2 rolls
2 tbsp butter	1 tbsp mayonnaise	2 tbsp butter
2 tbsp apple butter	½ c lime jello	½ c strawberry parfait
1 c milk, nonfat	Coffee or tea	Coffee or tea
Coffee or tea		

Midmorning snack	*Midafternoon snack*	*Evening snack*
1 c milk, nonfat	1 c milk, nonfat	1 c hot chocolate, made with
	2 brownies without nuts	nonfat milk

Bland diet

Purpose: Provision of a diet low in fiber, roughage, mechanical irritants, and chemical stimulants.

Use: Ulcers (gastric and duodenal), gastritis, hyperchlorhydria, functional GI disorders, gastric atony, diarrhea, spastic constipation, biliary indigestion, and hiatus hernia.

Foods allowed: Varied to meet individual needs and food tolerances.

Foods avoided: Fried foods including eggs, meat, fish, and seafood; cheese with added nuts or spices; commercially prepared luncheon meats; cured meats such as ham; gravies and sauces; raw vegetables; potato skins; fruit juices with pulp; figs; raisins; fresh fruits; whole wheats; rye bread; bran cereals; rich pastries; pies; chocolate; jams with seeds; nuts; seasoned dressings; regular coffee; strong tea; cocoa; alcoholic and carbonated beverages; and pepper.

Sample menu

Breakfast
1/2 c applesauce
1 egg, poached
1 slice white toast
1 tsp butter
1 tsp grape jelly
1 c whole milk
Coffee, decaffeinated
1 tsp sugar

Midmorning snack
1 c buttermilk

Lunch
1 c creamed tomato soup
Sandwich:
  3 oz cheese
  2 slices white bread
  1 tbsp mayonnaise
1/2 c sherbet
Coffee, decaffeinated

Midafternoon snack
1 vanilla milkshake

Dinner
6 oz white fish, broiled
1/2 c mashed potatoes
1/2 c green peas
1 dinner roll
1 tsp butter
1/2 c vanilla ice cream
Weak tea or decaffeinated
  coffee
1 tsp sugar

Evening snack
1 egg custard

Low-fat, cholesterol-restricted diet:

Purpose: Reduce hyperlipemia, provide dietary treatment for malabsorption syndromes, and patients having acute intolerance for fats.

Use: Hyperlipidemia, atherosclerosis, pancreatitis, cystic fibrosis, sprue, gastrectomy, and massive resection of the small intestine.

Foods Allowed: Nonfat milk, low-carbohydrate, low-fat vegetables; most fruits; breads; pastas; cornmeal; lean meats; unsaturated fats such as corn oil; desserts made without whole milk; and unsweetened carbonated beverages.

Foods Avoided: Whole milk and whole-milk or cream products, avocados, olives, commercially prepared baked goods as donuts and muffins, poultry skin, highly marbled meats, shellfish, fish canned in oil, nuts, coconut, commercially prepared meats, butter, ordinary margarines, olive oil, lard, pudding made with whole milk, ice cream, candies with chocolate, cream, sauces, gravies, and commercially fried foods.

Sample menu

Breakfast
1/2 grapefruit
3/4 c puffed wheat
1 tsp sugar
1 slice white toast
2 tsp safflower margarine
2 tsp jelly
1 c skimmed milk
Coffee or tea

Lunch
Sandwich:
2 slices whole wheat bread
2 oz sliced chicken
2 tsp mayonnaise
1/2 c coleslaw
1 small banana
Coffee or tea

Dinner
4 oz lamb chops (2)
1 baked potato
1 tsp safflower margarine
1/2 c cooked carrots
3/4 c tossed lettuce salad
Lemon wedge
1/2 c fruit sherbet
Coffee or tea

Diabetic diet

Purpose: Control the progression of diabetes mellitus.

Use: Diabetes mellitus.

Foods allowed: Foods are divided into groups from which exchanges can be made. Coffee, tea, broth, bouillon, spices, and flavorings can be used as desired. Vegetable A exchanges, one cup, contain mostly green vegetables while vegetable B exchanges, one-half cup contain the remaining vegetables. The amounts of the remaining exchanges depend on the food selected. Fruit exchanges are fruits without sugar or syrup. Meat, fat, and milk exchanges. The number of exchanges allowed from each group is dependent on the total number of calories allowed.

Foods avoided: Concentrated sweets or regular soft drinks.

Sample menu

Breakfast	*Lunch*	*Dinner*
$\frac{1}{2}$ c orange juice	1 hamburger with bun,	1 c tossed green salad
1 poached egg	2 oz broiled meat	4 oz roast lamb
1 slice toast	1 sliced tomato	$\frac{1}{2}$ c rice
$\frac{2}{3}$ c corn flakes	2 tsp mayonnaise	$\frac{1}{2}$ c cabbage
1 tsp margarine	1 tsp mustard	2 tbsp French dressing
1 slice crisp bacon	2 small carrots	1 tsp margarine
1 c milk, nonfat	1 medium apple	Diet gelatin with $\frac{1}{2}$ c
Black coffee or tea	Tab	Fruit cocktail
		Black coffee or tea

Bedtime: 1 c nonfat milk
2 graham crackers

Sample food exchange lists for diabetic diet*

Daily menu guide—1500 Calories

	Breakfast	Lunch	Dinner
Carbohydrate	1 fruit exchange (List 3)	2 meat exchanges (List 5)	2 meat exchanges (List 5)
150 gm	2 bread exchanges	2 bread exchanges	1½ bread exchanges
Protein 70 gm	(List 4)	(List 4)	(List 4)
Fat 70 gm	1 meat exchange (List 5)	Vegetable(s) as desired	Vegetable(s) as desired
	1 milk exchange (List 7)	(List 1)	(List 1)
	2 fat exchanges (List 6)	1 fruit exchange (List 3)	1 vegetable exchange
	Coffee or tea (any	1 milk exchange (List 7)	(List 2)
	amount)	1 fat exchange (List 6)	1 fruit exchange (List 3)
		Coffee or tea (any	½ milk exchange (List 7)
		amount)	1 fat exchange (List 6)
			Coffee or tea (any
			amount)

*Courtesy of Eli Lilly Company.

List 1 allowed as desired**

Seasonings: Cinnamon, celery salt, garlic, garlic salt, lemon, mustard, mint, nutmeg, parsley, pepper, saccharin and other sugarless sweeteners, spices, vanilla, and vinegar.

Other Foods: Coffee or tea (without sugar or cream), fat-free broth, bouillon, unflavored gelatin, rennet tablets, sour or dill pickles, cranberries (without sugar), rhubarb (without sugar).

Vegetables: Group A—insignificant carbohydrate or calories. You may eat as much as desired of raw vegetables. If cooked vegetable is eaten, limit

**Need not be measured

amount to 1 cup.

Asparagus	Lettuce
Broccoli	Mushrooms
Brussels sprouts	Okra
Cabbage	Peppers, green
Cauliflower	or red
Celery	Radishes
Chicory	Sauerkraut
Cucumbers	String beans
Eggplant	Summer squash
Escarole	Tomatoes
Greens: beet, chard,	Watercress
collard, dandelion, kale,	
mustard, spinach, turnip	

List 2 vegetable exchanges

Each portion supplies approximately 7 gm of carbohydrate and 2 gm of protein, or 36 calories.

Vegetables: Group B—One serving equals ½ cup, or 100 gm.

Beets	Pumpkin
Carrots	Rutabagas
Onions	Squash, winter
Peas, green	Turnips

List 3 fruit exchanges*

Each portion supplies approximately 10 gm of carbohydrate, or 40 calories.

	Household Measurement	Weight of Portion
Apple	1 small (2-inch diam)	80 gm
Applesauce	½ c	100 gm
Apricots, fresh	2 med	100 gm
Apricots, dried	4 halves	20 gm
Banana	½ small	50 gm
Berries	1 c	150 gm
Blueberries	⅔ c	100 gm
Cantaloupe	¼ (6-inch diam)	200 gm
Cherries	10 large	75 gm
Dates	2	15 gm
Figs, fresh	2 large	50 gm
Figs, dried	1 small	15 gm
Grapefruit	½ small	125 gm
Grapefruit juice	½ c	100 gm
Grapes	12	75 gm
Grape juice	¼ c	60 gm
Honeydew melon	⅛ (7-inch)	150 gm
Mango	½ small	70 gm
Orange	1 small	100 gm
Orange juice	½ c	100 gm
Papaya	⅓ med	100 gm
Peach	1 med	100 gm
Pear	1 small	100 gm
Pineapple	½ c	80 gm
Pineapple juice	⅓ c	80 gm
Plums	2 med	100 gm
Prunes, dried	2	25 gm
Raisins	2 tbsp	15 gm
Tangerine	1 large	100 gm
Watermelon	1 c	175 gm

List 4 bread exchanges

Each portion supplies approximately 15 gm of carbohydrate and 2 gm of protein, or 68 calories.

---

*Fresh, dried, or canned without sugar

	Household Measurement	Weight of Portion
Bread	1 slice	25 gm
Biscuit, roll	1 (2-inch diam)	35 gm
Muffin	1 (2-inch diam)	35 gm
Cornbread	1½-inch cube	35 gm
Flour	2½ tbsp	20 gm
Cereal, cooked	½ c	100 gm
Cereal, dry (flakes or puffed)	¾ c	20 gm
Rice or grits, cooked	½ c	100 gm
Spaghetti, noodles, etc	½ c	100 gm
Crackers, graham	2	20 gm
Crackers, oyster	20 (½ c)	20 gm
Crackers, saltine	5	20 gm
Crackers, soda	3	20 gm
Crackers, round	6-8	20 gm
Vegetables		
Beans (lima, navy, etc.), dry, cooked	½ c	90 gm
Peas (split peas, etc.), dry, cooked	½ c	90 gm
Baked beans, no pork	¼ c	50 gm
Corn	⅓ c	80 gm
Parsnips	⅔ c	125 gm
Potato, white, baked or boiled	1 (2-inch diam)	100 gm
Potatoes, white, mashed	½ c	100 gm
Potatoes, sweet, or yams	¼ c	50 gm
Sponge cake, plain	1½-inch cube	25 gm
Ice cream (omit 2 fat exchanges)	½ c	70 gm

List 5 meat exchanges

Each portion supplies approximately 7 gm of protein and 5 gm of fat, or 73 calories (30 gm equal 1 oz).

	Household Measurement	Weight of Portion
Meat and poultry (beef, lamb, pork, liver, chicken, etc.) (med. fat)	1 slice (3 × 2 × ⅛-inch)	30 gm
Cold cuts	1 slice (4½-inch sq., ⅛-inch thick)	45 gm
Frankfurter	1 (8-9 per lb.)	50 gm
Codfish, mackerel, etc.	1 slice (2 × 2 × 1-inch)	30 gm
Salmon, tuna, crab	¼ c	30 gm
Oysters, shrimp, clams	5 small	45 gm

Sardines . . . . 3 med . . . . . . .30 gm
Cheese, cheddar,
   American . . . . 1 slice (3½ × 1½ ×
                                   ¼-inch) . . . .30 gm
Cheese, cottage . . . . . ¼ c . . . . .45 gm
Egg . . . . 1 . . . . .50 gm
Peanut butter . . . . . . 2 tbsp . . . . . .30 gm

Limit peanut butter to one exchange per day unless allowance is made for carbohydrate in the diet plan.

List 6 fat exchanges

Each portion supplies approximately 5 gm of fat, or 45 calories.

	Household Measurement	Weight of Portion
Butter or margarine . . .	1 tsp	5 gm
Bacon, crisp	1 slice	10 gm
Cream, light	2 tbsp	30 gm
Cream, heavy	1 tbsp	15 gm

Cream cheese . . . . . . 1 tbsp . . . . . . 15 gm
French dressing . . . . . 1 tbsp . . . . . . 15 gm
Mayonnaise . . . . 1 tsp . . . . 5 gm
Oil or cooking fat . . . . 1 tsp . . . . 5 gm
Nuts . . . . 6 small . . . . . . 10 gm
Olives . . . . 5 small . . . . . . 50 gm
Avocado . . . . ⅛ (4-inch diam) . 25 gm

List 7 milk exchanges

Each portion supplies approximately 12 gm of carbohydrate, 8 gm of protein, and 10 gm of fat, or 170 calories.

	Household Measurement	Weight of Portion
Milk, whole	1 c	240 gm
Milk, evaporated	½ c	120 gm
Milk, powdered*	¼ c	35 gm
Buttermilk*	1 c	240 gm

*Add two fat exchanges if milk is fat free

Acid and alkaline ash diet

Purpose: To furnish a well-balanced diet in which the total acid ash is greater than the total alkaline ash each day.

Use: Retard the formation of renal calculi. The type of diet chosen is dependent on laboratory analysis of the stones.

Acid and alkaline ash food groups

Acid ash	*Alkaline ash*	*Neutral*
Meat	Milk	Sugars
Whole grains	Vegetables	Fats
Eggs	Fruit (except cranberries, prunes,	Beverages (coffee and tea)
Cheese	and plums)	
Cranberries		
Prunes		
Plums		

Foods allowed: You may eat all you want of the following foods.

1. Breads: any, preferably whole grain; crackers, rolls.
2. Cereals: any, preferably whole grain.
3. Desserts: angel food or sunshine cake; cookies made without baking powder or soda; cornstarch pudding, cranberry desserts, custards, gelatin desserts, ice cream, sherbet, plum or prune desserts; rice or tapioca pudding.
4. Fats: any, as butter, margarine, salad dressings, Crisco; Spry, lard, salad oils, olive oil, etc.
5. Fruits: cranberries, plums, prunes.
6. Meat, egg, cheese: any meat, fish or fowl, two servings daily; at least one egg daily.
7. Potato substitutes: corn, hominy, lentils, macaroni, noodles, rice, spaghetti, vermicelli.
8. Soup: broth as desired; other soups from foods allowed.
9. Sweets: cranberry or plum jelly; sugar, plain sugar candy.
10. Miscellaneous: cream sauce, gravy, peanut butter, peanuts, popcorn, salt, spices, vinegar, walnuts.

Restricted Foods: Do not eat any more than the amount allowed each day.

1. Milk: 1 pint daily (may be used in other ways than as beverage).

2. Cream: ¹/₃ cup or less daily.
3. Fruits: one serving of fruit daily (in addition to the prunes, plums, and cranberries); certain fruits listed below are not allowed at any time.
4. Vegetables including potato: two servings daily; certain vegetables listed below are not allowed at any time.

Foods avoided:

1. Carbonated beverages, as ginger ale, Coca-Cola, root beer.
2. Cakes or cookies made with baking powder or soda.
3. Fruits: dried apricots, bananas, dates, figs, raisins, rhubarb.
4. Vegetables: dried beans, beet greens, dandelion greens, carrots, chard, lima beans.
5. Sweets; chocolate or other candies than those listed above; syrups.
6. Miscellaneous: other nuts, olives, pickles.

Sample menu

Breakfast	*Lunch*	*Dinner*
Grapefruit	Creamed chicken	Broth
Wheatena	Steamed rice	Roast beef, gravy
Scrambled eggs	Green beans	Buttered noodles
Toast, butter, plum jam	Stewed prunes	Sliced tomato
Coffee, cream, sugar	Bread, butter	Mayonnaise
	Milk	Vanilla ice cream
		Bread, butter

FOOD LIST FOR READY REFERENCE IN MENU PLANNING

High-cholesterol foods—based on portions of 100 gm

Beef	70 mg
Butter	250 mg
Cheese	60–120 mg
Egg yolks	1500 mg
Fish	70 mg
Ice cream	45 mg
Kidney	375 mg
Liver	300 mg
Margarines, vegetable	0 mg
Milk, whole	11 mg
Milk, skim	3 mg
Pork	70 mg
Veal	90 mg

High-sodium foods—over 500 mg/100 gm portion

Bacon, cured	1021 mg
Bacon, Canadian	2555 mg
Baking powder	8220 mg
Beef, corned, cooked	1740 mg
Beef, corned, canned	540 mg
Beef, dried, cooked, creamed	716 mg
Biscuits, baking powder	626 mg
Bouillon cubes	24,000 mg
Bran, added sugar and malt	1060 mg
Bran flake with thiamine	925 mg

Bran flakes with raisins	800 mg
Breads	
Wheat	529 mg
French	580 mg
Rye	557 mg
White	507 mg
Whole wheat	527 mg
Butter	987 mg
Cheese	
Cheddar	700 mg
Parmesan	734 mg
Swiss	710 mg
Pasteurized American	1136 mg
Pasteurized American spread	1625 mg
Cocoa	525 mg
Cookies, gingersnaps	571 mg
Corn flakes	1005 mg
Cornbread	950 mg
Crackers	
Graham	670 mg
Saltines	1100 mg
Margarine	987 mg
Milk, dry, skim	532 mg
Mustard	
Brown	1307 mg
Yellow	1252 mg

Oat products . . . . 1267 mg	
Olives	
Green . . . . 2400 mg	
Ripe . . . . 803 mg	
Peanut butter . . . . 607 mg	
Pickles, dill . . . . 1428 mg	
Popcorn with oil and salt . . . . 1940 mg	
Salad dressing	
Blue and Roquefort . . . . 1094 mg	
French . . . . 1370 mg	
Thousand Island . . . . 700 mg	
Sausages	
Bologna . . . . 1300 mg	
Frankfurters . . . . 1100 mg	
Soysauce . . . . 7325 mg	
Tomato catsup . . . . 1042 mg	
Tuna, in oil . . . . 800 mg	

High-potassium foods—more than 400 mg/100 gm

Almonds . . . . 773 mg
Bacon, Canadian . . . . 432 mg
Baking powder, low-sodium . . . . . . 10,948 mg
Beans, white . . . . 416 mg
Beans, lima . . . . 422 mg
Beef, hamburger . . . . 450 mg
Bran with sugar and malt . . . . 1070 mg
Cake
Fruitcake . . . . 496 mg
Gingerbread . . . . 454 mg
Cashew nuts . . . . 464 mg
Chicken, light meat . . . . 411 mg
Cocoa . . . . 800 mg
Coffee, instant . . . . 3256 mg
Cookies, gingersnaps . . . . 462 mg
Dates . . . . 648 mg

RECOMMENDED DAILY DIETARY ALLOWANCES[a]

	Age (years)	Weight (kg)	Weight (lbs)	Height (cm)	Height (in)	Energy (kcal)[b]	Protein (g)	Fat-soluble vitamins Vitamin A activity (RE)[c]	Fat-soluble vitamins (IU)	Fat-soluble vitamins Vitamin D (IU)	Fat-soluble vitamins Vitamin E activity[e] (IU)
Infants	0.0–0.5	6	14	60	24	kg × 117	kg × 2.2	420[d]	1,400	400	4
	0.5–1.0	9	20	71	28	kg × 108	kg × 2.0	400	2,000	400	5
Children	1–3	13	28	86	34	1,300	23	400	2,000	400	7
	4–6	20	44	110	44	1,800	30	500	2,500	400	9
	7–10	30	66	135	54	2,400	36	700	3,300	400	10
Men	11–14	44	97	158	63	2,800	44	1,000	5,000	400	12
	15–18	61	134	172	69	3,000	54	1,000	5,000	400	15
	19–22	67	147	172	69	3,000	54	1,000	5,000	400	15
	23–50	70	154	172	69	2,700	56	1,000	5,000		15
	51+	70	154	172	69	2,400	56	1,000	5,000		15
Women	11–14	44	97	155	62	2,400	44	800	4,000	400	12
	15–18	54	119	162	65	2,100	48	800	4,000	400	12
	19–22	58	128	162	65	2,100	46	800	4,000	400	12
	23–50	58	128	162	65	2,000	46	800	4,000		12
	51+	58	128	162	65	1,800	46	800	4,000		12
Pregnant						+300	+30	1,000	5,000	400	15
Lactating						+500	+20	1,200	6,000	400	15

[a] *Reproduced with permission of the Food and Nutrition Board, National Academy of Sciences—National Research Council Recommended Daily Dietary Allowances, Revised 1974. The allowances are intended to provide for individual variations among most normal persons as they live in the United States under usual environmental stresses. Diets should be based on a variety of common foods in order to provide other nutrients for which human requirements have been less well defined.*

[b] *Kilojoules (kJ) = 4.2 × kcal.*

[c] *Retinol equivalents.*

[d] *Assumed to be all as retinol in milk during the first six months of life. All subsequent intakes are assumed to be half as retinol and half as β-carotene when calculated from international units. As retinol equivalents, three fourths are as retinol and one fourth as β-carotene.*

Garlic loaves . . . . 529 mg
Milk
  Dry, skim . . . . 1745 mg
  Powdered . . . . 720 mg
Peanuts, roasted . . . . 701 mg
Peanut butter . . . . 670 mg
Peas . . . . 1005 mg
Pecans . . . . 603 mg
Potatoes, boiled in skin . . . . 407 mg
Scallops . . . . 476 mg
Tea, instant . . . . 4530 mg
Tomato puree . . . . 426 mg
Turkey, light meat . . . . 411 mg
Veal . . . . 500 mg
Walnuts, black . . . . 460 mg
Yeast, brewers . . . . 1894 mg

Foods high in B vitamins

Thiamine	Riboflavin	Niacin
Pork	Liver	Liver
Dried beans	Poultry	Fish
Dried peas	Beef	Poultry
Liver	Oysters	Peanut butter
Lamb	Tongue	Lamb
Veal	Fish	Veal
Nuts	Cottage cheese	Beef
Peas	Veal	Pork

Foods high in C vitamins

Oranges	Grapefruit	Broccoli
Strawberries	Tomato	Melon
Dark-green, leafy vegetables	Cabbage	Liver
Potato		

Water-soluble vitamins							Minerals					
Ascorbic acid (mg)	Folacin[f] (μg)	Niacin[g] (mg)	Riboflavin (mg)	Thiamin (mg)	Vitamin B_6 (mg)	Vitamin B_{12} (μg)	Calcium (mg)	Phosphorus (mg)	Iodine (μg)	Iron (mg)	Magnesium (mg)	Zinc (mg)
35	50	5	0.4	0.3	0.3	0.3	360	240	35	10	60	3
35	50	8	0.6	0.5	0.4	0.3	540	400	45	15	70	5
40	100	9	0.8	0.7	0.6	1.0	800	800	60	15	150	10
40	200	12	1.1	0.9	0.9	1.5	800	800	80	10	200	10
40	300	16	1.2	1.2	1.2	2.0	800	800	110	10	250	10
45	400	18	1.5	1.4	1.6	3.0	1,200	1,200	130	18	350	15
45	400	20	1.8	1.5	2.0	3.0	1,200	1,200	150	18	400	15
45	400	20	1.8	1.5	2.0	3.0	800	800	140	10	350	15
45	400	18	1.6	1.4	2.0	3.0	800	800	130	10	350	15
45	400	16	1.5	1.2	2.0	3.0	800	800	110	10	350	15
45	400	16	1.3	1.2	1.6	3.0	1,200	1,200	115	18	300	15
45	400	14	1.4	1.1	2.0	3.0	1,200	1,200	115	18	300	15
45	400	14	1.4	1.1	2.0	3.0	800	800	100	18	300	15
45	400	13	1.2	1.0	2.0	3.0	800	800	100	18	300	15
45	400	12	1.1	1.0	2.0	3.0	800	800	80	10	300	15
60	800	+2	+0.3	+0.3	2.5	4.0	1,200	1,200	125	18+[h]	450	20
80	600	+4	+0.5	+0.3	2.5	4.0	1,200	1,200	150	18	450	25

[e] Total vitamin E activity, estimated to be 80% as α-tocopherol and 20% other tocopherols.

[f] The folacin allowances refer to dietary sources as determined by Lactobacillus casei assay. Pure forms of folacin may be effective in doses less than one fourth of the recommended dietary allowance.

[g] Although allowances are expressed as niacin, it is recognized that on the average 1 mg of niacin is derived from each 60 mg of dietary tryptophan.

[h] This increased requirement cannot be met by ordinary diets; therefore, the use of supplemental iron is recommended.

Foods high in iron, calcium, and residue

Iron	*Calcium*	*Residue*
Meat	Milk	Whole-grain cereals
Beef	Dry	Oatmeal
Pork	Skim	Bran
Veal	Whole	Shredded wheat
Liver	Evaporated	Breads
Organ meats	Buttermilk	Whole-wheat
Oysters	Cheese	Cracked-wheat
Clams	American	Rye
Egg yolk	Swiss	Bran muffins
Dried fruit	Hard	Vegetables
Prunes	Kale	Lettuce
Apricots	Turnip greens	Spinach
Peaches	Mustard greens	Swiss chard
Raisins	Collards	Carrots, raw
Dark-green		Celery, raw
leafy		Corn
vegetables		Cauliflower
Molasses		Eggplant
		Sauerkraut
		Cabbage
		Fruits
		Bananas
		Figs
		Apricots
		Oranges

Foods to be used in low-protein and low-carbohydrate diets

Protein*	*Carbohydrates*
Milk	All meats
Buttermilk	Cheese
Evaporated,	Hard

---

*These proteins are allowed in various amounts on controlled-protein diets for renal decompensation.

Protein—cont'd
  reconstituted
  Low-sodium
  Skim and dry
Meat
  Chicken
  Lamb
  Turkey
  Beef
  Veal
Fish
  Sole
  Flounder
  Haddock
  Perch
Cheese
  Cheddar
  American
  Swiss
  Cottage
Eggs
Fruits
  Apples
  Grapes
  Pears
  Pineapple
Vegetables
  Cabbage
  Cucumber
  Lettuce
  Tomato
Cereals
  Cornflakes
  Puffed rice
  Puffed Wheat
  Farina
  Rolled oats

Carbohydrates—cont'd
  Soft
  Cottage
Eggs
Shell fish
  Oysters
  Shrimp
Fats
  Bacon
  Butter
  French dressing
  Salad oil
  Mayonnaise
  Margarine
Vegetables
  Asparagus
  Green beans
  Beet greens
  Broccoli
  Brussel sprouts
  Cabbage
  Celery
  Cauliflower
  Cucumber
  Lettuce
  Green pepper
  Spinach
  Squash
  Tomatoes
Fruits
  Avocados
  Strawberries
  Cantaloupe
  Lemons
  Rhubarb

Appendix D   Intravenous Therapy

INTRAVENOUS THERAPY

1. Infusion systems

A. Plastic bag

  1. Contains no vacuum—needs no air to replace fluid as it flows from container

  2. Medication can be added with syringe and needle through a resealable latex port

    a. During infusion, administration set should be completely clamped before medications are added

    b. Prevents undiluted, and perhaps toxic, dose from entering administration set

B. Closed system

  1. Requires partial vacuum—however, only filtered air enters container

  2. Medication may be added during infusion through air vent in administration set

    a. Care must be utilized to maintain sterility during procedure

    b. Medications also may be added through a solid rubber stopper prior to infusion

C. Open system

  1. Requires partial vacuum—air is not filtered

  2. Medications are added into an outlet port before sterile latex disk is removed

    a. Vacuum check—latex disk should be depressed; if not, sterility will be questionable

    b. During infusion—medications added through designated area on rubber after infusion set is clamped

    c. Agitate and mix thoroughly before beginning administration

D. Administration sets

  1. Standard—deliver 10 to 25 drops/ml

  2. Pediatric or mini-drop sets—deliver 50 to 60 drops/ml

  3. Controlled-volume sets—permit accurate infusion of measured volumes of fluids

    a. Particularly valuable when piggybacked into primary infusion

    b. Solutions containing drugs can then be administered intermittently

  4. Y-type administration sets—allow for simultaneous or alternate infusion of two fluids

    a. May contain filter and pressure unit for blood transfusions

    b. Air embolism significant hazard with this type of administration set

  5. Positive-pressure sets—designed for rapid infusion of replacement fluids

    a. In emergency, built-in pressure chamber increases rate of blood administration

    b. Pump chamber must be filled at all times to avoid air embolism

    c. Application of positive pressure to infusion fluids is responsibility of physician

  6. Infusion pumps—utilized to deliver small volumes of fluid or doses of high-potency drugs

    a. Used primarily in neonatal, pediatric, and adult intensive-care units

    b. Have increased the safety of parenteral therapy and reduced nursing time

2. Fluid administration

A. Factors influencing rate

  1. Patient's size

  2. Patient's physical condition

  3. Age of patient

  4. Type of fluid

  5. Patient's tolerance to fluid

B. Flow rates for parenteral infusions can be computed using the following formula:

$$\frac{\text{gtt/ml of given set}}{60 \text{ (minutes in hours)}} \times \text{total hourly volume}$$
$$= \text{gtt/minute}$$

If 1000 ml are to be infused in an eight-hour period and the administration set delivers 15 gtt/ml, the gtt/minute is 31.2 gtt/minute.

$$\frac{15}{60} \times 125 = \frac{1}{4} \times 125 = 31.2 \text{ gtt/minute}$$

C. Generally the type of fluid administration set determines its rate of flow

  1. Fluid administration sets—approximately 15 gtt/minute

  2. Blood administration sets—approximately 10 gtt/minute

3. Pediatric administration sets—approximately 60 gtt/minute

4. Always check information on the administration set box to determine the No. of gtt/ml before calculating, varies with manufacturer

D. Factors influencing flow rates

1. Gravity—a change in the height of the infusion bottle will increase or decrease the rate of flow, for example, raising the bottle higher will increase the rate of flow and vice versa

2. Blood clot in needle—stopping the infusion for any reason or an increase in venous pressure may result in partial or total obstruction of needle by clot
   a. Delay in changing infusion bottle
   b. Blood pressure cuff on or restraints on or above infusion needle
   c. Patient lying on arm in which infusion is being made

3. Change in needle position—against or away from vein wall

4. Venous spasm—due to cold blood or irritating solution

5. Plugged vent—causes infusion to stop

3. Complications of intravenous therapy

A. Local complications

1. Thrombophlebitis—inflammation and thrombosis of vein
   a. Signs and symptoms—pain, redness, swelling, and heat along the length of the vein
   b. Contributing factors
      (1) Length of infusion—infusions in place over 24-48 hours most frequent factor
      (2) Infusion fluid—hypertonic glucose, drug additives, or solutions with pH significantly different from plasma
      (3) Infusion site—venous injury can occur due to motion of needles
      (4) Technique—maintenance of aseptic technique during venipuncture is essential
   c. Preventive nursing measures
      (1) Do not use veins in lower extremities
      (2) If irritating solution is to be infused, use vein with ample blood volume
      (3) Avoid infusion sites over joints
      (4) Tape needles securely to avoid motion

2. Infiltration—dislodgement of the needle with fluid flowing into surrounding tissue
   a. Signs and symptoms—edema of infusion site
   b. Nursing measures
      (1) If edema is present, the presence of blood return in adapter with negative pressure (lowering of IV bottle below infusion site) does not mean infusion is still entering vein
      (2) Confirm infiltration by applying a tourniquet proximal to infusion site, restricting venous flow; if infusion continues, extravasation is evident, and the needle should be removed immediately

B. Systemic complications

1. Infections—occur when pathogens are introduced into the bloodstream
   a. Signs and symptoms—chills, fever, general malaise, headache, backache, nausea, and vomiting
   b. Immediate nursing measures
      (1) Terminate infusion
      (2) Take vital signs
      (3) Notify physician
      (4) Send solution to lab for culture
   c. Preventive nursing measures
      (1) Utilize aseptic venipuncture technique
      (2) Inspect fluids for cloudiness or extra matter
      (3) Use open solutions within 24 hours
      (4) Change administration sets every 24 hours
      (5) Avoid irrigating plugged cannulas

2. Pulmonary embolism—substance, usually blood clot, enters pulmonary circulation and obstructs pulmonary artery
   a. Signs and symptoms—dyspnea, orthopnea, and signs of circulatory and cardiac collapse
   b. Preventive nursing measures
      (1) Infuse blood or plasma through adequate filters
      (2) Avoid venipuncture in lower extremities, as these veins are prone to trauma and thrombosis formation
      (3) Restart infusions that have become clogged—do not irrigate
      (4) Be sure all drugs are completely dissolved before adding to infusions

3. Air embolism—usually a complication of

blood infused under pressure; it is a complication that may occur with any infusion—small, tenacious bubbles of air block pulmonary capillaries

a. Signs and symptoms—cyanosis; hypotension; weak, rapid pulse; increased CVP; and loss of consciousness

b. Immediate nursing measures
   (1) Place patient on left side with head down (prevents air from entering pulmonary circulation)
   (2) Administer oxygen
   (3) Notify physician

c. Preventive nursing measures
   (1) Avoid allowing infusion bottles to run dry; pay particular vigilance to infusions in which the extremity is elevated above the heart or that are flowing through CVP catheter—the negative pressures in these veins facilitate air entering circulation
   (2) Closely observe infusions utilizing Y-type administration set; if one container empties, it becomes a source of air
      (a) Avoid running fluids simultaneously if possible
      (b) Check valves and microfilters

4. Circulatory overload—rapid infusion of fluids may result in increased venous pressure, cardiac embarrassment, and pulmonary edema (a hazard particularly for the elderly with decreased cardiac and renal reserves)

a. Signs and symptoms—dyspnea; orthopnea; hypotension; tachycardia; decreased pulse pressure; distended neck veins; cough; and frothy, bloody sputum

b. Immediate nursing measures
   (1) Reduce infusion rate to minimal
   (2) Sit patient in upright position
   (3) Administer oxygen if indicated
   (4) Notify physician

c. Preventive nursing measures
   (1) Maintain infusions at prescribed rate of flow
   (2) Do not apply positive pressure to increase flow rate
   (3) Discard solutions not infused in 24-hour period—do not add to next day's solutions or try to catch up

4. Fluid and electrolyte therapy

A. Types of therapy
   1. Maintenance therapy—provides water, electrolytes, glucose, vitamins, and, in some instances, protein to meet daily requirements
   2. Restoration of deficits—in addition to maintenance therapy, fluid and electrolytes are added to replace previous losses
   3. Replacement therapy—infusions to replace current losses in fluid and electrolytes

B. Types of intravenous fluids
   1. Isotonic solutions—fluids that approximate the osmolality (290 mOsm/liter) of normal blood plasma
      a. Sodium chloride (0.9%)—normal saline
         (1) Indications
            (a) Extracellular fluid replacement when Cl^- loss is equal to or greater than Na^+ loss
            (b) Treatment of metabolic alkalosis
            (c) Na^+ depletion
            (d) Initiating and terminating blood transfusions
         (2) Possible side effects
            (a) Hypernatremia
            (b) Acidosis
            (c) Hypokalemia
            (d) Circulatory overload
      b. 5% dextrose in water (5% D/W)
         (1) Provides calories for energy, thus sparing body protein and development of ketosis from fat breakdown
            (a) 3.75 calories are provided per gram of glucose
            (b) USP standards require use of monohydrated glucose, so only 91% is actually glucose
            (c) 5% D/W yields 170.6 calories; 5% D/W means 5 gm glucose/liter
               $$50 \times 3.75 = 187.5 \text{ calories}$$
               $$0.91 \times 187.5 = 170.6 \text{ calories}$$
         (2) Indications
            (a) Dehydration
            (b) Hypernatremia
            (c) Drug administration
         (3) Possible side effects
            (a) Hypokalemia
            (b) Osmotic diuresis—dehydration
            (c) Transient hyperinsulinism
            (d) Water intoxication

c. 5% dextrose in normal saline
  (1) Prevents ketone formation and loss of potassium and intracellular water
  (2) Indications
      (a) Hypovolemic shock—temporary measure
      (b) Burns
      (c) Acute adrenocortical insufficiency
  (3) Same side effects as normal saline
d. Isotonic multiple-electrolyte fluids—utilized for replacement therapy; ionic composition approximates blood plasma
  (1) Types—Plasmanate, Polysol, lactated Ringer's
  (2) Indicated in vomiting, diarrhea, excessive diuresis, and burns
  (3) Possible side effect—circulatory overload
  (4) Lactated Ringer's is contraindicated in severe metabolic acidosis and/or alkalosis and liver disease
  (5) Same side effects as normal saline

2. Hypertonic solutions—fluids with an osmolality much higher than 290 m0sm (+50 m0sm); increase osmotic pressure of blood plasma thereby drawing fluid from the cells
a. 10% dextrose in normal saline
  (1) Administered in large vein to dilute and prevent venous trauma
  (2) Utilized for nutrition and to replenish Na^+ and Cl^-
  (3) Possible side effects
      (a) Hypernatremia (excess Na^+)
      (b) Acidosis (excess Cl^-)
      (c) Circulatory overload
b. 3% and 5% sodium chloride solutions
  (1) Slow administration essential to prevent overload (100 ml/hour)
  (2) Indicated in water intoxication and severe sodium depletion

3. Hypotonic solution—fluids whose osmolality is significantly less than blood plasma (−50 m0sm); these fluids lower plasma osmotic pressures causing fluid to enter cells
a. 0.45% sodium chloride—utilized for replacement when requirement for Na^+ use is questionable
b. 2.5% dextrose in 0.45% saline, 5% dextrose in 0.45% saline, and 5% dextrose in 0.2% saline—these are all hydrating fluids
  (1) Indications
      (a) Fluid replacement when some Na^+ replacement is also necessary
      (b) Encourage diuresis in patients who are dehydrated
      (c) Evaluate kidney status before instituting electrolyte infusions
  (2) Possible side effects
      (a) Hypernatremia
      (b) Circulatory overload
      (c) Use with caution in edematous patients with cardiac, renal, or hepatic disease
      (d) After adequate renal function is established, appropriate electrolytes should be given to avoid hypokalemia

4. Alkalyzing agents—fluids used in the treatment of metabolic acidosis
a. ⅙ M lactate
  (1) Administration—rate usually not more than 300 ml/hour
  (2) Side effects—observe carefully for signs of alkalosis
b. Sodium bicarbonate
  (1) Indications
      (a) Replace excessive loss of bicarbonate ion
      (b) Emergency treatment of life-threatening acidosis
  (2) Administration
      (a) Depends on patient's weight, condition, and carbon-dioxide level
      (b) Usual dose is 500 ml of a 1.5% solution (89 mEq)
  (3) Side effects
      (a) Alkalosis
      (b) Hypocalcemic tetany
      (c) Rapid infusion may induce cellular acidity and death

5. Acidifying solutions—fluids used in treatment of metabolic alkalosis
a. Types
  (1) Normal saline (see Isotonic solutions)

(2) Ammonium chloride
b. Administration—dosage depends on patient's condition and serum lab values
c. Side effects
(1) Hepatic encephalopathy in presence of decreased liver function, since ammonium is metabolized by liver
(2) Toxic effects of irregular respirations, twitching, and bradycardia
(3) Contraindicated with renal failure
6. Blood and blood products
a. Indications
(1) Maintenance of blood volume
(2) Supply red blood cells to maintain oxygen-carrying capacity
(3) Supply clotting factors to maintain coagulation properties
(4) Exchange transfusion
(5) Prime oxygenating pump
C. Nursing responsibilities
1. Awareness of imbalance and appropriate therapy
2. Reporting pertinent observations
3. Knowledgeable regarding clinical parameters to be assessed
a. Vital signs
b. Weight
c. Intake and output
d. Skin texture and elasticity
e. Peripheral veins
f. Central venous pressure
g. Pulmonary artery pressure
h. Laboratory values

TRANSFUSION WITH BLOOD OR BLOOD PRODUCTS

Blood or blood product	Indications	Actions	Shelf life	Side effects	Nursing implications
Whole blood	1. Acute hemorrhage 2. Hypovolemic shock	1. Restores blood volume 2. Raises hemoglobin count and, therefore, oxygen-carrying capacity	21 days	1. Hemolytic reaction 2. Fluid overload 3. Febrile reaction 4. Pyogenic reaction 5. Allergic reaction	1. See surgical complications for complete discussion of nursing responsibilities (p. 163) 2. Protocol for checking blood before transfusion is begun varies with each institution; however, at least two people must verify that the unit of blood has been cross-matched for a specific patient

Continued

TRANSFUSION WITH BLOOD OR BLOOD PRODUCTS—continued

Blood or blood product	Indications	Actions	Shelf life	Side effects	Nursing implications
Red blood cells, packed	1. Acute anemia with hypoxia 2. Aplastic anemia 3. Bone marrow failure due to malignancy 4. Patients who need red blood cells but not volume	1. Raises hemoglobin count	1. 21 days in original container 2. 24 hours if container is opened	*see Whole blood*	*see Whole blood*
Red blood cells, frozen	1. *see Red blood cells, packed* 2. Patients sensitized by previous transfusions	*see Red blood cells, packed*	1. In frozen state, three years 2. Thawed state, 24 hours	1. Less likely to cause antigen reaction 2. Decreased possibility of transmitting hepatitis	*see Red blood cells, packed*
White blood cells (leukocytes)	Currently being used in severe leukopenia with infection (research still being done)	Elevates leukocyte count	Must be given when collected	1. Elevated temperature 2. Graft versus host disease	1. Careful monitoring of temperature 2. Must be given as soon as collected
Platelet concentrate	1. Severe deficiency 2. Bleeding thrombocytopenic patients with platelet counts below 10,000	1. Elevates platelet count 2. Aids hemostasis by facilitating clot formation	48 hours	1. Fever 2. Chills 3. Hives 4. Development of antibodies that will destroy platelets in future transfusions *Contraindications* 1. Idiopathic thrombocytopenic purpura 2. Disseminated intravascular coagulopathy	Monitor temperature

Blood product	Indications	Action	Dating	Side effects	Special considerations
Single-donor fresh plasma	1. Clotting deficiency—concentrates not available or deficiency not fully diagnosed 2. Shock	1. Elevates level of clotting factors 2. Expands blood pressure	Given within six hours of collection	1. Side effects rare 2. Congestive heart failure 3. Possible hepatitis	Use sterile, pyrogen-free filters
Plasma removed from whole blood (up to five days after expiration date, which is 21 days)	1. Shock due to loss of plasma 2. Burns 3. Peritoneal injury 4. Hemorrhage 5. While awaiting blood cross-match	Expands blood volume	Three years	*see Single-donor fresh plasma*	*see Single-donor fresh plasma*
Freeze-dried plasma	*see Plasma removed from whole blood*	Expands blood volume	Seven years	*see Single-donor fresh plasma*	Must be reconstituted with sterile water before use
Single-donor fresh frozen plasma	1. *See single-donor fresh plasma* 2. Inherited or acquired disorders of coagulation 3. Presurgical hemophiliac	1. Increases level of deficient clotting factor 2. Facilitates hemostasis	1. Six months without preservative 2. Twelve months with preservatives 3. Thawed just before use	*see Single-donor fresh plasma*	1. Freezing preserves various clotting factors, especially V and VIII 2. Increasing temperature causes destruction of factor VIII 3. Notify blood bank to thaw about 30 minutes before administration 4. Give immediately
Cryoprecipitate concentrate (factor VIII—antihemophilic factor)	For hemophilia patients 1. Prevention 2. Preoperatively 3. During bleeding episodes	Facilitates control of bleeding by elevating level of factor VIII	3–12 months	Rare	55 ml cryoprecipitate concentrate has same effect on serum level as 1600 ml of fresh frozen plasma
Superconcentrate of factor VIII, lyophilized	*see Cryoprecipitate concentrate*	*see Cryoprecipitate concentrate*	Manufacturer's dating	Rare	Commercially prepared

Continued

TRANSFUSION WITH BLOOD OR BLOOD PRODUCTS—continued

Blood or blood product	Indications	Actions	Shelf life	Side effects	Nursing implications
Factor II, VII, IX, and X compiled	Specific deficiencies	1. Elevates serum level 2. Facilitates hemostasis 3. Allows surgery	Manufacturer's dating	Hepatitis	Commercially prepared
Fibrinogen (factor I)	Fibrinogen deficiency	1. Elevates serum level 2. 2 gm equal to 12 units of whole blood	Five years—give within one hour after reconstitution	Increased risk of hepatitis since the hepatitis virus combines with fibrinogen during fractionation	1. Reconstitute with sterile water 2. *Do not* warm fibrinogen or use hot water to reconstitute 3. *Do not* shake 4. Must be given with a filter
Albumin or salt-poor albumin	1. Shock due to (a) hemorrhage, (b) trauma, (c) infection, (d) surgery, or (e) burns 2. Treatment of cerebral edema 3. Low-serum protein levels	Restores vascular volume by elevating oncotic pressure	Three to five years	None; these are heat-treated products	Commercially prepared
Plasma protein factor	*see Albumin*	*see Albumin*	Three to five years	Minimal risk	Commercially prepared
Dextran	Hypovolemic shock	Expands intravascular volume by elevating oncotic pressure	Some will last indefinitely	1. Rare allergic reaction 2. Patient's with heart or kidney disease susceptible to heart failure or pulmonary edema	Commercially prepared

HYPERALIMENTATION—TOTAL PARENTERAL NUTRITION

1. **Indications**
A. Negative nitrogen balance
B. Conditions that interfere with protein ingestion, digestion, and absorption
C. May be used up to six months to maintain nutritional requirements—average daily volume 3300 ml/day
2. **Types of solutions**
A. Hydrolyzed protein (Hyprotigen, Amigen)
B. Synthetic amino acids (Freamine)
C. Usual components
   1. 5% amino acid
   2. 10% to 25% glucose
   3. Multivitamins
   4. Electrolytes
D. Supplements may be added as needed
   1. Fructose
   2. Alcohol
   3. Fat emulsions
   4. Minerals—iron, copper, calcium
   5. Trace elements—iodine, zinc, magnesium
   6. Vitamins—A, C, and B
   7. Androgen hormone therapy
   8. Additional electrolytes
3. **Administration**
A. Dosage
   1. Dependent on patient's clinical status
   2. One liter q5-6h

   3. Solution should be mixed under laminar flow hoods—usually done by pharmacist
   4. Solution should be stored in refrigerator after mixing
      a. Solution expires in 24 hours if refrigerated
      b. Solution expires in 12 hours once removed from refrigerator
   5. Incompatible with antibiotics
   6. Keep flow rate constant—do not adjust rate to "catch up" IV
B. Routes
   1. Must be given through large veins, such as subclavian
   2. Confirmation of catheter placement by x-ray before infusion begins
C. Side effects
   1. Hyperosmolar coma
   2. Hyperglycemia
   3. Septicemia
   4. Thrombosis and sclerosis of vein
D. Nursing implications
   1. In-line filter should always be used
   2. Aseptic occlusive dressing should be changed at least every 48 hours
   3. Clinitest and Acitest q4h, with sliding-scale urine coverage
   4. The catheter is to be utilized for *nothing* except hyperalimentation—if the catheter has been used for CVP readings or to draw blood, hyperalimentation *must* be discontinued

ELECTROLYTE DISTURBANCES

Disturbance	Symptoms	Etiology	Nursing assessment and implications
Hypervolemia (increase in sodium and water)	1. Dyspnea 2. Edema 3. Jugular vein distention 4. Weight gain	1. Over-hydration 2. Excessive intake 3. Congestive heart failure (CHF)	1. Maintain fluid and sodium restrictions 2. Monitor intake and output 3. Weigh daily 4. Administer diuretics
Hypovolemia (decreased sodium and water)	1. Thirst 2. Weakness 3. Elevated hematocrit 4. Rapid weak pulse 5. Decreased urine output	1. Acute hemorrhage 2. Diuretics 3. Decreased intake 4. Gastric suctioning	1. Replace losses 2. Monitor intake and output 3. Weigh daily

Continued

ELECTROLYTE DISTURBANCES—continued

Disturbance	Symptoms	Etiology	Nursing assessment and implications
Hypernatremia	1. Thirst 2. Oliguria 3. Anuria 4. Elevated temperature	1. Excessive intake of salt 2. Excessive loss of water	Administer hypotonic solutions, as ordered
Hyponatremia	1. Headache 2. Apprehension 3. Abdominal cramps 4. Oliguria	1. Extended submersion in fresh water 2. Water intoxication	Administration of sodium containing solutions
Hyperkalemia	1. Weakness 2. Flaccid paralysis 3. Cardiac arrhythmias 4. Nausea	1. Kidney disease 2. Burns 3. Acidosis	Administration of calcium, glucose, insulin, cation-exchange resins, and polystyrene sodium sulfonate (Kayexalate) as ordered
Hypokalemia	1. ECG changes 2. Malaise 3. Anorexia 4. Vomiting	1. Diuretics 2. Gastric suction 3. Fistulas 4. Alkalosis	Administration of potassium replacements
Hypermagnesemia	1. Muscle weakness 2. Hyperventilation 3. Hypotension	1. Overuse of antacids 2. Renal insufficiency 3. Epsom salt enemas 4. Severe dehydration	Emergency—administration of 10% calcium gluconate solution treats underlying problem
Hypomagnesemia	1. Tremors 2. Hyperactive reflexes 3. Positive Chvostek 4. Convulsions	1. Rare 2. Severe renal disease 3. Stress	Administration of magnesium sulfate, as ordered
Hypercalcemia	1. Hypotonicity of muscles 2. Decreased neuromuscular irritability	1. Hyperthyroidism 2. Hyperparathyroidism 3. Thiazide diuretics 4. Bone tumors	1. Administration of steroids and parenteral normal saline, as ordered 2. Restrict calcium intake
Hypocalcemia	1. Carpopedal spasms 2. Tetany Chvostek 3. Positive	1. Parathyroid hormone 2. Deficiency 3. Peritonitis	Administration of calcium or vitamin D, as ordered

Appendix E Diagnostic Tests

LABORATORY VALUES*

Blood Values

1. **Hematocrit**—the volume of packed red blood cells per 100 ml of blood
A. Men—45% (38% to 54%)
B. Women—40% (36% to 47%)
C. Increase—polycythemia, dehydration
D. Decrease—anemia

2. **Hemoglobin**—measures the oxygen-carrying pigment of the red blood cells
A. Men—14-16 gm/100 ml
B. Women—12-16 gm/100 ml
C. Increase and decrease—*see Hematocrit*

3. **Red blood count (RBC)**
A. Men—5.0 (4.5-6.0) $\times$ 10^6/cu mm
B. Women—4.5 (4.3-5.5) $\times$ 10^6/cu mm
C. Increase—polycythemia vera, leukemia
D. Secondary—chronic obstructive lung disease, cyanotic congenital heart, diseases with hypoxemia

4. **Red blood cell indices**
A. Mean cell volume (MCV)—80-94 (cuμ)
   1. Increase—macrocytic anemia
   2. Decrease—microcytic anemia
B. Mean cell hemoglobin (MCH)—27-32 μg/cell
   1. Increase—macrocytic anemia
   2. Decrease—microcytic anemia
C. Mean cell hemoglobin concentration (MCHC) —33% to 38%
   1. Decrease—severe hypochromic anemia

5. **White blood count (WBC)**
A. Normal value—4500-11,000/cu mm
B. Mild to moderate increase—infections, mainly

bacterial; severe sepsis in the elderly
C. Marked increase—Severe sepsis

6. **WBC differential**
A. Neutrophils—1800-7000 cu mm
   1. Increase—bacterial infections, inflammations, tumors, physical and emotional stress, drugs
   2. Decrease—acute viral infections, anorexia nervosa, primary and secondary splenic neutropenia, drug-induced, and alcoholic ingestion
B. Eosinophils—50-300/cu mm, or 1% to 3%
   1. Increase—allergic disorders, parasitic infestation, eosinophilic leukemia
   2. Decrease—acute and chronic stress, excess ACTH, cortisone, and epinephrine, and endocrine disorders
C. Basophils—0-100/cu mm, or 0% to 1%
   1. Increase—myeloproliferative disease
   2. Decrease—anaphylactic reaction, hyperthyroidism, radiation therapy, acute and chronic infections, ovulation, pregnancy, and aging
D. Lymphocytes—1000-4000/cu mm
   1. Increase—Chronic lymphocytic leukemia, infectious mononucleosis, whooping cough, acute lymphocytosis, viral infections with eczemas, and chronic bacterial infections

7. **Platelets**—200,000-500,000/cu mm
   1. Increase—polycythemia, splenectomy status, essential thrombocytosis
   2. Absence—thrombocytopenia

8. **Prothrombin time**
A. Sensitive to deficiencies of the procoagulants— Factor I (fibrinogen factor), Factor II (prothrombin factor), Factor V (labile factor), Factor VII (stable factor), and Factor X (Stuart factor)
B. Increase—hepatic disease, anticoagulant therapy, malabsorption, and defibrination syndrome

9. **Partial thromboplastin**
A. Time 35-50 seconds
B. Measures deficiencies in stage II of coagulation—deficiency of Factors VIII, IX, and X

*Among the sources used to compile this information were Tilkian, S. M., and Conover, M. H.: Clinical implications of laboratory test, St. Louis, 1975, The C. V. Mosby Co.; Widmann, F. K.: Goodale's clinical interpretation of laboratory tests, ed. 7, Philadelphia, 1973, F. A. Davis Company; and The Lippincott manual of nursing practice, Philadelphia, 1974, J. B. Lippincott Company.

10. Bleeding time

A. 30 seconds to 6 minutes
B. Prolonged in hemorrhagic purpura and in chloroform poisoning

11. Sedimentation rate—speed at which RBCs settle in uncoagulated blood

A. Men—0-9 mm/hour
B. Women—0-20 mm/hour
C. a nonspecific screening test; normal value rules out significant inflammatory disease

Blood Chemistry

1. Alkaline phosphatase, total serum

A. Adults
   1. 1.4-4.1 units/100 ml (Bodansky method)
   2. 4-13 units/100 ml (King-Armstrong method)
   3. 20-48 IU/ml
B. Increased—early obstructive jaundice, Paget's disease of bone, Ca with bone metastasis, cholangiolitic hepatitis, cirrhosis, hyperparathyroidism, and osteomalacia

2. Amylase—60-160 units/ml

A. Increase—acute pancreatitis, mumps, duodenal ulcer, and carcinoma of the head of the pancreas
B. Decrease—chronic pancreatitis, cirrhosis, acute alcoholism, and toxemias of pregnancy

3. Ascorbic acid, serum—0.4-1.5 mg/100 ml

A. Decrease—rheumatic fever, collagen diseases, renal and hepatic disease, and congestive heart failure

4. Bilirubin, serum

A. Direct—0-0.3 mg/100 ml
B. Indirect—0.1-1.0 mg/100 ml
C. Total—0.1-1.2 mg/100 ml
D. Increase—Low-grade hemolytic diseases, massive hemolysis, cirrhosis, obstructive liver disease, hepatitis, cholangitis, and carcinoma or calculus of lower biliary tract

5. Sulfobromophthalein (Bromsulphalein) (BSP)

A. Less than 6% retention after 45 minutes
B. Increase—acute hepatic disease

6. Cephalin flocculation

A. No precipitate
B. Increase—severe liver disease, malaria, and infectious mononucleosis

7. Calcium, serum—9-11.5 mg/100 ml or 4.5-5.7

mEq/liter

A. Increased—hyperparathyroidism, sarcoidosis, multiple myeloma, malignancies with bone metastases, milk-alkali syndrome, hyperthyroidism, bone fractures, Paget's disease of the bone
B. Decreased—hypoparathyroidism, osteomalacia, rickets, acute pancreatitis, pregnancy, diuretics, respiratory alkalosis

8. Carbon dioxide combining power—50-65 vol% or 24-30 mEq/liter

A. Increased—alkali ingestion, serum alkalosis, and intracellular acidosis
B. Decreased—uremia, diabetic ketoacidosis, lactic acidosis, renal tubular necrosis, hyperventilation

9. Chloride, serum (as Cl)—95-106 mEq/liter or 355-376 mg/100 ml

A. Increased—renal tubular acidosis and inappropriate IV or tube feedings
B. Decreased—spironolactone and chronic obstructive lung disease

10. Cholesterol (total serum)—110-300 mg/100 ml

A. Increased—liver disease with biliary obstruction and nephrotic stage of glomerulonephritis, familial
B. Decreased—malnutrition, extensive liver disease, and hyperthyroidism

11. Creatinine, serum—0.6-1.2 mg/100 ml

A. Increased—kidney disease with greater than 50% nephron destruction

12. Creatine phosphokinase (CPK)

A. Men—55-170 U/liter
B. Women—30-135 U/liter
C. Increased—muscular dystrophy, myocardial infarction, dissecting aortic aneurysms, heavy exercise or surgical procedures with damage to skeletal muscles, CVAs, salicylate poisoning, and acute alcohol ingestion

13. Fatty acids, serum—250-390 mg/100 ml

A. Increase—diabetes mellitus, anemia, nephrosis, and hypothyroidism
B. Decrease—hyperthyroidism

14. Fibrinogen, serum—0.2-0.4 gm/100 ml

A. Increase—pneumonia, acute infections, and nephrosis
B. Decrease—cirrhosis, toxic liver necrosis, anemia, and typhoid fever

15. **Blood glucose (fasting)**—80-120 mg/100 ml

A. Increased—acute stress, pheochromocytoma, Cushing's syndrome, hyperthyroidism, acute and chronic pancreatitis, diabetes mellitus, and ketoacidosis
B. Decreased—pancreatic islet cell tumor, pituitary hypofunction, Addison's disease, extensive liver disease, and reactive hypoglycemia

16. **Iodine, protein-bound, serum (PBI)**—4-8 μg/100 ml

A. Increase—hyperthyroidism
B. Decrease—hypothyroidism

17. **Iron-binding capacity**—250-450 μg/100 ml

A. Increase—iron-deficiency anemia
B. Decrease—chronic infections

18. **Lactic dehydrogenase (LDH)**

A. 80-120 Wacker units
B. 150-450 Wroblewski units
C. 71-207 IU/liter
D. Increased—myocardial infarction, pernicious anemia, chronic viral hepatitis, pneumonia, pulmonary emboli, CVA, and renal tissue destruction

19. **Lipids, total, serum**—400-1000 mg/100 ml

A. Increase—hypothyroidism, diabetes, nephrosis, and glomerulonephritis
B. Decrease—hyperthyroidism

20. **Phosphatase, alkaline, serum**

A. King-Armstrong method—8-14 units/100 ml
B. Bodansky method—1-4 units/100 ml
C. Increase—rickets, liver disease, and hyperparathyroidism

21. **Phosphorus, inorganic, serum**—1.8-2.6 mEq/liter or 3.0-4.5 mg/100 ml

A. Increased—chronic glomerular disease, hypoparathyroidism, milk-alkali syndrome, and sarcoidosis
B. Decreased—hyperparathyroidism, rickets, osteomalacia, renal tubular acidosis, and malabsorption syndrome

22. **Potassium, serum**—3.5-5.0 mEq/liter

A. Increased—renal failure and Addison's disease
B. Decreased—thiazide diuretics, Cushing's syndrome, cirrhosis with ascites, hyperaldosteronism, steroid therapy, malignant hypertension, poor dietary habits, chronic diarrhea, diaphoresis, renal tubular necrosis

23. **Protein, serum—albumin/globulin**

A. Total—6.0-7.8 gm/100 ml
B. Albumin—3.2-4.5 gm/100 ml
C. Globulin—2.3-3.5 gm/100 ml
D. Decreased—chronic liver disease and myeloproliferative diseases

24. **Sodium, serum**—138-144 mEq/liter

A. Increased—Increased intake, either orally or IV
B. Decreased—Addison's disease, sodium-losing nephropathy, vomiting, diarrhea, fistulas, tube drainage, burns, renal insufficiency with acidosis, starvation with acidosis, paracentesis, thoracentesis, ascites, congestive heart failure, and hypothermia

25. **T_3 uptake**—25% to 38%

A. Increase—hyperthyroidism and TBG deficiency
B. Decrease—hypothyroidism, pregnancy, and TBG excess

26. **Thyroxin**—5-11 μg/100 ml

A. Increase—hyperthyroidism, pregnancy, and TBG excess
B. Decrease—hypothyroidism, and TBG deficiency

27. **Serum glutamic oxaloacetic transaminase (SGOT)**—up to 40 units/100 ml

A. Increased—hepatitis, severe liver necrosis, myocardial infarction, cirrhosis, skeletal muscle disease, pulmonary infarction, and shock

28. **Urea nitrogen, serum (BUN)**—10-18 mg/100 ml

A. Increased—acute or chronic renal failure, congestive heart failure, and obstructive uropathy

29. **Uric acid, serum**

A. Men—2.1-7.8 mg/100 ml
B. Women—2.0-6.4 mg/100 ml
C. Increased—gout, chronic renal failure, starvation, and diuretic therapy

30. **Vitamin B_{12}**—300-1000 pg/ml

A. Increase—hepatic cellular damage and myeloproliferative disorders
B. Decrease—alcoholism, vegetarianism, total or partial gastrectomy, sprue and celiac disease, and fish tapeworm infestation

31. **Zinc**—55-150 μg/100 ml

A. Increase—hyperthermia
B. Decrease—alcoholic cirrhosis, leukemia, and pernicious anemia

Blood Gases

1. **pH, serum**—7.35-7.45
A. Increased—metabolic alkalosis-alkali ingestion and respiratory alkalosis-hyperventilation
B. Decreased—metabolic acidosis-ketoacidosis, shock and respiratory acidosis-alveolar hypoventilation

2. **Oxygen pressure (PO_2), whole blood, arterial**—95-100 mm Hg
A. Increased—oxygen administration in the absence of severe lung disease
B. Decreased—chronic obstructive lung disease, severe pneumonias, pulmonary embolism, pulmonary edema, and respiratory muscle disease

3. **Carbon dioxide pressure (PCO_2), whole blood, arterial**—35-45 mm Hg (mean is 40)
A. Increased—alveolar hypoventilation, loss of H^+ through nasogastric suctioning or vomiting
B. Decreased—hyperventilation

Urinalysis

1. **pH**—4.8-8.0
A. Increased—metabolic alkalosis
B. Decreased—intracellular acidosis due to potassium depletion

2. **Specific gravity**—1.015-1.025
A. Decreased—distal renal tubular disease, polycystic kidney disease, and diabetes insipidus

3. **Glucose**—negative
A. Increased—diabetes mellitus

4. **Protein**—negative
A. Increased—nephrosis, glomerulonephritis, and lupus erythematosus

5. **Casts**—negative
A. Increased—nephrosis, glomerulonephritis, and lupus erythematosus

6. **Red blood cells**—negative
A. Increased—renal calculi, hemorrhagic cystitis, and tumors of the kidney

7. **White blood cells**—negative
A. Increased—inflammation of the kidneys, ureters, or bladder

8. **Color**—normal: yellow
A. Red to reddish brown—hematuria

B. Brown to brownish grey—bilirubinuria and urobilinuria
C. Tea-colored—possible obstructive jaundice

9. **Sodium**—80-180 mEq/24 hours
A. Increased—salt-wasting renal disease
B. Decreased—congestive heart failure and primary aldosteronism

10. **Chloride**—110-250 mEq/24 hours
A. Increased—chronic obstructive lung disease
B. Decreased—metabolic alkalosis

11. **Potassium**—40-80 mEq/24 hours
A. Increased—osmotic diuresis
B. Decreased—renal failure

12. **Creatinine clearance**—1.0-1.6 gm/24 hours
A. Decrease—renal disease

13. **Creatine**—1-2 gm/24 hours
A. Increase—typhoid fever, salmonella, and tetanus
B. Decrease—muscular atrophy, anemia, and leukemia

14. **Hydroxycorticosteroids**—2-10 mg/24 hours
A. Increase—Cushing's disease
B. Decrease—Addison's disease

15. **Ketosteroids**
A. Male—1-22 mg/24 hour
B. Female—6-16 mg/24 hours
C. Increase—hirsutism and adrenal hyperplasia
D. Decrease—thyrotoxicosis, Addison's disease, and myxedema

16. **Catecholamines (VMA)**
A. Epinephrine—10 mg/24 hours
B. Norepinephrine: 100 mg/24 hours
   1. Increase—pheochromocytoma

Urine Tests

1. **Schilling test**
A. One-third of absorbed Vitamin B_{12} should appear in urine
B. Decreased—gastrointestinal malabsorption and pernicious anemia

2. **Phenolphthalein (PSP)**
A. At least 25% excreted in 15 minutes, 40% in 30 minutes, and 60% in 120 minutes
B. Decreased—renal disease, low in nephritis; pyelonephritis; and congestive heart failure

COMMON PROCEDURES

1. **Noninvasive diagnostic procedures**—those procedures that provide an indirect assessment of organ size, shape, and/or function; these procedures are considered safe, are easily reproducible, need less complex equipment for recording, and generally do not require the written consent of the patient and/or guardian
   A. General nursing responsibilities in noninvasive techniques
      1. Reduce patient anxieties and provide emotional support by
         a. Explaining the purpose and procedure of test
         b. Answering questions regarding safety of the procedure as indicated
         c. Remaining with patient during procedure when possible
      2. Utilize procedures in the collection of specimens which avoid contamination and facilitate diagnosis—clean-catch urines and sputum specimens after deep breathing and coughing, for example
   B. Graphic studies of the heart and brain
      1. Electrocardiogram—graphic record of the electrical activity generated by the heart during depolarization and repolarization; utilized to diagnose abnormal cardiac rhythms and coronary heart disease
      2. Ballistocardiogram—graphic record of body movements that occur as the result of the force of the heart beat; utilized to measure cardiac output, strength of myocardial contraction, aortic elasticity and presence of coronary artery disease, mitral stenosis, or chronic constrictive pericarditis
      3. Phonocardiogram—graphic record of heart sounds; utilized to keep a permanent record of the patient's heart sounds before and after cardiac surgery
      4. Electroencephalogram—graphic record of the electrical potentials generated by the physiologic activity of the brain; utilized to detect surface lesions or tumors of the brain and presence of epilepsy
      5. Echoencephalogram—beam of pulsed ultrasound is passed through the head and returning echos are graphically recorded; detects shifts in cerebral midline structures caused by subdural hematomas, intracerebral hemorrhage, and tumors
   C. Roentgenologic studies (X-ray)
      1. Chest—utilized to determine the size, contour, and position of the heart; the size, location, and nature of pulmonary lesions; disorders of thoracic bones or soft tissue; diaphragmatic contour and excursion; pleural thickening or effusions; and gross changes in the caliber or distribution of the pulmonary vasculature
      2. Kidney, ureter, and bladder (KUB)—determine size, shape, and position of kidneys, ureters, and bladder
      3. Mammography—examination of the breast with or without the injection of radiopaque dye into the ducts of the mammary gland
      4. Skull—outlines configuration and density of brain tissues and vascular markings; utilized to determine the size and location of intracranial calcifications, tumors, abscesses, or vascular lesions
   D. Roentgenologic studies (fluoroscopy)—require the ingestion or injection of a radiopaque substance to visualize the target organ
      1. Additional nursing responsibilities include
         a. Administration of enemas or cathartics prior to or following the procedure
         b. Keeping the patient NPO 6 to 12 hours prior to examination
         c. Ascertaining patient history of allergies or allergic reactions
         d. Observing for allergic reactions to dye following procedure
         e. Providing fluid and food following procedure to counteract dehydration
      2. Common fluoroscopic examinations
         a. Upper GI—ingestion of barium sulfate, a white, chalky, radiopaque substance followed by fluoroscopic and X-ray examination; utilized to determine
            (1) Patency and caliber of esophagus; may also detect esophageal varices
            (2) Mobility and thickness of gastric walls, presence of ulcer craters, filling defects due to tumors, pressures from outside the stomach, and patency of pyloric valve
            (3) Rate of passage in small bowel and presence of structural abnormalities
         b. Lower GI—rectal instillation of barium sulfate followed by fluoroscopic and X-ray examination; determines the contour and mobility of the colon and the presence of any space-occupying tumors

c. Cholecystogram—ingestion of organic iodine dye Telepaque (iopanoic acid) followed in 12 hours by X-ray visualization; gallbladder disease is indicated with poor or no visualization of the bladder; accurate only if gastrointestinal and liver function is intact

d. Cholangiogram—intravenous injection of a radiopaque dye followed by fluoroscopic and X-ray examination of the bile ducts; failure of the dye to pass certain points in the bile duct pinpoints obstruction

e. Intravenous pyelography (IVP)—injection of a radiopaque dye followed by fluoroscopic and X-ray films of kidneys and urinary tract; identifies lesions in kidneys and ureters and provides rough estimate of kidney function

f. Cystogram—instillation of radiopaque medium into the bladder through a catheter; utilized to visualize bladder wall and evaluate ureterovesical valves for reflux

E. Pulmonary function studies
1. Ventilatory studies—utilization of a spirometer to determine how well the lung is ventilating
   a. Vital capacity (VC)—largest amount of air that can be expelled after a maximal inspiration
      (1) Normally 4000 to 5000 ml
      (2) Decreased in restrictive lung disease
      (3) May be normal, slightly increased, or decreased in chronic obstructive lung disease.
   b. Forced expiratory volume (FEV_T)—percentage of vital capacity that can be forceably expired in one, two, or three seconds
      (1) Normally 81% to 83% in one second, 90% to 94% in two seconds, and 95% to 97% in three seconds
      (2) Decreased values indicate expiratory airway obstruction
   c. Maximum breathing capacity (MBC)—maximal amount of air that can be breathed in and out in one minute with maximal rates and depths of respiration

   (1) Best overall measurement of ventilatory ability
   (2) Reduced in restrictive and chronic obstructive lung disease
2. Diffusion studies—measure the rate of exchange of gases across alveolar membrane
   a. Carbon monoxide single-breath, rebreathing, and steady-state techniques—utilized because of special affinity of hemoglobin for carbon monoxide; decreased when fluid is present in alveoli or when alveolar membranes are thick or fibrosed

F. Sputum studies
1. Gross sputum evaluations—collection of sputum samples to ascertain quantity, consistency, color, and odor
2. Sputum smear—sputum is smeared thinly on a slide so that it can be studied microscopically; determines cytologic changes (malignant cell) or presence of pathogenic bacteria such as tubercle bacilli
3. Sputum culture—sputum samples are implanted or inoculated into special media; used to diagnose pulmonary infections
4. Gastric lavage or analysis—insertion of a nasogastric tube into the stomach to siphon out swallowed pulmonary secretions; detects organisms causing pulmonary infections; especially useful for detecting tubercle bacilli

G. Examination of gastric contents
1. Gastric analysis—aspiration of the contents of the fasting stomach for analysis of free and total acid
   a. Gastric acidity is generally increased in presence of duodenal ulcer
   b. Gastric acidity is usually decreased in pernicious anemia and in cancer of the stomach
2. Stool specimens—examined for amount, consistency, color, character, and melena; utilized to determine presence of urobilinogen, fat, nitrogen, parasites, and other substances

2. **Invasive diagnostic procedures**—procedures that directly record the size, shape, or function of an organ and which are often complex, expensive, or require the utilization of highly trained personnel; these procedures may result in morbidity and occasionally mortality of the patient and therefore require the written consent of the patient or guardian

A. General nursing responsibilities
   1. Prior to procedure, institute measures to provide for patient safety and emotional comfort.
      a. Have patient sign permit for procedure
      b. Ascertain and report any patient history of allergy or allergic reactions
      c. Explain procedure briefly and accurately advise patient of any possible sensations such as flushing or a warm feeling, as when a contrast medium is injected
      d. Keep patient NPO 6 to 12 hours before procedure if anesthesia is to be used
      e. Allow patient to verbalize concerns and note attitude toward procedure
      f. Administer preprocedure sedative, as ordered
      g. If procedure done at bedside
         (1) Remain with patient offering frequent reassurance
         (2) Assist with optional positioning of patient
         (3) Observe for indications of complications—shock, pain, or dyspnea
   2. Following procedure institute measures to avoid complications and promote physical and emotional comfort
      a. Observe and record vital signs
      b. Check injection cutdown or biopsy sites for bleeding, infection, tenderness, or thrombosis
         (1) Report untoward reactions to physician
         (2) Apply warm compresses to ease discomfort, as ordered
      c. Encourage relaxation by allowing patient to discuss experience and to verbalize feelings
B. Procedures used in evaluating cardiovascular system
   1. Angiocardiography—intravenous injection of a radiopaque solution or dye for the purpose of studying its circulation through the patient's heart, lungs, and great vessels; used to check the competency of heart valves, diagnose congenital septal defects, detect occlusions of coronary arteries, confirm suspected diagnoses, and to study heart function and structure prior to cardiac surgery

   2. Cardiac catheterization—insertion of a radiopaque catheter into a vein to study the heart and great vessels
      a. Right-heart catheterization—catheter is inserted through a cutdown in the antecubital vein into the superior vena cava and through the right atrium, ventricle, and into the pulmonary artery
      b. Left-heart catheterization—catheter may be passed retrograde to the left ventricle through the brachial or femoral artery; it can be passed into the left atrium after right-heart catheterization by means of a special needle that punctures the septa; or it may be passed directly into the left ventricle by means of a posterior or anterior chest puncture
      c. Cardiac catheterizations are utilized to
         (1) Confirm diagnosis of heart disease and determine the extent of the disease
         (2) Determine the existence and extent of congenital abnormalities
         (3) Measure pressures in the heart chambers and great vessels
         (4) Obtain estimate of cardiac output
         (5) Obtain blood samples to measure oxygen content and determine presence of cardiac shunts
      d. Specific nursing interventions
         (1) Preprocedure patient teaching
            (a) Fatigue due to lying still for three or more hours is a common complaint
            (b) Some fluttery sensations may be felt—occurs as catheter is passed backwards into the left ventricle
            (c) Flushed warm feeling may occur when contrast medium is injected
         (2) Postprocedure observations
            (a) Monitor ECG pattern for arrhythmias
            (b) Check extremities for color and temperature and peripheral pulses (femoral and dorsalis pedis) for quality
   3. Angiography (arteriography)—injection of a contrast medium into the arteries to study the vascular tree; utilized to determine obstructions or narrowing of peripheral arteries

C. Procedures used in evaluating the respiratory system

1. Pulmonary circulation studies—utilized to determine regional distribution of pulmonary blood flow
   a. Lung scan—injection of radioactive isotope into the body, followed by lung scintiscan, which produces a graphic record of gamma rays emitted by the isotope in lung tissues; determines lung perfusion when space-occupying lesions or pulmonary emboli and infarction are suspected
   b. Pulmonary angiography—X-ray visualization of the pulmonary vasculature after the injection of a radiopaque contrast medium; used to evaluate pulmonary disorders such as pulmonary embolism, lung tumors, aneurysms, and changes in the pulmonary vasculature due to such conditions as emphysema or congenital defects

2. Bronchoscopy—introduction of a special lighted instrument (bronchoscope) into the trachea and bronchi; used to inspect the tracheobronchial tree for pathologic changes, remove tissue for cytologic and bacteriologic studies, remove foreign bodies or mucus plugs causing airway obstruction, assess functional residual capacity of diseased lung, and apply chemotherapeutic agents
   a. Prebronchoscopy nursing actions
      (1) Oral hygiene
      (2) Postural drainage if indicated
   b. Postbronchoscopy nursing actions
      (1) Instruct patient not to swallow oral secretions but to let saliva run from side of mouth
      (2) Save expectorated sputum for laboratory analysis and observe for frank bleeding
      (3) NPO until gag reflex returns
      (4) Observe for subcutaneous emphysema and dyspnea
      (5) Apply ice collar to reduce throat discomfort

3. Thoracentesis—needle puncture through the chest wall and into the pleura to remove fluid and, occasionally, air from the pleural space
   a. Nursing responsibilities prior to thoracentesis

      (1) Position patient in high-Fowler's position or sitting up on edge of bed with feet supported on chair—facilitates accumulation of fluid in the base of the chest
      (2) If patient is unable to sit up—turn on unaffected side
      (3) Evaluate continually for signs of shock, pain, cyanosis, increased respiratory rate, and pallor

D. Procedures used in evaluating the renal system

1. Renal angiograms—small catheter is inserted into the femoral artery and passed into the aorta or renal artery, radiopaque fluid is instilled, and serial films are taken
   a. Utilized to diagnose renal hypertension and pheochromocytoma and to differentiate renal cysts from renal tumors
   b. Postangiogram nursing actions include checking pedal pulse for signs of decreased circulation

2. Cystoscopy—visualization of bladder, urethra, and prostatic urethra by insertion of a tubular lighted telescopic lens (cystoscope) through the urinary meatus
   a. Utilized to directly inspect the bladder, collect urine from the renal pelvis, obtain biopsies from bladder and urethra, remove calculi, and treat lesions in the bladder, urethra, and prostate
   b. Nursing actions following procedure include
      (1) Observing for urinary retention
      (2) Warm sitz baths to relieve discomfort

3. Renal biopsy—needle aspiration of tissue from the kidney for the purpose of microscopic examination

E. Procedures used in evaluating the digestive system

1. Celiac angiography, hepatoportography, splenoportography, and umbilical venography—injection of a contrast medium into the portal vein or related vessel to determine patency of vessels supplying target organ or to detect lesions in the organs, which distort the vasculature

2. Esophagoscopy and gastroscopy—visualization of the esophagus, the stomach, and sometimes the duodenum by means of a

lighted tube inserted through the mouth

3. Proctoscopy—visualization of rectum and colon by means of a lighted tube inserted through the anus

4. Peritoneoscopy—direct visualization of the liver and peritoneum by means of a peritoneoscope inserted through an abdominal stab wound

5. Liver biopsy—needle aspiration of tissue for the purpose of microscopic examination; utilized to determine tissue changes, to facilitate diagnosis, and provide information regarding a disease course

6. Paracentesis—needle aspiration of fluid from the peritoneal cavity to relieve excess fluid accumulation or for diagnostic studies
   a. Specific nursing actions prior to paracentesis
      (1) Have patient void—prevents possible injury to bladder during procedure
      (2) Position patient—sitting up on side of bed with feet supported by chair
      (3) Check vital signs and peripheral circulation frequently throughout procedure
      (4) Observe for signs of hypovolemic shock—may occur due to fluid shift from vascular compartment following removal of protein-rich ascitic fluid
   b. Specific nursing actions following paracentesis
      (1) Apply pressure to injection site and cover with sterile dressing
      (2) Measure and record amount and color of ascitic fluid and send specimens to lab for diagnostic studies

F. Procedures used in evaluating the reproductive system in women

1. Culdoscopy—operative procedure in which a culdoscope is inserted into the posterior vaginal cul-de-sac; utilized to visualize the uterus, fallopian tubes, broad ligaments, and peritoneal contents

2. Hysterosalpingography—X-ray examination of the uterus and fallopian tubes following insertion of a radiopaque dye into the uterine cavity; determines patency of fallopian tubes and detects pathology in uterine cavity

3. Breast biopsy—needle aspiration or incisional removal of breast tissue for microscopic examination; utilized to differentiate between benign tumors, cysts, and malignant tumors in the breast tissue

4. Cervical biopsy and cauterization—removal of cervical tissue for microscopic examination and cautery to control bleeding or obtain additional tissue samples

G. Procedures evaluating the neuroendocrine system

1. Radioactive iodine uptake test (iodine 131 uptake)—ingestion of a tracer dose of ^{131}I followed in 24 hours by a scan of the thyroid for amount of radioactivity emitted
   a. High uptake indicates hyperthyroidism
   b. Low uptake indicates hypothyroidism

2. Eight-hour intravenous ACTH test—administration of 25 units of ACTH in 500 ml of saline over an eight-hour period
   a. Utilized to determine function of adrenal cortex
   b. 24-hour urine specimens are collected before and after administration for measurement of 17-ketosteroids and 17-hydroxycorticosteroids
   c. In Addison's disease, urinary output of steroids does not increase following administration of ACTH; normally steroid excretion increases three to fivefold following ACTH stimulation
   d. In Cushing's syndrome, hyperactivity of the adrenal cortex increases the urine output of steroids by tenfold in the second urine specimen

3. Cerebral angiography—fluoroscopic visualization of the brain vasculature after injection of a contrast medium into the carotid or vertebral arteries; utilized to localize lesions (tumors, abscesses, intracranial hemorrhages, and occlusions) that are large enough to distort cerebral vascular blood flow

4. Air studies
   a. Pneumoencephalogram—withdrawal of CSF and injection of air or oxygen into the spinal subarachnoid space by means of a lumbar puncture; used to visualize the ventricles and subarachnoid spaces of the brain; may also be used to relieve intractable headache or to diagnose degenerative cerebral atrophy and massive tumors

b. Ventriculogram—withdrawal of CSF and injection of air or oxygen directly into the lateral ventricles through a needle thrust through the brain and into the ventricle; utilized to visualize the patency of the ventricular system, localize brain tumors, and detect cerebral anomalies such as atrophy

c. Specific nursing responsibilities following air studies
   (1) Position patient flat in bed for at least 12 hours
   (2) Observe for signs of increased intracranial pressure, shock, prolonged headache, or vomiting
   (3) Turn from side to side every two hours to hasten passage of air from ventricles
   (4) Apply ice cap to head intermittently

5. Myelogram—through a lumbar-puncture needle, a contrast medium is injected into the subarachnoid space of the spinal column to visualize the spinal cord; utilized to detect herniated or ruptured intervertebral disks, tumors, or cysts that compress or distort spinal cord

6. Brain scan—intravenous injection of a radioactive substance followed by a scan for emission of radioactivity
   a. Increased radioactivity at site of pathology
   b. Utilized to detect brain tumors, abscesses, hematomas, and arteriovenous malformations

7. Lumbar puncture—puncture of the lumbar subarachnoid space of the spinal cord with a needle to withdraw samples of cerebrospinal fluid (CSF); utilized to determine intracranial pressures, evaluate CSF for infections, and to determine presence of hemorrhage

Appendix F   Drugs

TABLE OF COMMON DRUGS

Drug and dosage	Use	Action	Side effects	Nursing implication
1. ADRENERGIC DRUGS				
a. Epinephrine (Adrenalin), Isoproterenol (Isuprel) HCl, Levarterenol bitartrate (Levophed), and Metaraminol (Aramine)	Stokes-Adams disease, cardiac arrest, Paroxysmal atrial tachycardia, neurogenic hypotension and shock, cardiogenic shock following MI, and circulatory collapse	Increases rate and strength of heart beat and causes arterial and venous constriction	Palpitations, pallor, headache, hypertension, anxiety, insomnia, dilated pupils, nausea, vomiting, and glycosuria	Constant monitoring of blood pressure, pulse, and CVP; check infusion site frequently for signs of leakage and infiltration—will cause tissue sloughing
b. Epinephrine— inhalation of 0.3 mg; Isoproterenol SO_4— inhalation of 0.125 mg	Acute and chronic asthmatic states, pulmonary emphysema, and chronic bronchitis and bronchiectasis	Stimulates beta II receptors in smooth muscle of bronchi, resulting in relaxation and dilatation of bronchi	*see Epinephrine*	Teach patient to use nebulizer properly; patient's lips should be held tightly around mouth piece before medicated mist is released
2. ADRENOCORTICAL STERIODS				
a. Cortisone acetate— po or IM, 20–100 mg qd in single or divided doses	Adrenocortical insufficiency, rheumatoid arthritis, allergic diseases and reactions, ulcerative colitis, and nephrosis	Anti-inflammatory effect of unknown action, promotes fat storage and utilization of glucose during stress, and increases K^+ and Ca^{++} excretion and Na^+ retention	Moon facies, hirsutism, thinning of skin and striae, hypertension, menstrual irregularities, glaucoma, delayed healing, psychoses	Administer oral preparation pc and with snack at bedtime; administer deep IM into gluteal muscle (never deltoid—causes cutaneous atrophy); monitor vital signs; observe for euphoria, depression, and mania; promote skin care and activity to tolerance; salt-restricted diet, high in protein and KCl supplement; protect from injury

Continued

TABLE OF COMMON DRUGS—continued

Drug and dosage	Use	Action	Side effects	Nursing implication
b. Desoxycorticosterone acetate (hydrocortisone)—IM, 1–5 mg	Addison's disease, extensive burns, surgical shock, and adrenal surgery	Promotes reabsorption of sodium and restores plasma volume, BP, and electrolyte balance in adrenal cortical insufficiency	Edema, hypertension, pulmonary congestion, and hypokalemia	Adjust dietary salt with blood pressure readings, monitor vital signs, and weigh daily
c. Dexamethasone (Decadron)—po, 0.5–5 mg qd; IM or IV, 4–20 mg qd	Addison's disease, allergic reactions, leukemia, Hodgkin's disease, iritis, dermatitis, and rheumatoid arthritis	Anti-inflammatory effect and less sodium and water retention	see Cortisone acetate	Contraindicated in tuberculosis; see Cortisone acetate for nursing care
d. Prednisone—po, 2.5–15 mg qd	Rheumatoid arthritis and cancer therapy	Anti-inflammatory effect of unknown action and decreased sodium and water retention	Insomnia and gastric distress	see Cortisone acetate
3. ANALGESICS				
a. Aspirin or acetylsalicylic acid—po or R, 0.3–0.6 gm	Minor aches and pains, fever of colds and influenza, rheumatic fever, rheumatoid arthritis, and anticoagulant therapy	Selectively depresses subcortical levels of CNS	Erosive gastritis with bleeding, coryza, urticaria, nausea, vomiting, tinnitus, impaired hearing, and respiratory alkalosis	Administer with food or pc; observe for nasal, oral, or subcutaneous bleeding; push fluids; check Hct, Hb, and prothrombin times frequently
b. Meperidine HCl (Demerol)—po or IM, 50–100 mg q3–4h	Pain due to trauma or surgery and allay apprehension prior to surgery	Acts on CNS to produce analgesia, sedation, euphoria, and respiratory depression	Palpitations, bradycardia, hypotension, nausea, vomiting, syncope, sweating, tremors, and convulsions	Check respiratory rate and depth before giving drug; administer IM, as subcutaneous administration is painful and can cause local irritation
	Maternal use: Maternal relaxation may (a) slow labor or (b) speed up labor	Depresses CNS: maternal and fetal; allays apprehension, po peak action: 1–2 hours; IM peak action: first hour	As above; also, can depress fetus	Monitor maternal vital signs, contractions, progress of labor, and response to drug; monitor FHR; if delivery occurs during peak action, prepare to give narcotic

			antagonist to mother and/or neonate
c. Morphine SO₄— po, 8–20 mg; subq 8–15 mg; IV, 4–8 mg	Control pain and relieve fear, apprehension, and restlessness as in pulmonary edema Depresses CNS reception of pain and ability to interpret stimuli; depresses respiratory center in medulla	Nausea, vomiting, flushing, confusion, urticaria, depressed rate and depth of respirations, and decreased blood pressure	Check rate and depth of respirations before administering drug; observe for gas pains and abdominal distention; smaller doses for aged; monitor vital signs; observe for postural hypotension
	Maternal use: preeclampsia-eclampsia, uterine dysfunction, and pain relief Increases cerebral blood flow, provides antihypertensive action, and CNS depressant	Respiratory and circulatory depression in mother and neonate, may depress contractions	Observe for level of sedation, respirations, arousability, and deep tendon reflexes; give narcotic antagonist as necessary; Check I & O, urinary retention possible
d. Pantopium (Pantopon)—po, subq, or IM, 5–20 mg	*Maternal use:* control pain and relieve fear and apprehension Enhances sedative-analgesic effects of narcotics—used in place of morphine	Addictive, may depress fetus	*see Meperidine HCl*
e. Alphaprodine HCl (Nisentil)—subq, 40–60 gm	*Maternal use:* control pain, especially during labor Synthetic narcotic similar to meperidine (Demerol) HCl, subq peak action 1–2 hours, IV peak action first hour	Addictive; may depress fetus, especially if used with barbiturate; respiratory depression; dizziness; sweating; nausea; vomiting; and restlessness	*see Meperidine HCl*
f. Codeine—po or subq, 15–60 mg (gr ¼ to 1)	*Maternal use:* control pain; may be used during puerperium Nonsynthetic narcotic analgesic	Of little use during labor; allergic response	Note patient's response to the medication
g. Oxycodone HCl (Percodan)—po, 3–20, mg; subq, 5 mg	*Maternal use:* control pain; may be used during puerperium; five to six times more potent than codeine Less potent and addicting than morphine; for moderate pain: episiotomy, and "after pains"; peak action 1 hour	*see Morphine SO₄*	Administer per order and observe for effect

Continued

TABLE OF COMMON DRUGS—continued

Drug and dosage	Use	Action	Side effects	Nursing implication
4. ANTACIDS				
a. Aluminum hydroxide gel (Amphojel)—po, 5–10 ml q2–4h or 1h pc	Gastric acidity, peptic ulcer, and phosphatic urinary calculi	Buffers HCl in gastric juices without interfering with electrolyte balance	Constipation and fecal impaction	Shake well before administering; encourage fluids to prevent impaction and milk-alkali syndrome
b. Calcium carbonate (Titralac, Ducon)—po, 1–2 gm taken with H_2O pc and hs	Peptic ulcer and chronic gastritis	Reduces hyperacidity	None known	
c. Aluminum hydroxide and magnesium trisilicate (Gelusil)—po, 5–30 ml pc and hs	Peptic acid gastritis, heartburn, and esophagitis	Neutralizes and absorbs excess acid	Diarrhea and hypermagnesemia	Avoid prolonged administration to patients with renal insufficiency
d. Magnesium and aluminum hydroxides (Maalox suspension)—po, 5–30 ml pc and hs	Gastric hyperacidity, peptic ulcer, and heartburn	Neutralizes and binds acids	Constipation and fecal impaction	Encourage fluid intake; contraindicated for debilitated patients or those with renal insufficiency
5. ANTIARRHYTHMICS				
a. Quinidine SO_4—po, 0.2–0.6 gm q2h loading dose for 5 doses maintenance dose: 400–1000 mg tid-qid	Atrial fibrillation, PAT, ventricular tachycardia, and PVCs	Lengthens conduction time in atria and ventricles and blocks vagal stimulation of heart	Nausea, vomiting, diarrhea, vertigo, tremor, headache, abdominal cramps, AV block, and cardiac arrest	Count pulse before administering; report changes in rate quality or rhythm; give drug with food; monitor BP daily
b. Procaine amide HCl (Pronestyl)—po, IM 500–1000 mg 4–6 times qd; IV, 1 gm	Atrial and ventricular arrhythmias, PVCs, overdose of digitalis, and general anesthesia	Depresses myocardium and lengthens conduction time between atria and ventricles	Polyarthralgia, fever, chills, urticaria, nausea, vomiting, psychoses, and rapid decrease in BP	Check pulse rate before administering; monitor heart action during IV administration
c. Lidocaine HCl—IV or 50–100 mg bolus	Ventricular tachycardia and PVCs	Depresses myocardial response to abnormally generated impulses	Drowsiness, dizziness, nervousness, confusion, and paresthesias	Check apical and radial pulses for deficits; observe for signs of toxicity; monitor ECG for prolongation of PR interval

6. ANTIBIOTICS

a. Dia-mer-sulfonamides (Sulfonamides duplex), Sulfisoxazole (Gantrisin), Sulfamethizole (Thiosulfil), and Sulfisomidine (Elkosin)	Acute, chronic, and recurrent urinary tract infections	Bacteriostatic and bacteriocidal	Nausea, vomiting, oliguria, anuria, anemia, leukopenia, dizziness, jaundice, and skin rashes	Maintenance of blood levels very important; encourage fluids to prevent crystal formation in kidney tubules—push up to 3000 ml/day
b. Penicillin—Penicillin G, Penicillin G Potassium, and Penicillin G Procaine	*Streptococcus, Staphylococcus, Pneumococcus, Gonococcus,* and *Treponema pallidum*	Primarily bactericidal	Dermatitis and delayed or immediate anaphylaxis	Outpatients should be observed for 20 minutes postinjection; hospitalized patients should be observed at frequent intervals for 20 minutes after injection
c. Tetracyclines: Chlortetracycline (Aureomycin), Doxycyline (Vibramycin hyclate), Oxytetracycline (Terramycin), and Tetracycline HCl (Sumycin)	Wide spectrum antibiotic	Primarily bacteriostatic	GI upsets as diarrhea, nausea, and vomiting; sore throat; black hairy tongue; glossitis; and inflammatory lesions in anogenital region	Phototoxic reactions have been reported; patients should be advised to stay out of direct sunlight and medication should not be given with milk or snacks, as food interferes with absorption of tetracyclines

7. ANTICHOLINERGICS

a. Atropine SO₄—0.3–1.2 mg po, subq, IM, or IV; ophthalmic 0.5%–1% up to 6 times qd	Peptic ulcer, spasms of GI tract, Stokes-Adams syndrome, and control excessive secretions during surgery	Blocks parasympathomimetic effects of acetylcholine on effector organs	Dry mouth, dysphagic rash, skin flushing, urinary retention; *Contraindications:* glaucoma and paralytic ileus	Observe for postural hypotension in ambulating patients; administer cautiously in aged; and monitor vital signs for pulse and respiratory rate changes
b. Tincture of Belladonna—0.3–0.6 ml tid	Hypermobility of stomach and bowel, biliary and renal colic, and prostatitis	Blocks parasympathomimetic effects of acetylcholine	Dry mouth, thirst, dilated pupils, skin flushing, elevated temperature, and delirium	Administer 30 to 60 minutes before meals; observe for side effects; Physostigmine salicylate is antidote

Continued

TABLE OF COMMON DRUGS—continued

Drug and dosage	Use	Action	Side effects	Nursing implication
c. Propantheline bromide (Pro-banthine)—po, 15 mg qid; IM or IV, 30 mg	Decreases hypertonicity and hypersecretion of GI tract, ulcerative colitis, and peptic ulcer	Block neural transmission at ganglia of autonomic nervous system and at parasympathetic effector organs	Nausea, gastric fullness, constipation, and mydriasis	Give before meals; observe urinary output to avoid retention, particularly in elderly; mouth care pc will relieve dryness; and contraindicated in presence of glaucoma
8. ANTICOAGULANTS				
a. Heparin—initial dose: 30,000 units	Acute thromboembolic emergencies	Prevents thrombin formation	Hematuria, bleeding gums, and ecchymosis	Observe clotting times—should be between 20-30 minutes; heparin antagonist is Protamine sulfate
b. Warfarin sodium (Coumadin)—initial dose: po, 40-60 mg; po, 20-30 mg elderly; maintenance dose: po, 5-10 mg qd	Venous thrombosis, atrial fibrillation with embolization, and pulmonary emboli myocardial infarction	Depresses liver synthesis of prothrombin and factors VII, IX, and X	Minor or major hemorrhage, alopecia, fever, nausea, diarrhea, and dermatitis	Drug effects last three to four days; antagonist is Vitamin K
9. ANTICONVULSANTS				
a. Phenytoin, or diphenylhydantoin (Dilantin) SO_4—po, 30-100 mg 3-4 times qd; IM, 100-200 mg 3-4 times qd; IV, 150-250 mg	Psychomotor epilepsy, convulsive seizures, and ventricular arrhythmias	Depresses motor cortex by preventing spread of abnormal electrical impulses	Nervousness, ataxia, gastric distress, nystagmus, slurred speech, hallucinations, and gingival hyperplasia	Give with meals or pc; frequent and diligent mouth care; advise patient that urine may turn pink to red-brown; teach patient signs of adverse reactions
b. Valium (Diazepam)—po, 2-10 mg bid-qid; IM or IV, 5-10 mg	All types of seizures	Induces calming effect on limbic system, thalamus, and hypothalamus	Drowsiness, ataxia, and paradoxical increase in excitability of CNS	IV may cause phlebitis; inject IM deeply into tissue; give IV injection very slowly, as respiratory arrest can occur

Drug/dose	Use	Action	Side effects	Remarks
10. ANTIDIARRHEALS				
a. Paregoric or camphorated opium tincture—5–10 ml q2h, not more than qid	Diarrhea	Act directly on intestinal smooth muscle to increase tone and decrease propulsive peristalsis	Occasional nausea; prolonged use may produce dependence	Contains approximately 1.6 mg morphine or 16 mg opium and is subject to Federal Narcotics Regulations; Administer with partial glass of water to facilitate passage into stomach; observe number and consistency of stools—discontinue drug as soon as diarrhea is controlled; keep in tight, light-resistant bottles
b. Kaolin with pectin (Kaopectate)—adults: po, 60–120 ml after each BM; children: over 12, po, 60 ml; 6–12, po, 30–60 ml; 3–6, po, 15–30 ml after each BM	Diarrhea	Reported to absorb irritants and soothe intestinal muscle; usefulness of mixture supported by tradition rather than controlled studies	Granuloma of the stomach	Do not administer for more than two days, in presence of fever, or to children less than 3 years of age
c. Diphenoxylate HCl with atropine sulfate (Lomotil)—po, 5–10 mg tid-qid	Diarrhea	Increases intestinal tone and decreases propulsive peristalsis	Rash, drowsiness, dizziness, depression, abdominal distention, headache, blurred vision, and nausea	May potentiate action of barbiturates, opiates, and other depressants; closely observe patients receiving these drugs and administer narcotic antagonists such as levallorphan (Lorfan) tartrate, naloxone HCl (Narcan), and nalorphine (Nalline) HCl as ordered; administer cautiously to patients with hepatic dysfunction—may precipitate hepatic coma
11. ANTIEMETICS				
a. Trimethobenzamide HCl (Tigan)—25 mg qid, po, IM, R	Prevention and treatment of nausea and vomiting	Suppresses chemoreceptors in the trigger zone located in the medulla oblongata	Drowsiness, vertigo, diarrhea, headache, hypotension, jaundice, blurred vision, and rigid muscles	Inject deeply into a large muscle to prevent escape of solution; can cause edema, pain, and burning

Continued

TABLE OF COMMON DRUGS—continued

Drug and dosage	Use	Action	Side effects	Nursing implication
b. Prochlorperazine dimaleate (Compazine)—5–30 mg qid po, IM, R	Control of nausea, vomiting and retching	Suppresses chemoreceptors in trigger zone and diminishes some motor activity	Drowsiness, orthostatic hypotension, palpitations, blurred vision, diplopia, and headache	Use cautiously in children, pregnant women, and patients with liver disease
12. ANTIHISTAMINES				
a. Diphenhydramine HCl (Benadryl)—po, 25–50 mg tid–qid; IM or IV, 10–50 mg q4–6h	Allergic and pyrogenic reactions to blood transfusions and penicillin; motion sickness; radiation sickness; hay fever; and Parkinson's disease	Inhibits action of histamine on receptor cells and decreases action of acetylcholine	Sedation, dizziness, inability to concentrate, headache, anorexia, dermatitis, nausea, diplopia, and insomnia	Avoid use in newborn or premature infants and patients with glaucoma; supervise ambulation; caution against driving or operating mechanical devices that require alertness
b. Chlorpheniramine maleate (Chlor-Trimeton)—po, 2–4 mg tid–qid; subq, IM, or IV, 10–20 mg	Asthma, hay fever, serum reactions, and anaphylaxis	Inhibits action of histamine	Nausea, gastritis, diarrhea, headache, dryness of mouth and nose, nervousness, and irritability	Parenteral administration may drop blood pressure; administer slowly, observing for side effects; caution patient about drowsiness
c. Tripelennamine HCl (Pyribenzamine)—po, 25–50 mg bid–qid; IV or IM, 25 mg	Asthma, hay fever, pruritus, and motion sickness	Inhibits histamine and promotes sedation	Dry mouth, vertigo, headache, nervousness, frequency, and blood dyscrasia	Blurred vision and drowsiness; caution patient about driving or handling mechanical equipment that requires alertness
13. ANTIHYPERLIPEMIAS				
a. Cholestyramine resin (Questran)—po, 4 gm packet tid ac	Reduction of blood cholesterol	Binds bile acids in the intestine and prevents their reabsorption, thus reducing serum cholesterol 10%–20%	Mild nausea and constipation; occasionally epigastric distress and diarrhea	Administer vitamin A, D, and K (fat-soluble vitamins) to supplement deficiencies due to decreased absorption; give drugs such as digitalis, chlorothiazide, thyroid, iron, or warfarin sodium one hour before or four hours after cholestyramine resin (Questran) (drug may also absorb other drugs given concomitantly)

Drug/dose	Use	Action	Side effects	Nursing considerations
b. Clofibrate (Atromid-S)—po, 500 mg qid	Endogenous hyperlipemias	Inhibits hepatic synthesis of triglycerides, phospholipids, and cholesterol; also decreases platelet adhesiveness and displaces various plasma proteins	Urticaria, stomatitis, pruritus, leukopenia, nausea, elevation of SGOT and SGPT activity, and weight gain	Contraindicated in pregnancy, lactation, renal and hepatic impairment, and in children; administer reduced dose of warfarin (Coumadin) sodium and monitor prothrombin times of patients on anticoagulant therapy

14. ANTIHYPERTENSIVES

Drug/dose	Use	Action	Side effects	Nursing considerations
a. Reserpine (Serpasil)—po, 0.25 mg qd	Mild and moderate hypertension	Depletes catecholamines and decreases peripheral vasoconstriction, heart rate, and BP	Depression, nasal stuffiness, increased gastric secretions, rash, and pruritus	Watch for signs of mental depression; closely monitor pulse rates of patients also receiving digitalis
	Maternal use: preeclampsia-eclampsia	CNS depressant, tranquilizer, sedation is major effect; decreases neural transmission to nerves; decreases tone in blood vessels	Low level of toxicity; nasal stuffiness; weight gain; diarrhea; allergic reactions—dry mouth, itching, skin eruptions	Side rails up; must not stand up without assistance; observe carefully; and monitor B/P
b. Guanethidine SO$_4$ (Ismelin)—po, 10–150 mg qd in divided doses	Severe to moderately severe hypertension	Blocks norepinephrine at postganglionic synapses	Orthostatic hypotension, diarrhea, and inhibition of ejaculation	Postural hypotension is marked in the morning and is accentuated by hot weather, alcohol, and exercise; teach to rise slowly
c. Methyldopa (Aldomet)—po, 500 mg–2 gm qd in divided doses	Severe to moderately severe hypertension	Inhibits formation of dopamine, a precursor of norepinephrine	Initial drowsiness, depression with feelings of unreality, edema, jaundice, and dry mouth	Contraindicated in active and chronic liver disease; encourage not to drive car if drowsy
d. Hydralazine HCl (Apresoline)—po, 10–50 mg qid	Moderate hypertension	Dilates peripheral blood vessels	Palpitations, tachycardia, angina pectoris, tremors, and depression	Encourage moderation in exercise and identification of stressful stimuli
	Maternal use: preeclampsia-eclampsia	Relaxes peripheral blood vessels (opens vascular bed—physiologic dehydration)	Headache, heart palpitation, gastric irritation, coronary insufficiency, edema, chills, fever, and severe depression	Side rails up; must not stand up without assistance; may be given with diuretics; observe carefully; IM route only; and monitor BP

Continued

TABLE OF COMMON DRUGS—continued

Drug and dosage	Use	Action	Side effects	Nursing implication
e. Pentolinium (Ansolysen) tartrate—po, 60–600 mg qd in divided doses	Malignant hypertension, and hypertensive crisis	Blocks sympathetic stimulation at ganglion; dilates peripheral vasculature; very potent	Orthostatic hypotension, diarrhea, and inhibition of ejaculation	Teach to rise slowly
15. ANTILACTOGENICS				
a. Diethylstilbestrol (DES)—po or IM, 0.2–5.0 mg qd; vaginal supp 0.1–0.5 mg hs	*Maternal use:* synthetic estrogen to control postpartum breast engorgement, menopausal symptoms, and osteoporosis pain of mammary carcinoma	Functions as natural estrogen in its effect on pituitary, ovaries, myometrium, endometrium, and other tissues	Anorexia, nausea, vomiting, diarrhea, dizziness, and fainting—many side effects with long-term usage	Administer as ordered; observe for side effects; never give if woman is pregnant—predisposes to vaginal cancer in female offspring at puberty
b. Deladumone (testosterone enanthate and estradiol valerate)—IM, 200 mg x1	*Maternal use:* suppresses lactation; prevents breast engorgement when given immediately after delivery	Depresses production of lactogenic hormone by posterior pituitary	Rare, following one dose; masculinization and electrolyte imbalance following long-term therapy	Administer as ordered; observe for side effects
c. Testosterone cypionate—IM, 100 mg	*Maternal use:* suppresses lactation; treatment for breast engorgement; palliative therapy for breast cancer and menopausal symptoms	*see Deladumone*	*see Deladumone*	Administer as ordered; observe for side effects
16. BRONCHODILATORS				
a. Aminophylline—po, 250 mg, bid-qid; R, 250–500 mg; IV, 250–500 mg over 10–20 min	Rapid relief of bronchospasm; asthma; and pulmonary edema	Relaxes smooth muscles and increases cardiac contractility; interferes with reabsorption of Na^+ and Cl^- in proximal tubules	Nausea, vomiting, cardiac arrhythmias, intestinal bleeding, insomnia, and restlessness	Give oral with or after meals; monitor vital signs for changes in BP and pulse; and weigh daily
b. Ephedrine SO_4—po, subq, or IM, 25 mg tid-qid	Asthma, allergies, bradycardia, and nasal decongestant	Relaxes hypertonic muscles in bronchioles and GI tract	Wakefulness, nervousness, dizziness, palpitations, and hypertension	Monitor vital signs; avoid giving dose near bed time; check urine output in older adults
c. Isoproterenol HCl (Isuprel)—inhalation of 1:100 or 1:200 sol	Mild to moderately severe asthma attack, bronchitis, and pulmonary emphysema	Relaxes hypertonic bronchioles	Nervousness, tachycardia, hypertension, and insomnia	Monitor vital signs before and after treatment; teach patient how to use nebulizer

	Use	Action	Side effects	Nursing implications
17. CARDIAC GLYCOSIDES				
a. Digitoxin—digitalizing dose: po, 1.2–1.5 mg; IM or IV, 1.2 mg; maintenance dose: po, 1.2 mg qd	Congestive heart failure, atrial fibrillation and flutter, and supraventricular tachycardia	Increases force of cardiac contractility, slows heart rate, decreases right atrial pressures, and promotes diuresis	Arrhythmias; nausea; vomiting; anorexia; malaise; color vision, yellow or blue	Hold medication if pulse rate less than 60 or over 120; encourage juices high in potassium, such as orange juice; and observe for signs of electrolyte depletion, apathy, disorientation, and anorexia
b. Digoxin—digitalizing dose: po, 1.5–3.0 mg; IM or IV, 0.75–1 mg; maintenance dose: po, 0.25–0.75 mg qd	see Digitoxin for Use, Action, Side effects, and Nursing implications			
c. Lanatoside C (Cedilanid)—digitalizing dose: po, 6 mg; maintenance dose: po, 1 mg qd	see Digitoxin for Use, Action, Side effects, and Nursing implications			
d. Deslanoside (Cedilanid D)—digitalizing dose: IV or IM, 1.2–1.8 mg	see Digitoxin for Use, Action, Side effects, and Nursing implications			
e. Ouabain—digitalizing dose: IV or IM, 0.25–0.5 mg	see Digitoxin for Use, Action, Side effects, and Nursing implications			
f. Digitalis	Maternal use: cardiac decompensation	Increases force (efficiency) of cardiac contractions; promotes diuresis; indicated by signs-symptoms of cardiac failure	Symptoms of toxicity: slow pulse, nausea, headache, and malaise	Observe for toxicity; observe for improvement in symptoms
18. CHOLINERGIC DRUGS				
a. Bethanechol Cl (Urecholine)—po, 5–30 mg; subq, 2.5–5 mg; Neostigmine Br (Prostigmin)—po, 10–30 mg; IM or subq, 0.25–1 mg	Postoperative abdominal atony and distention; for bladder atony or for bringing on micturition; postsurgical or postpartum urinary retention	Increased tone and motility of GI musculature; increased bladder tone and decreased sphincter tone	Heartburn, belching, abdominal cramps, diarrhea, nausea, and vomiting, incontinence, profuse sweating, and salivation	Warn patient of some discomforting side effects; have urinal or bedpan close at hand and answer calls quickly; atropine SO_4 is the antidote for cholinergic drugs

Continued

TABLE OF COMMON DRUGS—continued

Drug and dosage	Use	Action	Side effects	Nursing implication
19. CHOLINERGIC MIOTICS				
a. Pilocarpine HCl—0.1 ml of 0.5%–4% sol; 1–6 times qd; physostigmine salicylate (Eserine)—0.1 ml of 0.25–1% sol not more than qid	Wide-angle glaucoma	Contraction of the sphincter muscle of iris resulting in miosis	Browache, headache, ocular pain, blurring and dimness of vision, allergic conjunctivitis, nausea, vomiting, and profuse sweating	Let patient know that initially the medication may be irritating; teach proper technique for instilling eye drops—all equipment for instilling eye drops should be kept sterile, discard cloudy solutions
20. CNS STIMULANTS				
a. Amphetamine SO_4—po, 5–10 mg od–tid; IM or IV, 10–30 mg	Mild depressive states, childhood neuroses, narcolepsy, postencephalitic parkinsonism, and obesity control	Raises blood pressure, decreases sense of fatigue, and elevation of mood	Restlessness, dizziness, tremors, insomnia, increased libido, suicidal and homicidal tendency, palpitations, and angina pain	Avoid administering drug after 4 PM; dependence on drug may develop; and contraindicated with MAO inhibitors, hyperthyroidism, and psychotic states
b. Pentylenetetrazol (Metrazol)—IV, 5 ml of 10% sol; po, 200 mg tid	Overdose of barbiturates	Respiratory stimulation	Convulsion and vomiting	Observe for hypoxia, muscular twitching, and convulsions
21. CNS DEPRESSANTS				
a. Magnesium SO_4—dosage and dosage schedule varies	*Maternal use:* treat preeclampsia-eclampsia, counteract uterine tetany (especially following oxytocin overdose), and counteract the abnormally contracting myometrium	Vasodilatation—therefore it acts as (a) BP depressor, (b) diuretic (by improving kidney perfusion), and (c) sedative and CNS depressant; depresses all forms of muscle (smooth, skeletal, and cardiac)	Toxic effects: (a) hyporeflexia, (b) lowered respirations, (c) oliguria; cardiorespiratory arrest; hypermagnesemia in neonate, and (d) extreme thirst, flushing, or hypothermia	Have 20 ml of calcium 10% gluconate available for cardiac respiratory arrest; repeat magnesium sulfate dose only if (a) deep tendon reflexes present, (b) respirations above 12/minute, and (c) urine output 100 ml/6 hours (at least); frequent BP and pulse; never leave patient alone
22. DIURETICS				
a. Thiazides (Diuril, Hydrodiuril, and	Edema, congestive heart failure, Na^+ retention in	Inhibits sodium chloride and water reabsorption in	Hypokalemia, nausea, vomiting, diarrhea,	Watch for muscle weakness; give

Drug/Dose	Indication	Action	Side effects	Nursing considerations
Esidrix)—po, 0.5–1 gm qd	steroid therapy, hypertension	the proximal tubules of the kidneys	dizziness, and paresthesias; may accentuate diabetes	well-diluted potassium chloride supplement; monitor urine for changes in S and A
	Maternal use: preeclampsia-eclampsia	Decrease fluid retention, eliminate Na⁺, control BP, and no acidosis	All diuretics must be used with caution since they produce fluid-electrolyte imbalance in mother-fetus; may cause allergic reaction	Weigh daily, accurate I & O, assess edema, and replace electrolytes per order; less electrolyte imbalance with proper precautions (replace K⁺ with orange juice, banana, etc.)
b. Spironolactone (Aldactone)—po, 25 mg bid-qid	Cirrhosis of liver and when other diuretics are ineffective	Inhibits effects of aldosterone in distal tubules of kidney	Headache, lethargy, diarrhea, ataxia, skin rash, gynecomastia	Potassium-sparing drug; *do not* give supplemental KCl; monitor for signs of electrolyte imbalance
c. Furosemide (Lasix)—po, 40–80 mg qd in divided doses	Edema and associated heart failure, cirrhosis, renal disease, nephrotic syndrome, and hypertension	Inhibits Na⁺ and water reabsorption in ascending Loop of Henle and distal renal tubule	Dermatitis, pruritus, paresthesia, blurring of vision, postural hypotension, nausea, vomiting, and diarrhea	Assess for weakness, lethargy, leg cramps, anorexia; peak action in 1 to 2 hours; duration 6 to 8 hours; do not give at bed time; supplementary KCl indicated; may induce digitalis toxicity
d. Ethacrynic acid (Edecrin)—po, 50–200 mg qd in divided doses	Pulmonary edema, ascites, edema of congestive heart failure	Inhibits the reabsorption of Na⁺ in the ascending Loop of Henle	Nausea, vomiting, diarrhea, hypokalemia, hypotension, gout, dehydration, deafness, and metabolic acidosis	Assess for dehydration—skin turgor, neck veins; hypotension; KCl supplement
e. Meralluride (Mercuhydrin)—IM, 1–2 ml; Mercaptomerin (Thiomerin)—IM, 1–2 ml; Mercurophylline (Mercuzanthin)—IM, 1–2 ml	Acute edematous states	Enhances sodium excretion in proximal renal tubules	Metabolic alkalosis due to hypochloremia or bone marrow depression	Closely observe urine output—mercurial salts may cause tubular necrosis and renal failure; watch for signs of chloride depletion—apathy, somnolence, weakness, and disorientation

Continued

TABLE OF COMMON DRUGS—continued

Drug and dosage	Use	Action	Side effects	Nursing implication
f. Osmotic diuretic 30% Urea, 10% Invert sugar, 20% Mannitol	Cerebral edema	Hypertonic solution that kidney tubules cannot reabsorb and thus causes obligatory water loss		
g. Acetazolamide (Diamox)	*Maternal use:* preeclampsia-eclampsia	Potent diuretic; produces acidosis; self-limiting effect	Electrolyte depletion symptomology—lassitude, apathy, decreased urinary output, and mental confusion; may be fetotoxic	Weigh daily; I & O; assess edema; give early in day to allow sleep at night; observe for side effects; replace electrolytes as ordered
h. Ammonium Cl	*Maternal use:* preeclampsia-eclampsia	Promote Na$^+$ excretion; may lead to acidosis; self-limiting effect	*see Acetazolamide*	*see Acetazolamide*
23. ENZYMES				
a. Chymotrypsin (Chymar)—po, 50,000–100,000 U qid; IM 0.5–1.0 ml qd	Inflammatory edema, hematomas from traumatic injuries	Accelerates healing by removing fibrinlike material which blocks capillaries and lymphatics	Pain, local edema, urticaria, allergic reactions	Institute hypersensitivity test before administration
b. Pancreatin N.F.—po, 0.5–1.0 gm	Pancreatic deficiencies, sprue, chronic pancreatitis, and cystic fibrosis	Contains pancreatic enzyme, amylase, lipase, and trypsin needed for amino acid digestion	None, used for differences in normal enzymes	Administer with meals
24. EXPECTORANTS				
a. Ammonium Cl—po, 300 mg	Stimulate secretory activity of respiratory tract; diuretic	Nh$_4$ ions cause gastric irritation, which reflexly stimulates respiratory tract secretions	Nausea, vomiting, and bradycardia	Monitor respirations; keep IV record to avoid dehydration and metabolic acidosis
b. Ipecac—po, 0.5–1 ml, for cough; po, 15–30 ml for emesis	Bronchitis, bronchiectasis, emergency emetic for poison ingestion	*see Ammonium Cl*	Violent emesis, tachycardia, decreased BP, and dyspnea	Contraindicated in liver and renal disease; if given for emesis, follow dose with as much water as patient will drink
c. Potassium iodide—po, 300 mg tid-qid	Bronchial asthma, bronchitis, actinomycosis, blastomycosis, and sporotrichosis	Reduces viscosity of bronchial secretions by stimulating flow of respiratory tract fluids	Sore mouth, throat, conjunctivitis, headache, mental depression, ataxia, fever, and sexual impotence	Administer diluted in milk or juice to decrease gastric irritation; observe for side effects and teach patient signs

Drug	Use	Action	Side effects	Nursing
d. Terpin hydrate—po, 5–10 ml q3–4h	Bronchitis, emphysema	Liquifies bronchial secretions	Nausea, vomiting, and gastric irritation	Administer undiluted; push fluids
25. HORMONES				
a. Testosterone—po, 5–10 mg qd; IM 25 mg bid	Replacement therapy in hypogonadism, eunuchism, climacteric impotence, and advanced cancer of breast	Promotes Na^+ and H_2O retention, primary and secondary male sex characteristics; counteracts excessive amounts of estrogen	Nausea; dyspepsia; masculinization; hypercalcemia; menstrual irregularities; renal calculi; and Na^+, K^+, and H_2O retention	Observe for edema; weigh daily; I & O; push fluids for bedridden patients to prevent renal calculi
b. Progesterone—subq or IM, 5–30 mg qd; subling, 10–25 mg	*Maternal use:* amenorrhea, dysmenorrhea, endometriosis, and habitual abortion	Converts endometrium into secreting structure, prevents ovulation, stimulates growth of mammary tissue	Nausea, vomiting, dizziness, edema, headache, protein metabolism	Administer deep IM and rotate sites; weigh daily to ascertain fluid retention
c. Estradiol—po, 0.2–0.5 mg od–tid; IM, 0.5–1.5 mg bid–tid	*Maternal use:* menopausal symptoms, osteoporosis, hypogenitalism, sexual infantilism, postpartum breast engorgement	Inhibits release of pituitary gonadotropins; promotes growth of female genital tissues	Anorexia, nausea, vomiting, diarrhea, fluid retention, and mental depression	Weigh daily; encourage frequent physical check-ups
d. Methallenestril (Vallestril), estrogen—po, 0.2–5 mg qd	*Maternal use:* similar to DES and Tace; advantage: ease of administration and cost	Antilactogenic; suppresses production of lactogenic hormone from posterior pituitary	*see Diethylstilbestrol, under Antilactogenics;* rare with dosage given for antilactogenic effect	Administer as ordered; observe for side effects
e. Chlorotrianisene (Tace), estrogen—po, 12–50 mg qd	*Maternal use:* suppresses lactation	*see Methallenestril*	Breast engorgement is common; side effects rare after one course of treatment	Administer as ordered; observe for side effects; initiate other measures for breast engorgement, see p. 243
f. Medroxyprogesterone (Provera)—po, 2.5—10 mg tabs	*Maternal use:* For amenorrhea, functional uterine bleeding, and threatened abortion and dysmenorrhea	Similar to progesterone but can be taken orally	Drowsiness	Administer as ordered; teach patient regarding self-administration
g. Hydroxyprogesterone caproate (Delalutin)—IM, 250 mg / 2 ml q4 wks	*Maternal use:* For menstrual disorders and ovarian and uterine dysfunction	Synthetic derivative of progesterone but has a longer duration of action if given by parenteral route	Requires priming with estrogen; GI symptoms, headache, and allergy	Administer as ordered; observe for effect

Continued

TABLE OF COMMON DRUGS—continued

Drug and dosage	Use	Action	Side effects	Nursing implication
h. Menotropins (Pergonal)—IM, 9–12 days, followed by 1 10,000 U HCG	*Maternal use:* purified preparation of gonadotropic hormones extracted from urine of postmenopausal women; treatment of secondary anovulation	Induces ovulation	Abortions occur in 25%; failure rate 55% to 80% of patients	Assist in collection of urine to assess estrogen levels; counsel regarding couple's need to have daily intercourse from day of HCG injection until ovulation
26. NARCOTIC ANTAGONISTS				
a. Levallorphan tartrate	*Maternal use:* reverses respiratory depression in mother and/or neonate	Weak narcotic that competes with strong narcotics for CNS receptor sites; relieves narcotic-induced respiratory depression without altering analgesic effect; may be given with a narcotic; does *not* relieve depression from other drugs or causes	May cause respiratory depression if narcosis is due to causes other than a stronger narcotic	Note time, type of narcotic, dosage mother received, administer to mother or neonate, as ordered follow with other resuscitation prn
b. Nalerphine (Nalline) HCl	*See Levallorphan;* for treatment of narcotic addiction, refer to pharmacology text	*see Levallorphan tartrate*	*see Levallorphan tartrate*	*see Levallorphan tartrate*
c. Naloxone (Narcan) HCl	*Maternal use:* reverses respiratory depression in mother and/or neonate	Reverses respiratory depression of morphine SO$_4$, meperidine HCl, and methadone HCl; does not cause respiratory depression, sedation, or analgesia itself	No known side effects	*see Levallorphan tartrate*
27. SEDATIVES AND HYPNOTICS				
a. Chloral hydrate—po, 250 mg tid; hypnotic: po, 0.5–1.0 gm; R supp, 0.3–0.9 gm	Sedation for elderly; delirium tremens, pruritus, mania, and barbiturate and alcohol withdrawal	Depresses sensorimotor areas of cerebral cortex	Nausea, vomiting gastritis; pinpoint pupils; delirium; rash; decreased BP, pulse, respirations, and temperature; hepatic damage	Caution—should not be taken in combination with alcohol; dependency is possible

Drug	Action	Use	Side effects	Nursing considerations
b. Phenobarbital Na—sedative: po, 20–30 mg tid; hypnotic: po, 100–300 mg; IV or IM, 100–200 mg Butabarbital Na (Butisol); Pentobarbital Na (Nembutal); and Secobarbital Na (Seconal)	Depresses central nervous system, promoting drowsiness	Preoperative sedation; emergency control of convulsions; petit mal epilepsy	Cough, hiccups, restlessness, pain, hangover, and CNS and circulatory depression	Observe for hypotension during IV administration; put up side rails on bed of older patients; observe for increased tolerance
c. Chlordiazepoxide (Librium) HCl—po, 5–10 mg; IM or IV, 50–100 mg	CNS depressant resulting in mild sedation, appetite stimulant, and anticonvulsant	Psychoneuroses, preoperative apprehension, chronic alcoholism, and anxiety	Ataxia, fatigue, blurred vision, diplopia, lethargy, nightmares, and confusion	Ensure anxiety relief by allowing patient to verbalize feelings; advise patient to avoid driving and alcoholic beverages
d. Hydroxyzine pamoate (Vistaril)—po, 25–100 mg qid	CNS relaxant with sedative effect on limbic system and thalamus	*see Chlordiazepoxide;* antiemetic in postoperative conditions	Drowsiness, headache, itching, dry mouth, and tremor	Give deep IM only; potentiates action of warfarin (coumadin) sodium, narcotics, and barbiturates
e. Meprobamate (Equanil, Miltown)—400 mg tid-qid	*see Hydroxyzine pamoate*	Anxiety, stress, and petit mal epilepsy	Voracious appetite, dryness of mouth, and ataxia	Older patients prone to drowsiness and hypotension, observe for jaundice

28. UTERINE CONTRACTANTS

Drug	Action	Use	Side effects	Nursing considerations
a. Oxytocin (Pitocin, Syntocinon)—IM, 0.3–1 ml; IV, 1 ml (10 U) in 1000 ml sol	Synthetic pituitrin of posterior pituitary; stimulates rhythmic contractions of uterus	(a) To induce labor, (b) to augment contractions, and (c) to prevent or control postpartum atony; and antidiuretic effect	Avoid when (a) cervix is unripe, (b) CPD, (c) abruptio placentae, and (d) cardiovascular disease; tetanic contractions; FHR deceleration; uterine rupture; and cardiac arrhythmias	Monitor FHR, and contractions, maternal BP, and pulse; under physician's supervision, monitor and record IV, dosage in IV, and I & O, (see discussion of water intoxication) postpartum: this oxytocic is drug of choice in presence of hypertension
b. Methylergonovine maleate (Methergine)—po, 0.2 mg; IV, (gr 1 / 320)	Stimulates stronger and longer contractions than Ergotrate	Primarily for control of postpartum hemorrhage	Nausea, vomiting, transient hypertension, dizziness, and tachycardia	Do not give if mother is hypertensive; do not use if solution is discolored; and *do not use in labor*

Continued

TABLE OF COMMON DRUGS—continued

Drug and dosage	Use	Action	Side effects	Nursing implication
c. Ergonovine maleate (Ergotrate)—po, 0.2 mg (gr 1 / 320)	Rapid sustained action for control of postabortal or postpartum hemorrhage; promotes involution	Stimulates uterine contractions of three or more hours	Nausea, and vomiting; occasional transient hypertension, especially if given IV	Store in cool place; monitor maternal BP and pulse; and *do not use in labor*
29. VASODILATORS				
a. Nitroglycerine— subling, 0.3–0.6 mg prn	Angina pectoris	Directly relaxes smooth muscle, dilating blood vessels; lowers peripheral vascular resistance; and increases blood flow	Faintness, throbbing headache, vomiting, flushing, hypotension, and visual disturbances	Instruct patient to sit or lie down when taking drug to reduce hypotensive effect; may take one to three doses at 5-minute intervals to relieve pain; up to ten per day may be allowed; if headache occurs instruct patient to expel tablet as soon as pain relief occurs; keep drug at bedside and on person; watch expiration dates and replace as needed—tablets lose potency with continued exposure to air and humidity; alcohol ingestion soon after taking nitroglycerine may produce shocklike syndrome due to sharp drop in blood pressure; advise patient not to smoke as nicotine has vasoconstrictive effect
b. Cyclandelate (Cyclospasmol)—po, 100–200 mg qid with meals and hs	Thrombophlebitis, intermittent claudication, frostbite, Raynaud's disease, and peripheral arteriosclerosis	Acts directly on smooth vascular muscle to relax it and enhance blood flow	Faintness, flushing, and hypotension	Administer with meals to reduce gastrointestinal symptoms or give with antacid; contraindicated in pregnancy, glaucoma, obliterative coronary artery disease or

cerebrovascular disease, and in patients with bleeding tendencies

Agent	Use	Action	Side effects	Nursing implications
c. Erythrityl tetranitrate (Cardilate)—po, 10 mg tid	Long-term treatment of angina pectoris	Acts directly to relax smooth muscle of coronary muscular; slow onset; long duration	Faintness, dizziness, headache, hypotension, and skin flushing	Protect drug from light and exposure, as this reduces potency; see *Nitroglycerine*

CHEMOTHERAPY

Agent	Use	Action	Side effects	Nursing implications
ANTIMETABOLITES Cytosine arabinoside 6-Mercaptopurine Methotrexate	Acute leukemia	Inhibits DNA synthesis; metabolized by liver and excreted by kidneys	Causes nausea, vomiting, diarrhea, GI ulcers, stomatitis, photosensitivity, and alopecia	Antiemetics, good oral hygiene, bland diet, and way of coping with no hair (caps or wigs)
CORTICOSTEROIDS Prednisone Cortisone acetate Hydrocortisone	Leukemia, hypercalcemia, anemia, and reduction of CNS edema	*see Adrenocortical steroids*	No acute toxicity; increased appetite, fluid retention; long-term effects include moon face, striae, trunk obesity, purpura, osteoporosis, muscle weakness, and psychosis; and possible hypertension, infection due to immunosuppression, gastric bleeding, and ulcers	Prepare patient and family for body changes and possible effects on behavior; avoid exposure to infection; avoid aspirin; and give medication with food or beverage to minimize gastric irritation
ALKALATING AGENTS (Chlorambucil Cyclophosphamide)	Chronic leukemia, Hodgkin's disease, and lymphomas	Alter property of DNAs, nucleic acid, preventing mitosis	Nausea, vomiting, dermatitis, leukopenia, thrombocytopenia, and fever	Watch for signs and symptoms of infection and administer antiemetic
NATURAL PRODUCTS Doxorubicin hydrochloride Dactinomycin or actinomycin D	Sarcomas, Wilm's tumor, acute leukemia, lymphomas, neuroblastoma, and	Proposed mechanism for action—inhibition of RNA and DNA	Nausea, vomiting, fever, stomatitis, anorexia, acne, alopecia, bone marrow depression, malaise, and	Good oral hygiene, bland diet, attractive meals in social atmosphere, antiemetic, and prepare

Continued

TABLE OF COMMON DRUGS—continued

Drug and dosage	Use	Action	Side effects	Nursing implication
(antibiotic) Vinblastine SO$_4$ Vincristine SO$_4$ Daunomycin (Daunorubicin) (antibiotic) BCG (Bacille Calmette-Guerin)	rhabdomyosarcoma		diarrhea or neurotoxia with constipation and urinary retention	child and parents for resulting hair loss
MISCELLANEOUS AGENTS Hydroxyurea Procarbazine HCl	Chronic leukemia, Hodgkin's disease, and sarcomas	Inhibits DNA synthesis; crosses blood-brain barrier, metabolized by liver, and excreted by kidneys	Nausea, vomiting, bone marrow depression, alopecia, rash, pruritus, GI toxicity	Antiemetic, bland diet, observe for infection, and prepare for loss of hair

ADMINISTERING MEDICATIONS TO PEDIATRIC PATIENTS

A. Clark's rule for computation

$$\frac{\text{Child's weight in pounds}}{150} \times \text{Adult dose}$$

= Approximate dose for child

B. Check recommended amount per kilogram of medication; action of drug being administered; possible side effects; and toxic effects of medication

C. Be honest with child; do not bribe or tell child medication is candy

D. Offer only allowable choices (ask which site child prefers, *not* "Are you ready for an injection?")

E. Do not mix medication with large amounts of food or liquid

F. Oral medications
  1. Infant
    a. Use plastic dropper or syringe or nipple
    b. Elevate head and shoulders
    c. Place thumb on chin to open mouth
    d. Place dropper on middle of tongue
  2. Toddler
    a. May use syringe, straw, or medicine cup
    b. Unwise to "hide" medicine in food
  3. School-age
    a. Teach child to swallow pill or capsule with fluid
    b. Offer choice of fluid with medication if appropriate, particularly if taste of the medication is unpleasant
  4. Adolescent
    a. Allow patient to take own medication if possible
    b. Explain action of medication to ensure cooperation and to teach health measures

G. Intramuscular injections (IM)
  1. Infants
    a. Lateral and anterior aspect of thigh are preferred sites
    b. Insert needle at 90° angle to surface on which child is lying
  2. Toddler, school-age, and adolescent
    a. Dorsogluteal, after child has been walking one year or more
      (1) Upper outer quadrant
      (2) Prone position, toes pointed inward
    b. Ventrogluteal
      (1) Child on back
      (2) Shield child from observing if upset
    c. Deltoid
      (1) Older or larger child
      (2) Bottom of muscle

INSULIN THERAPY

Type	Onset, peak, and duration	Indications
Rapid		
Crystalline zinc (clear)	Onset 1 hour or less Peak 2–4 hours Duration 6–8 hours	Poorly controlled diabetes, trauma, surgery, and coma
Prompt insulin zinc suspension (Semilente insulin) (cloudy)	Onset 1 hour Peak 4–10 hours Duration 12–16 hours	Patients allergic to crystalline; and in combination with longer-lasting insulin
Intermediate		
Globin zinc insulin injection (clear)	Onset 2–4 hours Peak 6–12 hours Duration 18–24 hours	Rarely used
NPH insulin (isophane insulin suspension) (cloudy)	Onset 2–4 hours Peak 6–12 hours Duration 24–48 hours	Patients who can be controlled by one dose per day
Insulin zinc suspension (Lente insulin) (cloudy)	Onset 2–4 hours Peak 6–12 hours Duration 24–36 hours	Patients allergic to NPH
Slow-acting		
PZI (protamine zinc insulin suspension) (cloudy)	Onset 3–6 hours Peak 12–20 hours Duration 24–36 hours	Rarely used; only if uncontrolled by other types
Extended insulin zinc suspension (Ultralente insulin) (cloudy)	Onset 2–4 hours Peak 12–24 hours Duration 36 hours	Often mixed with Semilente for 24-hour curve

REMINDER: To avoid dangerous error use U-40 syringe with U-40 insulin; U-80 syringe with U-80 insulin; and U-100 syringe with U-100 insulin.

INSULIN REACTION VERSUS DIABETIC COMA

	Insulin reaction	Diabetic coma
	Insulin shock is the result of overdose of insulin, reduction of diet, or increase in exercise	Diabetic coma (acidosis) is result of untreated diabetes, inadequate insulin coverage, failure to follow diet, or chronic or repeated infections
Onset	Sudden or gradual (minutes to hours)	Slow (days)
Cause	Delayed or missed meal, excessive exercise, or overdose of insulin	Untreated diabetes, neglect of treatment, or infectious or disease process
Signs	Pallor, shallow respiration, pulse normal, sweating, eyeballs normal, and dilated pupils	Cherry-red lips; flushed face; increased respiration; loud, labored breathing; rapid pulse; dry skin; and soft, sunken eyeballs
Symptoms	Nervousness, tremors, abnormal behavior, semiunconscious, convulsions, blurred or double vision, and hunger	Thirst, nausea, vomiting, headache, constipation, dim vision, abdominal pain, and shortness of breath
Urine	Sugar-free and acetone-free urine	Sugar and acetone in urine
Response to treatment	Rapid or slightly delayed	Slow

Appendix G   Immunizations

CHILDHOOD COMMUNICABLE DISEASES

Disease	Incubation period	Isolation of child	Observation of contact	Clinical manifestations	Nursing care
Varicella (chickenpox)	11 to 21 days	Until pustules and most of scabs have disappeared	11 to 17 days from first exposure	General malaise, slight fever, anorexia, headache; successive crops of maculae, papules, vesicles, and crust; pruritus	Prevent child from scratching and use lotions
Parotitis (mumps)	14 to 24 days	Duration of swelling	Three weeks from first exposure	Swelling and pain may occur in salivary, parotid, sublingual, and submaxillary glands; unilaterally or bilaterally; difficulty swallowing, headache, fever, and malaise	Liquid or soft foods; bedrest for duration of swelling; and heat or cold application to reduce discomfort
Roseola	10 to 15 days	Duration of rash	Two weeks from first exposure	Elevated temperature, drowsy, irritable, and anorexia; after temperature falls (two to four days), macular or maculopapular rash appears on trunk and neck	Symptomatic—cool clothing, tepid baths, and offer liquids frequently
Rubella (German measles)	14 to 21 days	Duration of rash	12 to 21 days from first exposure	Slight fever; mild coryza; rash of small pink or light red maculae, which fade in three days; *no Koplik's* spots	Bedrest until fever subsides; otherwise, symptomatic
Rubeola (measles)	10 to 14 days	five days after appearance of rash	Two weeks from last exposure	Coryza, conjunctivitis, photophobia, Koplik's spots in mouth,	Bedrest until fever and cough subside; dim lights in room; use

	2 to 4 days	About one week	One week from last exposure	hacking cough, high fever, rash, and enlarged lymph nodes; rash goes from maculae to papules, which fade with pressure, last five days	tepid baths and lotion for itching; encourage fluids
Scarlet fever	2 to 4 days	About one week	One week from last exposure	Headache, fever, rapid pulse, rash, thirst, vomiting, and red-strawberry tongue; often seen poststreptococcal sore throat	Penicillin usually administered; encourage fluid intake, bedrest, and mouth care
Pertussis (whooping cough)	7 to 14 days	One week from last paroxysm	Two weeks from last exposure	Coryza, dry cough becomes worse at night; cough is distinctive—paroxysms of sharp coughs in single expiration followed by deep inspiration with "whoop" sound; dyspnea, fever, and occasional vomiting	Bedrest with emotional support, warm humid air, offer frequent small feedings, and child may require small amounts of sedative to ensure adequate rest and relaxation to decrease coughing

IMMUNIZATION SCHEDULE[a]

Age	Immunizations	
2 months	DTP[b]	TOPV[c]
4 months	DTP	TOPV
6 months	DTP	
1-12 years	Measles	Tuberculin test
18 months[d]	Rubella	Mumps
4-6 years	DTP	TOPV
14-16 years and every ten years thereafter	TD[e]	

[a] *American Academy of Pediatrics.*
[b] *DTP: Diphtheria and tetanus toxoids combined with pertussis vaccine.*
[c] *TOPV: Trivalent oral polio vaccine.*
[d] *At 12–15 months measles-mumps-rubella (MMR) combined vaccines can be given.*
[e] *TD: Combines tetanus and diphtheria toxoids (adult type), in contrast to DT containing a larger amount of diphtheria antigen.*

SIDE EFFECTS AND CONTRAINDICATIONS

Immunization	Side effects	Contraindications
DT: diphtheria toxoids	Local tenderness and pain, fever, and swelling	Infectious process or history of febrile convulsions in child
PV: pertussis vaccine (whooping cough)	Local redness, swelling and tenderness, fever, convulsions, and thrombocytopenia	Not given to child over age 6 years because risk of complications from pertussis is decreased and risk of febrile and vaccine-induced convulsions is increased; child with brain damage or history of convulsive disorders—these children may receive a minute test dose, and if no reaction occurs, normal schedule is followed
Tetanus toxoid	Rare in childhood; itching; painful, swollen injection site; and fever	Child sensitive to horse serum and history of antitoxin formation
Polio vaccine	Virtually no side effects	Acute illness or gastroenteritis
Measles vaccine	Occur seven to ten days after administration—anorexia, rash, and fever	Not recommended for infants under 1 year unless epidemic present, then reimmunize after 1 year of age; acute infection; and skin rash
Rubella vaccine	Joint pain and arthritis, more common in older children	Child with egg allergy, child whose mother is pregnant, and child under one year of age
Mumps vaccine	Virtually no side effects	Child with egg allergy, with immune deficiency, with pregnant mother, on steroid therapy, or undergoing radiation therapy

TUBERCULIN SKIN TEST

A. Keep area dry for two to four hours after test
B. Positive reading—2 mm or more diameter of *raised* reaction; redness itself is not necessarily indicative of positive reaction
C. False negative reading may result from

   1. Recent vaccination with live vaccine (measles, mumps, or smallpox)
   2. Acute fever
   3. Child on steroid therapy
D. Contraindications
   1. Previous history of positive reaction
   2. Previous vaccination with BCG

Appendix H Oxygen Therapy

1. **Purpose**—to relieve hypoxia and provide adequate tissue oxygenation
2. **Clinical indications**
A. Shock
B. Cardiac disorders—myocardial infarction and congestive heart failure
C. Respiratory depression, insufficiency, or failure
D. Anemia
E. Supportive therapy for unconscious patients
3. **Precautions**
A. Patients with chronic obstructive pulmonary disease should receive low flow rates of oxygen to prevent inhibition of hypoxic respiratory drive
B. Excessive amounts of oxygen for prolonged periods of time will cause retrolental fibroplasia and blindness in premature infants
C. Oxygen delivered without humidification will result in drying and irritation of respiratory mucosa, decreased ciliary action, and thickening of respiratory secretions
D. Oxygen supports combustion, and fire is a potential hazard during its administration
   1. Ground electrical equipment
   2. Prohibit smoking
   3. Institute measures to decrease static electricity
E. High flow rates of oxygen per ventilator or cuffed tracheostomy and endotracheal tubes can produce signs of oxygen toxicity in 24 to 48 hours
   1. Cough, sore throat, decreased vital capacity, and substernal discomfort
   2. Pulmonary manifestations due to
      a. Atelectasis
      b. Exudation of protein fluids into alveoli
      c. Damage to pulmonary capillaries
      d. Interstitial hemorrhage
4. **Oxygen administration**
A. Oxygen is dispensed from cylinder or piped-in system
B. Methods of delivering oxygen
   1. Nasal catheter
      a. Effective and comfortable
      b. Delivers 30% to 40% oxygen flow rates of 6–8 liters/minute

c. Can produce excoriation of nares
   2. Nasal prongs
      a. Comfortable, simple, and allows patient to move about in bed
      b. Delivers 30% to 40% oxygen at flow rates of 6–8 liters/minute
      c. Difficult to keep in position unless patient is alert and cooperative
   3. Face tent
      a. Well tolerated and provides means for supplying extra humidity
      b. Delivers 30% to 55% oxygen at flow rates of 4–8 liters/minute
   4. Venturi mask
      a. Mask allows for accurate deliverance of prescribed concentration of oxygen
      b. Delivers 25% to 35% oxygen at flow rates of 4–8 liters/minute
   5. Face mask
      a. Poorly tolerated—utilized for short periods of time
      b. Delivers 35% to 65% oxygen at flow rates of 6–12 liters/minute
      c. Significant rebreathing of carbon dioxide at low oxygen flow rates
      d. Hot—may produce pressure sores around nose and mouth
   6. T-piece
      a. Provides humidification and enriched oxygen mixtures to tracheostomy or ET tube
      b. Delivers 40% to 60% oxygen at flow rates of 4–12 liters/minute
5. **Ventilators**
A. Indications
   1. Hypoventilation
   2. Hypoxia
   3. Counteract pulmonary edema by changing pressure gradient
   4. Decrease work of breathing
B. Contraindications
   1. Tuberculosis—may rupture tubercular bleb
   2. Hypovolemia—increased intrathoracic pressures decrease venous return
   3. Air trapping—increased because adequate

exhalation is not allowed
C. Complications
1. Decreased blood pressure
2. Atelectasis
3. Infection
4. Oxygen toxicity
5. Difficulties weaning
6. Gastric dilatation
D. Types of ventilators
1. Oscillating or rocking bed
   a. Indirectly aid respirations by using weight and gravity of abdominal contents to change position of diaphragm
   b. Used for patients with paralytic disease and as an aid in weaning
2. Iron lung and chest respirators
   a. Driven by motors that create negative pressure within tank or shell and thus allow air to enter patient's lungs
   b. Utilized for patients with neuromuscular disease
3. Intermittent positive-pressure breathing
   a. Produces pressures greater than atmospheric pressures, intermittently
   b. Improves tidal volume and minute volume and aids in overcoming respiratory insufficiency
   c. Produces more uniform distribution of alveolar aeration and reduces work of breathing
   d. Utilized to deliver both oxygen and medications to patients during treatment and rehabilitative pulmonary therapy
   e. Contraindicated in pneumothorax, active tuberculosis, and history of recent hemoptysis
4. Pressure-preset ventilators
   a. Bird—Mark VII
      (1) Pressure-cycled, pneumatic-powered
      (2) When preset pressure is reached, valve closes terminating inspiration
      (3) Flow rate, sensitivity, and pressure limit all adjustable
      (4) Adjustable flow rate allows for increasing tidal volume
      (5) Disadvantage—changes in compliance or airway resistance can affect oxygen concentration and tidal volume
   b. Bennett—PR II
      (1) Positive-pressure cycled, time-cycled, flow sensitive
      (2) May be triggered by patient's inspiration or controlled by pressure or time setting
      (3) Oxygen delivery variable, so frequent monitoring is a *must*

6. **Volume respirators**
A. Emerson
1. Delivers preset tidal volume
2. Oxygen concentration adjusted by lighter flow being fed into machine
3. No alarms—malfunctions can go undetected
4. Has a sigh mechanism but no positive end-expiration pressure (PEEP), which maintains lung inflation
5. Utilized for patients with decreased compliance (stiff lungs)
B. Bennett—MA-1 and Ohio 560
1. Similar function and capabilities to Emerson
2. Sophisticated alarm system
3. Excellent humidification systems
4. PEEP capabilities

Appendix I   Positioning the Patient

POSITION AND INDICATION

1. Prone—head trauma, special surgeries, decubitus, and hemorrhoidectomy

2. Supine (flat)—chordotomy, spinal anesthesia, cervical laminectomy, myelogram, spinal cord injuries, spica cast till dry, subarachnoid hemmorrhage, and lumbar puncture

3. Side lying—head trauma, unconscious patients, patient with decubitus, and craniotomy

4. Semi-Fowler's—radical neck surgeries, thyroidectomy, parathyroidectomy, radical mastectomy, acute pancreatitis, Cushing's syndrome, respiratory dysfunctions, cholecystectomy, nephrectomy, cardiac problems, peritonitis, low back pain, tube feeding, emphysema, and glaucoma

5. High-Fowler's—pulmonary edema, empyema, and asthma, pulmonary emboli, thoracentesis, and paracentesis

6. Low-Fowler's—above knee amputation, intestinal surgery, cerebral aneurysm, myasthenia gravis, and increased intracranial pressure

7. Elevation of extremities—thrombophlebitis, cast, shock, and bunionectomy

8. Turn to unoperated side—cataract surgery

9. Turn to operative side—pneumonectomy

10. Extremely flat—meniscectomy and above knee amputation (after 12 hours)

Index

Supplement Ethical and Legal Aspects of Nursing

NURSING ETHICS

Nursing ethics are rules, or principles, to guide right conduct in terms of moral duty and obligation to protect individuals' rights. They provide professional standards and formal guidelines for nursing activities to protect the nurse and the patient.

1. **Code of ethics**—serves as frame of reference in which judgment is required as to which priorities and course of action to take
A. **Purpose**
   1. Provides basis for regulating relationship between nurse, patient, co-workers, society, and profession
   2. Provides standard for excluding unscrupulous nursing practitioners and for defending nurses unjustly accused
   3. Serves as basis for nursing curricula
   4. Orients new nurse and public to ethical professional conduct

ANA CODE FOR NURSES*

1. The nurse provides services with respect for human dignity and the uniqueness of the client unrestricted by considerations of social or economic status, personal attributes, or the nature of health problems.

Illness is a universal phenomenon; therefore the need for nursing is also universal. Because nursing is required by the broad spectrum of people who make up society, the nurse should be free of value judgments about "good people and bad people"; it is necessary to accept each person, as well as

the person's attitudes, customs, and beliefs. In this way nurses can best provide support to people of varied backgrounds.

2. The nurse safeguards the client's right to privacy by judiciously protecting information of a confidential nature.

It is clearly the nurse's responsibility to keep confidential any information received from the patient, only conveying details about illness or the physical, social, or personal situation of the patient to other persons who are also professionally concerned directly with the patient's care.

In some instances, the nurse may be required to provide testimony in a court. In these instances, the court will advise the nurse as to what is admissible and to what the nurse must testify.

Because people can be seriously harmed and embarrassed by a breach in confidence of the nurse, all nurses must use good professional judgment in what they say, being sure that it is stated to the correct person and that what is conveyed could be of value in promoting the health of the patient. The basis of this ethical principle is also found in the law.

3. The nurse acts to safeguard the client and the public when health care and safety are affected by the incompetent, unethical, or illegal practice of any person.

Nurses themselves are responsible for maintaining their own competence, updating their knowledge and skills as it is appropriate. Not to do so would imply that a nurse could not provide as high a standard of practice as the profession considers necessary.

4. The nurse assumes responsibility and accountability for individual nursing judgments and actions.

The nurse has a responsibility to report to the appropriate authority or to the professional association any conduct

---

*American Nurses' Association. 1976. *Code for nurses with interpretive statements.* Kansas City, Missouri: American Nurses' Association. Reprinted with permission. Commentary (in italics) from Kozier, Barbara and Erb, Glenora Lea: *Fundamentals of Nursing,* © 1979 by Addison-Wesley Publishing Company, Menlo Park, Ca.

of other nurses or physicians that endangers patients. The priority of the nurse is the patient, patient safety, and patient care.

5.   The nurse maintains competence in nursing.

Maintaining competence in nursing practice is essential; nurses must keep abreast of new developments to ensure the best standards of patient care. An essential quality of the nurse is a zest for continued study, since knowledge and skills for nursing need to be continually updated. The nurse who pursues knowledge independently is undoubtedly more effective in practice than one who does not.

6.   The nurse exercises informed judgment and uses individual competence and qualifications as criteria in seeking consultation, accepting responsibilities, and delegating nursing activities to others.

Nurses need to recognize their own areas of competence and incompetence; they have a right to refuse to carry out responsibilities that they consider unethical. Policies of agencies and the law assist the nurse as to what practices are considered to be within the nurse's area of responsibility. In addition, if a nurse is not familiar with some nursing activity, it is the nurse's right to explain this and to refuse to carry it out.

7.   The nurse participates in activities that contribute to the ongoing development of the profession's body of knowledge.

Increasingly, nurses are becoming involved in research activities as individual practitioners and as employees of hospitals and community health agencies. Nurses themselves are conducting research into nursing practice as well as are a variety of health personnel such as physicians and biochemists.

The nurse who plans to participate should first make sure that the patient understands and agrees to be part of the research; second, the nurse should make sure that the research proposed has the approval of the agency research committee or the appropriate approving authority of the agency.

8.   The nurse participates in the profession's efforts to implement and improve standards of nursing.

Peer review and established nursing standards assist in improving nursing. The nurse has a responsibility to participate in these activities as well as to participate in educational programs.

Standards for practice must always change as the health care system changes. The professional nurse has a responsibility to assist in making these changes and implementing them.

9.   The nurse participates in the profession's efforts to establish and maintain conditions of employment conducive to high quality nursing care.

Each nurse, acting through the professional organization, needs to be concerned with the economic and general welfare of the members of the profession. These are important factors in both recruiting nursing students and in retaining nurses in the work force. Through the nursing association, nurses assist in the establishment of employment practices and in bargaining for economic and general benefits.

10.   The nurse participates in the profession's effort to protect the public from misinformation and misrepresentation and to maintain the integrity of nursing.

Nurses are generally held in respect by members of the public, who have confidence in their knowledge and their advice. Often when a nurse speaks, it is assumed that the opinion given is the opinion of all nurses. For example, to advertise or recommend a product might be harmful or misleading to the public. The nurse appears to have knowledge that the particular product is better than others on the market; this may not be true because that knowledge is usually beyond the nurse's qualifications and authority.

11.   The nurse collaborates with members of the health professions and other citizens in promoting community and national efforts to meet the health needs of the public.

A professional nurse, with specialized knowledge and skills, has a responsibility to contribute in such a manner as to assist people to meet the health needs of the community. Citizens are increasingly concerned and becoming involved in planning health care. A nurse can offer such a group information that would be pertinent and helpful. Nurses also have a responsibility to act on committees with other health members and other professionals such as teachers and social workers in meeting the health problems of the people in the community.

---

2.   Conflicts and problems between
A.   **Personal values and professional duty**—nurses have the right to refuse to participate in areas of nursing practice that are against their personal values (therapeutic abortions or euthanasia) as long as the patient's welfare is not jeopardized
B.   **Nurse and agency**—conflict regarding whether or not to give out needed information to patient or follow agency policy that does not allow it (emotionally upset teenager asks nurse about how to get an abortion, a discussion that is against agency policy)
C.   **Nurse and colleagues**—to ignore or to whom to report and when (a nurse sees another nurse steal medication, has knowledge that a peer is giving a false reason when requesting time off, or observes intoxicated colleague)
D.   **Nurse and patient/family**—conflict over to reveal or not reveal (patient or family member relates a vital secret to the nurse)
E.   **Conflicting responsibilities**—to whom is nurse responsible when nurse at the same time is responsible to the agency and to the patient when needs might differ (physician asks nurse not to list all hospital supplies used for patient care because patient cannot afford to pay the bill)

LEGAL ASPECTS OF NURSING

1. **Definitions**
   common law–accumulation of law as a result of judicial court decisions.
   civil law (private law)–law that derives from legislative codes and deals with relations among people.
   public law–law that deals with relationships between an individual and the state.
   criminal law–law that deals with actions against the safety and welfare of the public (such as robbery); it is part of the public law.
2. **Nursing licensure**—mandatory licensure required to practice nursing
A. **Nurse Practice Act**—each state has one to protect nurses' professional capacity, and to legally control nursing through licensing, to define professional nursing
B. **American Nurses' Association definition of nursing, 1980:**

   The practice of nursing means the performance for compensation of professional services requiring substantial specialized knowledge of the biological, physical, behavioral, psychological, and sociological sciences and of nursing theory as the basis for assessment, diagnosis, planning, intervention, and evaluation in the promotion and maintenance of health; the casefinding and management of illness, injury, or infirmity; the restoration of optimum function; or the achievement of a dignified death. Nursing practice includes but is not limited to administration, teaching, counseling, supervision, delegation, and evaluation of practice and execution of the medical regimen, including the administration of medications and treatments prescribed by any person authorized by state law to prescribe. Each registered nurse is directly accountable and responsible to the consumer for the quality of nursing care rendered.
   The practice of practical nursing means the performance for compensation of technical services requiring basic knowledge of the biological, physical, behavioral, psychological, and sociological sciences and of nursing procedures. These services are performed under the supervision of a registered nurse and utilize standardized procedures leading to predictable outcomes in the observation and care of the ill, injured, and infirm; in the maintenance of health; in action to safeguard life and health; and in the administration of medications and treatments

prescribed by any person authorized by state law to prescribe.

Comment
   The statutes of each state usually include a section on general definitions that will be used by the courts if certain general terms are not defined in a particular statute. These definitions indicate that the use of gender terms—for example, her, his, she, he—will be interpreted to include both sexes. In this suggested legislation, the term her *is used in that manner.*
   A board of nursing may be an autonomous agency of state government directly responsible to the governor of the state, it may be part of a department of state government, or it may be advisory to an individual department head or agency of state government.
   When a board of nursing is not autonomous, definitions should be included in the statute for the department, commission, or other applicable individual or group with an indication of the extent of its authority and responsibility for the activities of the board of nursing.
   The nursing practice act must contain a definition of the practice that it seeks to regulate. The definition should be stated in terms broad enough to permit flexibility in the utilization of nursing personnel, with accountability vested in the registered nurse. The "shopping list" approach to a definition of practice is inflexible and undesirable. The definition should recognize the singular element that distinguishes the nurse from other nursing personnel—the breadth and depth of educational preparation that justify entrusting overall responsibility for nursing services to the judgment of the registered nurse.
   When the law regulates a second type of nursing practice, the definitions must differentiate between the types of practice. The definition of the second type of nursing practice should recognize the difference in the educational preparation of the practitioner.
   These suggested definitions of practice are intended to reflect the educational preparation expected for entry into practice in the future, i.e. at least a baccalaureate in nursing for beginning practice as a registered nurse, and at least an associate degree in nursing for beginning practice as a licensed practical nurse or other titles identified by the profession.
   *These definitions utilize information provided in "Report of the Task Force on Development of a Policy for Nursing Resources," a report prepared for the Commission on Nursing Services, American Nurses' Association.**

C. **License Revocation**—Board of Examiners in each state and province of Canada has the power to revoke licenses for just cause, e.g., incompetence in nursing practice, conviction of crime, drug addiction, obtaining license through fraud, hiding criminal history
3. **Crime**—an act committed in violation of societal law and punishable by fine, imprisonment, or both;

---

*American Nurses' Association. 1980. *The Nursing Practice Act: Suggested State Legislation*. Kansas City, Missouri: American Nurses' Association. Reprinted with permission.

it does not have to be intended (such as giving client accidental overdose that proves to be lethal)

A. **Felony**—crimes of serious nature punishable by imprisonment (such as murder)

B. **Misdemeanor**—crimes of less serious nature and usually punishable by fines, short-term prison, or both (such as stealing)

4. **Tort**—a wrong committed by one individual against another or his or her property; negligence and malpractice are two kinds of torts (such as losing client's hearing aid or bathing him in water that burns him)

A. **Negligence**—"omission to do something that a reasonable person, guided by those ordinary considerations which ordinarily regulate human affairs would do, or doing something which a reasonable and prudent person would not do"*

1. Types of negligent acts

    a. Sponge counts—incorrect number or failure to count

    b. Burns—heating pads, solutions, steam vaporizers

    c. Falls—siderails left down, baby left unattended

    d. Failure to observe and take appropriate action—failure to take vital signs or to check dressing in newly postoperative patient

    e. Wrong medicine, wrong dose and concentration, wrong route, wrong patient

    f. Mistaken identity—wrong patient for surgery

    g. Failure to communicate—ignore, forget, fail to report complaints of patient or family

    h. Loss of or damage to patient's property (denture, jewelry, or money)

B. **Malpractice**—part of the law of negligence as applied to the professional person; any professional misconduct, unreasonable lack of skill, or lack of fidelity in professional duties (such as accidentally giving wrong medication or forgetting to give it)

C. **Fraud**—misrepresentation of fact with intentions for it to be acted on by another person (such as falsifying college transcripts when applying for a graduate nursing program)

D. **Invasion of privacy**—right of patient to withhold self and own life from public scrutiny

    Implications for nursing—avoid unnecessary discussion of patient's medical condition; patient has a right to refuse to participate in clinical teaching; obtain consent before teaching conference

E. **Libel and slander**—wrongful action of communication that damages person's reputation by print, writing, pictures (libel) or spoken word using false or unprivileged words (slander)

    Implications for nursing—make comments about patient only to another health team member caring for patient

5. **Privileged communications**

6. **Assault and battery**—right to refuse physical contact with another

A. **Definitions**

    assault–attempt to touch another or threaten to do so

    battery–physical harm through willful touching of person or clothing

    Implications for nursing—must obtain consent to treat, with special provisions when patients are minors, unconscious, or mentally ill

7. **Good Samaritan Act**—protects health practitioners against malpractice claims resulting from assistance provided at scene of an emergency (unless there was willful wrongdoing) as long as the level of care provided is the same as any other reasonably prudent person would give under similar circumstances

8. **Law-related nursing responsibilities**

A. Liable for nursing acts even if nurse is directed to do something by the physician

B. Not responsible for negligence of the employer (hospital)

C. Responsible for refusing to carry out an order for an activity believed to be injurious to the patient

D. Cannot legally diagnose illness or prescribe treatment for a patient (this is the physician's responsibility)

E. Legally responsible when participating in a criminal act (such as assisting with criminal abortions or taking medications for nurse's own use from patient's supply)

F. Should review confidential patient information with appropriate health care team members only

G. Responsible for explaining nursing activities but not commenting on medical activities in a way that may distress the patient or physician

H. Responsible to recognize and protect the rights of patients to refuse treatment or medication and to report their concerns and refusals to the physician or appropriate agency personnel

I. Needs to respect the dignity of each patient and family

---

*From Creighton, H. 1975. *Law Every Nurse Should Know,* 3rd ed., p. 119.

TWENTY-FIVE QUESTIONS MOST FREQUENTLY ASKED BY NURSES ABOUT NURSING

A. Taking orders

1. *Should I accept verbal telephone orders from physician?* Generally no. Specifically, follow your hospital's by-laws, regulations, and policies regarding this. Failure to follow the hospital's rules could be considered negligence.

2. *Should I follow physician's orders if (a) I know it is wrong or (b) I disagree with his or her judgment?* (a) No, if you think a reasonably prudent nurse would not follow it, but first inform the physician and record your decision. Report it to your supervisor. (b) Yes, because the law does not allow you to substitute your nursing judgment for a physician's medical judgment. Do record that you questioned the order and that the physician confirmed it before you carried it out.

3. *What can I do if the physician delegates to me a task for which I was not prepared?* Inform the physician of your lack of education and experience in performing the task. Refuse to do it. If you inform the physician and still carry out the task, both you and the physician could be seen as negligent if the patient is harmed by it. If you do not tell the physician and carry out the task, you are solely liable.

B. Obtaining patient's consent for medical and surgical procedures

1. *Is a nurse responsible for getting a consent for medical or surgical treatment?* Obtaining consent requires explanation of procedure and risk that the physician should give and be responsible for. A nurse may accept responsibility for witnessing a consent, which carries little legal liability other than to obtain the correct signature and describe the patient's condition at time of signing.

C. Patient's records

1. *What should be written in the nurse's notes?* All facts and information regarding person's condition, treatment, care, progress, response to illness and treatment. Purpose of record: factual documentation of care given to meet legal standards; in order to refute unwarranted claims of negligence or malpractice.

2. *How should data be recorded?* Entries should (a) state time given, (b) be written and signed by caregiver or supervisor who observed action, (c) be in chronological sequence, (d) be accurate, precise, clear, (e) be legible, and (f) be universal abbreviations.

D. Confidential information

1. *If I am called on the witness stand in court, do I have to reveal the confidential information?* It depends on your state; each state has its own laws pertaining to this. Consult a lawyer. Inform the judge and ask for specific directions before relating in court information that was given to you within a confidential, professional relationship.

2. *Am I justified in refusing (on the basis of "invasion of privacy") to give information about the patient to another health agency to which a patient is being transferred?* No. You are responsible for providing continuity of care when the patient is moved from one facility to another. Necessary and adequate information should be transferred to serve as a source of accurate and necessary information and as necessary communication between appropriate professional health care workers. The patient's consent for this exchange of information should be obtained. Circumstances under which confidential information can be released include by (a) authorization and consent of patient, (b) order of the court, and (c) statutory mandate (as in reporting child abuse or communicable disease).

E. Liability for mistakes (yours and others)

1. *Am I or the hospital liable for mistakes I make while following orders?* Both you and the hospital can be sued for damage if a mistake you make injures the patient. You are responsible for your own actions. The hospital would be vicariously liable.

2. *Who is responsible if a nursing student or another staff nurse makes a mistake—the supervisor or the instructor?* Ordinarily neither the instructor nor the supervisor would be responsible unless the court thought the instructor or supervisor was negligent in supervising or assigning a task beyond the capability of the other. No one is responsible for another's negligence unless he or she contributed to or participated in that negligence. Each person is personally liable for his or her own negligent actions and failure to act as a reasonable prudent nurse.

3. *Am I responsible for injury to a patient by a staff member whom I observed (but did not report) was intoxicated while giving care?* Yes, you may be responsible. You have a duty to take reasonable action to prevent a patient's injury.

F. Good Samaritan

1. *For what would I be liable if I voluntarily stopped to give care at the scene of an accident?*

You would be protected under the Good Samaritan Act and required to live up to reasonable and prudent nursing standards in those specific circumstances, not as if you were performing under professional standards of properly sterile conditions and with proper technical equipment.

G. Leaving against medical advice

1. *Would I or the hospital be liable if patient leaves AMA, refusing to sign the appropriate hospital forms for AMA?* None of the involved parties would ordinarily be liable in this case as long as (a) the medical risks were explained, recorded, and witnessed; and (b) the patient is a competent adult. The law permits patients to make decisions that may not be in their own best health interest. You cannot interfere with the right and exercise of the decision to accept or reject treatment.

H. Restraints

1. *Can I put restraints on a patient who is combative when there is no order for this?* Only in emergency, for a limited time, for a limited purpose of protecting the patient from injury, not for the convenience of personnel. Notify the attending physician immediately. Consult with another staff, obtain patient's consent, if possible, document facts and reasons, and get a co-worker to witness the record. Apply restraints properly; check frequently to ensure they do not impair circulation, cause pressure sores, or cause other injury. Remove restraints at the first opportunity, and use them only as a last resort after other reasonable means have not been effective. Restraints of any degree may constitute false imprisonment. Freedom from unlawful restraint is a basic human right protected by law.

I. Wills

1. *What do I do when a patient asks me to be a witness to his will?* You have no legal obligation to participate as a witness, but you have a moral and ethical obligation to do so. You should not, however, help draw up a will, because this could be seen as practicing law without a license. You would be witnessing that (a) the patient is signing the document as his last will and testament and (b) at this time to the best of your knowledge, the patient (testator) is of sound mind, is lucid, and understands what he is doing. The testator must not be under the influence of drugs or alcohol so that he does not know what he is doing, and (c) he must be under no overt coercion; that is, as far as you

can tell, he is acting freely, willingly, and under his own impetus.

J. Disciplinary action

1. *For what reasons may my RN license be suspended or revoked?* For (a) obtaining license by fraud (omission of information, false information), (b) negligence and incompetence, (c) substance abuse, (d) conviction of crime (state or federal), (e) practicing medicine without a license (f) practicing nursing without a license (expired, suspened), (g) allowing unlicensed person to practice nursing or medicine, (h) giving patient care while under the influence of alcohol or other drugs, (i) habitually using drugs, and (j) discriminatory and prejudicial practices in giving patient care (pertaining to race, color, sex, age, ethnic origin).

2. *What could happen to me if I am proven guilty of professional misconduct?* (a) license may be revoked, (b) license may be suspended, (c) behavior may be censured and reprimanded, or (d) you may be placed on probation.

3. *Who has the authority to carry out any of the above penalties?* The State Board of Registered Nursing that granted your license.

4. *I am the head nurse. One of my nurse's aides has a history of failing to appear to work and not giving notice of or reason for absence. How should this be handled?* The employee has the right to know hospital policies, to know what is expected of that employee, and to know what will happen if he or she does not meet the expectations stated in the job description and hospital policies and procedures. As a head nurse, you need to document behavior factually, clearly, and concisely as well as to document any discussion and decision about future course of action. The employee needs the chance to read and sign it. The head nurse then sends a copy to his or her supervisor.

K. Floating

1. *If I was hired to work in psychiatry, am I obligated to cover in ICU when the latter is unstaffed?* The issue is the hiring contract (implied or expressed). The contract is a composite of the mutual understanding by involved parties of rights and responsibilities, any written documents, and hospital policies. A nurse hired as a psychiatric nurse could legally refuse to go to the ICU. If a hospital intends to float personnel, such a policy should be clearly stated during the hiring process. Also, at this time,

the employer should determine the employee's education, skills, and experience. On the other hand, if emergency staffing problems exist, a nurse should go to the ICU and not refuse merely because he or she does not want to go.

L. Dispensing medication

1. *Can I legally remove a drug from a pharmacy when the pharmacy is closed (during the night) and the physician insists that I go to the pharmacy to get the specifically prescribed medication immediately?* Within the legal boundaries of the Pharmacy Act a nurse may remove one dose of a particular drug from the pharmacy for a particular patient during an unanticipated emergency within limited availability of time and resources. However, the hospital should have a written policy for the nurse to follow and designate an authorized person to use the services of the pharmacy under certain circumstances.

M. Illegible orders

1. *What should I do if I cannot decipher the physician's handwriting when he or she persists in leaving illegible orders?* Talk to the physician regarding dangers of your giving the wrong amount of the wrong medication via the wrong route and the wrong time. If that does not help, follow appropriate channels. Do not follow an order you cannot read. You will be liable for following orders you thought were written.

N. Heroic measures

1. *The wife of a terminally ill patient approached me with the request that the heroic measures not be used on him. She has not discussed this with him but knows that he feels the same way. Can I act on this request?* No. The patient is the only one who can legally make this decision as long as he is mentally competent.

O. Medication

1. *Am I legally covered if I give half of the pain medication dosage ordered as prn by the physician if in my judgment the patient's pain is not severe, although the patient asks for the pain medication but at the same time says that "it isn't so bad"?* You cannot substitute your judgment for the physician's. If you alter the amount of the medication prescribed by the physician without a specific order to do so, you may be liable for practicing medicine without a license.

P. Malfunctioning equipment

1. *At the end of shift report, the nurse going off duty tells me the tracheal suctioning machine is malfunctioning and tells me how to get it to work.*

Should I plan to use the machine in the evening shift and follow the nurse's suggestions about how to make it work? Do not plan to use equipment that you know is not functioning properly. You could be held liable since you could reasonably foresee that proper function of equipment is going to be needed for your patient. You have been put on notice that there are defects. Report this to the supervisor or person responsible for maintaining equipment in proper working order.

ETHICAL AND LEGAL CONSIDERATIONS AND ISSUES IN INTENSIVE CARE OF ACUTELY ILL NEONATE

1. **Necessary provisions**

   A. NICU—or transfer to another hospital

   B. Personnel—adequate number, trained in neonate diseases, special treatment, equipment

   C. Equipment—adequate supply on hand, functioning properly (especially temperature regulator in incubator, oxygen analyzer, blood gas machine)

2. **Dying infants**

   A. Decision regarding resuscitation in cardiac arrest, with brain damage from cerebral anoxia

   1. Difficult to predict in infancy the outcome of anoxia later in infant's life

   B. Decision to continue supportive measures

   C. Euthanasia (such as severe myelomeningocele at birth)

   1. Active euthanasia (giving overdose)

   2. Passive euthanasia (not placing on respirator)

3. **Extended role of nurse in NICU**—may raise issues of nursing practice versus medical practice (such as drawing blood samples for blood-gas determinations without prior order)

   A. For legal coverage

   1. Nurse must be trained to perform specialized functions

   2. Functions must be written into job description

4. **Issue of negligence** (such as cross contamination in nursery)

5. **Issue of malpractice** (such as assigning care of critically ill infant on respirator to untrained student or aide)

   A. May be liable for inaccurate bilirubin studies for neonatal jaundice; may be legally responsible if brain damage occurs in absence of accurate laboratory tests

   B. May be liable for brain damage in infant due to respiratory or cardiac distress; must make sure that there are frequent blood-gas determinations to ensure adequate oxygen to prevent brain damage;

must be sure the infant is not receiving too high oxygen content concentration, which may lead to retrolental fibroplasia

LEGAL ASPECTS OF PSYCHIATRIC CARE

1. Sets of criteria to determine criminal responsibility at time of alleged offense

A. **M'Naghten rule** (1832)—not guilty because
  1. Did not know the nature and quality of the act
  2. If did not know what he or she was doing, did not know it was wrong ("right from wrong")

B. **The irresistible test** (used together with M'Naghten rule)
  1. Knows right from wrong, but
  2. Driven by impulse to commit criminal acts regardless of circumstance
    a. Need to show lack of premeditation in sudden violent behavior

C. **American Law Institute's Test**
  1. Not responsible for criminal act if person lacks capacity to appreciate the wrongfulness of it or to conform his or her conduct to requirements of law
  2. Excludes "an abnormality manifested only by repeated criminal or antisocial conduct," namely, psychopaths

D. **Durham Test,** or Product Rule (1954)
  1. Accused not criminally responsible if act was "product of mental disease"

2. Types of admissions

A. **Voluntary**—person, parent, or legal guardian apply for admission; person agrees to receive treatment and follow hospital rules; civil rights are retained

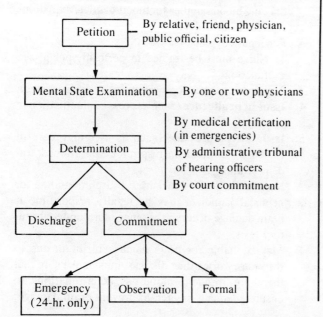

B. **Involuntary**—process and criteria vary among states

NURSING TRENDS

1. Overall characteristics
Some trends are subtle and slow emerging. Other trends are obvious and quickly emerging. Some trends are divergent and in conflict. Some prevail, whereas others get modified by social forces.

2. Trends

A. Broadened focus of care—from care of ill to care of sick and healthy, from individual to care of family
  1. Focus—prevention of illness, promotion of optimum level of health, holism

B. Increasing scientific base—in biosociophysical sciences, not relying on intuition, experience, and observation

C. Increasingly complex technical skills and use of technologically advanced equipment (such as monitors, computers)

D. Increased independence is use of judgment (such as teaching nutrition in pregnancy and providing primary prenatal care)

E. New roles
  1. Nurse clinician—advanced skills in particular area of practice
  2. Psychiatric nurse—consults with staff about problems
  3. Primary care nurse—takes medical histories, does physical assessment, coordinates 24-hour care during hospital stay
  4. Independent nurse practitioner—has own office in community where patients come for care

F. Community nursing services—rather than hospital-based; needs of the healthy as well as the ill are served

G. Development of nursing standards—reflects specific functions and activities of the nurse
  1. Purposes
    a. assure safe standard of care to patients and families
    b. Provide criteria to measure excellence and effectiveness of care

3. Four levels of nursing practice

A. Promotion of health—increase level of wellness (such as provide dietary information to reduce risks of coronaries)

B. Prevention of illness or injury (such as immunizations)

C. Restoration of health (such as teaching how to change dressing, care for wound)

STANDARDS OF NURSING*

1. The collection of data about the health status of the client/patient is systematic and continuous. The data are accessible, communicated, and recorded.
2. Nursing diagnoses are derived from health status data.
3. The plan of nursing care includes goals derived from the nursing diagnoses.
4. The plan of nursing care includes priorities and the prescribed nursing approaches or measures to achieve the goals derived from the nursing diagnoses.
5. Nursing actions provide for client/patient participation in health promotion, maintenance, and restoration.
6. The nursing actions assist the client/patient to maximize his health capabilities.
7. The client/patient's progress or lack of progress toward goal achievement is determined by the client/patient and the nurse.
8. The client/patient's progress or lack of progress toward goal achievement directs reassessment, reordering of priorities, new goal setting, and revision of the plan of nursing care.

*From American Nurses' Association. 1973. *Standards of nursing practice*. Kansas City, Missouri. Reprinted with permission. (Rationale for the above *Standards of nursing practice* are available from the ANA.)

D. Consolation of dying (such as assisting to attain peaceful death)
4. **Components of nursing care**
A. Nursing care activities—assist with basic needs, give meds and treatments; observe response and adaptation to illness and treatments; teach self-care; guide rehabilitation activities for daily living.
B. Coordination of total patient care—involve all health team to work together toward common goal
C. Continuity of care—when transfer location of care
D. Evaluation of care—flexibility and responsiveness (What needs are changing? How is patient reacting? What are patient's perceptions of his needs?)
E. Delegate and direct nursing care provided by others—based on particular patient/family needs and skills of other nursing personnel
5. **Three main nursing roles**
The emphasis of each nursing role in relation to care of patients and their families varies with the situation and with adaptation of skills and modes of care as necessary.
A. Therapeutic role (instrumental)

1. Function—work toward "cure" in acute setting
B. Caring role (expressive)
1. Function—provide support through human relations, show concern, demonstrate acceptance of differences
C. Socializing role
1. Function—offer distractions and respite from focus on illness

NURSING ORGANIZATIONS

1. **International Council of Nurses (ICN)**
A. Purpose—provide a medium through which national nursing associations can work together, share common interests (formed in 1899)
B. Functions
1. Serve as representatives and spokesmen of nurses at international level
2. Promote organization of national nurses' associations
3. Assist national organizations to develop and improve services for public health practice of nursing and social/economic welfare of nurses
2. **World Health Organization (WHO)**
WHO is a special intergovernmental agency of the UN and was formed in 1948
A. Purpose—Bring all people to the highest possible level of health
B. Functions—Provide assistance to countries in form of education, training, improved health standards, fighting of disease and water pollution
3. **American Nurses' Association (ANA)**
The ANA is a national professional association in the United States composed of the 50 states' nurses' associations and those in Guam, Virgin Islands, Puerto Rico, and Washington, D.C.
A. Purpose—Foster high standards of nursing practice, promote education and welfare of nurses
4. **National League for Nursing (NLN)**
The NLN is composed of both individuals and agencies.
A. Purpose—Foster development and improvement of all nursing services and nursing education
B. Functions
1. Provide educational workshops
2. Assist in recruitment for nursing programs
3. Provide testing services for both RN and LPN (LVN) licensure

PSYCHIATRIC NURSING
Prestudy answer form for review questions
1–116, pp. 49–61

NAME ___ LAST ___ FIRST ___ MIDDLE ___ DATE ___

SCHOOL ___ CITY ___

DIRECTIONS: Read each question and its numbered answers. When you have decided which answer is correct, blacken the corresponding space on this sheet with the special pencil. Make your mark as long as the pair of lines, and move the pencil point up and down firmly to make a heavy black line. If you change your mind, erase your first mark completely. Make no stray marks; they may count against you.

SAMPLE:

1—1 a country
1—2 a mountain
1—3 an island
1—4 a city
1—5 a state

1. Chicago is

BE SURE YOUR MARKS ARE HEAVY AND BLACK.
ERASE COMPLETELY ANY ANSWER YOU WISH TO CHANGE.

Printed by the International Business Machines Corporation, Dayton, N. J., U. S. A.

IBM FORM I.T.S. 1100 B 107

PSYCHIATRIC NURSING

Poststudy answer form for review questions

1–116, pp. 49–61

NAME _____
LAST   FIRST   MIDDLE   DATE _____

SCHOOL _____   CITY _____

DIRECTIONS: Read each question and its numbered answers. When you have decided which answer is correct, blacken the corresponding space on this sheet with the special pencil. Make your mark as long as the pair of lines, and move the pencil point up and down firmly to make a heavy black line. If you change your mind, erase your first mark completely. Make no stray marks; they may count against you.

SAMPLE:

1—1 a country
1—2 a mountain
1—3 an island
1—4 a city
1—5 a state

1. Chicago is

BE SURE YOUR MARKS ARE HEAVY AND BLACK.
ERASE COMPLETELY ANY ANSWER YOU WISH TO CHANGE.

Printed by the International Business Machines Corporation, Dayton, N. J., U.S.A.

IBM FORM I.T.S. 1100 B 107

MEDICAL NURSING
Prestudy answer form for review questions
1–102, pp. 130–138

NAME _____ LAST _____ FIRST _____ MIDDLE _____ DATE _____

SCHOOL _____ CITY _____

DIRECTIONS: Read each question and its numbered answers. When you have decided which answer is correct, blacken the corresponding space on this sheet with the special pencil. Make your mark as long as the pair of lines, and down firmly to make a heavy black line. If you change your mind, erase your first mark completely. Make no stray marks; they may count against you.

SAMPLE:

1. Chicago is

1—1 a country
1—2 a mountain
1—3 an island
1—4 a city
1—5 a state

BE SURE YOUR MARKS ARE HEAVY AND BLACK.
ERASE COMPLETELY ANY ANSWER YOU WISH TO CHANGE.

(Answer grid: questions 1–150, each with answer choices 1 2 3 4 5)

IBM FORM I.T.S. 1100 B 107

MEDICAL NURSING

Poststudy answer form for review questions 1–102, pp. 130–138.

NAME _____ LAST _____ FIRST _____ MIDDLE _____ DATE _____

SCHOOL _____ CITY _____

DIRECTIONS: Read each question and its numbered answers. When you have decided which answer is correct, blacken the corresponding space on this sheet with the special pencil. Make your mark as long as the pair of lines, and move the pencil point up and down firmly to make a heavy black line. If you change your mind, erase your first mark completely. Make no stray marks; they may count against you.

SAMPLE:

1—1 a country
1—2 a mountain
1—3 an island
1—4 a city
1—5 a state

1. Chicago is

	1	2	3	4	5
1					

BE SURE YOUR MARKS ARE HEAVY AND BLACK.
ERASE COMPLETELY ANY ANSWER YOU WISH TO CHANGE.

Questions 1–150 arranged in columns with answer spaces numbered 1 through 5 for each.

SURGICAL NURSING

Prestudy answer form for review questions

1–100, pp. 187–195.

NAME _____ DATE _____
    LAST   FIRST   MIDDLE

SCHOOL _____ CITY _____

DIRECTIONS: Read each question and its numbered answers. When you have decided which answer is correct, blacken the corresponding space on this sheet with the special pencil. Make your mark as long as the pair of lines, and move the pencil point up and down firmly to make a heavy black line. If you change your mind, erase your first mark completely. Make no stray marks; they may count against you.

SAMPLE:

1. Chicago is

1—1 a country
1—2 a mountain
1—3 an island
1—4 a city
1—5 a state

```
        1   2   3   4   5
1   :: :: :: :: ::
2   :: :: :: :: ::
3   :: :: :: :: ::
4   :: :: :: :: ::
5   :: :: :: :: ::
6   :: :: :: :: ::
7   :: :: :: :: ::
8   :: :: :: :: ::
9   :: :: :: :: ::
10
11
12
13
14
15
```

BE SURE YOUR MARKS ARE HEAVY AND BLACK.
ERASE COMPLETELY ANY ANSWER YOU WISH TO CHANGE.

(Answer grid: questions 1–150, each with columns 1 2 3 4 5)

Printed by the International Business Machines Corporation, Dayton, N. J., U.S.A.   IBM FORM I.T.S. 1100 B 107

SURGICAL NURSING

Poststudy answer form for review questions 1–100, pp. 187–195.

NAME _____
LAST   FIRST   MIDDLE

DATE _____

SCHOOL _____
CITY

DIRECTIONS: Read each question and its numbered answers. When you have decided which answer is correct, blacken the corresponding space on this sheet with the special pencil. Make your mark as long as the pair of lines, and move the pencil point up and down firmly to make a heavy black line. If you change your mind, erase your first mark completely. Make no stray marks; they may count against you.

SAMPLE:

1. Chicago is

1—1 a country
1—2 a mountain
1—3 an island
1—4 a city
1—5 a state

BE SURE YOUR MARKS ARE HEAVY AND BLACK.
ERASE COMPLETELY ANY ANSWER YOU WISH TO CHANGE.

Printed by the International Business Machines Corporation, Dayton, N. J., U.S.A.

IBM FORM I.T.S. 1100 B 107

MATERNITY NURSING

Prestudy answer form for review questions
1–120, pp. 272–284.

NAME _____ LAST _____ FIRST _____ MIDDLE _____ DATE _____

SCHOOL _____ CITY _____

DIRECTIONS: Read each question and its numbered answers. When you have decided which answer is correct, blacken the corresponding space on this sheet with the special pencil. Make your mark as long as the pair of lines, and move the pencil point up and down firmly to make a heavy black line. If you change your mind, erase your first mark completely. Make no stray marks; they may count against you.

SAMPLE:

1. Chicago is
1—1 a country
1—2 a mountain
1—3 an island
1—4 a city
1—5 a state

BE SURE YOUR MARKS ARE HEAVY AND BLACK.
ERASE COMPLETELY ANY ANSWER YOU WISH TO CHANGE.

Printed by the International Business Machines Corporation, Dayton, N. J., U.S.A.

IBM FORM I.T.S. 1100 B 107

NAME _____
LAST   FIRST   MIDDLE   DATE _____

SCHOOL _____ CITY _____

MATERNITY NURSING
Poststudy answer form for review questions
1–120, pp. 272–284.

SAMPLE:

1—1 a country
1—2 a mountain
1—3 an island
1—4 a city
1—5 a state

1. Chicago is

DIRECTIONS: Read each question and its numbered answers. When you have decided which answer is correct, blacken the corresponding space on this sheet with the special pencil. Make your mark as long as the pair of lines, and move the pencil point up and down firmly to make a heavy black line. If you change your mind, erase your first mark completely. Make no stray marks; they may count against you.

BE SURE YOUR MARKS ARE HEAVY AND BLACK.
ERASE COMPLETELY ANY ANSWER YOU WISH TO CHANGE.

PEDIATRIC NURSING

Prestudy answer form for review question 1–124, pp. 342–351.

DIRECTIONS: Read each question and its numbered answers. When you have decided which answer is correct, blacken the corresponding space on this sheet with the special pencil. Make your mark as long as the pair of lines, and move the pencil point up and down firmly to make a heavy black line. If you change your mind, erase your first mark completely. Make no stray marks; they may count against you.

SAMPLE:

1. Chicago is

1—1 a country
1—2 a mountain
1—3 an island
1—4 a city
1—5 a state

BE SURE YOUR MARKS ARE HEAVY AND BLACK.
ERASE COMPLETELY ANY ANSWER YOU WISH TO CHANGE.

PEDIATRIC NURSING

Poststudy answer form for review questio...

1–124, pp. 342–351.

NAME _____

LAST   FIRST   MIDDLE   DATE _____

SCHOOL _____ CITY _____

DIRECTIONS: Read each question and its numbered answers. When you have decided which answer is correct, blacken the corresponding space on this sheet with the special pencil. Make your mark as long as the pair of lines, and move the pencil point up and down firmly to make a heavy black line. If you change your mind, erase your first mark completely. Make no stray marks; they may count against you.

SAMPLE:

1. Chicago is

1—1 a country
1—2 a mountain
1—3 an island
1—4 a city
1—5 a state

BE SURE YOUR MARKS ARE HEAVY AND BLACK.
ERASE COMPLETELY ANY ANSWER YOU WISH TO CHANGE.

Columns of answer bubbles numbered 1–150, each with options 1 2 3 4 5.

Printed by the International Business Machines Corporation, Dayton, N. J., U.S.A.

IBM FORM I.T.S. 1100 B 107

NAME _____ DATE _____

LAST   FIRST   MIDDLE

SCHOOL _____ CITY _____

NURSING TRENDS

Answer form for review questions 1–20, p. 358–359.

DIRECTIONS: Read each question and its numbered answers. When you have decided which answer is correct, blacken the corresponding space on this sheet with the special pencil. Make your mark as long as the pair of lines, and move the pencil point up and down firmly to make a heavy black line. If you change your mind, erase your first mark completely. Make no stray marks; they may count against you.

SAMPLE:

1. Chicago is

1—1 a country
1—2 a mountain
1—3 an island
1—4 a city
1—5 a state

BE SURE YOUR MARKS ARE HEAVY AND BLACK.
ERASE COMPLETELY ANY ANSWER YOU WISH TO CHANGE.

Printed by the International Business Machines Corporation, Dayton, N. J., U.S.A.

IBM FORM I.T.S. 1100 B 107